COMMUNICATION

Making Connections

ELEVENTH EDITION

William J. Seiler
University of Nebraska-Lincoln

Melissa L. Beall
University of Northern Iowa

Joseph P. Mazer
Clemson University

Director, Portfolio Manager: Karon Bowers
Content Producer: Barbara Cappuccio
Content Developer: Ed Dodd
Editorial Coordinator: Dea Barbieri
Executive Product Marketing Manager: Christopher Brown
Senior Field Marketing Manager: Kelly Ross
Content Producer Manager: Ken Volcjak
Content Development Manager: Steve Rigolosi
Art/Designer: Integra-Chicago
Digital Studio Course Producer: Amanda Smith
Full-Service Project Manager: Integra-Chicago
Compositor: Integra-Chicago
Printer/Binder: LSC Communications, Inc.
Cover Printer: LSC Communications, Inc.
Cover Design: Lumina Datamatics, Inc.
Cover Credit: PeopleImages/E+/Getty Images

Acknowledgements of third party content appear within the text or on page 413, which constitutes an extension of this copyright page.

Library of Congress Cataloging-in-Publication Data

Names: Seiler, William J., author. | Beall, Melissa L., author. | Mazer, Joseph P., author.
Title: Communication : making connections / William J. Seiler, Melissa L. Beall, Joseph P. Mazer.
Description: Eleventh edition. | Hoboken, NJ : Pearson, [2020] | Includes bibliographical references and index.
Identifiers: LCCN 2018052712 | ISBN 9780134874722 (paper back)
Subjects: LCSH: Communication.
Classification: LCC P90 .S3994 2020 | DDC 302.2—dc23
LC record available at https://lccn.loc.gov/2018052712

Access Code Card
ISBN-10: 0-13-489037-X
ISBN-13: 978-0-13-489037-1

Revel Combo Card
ISBN-10: 0-13-525535-X
ISBN-13: 978-0-13-525535-3

Rental Edition
ISBN-10: 0-13-487472-2
ISBN-13: 978-0-13-487472-2

Loose-Leaf Edition
ISBN-10: 0-13-487457-9
ISBN-13: 978-0-13-487457-9

Instructor's Review Copy
ISBN-10: 0-13-487461-7
ISBN-13: 978-0-13-487461-6

Brief Contents

Contents

10 Organizing and Outlining Your Speech   202

11 Managing Anxiety and Apprehension When Delivering Your Speech   229

12 Informative and Persuasive Speaking   258

13 Connecting through Interpersonal Communication: Developing, Maintaining, and Dissolving Relationships   301

14 Connecting through Participating in Groups and Teams   341

15 Connecting through Workplace Communication: Preparing for Your Future 370

Preface

Facebook founder Mark Zuckerberg said, "The thing that we are trying to do at Facebook is just help people connect and communicate more effectively." This is exactly why we wrote *Communication: Making Connections*—to help students "make connections" in their daily lives, to communicate more effectively, and to strive to be successful and productive citizens. Imagine what life would be like without smartphones; iPads; wireless Internet access; GPS; or the many forms of social media such as Facebook, Twitter, Instagram, and Snapchat that we use every day. Perhaps we cannot imagine it because these tools are woven into the very fabric of our lives; we take them for granted as they become more and more an extension of who we are. It is clear that Zuckerberg and the founders of Google, Apple Computers, and many other high-tech companies have attained their ambitious goal of changing how we communicate and live.

Clearly our world, particularly our social world, has changed and will continue to change, perhaps more quickly and dramatically than at any time in our past. Further—and a key point we'll emphasize throughout the title—these changes have important implications for our communication and for the communication field. As in previous editions, we are committed to bringing readers the latest and most up-to-date information regarding communication and its importance to our everyday lives.

We continue to be gratified and grateful that so many instructors have chosen *Communication: Making Connections* for their students. With this new edition, we remain committed to our primary goal of helping students be more competent communicators. We also continue to strive for balance between thorough, straightforward explanations of basic communication principles and a solid theoretical foundation supported by the latest research findings.

Revel™

Revel is an interactive learning environment that deeply engages students and prepares them for class. Media and assessment integrated directly within the authors' narrative lets students read, explore interactive content, and practice in one continuous learning path. Thanks to the dynamic reading experience in Revel, students come to class prepared to discuss, apply, and learn from instructors and from each other.

Learn more about Revel
www.pearson.com/revel

Special Features in Revel for Communication Students

Revel offers students a way to study the content and topics relevant to communication in a whole new way. Rather than simply offering opportunities to read about and study communication, Revel facilitates deep, engaging interactions with the concepts that matter most. For example, in Chapter 1 in Revel, while learning about the basics of communication, students will encounter both the Personal Report of Communication Apprehension (PRCA-24) and the Personal Report of Public Speaking Anxiety (PRPSA).

In Chapter 2 they'll find the "Self-Perceived Communication Competence" self-assessment instrument to gauge their comfort in various communication scenarios ranging from presenting a speech to talking with a friend. After completing these surveys, the student is shown what his or her responses say about his or her level of communication apprehension, public speaking anxiety, and self-perceived communication competence. Interactive text and figures on topics like intentional and unintentional communication and mind mapping are designed to capture students' attention and engage them with the text. In addition, students are presented with video examples throughout the book on topics like perception barriers, intercultural communication, media multitasking, and the dangers of "sexting." By providing opportunities to read about and practice communication in tandem, Revel engages students directly and immediately, which leads to a better understanding of course material. A wealth of student and instructor resources and interactive materials can be found within Revel. Some of our favorites include:

- **Module Audio and Audio Excerpts** Students can listen to audio of the entire book while on the go. In addition, audio excerpts bring examples of speeches and interpersonal conversations to life; dialogue excerpts highlight effective as well as ineffective ways to communicate. These audio examples reinforce learning by increasing student comprehension and engagement.

- **Self-Assessments** Self-assessment instruments at the end of every module and chapter allow students to answer questions about the module's content, enabling them to learn and grow over the duration of the course.

- **Videos and Video Self-Checks** Video examples of sample conversations, presentations, and discussions as well as expert advice throughout the narrative boost mastery, and over 25 videos have correlating self-checks, enabling students to test their knowledge. More than 30 new videos (including many Sketchnote videos covering fundamental topics and key concepts) have been added to this edition.

- **Interactive Figures** Several interactive figures (such as Chapter 2's "Perceptual Differences" and Chapter 4's "Ladder of Abstraction") give students a hands-on experience, increasing their ability to grasp difficult concepts. For instance, by interacting with the "Perceptual Differences" figure, students are able to examine specific differences more closely to help provide a complete understanding of the concept. The interactive "Ladder of Abstraction" also serves a unique purpose, allowing students to take a step-by-step walk through the process of refining language use to lessen the chance for misunderstanding.

- **Integrated Writing Opportunities** To help students connect chapter content with personal meaning, each chapter offers two varieties of writing prompts: (1) the Journal prompt, which elicits free-form, topic-specific responses addressing content at the module level, and (2) the Shared Writing prompt, which encourages students to share and respond to one another's brief responses to high-interest topics in the chapter. Most of the journal prompts, which appear in every module, help students make connections between interpersonal communication topics and their own experiences. At the end of each chapter, a Shared Writing prompt allows students to see and respond to their classmates' comments, thereby facilitating discussion online as well as in the classroom. Instructors have access to students' responses to these writing activities and can also assign them as homework.

- **Making Connections for Success Writing Prompts** These boxes in each chapter (see "Unique Features") encourage students to think critically about communication in their lives and to reflect on issues and their own communication behavior. In Revel, these boxes appear as fill-in applications that provide students with the chance to respond to the questions posed in a low-stakes environment.

- **New Appendix on Mediated Public Speaking** This new Appendix, available only in Revel, prepares students so they are comfortable preparing, practing, and delivering the various kinds of mediated public speaking they may encounter, whether in school, in the workplace, or in the community.

For more information about all the tools and resources in Revel and access to your own Revel account for *Communication: Making Connections*, Eleventh Edition, go to www.pearson.com/revel.

What's New in the Eleventh Edition?

In addition to enhancing the the strengths of the interactive elements in Revel that resonate so much with students and instructors, we've refined and updated the content in this new edition. The introductory communication course, with a solid foundation of rhetorical tradition, is constantly evolving, but its central premise, that communication remains the number one skill that leads to success in both our professional and personal lives, remains a constant. We take each revision seriously to ensure that we make it fresher, more useful, and more readable. This edition is no exception, and we believe we have met our goal.

We also offer the following content enhancements:

- **We explore the influence of technologies on our communication** with a new Chapter 6 ("Connecting through Social Media and New Technologies") featuring an expanded discussion of communication and technology. The chapter includes updated information on communication technologies, from texting to online social networking, from blogging to streaming video.
- **We focus particularly on the implication of communication via social media.** We emphasize the implications of new communication technologies for the messages we send and receive, such as Facebook, Twitter, Instagram, Snapchat, and other social media tools; for how emotions are communicated online; and ultimately for our interactions and relationships.
- **We focus on the importance of culture and diversity in making connections with others.** The new Chapter 3 ("Connecting through Culture and Diversity") highlights connections among culture, diversity, and difference; summarizes how communication leads to cultural variations; explains how communication influences group affiliations; identifies intercultural communication obstacles; and helps students improve their cultural communication competence.
- **Streamlined coverage** We recognize the increased demands on time, so we have reevaluated every chapter and every line, streamlining, combining chapters, and editing to ensure that only the most relevant information and research findings are presented in the most useful and concise way.
- **Numerous new examples** In recognition of the need to continuously update and refresh the book to keep up with both the ever-changing world and the communication discipline, we have replaced, updated, or added examples to be relevant to today's students. Chapter-opening boxes called "Making Everyday Conncection" make communication come alive to students as they encounter real-world experiences.
- **New research findings** Every chapter is updated with the newest and most recent research findings and theoretical perspectives.

Chapter-by-Chapter Changes

In addition to the new content listed above, we have made specific changes in every chapter.

Part 1: Making Connections through Communication

- **Chapter 1** covers process and principles, and includes revised and updated content on social media and new communication technologies, with popular platforms—such as Snapchat—used as engaging examples. In Revel, a new animated video reviews the interpersonal communication models presented in the text, and students will also be able to complete the self-assessments Personal Report of Communication Apprehension (PRCA-24) and Personal Report of Public Speaking Anxiety (PRPSA) so they can see their level of communication apprehension and public speaking anxiety. Additional new inline self-quizzes on identifying types of communication and intentional and unintentional communication gauge students' grasp of important concepts at key points in the narrative.

- **Chapter 2** is new to this edition; it combines coverage of perception and self into one chapter. The chapter has been revised to include all the important aspects and effects of perception and self as they relate to how we send and receive messages. It also provides a more concise overview of self and how our perception of self affects our communication with others. In Revel, two new animated videos—one on perception barriers and the other on self-concept and intrapersonal communication—allow students who are visual learners to encounter key concepts in another presentation style. New inline self-quizzes in Revel include differentiating between self-concept, self-image, and self-esteem; identifying perceptual differences; and determining facts from inferences.

- **Chapter 3** is also new and focuses on the complex connection between culture and communication. The chapter highlights connections among culture, diversity, and difference; explains how communication influences group affiliations; identifies intercultural communication obstacles; summarizes how communication leads to cultural variations; and helps students improve their cultural communication competence. In Revel, three new animated videos explore the chapter's main focus on understanding diversity, understanding culture, and intercultural communication. Students also have the opportunity to complete new self-assessments on both cultural competence and communicating cultural competence.

- **Chapter 4** covers verbal communication and features a stronger connection between thinking and language choice. Our language choices reflect our thinking; thus we need to choose language carefully and be prepared to explain ourselves to others who may not think as we do. The distinction between language for the eye and for the ear is also discussed. In Revel, three new self-assessments allow students to test their grasp of the following key concepts: verbal immediacy, language that obscures meaning, and the ladder of abstraction.

- **Chapter 5** includes a revised and updated section on what nonverbal communication is and expands on the role of social media and new communication technologies in nonverbal communication, along with discussions of emojis and bitmojis and their influence on the communication process. In Revel, a new video showcases the diverse nonverbal communication messages present in hand gestures, and a new animated video addresses the concept of nonverbal messages. A new audio self-assessment asks students to select which emotion is being conveyed when the same sentence is read in different ways, while another new assessment asks students a series of 15 true/false questions regarding nonverbal communication.

- **Chapter 6** is new (as mentioned earlier) and offers a chapter completely devoted to social media and new technologies. The chapter offers a history of new technologies, highlights differences between social media and face-to-face communication, incorporates revelant theories of new technologies, addresses the dark side of social media, and helps students develop their communication competence via social media. In Revel, a new video focuses on the dangers of sexting, while three new animated videos highlight the key topics of media multitasking, synchronous and asynchornous communication, and cues. Two additional new videos present an overview of the important topic of electronically mediated communication. A new self-assessment asks students to rank different lean/rich communication channels, and Figure 6.1 presents the evolution of social media in the last 600 years.

- **Chapter 7** offers more coverage on the ways we take in information through all our senses and how our thinking preferences affect listening. A new model of listening, the *Harfield Cognitive Listening Model*, shows how different preferred modes of thinking affect the way we listen and respond to others. Students are encouraged to reflect on what they hear and analyze and to evaluate the conclusions they reach based on the information they processed.

Part 2: Connecting in Public and Relational Contexts

- **Chapter 8** on topic selection and audience analysis has a new emphasis on the thought process and discusses the effect of social media as we search for speaking topics. In Revel, a new animated video about finding and selecting topics reinforces the advice and guidance found within the chapter.
- **Chapter 9** covers gathering and using information. It has been reorganized and includes a section on the research plan. Students are encouraged to find credible sources that enhance information in their speeches. In Revel, a new animated video on supporting materials revisits this key concept.
- **Chapter 10** now places more emphasis on the analysis of organizing and outlining speeches. A new animated video in Revel on organization helps students tie together different concepts from across the chapter.
- **Chapter 11** covers managing communication anxiety and delivering the speech. Major changes include a discussion on using social media to enhance presentations and one on the use of Prezi and PowerPoint as presentational aids, with additional discussions on the cognitive aspect of managing anxiety. A new video has been added in Revel on using mental and physical preparation to overcome anxiety when speaking in public, along with a video overview of the types of presentation aids students can use when giving a speech.
- **Chapter 12** is new to this edition and streamlines content on informative and persuasive speaking into one chapter. This thoroughly revised chapter offers a more condensed presentation of content related to connecting with others in public contexts, including how technology and social media aid speech development. The chapter includes outlines, speeches, greater emphasis on analyzing and applying information, and strategies for putting it all together for effective finished presentations. In Revel, students have two new self-assessments available to test their understanding of the subgoals of persuasion and logical appeals. New videos in Revel present examples of different genres of speeches: speeches about an event ("Vietnam Donut Dollies"), a concept ("Fear of Public Speaking"), a question of fact ("Education of Youth"), a question of value ("Honey"), and a question of policy ("Texting and Driving"). A new animated video on persuasive appeals also features a new video self-check quiz, and two additional new animated videos break down the key concepts of Monroe's motivated sequence and Maslow's heirarchy.
- **Chapter 13** is also new to the eleventh edition and merges two interpersonal communication chapters from prior editions to offer a more streamlined approach to this topic. The chapter provides a solid understanding of the significant theories (uncertainty management theory, social exchange theory, interpersonal needs theory, dialectical theory, and social penetration theory) related to interpersonal communication and addresses interpersonal communication competence and relationship maintenance strategies. In Revel, two new animated videos revisit the key topic of interpersonal communication competence and the issue of romantic relationships and self-disclosure.
- **Chapter 14** is a combination and thorough revision of Chapters 15 and 16 found in the tenth edition. This new, streamlined chapter covers group and team communication

more precisely, with new examples related to group communication as well as up-to-date research related to leadership, how groups function, and the role of group or team members. In Revel, a new video on effective group meetings both highlights key ideas from the chapter and presents real-world examples of the dynamics of group meetings. Another new animated video focuses on the issue of problem solving in groups.

- **Chapter 15** is a new chapter entitled "Connecting through Workplace Communication." The chapter takes the major features of the Appendix from the tenth edition and expands them to include aspects related to communication in the workplace as well as prepares students to think about what they have accomplished or will need to accomplish in their college journey to help them achieve their career goals. It guides students to life beyond their college education by explaining what they need to communicate with future employers.

Unique Features

- **MAKING EVERYDAY CONNECTIONS** We reinforce our "making connections" theme by bringing in student and other real-life examples illustrating our connections in today's world. Each chapter opens with a **"Making Everyday Connections"** scenario that describes communication situations or issues likely to be part of students' real-life everyday communication encounters, such as what to disclose and not to disclose on Facebook and other social networking sites or how texting is affecting family relationships. Each scenario is followed by thought-provoking questions that ask students to think about the issues and apply them to their own lives.

- **MAKING CONNECTIONS FOR SUCCESS** We live in a connected world. Communication helps us make daily connections with each other and with events around the world as they unfold. Technology allows communication to take many forms and has changed the avenues through which communication occurs and how it occurs on the Internet.

    The ever-changing array of technological options has added to the challenge of presenting and receiving messages—of communicating effectively with others. The eleventh edition of *Communication: Making Connections* focuses not only on the different communication channels available but also on the implications of media for our communication and for the quality of the messages we send and receive.

    "Making Connections for Success" boxes in each chapter are designed to encourage students to think critically about communication in their lives. Each box contains skill-building activities and stimulating questions to help students reflect on issues and their own communication behavior, and become more competent communicators. Many of these boxes are designed to emphasize the role and importance of technology in our interactions. In addition, we've expanded our discussions of communication via social media and have emphasized technology and its influence in numerous other "Making Connections for Success" boxes and narrative discussions. These discussions allow students to see how technology influences the messages we send and how it can both help and hinder competent communication.

MAKING EVERYDAY CONNECTIONS

Carly slowly walks into her apartment. She looks as if she has just seen a ghost. Tears form as she sits down on the sofa, and she begins to cry openly and uncontrollably.

Her friend Dana puts her arm around her and pats her on the shoulder gently. Carly looks at Dana. Carly's face and demeanor tell Dana something is really wrong, as if Carly's whole world has just come crashing down. Dana doesn't know what to say, so she continues to comfort Carly by holding her hand. Carly is unable to control her emotions or speak. Finally, Carly looks at Dana. Dana looks back, her face showing concern as if to say, "What is going on?"

Neither uttered one word as they held each other tightly, yet their expressions and touch said everything.

QUESTIONS TO THINK ABOUT

1. How does nonverbal communication make communication easier? How does it make communication more difficult?
2. Why do we give little or no thought to our nonverbal communication?
3. Why do you think nonverbal communication is considered more believable than verbal communication?
4. Explain what nonverbal communication is and is not.
5. What are the challenges of communicating emotions online or via text message? Are there risks?

MAKING CONNECTIONS FOR SUCCESS

What You Say Can Hurt You! It's All about Perception

The following quotation was given in an interview and reported in the *New York Times* when a candidate for the U.S. Senate was asked why she believed she would make a good senator:

"So I think in many ways, you know, we want to have all kinds of different voices, you know, representing us, and I think what I bring to it is, you know, my experience as a mother, as a woman, as a lawyer, you know."[2]

1. Based solely on what the person said in the interview, what are your initial perceptions of the candidate?

2. In what ways would your initial perceptions of the person change if you learned that in the course of the interview, she said, "you know" 142 times?
3. How would your perceptions of the person's communication alter if you found out that she had written seven books, including two on the Constitution and two on American politics; that she had graduated from Harvard University and Columbia Law School; and her family name is well known in national politics?
4. In what ways, if at all, would your perceptions change if you knew it was her first major interview and she was extremely nervous?

- **MAKING CONNECTIONS AS YOU STUDY** Numerous pedagogical aids help students review, retain, and master important chapter concepts. Boxed features reinforce the "making connections" theme throughout, demonstrating how communication connects us in a variety of contexts: the workplace, family, network of friends, community, school, public communication settings, the Internet, and across cultures. They provide students with real-life examples and help them better understand how to send and receive communication more competently. In addition, each chapter contains one or more "Guidelines" box. These guidelines clearly and quickly summarize each chapter or section's key skill-oriented concepts.

- **GOAL-ORIENTED LEARNING OBJECTIVES** Learning objectives appear at the start of each chapter, and each learning objective is tied to a specific section within the chapter. Thus, student learning is guided by learning objectives, which highlight specific communication concepts, principles, and practices for students. In addition, chapter summaries highlight each objective and provide a handy way to review the chapter and ensure that objectives have been met.

- **PEDAGOGICAL AIDS** This edition, like previous ones, retains our commitment to the "making connections" theme—helping students understand communication as the means of connecting with others. We have added and updated research to support our theme, and we have also included several features:

  - **SAMPLE SPEECH EXCERPTS** In Chapter 10, a sample informative speech is used to illustrate both the full-sentence and the presentational outlines. In Chapter 11, a sample outline illustrates the effective use of PowerPoint for an informative speech. In Chapter 12, the sample speech from Chapter 10 is repeated, this time to illustrate an analysis and evaluation of informational speaking. In Chapter 12, a sample outline for a persuasive speech illustrates comprehensive analysis and evaluation of persuasive speaking.

  - **CHAPTER SUMMARIES AND DISCUSSION STARTERS** Chapter summaries are organized by learning objectives to help students focus on what they should have learned and understood in each chapter. They help students clarify what should be gained from reading each chapter. Discussion starter questions can be used as a springboard for classroom discussions as well as for individual study and review.

  - **GUIDELINES** Boxed guidelines succinctly summarize key skill-oriented concepts.

Guidelines

CHECK YOUR PERCEPTIONS: COMPETENT COMMUNICATORS DO!

1. **Separate fact from assumptions.** It is easy to accept assumptions, but we must realize that assumptions are not facts, nor are they always accurate. When we make assumptions, we are drawing conclusions with little or no basis in fact. Thus, we should label assumptions so that when we communicate them, they are differentiated from facts.

2. **Recognize your personal biases.** We all have biases that can influence our perceptions, and we must be careful that those biases don't inaccurately slant our perceptions. We should always qualify, when recognized, that our biases may have influenced our communication about events, objects, and people.

3. **Remember that perceptions, especially first impressions, are not always accurate.** This is important because when we make judgments based on limited information or our first impression, we may cling to that impression or perception as if that is all there is to know.

4. **Recognize that people from different cultural backgrounds do not always attach the same meanings to events, objects, and people.** It is important to recognize that not everyone sees the world

as you do, and this is especially true of people who come from different cultural backgrounds. For example, it is common for someone who lives in Europe or the Middle East to walk with someone of the same sex holding hands or kissing them on the cheek. How this might be perceived depends on differences in cultural norms or background.

5. **Remember that perceptions are a function of the perceiver, the perceived, and the situation in which the perception occurs.** To ensure accuracy, it is important to understand that perception is in the eye of the beholder, to understand what is perceived and why, and to take into account the situation or context of the perception.

6. **Don't be afraid to communicate to verify your perceptions.** It is important that you ask questions and seek additional information to ensure the accuracy of your perceptions. You do not want to leave yourself open to interpretations or misunderstandings that could be avoided.

7. **Be willing to admit misperceptions and to change them when necessary.** It is important to correct misperceptions and admit when perceptions are not accurate. It is also the responsibility of the perceiver to make changes when errors or misunderstandings occur.

Organization of the Content

As in all previous editions, the chapters are arranged to provide a practical and workable approach to teaching the fundamentals of communication. Part One, "Making Connections through Communication," provides the necessary background and basic principles for all communication. Part Two, "Connecting in Public and Relational Contexts," helps students develop their speaking skills as they learn to select a topic, analyze an audience, gather and use supporting and clarifying materials, organize and outline speech material, deliver a speech with confidence, and effectively inform and persuade an audience. It also describes communication in relationships, small groups, and teams, and prepares students' futures in the workplace.

Foundations are presented first. Then public communication and relational skills are discussed. We discuss public communication skills early, before interpersonal communication, because we believe the confidence and skills of public speaking are fundamental to all communication. To communicate effectively throughout life—whether socially, on the job, in one-to-one situations, in small groups, or before an audience—a person must be able to communicate with confidence, support and clarify his or her thoughts, organize information, analyze those with whom he or she is communicating, and inform and persuade effectively.

This sequence of concepts is also based on the recognition that students in an introductory communication course must master a great deal of information before they give a speech, but, because of time constraints, they need to begin preparing and presenting speeches as early in the term as possible. Introducing public speaking skills first provides a more even balance between speech presentations and other classroom activities, and curbs the tendency to focus exclusively on speech making at the end of the term.

Considerable demands are placed on instructors and students of introductory communication courses, and a wide variety of ways to teach these courses are available. Instructors should feel free to organize the course in whatever way is appropriate and meets the needs of their students.

Revel Combo Card

The Revel Combo Card provides an all-in-one access code and loose-leaf print reference (delivered by mail).

Instructor and Student Resources

Key instructor resources include an **Instructor's Resource Manual** (ISBN 978-0-13-487456-2), **Test Bank**, (ISBN 978-0-13-487459-3), and **PowerPoint Presentation Package** (ISBN 978-0-13-487458-6). These supplements are available at www.pearsonhighered.com/irc (instructor login required). MyTest online test generating software (ISBN 978-0-13-487460-9) is available at www.pearsonmytest.com (instructor login required).

For a complete listing of the instructor and student resources available with this product, please visit the *Communication: Making Connections* e-Catalog page at www.pearsonhighered.com/communication.

Pearson MediaShare

Share, assign, and assess a variety of media easily and meaningfully in Revel using Shared Media and VideoQuiz assignments.

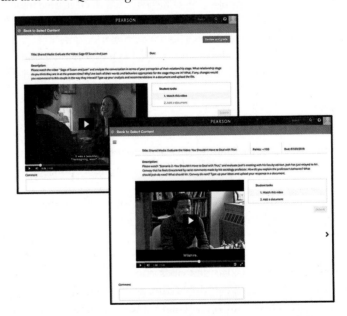

Using the best of MediaShare functionality and designed with learners and learning in mind, Shared Media assignments allow instructors and students to share and engage with videos and other media, including recorded performances in Public Speaking. And VideoQuiz assignments transform a typically passive activity into an active learning experience. Rather than watching a video and then answering questions, students engage with instructional content while it's being delivered.

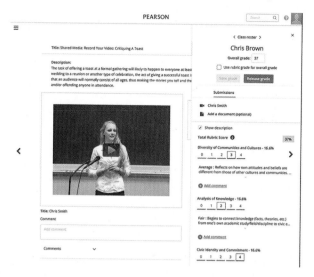

- Use Shared Media to assign or view speeches, video-based assignments, role plays, and more in a variety of formats, including video, Word, PowerPoint, and Excel.
- Assess students using customizable, Pearson-provided rubrics, or create your own around classroom goals, learning outcomes, or department initiatives.

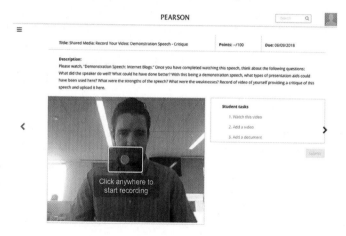

- Create assignments for students with options for full-class viewing and commenting or private comments between you and the student.
- Record video directly from a tablet, phone, or other webcam.
- Embed video from YouTube or Pearson Clips via assignments to incorporate current events into the classroom experience.

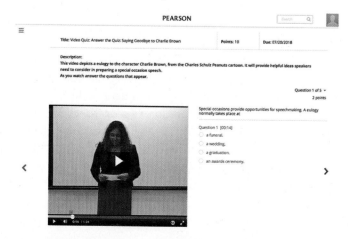

- Set up time-stamped quiz questions on video assignments to ensure students master concepts and interact and engage with the media.
- Import grades into most learning management systems.
- Ensure a secure learning environment for instructors and students through robust privacy settings.

Acknowledgments

Numerous people have contributed to previous editions as well as this current edition. First and foremost are the students who used this title and shared their time and learning experiences with us, the instructors who patiently taught us about communication and life, the colleagues who shared their expertise with us, and the many graduate students who worked in our basic communication courses over the years.

Any new edition requires the talents and hard work of many people. We extend our appreciation to Kelli Smith and Kriss Timmpast, Assistant Directors of Career Planning and Placement at the University of Nebraska–Lincoln, for their review and guidance in the writing of parts of Chapter 15, along with Bill Watts, the Director of Career Planning and Placement Services at the University of Nebraska, for his permission to use much of the materials in Chapter 15. A very special thanks goes to Jeff Child, at Kent State University, for his insightful review and suggestions regarding Chapters 8, 13, and 14. Special thanks go to Marilyn Shaw, instructor of the Introductory Communication course at the University of Northern Iowa, for assisting with the Instructor's Manual. We also wish to thank Tiffany Wang, University of Montevallo, along with Brigit Talkington, University of Nebraska, Lincoln, for their help in revising the Test Bank. In addition to Wang and Talkington, many other faculty and graduate students helped us by providing ideas and suggestions too numerous to mention here, but especially Jenna Abetz, Elissa Arterburn, Chase Aunspach, Diane Badzinski, Arleen Bejerano, Karla Bergen, Brandon Boatwright, Mary Bort, Dawn Braithwaite, Ann Burnett, John Caughlin, Kane Click, Susan Cusmano, Linda Dickmeyer, Sara Dirks, Josh Ewalt, Gus Friedrich, Marianne Glaser, Getachew Godana, Bobbie Harry, Haley Kranstuber Horstman, Christina Ivey, Adam Jones, Jack Kay, Jody Koenig Kellas, Karen Lee, Ronald Lee, Kristen Lucas, Rob Patterson, Drew McGukin, Michelle Maresh-Fuehrer, Carol Morgan, Bill Mullen, Richard Murphy, Emily Lamb Normand, Damien Pfister, Jack Sargent, Kaitlyn Dernovich, Paul Schrodt, Jordan Soliz, Sara Steimel, Blair Thompson, Shawn Wahl, William (Bill) Wilmot, and Nicole Zumbach.

A very special thank you goes to Sarah Johansen, a University of Nebraska student, for providing us with her informative and persuasive speeches, which appear in Chapters 10 and 12. Sarah not only provided outlines and transcripts of her speeches but also allowed us to video-record them.

We thank all the undergraduate and graduate students at University of Nebraska–Lincoln, University of Northern Iowa, and Clemson University who provided resources and examples. We are especially grateful to the following honor students at Wayne State College in Wayne, Nebraska, who provided scenarios and boxed information for this edition: Alyssa Bish, Lindsey Boyum, Spencer J. Bradley, Tabitha Burger, Kelsey Doht, Logan J. Fischer, Kylie Funk, Kjirsten Gedwillo, Amanda E. Gubbels, Alexander Hamilton, Ashley Nicole Hammond, Jessica Henderson, Brittany Hermsen, Cody Howser, Callie Jean Janke, Mitchell Tyler Johnson, Clarissa Kracl, Zachary D. Leitschuck, Cassie Minor, Sean Neal, Rachel Niedbalski, Sarah Plessing, Sydney G. Pokorny, Tiffinie Randall, Elisa Rempe, Michala Remund, Kella Rodiek, Molly B. Schroeder, Stephanie Ann Schumacher, Samantha Siewert, Bonnie Sisco, Chelsea Simmerman, Chris Varney, Stephanie Whitlow, Courtney Wiese, and Zachary J. Zobel.

We gratefully acknowledge all those at Pearson who had a hand in getting our manuscript into book form. We also thank Karon Bowers, Director-Courseware Portfolio Management, for her continued support, even though she continues to be a Longhorn, which is the only fault we have been able to identify! We extend a very special thank you and appreciation to Edward Dodd, our development editor, for his excellence and patience in working with each of us. He truly is a professional at his craft.

The publishing of any book requires people dedicated to high quality, and this edition of our book is no exception. We thank all those who participated in the review process of the first ten editions of the book:

Ritta Abell, Morehead State University; Bob Alexander, Bossier Parish Community College; David Allison, Liberty College; Philip M. Backlund, Central Washington University; William Patrick Barlow, Madison Area Technical College; Matt Barton, Southern Utah University; Marty Birkholt, Creighton University; Barbara L. Breaclen, Lane Community College; Scott Britten, Tiffin University; Allan R. Broadhurst, Cape Cod Community College; Michael Bruner, University of North Texas; Diane O. Casagrande, West Chester University; Patricia Comeaux, University of North Carolina at Wilmington; Juanita E. Dailey, University of Rio Grande; Linda Y. Devenish, Ithaca College; Carley H. Dodd, Abilene Christian University; Terrence Doyle, Northern Virginia Community College; Sean M. Dunn, Bridgewater College; Richard C. Emanuel, University of Montevallo; Skip Eno, University of Texas at San Antonio; Jeanine Fassl, University of Wisconsin at Whitewater; Julia Fennell, Community College of Allegheny County, South Campus; Mary C. Forestieri, Lane Community College; Robert E. Frank, Morehead State University; Joseph Ganakos, Lee College; Angela Gibson, Shelton State Community College; Anne Grissom, Mountain View College; Kelby K. Halone, Clemson University; Roxanne Heimann, University of Northern Iowa; Ted Hindermarsh, Brigham Young University; Colleen Hogan-Taylor, University of Washington; David D. Hudson, Golden West College; Mary Lee Hummert, University of Kansas; David A. Humphrey, College of DuPage; Stephen K. Hunt, Illinois State University; Karla Kay Jensen, Nebraska Wesleyan University; Kathryn C. Jones, Northern Virginia Community College, Annandale Campus; Erik Kanter, Virginia Tech University; Alyssa Kauffman, Suffolk County Community College; Thomas J. Knutson, California State University at Sacramento; Charles J. Korn, Northern Virginia Community College; Amy Lenoce, Naugatuck Valley Community College; Donald L. Loeffler, Western Carolina University; Louis A. Lucca, La Guardia Community College (CUNY); Mary Y. Mandeville, Oklahoma State University; Corinne E. Morris, Northeast Community College; William L. Mullen, Liberty University; Kay E. Neal, University of Wisconsin, Oshkosh; Dan O'Rourke, Ashland University; Nan Peck, Northern Virginia Community College; Kelly Petkus, Austin Community College; Sandra E. Presar, West Virginia Wesleyan College; Marlene M. Preston, Virginia Polytechnic Institute and State University; Richard G. Rea, University of Arkansas; Marc E. Routhier, Frostburg State College; Thomas Ruddick, Edison Community College; Jared Saltzman, Bergen Community College; Susan Schuyler, University of Wisconsin, La Crosse; Marilyn M. Shaw, University of Northern Iowa; Donald B. Simmons, Asbury College; Cheri J. Simonds, Illinois State University; Donald Smith, Northern Virginia College; Theresa Tiller, Rose State College; Charlotte Toguchi, Kapiolani Community College; Mary Anne Trasciatti, Hofstra University; Beth Waggenspack, Virginia Polytechnic Institute and State University; Catherine Egley Waggoner, Ohio State University; Gretchen Aggertt Weber, Horry-Georgetown Technical College; Kathie A. Webster, Northwest Missouri State University; Larry A. Weiss, University of Wisconsin at Oshkosh; Cherie C. While, Muskingum Area Technical College; Cora Ann Williams, Lone Star Kingwood; Karen Wolf, Suffolk Community College; David W. Worley, Indiana State University

Finally, thanks to those who provided analysis of the tenth edition and made recommendations and suggestions for this new edition:

Rachelle Biderman, Kirkwood Community College
Victoria Ellison, Henderson State University
Peter Galarneau, West Virginia Wesleyan College
LaKresha Graham, Rockhurst University
Darren Linvill, Clemson University
Jodi Hallsten Lyczak, Illinois State Univeristy
Jacki Brucher Moore, Kirkwood Community College
Whitney Pisani, Collin College
Elizabeth Ribarsky, University of Illinois Springfield

Some Concluding Comments...and a Request for Your Thoughts

It is time to ask for *your* help again. As we have in previous editions, we spared no effort to make this new edition the best ever. Although we are always striving for perfection, we more often than not fall short on some things. There is always room for improvement! We sincerely request your comments. If there's something you feel can be improved, please let us know. Write, call, fax, or email us at one of the contacts below. We will listen and respond to your comments as quickly as possible. Thank you in advance for your help.

William (Bill) J. Seiler
Department of Communication Studies
University of Nebraska
Lincoln, NE 68588-0329
Phone: 402-472-2197
Fax: 402-472-6921
bseiler@unl.edu

Melissa L. Beall
Department of Communication Studies
University of Northern Iowa
Cedar Falls, IA 50613-0139
Phone: 319-273-2992
Fax: 319-273-7356
Melissa.Beall@uni.edu

Joseph (Joe) P. Mazer
Department of Communication
Clemson University
Clemson, SC 29634-0533
Phone: 864-656-1567
Fax: 864-656-0599
jmazer@clemson.edu

About the Authors

Bill Seiler is a professor in the Department of Communication Studies, University of Nebraska–Lincoln, where he has taught since 1972. He was department chair for over 20 years and now teaches and was the director of the introductory course for over 45 years. The Undergraduate Leadership Award was renamed the William J. Seiler Undergraduate Leadership Award to honor him and his leadership of the department. Other honors include Outstanding Educator of America, Outstanding University and College Teacher by the Nebraska Communication Association, Outstanding Young Alumni and Distinguished Alumni Awards from the University of Wisconsin at Whitewater, and 2002 Boss of the Year Award. Bill received the 2013 National Communication Association's Basic Course Division's "Distinguished Faculty" award and was named to the 2013 Central States Association's "Hall of Fame." In 2015, he received the National Communication Associations' "Wallace A. Bacon Lifetime Teaching Excellence Award,"and in 2016 he received the "Robert J. Kibler Memorial Award" for personal and profession qualities of dedication to excellence, commitment to the profession, concern for others, vision of what could be, acceptance of diversity, and forthrightness. Bill earned a bachelor's degree in education from the University of Wisconsin at Whitewater, a master of arts from Kansas State University, and a doctorate from Purdue University. He is an experienced educator, consultant, researcher, and author in the area of communication and has an adjunct appointment in the Education & Human Sciences College.

He is an avid golfer who plays every chance he gets, which unfortunately for him is never enough. He loves his Nebraska Huskers. Bill and his wife Kathi's family includes two daughters, Dana and Dionne; two sons-in-law, Lee and Wade; two grandchildren, Grant and Will; and three step-grandchildren, Zach, Stephanie, and Taylor.

Melissa Beall is a professor in the Communication Studies Department and a member of the teacher education faculty at the University of Northern Iowa (UNI). Dr. Beall, a proud Husker fan, received all three degrees from the University of Nebraska–Lincoln. Her areas of expertise include listening, intercultural listening, intercultural communication, communication and technology, and communication theory. She teaches oral communication, listening, language and communication, public speaking, critical thinking, college teaching, communication and technology, intercultural communication, interpersonal communication, and communication theory.

Dr. Beall has served on many UNI committees and chaired the Graduate Faculty. Her honors include the 2007 Iowa Board of Regents Faculty Excellence recipient and the 2014 UNI Distinguished Scholar Award, she was inducted into the Central States Communication Association Hall of Fame in 2012, she was named the International Listening Association's Outstanding Listening Educator in 2008, and she was also inducted into the International Listening Association Hall of Fame. She was the recipient of the National Communication Association's (NCA's) Marcella E. Oberle Outstanding K–12 Teaching as a high school teacher, and in 2016 she received NCA's Donald H. Ecroyd Award for Outstanding Teaching in Higher Education. Dr. Beall was recognized as a Distinguished Faculty member by NCA's Basic Course Division and received the Iowa Communication Association Citation Award for contributions to Iowa and the communication discipline in 2014. She has served on numerous editorial boards; has presented over 700 papers, programs, and workshops; is a past president of the Iowa Communication Association and the Nebraska Speech Communication and Theatre Association; and is vice president of the World Communication Association, the Pacific and

Asian Communication Association, and the International Association of Communication Sciences. She is the current Executive Chair of the Global Listening Centre and speaks about listening all over the world. She was an officer in her local American Association of University Professors (AAUP) chapter and is a past president of the Central States Communication Association and of the International Listening Association; she has also served as an officer in many divisions of the National Communication Association.

Joseph Mazer is an associate professor and chair of the Department of Communication at Clemson University. At Clemson, he is Director of the Social Media Listening Center, an interdisciplinary research lab and teaching facility that provides a platform to listen, measure, and engage in more than 650 million sources of social media conversations. Joe's research interests include communication in teaching and learning contexts, social media and new technologies, communication in interpersonal relationships, and measurement issues and trends in communication research. He has authored or coauthored over 70 research articles, book chapters, and books and has been ranked in the top 1 percent of prolific scholars in the communication discipline for the past 10 years.

A July 2017 study named him among the top five influential scholars in instructional communication. His research has been funded by the National Science Foundation and discussed in media outlets, including *USA Today*, *Chronicle of Higher Education*, and *ESPN*. He has received international, regional, university-wide, and departmental recognition for outstanding teaching. Joe is a past recipient of the Outstanding New Teacher Award from the Central States Communication Association and the Outstanding Professor of the Year Award from Clemson University's Department of Communication undergraduate student body.

Joe is an active member of the National Communication Association and Central States Communication Association, where he has held several leadership roles. In addition to serving on editorial boards for several journals in the communication discipline, he is serving a three-year term as Editor of the *Basic Communication Course Annual* and recently completed a term as Consulting Editor for Forums for *Communication Education*. Joe received his Ph.D. in communication studies from Ohio University, a Master's degree in communication from Illinois State University, and a bachelor's degree in mass communication from Mansfield University. He is the inaugural recipient of the Outstanding Young Graduate Alumnus Award from the faculty in Illinois State University's School of Communication. Joe resides in Clemson, South Carolina, with his wife, Chrissy, and their children, Claire and Owen.

PART 1   MAKING CONNECTIONS THROUGH COMMUNICATION

CONNECTING PROCESS AND PRINCIPLES IN THE 21ST CENTURY

Fabio Formaggio/123RF

Smartphones, tablets, social media, and other technology allow us to communicate with friends and family and also make connections with people outside our usual social circle. In this chapter we define *communication*, explain the fundamental principles of communication, define the essential components of the communication process, and explore the different types of communication.

→ CHAPTER OUTLINE AND LEARNING OBJECTIVES

Communication: Making Connections

1.1 **Explain** how communication competence allows you to make connections with the outside world.

What Is Communication?

1.2 **Define** communication.

Why Should We Study Communication?

1.3 **Identify** four reasons for studying communication.

Principles of Communication

1.4 **Explain** the fundamental principles of communication.

Essential Components of Communication

1.5 **Define** the essential components in the communication process.

Types of Communication

1.6 **Differentiate** the various types of communication: intrapersonal, interpersonal (including group), public, mass, and communication via social media.

Misconceptions about Communication

1.7 **Summarize** five common myths about communication.

MAKING EVERYDAY CONNECTIONS

Think for a moment about how many social media tools you have at your fingertips: Snapchat, Facebook, Twitter, Tinder, LinkedIn, Pinterest, Tumblr, Instagram, and Flickr—the list could go on. Without a doubt, there are many benefits to these tools, but there are some drawbacks as well. Nearly all social media tools allow us to make fast connections with people. However, some social media require us to remain anonymous, which can cause some people to send messages that others may perceive as hurtful and offensive. Apps like Tinder allow for online dating, but the speed with which connections are made can lead to dangerous encounters with people who have ulterior motives for using the tool.[1]

While drawbacks to using social media exist, the benefits can often far outweigh its consequences. Presidents Barack Obama and Donald Trump each changed the nature of political campaigning. Obama's campaign made extensive use of YouTube, blogs, tweets, and other tools on the Internet to help Obama get elected. Trump used Twitter during the campaign to galvanize support and attack his opponents directly, which helped in his election. As president, Trump often uses Twitter to get more attention for his messages and to avoid the mainstream media's filtering of them. Pope Francis, head of the Roman Catholic Church, maintains Twitter accounts in several languages to connect with people around the globe. The pope justifies his use of social media because its key characteristic—is "a network not of wires but of people."[2]

U.S. presidents, a pope, and most students and professors are highly dependent on social media to communicate and connect in everyday life and remain in touch with family, friends, and others. Snapchat users create and send over three billion photos and videos each day[3] and view more than 10 billion videos daily.[4] Facebook has, on average, over two billion monthly active users worldwide with over one billion people using Facebook on their mobile device each day. Facebook users upload over 300 million photos each day. That's over two billion pictures per week![5] The Pew Research Center found that texting is the single most used feature on a smartphone; it also found that 18- to 24-year-olds, on average, send and receive almost four thousand text messages per month—or about 130 per day.[6] Where will this communication lead? How will it affect each of us as communicators?

QUESTIONS TO THINK ABOUT

1. Discuss both the positive and negative characteristics of technology on communication.

2. In what ways does the time you spend on social media affect your productivity?

3. How much time do you spend daily listening to others in face-to-face conversations? What does this tell you?

4. Explain the differences between an effective and ineffective communicator.

5. Create a set of rules for using technology in the classroom, in the workplace, and in social settings.

6. Describe why you believe you are an effective communicator in face-to-face situations and through social media.

Communication: Making Connections

1.1 **Explain** how communication competence allows you to make connections with the outside world.

We live in a connected world. Everywhere, we see others talking, texting, or listening to music on their cell phones. At work, at school, while doing homework, or while socializing, we are connected to the Internet. The Internet is *the* source of information on every aspect of our lives, from resources for class papers and presentations to emails that allow us to contact our professors, to Snapchat, which allows us to present ourselves in the ways we choose and to connect with our friends and family. In our free time, we are connected to the Internet, TV, cell phones, music, or video games. Life is a series of connections, mediated or face-to-face. Despite these connections, we do not really reflect much on how we make and maintain them. Communication is something we often take for granted. We talk or text, for example, therefore, we communicate. Nevertheless, can we *really* communicate effectively just because we can talk or text? What is competent communication? For our purposes, **communication competence** is the ability to communicate effectively and is characterized by skills and understandings that enable communicators to exchange messages accurately and successfully.

communication competence
The ability to communicate effectively, characterized by skills and understandings that enable communicators to exchange messages accurately and successfully.

Communication helps us *make connections* with each other and with our world. We communicate daily with many people in a variety of situations. We listen to professors, employers, coworkers, family members, friends, and many others every hour. We continually text our friends and family. Snapchat allows us to share quick videos with friends and family. With Facebook, we can tell the world how we're feeling and connect with others, whether close or distant. Twitter provides a way to stay socially linked in 280 characters or less. Whatever your cultural background, learning style, or geographical location, you will find that your communication proficiency can mean greater academic success, improved relationships, a better job, and greater satisfaction in your life.

When you stop to think about a typical day in your life, you will discover you spend a lot of time *making connections*. Moreover, you will realize communication allows you to make those connections. Communication takes many forms and you, as a communicator, must have a wide range of behaviors to allow you to adapt to the various situations in which you find yourself. In this text, we provide a variety of ideas and approaches to help you learn more about the exciting ways people make connections through communication in the 21st century. This chapter presents the concepts and processes of effective communication in everyday life. We examine the essential components and principles, the types and contexts, and the myths about communication. You will have the opportunity to think about the role communication has in an increasingly multicultural and technological world. We will provide hands-on activities and reflective questions to apply to your personal life and to use communication to *make connections* in all areas of your life.

What Is Communication?

1.2 **Define** communication.

What is communication? What do we mean when we say that communication occurred? How do we know when we have communicated effectively? How do we use communication to *make connections* in our lives? The answers to these questions require an understanding of the principles and process of communication as well as some guidelines for achieving success.

Generally, we can say communication is a process that allows us to share and create meaning. More formally, we define **communication** as the simultaneous sharing and creating of meaning through human symbolic interaction. It might seem obvious, but it bears repeating: Communication is complex. If it were simple, people would have few difficulties with it, and we would not need to study it! This complex and challenging process is critical, however, to making connections in all of our relationships, from the professional to the romantic and everything in between.

communication

The simultaneous sharing and creating of meaning through human symbolic interaction.

Communication as a discipline has existed for thousands of years. Scholars in ancient Greece and Rome recognized communication as a powerful means of influence. Classical rhetoricians studied the principles of effectively composing and delivering persuasive speeches. In the Middle Ages in Western Europe, religious leaders such as St. Augustine developed written and spoken communication, including letter writing and preaching, to spread the Christian faith. In the Western world, public speaking, storytelling, and debating have been important means of changing public opinion and persuading others to take political action. African, Eastern, and Middle Eastern cultures, too, have long emphasized the importance of effective communication. According to intercultural communication scholars Larry Samovar and Richard Porter, "the Buddha advised his disciples to avoid 'harsh speech.'"[7] Communication colleagues in China, Indonesia, Japan, Korea, Malaysia, Mexico, Peru, Portugal, and Spain confirm that the study of communication is an ancient and valued tradition in their cultures.

MAKING CONNECTIONS FOR SUCCESS

Communication Competence

Communication is central to our ideas of a "good" life. Communication is identified as a way to make the world a better, safer place. In the United States, numerous public figures are competent or effective communicators. For example, Presidents Ronald Reagan, Bill Clinton, and Barack Obama were considered strong and effective communicators. Reagan, on leaving the presidency, reportedly said, "I've been called 'The Great Communicator.' If I am it's because I have great things to communicate." Media figures such as Ellen DeGeneres, Rush Limbaugh, Anderson Cooper, and Dr. Phil have award-winning talk shows drawing large audiences because each knows how to connect with others. Think about these examples and then answer the following questions:

1. Create a list of five specific qualities of a "competent communicator."

2. Which of the five qualities on your list and the lists of others in your class are the most important for successful communication? Which of these qualities do you believe you possess?

3. How will the ability to communicate effectively affect your life socially, in the classroom, and in your career?

4. Whom do you consider a competent communicator? Describe what makes her or him competent.

communications

Generally used to denote the delivery systems for mediated and mass communication.

While *communication* refers to the process by which we create and share meanings, **communications** is the word generally used to denote the delivery systems for mediated and mass communication. People often confuse the two words, but they are quite different. Communication is what you and your friend do when you discuss the next speech assignment or what your plans will be for the weekend. Communications refers to the systems such as telephone lines used to disseminate information.

According to the definition used in this text, communication involves a range of behaviors and occurs in a variety of situations: public and private, business and social, home and school, formal and informal. The diverse situations are all linked by one common thread—*human symbolic interaction*, or people using a symbol system (language) to share thoughts, feelings, beliefs, attitudes, customs, and ideas. As you read this text, you will learn about human symbolic interaction as it occurs within and among individuals, groups, organizations, cultures, and co-cultures. You will discover more about the nature of the communication *process*: listening; thinking; speaking in public settings; speaking in small-group settings; and speaking with one, two, or a small number of people in social settings. Your ability to communicate effectively by using speech will be one of the determining factors for your success in the classroom, in the workplace, and in your personal life. Being an effective communicator saves time, makes life more enjoyable, allows people to establish and maintain relationships, and facilitates accomplishing personal goals.

Why Should We Study Communication?

1.3 **Identify** four reasons for studying communication.

Although you have communicated for many years, you probably have not had the opportunity to learn about communication competence. The ability to communicate might seem natural because, unless disabilities are present, most of us readily develop speaking skills. Nevertheless, the ability to *communicate* (not simply to utter words) is a learned ability; the process of becoming a competent communicator is a difficult, lifelong project. You can make progress quickly, however, if you work hard to learn the principles and concepts and then apply them in everyday situations. These skills will enable you to reap benefits in career development, ethical behavior, and the promotion of positive relationships among people of diverse cultural backgrounds.

In addition, technology is so much a part of our lives and its influence is constantly changing how we communicate.

Communication and Our Technological Society

Can you remember a time when you did not rely on some form of technology to communicate? Your answer to this question is most likely a definite no. Even if you reflect back to when you were an infant, your parents may have placed a two-way baby monitor by your crib to alert them when you started crying. In many ways, that two-way monitor was probably your first interaction with the rapidly developing world of communication and technology. Today, the baby monitor is gone, but you rely on a host of technological tools to remain connected with the people in your life. We use **social media**—highly accessible technologies that facilitate communication, interaction, and connection with others.

The way technology has sped up the pace of communication adds to the challenge of both presenting and receiving meaningful messages. We use social media to remain connected with others in our **social network**—a group of individuals who are connected by friendship, family, common interests, beliefs, or knowledge.

Our social networks are now larger than ever and significantly more complex than those of our ancestors. We rely heavily on Facebook to remain connected with our friends across the country and around the world. We text our friends to check in and maybe make plans for later in the day; we send videos to friends through Snapchat; we update the world (our followers) through tweets on Twitter; we may get breaking news alerts on our iPhones or other smartphones. Perhaps most fascinating, we can do *all* of these things in a matter of seconds from desktop computers, laptops, and smartphones. These social media may constitute the bulk of what we use to communicate with others. No matter where we are, we connected to social networks and world events.

Social media makes it possible for us to experience historic events just moments after they occur, sometimes even *while* they are occurring. In essence, social media enable us to experience events as they happen anywhere in the world. For example,

social media
Highly accessible technologies that facilitate communication, interaction, and connection with others.

social network
A group of individuals who are connected by friendship, family, common interests, beliefs, or knowledge.

MAKING CONNECTIONS FOR SUCCESS
How Do You Remain Connected?

Most of us cannot begin to imagine life without a smartphone. A tweeted image first captured the forced miracle landing of US Airways flight 1549 in the Hudson River. Biz Stone and Evan Williams conceived of Twitter as a basic communication tool providing social networking applications. It has grown into one of the "world's most valuable real-time information caches." Twitter has now evolved into a powerful new communication tool. Regional emergency preparedness organizations are looking at Twitter as a way to reach millions of people during a disaster. NASA is using it to update interested parties about the status of space shuttle flights. Through our Facebook profiles, we present what we want to the world. Snapchat lets us take photos and record videos and quickly share them with people—before they are automatically deleted. LinkedIn allows us to make contacts with people in our profession or those in the profession to which we aspire. It can help us get recommendations as well as networking

possibilities. Facebook was initially created for college students but is now populated by people of all ages (including your authors), who use it to maintain connections with friends and colleagues both near and far. With that in mind, answer the following questions and share them with friends and/or classmates to compare your stories:

1. In what ways do you use various social media platforms to communicate and maintain relationships?

2. What rules do you follow when communicating through social media to establish and maintain relationships?

3. Provide two or three specific recommendations you would give to someone using social media related to establishing and maintaining a relationship.

4. How is communication via social media easier or more difficult than face-to-face communication with family and friends?

David Grossman/Alamy Stock Photo

Technology allows us to make connections with each other and with the world. At the same time, the many communication tools available sometimes make our messages less personal than they would be in face-to-face communication. Social media are indeed changing our way of communicating and how we connect with and relate to others.

social media brings natural disasters such as hurricanes, earthquakes and tornadoes to us as the event or events are occurring. We use digital cameras on our computers or smartphones to send images or to visit face-to-face with people around the globe. If you happen to be in the right place at the right time, witnessing a news event with a smartphone camera, your image, words, or voice may be instantaneously transmitted to others. Consider Timothy McIntosh, who tweeted a photo of Texas nursing home residents in waist deep water in the midst of Hurricane Harvey. This was an eye-opening image of a storm that ended up dumping nearly 50 inches of rain in certain areas of southern Texas. McIntosh's tweet quickly went viral and led first responders to the stranded nursing home residents. His tweet saved their lives.

The sheer volume of communication presented through social media can seem overwhelming. How does a competent communicator choose the appropriate channel and materials from among many options? What does technology do to the quality of one's messages? Does social media harm or help the quality of interactions? These questions are some you will need to address, and this text will provide guidelines and ideas to help answer them. Those who take time to learn and practice the principles of sound communication will best utilize social media to develop and maintain connections with others.

Communication and Career Development

Most of us aspire to have successful and satisfying jobs in our chosen career fields. We enter college to better ourselves and to prepare for our future lives. Communication, whether we agree or not, plays an important role in our success. Leaders in education, business, and industry have identified several life skills critical to success in the workforce, and communication is one of the most valued areas of expertise. For example, several recent studies[8] reinforce what previous research had already shown: Employers want workers at all levels who know how to communicate and relate to others both verbally and in writing. They want workers who are good listeners; have nonverbal skills such as eye contact, hand gestures, and effective tone; show confidence; are concise and open-minded; and give appropriate feedback. Finally, employers want workers who are flexible and able to adapt to new situations on the job, and have a strong work ethic and initiative.

In other words, effective workplace communicators can explain ideas clearly and give clear directions. Effective communicators are good listeners who work harmoniously with others and represent their companies well in small- and large-group settings. Too often, employers believe these skills are lacking in their employees. Introductory courses in communication, such as this one, focus on these skills.

Employers want workers who can speak effectively, listen carefully and efficiently, and think critically. Strong communication skills are vital to today's global workplace.

Andrey_Popov/Shutterstock

Personnel directors have described their needs regarding prospective employees as follows: Send me people who know how to speak, listen, and think, and I will do the rest. I can train people in their specific job responsibilities, as long as they listen attentively, know how to think, and can express themselves well.[9] In fact, most careers involve contact with others and require the ability to communicate effectively. Business and industry often look for the most competent communicators when they hire new employees. Although some companies provide on-the-job training in communication skills, it is most advantageous to develop excellent

MAKING CONNECTIONS FOR SUCCESS
Your Communication Effectiveness in the Workplace

In the surveys cited in the text, executives indicate all employees need to improve their communication skills. The executives also noted greater flexibility and higher ethical standards should be a focus of career preparation. If a prospective employer asked you the following questions, how would you respond?

1. Describe the necessary skills of an effective communicator in the workplace.

2. Describe one instance in which you found yourself wishing that you were a better listener.

3. What areas of communication do you need to improve at school or work? How do you know you need to improve in these areas?

4. What anxieties about communication do you have? (James McCroskey and his colleagues developed the Personal Report of Communication Apprehension [PRCA] to help identify the strength of your communication anxiety. Try a web search on communication apprehension and complete a PRCA found on the web. We discuss communication apprehension more fully in the public speaking section, Chapters 8 through 12.)

---

speaking, listening, and analytical abilities before applying for a specific job that could launch or enhance your career.

Effective social media skills are vital for professional success. In fact, many employers and college professors acknowledge the ease of communication and access to information offered by electronic media. At the same time, some of those same people criticize the poor spelling and damage done to the quality of both written and oral messages. For text messages, "gr8" is fine. Using a similar message in work-related reports, memos, emails, or class papers, however, may result in a demotion, job loss, or a lower grade on a speech or paper. While some research suggests that communication through social media is as effective at building and maintaining relationships, given enough time,[10] other research indicates that it reduces social skills, harms society, and generally interferes with face-to-face communication.[11] Perhaps you share personal information via Facebook that you otherwise might not share face-to-face, but this is a double-edged sword in that employers search social networking sites to learn more about future employees and, on that basis, have rescinded interviews and job offers. A few tweets have cost some employees their jobs. Throughout this text, we provide suggestions on how to use social media effectively in your personal and professional life. For more in depth understanding of workplace communication and your future career see Chapter 15.

Communication and Ethical Behavior

All societies have ethical standards and ideals about what is right and what is wrong. In most societies, unethical behavior often carries a penalty when an ethical standard is violated. **Ethics** refers to an individual's system of moral principles. People have been removed from political office, lost their jobs, or been publicly chastised for violating ethical standards and codes. Such behaviors often involve unethical acts related to communication. Consider former White House communications director Anthony Scaramucci, who held his White House post for a mere 10 days. Days into the job, Scaramucci provoked controversy after an expletive-laden interview with *The New Yorker*, in which he made obscene and derogatory statements about several members of the Trump administration. Ten days after the announcement of his appointment, President Donald Trump fired him on the recommendation of the new White House chief of staff, General John F. Kelly.[12] As an additional example, financiers have received prison terms for participating in insider trading—using illegally obtained information to make money on the stock market. Sharing such information constitutes an illegal act of communication. Another unethical behavior is telling lies, whether

ethics
An individual's system of moral principles.

MAKING CONNECTIONS FOR SUCCESS
Communication Principles in the Workplace

Erin is working to build her professional brand. She developed a LinkedIn page and a professional Twitter account. She uses LinkedIn to connect with people who have similar professional interests. Since she works for an advertising agency, she typically shares news from the industry through her Twitter account. It's important for her to connect with colleagues across the country, so she regularly "favorites" and retweets the posts of those she follows. She is seeking opportunities to move up in her career and hopes that her social media connections with other advertising industry professionals helps her to do so:

1. How is Erin's drive to seek a new, higher-paying job likely to affect her communication with others through social media?
2. How might Erin change her online behavior? Is it ethical to do so?
3. What principles of communication are important in this example?
4. Compare some of your own workplace situations with those of others in your class. How did you see communication principles in these examples?

---

done to hurt someone else or to protect or enhance one's own position. Though politicians spring to mind as typical offenders in this category, the problem is more widespread: for instance, enhancing one's résumé to increase the chances of being hired or "borrowing" a friend's old term paper or speech to pass a course.

Sometimes people think they need to find so-called shortcuts to accomplish tasks, whether they involve questionable accounting procedures in business, insider trading to keep more money, or stealing ideas to complete a presentation or paper. **Plagiarism** is the use of another person's information, language, or ideas without citing the originator and making it appear the user is the originator. Technology allows us to find and use all kinds of information, but it also presents ethical dilemmas. Technology may tempt us to use someone else's work or perhaps information before carefully screening or evaluating it for authenticity or truthfulness. A quick search of the Internet provides numerous sources for A, B, or even C papers for a "minimal cost" and "minimal risks to you." While those papers can save time and effort, they can also cost you a passing grade or even a diploma from your institution.

plagiarism
The use of another person's information, language, or ideas without citing the originator and making it appear that the user is the originator.

The Internet creates more opportunity for plagiarism because of easy access to information. So many sites exist, with so much information, that people often believe they can go to a site, take what they want, use it as their own, and not get caught. Social media encourage plagiarism and make it more likely you will get caught. For example, on Twitter, communication is purposely short and fast. An initial tweet may properly attribute the original source, but as the message is retweeted, somewhere along the way the attribution can be lost. Plagiarism, in whatever form, is still unethical, and just as it has consequences in educational institutions, in the workplace, plagiarism and other unethical behaviors also come with consequences.

Ethical communicators speak responsibly and give credit to any sources contributing to their messages. An ethical communicator does not plagiarize and does not deceive. Aristotle, a Greek rhetorician (384–322 BC), suggested that communication was most powerful when the speaker's character, or *ethos* (ethical appeal), was engaged in presenting the truth.[13] (Chapter 12 further develops this concept.) Quintilian (ca. AD 35–100), another rhetorician, stated (before the days of inclusive language) that communication needed presentation by "a good man speaking well."[14]

An important distinction to make is that unethical communication may constitute effective communication, but it is not virtuous. For example, if a person persuades another to do something morally wrong, the communication has been effective but not virtuous. Unethical communication should never be condoned or accepted. We need a good deal of critical thinking in our attempt to be effective *and* ethical communicators who evaluate others' communication to determine its ethical content. Throughout this

MAKING CONNECTIONS FOR SUCCESS
Ethical Perspectives

Every few weeks, we hear examples of unethical behavior. In early 2017, Kellyanne Conway, counselor to President Donald Trump, participated in a *Fox News* interview where she urged consumers to buy fashion products marketed by Ivanka Trump, President Trump's daughter. Conway said, "Go buy Ivanka's stuff is what I would say. I'm going to give a free commercial here: Go buy it today, everybody; you can find it online." Federal ethics rules state employees of the government's executive branch cannot use their public office for personal gain or to endorse products or services on behalf of friends or relatives. The director of the Office on Government Ethics ruled in mid-February 2017 that "there is strong reason to believe" Conway violated the Standards of Ethical Conduct for Employees of the Executive Branch. The above example demonstrates not knowing the rules can easily lead to a violation of ethical standards by what is said.

1. Define in your own words what it means to be ethical.
2. Is ignorance of ethical standards an excuse for being unethical? Explain your response.
3. What actions have you taken when you discover someone has been unethical?
4. What policies does your college or university have when someone plagiarizes, cheats on an exam, or commits other breaches of ethics? What are the penalties for such ethics violations?

text, examples of ethical dilemmas and perspectives are presented to help you become more aware of the need for ethical communication behaviors.

Communication and Our Multicultural Society

Job transfers, changes in economic and political conditions, and numerous other factors cause people to move from place to place, often leaving their country of birth to settle elsewhere. Many countries are experiencing an increase in this trend. In the United States, for example, the population once characterized by a white majority with European roots is now a diverse mosaic comprising people of different ethnic and cultural backgrounds. In this environment, we can grow to appreciate the distinctions that make each culture unique as well as the interconnectedness shared by all, sometimes described as the global village. However, a great deal of knowledge, flexibility, and sensitivity is necessary if people of diverse cultural backgrounds are to communicate successfully and live well together.

Current demographic trends and projections in the United States create the necessity to interact successfully with people of all racial, ethnic, cultural, and religious heritages. See Table 1.1 for the 2010 and 2016 U.S. Census Bureau report about the demographic breakdown by race (all ages).[15,16]

Table 1.1   U.S. POPULATION BY RACE (2010 AND 2016)

Group	Population Numbers in 2010	Population Numbers in 2016
One Race	296,635,891	307,067,138
White	224,895,700	232,943,055
Black or African American	37,978,752	39,908,095
American Indian and Alaska Native	2,480,465	2,569,170
Asian	14,185,493	16,235,305
Hispanic or Latino/a	47,727,533	54,232,205
Native Hawaiian and Other Pacific Islander	491,673	546,255
Some Other Race	16,603,808	14,865,258
Two or More Races	7,329,381	9,447,883
Total Population	303,965,272	316,515,021

SOURCE: U.S. Census Bureau.

Table 1.1 translates to roughly the following 2016 percentages: 74 percent of the population is white, 17 percent is Hispanic or Latino or Latina, 13 percent is black or African American, 5 percent is Asian, and less than 1 percent is American Indian. Projections from the Census Bureau suggest a significant increase in Hispanic/Latino/a, black, and Asian numbers in the near future, with a decline or stable percentage for whites. The changes in "how we look" are already occurring in elementary schools and high schools, as well as college and university classrooms. Language differences complicate communication within many schools. Some kindergarten-through-twelfth-grade (K–12) schools on the East and West Coasts, as well as in other populous areas such as Chicago, Cincinnati, Dallas, and St. Louis, have students who speak 50 to 100 or more different native languages. College and university classrooms, too, have increasing numbers of students whose first language is not English, and each one's cultural and ethnic background affects the way these students communicate in the classroom, the residence hall, the supermarket, and the workplace.

Language structure influences and is influenced by culture. It takes a great deal of patience, understanding, and respect to learn to communicate effectively in situations involving different languages and social and conversational customs. Thus, it is important to discover all we can about the people with whom we associate at school, at work, or in the community. We should consider how our customs might seem unusual to others if they are of a different heritage We must embrace an open mind and a good sense of humor. These attitudes will facilitate communication and enrich our lives. Chapter 3 further discusses how we connect with others through culture and diversity.

Principles of Communication

1.4 **Explain** the fundamental principles of communication.

To appreciate the true nature of communication, it is important to understand four fundamental principles:

1. Communication is a process.
2. Communication is a system.
3. Communication is transactional.
4. Communication can be intentional or unintentional.

These principles apply readily to life beyond the classroom (and they improve interactions within the classroom as well). No doubt, situations from your personal life—family relationships; work experiences; interactions with others through social media; or your participation in sports teams, music groups, social clubs, or political or community action organizations—will come to mind as we discuss the dynamics of communication. An understanding of these principles should make a difference in your life, building greater understanding and cooperation into relationships at any level.

Communication Is a Process

process

A series of actions having no beginning or end and is constantly changing.

Communication is a **process** involving a series of actions having no beginning or end and is constantly changing.[17]

Communication involves variables that cannot be duplicated in exactly the same way. The interrelationships among people, environments, skills, attitudes, status, experiences, and feelings all determine communication at any given moment. Think about a relationship you developed with someone recently. How did it occur? It may have happened by chance (striking up a conversation with someone you met while walking to class), or it may have been a prearranged meeting (a business meeting with a prospective client). No two relationships develop in the same way. And like the weather, some relationships are warm while others are cool.

Communication is both ever-changing and capable of effecting change. Saying something you wish you had not said is an excellent example of this principle. No matter how hard you try to take back a poorly worded or insensitive comment, you cannot. It made its impact and, in all likelihood, affected your relationship with another person in some way. The change might not be immediate or significant, but it does happen because of your communication.

Furthermore, communication and the changes it produces might not have a clearly identifiable beginning or end. Certain events led up to it, and as we noted, results follow in its wake. Communication generally is not characterized by abrupt endings and beginnings; rather, it takes place within a flow. If you were to stop mid-conversation and walk away, that conversation would still affect you; it would not end. You would carry away some new information or at least a general impression, whether positive or negative. Understanding that communication is a process enables you to see how events and relationships constantly change yet also have continuity.

Communication Is a System

Simply stated, a **system** is a combination of parts acting interdependently to form a whole. The human body is an excellent example of a system. All parts of the body are interdependent and work together to form one complex system. If something is not functioning correctly, some response usually occurs either to correct what has gone wrong or to warn that something is going wrong. When you have a headache, it affects not only your head but also the rest of your body. You may find that you have trouble seeing or even walking. You may not wish to eat because your head pain seems to have taken over your body. If your headache is severe, you may experience trouble thinking clearly. You may also have difficulty explaining something to your coworkers or friends. Because all parts of the system are connected, your inability to think clearly, speak lucidly, or listen carefully will likely lead to ineffective communication.

system
Combination of parts acting interdependently to form a whole.

Systems also exist in the workplace, in the family, and in the classroom. If your supervisor had a fight at home, that event may affect his or her relationship with coworkers; the supervisor may be irritable and snap at you and others. Although you do not know what has caused the irritability, it does affect all who must deal with it. In other words, the supervisor's fight at home has an impact not only on the home system but also on the system at work. In a similar sense, the communication process is a system and occurs only when the necessary components interact. If components of communication malfunction or are absent, communication is prevented or ineffective.

Communication Is Transactional

Communication is often viewed as a highly complex and **transactional** process—the simultaneous sending (encoding) and receiving (decoding) of messages. In order to understand the transactional nature of communication, it is useful to compare it with the related ideas of *action* and *interaction*. If we view communication as strictly action, we would consider a source who sends a message to a receiver or audience. An action perspective does not consider the reaction from the receiver. Early communication research suggested communication was as simple as injecting receivers with messages.[18]

transactional
Exchange of communication in which the communicators act simultaneously; that is, encoding and decoding occur at the same time.

If we think about communication from an interaction perspective, we consider not only the source's message but also the receiver's reaction. Such a view marked a clear step forward in our concept of communication. The interaction perspective explains that communication is not a simple one-way process. An example of communication as an interaction is a phone conversation between Tomás and Kenja. Tomás speaks and Kenja listens, then Kenja speaks and Tomás listens, and so on. Each message is a separate action. Even though a reaction to each sent message does occur, the reaction and message are not simultaneous.

Most face-to-face communication does not occur as a series of distinctly separate actions. Today, nearly all communication scholars view communication as a transactional process. Much like the interaction view, the transactional perspective considers the listener's reaction to our message, but it goes further and explains how people simultaneously act as speaker and listener in communication situations. In any given interaction, people talk, offer feedback, and respond as each person contributes through constant participation. Consider an interaction between a professor and the student she suspects has committed plagiarism. If we view communication as an interaction, we would look first at what the professor says, then consider what the student says, then examine what the professor says, and so on. However, if we view the exchange as a transaction, we would look simultaneously at the professor and the student. The professor may vary the content or tone of the conversation based on the student's nonverbal behaviors. Simultaneously, the student may respond to the professor's communication cues by changing his behavior.

Without simultaneous actions, the communication transaction would be extremely limited, like sending a letter to someone and then having to wait a week or two for a response. In face-to-face communication, each person affects the other and shares in the process simultaneously. When you email or text someone, unlike in face-to-face communication, you are both sender and receiver, but not simultaneously. The lag time can be frustrating because you have to wait a bit to respond. The advantage is that the written message helps you follow the flow of ideas. The principle of transaction is more fully depicted in Figure 1.1.

The transactional nature of communication also considers the context or the setting in which interaction takes place. Not only do participants constantly influence each other, but the communication context also affects how they interact. For instance, a funny comment made by friends in the dining hall can take on a very different meaning in a professional work setting. In many ways, our understanding of the transactional nature of communication highlights the complexity of communication and enhances our competence as we interact with others.

FIGURE 1.1 Communication as Transaction

In a transaction, the persons communicate simultaneously. That is, both Tomás and Kenja are communicating at the same time. This does not mean they are both speaking at once. Instead, each is aware of and reacting to the other. The sender is also a receiver, and the receiver is also a sender. Each is actively involved in what is happening.

(*left*) Daniel M Ernst/Shutterstock;
(*right*) Leungchopan/Shutterstock

Communication Can Be Intentional or Unintentional

When a person communicates with another, he or she intends specific messages with specific purposes and meanings. Communication can occur, however, regardless of whether it is intended or not. **Intentional communication** is a message purposely sent to a specific receiver. **Unintentional communication** is a message not intended or not intended for the individual who received it. On the basis of intent or lack of intent, four possible communication situations can occur, as illustrated in Figure 1.2. Arrow 1 is generally the way communication takes place. Arrow 2 indicates a situation in which a person unintentionally communicates something to someone who is intentionally trying to receive a message or messages. This situation occurs every time someone reads more into a communication act than was intended by the source. For example, when a work supervisor frowns at everyone and generally speaks abruptly whenever anyone addresses her, the employees immediately begin to attribute meanings to her behavior. One worker may believe that the business has financial problems and his position is at risk. Another might believe that she has done something wrong and is going to face discipline for her behavior. A third person decides that the supervisor had an argument with her husband and is taking it out on everyone at work. In reality, the supervisor actually had a headache and did not intend to communicate anything negative about the job, but others read meaning into her behavior, whether intended or not.

Arrow 3 illustrates the opposite situation. Here the source intends to send a message, but the person for whom the message is intended is not consciously or intentionally receiving it. Such a situation happens in the classroom when students daydream while the instructor is lecturing.

Arrow 4 shows that communication can be unintentional for both the source and the receiver and can occur without anyone intentionally sending or receiving a message. Communication not intended, or not consciously sent and received, is usually nonverbal. For example, the clothing a person wears might not be worn to communicate any specific message, and persons observing the clothing might not intentionally or consciously receive any message, but they do see it. Thus, communication occurs even though neither the person nor the observer intended to

intentional communication

A message purposely sent to a specific receiver.

unintentional communication

A message not intended to be sent or was not intended for the individual who received it.

FIGURE 1.2 Types of Intentional and Unintentional Communication

Communication occurs both intentionally and unintentionally. Thus, we must be aware that even when we do not intend it, communication can occur. Can you recall any instances in which you unintentionally communicated to another person?

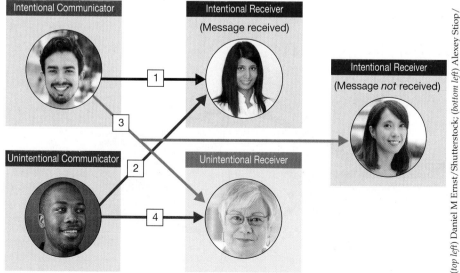

communicate any particular message. Think of a time when you received a message not intended for you but it upset you. Why were you upset?

Essential Components of Communication

1.5 **Define** the essential components in the communication process.

Although no exhaustive list of the components of communication exists, here are eight of the most basic elements worth examining in detail:

1. Source/sender
2. Message
3. Interference/noise
4. Channel
5. Receiver
6. Feedback
7. Environment
8. Context

Figure 1.3 illustrates how these components interact when two people are communicating, yet it depicts each element's movement and interdependence on the other elements only in a limited way. During actual communication, these components are constantly in flux as the communicators react to each other. The model also shows that communication is a process, where the components work together as a system, that interaction and transaction are both possible modes of communication, and that intentional and unintentional communication can occur—thus illustrating the principles of communication we have already discussed.

Now that you can see how these elements relate during communication, we discuss each separately.

Source/Sender

source

The creator of the message.

The **source** is the creator of the message. Because communication usually involves more than one person, more than one source can exist at one time. In the model in Figure 1.3, both persons function as a source. Likewise, both the teacher and the

FIGURE 1.3 Model of the Essential Components of Communication

The essential components of the transactional communication process are constantly changing, ongoing, and dynamic, and they affect one another.

(left) Daniel M Ernst/Shutterstock; *(right)* Pkchai/Shutterstock

students in a classroom can function as sources, sending messages simultaneously to one another—teacher to students, students to teacher, and students to students.

The communication source performs four roles: He or she determines the meaning of the communication, *encodes* the meaning into a message, sends the message, and perceives and reacts to a listener's response to the message. Tomás, when acting as source, also brings into play the communicative skills, knowledge, attitudes, and sociocultural background that make him a unique individual. No two communicators are identical in their abilities to communicate, nor do they see others, events, or situations in exactly the same way. The greater the differences between Tomás and Shenice, the more effort and skill it will take for Tomás to effectively communicate with Shenice. Respecting another person's views, even when they differ from one's own, is the first step to communicating effectively.

Determining Meanings   The meaning behind the message determines how you'll create the message. Your word choices and tone of voice, as well as other, nonverbal behaviors, will help convey your meaning to those with whom you communicate and will require careful choices on your part. When you tell your friends you're going to the Caribbean for spring break, you have to choose the ultimate intended meaning. Do you want them to be excited for you? Do you want them to be jealous? Do you want them to ask about going along? Or do you wish to let them know about the good deal on travel and lodging? On the other hand, perhaps you just want to express your pleasure about this destination. How do you choose words and behavior to convey the desired message?

Encoding   Once a source has chosen a meaning, she or he **encodes** it. In other words, a source translates the thoughts or feelings into words, sounds, and physical expressions, which make up the actual message. According to symbolic interactionism, a theory created by sociologist George Herbert Mead and his students, the most human and humanizing activity people engage in is talking with one another. Our conversations with others—our participation in the communication process in social settings—allow us to construct meaning. For example, the postal carrier rings your doorbell and asks you to sign for a package. Without looking at the return address, you tell her you have been anxiously waiting for your new laptop to arrive. Symbolic interactionism also explains that we talk to ourselves (intrapersonal communication) as we sort through difficult circumstances, solve problems, and make decisions.

encoding
Process by which the source translates thoughts or feelings into words, sounds, and physical expressions, which together make up the actual message that is to be sent.

Sending   The source then sends the message, which involves the source's ability to communicate overtly, that is, to use voice and body to express the intended meaning accurately. For example, if your internal meaning is to tell the other person how pleased you are to go to the Caribbean for spring break, you must use words and actions to illustrate what you are feeling and thinking.

Reacting   Finally, a source must interpret the receiver's response to the message. A source's perception of a receiver's response in most communication situations is simultaneous with the response. For example, the person you are telling about your trip to the Caribbean will send you messages (smiles, nods of the head, eye contact) as you speak, in reaction to what you are saying. If you interpret that response as positive, you will probably continue to tell more about your trip.

Message

A **message** is the communication produced by the source. Messages are composed of words, grammar, organization of thoughts, physical appearance, body movement, voice, aspects of the person's personality and self-concept, and personal style. Environment and noise can also shape the message. Any stimulus that affects a receiver is a message from the source, regardless of whether the source intended to

message
The communication produced by the source.

send it. Hence, if you ask a frowning friend what is wrong and the friend says, "Oh, nothing," you're sure to believe that there *really is* something wrong. The frown communicates that the words and actions do not fit together, and you're more likely to believe the frown than the words. Your friend may not want to discuss anything with you, but you still attach meaning to all that occurs.

Remember, each message is unique. Even if the same message were repeated several times, it would differ in each instance because messages cannot be repeated or received in exactly the same way or in the same context. To illustrate this, imagine reading the headline "The World Has Been Invaded by Small Green People!" in a comic book, in your local newspaper, and on an online news website. Although the words might be the same, the messages conveyed would be quite different.

Interference/Noise   Anything that changes the meaning of an intended message is called **interference**. It is included in our model because it is present, to one degree or another, in every communication environment.

Interference can be external and physical, such as noise caused by the slamming of a door, someone talking on a cell phone, or the blasting of music on an office computer. Other examples of external interference include an unpleasant environment, such as a smoke-filled room or a room that is too cool or too hot; an odor, such as that of overly strong perfume; or distracting characteristics of the speaker, such as too much makeup, talk that is too fast or too slow, mumbling pronunciation, or outlandish clothing or jewelry.

Interference can also be internal and psychological. For example, thoughts going through a person's mind can interfere with the reception or creation of a message. A person who speaks in a loud voice to get someone's attention may create both physical and psychological interference. If the receiver perceives the loudness as anger, the loud voice creates not only a distraction from attending but also a distortion of interpretation. If the receiver responds accordingly, the sender may be quite surprised. Essentially, interference is anything that reduces or distorts the clarity, accuracy, meaning, understanding, or retention of a message.

Channel

A **channel** is the means by which messages flow between sources and receivers. The usual communication channels are light waves and sound waves, which allow us to see and hear one another in face-to-face interactions. However, if a letter is sent from one person to another, the paper itself serves as the means by which the message is conveyed. If you settle in to watch the evening news on television, the television set serves as the channel. Books, movies, computers, radios, magazines, newspapers, and social networking sites are channels through which messages are conveyed.

We also receive communication by smelling, touching, and tasting. We sometimes take these senses for granted, but imagine walking into a bakery and not being able to smell the aromas or taste the flavors. Alternatively, all you have to do is hug someone you care about to recognize how important touch is. All five senses, therefore, contribute to communication.

Receiver

Both persons function as receivers in the model depicted in Figure 1.3. A **receiver** analyzes and interprets messages, in effect translating them into meaning. This process is called **decoding**. *You are simultaneously a receiver and a source.* As you listen to another person's message, you react with body movements and facial expressions, and the person sending the message receives the information conveyed by your

interference
Anything that changes the meaning of an intended message.

channel
The means by which messages flow between sources and receivers.

receiver
The individual who analyzes and interprets the message.

decoding
The process of translating a message into the thoughts or feelings that were communicated.

physical reactions. Like the source, a receiver has several roles: to receive (hear, see, touch, smell, or taste) the message; to attend to the message; to interpret and analyze the message; to store and recall the message; and to respond to the source, message, channel, environment, and noise. In addition, Shenice also has communication skills, knowledge, attitudes, and a sociocultural background that differ from those of Tomás. The greater the differences between Tomás and Shenice, the more effort Shenice must make to be a competent receiver.

Feedback

Another component in the communication process is **feedback**, the response to a message that a receiver sends back to a source. Feedback enables a sender to determine whether the communication sent was received and understood as intended. To share meaning accurately, the sender must correct faulty messages and misconceptions, repeat missed meanings, and correct responses as necessary.

Feedback is a natural extension of effective receiving. Receivers have the responsibility of attending to, decoding, and determining a message's intended meaning. The next logical step is to provide responses (feedback) that let the sender know the message was received and understood. It is then up to the sender to decide whether the feedback provides enough information to judge whether the receiver accurately interpreted the message. Thus, feedback serves as a kind of control mechanism in the communication process. Unfortunately, we often fail to monitor our own communication and, more important, others' reactions to it, so we are often not heard or are misunderstood. For example, consider the following scenario. Restaurant employees requested a pay raise or bonus because of an especially profitable and successful party. The boss told them they would get a bonus in the next paycheck but failed to tell payroll. The employees wondered what went wrong.

Feedback is an essential component of the communication process because it is both a corrective device and a means by which we learn about ourselves. It helps us adjust to others and assess ourselves. Giving feedback to others is just as important as receiving it, making communication truly a shared process.

Feedback offers other advantages. A classic study found that when feedback is increased, reception of information is enhanced.[19] The experiment required four groups of students to construct geometric patterns that were described by a teacher under conditions that differed for each group: (1) zero feedback—the teacher's back was turned to the students, and they were not allowed to ask questions or make noise; (2) visible audience feedback—the students could see the teacher's face but could not ask questions; (3) limited verbal feedback—the students were allowed to ask the teacher questions, but the teacher could respond only with yes or no; and (4) free feedback—all channels of communication were open, with no limits placed on the type of questions asked of the teacher or the depth of response the teacher could provide. Students provided with no opportunity to receive feedback from the teacher fared poorly, whereas each increasing level of feedback produced better results. This study resulted in two important findings: (1) As the amount of feedback increases, so does the accuracy of communication, and (2) as the amount of feedback increases, so does the recipient's confidence in her or his performance.

Environment

The **environment**, or atmosphere, refers to the psychological and physical surroundings in which communication occurs. The environment encompasses the attitudes, feelings, perceptions, and relationships of the communicators as well as the characteristics of the location in which communication takes place, for example, the size, color, arrangement, decoration, and temperature of the room.

feedback
The response to a message that a receiver sends back to a source.

environment
The psychological and physical surroundings in which communication occurs.

The environment affects the nature and quality of the communication. For example, it is much easier to carry on an intimate conversation in a private, quiet, and comfortable setting than in a public, noisy, and uncomfortable setting. Most of us find it easier to communicate with someone we know than with someone we do not know. Some environments appear to foster communication, whereas others seem to inhibit it. Consider these contrasting environments. One office is clean, is painted light blue, and has quiet music playing in the background. The office has a pleasant and inviting smell. Two people, seated in soft, comfortable desk chairs at clean and organized desks, are working alongside each other, smiling, and they take frequent breaks to share funny stories and family updates. They show genuine concern for each other. Their communication is open and caring. Another office is cluttered, is painted dark brown, and has no music playing in the background. The office has a musty odor. Desks are cluttered and set up in small cubicles. Two people sit in uncomfortable chairs in a cubicle, side-by-side. One person blasts his music at high volume on his computer and disrupts the other's work. They show little respect for each other. Their communication is guarded.

How does the appearance of the room ultimately affect the communication? Both effective and ineffective forms of communication are, in part, products of their environments. Effective communication can occur anywhere and under most circumstances, but pleasing, comfortable environments (along with open, trusting relationships) are more likely to produce positive exchanges.

Context

context

The broad circumstances or situation in which communication occurs.

The broad circumstances or situation in which communication occurs is called the **context**. Communication does not take place in a vacuum. It happens in formal and informal settings, such as between two friends; among five colleagues in a business meeting; or between a rabbi, priest, cleric, or minister and a group of worshippers. The number of people, the type of communication, and the situation in which the communication occurs all lend themselves to the context. Each context affects what we say and how we say it. Contexts also help determine the type of communication used.

Guidelines

UNDERSTANDING YOURSELF AND THE COMMUNICATION PROCESS

1. **Always strive to be a competent communicator.** Competent communicators do everything they can to help their listeners understand their communication as intended.

2. **Understand that interference can detract from your message.** Interference from both external and internal sources may make the communication difficult to interpret the way you, the sender, intend it.

3. **Recognize that you often cannot control environmental factors (heat or lack of it, outside noise, dim or too-bright lighting).** However, you can control your own speech rate, volume, use of pauses, use of gestures, and correct pronunciations, and these factors can increase your effectiveness.

4. **Carefully choose your words and the way you present your message (encoding).** If you do this, your listeners have a better chance of understanding you.

5. **Observe your listeners (receivers).** If you do this, you will learn how to read their nonverbal feedback and be able to adapt your message to them.

6. **Remember that listening is a critical aspect of the communication process.** Effective listeners communicate that they are active participants in the communication process.

Types of Communication

 Differentiate the various types of communication: intrapersonal, interpersonal (including group), public, mass, and communication via social media.

Type of communication is usually distinguished by the number of people involved, by the purpose of the communication, and by the degree of formality with which it occurs. Each type of communication involves appropriate verbal and nonverbal behaviors. Five types of communication discussed in this text are: intrapersonal, interpersonal, public, mass, and communication via social media. We also refer to small group and team communication here and throughout the text.

Intrapersonal Communication

To communicate with others, we must first understand how we communicate with ourselves. This process of understanding information within oneself is **intrapersonal communication**. As we mature, we learn a lot about our surroundings and ourselves. Much of what we learn is from our own experiences. Even though we learn many things from others, we must also learn many things through our own experiences and can learn those things in no other way.

intrapersonal communication
The process of understanding information within oneself.

Intrapersonal communication also occurs anytime we evaluate or attempt to understand the interaction occurring within us. We are involved in intrapersonal communication as we receive, attend to, interpret and analyze, store and recall, or respond in some fashion to any message.

Intrapersonal communication includes diverse internal activities such as thinking, problem solving, conflict resolution, planning, emotion, stress, evaluation, and relationship development. All messages we create first occur within us. Ultimately, all communication takes place within each of us as we react to communication cues. Intrapersonal communication may occur without the presence of other types of communication, but all other types of communication cannot occur without it. In fact, intrapersonal communication is always happening, yet we often don't think about it as a type of communication.

Interpersonal Communication

Interpersonal communication is creating and sharing meaning between persons who are in a relationship. It is similar to intrapersonal communication in that it helps us share information, solve problems, resolve conflicts, understand our perception of self and of others, and establish relationships with others. (In Chapter 13, interpersonal relationships and our relationships with friends and family members are discussed in more detail.)

interpersonal communication
The creating and sharing of meaning between people who are in a relationship.

A subcomponent of interpersonal communication is dyadic communication. **Dyadic communication** is simply an exchange of information between two people. It includes informal conversations, such as talks with a parent, spouse, child, friend, acquaintance, or stranger, as well as formal interviews. An **interview** is a carefully planned and executed question-and-answer session designed to exchange desired information between two parties.

dyadic communication
An exchange of information between two people.

interview
A carefully planned and executed question-and-answer session designed to exchange desired information between two parties.

Another subcomponent of interpersonal communication is **small-group communication**, an exchange of information among a relatively small number of people, ideally five to seven, who share a common purpose, such as completing a task, solving a problem, making a decision, or sharing information. (Chapter 14 discusses the purposes, characteristics, leadership, participation, decision making, problem solving, and evaluation of communication in small groups.)

small-group communication
An exchange of information among a relatively small number of people, ideally five to seven, who share a common purpose, such as completing a task, solving a problem, making a decision, or sharing information.

Public Communication

public communication
Transmission of a message from a person who speaks to a number of individuals who listen.

In **public communication**, a message is transmitted from a person who speaks to a number of individuals who listen. The most widely used form of public communication is a public speech. We find ourselves on the listening end of a public speech in lecture classes, political rallies, group meetings, and religious services.

Although many similarities exist between public speaking and other types of communication, some differences are noted here. Public speaking usually is more highly structured than the other types. It demands much detailed planning and preparation by the speaker. Unlike participants in other forms of communication, listeners do not regularly interrupt the speaker with questions or comments. It is the public speaker's responsibility to anticipate questions that listeners may have and to attempt to answer them.

Public speaking usually requires a more formal use of language and a more formal delivery style than the other types. The use of jargon, poor grammar, or slang is usually not accepted or tolerated in public speeches. The speaker must use language precisely and must speak clearly to ensure the message is heard and understood by the audience. This may require the speaker to eliminate distracting vocal and physical mannerisms usually tolerated in other types of communication.

Public speeches usually have three purposes: to inform, to persuade, and to entertain. There are also speeches presented to introduce, to pay tribute, to accept, and to welcome. (These purposes are discussed in detail in Chapters 8 through 12.)

Mass Communication

mass communication
When professionals communicate with or to a large number of people via radio, television, newspapers, magazines, books, or movies.

Mass communication generally signifies that professionals are communicating with or to a very large number of people via traditional media outlets such as radio, television, newspapers, and magazines. These channels constitute the means by which messages are directed to a large group (mass) of people. In these instances, the professional communicator—news reporter, anchor, or book author—acts as the source. The large audience functions as receivers. In mass communication, opportunities for feedback are often minimal, given the one-way nature of communication. In some situations, though, an individual audience member (receiver) may write a letter to the editor of a newspaper, send an email to a news reporter, or call in to a radio show.

Communication via Social Media

communication via social media
Any communication transmitted through digital devices or platforms (smartphones, text messaging, Facebook, Twitter, Snapchat, etc.).

Communication via social media is any communication transmitted through digital devices or platforms (smartphones, text messaging, Facebook, Twitter, Snapchat, and so on). These technologies, as you know, are often highly accessible and allow us to accomplish multiple objectives. For example, you use your smartphone to text with a friend, review your Facebook and Twitter feeds, tweet to your followers, send and receive emails, snap a picture and post it to Facebook, and record a video and post it to Snapchat or YouTube. (Chapter 6 discusses differences between social media and face-to-face communication, offers a brief history of new technologies, and highlights new technology theories that further explain how communication functions via social media.)

As technology continues to develop and change, one thing remains consistent: Communication is the process that helps us *make connections*. Communication is a learned tool that enables us to function in our personal and family lives, in our social and work lives, and in our roles as citizens of the world. Many people are concerned that technology negatively affects the way we interact with each other on a one-to-one basis. Therefore, it becomes increasingly important to search for ways to use it in a positive manner. If you email a campus administrator, your professor, or future employer, remember to use appropriate grammar, spelling, and punctuation. Do not use emoticons, which are so common in texting. If you're making a request by mail or phone, be sure you are courteous and clear about who you are and what you seek. Your communication is judged via whatever means you choose. So, consider the receiver, the context, and the perception of your message.

Misconceptions about Communication

1.7 **Summarize** five common myths about communication.

Several misconceptions keep many of us from examining *our own* communication more closely. Notice the emphasis on *our own*! Most of us who have problems communicating tend to look for the fault in places other than ourselves. Becoming aware that these misconceptions exist and that many people accept them as truths should help us understand why the study of communication is necessary. Here are some of the most common myths that interfere with the improvement of personal communication skills.

Myth 1: Communication Is a Cure-All

The first misconception is that communication has the magical power to solve all our problems. The act of communicating with others does not carry any guarantees. Obviously, without communication, we cannot address problems, but sometimes communication can create more of them than it solves.

Here is one example: Andrew's neighbor, Erin, is a realtor. Erin created a flyer for distribution in the neighborhood and asked Andrew to read it and tell her what he thought about it. Erin had obviously spent a great deal of time on the project. After Andrew looked it over, he said: "I really don't think your message is going to reach who you want to reach." Erin became quite agitated and said that Andrew was the only one who had anything negative to say. Andrew had taken Erin's message literally, when she really wanted affirmation that she had done a good job. How might Andrew have avoided angering Erin?

Communication can help to eliminate or reduce our problems, but it is not a panacea. Communicating itself does not make the difference; the message communicated does.

Myth 2: Quantity Means Quality

We often assume that the more we communicate, the better. People who communicate effectively a great deal are often perceived as more friendly, competent, and powerful and as having greater leadership potential than those who do not. However, quantity of communication is not the same as quality. A mother tells her high school son that he cannot wear a certain shirt to his older brother's college graduation ceremony. The younger son likes the shirt and feels that it is appropriate and that everyone else wears similar shirts. Neither mother nor son will change their respective views, and they continue to argue. Each becomes more defensive and louder until another family member steps in to stop the argument. In this case, as in the one described in the section about the first myth, it isn't the act or the amount of communication but the content of communication that makes the difference.

The convenience of social media allows us to send email messages, tweets, and text messages in rapid succession. Have you ever received multiple texts from a friend within seconds? Perhaps the initial text autocorrected to a word your friend did not intend to send and, as a result, your friend fired off a text to correct the error and then a series of others to apologize and add on to the conversation. One carefully composed text message would have been much more effective than a series of short texts with typographical errors.

Competent communication is essential in all aspects of our everyday lives. Effective communication enhances our personal, social, and career relationships and allows us to make connections with people from other cultures.

Myth 3: Meaning Is in the Words We Use

If your friend tells you that she doesn't feel well, what would that mean to you? That she is sick? That she has a cold? That she has an upset stomach? That her feelings have been hurt? It could mean any number of things because, without context and more information, the statement is not clear. If she tells you she has a cold and doesn't feel well, is the message clear? Well, at least it would narrow the choices a little. Confusion may arise because the statement "I don't feel well" is relative; that is, it might not signify the same thing to you as it does to her. Some people use this statement to refer to a minor discomfort, whereas others mean they are more seriously ill. The words themselves could refer to many degrees or types of conditions. Thus, *meanings are in people and not in the words they use.* This is truer today than ever because of diversity of opinions on so many subjects and levels.

The notion that words contain meanings is probably the most serious misconception of all. Words have meaning only when we give them meaning. *No two people share the same meanings for all words because no two people completely share the same background and experiences.* Thus, the meaning of a word cannot be separated from the person using it.

Myth 4: We Have a Natural Ability to Communicate

Many people believe that, because we are born with the physical and mental equipment needed for communication, it must be a natural ability. This simply is not true. The capacity to communicate, like almost everything we do, is learned. Most of us possess the physical ability to tie our shoes, but we still have to learn how the shoelaces go together. Similarly, most of us are born with the ability to see, but that does not make us able to read. Reading requires knowledge of the alphabet, the acquisition of vocabulary, and practice. The ability to communicate requires not only capability but also an understanding of how human communication works and an opportunity to use that knowledge. By taking this class, you are working toward improving very important communication skills that comprise your communication **repertoire**, a range of communication behaviors from which to choose when connecting with others.

repertoire

Wide range of communication behaviors from which effective communicators make choices.

Myth 5: Communication Is Reversible

All of us sometimes make a mistake in communication. We might think that we can take something back, but that is impossible. Once something is said, it is out there; the listener will have to deal with that message, and the speaker will have to try to explain and compensate for what was said. For example, in a moment of anger, we say something that we regret and later ask the other person to "forget I even said that." Although the other person may forgive us for speaking in anger, it is not likely that he or she will forget what was said. When we communicate through writing, we can take things back until we let someone else see what we've written. When we send oral messages, others can hear and will respond to what we say, even if we don't really mean to say things the way they come out.

If you are exchanging email messages with a manager or colleague, it is important to remain aware of your receivers. If you raise a sensitive workplace issue in an email and quickly click "send," you might later notice your supervisor received a copy. If you did not intend to send this email to your supervisor, you may have some explaining to do. Always remember that communication is irreversible. Usually this is also true for communication that occurs via social media. As in face-to-face communication, the moment we send a tweet through Twitter, that message is out there for the world to see and for its reaction. It is important, therefore, to organize our thoughts and choose our words carefully before we utter (or type) them to others.

Guidelines

IMPROVING COMMUNICATION COMPETENCE

1. **Understand the role of communication in your life.** Be aware of the complexity of the communication process and different types of communication, and understand how face-to-face communication is different from communication via social media.

2. **Recognize the many misconceptions about effective communication.** We need to realize that myths about communication may hinder our ability to develop effective communication.

3. **Increase your knowledge of effective communication behaviors.** Good communicators have developed a broad communication repertoire, a range of communication behaviors from which to choose.[20]

4. **Competent communicators possess the ability to coordinate several communication tasks simultaneously.** For example, a competent communicator will, at the same time, choose a way of conveying a message, consider what the receiver's various responses might be, and plan a way to restate the message if the first attempt is not effective.

5. **Background knowledge about communication, practical experience, and feedback given in the classroom will help you think on your feet and make better decisions as you communicate.** You will also gain confidence and the ability to evaluate your skills as your work in this course progresses.

⟩ SUMMARY

Communication: Making Connections

1.1 **Explain** how communication competence allows you to make connections with the outside world.

Communication competence is the ability to take part in effective communication that is characterized by skills and understandings that enable communicators to exchange messages successfully.

What Is Communication?

1.2 **Define** communication.

Communication is the simultaneous sharing and creating of meaning through human symbolic interaction. It involves a range of behaviors and occurs in a variety of situations.

Why Should We Study Communication?

1.3 **Identify** four reasons for studying communication.

The ability to *communicate* (not simply to utter words) is learned; learning to be a competent communicator is a difficult, lifelong project.

- We live in a technological society and use *social media* to interact with others in our social network.
- Communication plays a vital role in career success.
- Communication involves a high degree of ethical behavior.
- We live in a multicultural society and interact with people from different cultures.

Principles of Communication

1.4 **Explain** the fundamental principles of communication.

To appreciate the true nature of communication, it is important to understand four fundamental principles. These principles are readily applicable to life beyond the classroom.

- Communication is a process because it involves a series of actions that has no beginning or end and is constantly changing.
- Communication is a system, a combination of parts interdependently acting to form a whole.
- Communication is *transactional* because messages are simultaneously sent and received between people.
- Communication can be *intentional* or *unintentional*.

Essential Components of Communication

1.5 **Define** the essential components in the communication process.

Several components interact when two people are communicating. These components are constantly in flux as communicators react to each other.

- The *source*/sender is the creator of the message.
- A *message* is the communication produced by the source.

- Anything that changes the meaning of an intended message is called *interference*.
- A *channel* is the means by which messages flow between sources and receivers.
- A *receiver* analyzes, interprets, and translates messages into meaning.
- *Feedback* is the response to a message that a receiver sends back to a source.
- The *environment* includes the psychological and physical surroundings in which communication occurs.
- The broad circumstances or situation in which communication occurs is referred to as the *context*.

Types of Communication

1.6 **Differentiate** the various types of communication: intrapersonal, interpersonal (including group), public, mass, and communication via social media.

The type of communication is distinguished by the number of people involved, by the purpose of the message, and by the degree of formality with which it occurs.

- *Intrapersonal communication* is the process of understanding information within oneself.
- *Interpersonal communication* is creating and sharing meaning between persons who are in a relationship.
- *Public communication* occurs when a message is transmitted from one person to a number of individuals who listen.

- *Mass communication* means that professionals are communicating with or to a very large number of people via radio, television, newspapers, magazines, books, or movies.
- *Communication via social media* is any communication transmitted through digital devices or platforms such as smartphones, text messages, Facebook, Twitter, Skype, and so on.

Misconceptions about Communication

1.7 **Summarize** five common myths about communication.

Several misconceptions keep many of us from examining *our own* communication more closely. Many people who have problems communicating tend to look for the fault in places other than themselves.

- Communication has the magical power to solve all of our problems. It does not.
- We often assume that the more we communicate, the better. However, the quantity of communication is not the same as the quality.
- Meaning is in the words we use. Actually, meanings are in people and not in the words they use.
- We have a natural ability to communicate. That ability, like almost everything we do, is learned.
- Communication is reversible. In truth, once something is said, it is out there. We cannot take it back.

> DISCUSSION STARTERS

1. Why is communication sometimes difficult for us?

2. Based on what you read in this chapter, describe an effective communicator in your own words.

3. Explain what it means when we say that communication is a process.

4. How does feedback motivate you to be more effective?

5. Provide several suggestions to improve communication with people from other cultures.

6. How might text messaging, Snapchat, and Twitter individually influence our communication and the quality of the messages we send and receive?

7. Choose one thing that you believe is the most important idea, concept, or principle to have learned from the chapter that will help you become a more competent communicator.

CHAPTER 2

CONNECTING PERCEPTION, SELF, AND COMMUNICATION

LightField Studios/Shutterstock

Perception is reflection of the world around us as well as how we see ourselves. Each of us chooses what we pay attention to and how we interpret the world. In this chapter, we discuss the role of perception in our everyday communication, how it specifically relates to understanding who we are, the world around us, and the people in it. We will first discuss what perception is and how it forms meaning for our surroundings and ourselves. Second, we will examine what self-concept is, and its effects on how we communicate and how we manage our public image.

→ CHAPTER OUTLINE AND LEARNING OBJECTIVES

Perception and Communication
2.1 Explain the connection between perception and your communication competence.

The Perception Process
2.2 Understand the effect of the three stages of perception on your communication.

Perceptual Differences
2.3 Identify seven reasons why different people may perceive the same situation in different ways.

Improving Perception Competencies and Perception Checking
2.4 Accurately **interpret and check** your perceptions to improve your communication competence.

Perception and Self-Concept
2.5 Understand the role perception has in determining self-concept.

Understanding Self-Concept
2.6 Differentiate among self-concept, self-image, and self-esteem.

Social Media and Perceived Self-Concept
2.7 Identify social media factors that influence self-concept.

Culture and Perceived Self-Concept
2.8 Characterize the role of culture in determining self-concept.

Gender and Perception of Self-Concept
2.9 Characterize the role of gender in determining self-concept.

Self-Fulfilling Prophecy and Impression Management
2.10 Explain the roles of self-fulfilling prophecy and impression management as they relate to self-concept.

Enhancing Self-Concept
2.11 Identify six ways to improve self-concept.

MAKING EVERYDAY CONNECTIONS

Social media as discussed in Chapter 1 plays a predominant role in our everyday lives. We readily post information electronically about ourselves to share with family and friends. We assume that everyone who sees our posts will interpret them exactly as we intended. It is true that those who see our posts see the exact same messages, yet more often than not, they interpret them differently. How is it that no two individuals interpret our posts in the exactly the same way? It is because each of us chooses what we pay attention to, and then we give those things meaning by how we perceive and communicate about them to others. For example, you post a picture of yourself having a good time at party. Your friends see it and think that you were at a great party, your parents see it as nothing but trouble, and a coworker sees it and thinks you are very irresponsible. Who is right?

Most of us fear that others perceive us incorrectly or negatively. We think that no matter how hard we try or how successful we are—no matter how highly we rate ourselves as a student, friend, coworker, teammate, person, lover, and so on—our efforts may not be good enough. We may see others as smarter, more attractive, thinner, more muscular, faster, or more powerful than we are. High self-esteem usually requires us to feel special and above average. Even the most successful of us often consider "average" an insult and see the label "average" as a failure. One way to deal with this is to constantly make social comparisons in which we try to inflate our image at the expense of others; another is accepting that we just aren't as good as others. Neither of these approaches seems to satisfy our perception of self in a positive way.

We have been told, more or less, that what others say about us, either in person or on social media, influences our self-esteem—especially if what is communicated is from someone we hold in high esteem and admire. For example, imagine if a close friend, romantic partner, parent, professor, music instructor, coworker, or coach whom you admire says one of the following to you:

"You're talented. You are amazing—you are doing great."

"Wow, you're not very bright. How you ever got this far, I'll never know."

"You're a lot of fun; you make me laugh."

"You don't know what you're talking about. You simply don't get it."

"You sure have gained a lot of weight."

These comments or actions, whether on social media or said in person, influence temporarily, and sometimes permanently, how we perceive ourselves and how we communicate about ourselves to others.

QUESTIONS TO THINK ABOUT

1. What do you think influences our perceptions more— what we see or what we hear? Explain.

2. What lessons can we learn from the above about perception and its role in communicating with others?

3. Describe a situation or situations in which technology, such as a social networking site, a text, a tweet, Snapchat, or even broader media, influenced your perceptions of others or an event.

4. Describe how one's view of self can affect communication with others. Discuss both positive and negative effects.

5. How can the understanding of one's self help a person to become a more competent communicator?

6. How does our ability to control what others learn about us through social networking sites and other Internet venues affect how we see ourselves?

Perception and Communication

 Explain the connection between perception and your communication competence.

perception
The process of selecting, organizing, and interpreting information to give personal meaning to the communication we receive.

Perception involves selecting, organizing, and interpreting information to give meaning to our communication and lives. Our perceptions, based on our experiences, give meaning to our communication and influence what and how we communicate with others.

Perception is at the heart of our communication. Some scholars argue that, without communication, perceptions could not exist. Thus, equally true is the statement that communication lies at the heart of our perceptions. Robert L. Scott, a communication scholar, writes, "Nothing is clear in and of itself but in some context for some person."[1] A difference between two people's perceptions, for example, does not necessarily make the perception of one person more correct or accurate than that of the other. What this does mean is the communication occurring between individuals who see things differently may require more understanding, negotiation, persuasion, and tolerance of those differences.

Perception, like communication, is a complex phenomenon. To receive stimuli from our surroundings and to form perceptions requires use of at least one of our five senses: hearing, touching, smelling, seeing, and tasting.

Our perceptions—whether complete or incomplete, accurate or inaccurate—influence our communication and decisions. Our perceptions of people, situations, events, and objects and how they communicate represent our reality. However, our perception of reality may not be the same as someone else's. For example, when one person says to another, "I understand how difficult this might be for you," the statement is an illustration of one person's perception of another's reality. It does not mean he or she actually knows what the other person is experiencing. Competent communicators understand the role of perception and its influence on communication, and vice versa. Competent communicators also know that their perception of a single communication, event, or situation may be only part of the story and that they often need more information before drawing conclusions. They also are not afraid to seek out more information or to ask questions before coming to any conclusions.

John G Mabanglo/epa european pressphoto agency b.v./Alamy Stock Photo

Our perceptions do influence our reactions and our communication. It is virtually impossible for our feelings about things to be the same as others'. We perceive feelings based on experiences and communication. How do you interpret what these National Football League (NFL) players shown in the picture are doing? As most of you know, they were kneeling during the playing of the national anthem. Describe why you think they were kneeling and discuss it in class. Their kneeling has created a great deal of controversy—how would you explain the controversy as it relates to perception?

The Perception Process

2.2 **Understand** the effect of the three stages of perception on your communication.

Perceiving, in and of itself, appears simple enough. After all, we do it all the time, and it seems so natural that we hardly give it much thought. But perceiving is a complex thought process that, if not understood, could lead to communication misunderstandings—some quite costly—such as losing an internship, a promotion, or a friend. The first stage of perception is awareness of our surroundings and selecting what we attend to out of all of the stimuli before us. Second, we organize the information we perceive in a way that makes sense to us. Third, we interpret or assign meaning to the information we perceive. Finally, we must be able to communicate our perceptions to others. Table 2.1 illustrates this process.

Selection

Many people imagine the brain to be similar in operation to a video camera; information enters through one of the senses and is stored in the brain. Actually, the environment has far too much information for the brain to absorb at once, so the brain

Table 2.1 THE PERCEPTION PROCESS

Term	Definition	Example
Selection	Sorting one stimulus from another	Selective exposure Selective attention Selective retention
Organization	Sorting, organizing, or categorizing	Closure Proximity Similarity
Interpretation	Assigning meaning to stimuli	Based on past experience Based on new situations Based on opinions of others

ignores much of it. It accepts a certain amount of information and organizes it into meaningful patterns. All of these connections happen in milliseconds. For example, the first time you walked into a classroom, what did you notice? More than likely, you engaged your senses fully or at least partially and you observed who else was in the room. You saw and heard other students, some of whom you may have known from other classes, and others whom you didn't know. You may have seen a smart board, the teacher, and other aspects of the classroom. The question is, what did you take away from the experience and why? What did you communicate, if anything, to others you know?

We process and catalog each person, sound, object, or surrounding, especially when new or novel. However, we all are creatures of habit, and when others behave in routine or predictable ways, we are more likely to gloss over or ignore important details, which can lead to misunderstandings, missed communication, or inaccurate communication. Competent communicators are *aware* of what is happening so that they make good choices about what to ignore and what to attend to. Because competent communicators know it is impossible to attend to, sense, perceive, retain, and give meaning to every stimulus or message they encounter, they *select* the relevant information and narrow their focus. **Selection** occurs when we mentally sort one thing from another, based on our previous experiences. Selection is of three types: selective exposure, selective attention, and selective retention.

selection
Sorting of one stimulus from another.

Selective Exposure   When we make deliberate choices to experience or to avoid particular stimuli, we are using **selective exposure**. When we choose to attend to one thing over another, we are using selective exposure, for example, choosing to respond to an iPhone text over greeting a friend who walks by us. Taking in the sights, sounds, smells, and so on, occurs only if we are paying attention to them.

selective exposure
Making deliberate choices to experience or to avoid particular stimuli.

Selective Attention   We at times give **selective attention** to a specific message while ignoring or downplaying others. That is, we concentrate on something or someone of interest, and we eliminate or reduce the effects of all extraneous messages. For example, we can focus on the accent and ignore the message. Attending to something usually requires a decisive effort, but interruptions occur even when we attempt to concentrate. For example, a cell phone going off in a quiet classroom, a loud sneeze, background talking, a siren, a baby's cry, a call for help, an odor, or a movement easily averts our attention. Continuing to attend to the original task usually requires extra effort. Similarly, when we converse with someone in a crowded lounge with loud music in the background, we focus on each other's words more attentively and ignore the other sounds. This blocking out of all extraneous stimuli to retain concentration (known as the *cocktail party effect*) is an instance of selective attention. Competent communicators quickly determine what is important to focus on and ignore extraneous stimuli so that their communication is accurate.

selective attention
Attending to a specific message while ignoring or downplaying another.

Selective Retention   Because we cannot possibly remember all the information that we encounter, we also are selective in what we retain. **Selective retention** occurs when we choose to process and store specific information we want to eventually retrieve and use again. We are more likely to remember for a longer time any information that agrees with our views and selectively forget information that does not. In addition, after perceiving and selecting certain stimuli, we may retain only a portion of them. For example, how many times have you listened to an instructor tell how to prepare an assignment and then, several days later, asked a classmate or the instructor about the assignment, only to discover that, thinking you had completed it, you had actually finished only a portion? This happened because you selectively retained the pleasant parts and forgot the not-so-pleasant parts. Selection plays an important role in what, why, and how we communicate.

selective retention
The processing, storing, and retrieving of information that we have already selected, organized, and interpreted.

Organization

To help understand how we organize the information we receive and its effect on communication, consider what happens when you enter a room filled with people. When you first walk in, you begin to sort and organize people into groups or categories. Chances are you will initially look for people you know; by doing so, you are categorizing the people in the room according to those you know and those you don't. You will be most likely to communicate with those you know or those who happen to be nearest to you. You will also probably spend more time with people you perceive to be like you than with those who are not.

Organization is the sorting, organizing, or categorizing of information. The way our minds organize information has a profound effect on how we perceive others, how we talk with them, and how they respond to us. We perceive things, places, and people because of who we are, our backgrounds and experiences, and how we see ourselves. We are also likely to focus on concrete aspects, such as a person's height, attractiveness, age, or race, rather than on abstract psychological aspects, such as sincerity, honesty, and so on.

organization
Sorting, organizing, or categorizing.

Cognitive complexity is a term used by psychologists to measure and explain our ability to process, interpret, and store simple to intricate information. The more cognitively complex we are, the more sophisticated our perceptions. For example, as a cognitively complex person, you will notice several attributes about a person at the same time: talks a lot, dresses well, tells good jokes, and is attractive. A person who is less cognitively complex may only notice one of these characteristics. At an abstract psychological level, you might infer that the behaviors you observe reflect an extroverted, sincere, and self-confident personality. This level of assessment is a sophisticated explanation because it involves perceptions of why the person acts as he or she does determined solely on observations.

cognitive complexity
A measure of our ability to process and store simple to complicated information.

People with high levels of cognitive complexity are likely to be flexible in interpreting complicated events and situations and are able to integrate new information into their perceptions. Such people are also likely to use "person-centered" messages and consider multiple attributes when communicating with others. For example, they are able to incorporate others' values, beliefs, appearance, and emotional needs into their messages. This ability allows those with high levels of cognitive complexity to be effective communicators because they are able to understand and process multiple perspectives at one time.

Closure One way to organize the stimuli around us is to fill in missing pieces and words, and to extend lines in order to finish or complete a figure or message. **Closure** is the filling in of details in order to complete a partially perceived entity or message. Closure occurs because we are always trying to make meaningless or incomplete information meaningful.

closure
Filling in of details so a partially perceived entity or message is complete.

Filling in the blank spaces or missing information helps us categorize, label, and make sense of the things we see and hear. We sometimes do the same thing as we try to understand people. For example, if we meet a Muslim student wearing a burka in one of our classes, we may fill in unknown information, such as the person's value system, beliefs, political views, or whether she is well educated or affluent, to help us understand the person. Unfortunately, we sometimes fill in what is missing with our own biases or ignorance.

When supplying missing information, competent communicators remain aware of what they are doing and remember to distinguish between what they know and what they don't. Otherwise, they increase their chances of forming a wrong or inaccurate perception of the person. Inaccurate perceptions can adversely affect communication and can cost you a relationship, a job, or a new experience. For example, you decided, without complete information and based on a casual comment, that the Muslim student in the above example does not share your religious or political views, and so you do not listen, lose interest, or disregard the information because you see it as counter to your views. It may also be you haven't probed adequately to know the person's views, and thus you may have lost a possibly rewarding relationship.

proximity
The grouping of two or more stimuli that are close to one another.

Proximity   **Proximity** is the grouping of two or more stimuli that are close to one another based on the assumption that, because objects or people appear together, they are similar. It is not unusual to think that people whose appearance, nationality, race, and origin are similar and who reside in the same community or belong to the same organization (fraternity, sorority, club, church, etc.) perceive others, events, and activities in the same way. For us to assume that they do would not only be inaccurate, but also wrong. Thus, we must be careful not to categorize or to communicate as if those who appear together think, behave, and believe the same way on every issue or situation. Competent communicators verify and do not categorize individuals based on their proximity to one another.

similarity
The grouping of stimuli that resemble one another in size, shape, color, or other traits.

Similarity   Organization based on **similarity** involves the grouping of stimuli that resemble one another in size, shape, color, or other traits. For example, Shelley, a sophomore who likes to party, might believe that others who enjoy partying resemble her in other ways as well. Thus, if Shelley likes both partying and hiking, she might assume that others who like to party will also like hiking. Of course, this may be wishful thinking on her part; just because two people are similar in one attribute doesn't automatically mean they will be similar in another. We sometimes make perceptual assumptions, much as Shelley did, when we see people from different cultures. We tend to assume that, because people are similar in appearance, they must behave and think similarly as well. When we perceive people, events, or objects as similar, it is difficult to see differences, and thus our communication with others often does not distinguish them from one another. This in turn makes discussion of differing perceptions difficult, if even possible.

Interpretation

Interpretation of what we see, hear, taste, touch, and smell is an integral part of who we are and how our perceptions influence our communication. **Interpretation** is the assigning of meaning to stimuli. We use our experiences, both past and present, as well as the opinions of others to help interpret the meaning of stimuli.

interpretation
Assigning of meaning to stimuli.

Interpretation Based on Experiences   Our interpretations of stimuli depend on our experiences. For example, when you first arrived on campus, you probably either

MAKING CONNECTIONS FOR SUCCESS

The Web and Perception

Wade, a farm kid, is a senior whose Facebook page is loaded with pictures of him hunting, including pictures of animals he has shot over the years. He spends hours making sure his page lets others know he is an avid hunter, an environmentalist, and of his love of nature. Almost every picture he posts or is tagged in shows him with a rifle or bow in his hands.

In his LinkedIn bio, Wade indicates that he has a 3.87 GPA and that he is president of the Honors Club in Biochemistry, which is his major; vice president of the Ecosystem Science and Sustainability Club; and a member of Future Farmers of America. He also indicates that he plans to go to medical school after he graduates next month. Wade has been extremely active in a variety of campus and community organizations and is a member of the debate team.

1. Based only on the description of Wade in the first paragraph, how would you describe him?
2. You are on LinkedIn and you happen to come upon Wade's bio. Again, having never met him in person, how would you describe him?
3. You meet Wade at a party and find him to be wild in terms of his behaviors, but you have also seen his LinkedIn bio. How would you describe him?
4. Describe what you learned about perception and communication from this exercise.

asked for help or consulted a map to locate various buildings and classrooms. With each passing day, however, you found it easier to get around and even discovered shortcuts from one place to another. As we become familiar with our surroundings, we do not have to think about where we are going; we just go. When we give directions to someone on how to get from one place to another on campus, it seems intuitive because we have done it so many times. We falsely assume that the person we are giving directions to will understand exactly what we are telling them. A distinct relationship exists between our perceptions and communication.

Interpretation Based on New Situations   Although experiences form a basis or foundation for interpreting our environment, we must be careful not to let them keep us from finding fresh meanings in new situations or events. For example, a bad experience with one professor does not automatically mean it will be the same with another. The competent communicator will view the previous experience as a lesson to ask more questions and do more research before he or she reaches a final opinion.

Competent communicators know that information, regardless of its source or form, must be interpreted to have meaning. They also know that their first interpretation may not always be accurate or complete. It should be clear that each of us perceives the world through a personal set of "lenses" or "filters." Therefore, we can never see a river, tree, mountain, person, or event, or hear and interpret a message in exactly the same way as others. Because others' perceptions are different, does that make their interpretation wrong? Not at all; it is just different.

Interpretations Based on Others' Opinions   Our perceptions are influenced by others' communication. Much of what we learn about our world comes from magazines, newspapers, television, social media, and the Internet. These media often form our perceptions. For example, tweets or blogs such as Perezhilton, Daily KOS, Gizmodo, and AMERICAblog.com influence our perceptions and affect our communication in ways we may not question, as we should.

Interpretation Based on Verbal Communication   When we think of perception, most of us associate the term with what we see, but we also form perceptions based on the sound of individuals' speech patterns, which include voice, grammar, and word choices. Speech patterns create images of age, competency, intelligence, cultural or ethnic background, and gender, for example, the perception of a soft-spoken voice as timid or lacking in confidence, a loud voice as overbearing or controlling, a squeaky voice as annoying, or a deep voice as masculine. We also form images from the accent, speed, fluency, and quality of people's voices. How people use their voices produces a variety of images, both positive and negative. Think about how a person's voice or use of language influences your perception of that person's credibility, competency, intelligence, age, or gender.

A college student says, "Okay, I don't understand what you *was* saying"; a coach being interviewed responds, "We got our butts kicked, like *you know*"; a storeowner says, "We don't *got* any more of these"; or a homeless person says, "Our capitalistic society is the best economic system in the world." How might these statements affect your perception of those making them? If the college student were dressed in a suit and tie, would that change your perception? If the coach had won the most games in the country, would that make a difference in your view? Would knowing that the storeowner just became a U.S. citizen affect your perception of her? Would learning that the homeless person had a college education and recently lost his job change how you see him? Would this additional information change your perceptions at all?

Most of us believe that actions speak louder than words, but do they? It depends! The perceptions created by what we *see* and *hear* have a powerful influence. However, someone you respect tells you to avoid a certain course or professor because it is a waste of time, and the professor speaks with a terrible foreign accent and

MAKING CONNECTIONS FOR SUCCESS

What You Say Can Hurt You! It's All about Perception

The following quotation was given in an interview and reported in the *New York Times* when a candidate for the U.S. Senate was asked why she believed she would make a good senator:

> "So I think in many ways, you know, we want to have all kinds of different voices, you know, representing us, and I think what I bring to it is, you know, my experience as a mother, as a woman, as a lawyer, you know."[2]

1. Based solely on what the person said in the interview, what are your initial perceptions of the candidate?

2. In what ways would your initial perceptions of the person change if you learned that in the course of the interview, she said, "you know" 142 times?

3. How would your perceptions of the person's communication alter if you found out that she had written seven books, including two on the Constitution and two on American politics; that she had graduated from Harvard University and Columbia Law School; and her family name is well known in national politics?

4. In what ways, if at all, would your perceptions change if you knew it was her first major interview and she was extremely nervous?

---

is impossible to understand. You may avoid the course and professor based on your friend's experience and your perception of that experience. You might also tell someone else what you heard from a reliable source about the course and professor. You formed your perception of the course and professor on what you heard and not what you personally experienced. A couple of weeks later, you talk to another friend whom you also respect and who had the same professor in another course and absolutely loved it. Now you are thinking you may have missed a good course and professor. Competent communicators not only verify their perceptions before drawing conclusions but also are also willing to alter them should new information suggest they do so. Later you will learn some techniques for verifying new information.

Perceptual Differences

 Identify seven reasons why different people may perceive the same situation in different ways.

Our experiences, our physical makeup, our cultural background, and our current psychological state determine what we perceive, and how we interpret, evaluate, and organize our perceptions and our actions in response to them. The following sections discuss how these factors influence our perceptions.

Perceptual Set and Stereotyping

perceptual set
A fixed, previously determined view of events, objects, or people.

stereotyping
The categorizing of events, objects, and people without regard to unique individual characteristics and qualities.

When we ignore new information and instead rely solely on our experiences—fixed, previously determined views of events, objects, and people—to interpret information, we are using a perceptual set.[3] A **perceptual set** allows our experiences to control or focus our perceptions so that we ignore information that is different or has changed about an event, object, or person. It is a form of stereotyping. **Stereotyping** refers to the categorizing of events, objects, and people without regard to unique individual characteristics and qualities. Stereotyping, for example, exists in nearly every intercultural situation, usually because of people's unfamiliarity with the other culture. Stereotyping is pervasive because of the human psychological need to categorize and classify information. Through stereotyping, we profile people and their behaviors. This tendency may hamper our communication by causing us to overlook individual characteristics and differences.

Stereotypes often oversimplify, generalize, or exaggerate traits or qualities and thus are based on half-truths, distortions, and false premises—hardly fertile ground for successful communication. Stereotypes repeat and reinforce beliefs. For example, for some of us to assume that student athletes go to college only because they want to participate in their sport is a typical assumption. Stereotypes ultimately perpetuate inaccuracies about people and thus may impede or reinforce our communication about those whom we stereotype. Although many stereotypes are negative, positive stereotypes exist as well. When we stereotype male students as decisive or female students as sensitive, for instance, we project positive images that should apply equally to both genders.

Perceptual sets, like stereotypes, do not always limit or hinder us. Sometimes they help us make decisions more efficiently. They provide us with expectations of how things, events, or people should be, and they enable us to compare our expectations with the reality of the moment and to respond accordingly. For example, when a student from China comes to the United States to attend college, many of us would expect the student to lack fluency in English. However, after talking with the student for just a few minutes, you find that not only is she fluent in English, but she also sounds more American than many of us who were born in the United States. You ask her where she learned to speak English so well, and she tells you that she has studied English most of her life, that she studied in England for five years while growing up, and that she is a translator of Chinese to English for government officials in China. A competent communicator avoids the assumption that perceptual sets or stereotypes will always be complete or accurate. Many communication scholars believe that *the greatest single problem with human communication is the assumption that our perceptions are always correct.*[4]

Attribution Error

It is human nature to attribute, or assign, causes to people's behavior. **Attribution** is the complex process through which we attempt to understand the reasons behind others' behaviors. Two factors influence our assumptions about our own and others' behavior: the *situation* (environment/external factors) and the *disposition* (traits of the person/internal factors). We are always trying to explain why people behave the way they do, but to seek an explanation, we must make assumptions. For example, imagine that you witness the following scene. A classmate arrives over an hour late for a study session. He walks in and drops his iPad on the floor. While trying to pick it up, his glasses fall out of his coat pocket and break. Reaching for his glasses, he spills his Coke all over the floor. How would you explain these events? The chances are good that you would reach conclusions such as, "He is disorganized and clumsy." Are your attributions accurate? Perhaps. However, it is also possible that he was late because his car would not start, dropped his iPad because it had a slick cover, and spilled his Coke because he was picking up his glasses. Research shows that we are more likely to overestimate dispositional causes and underestimate situational causes of others' actions. This is a **fundamental attribution error**.[5] Fundamental attribution errors occur when we perceive others acting as they do because they are "that kind of person" rather than because of any external factors that may have influenced their behavior.

Suppose you come across a fellow student who is having trouble starting her car. You decide to help by giving her some suggestions on how to start it. She looks at you as though you were an idiot, snaps at you, and ignores you. You get a bit angry and think to yourself, "*She's* the idiot; she is rude, insensitive, and self-centered, and doesn't value my help." Is it possible that several others had already offered the same advice and it failed? Or that she has had an extremely rough day, having failed an exam and broken up with her boyfriend, and the car problem was the last straw? This is another example of a fundamental attribution error. The error occurs because we have no other reference point except the observable behavior of the person in question; thus, we are likely to make a judgment about the person to appease ourselves. It

attribution
The complex process through which we attempt to understand the reasons behind others' behaviors.

fundamental attribution error
Perceiving others as acting as they do because they are "that kind of person" rather than because of any external factors that may have influenced their behavior.

also can lead to faulty and inaccurate communication, especially if we communicate without verification of the facts or situation.

In our own case, we know the situation, so we know what accounts for our behavior. It is often easier to "assume" rather than determine what actually causes someone to behave the way he or she does. For example, a student who speaks with an accent and has trouble expressing himself in class might be perceived as not very intelligent. However, after the first exam you learn that the same student scored the highest grade on the exam. This surprises you because of your first impression of the student; but then, in talking with the student, you discover that he is a biological science major with a straight-A GPA. What you didn't know is that the student suffers from communication apprehension. It is common to make this attribution error and make judgments that are inaccurate based on a person's ability to express her- or himself. This is a fundamental attribution error based on the assumption that, because the student does not speak fluently, he lacks intelligence.

As competent communicators, we need to learn how to avoid making fundamental attribution errors and taking too narrow a perspective. We should stop and think before making judgments about other people's behavior and at least ask ourselves if we are possibly overreacting or misjudging the situation. Through such questioning, we will improve our ability to form accurate perceptions, as well as improve our communication.

Physical Characteristics

Our weight, height, body shape, health, strength, and ability to use our five senses can account for differences in what we perceive. For example, if you are visually impaired, you likely experience the world in ways that a sighted person may find difficult to comprehend or even imagine. Sighted people might not automatically consider such differences, thus making communication a bit awkward.

When we meet someone for the first time, we usually react to a variety of factors, no matter how superficial, resulting in emotional reactions that lead to a positive or negative image of that person. One such factor is the clothing the person is wearing. Beyond such factors as neatness or perceived cost, clothing color and style appear to have an effect on our perception. It seems that we automatically conclude that bright is good and dark equals bad.[6] Other influences on our perceptions are observable disabilities, the presence of eyeglasses, a person's height and physique, and facial hair on men.[7] Once again, perceptions can lead to assumptions, and those assumptions can influence how and what we communicate with others.

Psychological State

Another factor that influences or alters our perceptions of people, events, and things is our state of mind. All information coming to us passes through various filters and screens that sort and color what we receive and how we perceive it. Obviously, when everything is going well and we are in a positive frame of mind, we view things, events, and people much more positively than when our mind-set is negative. When we are under a great deal of stress or if we have a poor self-image, these conditions will influence how we perceive the world around us. Sometimes this distortion is small and temporary and has no appreciable effect on communication. At other times, our state of mind can actually reverse meaning or alter a message, changing how we select, organize, and interpret it. It is undeniable that psychological disposition can color or alter perceptions and ultimately communication. Think about how you feel when you are upset, angry, or frustrated with someone or something and when you are not. How does your disposition affect your communication with others? Later in this chapter, we discuss the connections between self-concept and perception in more detail.

Cultural Background

Cultural background can also affect the perception of other people, events, and things. Culture has well over a hundred different definitions, each taking a different perspective. For our purposes, **culture** is "a set of interpretations about beliefs, values, norms, and social practices that affect behaviors of a relatively large group of people."[8] A culture evolves through communication, beliefs, artifacts, and a style of living shared among people. A group's culture usually includes similarities in religion, language, thinking, social rules, laws, perceptions, communicative style, and attitudes, all of which contribute to a group's identity as distinct from that of other cultural groups.

Culture evolves through communication, beliefs, artifacts, and a style of living shared by others. Traditions and customs also play a role in shaping a culture and communicating it to future generations, such as this Indian celebration with special food, dress, and rituals.

J.Paul Guilloteau/EXPRESS-REA/Redux Pictures

Take a moment and reflect on the cultural beliefs you hold that influence how you perceive the world and interact in it. Your views on work, education, freedom, age, competitiveness, personal space, cleanliness and hygiene, gender, loyalty, death and mourning, etiquette, health, status differentiation, bodily adornment, courtship, family, art, music, technology, and the like, all play a role in your cultural identity. Your views also affect how you communicate and interact with others.

Cultural identity has little or nothing to do with physical features, such as skin color, shape of eyes, or sex, because these characteristics are passed on genetically and not by communication. Because people of a particular race or country are often taught similar beliefs, values, and attitudes, those similarities have created labels such as "African American," "Latino," "Native American," or "European American." Each of these labels, by definition, suggests that cultural differences exist among these groups, but the labels do not suggest differences exist within the groups. Most of us believe people who are similar in race or nationality think and behave in the same way. This way of thinking, however, is likely to lead to misunderstandings and perceptual errors. For example, two Latino business owners, one in New York City and the other in rural Nebraska, while labeled "Latinos," could have different values, beliefs, and lifestyles because of where they live. Yet both are Latino. Therefore, to assume that they think and act similarly because they both are Latino or because of their physical features is an assumption that could prove wrong. The competent communicator does not rely on labels or physical characteristics to make assumptions about people's values, attitudes,

culture

A set of interpretations about beliefs, values, norms, and social practices that affect behaviors of a relatively large group of people.

MAKING CONNECTIONS FOR SUCCESS

Perceptual Differences

Create a list of groups, such as law enforcement officers, athletes, teachers, bankers, middle class, supervisors, business owners, corporate leaders, accountants, and so on. You can use these groups if you wish, but you could also create your own list of three to five groups. Select two groups and list traits that describe each. For example, for athletes, you might list traits such as competitive, aggressive, dedicated, skilled, strong, fast, and so on.

1. What role does perception have, if any, in creating your list of traits?

2. In what ways would the list of traits and characteristics influence how you communicate about or with individuals in these groups?

beliefs, or behaviors. The competent communicator, however, does learn about others through communication and perceptions of their behaviors. They also ask questions to ensure the accuracy.

Gender

gender
A socially constructed concept related to masculine and feminine behaviors that are learned.

androgyny
A socially constructed concept related to having both masculine and feminine traits.

Another factor that affects the way we perceive our world is gender. Unlike biological sex, **gender** is socially constructed. It involves learned behaviors related to masculinity, **androgyny**, and femininity. Some theorists believe that where we fall on the masculine-and-feminine scale determines how we learn to understand the world around us, resulting in the way we perceive and communicate.

An interesting study on voice pitch and perceived affection in initial interactions by Kory Floyd and George B. Bay, two communication scholars, found that men whose voices were higher pitched were perceived as weak or effeminate and would therefore not be regarded by women as a good relational fit.[9] However, with women, the opposite was found to be true. Women with higher-pitched voices were perceived to be more affectionate than women with lower-pitched voices.[10] There is a more detailed discussion of gender found on pages 51–53 of this chapter.

Media

Sometimes other people influence our perceptions deliberately. Advertisers, government leaders, political advocates, and many others attempt to shape our views. Advertisers have mastered techniques to encourage us to think and behave in ways that will benefit their clients.

Have you ever wondered how much the media influences our perceptions? In recent elections, candidates have hired people often referred to as "handlers" or "spin doctors." Their job is to create a positive image of their candidates and to protect them from any exposure that might create a negative image. In addition to trying to create favorable impressions by using positive messages related to their candidates, they also try to create negative messages and images of their candidates' opponents. Most of us perceive negative ads as unfavorable; however, they do have more of a persuasive effect on most of us than positive ads.

Many of us who use social media believe that our messages do not create perceptions or, if they do, the perceptions are not interpreted. However, as with anything we communicate, including our use of emails, Snapchat, Instagram, or tweets, perceptions are created, and at times our message is interpreted in ways we did not intend. Therefore, we need to be careful about what and how we write and what we show or

MAKING CONNECTIONS FOR SUCCESS

Communication Style Dictated by Gender?

Dr. Carol Kensey Goman, president of Kensey Consulting Services, conducted a research study to see how gender differences in communication are perceived in the workplace. Create a list of what you believe are the top three communication strengths and the top three weaknesses of women and men. Then discuss your list with several others in your class to determine an agreed-upon list.

1. What role did perception have, if any, in creating your list? Explain.

2. Do the perceptions of males and females in your class/group differ as to the strengths and weaknesses they listed? If so, in what ways?

3. To learn what Carol Kinsey Goman found in her research, go to: https://tinyurl.com/ybuk9efw. Do you agree or disagree with what she found? Explain.

4. Explain why her findings may or may not be accurate for all men and women.

MAKING CONNECTIONS FOR SUCCESS

Perceptions and Ethics

Bob, a photographer, is hired by your college to take pictures to make the college appear as attractive as possible for its Internet web page. When he gets to campus, Bob notices right away that it is located in an undesirable part of the city, parking is difficult, and the campus is in dire need of maintenance. Therefore, he does not take any photos that show the surroundings. He does take a photograph of a student dressed to look like a successful businessperson approaching the newly remodeled entrance of the administration building. He takes close-up photos of a diverse group of students to show the diversity on campus. He takes a shot of a small pond in front of one of the campus buildings, using a wide-angle lens to give the illusion of a lake. Bob has

created the impression on the Internet that the college attracts a variety of students, has a modern campus, and has a lake.

1. What has Bob done regarding the perceptions he has created through the photos he took?

2. Because the area around the campus is a blighted and poor neighborhood, Bob decides to take photos of attractions and homes in another part of the city and use them, giving the impression that they are close to the campus. Is the use of Bob's photos ethical in your opinion? Why or why not?

3. How can you be sure that the Internet sites you view are presenting images and messages in a truthful way?

---

don't show. Those who receive our emails or view our Twitter feeds form impressions and make inferences based on the language we use, spelling accuracy, the tone in which we write our messages, or the photos we post.

We must also keep in mind that the information we receive via the Internet and social media is only as good or reliable as the sources. What we see, hear, or read on the Internet, in emails, on Facebook pages, in tweets, or on other media does affect our perceptions and ultimately our view of the world. The Internet and social media are powerful tools and, as with other media, do not always contain reliable information.

The example of the media's influence on the public perception of the killing of blacks by white police officers or sexual harassment incidents of celebrities or politicians shows how the media can mold and reinforce perceptions in powerful ways. You might believe there is nothing wrong with this, but think about how we depend on the media for information and how people often accept what is presented to them by the media without question. The gap between our perceptions and what is actually real can be huge. Competent communicators check the information they receive—especially when the source is unknown to them—to determine its truthfulness and accuracy.

Sion Touhig/Getty Images Entertainment/ Getty Images

What is in print or seen on the Internet is often misleading and inaccurate. It is important that as competent communicators we double check information, especially when it seems sensational or not mentioned anywhere else.

Improving Perception Competencies and Perception Checking

2.4 Accurately **interpret and check** your perceptions to improve your communication competence.

To be competent communicators, we must understand the impact perceptions have, how we communicate with others, and what we accept as reality or truth. We tend to take the validity of our perceptions for granted and fail to look beneath the surface. For example, you and Stephanie are taking the same biology class. You have heard from another student that Stephanie goes out a lot and really likes to party. Her Facebook page is loaded with off-color photos, and she is usually holding a beer. You see her as a party girl and assume her only motivation to be in college is to have a good time. She seldom is on time for class, misses class more than most, and doesn't say much unless she is called on, but she always seems to know the correct answer. The midterm exam is coming up and you have heard from her roommate that, not only does Stephanie go out a lot, but also she hardly cracks a book, let alone studies. You see Stephanie shortly after the exam and ask her how she did. She tells you she aced it and that it was easy. You say you thought the exam was darn hard. Later you find that Stephanie received the second-highest grade in the class. You could infer that Stephanie cheated because there is no way, from what you know, that she could have done that well on the exam. No matter what reason you choose, you are making an inference, and if you communicate that inference without labeling it as such, you may be communicating false—or, at the very least, misleading—information about Stephanie. To become a more competent communicator, you must realize that your perceptions are partial, often subjective, and could be wrong.[11] To avoid misperceptions, you must be an active perceiver; recognize your perceptions might differ from others; be aware that facts differ from inferences; understand the role of perception in communication; keep an open mind; and, when possible, perception check.

Become an Active Perceiver

First, we must be active as perceivers. We must be willing to seek out as much information as possible about a given person, subject, event, or situation. The more information we obtain, the deeper our understanding, and the more accurate our perceptions will be. We must question our perceptions to determine how accurate they are. By acknowledging that we may misinterpret information, we prompt ourselves to confirm facts and impressions before we draw conclusions. Taking time to gather more information and recheck the accuracy of our perceptions is well worth the effort. For example, is Stephanie late for class because she is lazy or because she has another class across campus right before biology? Does she miss class because she is not interested or because the bus sometimes doesn't run? An active perceiver will ask Stephanie why she is often late or misses class and will not make attribution errors.

Recognize That Each Person's Frame of Reference Is Unique

Second, we must recognize the uniqueness of our own frame of reference. We must remember that our view of things may be only one of many views. Each of us has a unique window to the world, as well as a unique system of understanding and storing data. Some of us make judgments about people based on appearance, whereas others base their judgments on ability, income, education, gender, ethnicity, or other factors. This variety of approaches shows that all of us operate according to different perceptual systems, and it is wrong to assume that one system is better than another.

Distinguish Facts from Inferences

A third way to improve our perceptions and interpretations is to distinguish facts from inferences or assumptions. A fact is a statement put forth objectively and is easily verified. For example, it is a known fact which science building on campus is the tallest, that Gina has been late to class five times this semester, and that the volleyball team has won its last eight home games. These events or behaviors are what you have observed and are verifiable; therefore, they are facts. An inference is an interpretation that goes beyond what we know to be factual. For example, when you say Stephanie is lazy, unprepared, disorganized, and unmotivated to learn, you are making inferences that may or may not be factual.

Because facts and inferences are often extremely difficult to distinguish, it is easy to confuse them. We sometimes treat inferences as if they are facts. A statement such as "Stephanie is lazy" sounds factual, and we tend to accept those types of statements

MAKING CONNECTIONS FOR SUCCESS
Just the Facts and Nothing but the Facts

Competent communicators can distinguish facts from inferences—can you?

1. College students who party are less likely to do well on exams—fact or inference?

2. More females go to college today than males—fact or inference?

3. College graduates, on average, make more money than non–college graduates—fact or inference?

4. Students who use social media during their classes have low motivation to learn—fact or inference?

5. Athletes who use special equipment to enhance their performance are unethical—fact or inference?

For answers, see page 59.

Competent communicators qualify inferences by labeling them as such. How would you qualify the above statements that are not factual?

---

as truth rather than communicating to find out what is fact and what is inference. We need to label our statements as inferences when we communicate them. For example, saying "Stephanie seems to be lazy" is much more tentative and is not stated as a fact or with certainty. A next step might be to learn more about Stephanie, try to draw her out, and find out if anything is affecting her life or discover more about her background before making a judgment about her.

Become Aware of the Role of Perceptions in Communication

A fourth way to improve our perceptions and interpretations is to be aware of the role of perceptions in communication, to consider others' perceptions, and to avoid the tendency to assume too much about what we perceive. To make the most of the information we receive, we must first evaluate it. We should check the source and context of the information. To help ensure the accuracy of our perceptions, we should ask questions and obtain feedback whenever possible. We cannot determine whether our perceptions are accurate without questioning them.

Keep an Open Mind

A fifth way to improve our perceptions and interpretations is to keep an open mind and remind ourselves that our perceptions may not be complete or accurate. Thus, we must continue to make observations, seek out additional information, be willing to describe what we observe both mentally and verbally, state what a given observation means to us. Finally, we should put our perceptions into words to test their logic and soundness. For example, is it possible that Stephanie doesn't communicate much in class because she is shy, or is it because she hasn't come prepared, or is there some other reason? If she didn't cheat, then either she is very smart or she studies a lot. We need a perception check to ensure the accuracy of what we are thinking and communicating.

Perception Checking: Being a Competent Communicator

Finally, to improve the accuracy of our perceptions and interpretations, we must learn to check perceptions. When it comes to interpreting perceptions, the variables and possibilities for misunderstanding are abundant; therefore, the potential for jumping to conclusions without fully knowing all of the information is large. For example, a friend of mine and I exchange texts periodically, but if I don't respond within 10 to 20 minutes or so of receiving his text, he assumes that I am upset with him. Of course, I am not upset with him, but that is what he perceives when he does not receive an

MAKING CONNECTIONS FOR SUCCESS

Competent Communicators Check Their Perceptions for Accuracy

In this chapter so far, we have discussed perception, its relationship to communication, and our competence as communicators. To check our perceptions, we should (1) try to state what we observed as best we can, (2) recognize that what we observe is a possible explanation, (3) consider other possible explanations, and (4) ask or check on the accuracy of the possible explanation(s).

Example: You saw Jason, an athlete friend, walking out of a clinic known for its distribution of steroids; Jason has shown a significant improvement in his athleticism over the past several months.

Perception-checking steps: I saw Jason, a good friend and athlete, coming out of a clinic that has been rumored to sell steroids. [(1) This is what was observed—describe, don't infer.] Jason was there to buy steroids. [(2) This is one possible explanation.] Jason was at the clinic to get his sprained ankle checked out, to check on a friend who was hurt, or to get

painkillers for his ankle sprain. [(3) These are other possible explanations.] Which explanation is the correct one, if any? [(4) Check on the accuracy or qualify the observation by stating that you don't know the reason Jason was coming out of the clinic.]

Now create your own perception-checking statements based on the following scenario:

Debra is a friend of yours who has been struggling in her speech class and receiving Cs on her speeches. She borrows an outline of a speech for which you received an A grade last semester. You overhear her bragging to another friend that she received an A on her last speech. How would you use perception-checking steps in the above example?

1. Describe the observed behavior.
2. Think of at least two interpretations of the observed behavior.
3. Verify your interpretation.

---

instant response from me. Think about this example and of how many times others have jumped to inaccurate conclusions about your thoughts, feelings, or motives.

Developing the skill of perception checking should help prevent jumping to the wrong conclusions about others' thoughts, feelings, or motives. For example, when a favorite professor walks by, you say "Hi" and smile, but the professor does not even acknowledge your presence, although you believe she looked directly at you. It would be very easy to assume that the teacher ignored you because she doesn't think much of you or you are unimportant to her. A competent communicator would employ perception-checking skills, which would include the following:

1. Describe the observed behavior—a fact: Your teacher ignores your presence.
2. Think of at least two interpretations of the teacher's behavior—inferences: (1) She was ignoring you because she doesn't think much of you, or (2) she was ignoring you because her mind was preoccupied and she didn't hear or see you.
3. Finally, verify your interpretation: You might ask the teacher, "What's going on? Is something wrong?" This would immediately clarify any possible misunderstandings.

By using such checking as a means of verifying your perceptions, you are less likely to assume that your first interpretation is the only one or the correct one. To prevent misunderstandings or misinterpretation of perceptions requires cooperation and willingness to communicate, as well as being open-minded about the communication received.

Perception and Self-Concept

2.5 **Understand** the role perception has in determining self-concept.

A question that most of us have asked or at least thought about asking at one time or another is, "Who is the real me?" When college students are asked, "Who are you?" or "How do you describe yourself?" their answers typically consist of references to relationships (e.g., Melissa's boyfriend, son of Bill and Frances), social identities

Guidelines

CHECK YOUR PERCEPTIONS: COMPETENT COMMUNICATORS DO!

1. **Separate fact from assumptions.** It is easy to accept assumptions, but we must realize that assumptions are not facts, nor are they always accurate. When we make assumptions, we are drawing conclusions with little or no basis in fact. Thus, we should label assumptions so that when we communicate them, they are differentiated from facts.

2. **Recognize your personal biases.** We all have biases that can influence our perceptions, and we must be careful that those biases don't inaccurately slant our perceptions. We should always qualify, when recognized, that our biases may have influenced our communication about events, objects, and people.

3. **Remember that perceptions, especially first impressions, are not always accurate.** This is important because when we make judgments based on limited information or our first impression, we may cling to that impression or perception as if that is all there is to know.

4. **Recognize that people from different cultural backgrounds do not always attach the same meanings to events, objects, and people.** It is important to recognize that not everyone sees the world as you do, and this is especially true of people who come from different cultural backgrounds. For example, it is common for someone who lives in Europe or the Middle East to walk with someone of the same sex holding hands or kissing them on the check. How this might be perceived depends on differences in cultural norms or background.

5. **Remember that perceptions are a function of the perceiver, the perceived, and the situation in which the perception occurs.** To ensure accuracy, it is important to understand that perception is in the eye of the beholder, to understand what is perceived and why, and to take into account the situation or context of the perception.

6. **Don't be afraid to communicate to verify your perceptions.** It is important that you ask questions and seek additional information to ensure the accuracy of your perceptions. You do not want to leave yourself open to interpretations or misunderstandings that could be avoided.

7. **Be willing to admit misperceptions and to change them when necessary.** It is important to correct misperceptions and admit when perceptions are not accurate. It is also the responsibility of the perceiver to make changes when errors or misunderstandings occur.

(e.g., a sophomore at Clemson; a major in Communication Studies; a member of the swim team; part of the Christian Student Fellowship; Nebraskans for Peace member; member of Utah Young Republicans; member of Sigma Lambda Chi; from Charleston, South Carolina; graduate from Central High School in Chicago), or personal traits (e.g., good student, hard worker, organized, athletic, kind, friendly, sincere, and trustworthy). However, do these descriptions really tell who you are or describe the real you? We know our perceptions of others, events, and things are usually subjective. We learned, so far in this chapter, the accuracy of our perceptions is often questionable because what we perceive may not be the same as what others perceive or what actually is real or true. Therefore, who is the real you?

Barbara Corcoran, real-estate mogul, wrote, "The best mistake I ever made was believing that I was stupid." Corcoran tells the story of a teacher who changed her life. The teacher saw her inattentiveness and pulled her right out of her chair. The teacher looked directly into her eyes and said, "If you don't learn to pay attention, you will always be stupid." As an 8-year-old, Corcoran was dramatically affected by the incident in two ways: She hid her true self, and she became the quietest kid in class. Corcoran says her insecurity made her a meticulous preparer; it made her work twice as hard, and she was constantly trying to prove she wasn't stupid. She knew she could succeed, but still she doubted herself. In 2001, she sold her business, which employed 1,000 people and was worth $66 million. In 2008, she became a real-estate expert for the *Today Show*, and in 2012 she began counseling entrepreneurs on ABC's reality show *Shark Tank*. So who is the real Barbara Corcoran?[12] On her website (www.barbaracorcoran.com), you will learn more about her and why she says "taking chances almost always makes for happy endings."

Each of us is extremely complex. Early in life, we begin to learn who we are—or at least who we think we are. We develop a social identity, or self-definition, that includes how we see and evaluate ourselves. Most of us manage to maintain a coherent image of our respective selves, yet we recognize that we define ourselves and behave differently in different situations. For example, when you are at home with your parents, your self-image as a responsible adult might at times come into question. You might not pick up after yourself, or you might even expect that someone else will do your laundry. However, when you are away at college, you perform these tasks competently and see yourself as a responsible adult. Despite such readily admitted pockets of irresponsibility, do you see yourself as irresponsible? No, of course not! Our self-concept and our communication with others depend on the context, the situation, and the other person or people involved; how we evaluate ourselves in that context or situation; and how we compare ourselves to the other person or people. The way others act toward us and communicate with us, and how we believe they will act toward and communicate with us in the future, have important implications as to how we see ourselves. When it comes to self-perception, no person is an island. When we suspect that others might reject us because of some flaw or inadequacy we believe they see in us, we could choose to change only that particular flaw or inadequacy. In other words, people can attempt to hide some aspects of the self from others who disapprove. To become competent communicators, we must understand that our image of self has a significant role in how we communicate and how others communicate with us. Therefore, we must try to understand the idea of self-concept and its connection to perception and our communication.

Understanding Self-Concept

2.6 **Differentiate** among self-concept, self-image, and self-esteem.

self-concept
A person's perceived self, which consists of an organized collection of beliefs and attitudes about self.

self-image
A person's mental picture of him- or herself.

self-esteem
A person's feelings and attitudes toward him- or herself.

Our **self-concept**, or self-identity, is our perceived self, which consists of an organized collection of beliefs and attitudes about self. Our experiences and communication with others, the roles and values we have selected for ourselves, and how we believe others see us determines our perceived self. Self-concept consists of two subcomponents: **self-image**, how we see ourselves or our mental picture of self (for example, I see myself as not very attractive, an athlete, a student, a worker, a female, a daughter, and a first-year student), and **self-esteem**, our feelings and attitudes toward ourselves or how we evaluate ourselves (for example, I feel that I am liked, lonely, confident, successful, unappreciated, alone, respected) (see Figure 2.1). Both self-image and self-esteem determine our self-concept.

FIGURE 2.1 Self-Concept

Our experiences and communication determine our self-concept, the roles and values we have selected for ourselves, our perception of how we think others see us, and how we evaluate ourselves.

self-esteem

Our feelings and attitudes toward ourselves or how we evaluate ourselves

How we see ourselves

self-image

SELF-CONCEPT

Our perception of how others see us

The relationship between self-concept and perception is extremely close, so it is difficult to separate them. They constantly interact. For example, what you think about yourself shapes and, in many ways, determines what you do and say. The information you receive from others influences how you see and feel about yourself, which creates a perception of who you are. If you regard yourself as a good speaker, you would take positive comments made about your communication as affirmation of your ability. If someone made a disparaging comment, however, you probably would dismiss it as not a reflection of your ability to communicate. In fact, you might interpret the comment as a sign of jealousy or humor; you might simply feel that the person making the comment isn't very knowledgeable about communication or you, or they are trying to improve your already excellent speaking ability to make it better.

Why is it important for us to understand the connection between communication, perception, and self-concept? Think about this question and read on to find an answer.

Development of Self-Concept

When we were children, our first communication involved sensing our environment—all the sights, sounds, tastes, and smells that surrounded us. We learned about ourselves as others touched us and spoke to us. Their responses helped to determine how we view ourselves. Parental communication, both verbal and nonverbal, generally has an extremely strong impact on the initial development of self-concept. For example, the clothes and toys they provided and what and how they communicated to us affected who we have become in some way. As we age and expand our environment and relationships, the communication of others may reinforce or alter our perceptions of self. In her book *Old Is Not a Four-Letter Word: A Midlife Guide*, Anne Gerike writes that aging has its advantages. For example, she says that aging brings increased self-confidence, a more reliable inner voice or "gut feeling," an acceptance that we are not perfect, a sense of perspective that difficult situations get worked out, an acceptance that life isn't always fair, and a willingness to take responsibility instead of directing the blame elsewhere.[13]

Assuming Gerike's observations are correct, why do you think such developments occur with age?

Social psychologist Daryl J. Bem believes sometimes we don't know or understand our own attitudes, feelings, or emotions. We therefore focus on others to obtain such information.[14] Bem indicates, however, that we learn a great deal about ourselves by observing our own behaviors. He suggests that what we do or how we act is a guide to what is happening inside us and how we feel about ourselves. Further, according to Bem, we draw inferences about ourselves in the same manner that we do about others. Thus, the process through which we come to know ourselves is very similar to the one we use to learn about others.

How we perceive ourselves is not only affected by our self-concept but also by how we perceive others and how we think others perceive us. Our past and present experiences affect how we will perceive ourselves in the future. The values, attitudes, and beliefs we possess; how we attribute these qualities to others; and how they connect them to us further determines our self-concept.

Values   Relatively long-lasting principles or standards that guide our behavior or judgment of what is important in our lives are called **values**. Values can be classified into broad categories, such as aesthetic, religious, humanitarian, intellectual, and material. Each category determines our behavior as well as our communication, and is often reflected in who we are as a person.

values

Relatively long-lasting principles or standards that guide our behavior or judgment of what is important.

We develop our self-concept early in life based on how others react to us and how we perceive their reactions.

Image Source/Getty Images

Values, Attitudes, and Beliefs about People with Disabilities

Words and phrases such as "handicapped person confined to a wheelchair" or "young woman stricken with cerebral palsy" can shape incorrect perceptions of people with disabilities. Stigma and negative attitudes are often the greatest barriers those with disabilities must overcome. Most people with disabilities don't see their disability as a liability or limitation; rather, they view it as who they are. For most of us, the problem is the visible characteristics and appearance of others strongly influence our perceptions and thus our communication. We might not be conscious of our behaviors until someone points them out. However, our actions, whether conscious or not, communicate our values and attitudes, and ultimately affect our beliefs as well.

1. Why do phrases like the previous examples form our values, attitudes, and beliefs about people with disabilities?

2. Create a list of behaviors you should and should not do when interacting with people with disabilities. Develop your own list first and share with either a small group of your classmates or the entire class.

3. Now search on the Internet, using the keywords "interacting with people with disabilities" to compare your list with those on the Internet. Are there suggestions you didn't discuss or list?

An excellent resource on communicating with people with disabilities is the *Handbook of Communication and People with Disabilities: Research and Application*, edited by Dawn O. Braithwaite and Teresa L. Thompson (Mahwah, NJ: Lawrence Erlbaum Associates).

---

attitude

An evaluative feeling or way of thinking about oneself, others, events, ideas, or objects.

belief

A conviction or confidence in the truth of something that is not based on absolute proof.

Attitudes   An evaluative judgment in terms of likes and dislikes about oneself, others, events, ideas, or objects is called an **attitude**. Attitudes help determine self-concept, but unlike values, they are more narrowly defined. The relationship between values and attitudes is close because values are reflected in our attitudes.

Beliefs   Closely related to attitudes are beliefs. A **belief** is a conviction or confidence in the truth of something that is not based on absolute proof. We have beliefs, for example, about history, religion, schools, events, people, and ourselves. Our beliefs, like our attitudes and values, have a hierarchy of importance. That is, some are much more important than others. Our most important beliefs, such as those about religion, education, and family life, do not change easily, but the less important ones, such as those about today's weather, the outcome of a sports event, or a grade, are only temporary and exist until the outcome is known.

Making clear and absolute distinctions among values, attitudes, and beliefs is difficult because they are interrelated. Consider, for example, how closely related the following three statements are:

Value (ideal): A college education will be beneficial to our society's success.

Attitude (feeling or position): A college education is good for our society.

Belief (conviction): A college education will make our society better.

Attitudes differ from beliefs in that attitudes include an evaluation of whether someone or something is good or bad. Beliefs, in turn, reflect the perception of whether something is true or false. Your attitudes and beliefs about college may change because of your experiences, but the value you place on education endures. Table 2.2 provides definitions and examples of values, attitudes, and beliefs, with space in the last column for you to add your own examples.

Communication and Self-Concept

Self-concept and the way we communicate have a direct connection to how others perceive us: Communication affects our self-concept, and our self-concept influences how and what we communicate. A model developed by social psychologist John W. Kinch[15] illustrates this relationship (see Figure 2.2). Our perceptions of how others respond to us (P) affect our self-concept (S). Our self-concept affects how we behave (B).

Table 2.2 VALUES, ATTITUDES, AND BELIEFS

Term	Definition	Example	Your Examples
Values	Broad-based ideals that are relatively long-lasting	Social media have made our lives more convenient.	
Attitudes	Evaluative dispositions, feelings, or positions about ourselves, other persons, events, ideas, or objects	Social media users are more tech savvy than nonusers.	
Beliefs	Convictions or confidence in the truth of something that lacks absolute proof	Social media are the only way to communicate effectively with others.	

Our behavior is directly related to how others react to our behavior (A). The actual responses of others relate to our perceptions of others' responses (P), and so we have come full circle.

According to Kinch, our conception of self emerges from our social interaction, which in turn guides or influences our behavior.[16] His theory postulates the way others react and how we perceive those reactions function to direct or alter our behavior. To test whether or not the Kinch theory is correct, four male students in one of his classes decided to see if they could actually change one's self-concept. One woman in class was rather plain looking but not unattractive. The four students selected her to run their experiment. The four, one at a time over a period of a few weeks, began interacting with the female student as if she were one of the most beautiful women on campus. They agreed to do this as naturally as possible so that she would not be aware of what they were doing. One after the other asked her for a date. Whenever they were with her, they behaved and interacted with her as if she were extremely attractive. After a few weeks, the results of their efforts began to show. She dressed more neatly, wore her nicest clothes, had her hair styled, and was more outgoing in her interactions with those around her. In fact, by the time the fourth male asked her out, she informed him that she would not be available for some time because of other dates she had.

According to Kinch, because of how the student perceived the behavior and responses of these male students, she changed her self-concept, which in turn changed her behavior. The interesting aspect of the experiment is that male students also

FIGURE 2.2 Kinch's Model of the Connection between Self-Concept and Communication

Kinch illustrates the relationship between self-concept and communication. Our self-concept is based on our communication with others.

Source: J. Kinch, "A Formalized Theory of the Self-Concept," *American Journal of Sociology* 68 (January 1963): 481–486. University of Chicago Press.

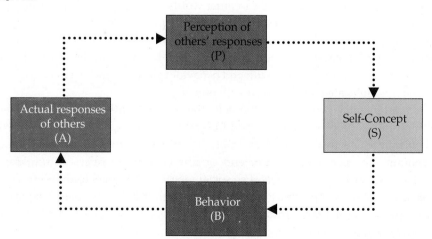

MAKING CONNECTIONS FOR SUCCESS

The Excuse?

Suppose that you are meeting a good friend for dinner, and she is late. You receive the following text message: "@ party, good time, leaving soon." However, after an hour, you begin to suspect that your friend will not arrive. Finally, she appears on the scene and says, "Sorry, I just got so involved with some friends at the party that I completely lost track of time!" What is your friend's perception of you?

Now imagine that she instead texts you, "OMG car accident, HUGE backup, CUL8R." Now what is her message saying about you?

If this is the first time your friend has been late, and this type of excuse has never surfaced before, you may perceive the explanation as true.

Now suppose that your friend is always late when it comes to meeting you and has used similar excuses all the time, but when she meets others, she is the first to arrive. In addition, this time she doesn't call or send you any message—she just doesn't show up.

1. Describe what you think is your friend's perception of you.
2. How might her behavior affect your self-concept? Or will it?
3. Is it easier to "get away with" excuses by texting or using Facebook or email than if you had to explain a situation in person?
4. Has technology changed how we perceive excuses for our inconsiderate behavior?

---

changed how they viewed the female student. They no longer regarded her as "plain Jane" but now as a more desirable and beautiful young woman, thus confirming Kinch's theory as circular.[17] In other words, how others behave and interact with us affects how we see ourselves, and our behaviors and interactions with others influence how they see themselves.

Personality theorists, such as Carl Rogers, believe that self-concept is the single most important aspect of our personalities. Our image of self forms our personality, which in turn determines our communication style and how we do or don't communicate with others. For example, Simon Cowell is a music mogul, television personality, and producer of many TV shows including *American Idol* and *America's Got Talent*. Simon is known for his blunt and often controversial criticisms, insults, and wisecracks about contestants and their abilities. He thinks of himself as competent and important, the ultimate judge of talent, who doesn't care much what others think of him. As a result, he regards himself as better than others and therefore believes he can say what he wants, even if it's self-serving or offensive to others. Furthermore, because he perceives that others don't know what he knows about talent, his perception of himself influences how and what he communicates to others. With respect to self, it becomes necessary to take into account the context and the person or people with whom you are communicating.

It is generally agreed people with high social self-concepts function better in most interpersonal situations than do those with low social self-concepts. The question here is not so much, "How do you perceive yourself?" but rather, "Who are you when you are with your best friend, your mother, your father, both your mother and father, people you don't know, and so on?" In other words, our image of self determines our communication style as perceived by others and as internalized by us, which in turn affects our perception and how we communicate with others. Kinch's experiment, described above, illustrates this notion clearly, when the female student began to internalize the men's communication with and behavior toward her, which in turn affected how she communicated and behaved with others.

personal-social identity continuum

The two ways the self can be categorized: at a personal level, in which the uniqueness of the individual is emphasized; and at the social identity level, in which the self is thought of as a member of a group.

A fundamental principle of the self, the social identity perspective,[18] says that individuals perceive themselves differently depending on where they are at a particular moment in time. This principle illustrates the **personal-social identity continuum**. The personal identity end of this continuum refers to thinking of ourselves primarily as *individuals*. The social identity end refers to thinking of ourselves as members of specific *social groups*. Because it is impossible to experience all aspects of our self-concept simultaneously, the specific aspect of our identity that is prominent at any given moment influences how we think about ourselves, and this in turn has consequences for our behavior. This idea is evident when we think of ourselves as unique individuals. Our personal identities are prominent, and this is likely to result in self-descriptions that emphasize how we are different from others. For example, you might describe yourself as a fun-loving person when thinking of yourself at the personal identity level—you are emphasizing your self-perception as a person who has more fun than those individuals with whom you compare yourself.

Personal identity self-description as an intragroup comparison involves comparisons with other individuals with whom you share a group membership. For this reason, our description of ourselves depends upon which group we are using for the comparison.[19] For example, how might you perceive yourself if you were asked to describe how you differ from others? You could label yourself as liberal when comparing yourself to your parents, but if you were indicating how you differ from other college students, you might say that you are more conservative. The point is that when we characterize ourselves we depend upon comparisons to others. According to Kristen Neff, an education psychologist, the need to positively evaluate ourselves often comes at a high price. High self-esteem generally requires feeling special and above average. Most of us consider being thought of as *average* by others is an insult. For example, "How did you like my speech yesterday?" "It was okay." "Just okay, ouch." Why is it that we all have to feel that we are better than average? According to Neff, it is impossible for every one of us to be above average at the same time.[20]

At the other end of the personal-social identity continuum, we can perceive ourselves as members of a group, which means we emphasize the ways we are similar to other group members. At the social identity level, we describe ourselves in terms of the attributes shared by members of our group as well as what differentiates "our group" from other groups. That is, descriptions of the self at the social identity level are intergroup in nature and usually involve contrasts between groups. For example, you may see yourself in terms of your social identity as a member of the school band, and you may describe yourself as musically talented and extroverted, attributes you perceive you share with other members of the band. Simultaneously, you differentiate the band group from other groups, such as members of the debate team, whom you see as studious and scholarly.

On other occasions, you might think of yourself in terms of your gender group. For example, if you are a female, you might emphasize what attributes you share with other females (e.g., being warm and caring) and what you perceive as differentiating women from males. What's noteworthy is when you think of yourself as an *individual*, the *content* of your self-description is likely to differ from when you regard yourself as a member of a *category* that you share with others.

Of course, most of us belong to a variety of groups (e.g., groups defined by age, religion, nationality, ethnicity, sexual orientation, occupation, sports, artistic ability), but all of these will not be prominent at the same time. When any particular social identity is prominent, people are likely to communicate in ways reflecting aspects of their self-concept. Can we say one of these "selves" is the "true" self—either the personal self or any one of a person's potential social identities? No, not really. Each view of self contributes to a larger general perception of self, which in essence identifies us.

So in any given context or time, we might perceive ourselves differently, thus creating many different "selves." Which of these descriptions can we say is the "true" self? We can't. All of the perceptions potentially reveal the true self, but they depend on the context and comparison dimension.[21] Therefore, how we perceive ourselves from one context to another could result in opposite self-descriptions (e.g., fun versus reserved; open versus closed; liberal versus conservative, and so on).

Social Media and Perceived Self-Concept

2.7 **Identify** social media factors that influence self-concept.

Our attitude toward online communication is another important factor that influences our perception of self. Attitude shapes how we interact with other people and how we present ourselves through social media. This orientation toward social media is our **online communication attitude** and it influences our media and message choices. Researchers have identified five attitudes toward online communication that shape how we approach or avoid opportunities to communicate through social media: online self-disclosure, online social connection, convenience, online apprehension, and miscommunication.[22] As you read about these attitudes, consider how they relate to your own experience.

online communication attitude
An attitude that shapes how we interact with other people and how we present ourselves through social media.

Online Self-Disclosure

Online self-disclosure is the degree to which individuals self-regulate what they reveal about themselves using social media. People using social media vary widely in this regard. Some people reveal nothing more than their name and location. Others use Facebook to display their personal philosophy, gender preferences, interests, and other private details. Still others go further by posting photos of everything from pets to the latest party they attended. All of these examples represent a different comfort level with online self-disclosure. Research has found that many people who share a great deal of personal information through social media are less likely to do so in face-to-face interactions with their friends. In some cases, these individuals come to depend on social media as an important outlet for sharing significant details in their lives. As a result, their communication through social media can affect perception of their self-concept.

online self-disclosure
The degree to which individuals self-regulate what they reveal about themselves using social media.

Online Social Connection

Those who use social media generally assume that this is an effective means of connecting with one's social network. **Online social connection** is the belief that online communication enables social contact. Research indicates that a person's communication competence is positively associated with his or her attitude toward online social connection.[23] In turn, their online communication and tendency to connect with others through social media can influence their perception of self.

online social connection
The belief that online communication enables social contact.

MAKING CONNECTIONS FOR SUCCESS

Social Media and Your Perceived Identity?

Jot down what you perceive your Instagram page communicates about you. Then show your page to a classmate who knows very little, if anything, about you. Then ask the classmate to describe your social identity or image based on what he or she perceives. Ask the following questions:

- How would you describe me? For example, does what you perceive communicate that I am a good student, a professional, a party animal, a family person, disorganized, an airhead, a typical Greek member?

- What did my social media page specifically communicate that formed your conclusion?

1. Now reflect on the other person's description. How does it compare to how you want others to perceive you?
2. What, if anything, surprised you about how the classmate perceived you?
3. What changes, if any, will you make to your Instagram page?

Convenience

Another dimension of online communication attitude is the ease with which people connect with others through social media. We call this **convenience**, and it encompasses the level of appreciation and enjoyment a user associates with social media. How long a person has been an active user of communication technology, as you might expect, provides a sense of ease for most with social media use. The convenient nature of social media can carry implications for how you present yourself to others. You can easily snap a picture or video with your smartphone at a party, and, within seconds, post it to your Facebook page or Snapchat account and tag your friends. Within seconds, you not only alter your online image but also that of your friends. Although the use of social media is quite convenient, it can quickly affect how others perceive your interpersonal communication competence, which can also affect your self-concept.

convenience
The ease with which people connect with others through social media.

Online Apprehension

Online communication apprehension is anxiety and nervousness associated with communicating through social media. Individuals who are nervous about the opportunities and challenges associated with social media often develop negative attitudes toward online communication in general. One's reluctance to use online media may stem from a general lack of familiarity with social media or it may be limited to certain communication contexts. For example, some people feel little anxiety in using social media for communicating with friends but totally avoid using it in the context of their work environment. Many people avoid social media in the workplace because how they present themselves online can have implications for their careers. Seeing your photos from a friend's bachelorette weekend can influence whether your supervisor promotes, disciplines, or fires you.

online communication apprehension
Anxiety and nervousness associated with communicating through social media.

Miscommunication

Another attitude related to online communication is the understanding that social media may naturally inhibit the clarity of communication. This belief is called **miscommunication**, and it could apply to many inherent aspects of social media, from sending messages with misspellings or unintended emotional inferences to wondering why a friend didn't get back to you as quickly as you got back to him or her. Experienced users learn to anticipate miscommunication and manage ways to prevent it. You can improve your communication competence by assuming that online communication can inhibit understanding of a message's meaning.

miscommunication
The understanding that social media may naturally inhibit the clarity of communication.

Culture and Perceived Self-Concept

2.8   **Characterize** the role of culture in determining self-concept.

The development of self-concept varies from one culture to another. Because our self-concept forms in a cultural context, one would expect differences across cultures. Specific cultural factors can influence the development and perception of self. For example, researchers have found that young Palestinians living in Jordanian refugee camps often have a low positive self-concept because they are raised in an autocratic setting of traditional Arab families and schools, and have little independence and responsibility.[24] However, among Chinese secondary school students, a cohesive, "achiever" family environment is found to be associated with a more positive perception of self.[25]

Aging is a certainty for most all of us, and how it is perceived and how it affects our perception of self as well as communication are not often discussed as it relates to culture. Howard Giles, Shardé Davis, Jessica Gasiorek, and Jane Giles in their book *Successful Aging: A Communication Guide to Empowerment* write that aging is not only a biological inevitability, but it also can be a social construct. According to Giles et al., people look at the aging process differently, for example, depending on the country in which they live. They point out that when "young adulthood" begins and ends depends upon the country: For example, in the United States it begins at 17 and ends at 28, while in Bulgaria it begins at 16 and ends at 32. Middle age in the United States begins at 33 and ends at 59, while in Mongolia it begins at 29 and ends at 45. Elderly age begins in the United States at 61 and in Ghana at 50.[26]

In Western societies, it is common to hold negative attitudes about people perceived as old. This seemingly unfavorable perception often translates for some into stereotypes that can be harmful because they shape our expectations of aging as well as how younger people behave and treat older people. For example, some stereotypes imply older people are less competent, slow-thinking, hopeless, naïve, selfish, lonely, depressed, and so on. These stereotypes can potentially affect older people's self-concepts and ultimately how they communicate and see themselves.[27]

Much research related to cultural differences has focused on the effects of individualism versus collectivism on the self-concept. An **individualistic orientation** stresses self or personal goals and achievements over group goals, an "I" consciousness, and a tendency to focus on individual accomplishments. Unique to the Western world are cultures that stress individualism and prescribe self-interest as a central determinant of one's behavior.[28]

A **collectivistic orientation** tends to put aside individual goals for the well-being of the group. Researchers have examined the influence of specific situational arrangements of Japanese and American students in which the students were asked to describe themselves as: in a group, with a faculty member, with a peer, and alone.[29] They found self-concept variations as a function of culture, of the situation, and of the interaction between the two. For example, Japanese students were not only more self-critical but also more affected by the situation than were American students. While American students were more likely to provide self-descriptions in terms of abstract, internal attributes, as well as to refer to friends and family with statements such as, "I love my family." Japanese students tended to describe themselves in terms of physical attributes and appearance, activities, the immediate situation, and possessions, saying, for example, "I am the youngest child in my family." Americans overall tended to generate more positive self-descriptions than did the Japanese. Why do you think Americans are more likely to express positive self-descriptions?[30]

Our ability to communicate with individuals from different cultural backgrounds requires an understanding both of their culture and of their culture's influence on self-concept and the skill to adapt perceptions to accommodate differences. One African American woman stated one reason such communication is difficult: "If people don't share the same life experiences, they can't be expected to understand each other. If whites haven't been exposed to blacks, there will be a 'fear of the unknown.'"[31] This same fear or potential for misunderstanding can arise whenever people from different backgrounds or experiences come together. In today's global society, our self-concept is generated in part through social interaction with others both inside and outside our culture. Contact with other cultures in the early development of self-concept might help us to avoid some of the communication problems between people of different backgrounds.

individualistic orientation
Tendency to stress self or personal goals and achievements over group goals and achievements.

collectivistic orientation
Tendency to put aside individual goals for the well-being of the group.

Self-concept variations are a function of culture. Those in collectivistic-oriented societies usually put individual goals aside for the well-being of the group or whole of society.

Ababsolutum/E+/Getty images

Gender and Perception of Self-Concept

2.9 **Characterize** the role of gender in determining self-concept.

Gender is a crucial element in our personal and social identity. That is, you might or might not pay much attention to your social class or ethnic identity, but it would be extremely rare for you to be unaware and unconcerned about being male or being female. Each day we are reminded of our gender in hundreds of ways: by how we dress, how we act, and how others respond to us.

Sex and Gender

The terms *sex* and *gender* are often used interchangeably. We defined gender earlier as socially constructed masculine and feminine behaviors that are learned. **Sex** is, in biological terms, the anatomical and physiological differences between males and females that are genetically determined.[32]

sex

The anatomical and physiological differences between males and females that are genetically determined.

The origin of gender differences is sometimes a matter of dispute, but most researchers agree that gender attributes are based entirely on what one learns and perceives (such as an association between hairstyle and femininity), whereas other attributes may be based entirely on biological determinants (such as the presence of facial hair). Each of us has a gender identity: A key part of our self-concept is the label *male* or *female*. According to Julia Wood, a communication scholar, for the vast majority of people, biological sex and gender identity coincide, though for a relatively small proportion of the population, gender identity differs from biological sex, such as for a female who has always thought of herself as male.[33]

The explanation for some male and female differences are biological differences in brain structure and development. Research—not conclusive, however—indicates that, although both men and women use both hemispheres of the brain, each tends to specialize in one. Men generally exhibit greater development of the left hemisphere of the brain (the locus of mathematical abilities, analytical thought, and sequential information processing), whereas women manifest greater development of the right hemisphere (the locus of intuitive thought, imaginative and artistic activity, and some visual and spatial tasks).[34] Research suggests that women are more likely to use both sides of the brain to do language tasks, whereas men are more likely to depend on the left side. Women's brains don't seem, according to the research, to work as hard as men's to understand emotions.[35]

From the moment of birth, our biological sex slants the treatment we receive, such as wrapping a baby in a blue or pink blanket or dressing a child in "feminine" or "masculine" clothing. The types of toys children are given or the types of games they are encouraged to play can shape their behavior. It appears these initial influences lead to gender stereotyping and expectations that strongly influence a person's perception of self.

Gender identity thus occurs when gender becomes part of one's self-concept. We develop a sense of self that includes maleness and femaleness,[36] and somewhere between the ages of four and seven, the concept of gender consistency (the sense that one is permanently male or female) develops. We become aware of our bodies and of the differences between us and the "other" sex. We may even view the other sex, for a short time at least, as "icky" and choose to play only with all girls or all boys. We may communicate in different ways as well; for example, boys use communication to assert themselves and their ideas or to achieve something. Girls use collaborative, cooperative talk to create relationships and generally try to avoid criticism or put-downs.[37] We begin to accept the principle that gender is a basic attribute of ourselves. As soon as these attributes become known to us and are firmly in place, our perceptions of self are affected by what we believe about our gender as well as how we communicate with others.

Gender Stereotypes

A research study found that when children (ages 5 to 9) and adolescents (ages 15 to college age) were shown videos of four 9-month-old infants, both age groups agreed that the babies identified as female (named Karen or Sue) appeared to be smaller, more beautiful, nicer, and softer than those identified as male (named William or Matthew).[38] Actually, the experimenters had assigned a male or female name to infants of either sex. For example, half of the participants correctly identified each male baby as male and half incorrectly identified each male child as female; similarly, half of the participants identified each female baby as a girl and half as a boy. The findings illustrate how perception of male and female names leads to gender stereotypes.

Even though societies have made great strides in reducing stereotypical thinking about males and females, stereotypes and narrowly defined role expectations are still accepted by many in Western culture and even more so in certain other cultures. These stereotypes affect communication behavior. There are many similarities in the communication behaviors of men and women. For example, there are soft-spoken men and verbally aggressive women. Females have often been the objects of stronger and more persistent stereotypes than males. Female stereotypes are often more negative in content than those applied to males. The positive stereotypes of feminine behaviors include characteristics such as nurturance, sensitivity, and personal warmth. There are those who believe these traits are less desirable and less suited for the valued roles of leadership and authority than are the gender stereotypes for males.[39] This issue is complex because such gender differences, even if observed, may be more a reflection of our stereotyping and their self-confirming nature than of actual differences between females and males.[40] Research and evidence, however, point to the following: Some differences between males and females do exist with respect to some aspects of behavior and aging; but, in general, the magnitude of these differences is much smaller than past and prevailing gender stereotypes might suggest.[41]

Gender Expectations

An overwhelming body of evidence demonstrates that differences in communication result from gender expectations. According to psycholinguist Deborah Tannen, men and women do see themselves as different and, as a result, they communicate differently. She implies, in a man's world conversations tend to be negotiations in order to gain an upper hand. It can be seen as a contest or struggle to "maintain independence and avoid failure."[42] The man's world is a hierarchical social order in which people are either up one or down one. In the woman's world, according to Tannen, conversations are negotiations in order to seek and give confirmation as well as support to reach consensus. Women want to protect themselves from attempts to push them away. Women seek community to obtain intimacy and avoid loneliness. The woman's world is also hierarchical, but it is organized more toward friendship than to power and accomplishment.[43]

MAKING CONNECTIONS FOR SUCCESS

Women and Body Image

A headline in the *Lincoln Journal Star* read, "Dying to Be Thin." The newspaper ran a three-day series on the pressures of being thin in American culture. It is clear that we focus on weight and body image. The image of thinness on television, in movies, on the Internet, in magazines, and in store catalogs is quite evident. Probably the most famous such representations are the Victoria's Secret swimwear summer catalog and the *Sports Illustrated* swimsuit issue.

1. How do the media affect women's perception of themselves?

2. How does technology influence how women communicate about themselves?

3. How, in your opinion, does personal information on social media differ from face-to-face communication?

Are males and females socially and psychologically different?

According to sociologist Dr. Cynthia Fuchs Epstein, "the two sexes are essentially similar and . . . the differences linked to sexual functions are not related to psychological traits or social roles."[44] She further believes that most gender differences are relatively superficial. The perceived differences in male and female behaviors therefore are socially constructed in one's cultural upbringing.

When asked to describe themselves, males and females differ in their descriptions. Males tend to mention qualities such as ambition, energy, power, initiative, and control. They are likely to discuss their success in sports and with females. Females, however, typically list attributes such as generosity, sensitivity, consideration, and concern for others.[45] Males, it seems, are expected to be powerful and authoritative, whereas females are expected to be concerned with relationships and expressiveness.

If men and women are to break the stereotypes and expectations applied to them, we must avoid categorizing behaviors as exclusively male or female. Psychologists indicate women and men who are androgynous—have both male and female traits—are more likely to be successful in their interactions and careers than are those who are totally masculine or feminine in their behaviors. For example, as you move from interactions with coworkers to those with your family, you might move from behaviors that are more "masculine" to behaviors that are more "feminine." If you are a supervisor or owner of a business, for example, you are to be assertive and task oriented, but when you take care of your children, you are, instead, to be patient and caring.

Self-Fulfilling Prophecy and Impression Management

2.10 **Explain** the roles of self-fulfilling prophecy and impression management as they relate to self-concept.

In addition to values, attitudes, and beliefs, expectations determine how we behave, who we eventually become, and what we communicate to others and ourselves. Our own expectations and those of others influence our perceptions and behavior. Thus, our experiences, our interactions with others, the expectations others have of us, and how we present ourselves to create an image affect our self-concept.

Self-Fulfilling Prophecy

Our own and others' expectations lead us to act in predictable ways. The expectation becomes a **self-fulfilling prophecy**.[46] It can be a powerful force for shaping our self-concept. A research study asked college students who were either characteristically optimistic or generally pessimistic to describe their future selves.[47] According to the research, both types of students could imagine a positive future, but the optimistic students had higher expectations about actually attaining a positive self than did those who were pessimistic. Thus, we are more likely to succeed if we have positive expectations and believe that we have the potential to be successful. Similarly, we are more likely to fail if we believe ourselves to be failures.

self-fulfilling prophecy
Expectations we have of ourselves or that others have of us that help to create the conditions that lead us to act in predictable ways.

Self-esteem can affect the predictions people make about themselves. It is a matter of attribution: People with positive, high self-esteem confidently attribute their success to past successes; therefore, they expect to succeed in the future. People with low self-esteem, however, attribute any success they might have had to luck and so predict they will not necessarily succeed again unless they are lucky. How we describe ourselves is a powerful influence on our expectations. Our expectations therefore are a potent force for shaping our self-concept.

Most of us set positive expectations for ourselves, and most of us manage to perceive ourselves favorably much of the time. The fact that the majority of us show

A performer's success or lack of success often relates to their image and self-esteem, which are influenced by their self-expectations. These expectations become a self-fulfilling prophecy, leading to success or, sometimes, disappointment.

Darrin Henry/Shutterstock

the *above-average effect*—which is thinking we are better than the average person on almost every dimension imaginable—is strong evidence of our desire to perceive the self in a relatively positive light.[48] Even when others communicate negative social feedback that contradicts our rosy view of ourselves, we often forget such instances and instead communicate information that supports our positive self-perceptions.[49]

We easily accept communication that suggests we are responsible for our successes. This acceptance is especially true for those with high self-esteem.[50] Culture-based limits on our willingness to "grab the credit" do exist, however. For the Chinese, for example, modesty is an important basis of their self-esteem.[51] Accordingly, Chinese students attribute their success in school to their teachers, whereas American students credit it to their own skills and intelligence. Conversely, when it comes to failure, Chinese students are more likely to explain their failure as stemming from their own flaws, while Americans tend to think of them as someone else's fault.

You can probably think of many times when the expectations you had for a certain outcome didn't come to pass. Thus, the more we understand about the role of expectations in our lives and recognize their influences on our perception of self, the better we will be able to set realistic expectations not only for others but for ourselves as well.

The self-fulfilling prophecy is a communicative force that influences self-concept; however, it cannot explain all outcomes. It is important to communicate high expectations for others rather than place unnecessary limitations on them, but the expectations we communicate should be realistic and obtainable.

Impression Management

Do you care if you make a good first impression on others? You should, according to the research findings, because such impressions seem to exert strong and lasting effects on others' perceptions of us. A study of 10,526 participants in HurryDate sessions—in which men and women interact with each other for very short periods, usually less than three minutes, and then indicate whether they are interested in future interaction—found that individuals know almost instantly if a person appeals to them when they see them. Men and women in the study assessed potential compatibility within moments of meeting. They based their compatibility on physically observable attributes such as age, height, attractiveness, and physique, instead of harder-to-observe attributes such as education, religion, and income, which seemed to have had little effect on their choices.[52] It is clear the way others first perceive us strongly influences their behavior toward us and if they want to interact with us.

So what, exactly, are first impressions? In addition, what steps can we take to make sure our first impressions are favorable? The desire to make a favorable impression on others is strong, so most of us do our best to "look good" to others when we meet them for the first time. The creation of a positive image of oneself to influence the perceptions of others is **impression management** (or self-presentation).

As your own experiences have probably suggested, impression management can take many forms. Most fall into two major categories: **self-enhancement** a type of motivation to make people feel good about themselves in order to maintain self-esteem (efforts to boost your own image) and **other-enhancement** when others compliment individuals in order to make them feel good about themselves (efforts to make a target person feel good in your presence).

impression management

Creating a positive image of oneself to influence the perceptions of others.

self-enhancement

A type of motivation to make people feel good about themselves in order to maintain self-esteem.

other-enhancement

When someone compliments individuals in order to make them feel good about themselves.

To better understand impression management, we have to know more about "self." Our *perceived self* is a reflection of our self-concept. This self is the person we believe ourselves to be at any given moment of self-examination. We keep many aspects of our perceived self private because we don't wish to tell others; for example, we might perceive ourselves as too fat even though everyone else tells us we are too thin, as inept in social settings with people we don't know well, or as smarter than everyone else.

Our *presenting self* is the public image, or the way we want to appear to others. A research study asked college students to self-select 15 adjectives from a list of 108 possible adjectives describing their perceived self and presenting selves. Men and women described themselves similarly in 12 of 15 choices, differing in only 3. Both men and women were most likely to select active, attractive, busy, capable, curious, faithful, friendly, generous, happy, independent, polite, and responsible. Men also selected able, funny, and smart, whereas women also selected careful, sensible, and special.[53] When describing their most commonly presented characteristics, men and women were similar in the following characteristics: able, active, proud, and responsible. Men listed wild, strong, smart, brave, capable, and rough, whereas women more commonly presented the qualities of bright, funny, independent, sensible, and warm.[54] How would you describe your presenting self?

A question some researchers have asked is, "Does the use of social media enhance or diminish our self-esteem?" Social networking sites are, according to communication scholars Amy Gonzales and Jeffrey Hancock, designed to share information about ourselves with others, including likes/dislikes, activities we participate in, personal musings described on "wall posts," and "status updates."[55] The researchers concluded from their findings that when participants in their study viewed their Facebook profiles, their self-esteem was enhanced, and when participants updated their profiles and viewed them during the experiment, self-esteem was reported to be greater.[56] Remember that self-esteem comprises our feelings and attitudes toward ourselves, which function to determine our self-concept. Therefore, what you communicate about yourself on social networking sites can influence your self-esteem. Is this due to the selective nature of the information we provide on our social networking site and how we impression-manage it? Probably. According to Gonzales and Hancock, self-esteem may rise because the selectivity of the site gives us the opportunity to present positive information about ourselves. While at the same time eliminating or not including any negative information.[57]

Facework is the specific tactics used when presenting self to others. **Facework** is a term first used by sociologist Erving Goffman to describe the verbal and nonverbal ways we act to maintain our own presenting image.[58] Goffman says each of us creates various roles or characters that we want others to believe represent us. He also suggests that we maintain face by putting on a front when we desire to impress others.

facework

A term used to describe the verbal and nonverbal ways we act to maintain our own presenting image.

MAKING CONNECTIONS FOR SUCCESS
Self-Respect, Ethics, and Self-Image

We express our values and image in a thousand different ways. Most of us try to "do the right thing" because we care about how others perceive us. This is especially true when it comes to our family, friends, fellow students, teachers, and coworkers.

1. Define in your own words what it means to have personal integrity.

2. Describe what it means to be an ethical person.

3. How might social media influence or affect our integrity? Our ethics?

4. What can you do, if anything, to ensure that others see you as a person of integrity? Of high moral standards?

Does impression management work? The answer provided by an overwhelming body of research indicates yes, provided the tactics are correctly used. For example, a 2009 review of research studies related to impression management found that the tactics work in job interview situations.[59] It seems, according to the study, those who used impression management effectively were quite successful in obtaining high ratings from the interviewers and thus were more likely to be hired.

Many other studies achieved similar results with impression management tactics, but if they are overused or incorrectly used, they can backfire and elicit negative rather than positive reactions from intended targets. For example, one study reported that overuse of different tactics of impression management (especially too much flattery of others) can lead to suspicion and mistrust rather than an increase in liking or higher evaluation.[60] It is clear from the findings that, while impression management usually succeeds, this is not always the case, and sometimes it may have the opposite effect.

Enhancing Self-Concept

2.11 **Identify** six ways to improve self-concept.

Throughout the previous part of this chapter, we discussed what self-concept is, how it's developed, and how it connects to perception and communication. Most of us already have a good image of ourselves, but most of us also have areas we would like to improve or change. Almost everyone wants a positive self-image and wishes others to view them as positively as possible. Building on these ideas of self-concept, we now explore possible ways to enhance or change self-concept and to grow as a communicator. The feature "Guidelines: Improving Self" should help you begin the process.

Guidelines

IMPROVING SELF

1. **Decide what you would like to change or improve about yourself.** For change to occur, you must know or state what needs to be changed. Describe, as accurately, specifically, and completely as you can, what you would like to change or improve about yourself. If you are unhappy about something or don't like something about yourself, identify it and make a statement about it—for example, "I don't want to be afraid when I speak in public," "I want to be taken seriously by my friends," or "I want to be better organized."

2. **Describe why you feel the way you do about yourself.** Is your problem or shortcoming brought on by you or by others? Many students, for example, do not want to be in college or in a certain major. They go to college or take a major because that is what their parents or friends expect or pressure them to do. Although many of these students would rather do something else, they are afraid to take a stand or do what they really want to do. Before you can begin to feel better about yourself, you must recognize why you are unhappy and who contributes to your problem. You might think that you can't change majors, that you are not capable of earning good grades in

a particular subject, or that you are too shy to make new friends. If you want to change something about yourself, you must first ask yourself why you feel that way. For example, are you living out a self-fulfilling prophecy?

3. **Make a commitment to improve or change.** Changing our self-concept or aspects of ourselves is not easy, especially if what we want changed has been with us for a long period. However, nothing ever changes by itself; thus, to make a change, we must begin with a concentrated effort, a strong commitment, and a belief that changes can occur. For example, on the TV show that aired from 2004 to 2016 *The Biggest Loser*, which involved a competition to lose the most weight, the people on the show, in spite of external rewards, did not reach their goal unless they had made a personal commitment to do so. Wishing or thinking something should change may be the first step, but only wishing or thinking won't make it happen—you have to commit to the change before it can occur. The process requires that you state what you want changed and decide you are going to make the change.

4. **Set reasonable goals for yourself.** You must be reasonable in setting your goals. You may be able to change

some things overnight, but others may require long-term effort. For example, you might decide that you are going to improve your grades by studying for several hours every night. You can begin your new study schedule immediately, but actually raising your grades could take much longer.

5. **Decide on the specific actions you are going to take.** Determine an action plan that will lead to the outcome you want. Of course, anytime you act, you run the risk of failure, but successful people learn most accomplishment cannot occur without some risk. When you understand your shortcomings, learn how to deal with them, believe and commit yourself to making changes, and then take the appropriate actions, you will accomplish your goals. It is important to realize that changing your self-concept not only requires commitment and action but also time.

If you feel unsure about, or lack confidence in, communicating with others, you might overcome or manage these feelings by approaching them in small steps. For example, you might feel hesitant to visit your professor in his or her office. You could start by briefly speaking with your professor before or after class. You might begin by asking a question about your progress, an assignment, or something relevant to the class. Once you begin to feel more comfortable, ask for an appointment or stop in to visit during office hours. To start the conversation, you might have a few questions prepared. If you continue such visits, you will gradually gain more confidence.

6. **Associate with positive people whenever possible.** Try to surround yourself with people you like and trust. This will make it much easier to discuss any problems you have and to ask for support. When others know what you are trying to do, they can provide support to help you make the changes you desire.

⟩ SUMMARY

Perception and Communication

2.1 **Explain** the connection between perception and your communication competence.

Perception is the process of selecting, organizing, and interpreting information to give it personal meaning. It lies at the heart of the communication process and is part of everything we do.

The Perception Process

2.2 **Understand** the effect of the three stages of perception on your communication.

Perception involves selecting, organizing, and interpreting.

- *Selection* is the process of mentally sorting one stimulus from another.
- *Organization* is the sorting, organizing, or categorizing of stimuli so that we can make sense of them.
- *Interpretation* is the assigning of meaning to stimuli.

Perceptual Differences

2.3 **Identify** seven reasons why different people may perceive the same situation in different ways.

Because everyone is different, their perceptions of an identical situation may vary.

- The *perceptual set*—a fixed, previously determined view of people, things, or events—can distort our perception of reality. *Stereotyping*, a form of perceptual set, can also lead to inaccuracies in our perception and, ultimately, in our communication.

- *Attribution error* can occur when people perceive others as they do because of the kind of people they are rather than through external factors that may have influenced their behavior.
- Physical characteristics can account for differences in perception.
- Psychological state or our state of mind can alter our perceptions of people, events, and things.
- Cultural backgrounds can affect the way people perceive others, as well as events and things.
- *Gender* is socially constructed and can affect the way we perceive the world around us.
- Media, including newspapers, magazines, television, and all forms of social media, can and do influence our perceptions of people, places, events, and things.

Improving Perception Competencies and Perception Checking

2.4 Accurately **interpret and check** your perceptions to improve your communication competence.

To be competent communicators, we must recognize the effect of differences in perception.

- An active perceiver seeks out information.
- Perceptions are not always the same for everyone.
- Facts are objective; inferences are subjective.
- Perception plays a role in communication.
- Another perception may be valid.
- It is always wise to check your perceptions.

Perception and Self-Concept

2.5 **Understand** the role perception has in determining self-concept.

Perception and *self-concept* affects how we see ourselves. This in turn affects how we learn who we are, or at least who we think we are.

- Social identity or self-definition includes how we perceive and make judgements about ourselves.
- How others act toward us and communicate with us has implications for how we perceive ourselves.
- In order to become a competent communicator, we need to understand that our image of self has a significant effect on how we communicate and how others communicate with us.

Understanding Self-Concept

2.6 **Differentiate** among self-concept, self-image, and self-esteem.

Self-concept (or *self-identity*) is how we perceive ourselves, which consists of our beliefs and attitudes about self. *Self-image* is how we see ourselves—our mental picture of self. *Self-esteem* is our feelings and attitudes toward ourselves or how we evaluate ourselves.

- Self-concept is based on our *values* (long-lasting ideals that guide our behavior), *attitudes* (evaluative dispositions, feelings, or positions about oneself), and *beliefs* (convictions that we hold or confidence in the truth of something that is not based on absolute proof).
- Our self-concept determines our behavior and the related communication.

Social Media and Perceived Self-Concept

2.7 **Identify** social media factors that influence self-concept.

- *Online self-disclosure* is the degree to which individuals self-regulate what they reveal about themselves using social media.
- The belief that online communication enables social contact is known as *online social connection*.
- *Convenience* is the ease with which people connect with others through social media.
- Anxiety and nervousness associated with communicating through social media is known as *online communication apprehension*.

- *Miscommunication* is the understanding that social media may naturally inhibit the clarity of communication.

Culture and Perceived Self-Concept

2.8 **Characterize** the role of culture in determining self-concept.

Competent communicators know that communicating with people from different cultural backgrounds requires an understanding of other cultures as well as an ability to adapt to each.

Gender and Perception of Self-Concept

2.9 **Characterize** the role of gender in determining self-concept.

Those who understand gender roles are more likely to be successful in their interactions and careers than are those who do not.

- Gender identity, not the biological *sex*, becomes part of a person's self-concept.
- Gender stereotyping can affect communication behaviors of both males and females.

Self-Fulfilling Prophecy and Impression Management

2.10 **Explain** the roles of self-fulfilling prophecy and impression management as they relate to self-concept.

Our own and others' expectations determine how we behave.

- *Self-fulfilling prophecy* is a communicative force that influences self-concept.
- Behaviors intended to create a positive self-image to influence others is referred to as *impression management*.

Enhancing Self-Concept

2.11 **Identify** six ways to improve self-concept.

- Decide what you would like to change or improve about yourself.
- Describe why you feel the way you do about yourself.
- Make a commitment to improve or change yourself.
- Set reasonable goals for yourself.
- Decide on the specific actions you will take.
- Associate with positive people whenever possible.

⟩ DISCUSSION STARTERS

1. Why does perception play such a huge role in our communication with others?

2. Explain the connection between perception and communication competence.

3. Given what you have read, what is the influence of social networking sites on perception? What advice would you give regarding communication on these sites?

4. Describe a personal experience that illustrates attribution error. How did the error affect communication?

5. How has technology affected our perceptions and how we communicate with others?

6. Explain the role Hollywood media has in shaping our perceptions and ultimately how we perceive the world around us.

7. How does understanding the influence of self-concept improve communication competency?

8. What does your use of social networking sites—profile, photos, and wall posts—communicate to others about how you view yourself and about the image you wish to convey?

9. Discuss the influence of culture on self-concept.

10. Discuss how we use impression management techniques to create a positive image of ourselves.

⟩ ANSWERS

Making Connections for Success: Just the Facts and Nothing but the Facts (p. 39)

Numbers 2 and 3 are facts; numbers 1, 4, and 5 are inferences.

CHAPTER 3

CONNECTING THROUGH CULTURE AND DIVERSITY

Cathy Yeulet /123RF

Culture is an integral part of who we are as individuals and as a society. It shapes who we are and influences our biases.

⟶ CHAPTER OUTLINE AND LEARNING OBJECTIVES

Connecting with Others through Difference
3.1 **Define** intercultural communication.

Understanding, Culture, Diversity, and Difference
3.2 **Explain** connections among culture, diversity, and difference.

Communication and Cultural Variations
3.3 **Summarize** how communication leads to cultural variations.

Making Connections through Group Affiliations
3.4 **Explain** how communication influences group affiliations.

Intercultural Communication Obstacles
3.5 **Summarize** intercultural communication obstacles.

Communicating Cultural Competence
3.6 **Identify** ways to communicate cultural competence.

MAKING EVERYDAY CONNECTIONS

Mark, an American business executive, is on a business trip to El Salvador. He told his American business partners that he understood and spoke Spanish and said he had few problems communicating while in El Salvador on past trips. Mark and his team were invited to a Salvadoran business executive's home to socialize with him and his family. Throughout the evening, Mark kept talking business. His Salvadoran host seemed mildly annoyed at discussing business and would promptly move the conversation from business to more social topics such as amazing places to visit, foods to eat, and so on. Upon returning to the United States, Mark learned his company lost the business of the Salvadoran company.

QUESTIONS TO THINK ABOUT

1. What should Mark have done prior to leaving on his business trip to El Salvador?

2. Why do you think Mark's company lost the business of the Salvadoran company?

3. What concerns do you have about communicating with people from different cultures?

4. How often do you interact with people from different cultures? How has this influenced your view of the world?

Culture is an integral part of each of us and determines many of our individual characteristics. As we discussed in Chapter 2, culture identifies us as members of a particular group and shapes our values and biases. Much cultural influence occurs without our realizing it: Typically, we are not conscious of how much of our behavior is conditioned by culture. The way we greet others, the way we use language, our opinions about what and when to eat, and many of our personal preferences are all culturally conditioned.[1]

The connection between culture and communication is extremely complex. In fact, because of culture we learn to communicate. For example, a Korean, an Egyptian, or an American learns to communicate like other Koreans, Egyptians, or Americans, respectively. Each knows certain behaviors convey certain meanings because they are learned and shared in their respective cultures.[2] Just as they behave in a certain way, people also perceive and organize their thoughts, observations, and values according to the dictates of their culture. For instance, in a purely scientific sense, the moon is a rocky sphere; yet when they look at the moon, many Americans see the "man in the moon." Some Native Americans view this same image as a rabbit, the Chinese interpret it as a woman fleeing her husband, and Samoans see in it the shape of a woman weaving.[3] These particular differences might not seem significant, but they point to the way people from different cultures can view or perceive the same phenomenon differently. When cultural differences are apparent, sensitivity, patience, and tolerance are required to avoid or reduce misunderstandings that can create barriers to effective communication and to relationship development.

Connecting with Others through Difference

3.1 **Define** intercultural communication.

To be part of any team, to be a good neighbor and informed community citizen, and to be an effective manager at work, you need to understand the importance of connecting with others through difference. Whether you're seeking to learn how to communicate better with your older relatives, understand the way your roommate's faith influences her communication, or think through your stance on current national debates on issues like immigration, it is important to understand cultural differences and similarities to increase your competence and ability to connect with others in intercultural encounters.

The fact that people from different cultures perceive the world quite differently can lead to misunderstandings, hurt feelings, isolation, and other challenges when they

intercultural communication
Communication between people who are unlike culturally and have different views of the world.

interact. Because of these challenges, communication scholars invest time and energy studying intercultural communication. **Intercultural communication** is communication between people who are unlike culturally and have different views of the world.

Communication is intercultural when people with differences because of their cultural backgrounds create different interpretations and expectations.[4] The answer to addressing intercultural misunderstanding and misconnections is *not* to limit yourself to interactions with people who perceive exactly as you do. Imagine how boring the world would be! Instead, in our technologically rich society, you work, study, and socialize with people who are different in many ways. So why is it so important to study intercultural communication?

Intercultural communication is important because of our increasing exposure to people from within and outside of our own culture and perception of the world around us. People are exposed to a variety of cultures through military and humanitarian service, jobs requiring global travel, vacations, and today's interconnected global community. Most of us are curious about others who don't look like us, sound like us, or live like us. You might wonder why one woman wears a long dress and veil, while another woman wears skinny jeans and a backward baseball cap. You might ask why one man does not eat meat, while another is always first in line for hamburgers in the dining hall. We are curious about arranged marriages and how funerals and weddings are different from country to country. Intercultural communication involves the process of connecting with others to better understand their culture. After all, you can communicate better with others from different cultures if you know something about theirs.

Understanding Culture, Diversity, and Difference

3.2 **Explain** connections among culture, diversity, and difference.

As you recall from Chapter 2, culture is a learned system of thought and behavior belonging to and typifying a relatively large group of people. In many ways, it is the composite of their shared beliefs, values, and practices. We might often think of an individual's culture as simply her or his nationality. Culture comprises much more.

Culture Is Learned

You are not born with your culture; you are born into a culture, which you have learned through communication. As a child, you observed the behaviors of your family, including your parents, siblings, grandparents, and others. They taught you words that were polite or inappropriate, how to make eye contact during a conversation, and when to use your "inside voice." As you entered school, you interacted with and observed the behaviors of your teachers and fellow classmates. You learned the types of conversational topics that were appropriate to discuss with your peers rather than adults. You also learned the intricacies of interacting with members of the same or opposite sex. In college, you are exposed to hundreds (maybe thousands) of different people, each having an upbringing and experiences unique to them. Your communication with college friends continues to influence your understanding of culture.

Through communication, most of us develop an awareness of what constitutes appropriate behavior in various situations. Many of your nonverbal behaviors like gestures, eye contact, and vocal tone (which you will learn more about in Chapter 5) are communicated often at an unconscious level.[5] This means that you don't even notice them until another person behaves in a way that doesn't meet your expectations. For example, you may not notice that you always make eye contact during a conversation until another person fails to do the same with you. You may yield a conversation to another person, until you notice the person is constantly interrupting you.[6]

(*left*) Lady Gaga was the target of offensive social media posts about her physical appearance during her 2017 Super Bowl halftime show performance. (*center, right*) Advertisements from different countries often reflect different cultural values.

Culture Is Expressed through Communication

Just as you learn about your culture through communication, you also use communication to express your culture. Your culture affects topics you discuss in personal and professional settings. It also affects how you perceive others' communication.

In many Western cultures, including the United States, a woman's thin body type is often equated with beauty. This perception is in the messages sent and received via media. If you're not convinced, pick up a magazine, watch a television commercial, or view advertisements through social media. Traditional and social media are filled with judgments about celebrities and their weight. Consider Lady Gaga's 2017 Super Bowl halftime show performance. Gaga was *trolled* (made the target of a deliberately offensive online post) and called "fat," among other things, after she donned multiple outfits during the show, including one which exposed her abdomen.[7] In many other cultures, perceptions about weight and physical attractiveness differ greatly. For example, in Uganda, larger women are considered desirable, and so some women in that country prepare for marriage in a "fattening hut."[8] This cultural practice communicates to the people of Uganda the value for women of *gaining* weight, just like traditional and social media in the United States promotes the desirability of *losing* it.

Culture Is Comprised of Rituals

When you began your college experience, you had to learn an entirely new set of **cultural rituals**, or practices, behaviors, celebrations, and traditions common to people, organizations, and institutions. For example, on the first day of class, your professor likely passed out a course syllabus that explained the course assignments, readings, and due dates for assignments, and so on. Rushing Greek organizations is an important campus ritual for some. Another campus ritual you will participate in someday is your college or university's graduation ceremony, one of the proudest cultural rituals of your life! Indeed, your campus is made up of many rituals that allow you to experience the day-to-day life of its culture.

Many of us are so entrenched in our own culture—its rituals, language, and norms—that when those expectations are contradicted or disrupted, we may experience anxiety preventing us from communicating. This may occur when we interact with people from cultures different than our own. **Culture shock** is the psychological discomfort experienced when interaction occurs in a different culture or when one's current cultural experiences are contradicted or disrupted. You are likely to feel it

cultural rituals

Practices, behaviors, celebrations, and traditions common to people, organizations, and institutions.

culture shock

The psychological discomfort experienced when interaction occurs in a different culture or when one's current cultural experiences are contradicted or disrupted.

Cultural Rituals and Your University: What Do They Tell You about the Culture?

Most college and universities feature a wide array of cultural rituals. At some universities, Greek life is very popular; at other schools, it is not. Some universities have very popular and successful athletics programs involving tailgating, spirit sections, and well-attended games. Take a moment to reflect upon the cultural rituals at your college or university.

1. Select a cultural ritual that you think is unique to your university and explain why it is unique.
2. What other types of cultural rituals are common at your university? What do you they tell you about its culture?
3. What stories have you heard that explain the culture of your campus?

Ed Endicott/Alamy Stock Photo

Tailgating before a U.S. sporting event—such as a football game—is a popular American cultural ritual.

most profoundly when you are thrust into another culture as part of international travel for your study abroad program or for a job. But you can also experience culture shock when you interact with people from within your home country. Consider Jan, a young woman who was raised in a very small town with one traffic light. She sets off to visit a friend who recently moved to New York City. The traffic jams, city smells, loud noise, large crowds, and confusing subway system may overwhelm her. If Jan is going to overcome her culture shock and enjoy her time in New York City, she will need to become accustomed to this new culture quickly.

Communication and Cultural Variations

3.3 **Summarize** how communication leads to cultural variations.

We can begin to understand people's culture based on their language, dress, or personal artifacts, such as religious markers worn as jewelry or displayed in the home. For example, when people meet Prabhjot Singh, his turban tells them that he is a Sikh. While these things may help you recognize that someone belongs to a specific culture, they do not help you understand her or his values or communication practices. Appearance alone does not explain people's values, attitudes, or beliefs; how they perceive the world; or how they connect and communicate with others both within and outside their culture.

Research conducted by Geert Hofstede and Edward T. Hall provides a way to understand how cultures are similar to and different from one another and how cultural variation affects communication. As a manager at IBM Europe, Hofstede conducted a large-scale research project involving 50 countries and 3 regions. His research identified four ways cultures differ in how people connect and communicate through culture:

1. The extent to which the individual is valued versus the group;
2. The extent to which predictability is valued versus tolerating uncertainty;
3. The extent to which the norms of the culture support equality or uneven distribution of power; and

4. The extent to which the culture is oriented toward an achievement culture or a nurturing one.[9]

Hall further identified two ways cultures differ, each having important implications as to how cultures connect with other cultures.

1. Cultural norms related to time and

2. The importance of context for understanding a message.[10]

People and nations themselves fall onto a continuum of sorts when it comes to the variations we discuss in this section. It would be incorrect to assume that if a person is from any particular country or culture that she or he would behave when communicating in any one particular way simply because she or he is from a certain country. The ideas we discuss below provide a structure for understanding the cultural variations that make our world a vibrant planet of cultural difference.

Individualistic and Collectivistic Cultures

Recall the discussion in Chapter 2 (page 50) about individualistic and collectivistic cultures. Much research related to cultural differences has focused on the effects of individualism versus collectivism. An *individualistic orientation* stresses self or personal goals and achievements over group goals, an "I" consciousness, and a tendency to focus on individual accomplishments. Individualistic cultures value each person's autonomy and privacy. They pay relatively little attention to status and hierarchy based on age or family connections.

A *collectivistic orientation* tends to put aside individual goals for the well-being of the group. Collectivistic cultures value group goals and emphasize group harmony and cooperation. Communication in collectivistic cultures is often clearly based on the status and hierarchy among group members, loyalty to the group, and honor for one's family.

Comfort with Uncertainty

Cultures differ in the degree of anxiety that individual members feel about the unknown. All cultures adapt their behaviors to reduce uncertainty, a process called **uncertainty avoidance**. Cultures that are more anxious about the unknown are said to be *high uncertainty avoidance cultures*. People from these cultures strive to minimize risk and uncertainty. In high uncertainty avoidance cultures, communication is usually governed by formal rules to satisfy a need for absolute truth, correct answers, and stability. People value consensus and have little tolerance for differences of opinion. By following social rules and minimizing dissent, they reduce uncertainty and anxiety in prescribed communication situations.[11]

uncertainty avoidance
The process through which cultures adapt their behaviors to reduce uncertainty.

Cultures with a higher tolerance for ambiguity are considered *low uncertainty avoidance cultures*.[12] Their lower level of anxiety about the unknown generally means that individuals in these cultures are more comfortable with a variety of communication styles, are more tolerant of differences of opinion, and have fewer formal rules for behavior.[13] As you might expect, the more diverse the people in a society, the more likely the dominant culture will be low on uncertainty avoidance. How our culture has taught us to view uncertainty affects our communication with others.

Perspectives on Power Distribution

How members of a culture view unequal distribution of power affects communication with others. **Power distance** is the extent to which members of a culture expect and accept that power will be unequally shared. Status differences in a culture result in some groups or individuals having more power than others. But a person's position in the cultural hierarchy can come from sources such as social class, age, job title, or life

power distance
The extent to which members of a culture expect and accept that power will be unequally shared.

experiences. In *high power distance cultures*, people with less power accept their lower position as a basic fact of life. They might experience more anxiety when they communicate with those of higher status. They also tend to accept coercion as normal and avoid challenging authority. People in *low power distance cultures* tolerate less difference in power between people and communicate with those higher in status with less anxiety. They are more likely to challenge the status quo, consider multiple options or possibilities for action, and resist coercion.

Our cultural beliefs about power distance naturally affect how we interact with others in authority. If you are a student, an unskilled worker, or an average citizen in a high power distance culture, you would not challenge a person who holds a position of authority. You would expect the more powerful person to lead the interaction, you would listen attentively, and you would do what the person asked of you without question. In contrast, in a low power distance culture, you might be more comfortable arguing with those in authority. When interacting with a powerful person, you will likely feel comfortable taking the conversational lead and challenge the person if necessary.

Achievement and Nurturing Culture

achievement culture
A culture that values assertiveness, achievement, ambition, and competitiveness.

nurturing culture
A culture that places value on relationships and quality of life.

Cultural differences affect communication through the extent to which traditionally masculine or feminine orientations are valued in a particular culture. Cultures differ in how strongly they value traditional sex role distinctions. An **achievement culture** often values assertiveness, achievement, ambition, and competitiveness.[14] Men and women in these cultures usually make very clear distinctions between the sexes, such as expecting more aggressiveness in men and more passivity in women. In a **nurturing culture**, people place value on relationships and quality of life. These cultures highly value affection, friendliness, and social support over assertiveness and aggressiveness.

Time Orientation

Each culture teaches its members about time expectations, and these expectations vary. In some cultures, punctuality is expected; in others, it is not important, and, in fact, people are expected to be late. In U.S. culture, for example, you are expected to be on time for a dinner party, but being up to 20 minutes late may still be socially acceptable and still considered "on time." In some countries, such as Japan, arriving late for a dinner party is considered an insult.[15] Our use of time communicates messages about us, so it is important to adhere to the time-related norms of the culture in which we communicate.

monochronic culture
A culture that sticks to a schedule and values punctuality, uninterrupted task completion, meeting deadlines, and following plans.

polychronic culture
A culture that is comfortable dealing with multiple people and tasks at the same time.

In **monochronic cultures**, time is treated as a limited resource. People in monochronic cultures stick to a schedule and value punctuality, uninterrupted task completion, meeting deadlines, and following plans. **Polychronic cultures** are comfortable dealing with multiple people and tasks at the same time. In polychronic cultures, people are less concerned with making every moment count. They do not adhere to strict schedules, are less likely to make appointments, and change plans often and without hesitation.

High-Context and Low-Context Cultures

high-context culture
A culture in which the meaning of the communication act is inferred from the situation or location.

Anthropologist Edward T. Hall suggests that, for some cultures, the situation in which a particular communication occurs tells us a great deal about its meaning.[16] In a **high-context culture**, the meaning of the communication act is often inferred from the situation or location. In Japan (a high-context culture), for example, businesspeople do not conduct business in a social setting, although they might refer to their business interests. If one visits Japan on business and is invited to dinner, there is no hidden agenda—the objective for the evening is to eat a meal together, not to

MAKING CONNECTIONS FOR SUCCESS

Understanding High- and Low-Context Cultures

One aspect of culture and language that global travelers or those who interact with people from other cultures—whether face-to-face or through social media—need to know is how time is identified. People in high-context Central and South America tend to be polychronic and have views of time and its importance that differ from what most people in the monochronic and low-context nations of Western Europe and North America have. In North America, students expect to receive a detailed syllabus for their classes and assignments. In polychronic countries, students may never get complete explanations directly. They expect to discover the rules and expectations for each class.

A staff lounge in a low-context country may have signs on the microwave or refrigerator reminding users to clean up before they leave. People from high-context cultures do not need to be reminded. They know what is expected of them.

1. Now that you are aware of the differences between high- and low-context cultures, identify possible sources of conflict between people from two different context cultures.

2. What are the differences between high- and low-context cultures in terms of language use?

3. How would you be able to tell if listeners understand your message?

conduct business. Business is saved for the office or the meeting place. A dinner is a social event at which business is not conducted. Also, in a high-context culture, language is indirect, nonspecific, and not assertive. In a **low-context culture**, the meaning of the communication act is inferred from the messages being sent and not the location where the communication occurs. According to Hall, the United States is a low-context culture in which businesspeople are as likely to conduct business on the golf course, in a restaurant, or at a reception as they are in the workplace. People in a low-context culture typically are more assertive and more direct. They get to the point immediately. Because understanding such distinctions is essential to sending and receiving messages successfully, the competent communicator will learn as much about language and cultural differences as possible.

low-context culture
A culture in which the meaning of the communication act is inferred from the messages being sent and not the location where the communication occurs.

You should also be aware that some cultures have greater or lesser expectations for an individual's involvement in communication events. Students in China, Finland, France, Japan, Korea, Mexico, most of South America, Indonesia, and Thailand are expected to listen to their professors and not ask questions during class unless the professor gives them permission. These cultures seem to prefer low involvement on the part of students. In Russia, Denmark, Canada, and the United States, however, students are expected to have high involvement in the learning process and are encouraged to ask questions and otherwise participate.

Making Connections through Group Affiliations

 Explain how communication influences group affiliations.

Oprah Winfrey is an American, a woman, and a baby boomer. She is African American and was born into poverty in rural Mississippi. She is a talk show host, actress, businesswoman, philanthropist, and one of the most influential women in the world. All of these characteristics and many others form Winfrey's unique identity. These attributes also make her a member of various groups. Some of these groups might be formal, such as her affiliation with mainstream media. However, most are informal and reflect the more general ways we all group ourselves and others based on particular characteristics.

You too have multiple aspects to your identity, including the many groups to which you belong. Of course, some of your group memberships may be more important to you than others, and these group affiliations powerfully shape your communication and ability to connect with others—and they affect how others communicate with and about you. Here we will examine communication across cultures and review social identity theory and intergroup communication.

Co-Cultures

Differences among people are often based upon a variety of factors such as race, ethnicity, religion, gender, sexual orientation, age, social class, and others. These terms are often understood in relation to intercultural communication. Many students describe culture by referencing national borders and language, but a person can be a member of many different cultures, most of which have little to nothing to do with boundaries or nationalities. If you think about your own college or university campus, there is likely a sense of culture.

dominant culture

The learned system of values, beliefs, attitudes, and orientations held by people who are in power in a society.

Although the United States is a diverse society, there are many attitudes, values, beliefs, and customs that the majority of people hold in common and that the minority feel they must follow. The **dominant culture** is the learned system of values, beliefs, attitudes, and orientations held by people who are in power in a society. In the United States, the dominant culture has evolved over time but once reflected and privileged the values of white, Western European, English-speaking, Protestant, heterosexual men. Since the 1960s, the United States has experienced a cultural revolution that has resulted in an adjustment of the dominant cultural perspective to be more reflective of the diverse cultures with which its citizens identify. We have come to understand and expect that different people may follow different communication patterns and that to connect with others, we need to be able to adjust to diversity.

co-culture

A group that exists within a larger, dominant culture but differs from the dominant culture.

While there is a dominant culture, many Americans also identify with one or more **co-cultures** that exist within a larger, dominant culture but differ from the dominant culture. Co-cultural groups form around one or more shared characteristics such as gender, race, ethnicity, religion, sexual orientation, gender identity, generation, interest, activities, opinions, or group membership. For example, a group of people born during a specific time frame might develop different ideas about how relationships work. Americans who lived through World War II share common memories, as do Americans who lived through the assassination of President Kennedy and the 9/11 terrorist attacks. Those memories have shaped their worldviews in similar but not necessarily identical ways, and the memories affect how they communicate.

Social Identity

social identity theory

Specifies that we have a *personal identity*, which is our sense of our unique individual personalities, and a *social identity*, the part of our self-concept that comes from our group memberships.

Without doubt, our co-cultural group memberships influence our communication and ability to connect with others. This is because our group memberships are such a large part of who we are. **Social identity theory** teaches us that we have a *personal identity*, which is our sense of our unique individual personalities, and a *social identity*, the part of our self-concept that comes from our group memberships.[17] We divide ourselves into "us" and "them" partly based on our affiliations with various co-cultural groups. The groups with which we identify and to which we feel we belong are our *in-groups*; those we define as "others" are *out-groups*. We want "us" to be distinct and better than "them," so we continually compare our co-cultures to others in the hope that we are part of the more desirable group. Members of fraternities and sororities often consider themselves as part of an in-group. The same goes for college students who join other organizations, clubs, and activities. For instance, a university with a large, popular, and well-directed marching band program may lead its band members to view themselves as part of an in-group.

Intercultural Communication Obstacles

 Summarize intercultural communication obstacles.

With all of the cultural variations possible in the many co-cultures to which each individual belongs, it is easy to understand that communication difficulties arise. Even with people who you think you know very well or who are similar to you in many ways, you can often experience obstacles to connecting and communication through culture. The most common obstacles to communicating with members of different cultures include anxiety, ethnocentrism, and discrimination.

Anxiety

It is normal to feel some degree of discomfort or nervousness when you recognize that you are different from most everyone else or when entering a culture whose customs are unfamiliar. Most people experience fear, dislike, and distrust when they first interact with someone from a different culture.[18] If you have ever traveled to a foreign country, been the only member of your cultural group in some setting, or began your college adventure at a large university in a huge city unlike your small hometown, you probably experienced **anxiety**, a feeling of worry, nervousness, or unease.

anxiety
A feeling of worry, nervousness, or unease.

Ethnocentrism

Being unable to appreciate ideas, customs, or beliefs that differ from those of one's own cultural background and automatically assuming that one's own view is superior to that of any other culture is referred to as ethnocentrism. **Ethnocentrism** is a learned belief that our own culture is superior to all others.[19] Those who lack interaction or contact with other cultures may find it difficult to understand that other cultures and their practices may be as acceptable as our own. Even if we know of weaknesses in our own culture (too competitive, too materialistic, too informal, and so on), we are unlikely to criticize our own culture when comparing it to others.

ethnocentrism
A learned belief that our own culture is superior to all others.

Ethnocentrism is not necessarily a bad thing, but it does alter our perceptions and often colors how we regard others who are different from us. We learn to behave through culture, and the way we behave, most of us believe, is the way everyone else should behave. We use our culture and our cultural behaviors as a yardstick by which to judge all other cultures and people. The difference between a person's own culture and other cultures is often judged on a superiority–inferiority scale. People often view cultures different from their own as inferior. The greater the differences seen between cultures, the greater the degree of perceived inferiority.

Discrimination

Ethnocentrism can lead an individual down a destructive path toward **discrimination**, the verbal or nonverbal communication behaviors that foster prejudiced attitudes including the act of excluding or denying people access to products, rights, and services based on their race, gender, sexual orientation, disability, and so on. Discrimination arises when attitudes about superiority of one group lead to rules and behaviors that favor that group and harm another group. Discrimination can be shown in obvious ways, for example when a person uses a racial epithet to refer to a boss or coworker; it can also be quite subtle, such as not inviting a wheelchair-bound person to a party at an apartment for fear his or her wheelchair will take up too much space.

discrimination
The verbal or nonverbal communication behaviors that foster prejudiced attitudes including the act of excluding or denying people access to products, rights, and services based on their race, gender, sexual orientation, disability, and so on.

Discrimination can be explained in part by research on intergroup communication. Research shows that we have a bias tendency to treat fellow in-group members better than we treat members of out-groups.[20] In fact, we tend to interpret in-group behaviors more favorably than out-group behaviors. For example, if you discovered that someone in your sorority was caught cheating on an exam, you would likely explain the behavior as an unusual situation brought on by challenging circumstances. But if you heard about someone from another sorority (an out-group) cheating, you would be more likely to label that person as dishonest.

Communicating Cultural Competence

3.6 **Identify** ways to communicate cultural competence.

As you have read this chapter, you have probably begun to realize how difficult it is to communicate effectively with someone from a different culture. Yet you know that immigration, the Internet, and increasing globalization of business require effective intercultural communication. Communicating your cultural competence requires that you take action and remain aware, learn, overcome bias, show mutual respect, and practice your skills.

Be Aware

As you learned in Chapter 2, it is important to always remain aware of your behavior and others' behavior. Indeed, many of your communication attitudes and behaviors are so rooted in your own culture that they are unconscious. When someone stands a bit too close to you, you might feel slightly uncomfortable. You might interpret a person's direct eye contact as a sign of aggression rather than merely a cultural difference. Of course, not all uncomfortable interactions stem from cultural differences, but being mindful of the possibility gives you a wider range of effective ways to respond.

You should also ask yourself whether you might be interpreting another person's behaviors based on whether the individual shares your group memberships. Remaining aware of your behavior involves practicing **intercultural sensitivity**, or awareness of behaviors that may offend others.[21] Being sensitive does not necessarily mean that you have to give up your own beliefs and practices, but it does mean not forcing them blindly on others.

intercultural sensitivity
Awareness of behaviors that may offend others.

Learn

Learning about a new culture can prepare you to adapt as you think about the many factors that influence intercultural communication. But how should you go about learning about another culture or co-culture? How can you understand members' communication preferences? In the new culture, is it okay to ask questions or seek clarification? Do you need a close friend from that culture to understand aspects of that culture's communication? As you grow as a communicator, you should ask

MAKING CONNECTIONS FOR SUCCESS
Practicing Intercultural Sensitivity

After Jayla, an American-born and -raised businesswoman, opens an office in Japan, she is preparing for her first meeting in the new space. Jayla has several Japanese assistants working with her to help her get ready. She tries to beckon one of the assistants to come into her office. Instead of pointing her index finger at the assistant, Jayla walks over to her assistant and politely asks her to join her in the office. While it is okay to beckon someone in the United States by curling or pointing your index finger at them, in Japan this behavior is seen as offensive.

1. How is Jayla being culturally sensitive?
2. What else could Jayla do to practice intercultural sensitivity?
3. Given what you know about high power distance cultures, how would Jayla be able to tell if she offended one of her assistants?

respectful and sincere questions and experience other cultures in various ways—you might research, try foods outside your own culture, study the speeches or writings of leaders from other cultures, or think about studying abroad. In fact, new technologies allow you to engage with cultures through online communities, even if you cannot personally travel around the world.

Overcome Bias

As you learn about other cultures in an effort to improve your ability to connect with others through culture, you might also actively seek to spend time with members of other cultures and co-cultures. Part of the problem is that when different groups get together, we often engage in **behavioral affirmation**, seeing or hearing what we want to see or hear. For instance, if you think fraternity guys are lazy and only like to party, then regardless of how hard your roommate studies during Rush Week, you do not see that effort. Instead, you notice that he is always making time for his new fraternity buddies, so you still perceive him as a poor student. We may also engage in **behavioral confirmation**, when we act in a way that makes our expectations about a group come true.[22] Again, if you think your fraternity-pledge roommate is a poor student, you will more than likely not ask him to clean the apartment and take out the trash because you know he should focus on studying. When you learn your roommate recently failed his accounting exam, you confirm to yourself, "I knew he wouldn't do well on that test."

If you attended a few fraternity events and got to see your roommate and several of his brothers more regularly in their fraternity setting, you might learn that many of them are serious students and that some of them are not really into the party scene. We all need to be aware of our own behaviors and biased perceptions when interacting with members of other cultures and groups so that we do not simply confirm our existing expectations.

Show Mutual Respect

You foster connections with people who are different in terms of race, ethnicity, religion, gender, and sexual orientation by coming to understand those differences. When individuals and groups communicate with a goal of mutual respect, cultural tensions, misunderstandings, and conflict can be avoided.[23] Mutual respect develops when a person seeks to understand another with an open attitude and dialogue; doing so encourages others to respond in a similar way.

We can show respect by adjusting our language and style of speaking toward the people with whom we are communicating through a process called **accommodation**. When you squat down to make eye contact with a child, and use basic vocabulary to speak to her, you are practicing a form of accommodation. Police officers practice accommodation by using the language commonly used in neighborhoods they patrol. When speakers shift their language or nonverbal behaviors toward each other's way of communicating, they are engaging in **convergence**. We typically converge to show respect and gain approval from others and show a shared group identity.[24] Convergence is one method of displaying mutual respect; it usually results in positive reactions. In essence, if I speak like you, it is a way of saying "I am one of you."

It is important to be careful not to **overaccommodate**, which means going too far in changing your language based on an incorrect or stereotypical notion of another group.[25] For example, your elderly grandmother might find it patronizing and insulting when you speak "down" to her using slow speech, an increased volume, and childish words. Be cautious if you attempt to adjust your

behavioral affirmation

Seeing or hearing what we want to see or hear.

behavioral confirmation

When we act in a way that makes our expectations about a group come true.

accommodation

A process through which people adjust their language and style of speaking toward the people with whom they are communicating.

convergence

When speakers shift their language or nonverbal behaviors toward each other's way of communicating.

overaccommodate

Going too far in changing your language based on an incorrect or stereotypical notion of another group.

Communicating mutual respect is essential for effective communication and creating meaningful connections with others.

AZemdega/E+/Getty Images

language and style of speaking; conveying mutual respect is a vital requirement for effective communication between and among cultures and co-cultures.

Practice Your Skills

This chapter has made clear that you need to use verbal and nonverbal behaviors effectively and appropriately to connect with others in intercultural contexts. During your study abroad trip, this might mean using the language of your new culture well enough to get by. In other situations, it might mean communicating care, concern, and appreciation for another person's life experiences and opinion. Research tells us that people with fewer social skills experience greater challenges with managing the complexities of intercultural interactions.[26] Therefore, it is important to develop the following skills to effectively connect with others through culture.

- **Listen effectively.** You cannot remain fully aware without first listening to what people say and taking note of what they do not say. Knowing when to talk and when to listen is crucial to connecting with others through culture. You will learn more about how to be an effective listener in Chapter 7.

- **Think before you speak.** Imagine that someone fails to make eye contact with you during a face-to-face conversation or speaks very directly on a sensitive issue. When someone communicates in a way that seems strange to you, take a moment to think about whether her or his behavior is a cultural difference rather than a hostile message. You will learn more about how language and nonverbal communication in Chapters 4 and 4.

- **Practice empathy.** People who practice empathy are able to picture themselves in another person's shoes so they can better understand that person's experience. When you practice empathy, you can change your perceptions and improve your understanding of the ways in which another person's culture affects his or her communication.

- **Advocate for effective communication.** When someone is being mocked for his or her race, religion, or sexual orientation, stand up for that person. When a friend makes a remark that you perceive as culturally insensitive, simply remind your friend of his rude statement. This will go a long way in advocating for effective communication and send a powerful message that helps your friend learn what constitutes effective and appropriate communication that fosters connections among others.

〉 SUMMARY

Connecting with Others through Difference

 Define intercultural communication.

Intercultural communication refers to the communication between people who are unlike culturally and have different views of the world.

Understanding, Culture, Diversity, and Difference

3.2 **Explain** connections among culture, diversity, and difference.

We might often think of an individual's culture as simply her or his nationality. Culture comprises much more than that.

- Culture is learned.
- Culture is expressed through communication.

- Culture is comprised of rituals.

Communication and Cultural Variations

3.3 **Summarize** how communication leads to cultural variations.

Appearance alone does not explain who people are inside, how they perceive the world, and how they connect and communicate with others.

- *Individualistic* cultures stress self or personal goals and achievements over group goals, an "I" consciousness, and a tendency to focus on individual accomplishments, while *collectivistic* cultures tend to put aside individual goals for the well-being of the group.

- Cultures that are more anxious about the unknown are said to be high *uncertainty avoidance* cultures, while cultures with a higher tolerance for ambiguity are considered low uncertainty avoidance cultures.

- In high *power distance* cultures people with less power accept their lower position as a basic fact of life, while people in low power distance cultures tolerate less difference in power between people and communication with those higher in status with less anxiety.

- *Achievement cultures* value assertiveness, achievement, ambition, and competitiveness, while *nurturing cultures* place value on relationships and quality of life.

- In *monochronic cultures*, time is treated as a limited resource. *Polychronic cultures* are comfortable dealing with multiple people and tasks at the same time.

- In a *high-context culture*, the meaning of the communication act is often inferred from the situation or location. In a *low-context culture*, the meaning of the communication act is inferred from the messages being sent and not the location where the communication occurs.

Making Connections through Group Affiliations

3.4 **Explain** how communication influences group affiliations.

Some of your group memberships may be more important to you than others, and these group affiliations powerfully shape your communication and ability to connect with others.

- *Co-cultures* that exist within a larger, dominant culture but differ from the dominant culture.

- *Social identity theory* teaches us that we have a personal identity, which is our sense of our unique individual personalities, and a social identity, the part of our self-concept that comes from our group memberships.

Intercultural Communication Obstacles

3.5 **Summarize** intercultural communication obstacles.

With all of the cultural variations possible in the many co-cultures to which each individual belongs, it is easy to understand that communication difficulties arise.

- It is normal to feel some degree of *anxiety* when you recognize that you are different from most everyone else or when entering a culture whose customs are unfamiliar.

- *Ethnocentrism* is a learned belief that our own culture is superior to all others.

- *Discrimination* involves verbal or nonverbal communication behaviors that foster prejudiced attitudes including the act of excluding or denying people access to products, rights, and services based on their race, gender, sexual orientation, disability, and so on.

Communicating Cultural Competence

3.6 **Identify** ways to communicate cultural competence.

Communicating your cultural competence requires that you take action and remain aware, learn, overcome bias, show mutual respect, and practice your skills.

- It is important to always remain aware of your behavior and others' behavior.

- Learning about a new culture can prepare you to adapt—or not adapt—as you think about the many factors that influence intercultural communication.

- As you learn about other cultures in an effort to improve your ability to connect with others through culture, you might also actively seek to spend time with members of other cultures and co-cultures.

- You foster connections with people who are different in terms of race, ethnicity, religion, gender, and sexual orientation by coming to understand those differences.

- You need to use verbal and nonverbal behaviors effectively and appropriately to connect with others in intercultural contexts.

⟩ DISCUSSION STARTERS

1. Other than your own, which culture or cultures do you most identify with or prefer?

2. Based on what you read in the chapter or in your own personal experience, what recommendation would you make to improve your or others' competencies to communicate across cultures, both within and outside of your culture?

3. Explain a time when you experienced an awkward social situation involving race, religion, sexual orientation, or any other topic. How did you react?

4. What issue covered in this chapter resonates most with your lived experience related to communication and culture?

5. Identify at least two co-cultures that you belong to and describe how each affects how you behave and communicate differently within each co-culture.

CHAPTER 4

CONNECTING THROUGH VERBAL COMMUNICATION

Olivier Douliery / dpa picture alliance / Alamy Stock Photo

In his first appearance as press secretary for the president, Sean Spicer asserted that President Donald Trump's inaugural crowds were the largest ever. Members of the press said his remarks were untrue. After his resignation, he said Trump's views were what was important to convey to the world.

→ CHAPTER OUTLINE AND LEARNING OBJECTIVES

The Power of Language

4.1 **Assess** the power of language in communication events and our lives.

The Elements of Language

4.2 **Use** the elements of language (sounds, words, grammar, and meaning) in effective communication.

Language-Based Barriers to Communication

4.3 **Explain** how language can create barriers to effective communication.

Language and Social Influences

4.4 **Illustrate** the impact of social influences on language.

How to Use Language Effectively

4.5 **Describe** how accurate, vivid, immediate, and appropriate language can help you be a more effective communicator.

MAKING EVERYDAY CONNECTIONS

Language is power. Karen Tracy and Nancy Robles, in *Everyday Talk* suggest there is an inextricable link between language use and our identities.[1] Because we use language constantly each day, we often do not recognize its power and significance and take it for granted. Events in the political arena, the past few years reinforce the power of language. The 2016 U.S. presidential campaign, speeches, rallies, and tweets provide a clear view of the role of language in swaying opinion and reinforcing people's own views. Donald Trump's campaign theme "Make America Great Again" and his constant repetition of key issues in the form of "sound bites" appealed to his voter base and reinforced his position as an outsider who would go into Washington, DC, and "drain the swamp." The strategy won him the necessary electoral college votes and thus the election. Trump since asserts this as proof of the mandate he has from the U.S. public to do what he wishes, even when his language and actions are unprecedented and go against the normal approach to government policies and procedures. His rejection of the language and approaches of his predecessors works well for those citizens who feel disenfranchised. A December 31, 2017, *New York Times* headline read, "President Trump has brought a reality-show accessibility to a once-aloof office, invigorating voters who felt alienated by the establishment."[2]

Trump conducts business through tweets. He announced personnel decisions regarding several of his cabinet members and proclaimed policy not previously discussed with the affected departments on Twitter. His concern with how he is perceived when various media outlets challenge his assertions with evidence or facts brought new phrases into our everyday talk. When he and then press secretary Sean Spicer claimed the 2017 inaugural crowd was the largest ever,[3] news media posted National Parks Service photos of both former President Barack Obama's and President Trump's crowds where it was clear that Trump's attendance was smaller. Spicer responded that Trump's view was that his crowd was larger. Other close advisors also use language to justify his view of the world. "Alternative facts" and "fake news" are two of the phrases used to demonstrate how Trump takes on anyone with whom he disagrees and asks his supporters to discount views other than his own. Anything he disagrees with in the media is automatically ridiculed as "fake news." When one of his advisors is challenged with facts about any issue, the Trump administration points out "the liberal press and media" differ greatly on their perceptions of what is happening; thus "alternative facts" explain how the biases of "fake news" sources interfere with their reality. For his surrogates, Trump's views are, or should be, accepted as the "real truth." When Kellyanne Conway was challenged on this issue, she said, "[He] provided 'alternative facts' about what he believed to be true."[4]

QUESTIONS TO THINK ABOUT

1. Where do you hear language using "alternative facts" (identified as such or not) around you?

2. In what ways are you concerned that language creating suspicion about the press and media will erode the importance of separating what is real and what is fake?

3. What role do newspapers and television play in providing a variety of views for informed citizens?

4. How can seeking information from a variety of sources allow you to think critically about truth and distorted actions or events and help you make informed judgments?

Language is a powerful tool we use to share meaning. Every culture has one or more languages that help them share meaning with others. Some linguists estimate there are more than 6,000 languages in the world today; there were only an estimated 60 languages 70 to 80 years ago. As global reach increases because of the prevalence of 24-hour news reporting on even the most trivial of stories and speculating on both meaning and impact, language becomes even more powerful and significant. Many people, for example, tweet on a regular basis, and many others follow the tweets as observers rather than as participants. As a result, media changes language and bring new words into use. (Please see Chapter 6 for more examples.)

Research provides information on the specialization of different areas of the brain. One specialized component of our brain is language, and each part of the brain has its own language. People are attracted to other people speaking the same language. Have you ever heard someone say, "It's like we speak the same language"? Chances are, that is *exactly* what is happening—the persons in dialogue are speaking from the same thinking preference. How we give information, how we listen, and our perspective on the information we give and receive are, in good part, shaped by our thinking preferences.[5]

The Power of Language

4.1   **Assess** the power of language in communication events and our lives.

language
A structured system of signs, sounds, gestures, or marks used and understood to express ideas and feelings among people within a community, nation, geographic area, or cultural tradition.

Language is a structured system of signs, sounds, gestures, or marks used and understood to express ideas and feelings among people within a community, nation, geographic area, or cultural tradition. Language has the power to influence our perceptions of others (and theirs of us) as we use language to share who we are. It affects our emotions and allows us to make connections. Language helps us gain and maintain relationships with loved ones, family, friends, and strangers. Without language, little or no human communication as we now know it would exist. Language allows us to encounter our world in significant ways because it enables us to share meaning with others. Can you imagine what it would be like to be unable to tell someone what you know or think or feel? Language is a powerful tool. But it is only as effective and efficient as the people using it. Although we often believe that language is neutral, in actuality it communicates much about what we are and what we think; therefore, language is subjective, must be carefully used, and should be chosen according to the context. Furthermore, language for writing differs from language for the ear.

A short YouTube clip called "The Power of Words" shows a blind man sitting on the sidewalk with a sign that reads, "I'm blind. Please help."[6] He received few donations until a young woman changed the sign to read, "It's a beautiful day and I can't see it," and most passing people threw money into his container. This example demonstrates the power of the right words.

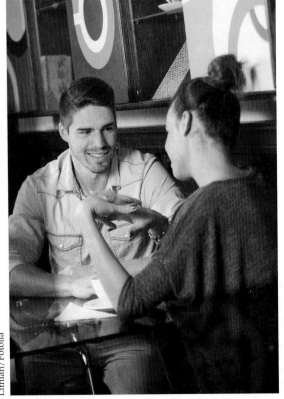

Conversations are a vital part of our everyday lives. Language allows us to share our thoughts and feelings with others in meaningful ways.

Lithian / Fotolia

Words create images in our minds. We attribute meaning to what we hear, and we can accept or reject a speaker's message just because we don't attribute the same meaning to the message. Social theorists raise issues about perspectives on language because they want an inclusive world. In her book *Fighting Words*, Patricia Hill Collins, black feminist and author, investigates how effectively black feminist thought confronts the injustices African American women currently face. Her book examines poverty, mothering, white supremacy and Afrocentrism, the resegregation of American society by race and class, and the ideas of Sojourner Truth and how they can serve as a springboard for more liberating social theory.[7]

Language has the power to create biases for everyone. For instance, when you hear the word *doctor*, what image comes to mind? What about a *strong leader*? When you hear *nurse*, what is the image? Many people think of leaders and medical doctors as men and nurses as women, but increasingly that's not the case. People choose the careers they prefer, despite whatever labels were previously given to those professions. We need to share with each other and accept people for who they are. Language does that for us when we choose words carefully. Effective language has the power to allow everyone in the conversation to have similar views of what is happening.

What Did I Say?

Have you ever heard someone describe a situation you also witnessed and wondered how their impression was so different from yours? Why do three people who witness the same event see and describe it in various ways? People have vastly different perspectives and attach different meanings to the words they use to describe those perspectives. In fact, differences in thinking preferences can be so great they create separate and distinct "languages"; thus, we can understand the explosion of the number of languages in the world. While superficially using the same vocabulary, these preferences allow us to assign different meanings to the same words, thereby describing worlds seen from vastly different perspectives.[8]

1. Describe some of your effective communication interactions.
2. What kinds of problems do you encounter when communicating with others?
3. How do you get around problems or reach understanding with others?
4. What unique circumstances are created when the conversation partners come from different cultures including different age groups?
5. Identify a time when you heard or used the same language for a written exchange as for an oral one with negative results. Why do you think this happened?

The Elements of Language

 Use the elements of language (sounds, words, grammar, and meaning) in effective communication.

Language, talk, speech, and communication are four different but related phenomena. *Language*, as noted earlier, is a shared structured system of signs, sounds, gestures, or marks (in other words, *symbols*) that allows people to express ideas and feelings to others; *talk* is what we do every day; *speech* is one vehicle used to transmit language; and *communication* involves the exchange of meanings. Language is one means by which we communicate, and speech is one way we use language. The fact that we process language does not automatically mean we communicate well, but we cannot verbally communicate without some language, and all language would be useless if it did not help us convey meanings. Of course, nonverbal communication also allows us to express ourselves.

The goal is to coordinate language and speech to produce effective communication, or transfer the meaning intended. You can learn more about language by examining four of its key elements: *sounds*, *words*, *grammar*, and *meaning*.

Sounds

Most of us learn to speak a language before we learn to write it, and most of us are born with the physical mechanisms that enable us to make speech sounds. However, we do not all learn to produce sounds in exactly the same way. Though using the same language, people of certain geographic regions or cultural groups may speak quite differently. Dialects and other speech patterns can complicate communication between people who speak the same language.

Words

Words are symbols that stand for objects and concepts. A word can represent an object or an abstract concept: The word *desk* represents an actual piece of furniture, an object, while the word *anger* represents a whole range of emotions associated with our feelings when we are extremely upset and unhappy.

word

A symbol that stands for the object or concept it names.

MAKING CONNECTIONS FOR SUCCESS

The Power of Words

Arabs have a great appreciation of the power of language. An ancient Arab proverb clearly illustrates this power: "A man's tongue is his sword." In the Arab culture, words used to describe events can become more significant than the events themselves. Communication scholars Samovar and Porter suggest that, in Arabic, "Words are used more for their own sake than for what they are understood to mean. Whereas North Americans can adequately express an idea in ten words, the Arabic speaker may use one hundred."[9]

People in the Arab culture know language is powerful. But other cultures also share that view. African cultures often use the spoken word over the written word, and they use proverbs to demonstrate issues. African Americans also place a high value on talk, conversation, and the oral storytelling tradition.[10] An example from Kenya is: "Having a good discussion is like riches." This proverb demonstrates that both history and news are shared in the oral tradition.[11] People in El Salvador have at least five specific forms of the English word "you." For example, *usted* is used when speaking to an elder or a superior, while *tu* is used for informal situations, but not with elders or superiors.[12]

1. Identify an instance where you learned about the power of words.

2. If you speak another language in addition to your first language, what have you learned about using your second language among people for whom that language is the first language?

3. How have social media affected your own language in everyday conversation?

---

idioms
Words whose meanings cannot be understood according to ordinary usage.

Words have meanings because communities and cultures give them meaning. People agree that certain sound combinations signify certain things. One of the intriguing aspects of languages is the **idioms**, or words whose meanings cannot be understood according to ordinary usage. If you hear someone say "that happens once in a blue moon," you may realize that something is a rare event, but someone from another culture who uses English as a second language may be totally lost because the phrase cannot be literally translated. All parties in the communication event must agree on meanings if they wish to understand each other.

Grammar

grammar
Rules that govern how words are put together to form phrases and sentences.

Just as language has rules that govern how sounds may be joined into words, it also has rules that govern how words may be joined into phrases and sentences. This set of rules is called **grammar**. For example, the English grammar system requires that singular nouns take singular verb forms and plural nouns take plural verb forms (*friend is; friends are*).

As we join sounds together to form words and join words together to form phrases, sentences, and paragraphs, we use language's sound and grammar systems simultaneously. The ability to use sounds and grammar correctly is crucial to competent communication. Grammar enables us to make complete sentences and to understand sentences made by others.

Despite the many rules governing language, the number of different messages that can be created is nearly limitless. It has been estimated that in the English language, it is possible to create 10 quintillion 20-word sentences.[13] This does not include sentences either shorter or longer than 20 words. Thus, the number of possible sentences and messages is nearly infinite.

Meaning

semantics
The study of meaning, or the association of words with ideas, feelings, and contexts.

The study of meaning, or the association of words with ideas, feelings, and contexts, is called **semantics**. If language did not have meaning, it would serve little or no purpose. Because words and word patterns can be used to exchange meanings between people, language is a necessary tool for communication.

Do Words Contain Meaning?   We tend to associate language symbols (words) with specific meanings and to take that relationship for granted. But it is important to understand that, in fact, language by itself has no meaning.

This notion might seem to contradict our entire discussion so far. You might wonder how language can be a system involving rules and meanings, yet it still has no meaning itself. Actually, it is entirely arbitrary, for instance, that the word *desk* represents a piece of furniture where one may sit and write. A desk in a classroom is quite different from a desk in an office or one's home. Nothing about the letters *d*, *e*, *s*, and *k* is essentially related to the actual desk. When we see or hear the symbol, we fill in the meaning.

Look at this photo and think about how mediated communication has changed the way we communicate, especially in shortcuts with language.

Words are symbols that represent people, objects, concepts, and events; the word is not actually the person, object, concept, or event. For example, *democracy*, *freedom*, *music*, and *friends* are only words, not the entities they symbolize. It is easy to miss this distinction. Even though words are symbols, try screaming, "I'm bleeding!" in front of someone who gets nauseous at the sight of blood, and you will quickly see how words cause reactions—as if the words were actually the things they were depicting.

The belief that words hold specific meaning is widespread. During the past several years, we have asked students in communication classes whether words have meaning. The data, though not scientifically collected, suggest that more than 75 percent of the students believe words do have meaning. But the simple fact is words only have the meaning we give them. Words acquire meaning only through the context in which they are used and by the fact that those who use them give them meaning. Meanings are in people. Figure 4.1 shows how two different people attach different meanings to the word *house*.

FIGURE 4.1 Meanings Are Not in Words but in People

We cannot assume that using words we consider appropriate and adequate to convey a particular message will succeed with every listener. As this figure illustrates, different people associate different meanings with even the simplest words because words are symbols only—people fill in the meaning.

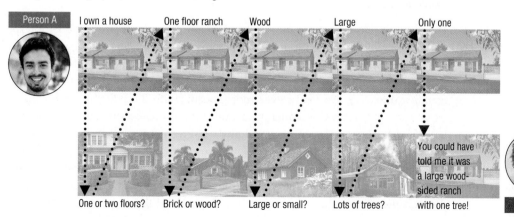

The following dialogue from Lewis Carroll's *Through the Looking Glass* illustrates this idea. Humpty Dumpty and Alice become involved in an argument about language and meaning:

> "I don't know what you mean by 'glory,'" Alice said.
>
> Humpty Dumpty smiled contemptuously. "Of course you don't—till I tell you. I meant there's a nice knock-down argument for you!"
>
> "But 'glory' doesn't mean 'a nice knock-down argument,'" Alice objected.
>
> "When I use a word," Humpty Dumpty said, in a rather scornful tone, "it means just what I choose it to mean—neither more nor less."
>
> "The question is," said Alice, "whether you can make words mean so many different things."
>
> "The question is," said Humpty Dumpty, "which is to be master—that's all."[14]

Who determines meaning? *You.* You control which words you use; the meaning you wish to give them; and, if you have mastered communication, how people react to them. Although everyone has the ability to impart meaning to words, not everyone does so in the same way. Thus, a sender might intend one meaning, but the receiver might either intentionally or unintentionally give the message a different meaning. Disparity between the meaning sent and the meaning received can be a greater problem when the sender and receiver have different cultural backgrounds or different experiences and knowledge. For example, people who keep up with computers and technology often use specialized language unfamiliar to someone who doesn't have much knowledge about computers. Care in choosing words is especially important in such situations.

denotation

The objective meaning of a word; the standard dictionary definition.

Words Have Denotative and Connotative Meanings   **Denotation** is the common meaning associated with a word—its standard dictionary definition. Denotative meanings are usually readily understood. Many people use words as if they had only a denotative or specific meaning, but this is not the case. Although commonly understood dictionary definitions (denotative meanings) exist, when we communicate we usually use words connotatively.

connotation

The subjective meaning of a word; what a word suggests because of feelings or associations it evokes.

Connotation is the subjective meaning of a word, what a word suggests because of feelings or associations it evokes. The connotative meaning is based on the context in which the word is used, how the meaning is expressed nonverbally (tone of voice, facial expression of the speaker, and so on), and the understanding of the person who is receiving it. The competent communicator can differentiate between denotative and connotative meanings and understands which is being used in a given situation. Connotative meanings may be generally accepted by most people who use the language, by people within a particular group, or by an individual. To someone who lives in the South, a glass of *tea* is understood to mean "sweet tea," while to one from the Midwest it means "unsweetened tea," and to most Canadians it means "tea with lemon." Thus, when Midwesterners order tea in the South or in Canada, they will likely be surprised by the drink they receive.

concrete word

A symbol for a specific thing that can be pointed to or physically experienced.

Words Can Be Concrete or Abstract   **Concrete words** are symbols for specific things that can be pointed to or physically experienced (seen, tasted, smelled, heard, or touched). For example, words such as *car*, *house*, *food*, and *soda* (*pop*) are concrete words. They represent specific, tangible objects, and therefore their meanings are usually quite clear. We can be even more specific with *Buick Enclave*, *ranch-style home*, *pizza*, and *Dr. Pepper*. Consequently, communication based on concrete words leaves less room for misunderstanding, and any disagreement can typically be resolved by referring to the objects themselves.

abstract word

The symbol for an idea, quality, or relationship.

Abstract words, however, are symbols for ideas, qualities, and relationships. Abstract words represent intangible things, or things that cannot be experienced through the senses; thus, their meanings depend on the experiences and intentions of the persons using them. For instance, words such as *beauty*, *love*, *ethics*, *music*, and *determination* stand for ideas or symbols that signify different things to different people.

FIGURE 4.2 The Ladder of Abstraction

Word meanings become more concrete when they refer to a specific person, place, or thing. Concrete language helps to reduce the number of possible interpretations of messages, leaving less chance for misunderstanding.

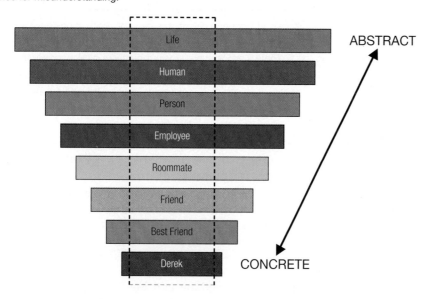

The "ladder of abstraction" (Figure 4.2), first described by Alfred Korzybski in 1933 and expanded on by S. I. Hayakawa in 1964,[15] remains a useful way to explain concrete and abstract words and meanings. Figure 4.2 illustrates the varying degrees of concreteness among related words. *Derek* is the most tangible word because it refers to a specific individual named Derek. You can see that, as words move from concrete to abstract, they refer to more general and more intangible ideas that are open to differing views.

Words Can Be Specific or Vague   Just as abstract words provide little in the way of tangible things, specific and vague words can interfere with the meaning you intend. Someone who says, "Call me later" when she leaves the meeting at 5 p.m. gives an open time frame. So if you call after 9 p.m. and are confronted with a grumpy person who answers the phone, "You're calling too late—it's my child's bedtime," the lack of specificity makes for hurt feelings. You can see how misinterpretations can easily occur. The use of vague words confuses the issue and sends unclear messages. Specific words allow the listener to share in the meaning you intend. Vague language can easily lead to misunderstandings and result in ineffective communication, as illustrated by the following conversation:

> **Shar:**   Julian, you said you would meet me at the Book Nook in the library after class last night. I went there right after class and waited for an hour. Where were you? Did you forget?
>
> **Julian:**   I meant tonight after class—this is the class we both attend.
>
> **Shar:**   Why didn't you say tonight when we talked yesterday?
>
> **Julian:**   I thought you'd understand it was tonight and not last night. We don't have classes together on Tuesdays.
>
> **Shar:**   Next time, be specific!
>
> **Julian:**   Next time, ask if you're not sure!

This conversation is problematic because Julian is vague and Shar didn't ask for clarification. While this is not earth-shattering, real communication did not occur because neither was aware of the other's meaning. It's always a good idea to explain, define, or illustrate any vague words that may be misunderstood.

Meaning Depends on Commonalities   The more communicators have in common in terms of background, experience, and attitudes, the more likely they are to hold similar meanings for the words they exchange. However, competent communicators do not assume too much about how others will interpret their messages; they

MAKING CONNECTIONS FOR SUCCESS
What Do Words Really Mean?

The conversation between Shar and Julian illustrates much more than the use of vague or specific words. Culture, educational background, social status, age, the nature of the relationship, and gender are only a few of the factors that influence language choice and word meanings. Numerous communication scholars have discussed gender and cultural differences in the way people use language to communicate. Psychologist Deborah Tannen became a pop culture phenomenon for her books and assertions that men and women are different in their communication styles and language choices. Think about language choice in the following situations:

1. Identify two specific instances in which you and a person of the opposite sex had different views of language. What was the result of each?

2. What language differences between generations have you noticed? Would you talk or write to your grandmother the same way you would to your best friend? Why or why not?

3. List the characteristics of language appropriate to writing a class paper or work report. Then list the characteristics of language appropriate for making an oral presentation in class or at work.

4. Together with your classmates, compare and contrast the two lists you came up with in number 3. What are the similarities and differences?

5. How would making a presentation to a group of high school students versus a group of retired professionals affect your language choices?

---

continuously refine their messages. Shing-Ling and Maddie are roommates. They have trouble budgeting for household expenses. Shing-Ling wants to buy the economy sizes of dish and laundry soap because they can save money over the semester. Maddie becomes upset because she doesn't want to spend her entire budget the first week of the month. *Economy*, *budget*, and *careful spending* mean different things to the two, and stating those words usually causes a major conflict.

Instead of talking things through, each person goes her own way and spends the joint budget in ways she thinks best. The roommates have never taken the time to try to understand the other's position. Their own backgrounds and experiences make a difference in the way they choose and use language and meaning, and unless they can talk about it, they will not achieve a common understanding.

Language Can Obscure Meanings   Words mean different things to different people, based on each person's experiences and the direct relationship of those experiences to particular words. *Unfamiliar words*, such as technical medical terms, can negatively influence a listener's views. When you have no frame of reference for certain words, you're lost in a conversation when they are used and not explained. When you choose more understandable words, you help listeners comprehend the nature of the issue, and you reduce some of the frustration about lack of knowledge and information.

In addition, the *meanings of words*, like words themselves, change from time to time and from place to place. It is easy to forget that the meaning we have for a word might not match one held by others. For example, ask a person over age 80 the meanings of *hashtag*, *viral*, *digital detox*, *girl crush*, or *bromance* and see what response you get. We constantly add words to our language, especially technology-related words. How many new words have been added to the language because of these advances? *Blogging*, *texting*, *googling*, *Twitter* and *tweet*, *gaslighting*, *spamming*, *catfishing*, *emoji*, and *phishing* are some fairly recent examples.

Regional differences exist. Word meanings vary from region to region. For example, in some regions of the United States, if you ask for *pop* at a store, the clerk will not understand you until you rephrase your question and ask for *soda* or a Coke. In Wyoming and Ohio, people get a drink of water from the drinking fountain, but in Wisconsin and Massachusetts, people use a bubbler.

Language, or jargon, used by a particular group or discipline may be too specialized or technical to be understood by the general public. In such a situation, one would need specific knowledge about the subject and the cultural differences to understand what is being said.

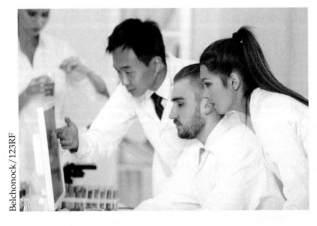

Belchonock/123RF

Regional word use can lead to misunderstandings, and we must be sensitive to such potential differences. In addition, cultures and co-cultures hold differing meanings for certain words. For example, for most in the United States, *very dear* means something highly valued or loved, whereas in Canada and Ireland, *very dear* means very expensive and has nothing to do with personal value or love.

Co-cultures within a language community sometimes use words or phrases in ways unique to their group. Scientists, engineers, and health-care providers use language that might be too specialized to be understood by the general public. This unique language use is referred to as **jargon**. Other co-cultures, such as students, might use **slang** or words used to communicate only with those who know the words, and the words and meanings change quickly. Sometimes those words become so known and accepted they end up in the dictionary. *Twerking* was a relatively unknown word until Miley Cyrus twerked and got media attention for her performance; then the word and the image went viral. In newspapers and house-for-sale advertising, a real estate agent might use the term *handyperson's special* to refer to a house in need of repair.[16]

Numerous colleges have created slang projects they regularly update. You might want to go to your browser and key in "slang terms" to see if other schools have slang terms similar to those in your school. This search provides an opportunity to add new slang terms as well as learn whether we use specific terms unique to our geographical location. Slang words are constantly discarded and new ones invented or refined— sometimes just to make sure that people outside a particular group will not catch on to their meanings. All kinds of groups, including members of a given profession, college students, ethnic groups, and gangs, develop and use slang terms.[17]

Language is used to share meaning, but it also can be used to obscure, distort, or hide meaning. One way to obscure meaning is to use a euphemism. A **euphemism** is an inoffensive or mild expression given in place of one that may offend, cause embarrassment, or suggest something unpleasant. Our society also uses euphemisms to avoid taboo subjects or words that can trigger negative reactions. Euphemisms can defuse the emotional charge associated with controversial or difficult concepts. For example, when a person dies, we often use a euphemism such as "passed away" instead of "died." The phrase "passed away" seems to make an emotional situation more approachable.

Euphemisms can also be used to enhance something, to make it seem a little more glamorous than it actually is. In our society, we have become so concerned with labels that we rename many things to give them a more positive connotation. For example, we rarely use the term *salesman* because, apart from being sexist, it may conjure a negative image characterized by unscrupulous business ethics. This unfavorable connotation is fostered by the media and sometimes by personal experience. Thus, referring to a person who sells merchandise as a sales associate, sales consultant, or sales representative sounds more positive. Also, the terms *trash* or *garbage collector* are recast as *sanitation engineer*, seemingly to make the job more attractive.

Language can also be used to create **doublespeak**, or deliberately ambiguous messages. William Lutz, a professor at Rutgers University who wrote a book, *Doublespeak*, denounces the use of words to conceal meaning. He says he can live with ordinary euphemisms, but his teeth are set on edge when a worker is told he has been "dehired" because the firm is experiencing "negative employee retention." Actually, the employee has been fired in a layoff, but no one is willing to say so, laments Lutz.[18] SourceWatch is an online project of the Center for Media and Democracy and provides a list of doublespeak terms and their meanings. Examples are "shock and awe" for the massive bombing in Iraq and "security contractors" for mercenary troops or agencies that provide them.[19] Lutz thinks the practice of doublespeak is "disgraceful, dangerous to democracy, perverse, and pervasive." It's hard work, too. Doublespeak isn't just the natural work product of the bureaucratic mind, painstakingly invented by committees to cloak meaning. Doublespeak is not a slip of the tongue or language

jargon
Language used by certain groups or specific disciplines that may be technical or too specialized to be understood by the general population.

slang
Language used by groups to keep the meaning of the communication within the group. Slang words change frequently and are specific to regions and/or groups.

euphemism
The use of an inoffensive or mild expression in place of one that might offend, cause embarrassment, or suggest something unpleasant.

doublespeak
The deliberate misuse of language to distort meaning.

used improperly because of ignorance. It is a tool that the powerful use to achieve their ends without clearly communicating with those who may be affected by their actions or who may foot the bill for them. According to Lutz and other scholars, doublespeak is particularly harmful when it makes something inappropriate or negative appear appropriate or positive.

As you can see, language and meaning are inseparable parts of communication. They mesh smoothly in successful communication. Unfortunately, a type of communication also occurs when a message is misunderstood.

Language-Based Barriers to Communication

4.3 **Explain** how language can create barriers to effective communication.

Although it takes little physical effort to say something to someone, it does take mental effort to ensure that what we say conveys our intended meaning. Even if we create what we *think* is the perfect message, there's always a possibility the receiver will misinterpret the message or find it ambiguous. Remember, the receiver must also make an effort to understand the intended message.

"There are over 300 different languages in everyday use in the United States. This number includes more than 160 Native American languages, the languages of the colonizers (English, French, and Spanish), languages of immigrants—both old and new—and a variety of dialects spoken in various regions of the country."[20] We must recognize that communication is a symbolic interaction rich in subtlety. It will never be strictly concrete or objective and thus always carries the potential for misunderstanding. Misunderstandings occur for numerous physical, mental, and cultural reasons. Ineffective use of language is one reason. Among the most common language-based barriers to effective communication are bypassing, indiscrimination, and polarization.[21]

Meanings Can Be Misunderstood

What a speaker means and what is *heard* and *understood* by the listener often differ. Such misunderstanding between a sender and a receiver is called **bypassing**. How many times have you said to someone, "But that's not what I meant"? Here is an illustration of bypassing:

> Your supervisor says, "Get the figures on how much space there is in the new office complex and give me a report as soon as you can." You find the information, make the calculations, make comparisons, identify advantages and disadvantages, and three days later take the report to your supervisor. You're dismayed when you're told, "What took you so long? I wanted that information two days ago. It's too late now." The supervisor never said the information was needed or wanted the next day, and you worked hard to get a polished report. Who's at fault? Was the supervisor not clear? Did you ask any questions?

Bypassing occurs in similar situations every day.

Bypassing usually results from the false belief that each word has only one meaning and that words hold meaning. A glimpse at our everyday language quickly illustrates that most words have multiple uses and meanings. Words acquire many meanings because they change over time, are used and understood differently in various cultures and regions, and often reflect the knowledge and situation of the user. It is therefore crucial for all communicators, both senders and receivers, to stay alert and recognize this: Different people can and do interpret words differently.

bypassing
A misunderstanding that occurs between a sender and a receiver because of the symbolic nature of language.

The interpretation of words becomes even more complex when people from different cultures exchange everyday communication. The problem is magnified when someone uses common phrases unfamiliar to non-native speakers of English. For example, consider this sentence: "Won't you have some tea?" The non-native speaker of English listens to the literal meaning of the question and would answer no if they did in fact want tea. Because they use this wording so frequently, native English speakers forget it contains a negative. But a non-native speaker might not know that, in practice, "Won't you have some tea?" and "Will you have some tea?" mean the same thing. In this situation, bypassing occurred because of cultural differences between the two speakers

Some speakers deliberately invite bypassing and use euphemisms or doublespeak to soften or distort meanings. It is important to be aware of this. Politicians and advertisers sometimes say one thing to get people to believe or accept something else. President Obama was surprisingly candid in the early weeks of his presidency in 2009 when he admitted, "I screwed up." Listeners should critically examine what is said. Both speaking and listening involve ethical considerations. Issues of conscience—what is right or wrong and what is beneficial or harmful—are everyone's responsibility.

Language Can Shape Our Attitudes

Indiscrimination is the neglect of individual differences and the overemphasis of similarities. Indiscrimination is a type of perceptual set in which a person chooses to ignore differences and changes in events, things, and people. Language plays a significant role in our tendency to see similarities between things, even when they don't exist. Nouns categorizing people (*teenager, divorcé, student, professor, Latino, conservative, Southerner, friend, government official, politician, athlete, salesperson*) encourage us to focus on similarities. Statements such as "Professors are unfair" and "People in my parents' generation and older know very little about computers and social media" may be interpreted to include all people over 50, instead of some parents and some grandparents. They fail to distinguish among individuals. Such categorization often results in stereotyping.

indiscrimination
The neglect of individual differences and overemphasis of similarities.

Guidelines

REDUCING BYPASSING[22]

1. **Be person-minded, not word-minded.** Think about words and their meanings but also consider the persons using the words and the meanings they might give to them. Constantly question your own interpretation: "This is what the word means to me, but what does it mean to others?"

2. **Query and paraphrase.** Ask questions and paraphrase your message or the meaning you've derived from others' messages whenever there is potential for misunderstanding. Differences in background, age, gender, occupation, culture, attitudes, knowledge, and perceptions may affect communication. If you are uncertain, ask others to explain. Restating a message in your own words gives you and the sender a chance to check that you received a message similar to what was sent. As the importance and complexity of a message increase, so does the need to ask questions and paraphrase.

3. **Be approachable.** Encourage open and free communication. The most frequent barrier to effective communication is an unwillingness to listen to others. Allow others to question and paraphrase your messages and show respect for what they say. It is not always easy to listen for specific meaning, but the effort will ensure a clear exchange of information.

4. **Be sensitive to contexts.** Consider the verbal and situational contexts of your communication interactions. The meaning of a word can be interpreted more precisely when you consider the words, sentences, and paragraphs that precede and follow it and the setting in which communication takes place.

5. **Consider the impact of social media.** Many students in your classes are the digital generation, while your parents and grandparents may have no clue as to your meaning when you use words or phrases associated with mediated forms of communication.

When we stereotype, we categorize events, objects, and people without regard to unique individual characteristics and qualities. Stereotypes are often negative, but they may also be positive—for example, "All liberals are hardworking," "All conservatives want peace," "All teachers are dedicated professionals," and "All environmentalists are concerned citizens." Whether the stereotype is negative or positive, the problem is the same: Individual qualities are ignored. It is too easy to stereotype because it does not require analysis, investigation, or thought. When we preclude distinctions, stereotypes give us neat, oversimplified categories that facilitate but also distort our evaluation of people, situations, and events.

indexing

A technique to reduce indiscrimination by identifying the specific persons, ideas, events, or objects a statement refers to.

There are ways to reduce indiscrimination in our communication. **Indexing** is one way to point out differences that distinguish various members of a group and thus reduce indiscrimination. Indexing identifies the specific person, idea, event, or object to which a statement refers. When you hear someone say something that lumps people, ideas, events, or objects into a single category, such as, "All professional athletes are egotistical," "All professors are liberal," "Feminists don't care about family values," or "All Republicans are Tea-Party thinkers," you need to analyze and ask, "Which people are you talking about?" Everyone is unique. None of us is all one thing or another, and none of us is exactly like anyone else. Even though the media play up politicians who are greedy, sell their votes, or are influenced by lobbyists, each politician is different. The same is true of professional athletes, professors, feminists, and Republicans. They may belong to a class or a group with an identity and whose members have similarities, but the group is composed of unique individuals.

dating

A form of indexing that sorts people, events, ideas, and objects according to time.

Dating, another technique for reducing indiscrimination, is a form of indexing that sorts people, ideas, events, and objects according to time. By telling when something occurred, we acknowledge that things change over time and add specificity to a statement. As an example of how important dating is, indicate the year in which you think each of the following news bulletins was probably made:

> **Pope Condemns Use of New "Horror" Weapons**
>
> Vatican City—Prompted by widespread fears that new weapons of mass destruction might wipe out Western civilization, the Pope today issued a bulletin forbidding the use of these weapons by any Christian state against another, whatever the provocation.

> **Moral Rot Endangers Land, Warns General**
>
> Boston—The head of the country's armed forces declared here today that if he had known the depth of America's moral decay, he would never have accepted his command. "Such a dearth of public spirit," he asserted, "and want of virtue, and fertility in all the low arts to obtain advantages of one kind or another, I never saw before and hope I may never be witness to again."[23]

The thoughts expressed in these two paragraphs could easily apply to today's events, but, in fact, the first paragraph pertains to a statement made by Pope Innocent II in 1139, and the second is a comment made by George Washington in 1775. Did you think that these news bulletins referred to recent events? If so, you fell victim to indiscrimination. Why do such errors occur? How can we avoid or prevent them? The contexts of the statements in these news bulletins could be greatly clarified merely by adding dates: Vatican City, 1139, and Boston, 1775. Dating gives listeners valuable information that can increase their understanding of the intended message.

Language Can Cause Polarization

polarization

The tendency to view things in terms of extremes.

Polarization is the tendency to view things in terms of extremes—rich or poor, beautiful or ugly, large or small, high or low, good or bad, intelligent or stupid—even though most things exist somewhere in between. This either–or, black-or-white way of thinking is aggravated by aspects of language.

Polarization can be destructive, escalating conflict to the point at which two parties simply cannot communicate. This escalation is referred to as the **pendulum effect**. The pendulum represents a person's perception of reality, which includes feelings, attitudes, opinions, and value judgments about the world. When the pendulum hangs in the center, a person's perception is considered realistic, virtuous, intelligent, sane, honest, and honorable. Of course, most of us believe that our pendulums are at or near the center most of the time. When two individuals disagree in their perceptions of reality, their pendulums begin to move in opposite directions. The distance the pendulum swings represents their differences in opinion or conviction. As the conversation intensifies, each remark provokes a stronger reaction from the party to whom it is directed until both parties are driven to positions at opposite extremes. For example, when two roommates argue over whose turn it is to clean, one might begin by saying, "It's your turn. I did it last time." The other is likely to respond, "No, I did it last time. Now it's your turn." If the disagreement continues and no solution is found, both will become more entrenched in their positions, and their comments may turn into personal attacks: "You're always so messy and lazy." "And you're always so picky and critical." The situation can degenerate to such a degree that one or the other threatens to move out. Such an extreme outcome is typical of a discussion driven by the pendulum effect. Emotions can eventually run so high that differences between the parties seem insurmountable and a mutually agreeable settlement seems unattainable.

Speakers can avoid the dangers of polarization if they recognize the potential for misunderstanding and avoid statements that represent general extremes. For example, a noncontroversial statement such as "Iowa is hot in the summer" is not as meaningful as it could be because the word *hot* represents a generalized extreme. Further information prevents misunderstanding: What is the basis of comparison (Arizona or Manitoba)? Are Iowa summers all the same, or do they vary from year to year? Is an Iowa summer the same in all parts of the state, or does it vary from north to south? What is the average summer temperature? The problem of an incorrectly overgeneralized and extreme statement is avoided here: "Iowa summers can be hot. The average temperature is 85 degrees Fahrenheit, with lows around 74 degrees and highs around 105 degrees." Such clarification is especially important when the topic is likely to provoke emotional, defensive, or unpredictable reactions.

This photo exemplifies cultural differences in the way people dress. People from all cultures can still communicate effectively if they take cultural and language differences into account.

pendulum effect
Escalating conflict between two individuals or groups that results from their use of polar terms to describe and defend their perceptions of reality.

Language Can Be Sexist or Homophobic

Men and women show a difference in how they use language and converse with one another. Psychologist Deborah Tannen, for example, suggests that men tend to use language to assert status, whereas women tend to use language to establish and maintain social relationships.[24] Tannen says that, rather than using language to dominate another, women tend to establish closeness and support with it. Men, by contrast, tend to dominate or compete via language. The result, according to Tannen, is that the game of communication for men and women is the same, but the rules are different. When men and women communicate with each other, the potential for clash and conflict arises because of different language use. The problem is magnified when sexist language is used either consciously or unconsciously. Our goal should be to use **gender-inclusive language**—language that does not discriminate against males or females.

Unfortunately, the English language was structured with an inherent bias in favor of men. For example, English has no singular gender-neutral pronouns. Therefore, traditionally, the masculine pronouns (*he, him, his*) have been used to refer to people in general, even if the referent could be a male or female. Use of the masculine

gender-inclusive language
Language that does not discriminate against males or females.

pronoun is not incorrect grammatically, but its use in generic situations is a social issue. Language sets expectations that at times discriminate against and stereotype people. According to traditional usage, the omnipresence of *he* and *him* and the general absence of *she* and *her* subtly but powerfully give the impression that men hold important roles but women do not. Thus, our language creates the expectation that males are active and have important roles, while females are inactive and do not hold important roles. Furthermore, sexist language can be misleading. When a speaker constantly uses only female or only male pronouns such as "she can expect this," or "it is in his best interests," members of the excluded sex believe that the message has little or no relevance to them. When that happens, about 50 percent of listeners may not pay attention to vital information. If it's a medical situation, those who think that it doesn't affect them might not heed the precautions and may expose themselves to greater danger because "it doesn't apply." The pronouns *they* and *their*, for example, are inclusive and acceptable and clearer to all.

sexist language
Language that creates sexual stereotypes or implies that one gender is superior to another.

Sexual stereotypes and the assumption that one gender is superior characterize **sexist language**.[25] Sexist language involves an attitude as much as the use of specific words. Words with a positive connotation are often used to describe males—*independent*, *logical*, *strong*, *confident*, and *aggressive*; females are often associated with words having negative connotations—*dependent*, *illogical*, *weak*, *gullible*, and *timid*. Sexist language suggests that one gender is more important than, and superior to, the other. Language used to discriminate can be quite subtle. We barely register the comment, "He's president of the company." Consider, however, these statements: "She is president of the company, and she's a woman"; "Susan got that position because she's a woman." They describe women who have risen to high authority positions, but they also imply that women do not typically hold these positions or that the only reason Susan got the position was because she's a woman. In other words, they imply that women are less qualified than men.

Stereotypes do not occur in a social vacuum. On the contrary, they often exert a powerful influence on the lives of those who are stereotyped. Gender stereotypes influence perceptions and behaviors of both men and women. Stereotypes affect both how people are treated in society and how they think of themselves. Language is one significant means of perpetuating these stereotypes. There's a significant scene in the movie *Hidden Figures* when one of the male characters says that he didn't realize they hired women for the computers. The woman lets him know he's being sexist and out of line and walks away. If you refer to your female professors who have a Ph.D. as Ms. or Mrs. but refer to male professors as Dr., you are using sexist language. *You* make positive steps to rid your language of stereotypes when you avoid sexist language and substitute gender-inclusive terms.

homophobic language
Language that denigrates or places lesser value on someone from the lesbian, gay, bisexual, or transgender community.

Other stereotypes are reinforced when we use **homophobic language**. When we use negative or pejorative words, we devalue the person we label. When a speaker demonstrates both insensitivity to individuals and a general negative categorization of a group of people, each of whom is unique, their insensitivity is bothersome. Some in the gay, lesbian, bisexual, and transgender community do not want to be identified by gender terms; because they don't identify with any gender labels, use of such terms would not be appropriate. Honor people's wishes when they tell you they don't accept the pronouns *he* or *she* to identify them. Many wish to be referred to as "they" rather than "he" or "she." Ask them how they prefer to be referred to in conversations. A national speaker on the University of Northern Iowa campus was conducting a workshop and asked for student volunteers. She asked each person some questions and made some comments, and then referred to one of the persons as "she"—the student politely asked her not to use "she" as a referent, to no avail. Such language demonstrated that the workshop speaker was not really listening and also indicated her unwillingness to avoid pronouns when speaking about this particular student.

Guidelines

USE GENDER-INCLUSIVE LANGUAGE AND AVOID HOMOPHOBIC LANGUAGE

1. **Remove sexism and homophobia from your communication.** Use *they* and *their* instead of *he* or *she* when referring to others.

2. **Practice and reinforce nonsexist communication patterns.** The ultimate goals are to use nonsexist, inclusive language effortlessly in private conversation and to think in nonsexist terms.

3. **Use familiar language whenever possible.** When you must choose between sexist language and an unfamiliar phrase, choose the unfamiliar phrase and practice it until it becomes familiar.

4. **Do not arouse negative reactions in listeners by using awkward, cumbersome, highly repetitious, or unnecessary words.** There are so many graceful and controlled ways to state your message inclusively that you need not use bland or offensive constructions.

5. **Not all words need to be changed.** Be sure to carefully analyze whether meanings of words need to be changed before doing so.

6. **Check every outgoing message**—written, oral, nonverbal, and email—for sexism or homophobia before sending it.[26] Refer to the person and not the gender whenever you can.

7. **Honor the wishes of those who do not use *he* or *she* to describe themselves.** Ask questions to determine what they prefer or simply refer to them by name.

Competent communicators use inclusive language and avoid demeaning others. Language influences how we see others around us. Inappropriate language causes perceptual and social problems that should not be tolerated in our society.

Culture Affects Language Use

Just as gender differences characterize language use, so, too, do cultural differences. Each language has its own grammatical rules, and some seem very strange to new speakers of a language. Anthropologist Edward T. Hall asserted "all people are captives of the language they speak."[27] Intercultural communication scholars and linguists look at how different cultures use words. The multiple meanings of words and the use of slang that may or may not sound like dictionary words are confusing. Add to that mixture a different culture and a different set of language rules as well as numerous new experiences, and it's easy to see why non-native speakers of U.S. English have concerns about their language use. Linguist Guy Deutscher suggests that while we reject the view that language determines our thoughts and our perception of reality, we do need to recognize "when we learn our mother tongue, we do…acquire certain habits of thought that shape our experiences in significant and often surprising ways."[28] Deutscher further suggests that since habits of speech are cultivated from the earliest age, it is only natural that they can settle into habits of mind that go beyond language itself, affecting your experiences, perceptions, associations, feelings, memories, and orientation in the world.[29] Spanish, French, German, and Russian languages assign a male or female gender to a whole range of inanimate objects, and an object that is male to a speaker of Spanish may be female to a German language speaker. Deutscher provides examples from a language used by certain Indigenous people in Australia, Guugu Yimithirr, where directions determine space. They always describe where cardinal directions locate things: north, east, south, west. They might warn you to "look out for that big ant just north of your foot."[30]

Contemporary linguists suggest that the habits of mind our culture instills in us from infancy shape our orientations to the world and our emotional responses to the objects we encounter. Thus, our first step to understand others is to remember that not everyone thinks or speaks the same.[31]

When we communicate, we first form thoughts and then decide how we're going to express them. Competent communicators begin with clear thinking and then make careful language choices that reflect an understanding of what language is, how it is used, and what effects it might have on listeners.

James Neuliep, a communication scholar, connects language and culture in this way:

> Our ability to put thoughts into a code in order to communicate with someone else empowers us beyond imagination.... If how we think is a reflection of the language we speak, then the speakers of two very different languages must think very differently. This could render effective and successful intercultural communication extremely difficult, if not insurmountable.[32]

The Sapir-Whorf hypothesis explains how language, culture, and thought are inextricably bound together. In this view of culture and language, Benjamin Whorf suggests that the language one speaks affects how one thinks.[33] The hypothesis shows that language options (word and grammatical choices) shape both meaning and how we understand words. Tracy and Robles, in *Everyday Talk*, suggest that if we change words we routinely use, we can sometimes make a difference in our own thoughts and actions. They give an example of people who think of themselves as "guardians of their pets" rather than "pet owners" and suggest those who think they are guardians of their pets actually treat their pets better.[34] The significance of the hypothesis is that language does not operate in a vacuum. We and our language choices are influenced by many things, especially by their link to identity, thought, and culture.

muted group theory

A theory suggesting that underrepresented groups (women, the poor, people with disabilities, seniors, gays, blacks, Latinos, etc.) often are not as free or as able to say what they mean, when and where they wish.

Communication scholar Cheris Kramerae suggests that people who do not have the power of "correct or appropriate" language have little voice in their worlds. Her **muted group theory** suggests status and power are clearly linked.[35] Kramerae says that muted groups often include women and ethnic minorities or out-groups, including lesbian, gay, bisexual, transgender, and queer (LGBTQ) people; people with disabilities; the elderly; and the poor. When people are muted, they have neither the requisite language nor the perceived status to be heard. One often sees someone constantly interrupt or talk over someone from an underrepresented group, giving the impression that person's views are unimportant. Effective communicators avoid such muting and ensure that others also do not mute another.

code-switch or style-switch

For people from co-cultures, to speak the language of their own culture but switch to that of the dominant culture when needed and appropriate.

Another communication scholar, Marsha Houston, reports women of color and other out-groups **code-switch** or **style-switch**, or move between "dominant culture" language and the language of their own coculture, to operate successfully in both the dominant society and their own co-culture.[36] When people code-switch or style-switch, they use appropriate language when speaking with their own group and know when to choose words to communicate effectively with those from other cultures or groups. Michelle Obama is a role model and a popular speaker both in the United States and around the world who clearly demonstrates her ability to function effectively in any culture. She communicates effectively with majority audiences as well as with people of color and other underrepresented groups. Her ability to connect with others has landed her in the top ten lists of "most admired women" several years running and makes her a popular commencement speaker.

Language allows us to share our thoughts and ideas with others. We can name things and converse with others to learn what we have in common. Words can cause us to take up specific causes or create a better environment. Sometimes, however, we don't have the words to explain our thoughts fully, but we can usually reach the point where we understand each other fairly well. For these and other reasons, communicators need to make careful choices in the language they use to communicate.

Language and Social Influences

4.4 **Illustrate** the impact of social influences on language.

Media communication scholar Neil Postman once wrote that use of technology creates "a bargain with the devil."[37] In *Technopoly*, he says that technology redefines culture through its control over and elevation of information, and he claims that for every good thing technology provides, it also gives us negatives or disadvantages. Postman is concerned that technology will take over the world and remove too many of the face-to-face interactions as we "amuse ourselves to death."[38] Given the rapid growth of technology, it is likely that some changes will occur simply because of technological advances. Reddit, YouTube, Instagram, Snapchat, Pinterest, Facebook, Twitter, and other social media outlets already enhance awareness of personal, social, and political issues and people's responses. Jeff Child, Joseph Mazer, and other communication scholars research how social media affect people, especially our language choices, and the lack of privacy that result from our use. (For more information, see Chapter 6.)

Government and elected officials are often concerned about words and actions they feel are either conducive to running the country or counterproductive when someone questions those words and actions. Since the early days of his presidency, Donald Trump has taken on individuals and the media. He tweets about the media being "unfair" to him and fails to tell the truth. Twitter is his platform for staying in touch with the people who elected him and for gaining agreement with his actions and views. Twitter is also the platform for those who disagree with his words and policies, and the running threads of arguments against him can be lengthy. Fortunately, in the United States, the First Amendment to the U.S. Constitution guarantees the right to thoughtfully use language to express views about the world, especially through freedom of speech and freedom of the press. This is a clear demonstration of how social media have become significant in our lives and in the ways we talk and think.

MAKING CONNECTIONS FOR SUCCESS

Language and the First Amendment

"Only a free and unrestrained press can effectively expose deception in government." These words were included in Justice Hugo Black's majority decision of the Supreme Court to allow publication of the "Pentagon Papers" detailing U.S. involvement in Vietnam from 1945 to 1967 (the subject of numerous films, including 2017's *The Post*, starring Meryl Streep and Tom Hanks).[39]

The First Amendment to the U.S. Constitution guarantees citizens freedom of speech, freedom of the press, freedom of assembly, freedom to exercise the religion of their choosing, and the freedom to address the government for redress of grievances. Numerous situations and events in the public eye in 2017 and 2018 placed increased scrutiny on language in social media and media and print sources. When differences of opinion and differing views were brought to light, President Trump argued that news sources were guilty of peddling "fake news" and went so far as to threaten to shut down "fake news" organizations such as CNN when they questioned his words. When National Football League (NFL) players knelt during the national anthem before games to protest the treatment of black people and people of color by police in the United States,[40] President Trump stated that they should be fired for not honoring the country and its flag. Some saw those actions as Trump did; others felt the football players displayed freedom of speech concerning their views about the treatment of people of color by police. When Michael Wolff, a journalist, wrote a book *Fire and Fury* chronicling Trump's actions and questioned his ability to lead the country effectively, Trump demanded that Macmillan Publishers cease publication of the book. Macmillan's president responded that the First Amendment guaranteed the right to publish the book.[41] Twitter users and news sources continued to express their views, and Trump and his advisors continued to push against the words and actions. As you consider language and First Amendment rights, answer the following questions:

1. What are your views on the First Amendment?

2. Are you concerned about freedom of speech when numerous people try to stifle views different from their own?

3. What other words or actions might be perceived as either upholding or violating the First Amendment?

How to Use Language Effectively

4.5 **Describe** how accurate, vivid, immediate, and appropriate language can help you be a more effective communicator.

People of all ages, cultures, and educational levels use language every day. Nevertheless, the ability to use language efficiently and successfully requires years of practice and study. Although many variables influence the effectiveness of language, five aspects merit special attention. They are *accuracy*, *vividness*, *immediacy*, *appropriateness*, and *metaphor*.

Use Accurate Language

Use of accurate language is as critical to a speaker as accurate navigational directions are to an air traffic controller. A wrong word can distort your intended message, misguide your receiver, and undermine your credibility. When you speak, your goal should be precision. Don't leave room for misinterpretation. You should constantly ask, "What do I want to say?" and "What do I mean?" When necessary, look to what others say to be sure you choose the correct word to express your message.

The more words you can use accurately, the greater the likelihood you will find the one you need to make your meaning clear. You must expand your vocabulary. Two of the best ways to do this are through listening to others and reading. Pay attention to words you don't understand. Whenever you come across an unfamiliar word, determine the context in which it is used and ask questions when appropriate. The dictionary or thesaurus function in your computer software can help you increase word choice possibilities. Once you have learned a new word, try to put it to use. Unused words are typically forgotten.

One word of warning: As you continue to develop your vocabulary, avoid the temptation to use long or little-known words when short or common words serve the purpose. Be sure, also, that you know the shades of meaning and connotations of new words before you use them, and remember that words may have different meanings for different people.

Sometimes a message is unclear because it was not constructed effectively. Poor sentence structure and word usage can wreak havoc on a statement's clarity. For example, classified ads in newspapers frequently are so condensed that their intended meaning becomes distorted or obscured. The result might be "TV ads boost eating of obese children" and "Baby born 10 months premature." We hope these headline writers knew what they wished to communicate, but their failure to phrase their messages accurately interfered with their intended meaning.

When we converse, we can usually clear up misunderstandings caused by scrambled sentence structure or poor word choice. But to do so, we must first be aware of listeners' reactions to what we are saying. If they appear confused or ask a question, we should rephrase the message more clearly.

Effective speakers do not assume what is clear to them will necessarily be clear to listeners. They are especially aware of this potential problem in situations such as public speeches, during which listeners might not be able to ask questions. To ensure comprehension, such speakers strive to make their meaning clear by, among other tactics, using familiar and concrete, rather than abstract, language and by being aware of the connotations associated with particular words. (Review the section in this chapter entitled "The Elements of Language.")

Use Vivid Language

To communicate effectively, make your message animated and interesting. Direct, fresh language conveyed in the active voice can bring a sense of excitement, urgency, and forcefulness to what you say. Such **vividness** tells your listeners they better listen because what you have to say is important.

vividness
Active, direct, and fresh language that brings a sense of excitement, urgency, and forcefulness to a message.

MAKING CONNECTIONS FOR SUCCESS
Using Vivid Language

Compare the following two messages. President Franklin D. Roosevelt said the first. The second expresses a similar thought, though in a different way.

> I see one-third of a nation ill housed, ill clad, ill nourished.

> It is evident that a substantial number of persons within the continental boundaries of the United States have inadequate financial resources with which to purchase the products of agricultural communities and industrial establishments. It would appear that, for a considerable segment of the population, perhaps as much as 33.333 percent of the total, there are inadequate housing facilities, and an equally significant proportion is deprived of the proper types of clothing and nourishment.

1. How would you describe the word choice in each message?
2. How does each message affect your emotions?
3. How does the vivid (and succinct) language used in the first example create an impression of the speaker that differs from that of the second speaker?

For example, suppose an organization is trying to raise money for homeless people. It could take one of two approaches in seeking a donation from you. It could present (1) statistics to illustrate the number of people who are believed to be homeless or (2) cases of actual individuals who are homeless, including children and their families. The first approach is rational, informative, abstract, and emotionally distant. The second approach is emotional, urgent, concrete, and forceful. The vividness of the second approach is at least likely to get your attention and perhaps influence you to contribute.

According to social psychologists, vivid language affects us in several ways. It is more persuasive than a flat, pallid presentation of information because it is more memorable and has an emotional impact. Vivid messages are more likely to create readily retained and recalled mental images. Finally, people tend to listen more attentively to vivid messages than to uninspiring or uninteresting messages.[42]

Effective communicators use vivid language in all their interactions, whether it's one-to-one with friends or family, in small groups, or in the public arena. Use interesting words, try to include active verbs, and provide variety in the length of your sentences. Whenever possible, avoid clichés and use slang appropriately and with the appropriate audience. You are more likely to keep your listeners interested in what you say if you use fresh language to present your ideas in new and exciting ways.

verbal immediacy

Identifies and projects the speaker's feelings and makes the message more relevant to the listener.

Use Immediate Language

Verbal immediacy identifies and projects the speaker's feelings and makes the message more relevant to the listener. Verbal immediacy draws listeners in and involves them in the subject at hand. The following statements illustrate different levels of verbal immediacy. The first sentence displays a high immediacy level, and the last displays a low immediacy level:

1. I am a social constructionist who believes we create and share meaning as we interact with each other; thus, we will share ideas about effective communication in this class—all of us contribute and we learn together.
2. You and I will share ideas about effective communication.
3. I think you and I may enjoy talking about effective communication.
4. People often enjoy talking about effective communication.

The first statement is directly related to the speaker, the listener, and the situation. It is assertive, and the speaker makes a

Communicators would do well to create vivid messages through the imagery of language. Vivid images are apparent to the viewer in the vibrant, attention-grabbing decorations in this photo.

Sean Motola/Fotolia

connection with the listener by using the word *we*. In each successive statement, the speaker decreases the intensity of this association with the listener and the event. The language becomes less immediate, more distant in tone.

Verbal immediacy also makes the speaker appear relaxed, confident, competent, and effective. In addition, receivers tend to view messages characterized by immediacy as more similar to their own beliefs than those cast in language unrelated to the speaker, topic, or receiver.

Use Appropriate Language

Each time you speak, your listeners have specific expectations about the kind of language you use. Different kinds of words or language are appropriate to different situations. For example, the words you use to address the president of your college or university would be much more formal than the language you would use when chatting with friends. You would be unlikely to call the president by a nickname, and you would be equally unlikely to call a friend Dr. or Mr. or Ms., except in professional settings or in jest.

Use of inappropriate language for a given situation damages your credibility, and your message might be misinterpreted or disregarded as disrespectful. Words we use in writing can sound stilted, formal, and unnatural when spoken. Words for the ear should be vital and natural. It is crucial to assess each communicative situation and adjust your language accordingly. In public situations, profanity and improper grammar are always inappropriate.

Use Metaphorical Language

metaphor
A figure of speech that associates two things or ideas, not commonly linked, as a means of description.

According to some language scholars, our way of looking at the world around us is fundamentally metaphorical. A **metaphor** is a figure of speech that associates two things or ideas, not commonly linked, as a means of description. Metaphors help us to structure what we think, how we perceive the world, and what we do. Metaphorical language pervades our everyday language and our thoughts.

Metaphorical language is culture-bound, and most metaphors have meaning only within a specific language community. If your receivers cannot identify with a particular metaphor you use, it will be meaningless to them. Also, as we pointed out earlier in the chapter, avoid metaphors that negatively or unfairly categorize a specific person or group of people.

As a student, you probably can think of many metaphors to describe your college experiences. For example, some students have said college life is a roller-coaster ride: There are many ups and downs, as well as turns. What are some other metaphors you use to vividly express your college experiences?

The misuse of language involves more than misuse of words. Misused language affects our ability to think. Thought and language are inseparable. Most scholars agree that words help us form thoughts. How many times have you found yourself struggling to find *the* right word and, without it, a frustrating inability to express what you really meant? When you take the time to think for a minute, however, the word usually appears. It is important to carefully consider language choices before we speak. We cannot erase what we said. We can correct or retract a statement and apologize for it, but we cannot eliminate the fact that we said it.

Those whose career success is profoundly affected by the ability to communicate expend great effort in evaluating the potential effects of using certain words. Many songwriters have examples of songs that didn't quite come together for years until they were inspired and found the words that previously eluded them. President Obama, normally a fluent speaker, made verbal gaffes. When in Austria in March 2009, he said "I don't know what your Austrian word is, but…". This was considered a blunder because in Austria (once a part of Germany) the official language is Austrian German. Leaders are supposed to think things through very carefully, and this example might be attributed to a failure to think. Such a mistake has the potential to affect a politician's political life, especially on the world stage. Language also has the potential to create positive or negative impressions. Lord Chesterfield, 18th-century British statesman and "man of letters," once said, "Words, which are the dress of thoughts, deserve surely more care than clothes, which are only the dress of the person."[43]

⟩ SUMMARY

The Power of Language

4.1 **Assess** the power of language in communication events and our lives.

- *Language* is the way we create and share meaning with others.
- Language is powerful in every aspect of our lives.
- Language allows us to make connections with others.
- Language has the power to influence our perceptions of others and theirs of us.
- Language affects our emotions.
- Language affects our relationships

The Elements of Language

4.2 **Use** the elements of language (sounds, words, grammar, and meaning) in effective communication.

- The four elements of language are sounds, words, grammar, and meaning.
- Most of us are born with the ability to make speech sounds, but people do not all learn to produce the sounds in the same ways.
- *Words* represent objects and concepts.
- *Grammar* is the set of rules we use to join words into phrases and sentences.
- Meaning allows us to use words and patterns to exchange messages between people.

Language-Based Barriers to Communication

4.3 **Explain** how language can create barriers to effective communication.

- Language can be misunderstood because meanings depend on commonalities.
- Language can be misunderstood because people believe words have meanings in themselves.
- Language can shape our attitudes.
- *Indiscrimination* occurs when we neglect individual differences and lump things together.
- When we fail to identify people, objects, ideas, and events by time, we are open to misunderstanding.
- Language can cause *polarization* when we view and use extremes. This either–or language leads to failure to communicate.

- We should avoid *sexist* or *homophobic language* if we wish to avoid stereotypes and use language to help us make connections with others.

Language and Social Influences

4.4 **Illustrate** the impact of social influences on language.

- Advances in technology have created a faster, global means of communicating.
- Social media outlets have a tremendous impact on our lives and our communication with others.
- The First Amendment of the U.S. Constitution guarantees people's right to use language thoughtfully under freedom of speech and freedom of the press.

How to Use Language Effectively

4.5 **Describe** how accurate, vivid, immediate, and appropriate language can help you be a more effective communicator.

- Accurate language allows you to be precise and to eliminate misinterpretations.
- *Vivid* language allows you to be animated and interesting.
- *Immediate* language identifies the speaker's feelings and allows the message to be more relevant to the listener.
- Language is used differently in varying situations. You should choose language that is appropriate for the listener and the context. Remember, too, language for the ear is different from language for the eye. Writing and speaking require different choices.
- Metaphorical language can help you create shared meanings when you compare the known and the unknown. *Metaphors* allow us to structure and describe what we think, how we perceive the world, and what we do.
- Technology has created new words and affected the ways we connect with others on a global level, but, again, we need to make effective choices in order to share meaning with others.
- Language is culture-bound, so we need to be especially aware of effective language in order to communicate clearly.

〉 DISCUSSION STARTERS

1. Provide two personal examples of the power of language.

2. Explain the relationship between language and thought.

3. Why are language, communication, talk, and speech defined separately and not considered synonymous?

4. We say that language has rules, but we also say that language is arbitrary. Why might this be a contradiction in terms?

5. How and why should we defend against the use of inappropriate language?

6. What do we mean when we say "meanings are in people"? Identify an example of a conversation where a person's different meaning was the cause of confusion or a failure to communicate.

7. Which of the language barriers discussed is most likely to occur in your interactions?

8. How do competent communicators use indexing and dating in their communication efforts?

9. Create a list of words commonly used in conversations brought to us from technology.

10. In what ways have current political and social events affected our use of language?

11. Identify four differences between spoken and written language.

12. How does language help us identify who we are, recognize others' identities, and also help us connect with others?.

CHAPTER 5

CONNECTING THROUGH NONVERBAL COMMUNICATION

Medioimages/Photodisc/Getty Images

Nonverbal communication describes all communication behaviors that transcend spoken or written words. Although it is difficult to quantify its contribution to the communication process, nonverbal communication often provides much more meaning than people realize.

→ CHAPTER OUTLINE AND LEARNING OBJECTIVES

What Is Nonverbal Communication?

5.1 **Differentiate** nonverbal communication from verbal communication.

Characteristics of Nonverbal Communication

5.2 **Explain** the six key characteristics of nonverbal communication.

Functions of Nonverbal Communication

5.3 **Identify** the five common functions of nonverbal communication.

Types of Nonverbal Communication

5.4 **Compare and contrast** different types of nonverbal communication and the ways competent communicators are aware of their nonverbal communication.

Improving Our Ability to Send and Interpret Nonverbal Communication

5.5 **Explain** why it is difficult to interpret and understand nonverbal communication and how to ensure that the message received is accurate.

MAKING EVERYDAY CONNECTIONS

Carly slowly walks into her apartment. She looks as if she has just seen a ghost. Tears form as she sits down on the sofa, and she begins to cry openly and uncontrollably.

Her friend Dana puts her arm around her and pats her on the shoulder gently. Carly looks at Dana. Carly's face and demeanor tell Dana something is really wrong, as if Carly's whole world has just come crashing down. Dana doesn't know what to say, so she continues to comfort Carly by holding her hand. Carly is unable to control her emotions or speak. Finally, Carly looks at Dana. Dana looks back, her face showing concern as if to say, "What is going on?"

Neither uttered one word as they held each other tightly, yet their expressions and touch said everything.

QUESTIONS TO THINK ABOUT

1. How does nonverbal communication make communication easier? How does it make communication more difficult?
2. Why do we give little or no thought to our nonverbal communication?
3. Why do you think nonverbal communication is considered more believable than verbal communication?
4. Explain what nonverbal communication is and is not.
5. What are the challenges of communicating emotions online or via text message? Are there risks?

What Is Nonverbal Communication?

5.1 **Differentiate** nonverbal communication from verbal communication.

nonverbal communication

Behaviors, symbols, attributes, or objects—whether intended or not—that communicate messages with social meaning.

Nonverbal communication includes all behaviors, symbols, attributes, or objects—whether intended or not—that communicate messages with social meaning. Nonverbal communication includes tone of voice, facial expressions, posture, gestures, and appearance, all of which communicate messages. Nonverbal communication can enhance or change the meaning of words, such as when tone of voice, volume, or facial expression adds emphasis to meaning. According to communication scholar Mark Knapp and social psychologist Judith Hall, it is important to understand that the division of "verbal and nonverbal behavior into two separate and distinct categories is virtually impossible."[1] Unfortunately, nonverbal communication can also change the intended meaning of a message or make it confusing and unclear.

We tend to take nonverbal communication for granted because it is so basic, but its importance is unmistakable, and its connection to communication is undeniable. In most communication situations, we spend more of our time communicating nonverbally than verbally, and our nonverbal messages can carry more meaning than our verbal messages.

A review of nonverbal communication research by Knapp and Hall concluded that some people depend more heavily on verbal messages, whereas others seem to rely more on nonverbal messages.[2] Another research study found that nonverbal behaviors were 12 to 13 times more powerful in impact than the accompanying verbal message.[3] These findings indicate the importance and impact of nonverbal behaviors.

Without realizing it, we often base many daily decisions on nonverbal communication. When are others more likely to do favors for you—when they are in a good mood or a bad one? Can you think of recent decisions you made on the basis of another's nonverbal communication? For example, your professor's facial expression suggests that she is in a really good mood, so you decide that now is a good time to ask her whether you can miss next week's class to get an early start on your spring break trip. In situations like this, as well as ones where we can't ask others how they feel, we are more likely to pay careful attention to nonverbal cues, such as changes in facial expressions, eye contact, posture, body movements, and other expressive actions to determine mood. According to psychologists, such behavior is extremely difficult to repress or control, so even when others try to conceal their inner feelings from us, they express those feelings through their nonverbal cues.[4]

Characteristics of Nonverbal Communication

5.2 **Explain** the six key characteristics of nonverbal communication.

Students often ask, "Why study nonverbal communication?" Of the many reasons, the primary one is the pervasive effect of nonverbal communication on what and how we communicate; we always communicate something nonverbally. In addition, nonverbal communication depends on context, is more believable than verbal communication, is a primary means of expression, is related to culture, and is at times ambiguous or easily misunderstood.

Nonverbal Communication Occurs Constantly

When another person is aware of you, or you of her or him, communication occurs whether something is said or not. If you make eye contact, smile, frown, or totally ignore the other person, you are communicating. Sometimes what is said is less important than what is not said. For example, if you did not attend a meeting when you were expected, you came late to an employment interview, you wore jeans when you were expected to dress formally, you wore a suit when jeans were expected, you talked about a sad situation with a smirk on your face, or you spoke to someone but never looked him or her in the eye, these all convey strong messages. Facial expression, appearance (sex, race, physique), clothing, willingness to make eye contact, body movements, and posture all communicate.

To illustrate that we always communicate, whether intentionally or unintentionally, consider the two students pictured: Sam dresses as a perfectly groomed professional and wears expensive cologne. Oliver wears a hat to cover his hair and an old T-shirt. If we only look at them, we cannot tell what these two actually intend to communicate. Sam might simply be neat and use cologne because it gives him confidence, or he might really want to communicate that designer clothes and expensive cologne are important to him, or he wants to let everyone know he's got money. Oliver might simply like to show that he will not conform to everyone else; alternatively, he may communicate that he disdains society's obsession with outward appearances. Ultimately, it's not so much what Sam and Oliver intend to "say" as what others perceive. Both indicate something about themselves through their appearance, whether intentional or not.

Val Lawless/Shutterstock

Sigrid Olsson / PhotoAlto Agency RF Collections/Getty Images

The messages you send via your appearance, facial expressions, clothing, eye contact, body movements, and posture may not always be clear or what you intended. What is perceived, however, is what is communicated, whether it's intended or not.

Nonverbal Communication Depends on Context

The context in which nonverbal communication occurs plays a crucial role in its interpretation. Pounding on a table to make a point during a meeting means something entirely different from pounding on the table in response to being called a liar. Direct eye contact with a stranger can mean something entirely different from such contact with a close friend.

When you communicate, nonverbal and verbal cues usually supplement and support each other. Your appearance, tone of voice, eye movement, posture, and facial expression provide cues about the communication relationship. For example, when you talk to a friend, your relaxed tone of voice, eye contact, and posture reveal much about your friendship. Your nonverbal cues can tell your friends how much you value them, how comfortable you feel, or how intimate your relationship is. Such nonverbal communication is interpreted within the context of your friendships and is complemented by casual and personal conversations.

Nonverbal Communication Is More Believable Than Verbal Communication

Most of us tend to believe nonverbal communication, even when it contradicts the accompanying verbal message. Consider this conversation between a mother and her daughter regarding the daughter's husband:

JESS'S MOTHER:	What's wrong? Are you upset with Chad?
JESS (STARING AND FROWNING):	Whatever. I'm not upset; why should I be?
JESS'S MOTHER:	You seem to be in a funk, and you are avoiding talking to me. So what's wrong? Did you and Chad have a fight?
JESS (SHOUTING ANGRILY):	*I said nothing is wrong! Please leave me alone! Everything is fine!*

Throughout the conversation, Jess seems upset and is snappy in tone; she sends a signal to her mother that there's more to the story. It seems clear from the interaction and the mother's intuition that Jess is hiding something—hence, the second inquiry. Indeed, the real story is that Jess and her husband have problems. They fight over money, and the mother senses that something is on Jess's mind. Nonverbal messages are much more difficult to control than verbal messages because nonverbal cues are more representative of our emotions, which are also more challenging to control.

Is nonverbal or verbal communication more likely to be true or more accurate? Verbal communication is more conscious; it involves more processing of thoughts and impulses into words. Although nonverbal messages can be conscious and deliberate, they are often, as we have suggested, unintentional and subconsciously generated. It is almost always easier to determine what you are going to say, but it is very difficult for most of us to control our voices, facial expressions, and other body movements when we are upset, hurt, or angry. Jess's mother interpreted her daughter's nonverbal communication as a more accurate reflection of Jess's feelings than her verbal communication.

Nonverbal Communication Is a Primary Means of Expression

We can often detect other people's feelings of frustration, anger, sadness, resentment, or anxiety even when they actually say nothing. We can detect others' emotions because nonverbal communication is powerful. Almost all of our feelings and attitudes are expressed through our nonverbal behaviors. For example, at a large party, a woman enters with her friend and spots a former roommate. She turns up her nose and walks away. Her friends, running after her, ask why she had suddenly left, to which the woman replied, "I don't like that girl over there. We were roommates during our first semester. She's crazy." The nonverbal communication really didn't need much explanation; it was obvious what the woman was saying through her actions.

Nonverbal Communication Is Related to Culture

Culture contributes significantly to differences in nonverbal behavior. Norms and rules that govern the management of behavior differ from culture to culture. Yet because human beings around the world share common biological and social functions, it should not be too surprising to also find areas of similarity in nonverbal communication. For example, studies comparing facial expressions have found that certain universal expressions, such as those indicating sadness and fear, are easily understood across various cultures. Although much outward behavior is innate (such as smiling, touching, eye contact, moving), we are not born knowing what meanings such nonverbal messages communicate.[5]

Most scholars agree that cultures formulate rules that dictate when, how, and with what consequences nonverbal expressions are exhibited. For instance, the way people sit can communicate different and important messages across cultures. In the United States, being casual and open is valued; thus, people, consciously or unconsciously, convey this quality by the way they sit. Males in the United States often sit in a slumping and leaning-back position, as well as sprawled out, so they occupy a lot of space (also called "manspreading").[6] However, in other countries, such as Germany and Sweden, where more formality prevails, slouching is considered a sign of rudeness and poor manners. The way your legs are positioned also has cultural meaning. For example, the innocent act of ankle-to-knee leg crossing, typical of the way many American males sit, could be interpreted as an insult in Saudi Arabia, Singapore, Thailand, or Egypt.[7] Many sexual connotations for gestures are tied to culture as well. In the United States, the middle finger is used to send an insulting, obscene message. This gesture, however, is not universal. In some cultures, the gesture used to represent the same insult is the forming of an O with the thumb and index finger, which means "A-OK" in American culture. The same gesture in France means "zero" or "worthless," in parts of Latin America and the Middle East, it indicates "a**hole," and in Japan it signifies "money."

People from different cultures also infer emotions in somewhat different ways.[8] For example, Americans typically look at facial expressions, body posture, and other nonverbal cues. Japanese, in contrast, might consider not only those same cues but also the relationship the person has with other people. In other words, in the Japanese culture, a smiling person can't really be happy unless other important people in that person's life also experience positive reactions.[9] Although nonverbal cues provide important information about others' emotions in all cultures, the extent to which they are used to infer others' feelings can and does vary across cultures. Because the United States is an individualistic culture, facial expressions, body movements, eye contact, and other nonverbal cues are a primary source of such information. In contrast, in collectivist cultures, relationships and status between people are significant. So where does emotion reside: inside people or between them? The answer appears to depend on your culture.

Nonverbal Communication Is Ambiguous

Although nonverbal channels are absent, many people prefer text messaging to talking on the phone or face-to-face-communication. A focus-group study[10] revealed that people might feel a greater level of control in asynchronous communication (such as texting) than in synchronous communication (responding to others immediately). The reasons people favor the asynchronous type include greater control and the opportunity to think through their responses; thus they can better control how they will be perceived.

Although using forms of asynchronous communication, such as email and texting, may seem advantageous, these can actually lead to miscommunication and misunderstandings. Research shows that email receivers often fail to understand the sender's expressions of sarcasm or humor (even with emojis). For example, nonverbal expressions (such as tone of voice) used to detect sarcasm are absent in texts, social media, and email; thus these messages may be misunderstood and possibly offensive. Emojis help to make the meaning in our texts clearer; bitmojis bring a sender's cartoon avatar into the message, and can allow for messages to be personalized and communicated clearly and succinctly.

Unless we understand the context of the communication, it is almost impossible to tell what a specific nonverbal behavior may mean. In fact, misunderstandings can occur even when the context is fully understood. That is why we must think twice about our interpretation of others' nonverbal behavior and their possible interpretations of ours. When you see and hear nonverbal communication without a complete understanding of the context, you might not receive the intended message. When you assume too much about a nonverbal message, further miscommunication and misunderstanding can result.

Because nonverbal messages are always present, we must recognize their importance or impact and also exercise care when interpreting them. Like verbal communication, nonverbal behavior can be ambiguous, abstract, and arbitrary. We cannot assume that nonverbal messages have only one meaning. For example, does crying always signify grief or sadness, or does it also express joy or pain? If we effectively interpret nonverbal behavior we need to understand the context in which it takes

MAKING CONNECTIONS FOR SUCCESS
Body Language and Facial Expressions: It's All about Culture and Meaning

Examine the photos below and interpret what the gestures mean. Each gesture has a specific meaning in the United States and most other Western cultures.

1. What are the gestures/behaviors communicating to you?

2. Show the photos to people from other cultures (especially non-Western cultures) to determine whether they interpret the gestures as you do.

3. What advice would you give to someone about nonverbal communication and traveling to different cultures?

Daryl Visscher/arabianEye/Getty Images

Image Source/Stockbyte/Getty Images

place and the cultural norms governing it. But even when a person understands these dynamics, it is still easy to misinterpret nonverbal behaviors. For example, does a fellow student's yawn signal boredom or fatigue? Does a speaker tremble because of nervousness or excitement? Most nonverbal behaviors have a multitude of possible meanings, and to automatically assume that you have grasped the *only* possible meaning could lead to a serious misunderstanding. No consistent rules are in place for using or interpreting nonverbal communication.

Why Should You Know about Nonverbal Communication? An Overview

You should understand nonverbal communication for many reasons. The following are some of the more important ones. Nonverbal communication:

- carries most of the meaning of a message, particularly feelings and attitudes toward others.
- is a frequent source of misunderstanding.
- is not governed by a set of universal rules.
- is multichanneled, complicated, and ever-changing.
- is bound to context and culture.
- is more likely than verbal communication to be spontaneous and unintentional.
- is powerful and more believable than verbal communication.
- is learned (not always consciously).
- is critical in relationship initiation, development, and termination.

Functions of Nonverbal Communication

5.3 **Identify** the five common functions of nonverbal communication.

Nonverbal communication adds life to our exchanges by complementing, repeating, regulating, and substituting for our words. Sometimes we even use it to deceive others (see Table 5.1).

Complementing Verbal Behavior

The use of nonverbal cues to complete, describe, or accent verbal cues is called **complementing**. For example, after shooting a chip shot from about 75 yards, a golfer tells her partner that she missed the cup by inches and uses her thumb and index

complementing
The use of nonverbal cues to complete, describe, or accent verbal cues.

Table 5.1 FUNCTIONS OF NONVERBAL COMMUNICATION

Category	Characteristic	Example
Complementing	Completes, describes, or accents a verbal message	A person needs help immediately, so he yells as loudly as possible.
Repeating	Expresses a message identical to the verbal one	A person says yes and nods her head up and down.
Regulating	Controls flow of communication	A person nods his head as a way of communicating, "I am interested in what you are saying," implying "tell me more."
Substituting	Replaces a verbal message with nonverbal signals to exchange thoughts	Two people use hand signals to communicate because the environment is too loud to hear each other's voices.
Deceiving	Nonverbal cues that purposely disguise or mislead to create a false impression	A doctor examining a patient discovers a serious problem, but the doctor's facial expressions remain neutral to avoid alarming the patient.

finger to show the distance. When you say hello to a friend, you show your genuine interest with a warm smile, steady eye contact, and holding the friend's hand.

We use complementary nonverbal cues to accent verbal behavior by emphasizing or punctuating our spoken words. For example, a mother tries to get her children to be quieter and softly asks, "Will you please keep it down?" If that doesn't work and the noise really bothers her, she might raise her voice to indicate that she wants quiet immediately.

People who are excited or enthusiastic are more likely to use nonverbal cues to accent their messages than are people who are restrained, have a difficult time expressing themselves, do not pay attention, or do not understand others' meanings.

Repeating Verbal Behavior

Repeating behavior expresses a message identical to the verbal one. For example, a father attempts to keep his child quiet in church and places his index finger to his lips and says, "Shh!" A speaker states she has two points to make and holds up two fingers. The actions of the father and the speaker are called **repeating** because they convey the same meaning as the verbal message.

Such repetition is especially common in sports. For instance, a referee on a basketball court shouts, "Traveling!" while rolling her arms in a circular motion, or a baseball umpire cries "Strike!" while raising his right arm. These repeating nonverbal signals are deliberately planned so that all players and spectators know the official's call.

repeating
The use of nonverbal cues to convey the same meaning as the verbal message.

Regulating Verbal Behavior

As illustrated in the introductory "Making Everyday Connections," nonverbal cues can also be used to control the flow of communication, a behavior known as **regulating**. For example, we frequently use nonverbal signals to indicate that we want to talk, to stop another person from interrupting us when we are talking, or to show that we are finished and that the other person may take a turn. When we truly listen, we might nod our heads rapidly to suggest that the speaker hurry up and finish, or we might nod slowly to show that we want to hear more.

Senders might not even realize when they send regulating cues, but receivers are usually aware of such signals. In class, for example, a professor receives a clear message when students put on their coats or close their notebooks to indicate class is over. The students may demonstrate their recognition of the clock—it's time to leave—but the professor may receive an entirely different message. If your friend interrupts you during a conversation, you might extend your hand with an outward palm to indicate to your friend that she should stop cutting you off in mid-sentence.

regulating
The use of nonverbal cues to control the flow of communication.

Substituting for Verbal Behavior

When we use nonverbal messages in place of oral messages, we are **substituting**. It is common when speaking is impossible, undesirable, or inappropriate. For example, ramp controllers at airports use hand signals to guide planes to their unloading positions because the noise level is too high for spoken communication; friends often exchange knowing looks when they want to communicate something behind another person's back; some people with hearing impairments use a sophisticated formal sign language in place of the spoken word. When we include symbols, emojis, or bitmojis in our communication, they serve as substitutes for oral messages. You may use hashtags in social media to stand in the place of oral messages and convey emotion. Consider the following tweet: "Just got to my 8am class only to learn the professor canceled class! #annoyed #8amclassessuck."

substituting
The use of nonverbal cues in place of oral messages when speaking is impossible, undesirable, or inappropriate.

Deceiving

When we purposely mislead others with nonverbal cues to create false impressions or to convey incorrect information, we are **deceiving**. Among the most common of such *deceiving* nonverbal behaviors is the poker face that some use when playing cards. By masking their facial expressions, they try not to let the other players know what they have in their hand. Masking is a form of deceiving. We might try to appear calm when we are really nervous or upset, and we often act surprised, alert, or happy when, in fact, we are feeling quite the opposite.

Research suggests that most people lie at least once a day[11] and use deception about 20 percent of the time in their social interactions. Deception occurs for many reasons, such as to avoid hurting someone's feelings, to conceal our real feelings or reactions, or to avoid being caught for some misdeed. This apparent fact raises a couple of questions: (1) How good are we at recognizing when someone deceives us? (2) How can we do a better job at detecting when someone tries to deceive us? The answer to the first question is not very promising. The research seems to suggest that we do slightly better than 50/50 in determining if someone deceives us.[12] Many reasons account for our inability to detect deception, the least of which is that we want to believe that people tell the truth; another is our lack of attention to nonverbal cues that might reveal that someone is deceiving us.[13] One more reason has come to light—most of us assume that if people are truthful in one situation or context, they are likely to be truthful in all others, and this may prevent us from recognizing they might lie on some occasions.[14] One study found that people who lie make fewer hand movements and tend to look away from a person when they tell untruths. The research further found that liars' voices could also be a telling sign; there is a tendency to hesitate and to shift pitch more often than when telling the truth.[15] Another study found that liars often try to control their voices, which often leads to sounding over-controlled or undercontrolled, indicating anxiety or deception.[16]

Recent research indicates that when people find themselves on the receiving end of lies, they react with mistrust of, and dislike toward, the liar.[17] In fact, the more lies a stranger tells, the more that person is disliked and the less he or she is trusted. Once exposed to someone who has lied, most people are more willing to engage in such behaviors themselves.[18] The researchers told participants in their study that a person in the video they were about to watch was lying. Some lies involved exaggerations (e.g., the liar said that he had been an honor student in high school when this was not true), and others involved mini-mizations (e.g., the liar indicated that her academic record was worse than it really was). The researchers also varied the number of lies so that the liars engaged in deception only once in four times. When participants rated the liars, they gave lower scores for likeability and trustworthiness to the frequent liars and to the liars who had exaggerated rather than mini-mized their own achievements. This finding seems to suggest that some lies are worse than others.

In spite of what we know about nonverbal behaviors when people do not tell the truth, very few of us are able to de-tect or interpret these behaviors as signs of deception. People who can detect untruthfulness usually consider more than one nonverbal cue to determine whether someone tells the truth. A very fine line divides the nonverbal behaviors of someone who is legitimately anxious from those of someone who is not being truthful. Therefore, lying cannot be confirmed on the basis of nonverbal behaviors alone.

Haraz N Ghanbari/AP Images

Former President Obama and former Arizona Republican governor Jan Brewer's greeting of each other appears to be less than cordial. By pointing her finger at him, she communicates her anger and frustration toward him.

deceiving

Purposely misleading others by using nonverbal cues to create false impres-sions or to convey incorrect information.

Iakov Filimonov/123RF

Detection of deception usually results from nonverbal cues such as facial expressions, eye contact, and body language that can help us decide whether a person is lying.

MAKING CONNECTIONS FOR SUCCESS

Telling the Truth: It May Not Be What You Say; It's How You Behave

If deception is an all-too-common aspect of social life, what are its effects? As you might guess, they are largely negative. Often, we make assumptions about people's truthfulness based on the inconsistencies of their nonverbal and verbal messages. A student's eyes wander during a test, but he claims that he's not looking at his neighbor's test; a student smiles as she looks at her laptop screen, and, when asked what she is looking at, claims she is taking notes; a student has his head down, peering at his cell phone, but when asked about texting, he claims he was just checking the time.

1. What nonverbal cues can signal that a person is not being truthful?

2. On a scale of 1 to 10 (with 10 being extremely confident), how confident are you to conclude, on the basis of nonverbal cues, that a person is not being truthful? Explain your rating.

3. When, if ever, is it appropriate to be deceptive?

Are men really clueless about nonverbal cues? The answer, as revealed by research on gender differences, is somewhat mixed. Overall, there is no clear evidence that women are better than men at all aspects of nonverbal perception. But they do seem to be superior in performing several important tasks, such as judging another's specific personality characteristics,[19] recognizing their current moods, and both sending and interpreting nonverbal cues.[20]

Women are clearly superior in their ability to read facial expressions; they also have the edge in interpreting body movements and gestures.[21] However, they have a lesser ability for interpreting voice tone and for noticing discrepancies between nonverbal cues—for instance, inconsistencies between facial expressions and body cues.

While the research is not completely conclusive, it does suggest that women are better than men at both sending and interpreting nonverbal cues, and better at remembering details. This gives women an important advantage in many situations and may account for the widespread belief in women's intuition and their ability to recognize when someone's nonverbal communication is consistent with what that person is saying.

Types of Nonverbal Communication

5.4 **Compare and contrast** different types of nonverbal communication and the ways competent communicators are aware of their nonverbal communication.

When you dress in a suit for a meeting, smile at someone, sit in a specific seat in class, use hand gestures as you talk, play with a pen or pencil as you listen, dim the lights to create a romantic atmosphere, play music loudly, look someone directly in the eyes, or burn incense to create a pleasant scent, you are communicating nonverbally. We perform a wide range of nonverbal behaviors every day without even thinking about them. Because nonverbal communication is so diverse, complex, common, and informative, we need to be sensitive to its many manifestations. In the following sections, we examine some of the more significant forms of nonverbal communication, such as kinesics (body movements, including gestures, facial expressions, and eye behavior), physical characteristics, haptics (touch), proxemics (space), chronemics (time), vocalics or paralanguage (use of voice), silence, artifacts, and environment.

Facial Expressions and Body Movements

kinesics
Sometimes referred to as "body language"; any movement of the face or body that communicates a message.

We use body movements—gestures, facial expressions, and eye behavior—to create an infinite number of nonverbal messages. **Kinesics**, sometimes referred to as *body language*, is any movement of the face or body that communicates a message. Two particularly significant categories of kinesics are eye behavior and facial expressions. **Eye behavior** is a subcategory of facial expressions that includes any movement or behavior of the eyes; it is also referred to as **oculesics**, the study of eye movement or eye behavior. The eyes, through eye contact with others, have the primary function of establishing relationships. **Facial expressions** include configurations of the face that can reflect, augment, contradict, or appear unrelated to a speaker's message.

Eye Behavior Or Oculesics

According to some researchers, eye behavior is the first and primary characteristic we notice about others. Researchers found that, during interactions, people spend about 45 percent of the time looking at each other's eyes.[22] Through eye behavior, we establish relationships. Eye behavior also conveys a variety of other important messages. For example, we notice a speaker's eye contact, share mutual glances with friends, and feel uncomfortable when others stare at us. Eye behavior, according to communication scholar Dale Leathers, can serve one of six important communicative functions: (1) influence attitude change and persuasion; (2) indicate degree of attentiveness, interest, and arousal; (3) express emotions; (4) regulate interaction; (5) indicate power and status; and (6) form impressions in others.[23]

Eye gaze at the interpersonal level communicates sincerity, trustworthiness, and friendliness. Romantic partners are more likely to gaze into each other's eyes for prolonged periods when they express their affection for one another.[24] Members of groups or teams use eye contact to build their relationships and to show unity or a sense of belonging to the group or team. In Chapter 11, we discuss the importance of eye contact between a speaker and an audience. In general, effective speakers use more frequent eye contact with their audiences than do less effective speakers. Eye contact is also important for listeners because looking at the speaker indicates interest in what is said and is a sign of respect for the speaker.

Have you ever had a conversation with someone wearing dark glasses? If you have, you know that it is a bit uncomfortable because you can't completely see how the other person reacts to you. We learn much about others' feelings and emotions from their eyes. For example, we associate a high level of gaze or direct eye contact from another as a sign of liking or friendliness.[25] In contrast, if others avoid eye contact with us, we are likely to conclude that they are unfriendly, don't like us, or are simply shy.[26] Although a high level of eye contact can be interpreted as positive, some exceptions to this rule occur. If people look at us continuously and maintain eye contact regardless of actions we take, they are said to be staring. When confronted by unwanted staring, most of us tend to withdraw from the situation.[27] Generally, people find being stared at an unpleasant experience; it makes most of us nervous and tense.[28] This is especially true of what is referred to as a "cold stare" because it is a form of intimidation, and unwanted stares are often interpreted in our society as a sign of hostility and anger.[29] This is one reason experts on road rage—highly aggressive driving by motorists, sometimes followed by actual assaults—recommend that drivers avoid eye contact with people who disobey traffic laws and rules of the road.

Facial Expressions

Facial expressions are windows to our emotions. They provide clues about our and others' emotional states, which at times can be very complex and difficult to interpret accurately.

More than 2,000 years ago, the Roman orator Cicero stated, "The face is the image of the soul." By this, he meant that human feelings and emotions are often reflected in our faces. Modern research suggests that Cicero and others who observed human behavior were correct: It is possible to learn much about others' current moods and feelings from their facial expressions. Researchers have found that from a rather early age, our faces clearly depict six different basic emotions: anger, fear, happiness, sadness, surprise, and disgust.[30] Other research suggests that contempt may also be a basic emotion.[31] However, agreement on what specific facial expression represents contempt is less consistent than is the case for the other six emotions.

eye behavior
A category of kinesics and a subcategory of facial expressions that includes any movement or behavior of the eyes.

oculesics
Study of eye movement or eye behavior.

facial expressions
Configuration of the face that can reflect, augment, contradict, or appear unrelated to a speaker's vocal delivery.

Our facial expressions typically display our emotions, but because of their complexity, these emotions can be difficult to interpret. Researchers have identified more than 1,000 different expressions made by the human face.

It is important to realize that the relatively small number of basic facial expressions in no way implies that human beings are limited to them. The human face is said to produce more than 1,000 different expressions. Emotions often occur in many combinations (for example, joy tinged with sorrow, surprise combined with fear), and each of these reactions can vary greatly in emphasis. Thus, while facial expressions may have only a small number of basic themes, the range of variations on these themes is immense.

Facial expressions play an extremely powerful role in communication and relationships. Of all body motions, facial expressions convey the most information. In examining the judgments we make about another's facial expressions, researchers found that we judge not only emotions but also personality—such as the tendency to be friendly or unfriendly, harsh or kind—on the basis of facial expressions.[32] We perceive people with relaxed facial expressions as people with more power who are more controlled than those whose facial expressions seem nervous.[33]

Overall, then, it seems safe to conclude that, although facial expressions are not completely universal—cultural and contextual differences exist about precise meaning—they generally need very little translation compared to spoken language. However, despite cultural rules, our faces often communicate feelings and emotions spontaneously in reaction to a situation. For example, if you open the door to your house and a group of your friends hiding in the dark turn on the lights and yell "Surprise!" your face will probably automatically and unconsciously express shock and surprise. If you open the door and they yell "Boo!" your face will probably show fear or anxiety.

Although many facial expressions are unconscious and involuntary reactions to certain stimuli, researchers found that facial cues may be only partially reliable in terms of what they express. In a study of facial expressions in everyday conversations, communication researcher Michael Motley found they are extremely difficult to interpret and may be relevant only as they relate to specific conversations or situations in which they occur.[34] This is in part because most of us have learned to conceal our real feelings from others.[35] Most of us have learned how to control our facial muscles in order to hide inappropriate or unacceptable responses. Such controlling behaviors regarding our facial expressions are referred to as **facial management techniques**. Facial management techniques may be used to intensify, deintensify, neutralize, or mask a felt emotion[36] (see Table 5.2).

facial management techniques

Control of facial muscles to conceal inappropriate or unacceptable responses.

Body Movements To make sense of thousands of different body movements, psychologists Paul Ekman and Wallace Friesen devised a classification system based on the origins, functions, and coding of nonverbal behavior.[37] Their system divides body motions into five categories: emblems, illustrators, regulators, affect displays, and adaptors (see Table 5.3). Because there are so many body motions, and many are

Table 5.2 FACIAL MANAGEMENT TECHNIQUES

Technique	Definition	Example
Intensifying	Exaggeration of reactions to meet others' expectations	You receive a gift and try to look completely surprised, excited, and delighted.
Deintensifying	Understatement of reactions to meet others' expectations	You receive an A on a speech; a friend receives a C. You tone down your excitement, just in case your friend feels bad about receiving a lower grade.
Neutralizing	Avoidance of any emotional expression in a situation; "poker face" shows no emotion	You show no fear or sadness when you don't want to show your emotions, even if fear or sadness may be justified.
Masking	Replacement of one expression with another considered more appropriate for the situation	You smile when a friend wins a scholarship and you don't, even though you think you deserve it.

Table 5.3 CATEGORIES OF BODY MOVEMENTS AND FACIAL EXPRESSIONS

Category	Characteristics	Examples
Emblems	These translate directly into words and are used for specific words or phrases. Meanings of emblems are like those of words—arbitrary, changeable with time, learned, and culturally determined.	A hitchhiker's extended thumb, the thumb and circle sign for "OK," the peace sign
Illustrators	These accent, reinforce, or emphasize a verbal message.	A child holding up his hands to indicate how tall he is while saying, "I'm a big boy"; an instructor underlining a word on a PowerPoint slide to emphasize it
Regulators	These control, monitor, or maintain interaction between or among speakers and listeners. These are cues that tell us when to stop, continue, hurry, elaborate, make things more interesting, or let someone else speak. The dialogue at the beginning of the chapter is a good example of the need for regulators.	Eye contact, shift in posture, nod of the head, looking at a clock or wristwatch
Affect displays	These are body movements that express emotions. Though your face is the primary means of displaying affect, your body may also be used.	Sad face, slouching, jumping up and down
Adaptors	These help one feel at ease in communication situations. They are difficult to interpret and require the most speculation.	Scratching, smoothing hair, playing with coins, putting hands in front of the face, moving closer to someone

interdependent, it is important to understand that categories are not mutually exclusive. Some body motions may fall into more than one category.

Finally, body movements and posture can reveal much about our physical states (vigor, age) and perhaps the extent to which we possess certain traits.[38] Evidence from several research studies supports these conclusions. For example, one study investigating males and females in four age groups (5 to 7, 13 to 14, 26 to 28, and 75 to 80 years old) asked participants to walk back and forth at a pace they felt was comfortable.[39] The walkers were recorded, and then the video was shown to others, who rated the walkers on various dimensions, such as gait, traits, age, and sex. By using adjustments and lighting techniques, the researchers were able to disguise the walkers so that the subjects saw only their gait.

The subjects made judgments about the walkers two different times. The first time, they rated the walkers' gait in terms of revealing certain traits (submissive or dominating, physically weak or physically strong, timid or bold, sad or happy, unsexy or sexy). The second time, they rated the walkers' gait in terms of several other characteristics (amount of hip sway, knee bending, forward or backward lean, slow or fast pace, stiff- or loose-jointed gait, short or long strides). In addition, the subjects were asked to estimate each walker's age and guess whether each was female or male.

The results were interesting and clearly indicate that people's gaits provide important nonverbal cues. For example, as predicted, ratings of traits and gaits did vary according to age. Further analysis revealed that possession of a youthful gait (one characterized by hip sway, knee bending, arm swing, loose-jointedness, and more steps per second) was strongly related to ratings of the walkers' happiness and power. Thus, persons with a youthful gait—regardless of their actual age—were rated more positively along several dimensions than persons with an older gait. Can you think of a situation or time when the way a person walked influenced what you thought of him or her? In what ways did the style of walking affect your perception?

Physical Characteristics

Whereas body movements and facial expressions change quickly and can be controlled to some extent, physical characteristics, such as body type, attractiveness, height, weight, and skin tone, are fairly constant and more difficult to control, especially in the course of a single interaction. In our culture, physical appearance plays a significant role in communication and relationships. Segments of our society have become obsessed with physical appearance and general health, and spend billions of dollars each year to modify, preserve, and decorate their bodies. We might say "beauty is only skin deep," but we are likely to respond positively to those who are attractive and negatively to those who are unattractive.[40]

Physical attractiveness is an extremely powerful influence on everyday communication. It appears that both males and females are strongly influenced by attractiveness, though males seem to be more responsive to appearance than are females.[41] Overall, though, an appealing physical appearance is perceived as a positive characteristic that influences interpersonal attraction (see Chapter 13 for more on interpersonal attraction) and interpersonal preferences. Numerous stereotypes are consistently associated with physical appearance, and it would not be surprising if you hold some of them. Consider how you respond to the photos of the young woman before and after a makeover in the next "Making Connections for Success" box.

Numerous research studies have indicated that attractive people are perceived to be more popular, successful, sociable, persuasive, sensual, and happy than unattractive ones. Attractiveness affects credibility and a person's ability to persuade others, to get a job, and to gain a higher salary. Handsome men are likely to be viewed as more masculine, and beautiful women as more feminine, in comparison with those perceived as less attractive.[42]

Touch

haptics
Tactile, or touch, communication; one of the most basic forms of communication.

Touch is referred to as either tactile communication or **haptics**. Haptics is one of the most basic forms of communication. You talk with someone, and he or she touches you. How would you react? What does the person's touch communicate? The answer to both questions most likely depends on several factors relating to *who* touches you (a friend, a stranger, a member of your own or the other gender), the nature of contact (brief or prolonged, gentle or rough, what part of the body is touched), and the context in which the touch took place (at school, work, a social setting, a doctor's office). Depending on the person and context, touch can suggest caring, affection, sexual interest, dominance, or aggression. Despite such complexities regarding what touch communicates, existing evidence suggests that when touch is appropriate, it is likely to produce positive reactions in recipients.[43] To be seen as positive, however, it must be viewed as appropriate.

As one of our most primitive and yet sensitive ways of relating to others, touch is a critical aspect of communication. It plays a significant role in giving encouragement,

MAKING CONNECTIONS FOR SUCCESS
You Can't Judge People by Their Appearance, or Can You?

Look at the young woman in the photographs that follow and think about what she might be like. Look at the "before" photo and respond to number 1 below; then look at the "after" photo, taken after she had a makeover, and respond to number 1 below; then respond to 2, 3, and 4.

1. Make a list of the physical characteristics that describe this person. Then, on the basis of those characteristics, describe the person in terms of her sociability, intelligence, poise, independence, masculinity or femininity, popularity, vanity,

potential for success, integrity, concern for others, temperament, and other features.

2. How do you think your or others' interactions with the person shown in the "before" photo might differ from those with the person shown in the "after" photo?

3. Do you think men and women differ in their responses to the above questions? Why or why not?

4. Given the two photos, do any stereotypes emerge? If so, describe them.

Pietro Scozzari / age fotostock / Alamy Stock Photo

expressing tenderness, and showing emotional support, and it can be more powerful than words. For example, when you receive some bad news, a pat on the shoulder from a friend can be far more reassuring than any number of understanding words.

The kind and amount of appropriate touch varies according to the individuals, their relationship, and the situation. Researchers identified categories to describe variations of touch as it relates to the dominant culture of the United States. The categories are functional–professional, social–polite, friendship–warmth, love–intimacy, and sexual arousal.[44] Definitions and examples are given in Table 5.4.

The meaning of a particular touch depends on the type of touch, the situation in which the touch occurs, who is doing the touching, and the cultural background of those involved. Some cultures are more prone to touching behavior than others. Research states that people in the United States are less touch oriented than persons in other cultures. For example, a classic study of touching behavior during a one-hour period in a coffee shop found that people in San Juan, Puerto Rico, touched 180 times in an hour; those in Paris, France, touched 110 times; and those in Gainesville, Florida, touched only twice.[45]

Gender differences in touching behavior are also noteworthy. Men tend to touch more than women do, women tend to be touched more often than men, and women seem to value touch more than men do. Little research exists regarding sex differences in touching behavior. One study found that a light, comforting pat on the arm can create feelings of security among both men and women—but only if women do

Table 5.4 TOUCH/HAPTICS

Category of Touch	Definition/Explanation	Example
Functional–professional	Unsympathetic, impersonal, cold, or businesslike touch	A doctor touches a patient during a physical examination or a tailor touches a customer while measuring.
Social–polite	Acknowledges another person according to the norms or rules of a society	Two people shake hands in American culture or kiss in other cultures to greet one another.
Friendship–warmth	Expresses an appreciation of the special attributes of another or warm feelings for another; the most misinterpreted type of touching behavior	Two men or two women meet in an airport, hug, and walk off with their arms around each other. Athletes touch a shoulder or pat each other on their buttocks.
Love–intimacy	Occurs in romantic relationships between lovers and spouses; highly communicative and usually requires consent between both parties, even though one party might not reciprocate	Two people hug, embrace, and kiss.
Sexual arousal	The most intimate level of personal contact with another; expresses physical attraction between consenting individuals	Sexual touch behavior includes foreplay and intercourse.

the touching.[46] Another study investigated sex differences in amounts, types, and factors influencing same-sex touch in a sports context. The study found that females performed more touch behaviors than males overall, but that males performed more touch behaviors at away games than home games, while females performed more touch behaviors than males after negative game events.[47] Gender differences in touch behavior may be partially attributed to men's sexual aggressiveness in U.S. culture and their expression of power and dominance.

Space

Statements such as "Give me some room to operate," signs that say "Keep Out," and the bumper sticker that reads "Keep Off My" followed by a picture of a donkey are all attempts to regulate the distance between people. Such behaviors are of special interest to researchers in **proxemics**, the study of how we use space and the distance we place between ourselves and others when we communicate. Edward T. Hall, anthropologist and author of two classic books, *The Silent Language* and *The Hidden Dimension*, coined the term *proxemics*.[48] Hall was a pioneer who explained how space is used in North American culture. In his study of proxemics, Hall identified four zones. *Intimate space* is defined as the distance from no space between two individuals to 1½ feet between two individuals. This zone is the most personal, and it is usually open only to those with whom we are well acquainted, unless such closeness is physically forced on us, such as in a crowded train or elevator.

The second zone is referred to as *personal space* and ranges from distances of 1½ feet to 4 feet between people. It is not unusual for us to carry on conversations or other activities with close friends and relatives in this zone. If someone we don't know enters this zone, we are likely to feel uncomfortable or violated. The third zone is called *social space*. It ranges from 4 to 12 feet and is where most professional conversations occur, as well as group interactions, such as meetings. *Public space*, the fourth zone, is 12 feet or more. This distance is common for public speaking situations or other formal presentations.

The need to identify certain amounts of space as our own is an aspect of proxemics called **territoriality**. We often position markers such as books, coats, pencils, papers, and other objects to define our space. Some students become upset when someone else sits in a seat they usually occupy, even when seating is not assigned. This uneasiness

proxemics
The study of the use of space and of distance between individuals when they are communicating.

territoriality
The need to identify certain areas of space as one's own.

MAKING CONNECTIONS FOR SUCCESS

When Doing International Business, What Should You Know about Nonverbal Communication?

Doing business in another country requires more than just knowledge of the language or an effective translator. Communication between cultures requires knowledge of basic business etiquette in the country where you are doing business. Business etiquette in England is quite formal. Be friendly, but get to the point quickly. Always be on time to appointments. In Japan, be prepared to dress up when doing business. Always wait to be directed to your seat, as the seating arrangement often indicates the status of the meeting's participants. Always give a small gift to the host. Punctuality may not be as important in Spanish culture, so do not be upset if your host is late. Interruptions are common and acceptable. The bottom line is this—if you are preparing to do business in another country, be sure to research the cultural practices well. Differences in cultural interpretations can lead to misunderstanding and lost business. With that in mind, answer the following questions:

1. What are important nonverbal communication behaviors to keep in mind when someone is preparing to communicate in the international business environment?
2. What nonverbal communication advice would you give to someone doing business internationally?
3. What are some of the common nonverbal mistakes Americans might make in international business situations?

stems from a strong desire to stake out and protect territory. Similar reactions occur when someone enters a room without knocking or tailgates when driving; it seems like an invasion of our territory.

We usually give little conscious attention to the role of space in our communication, yet the way others use space gives strong clues to their thoughts and reactions to us. Many variables influence our use of space when we communicate; status, sex, culture, and context are but a few.

Status affects the distance maintained between communicators. Research shows that people of different status levels tend to stay farther apart than do individuals of equal status. Furthermore, people of higher status tend to close the distance between them and people of lower status, but seldom do people of lower status move to close the distance between them and a person of higher status.

Men and women tend to differ in their proxemic patterns, but the differences in part hinge on whether the interaction is with someone of the same or opposite sex. In same-sex situations, men prefer, expect, and usually establish greater conversational distance than women do. Opposite-sex distancing depends on how intimate the relationship is.

Culture creates a wealth of differences in the way individuals use distance for communication. For example, people from the United States tend to stand farther apart during conversations than do those from many European and Middle Eastern countries. Arab males, for example, consider it polite to stand close to other males with whom they are communicating. There are as many culture-based differences as there are cultures, and it is not unusual for one group of people to be perceived as cold and unfriendly and another as pushy and forward because of their use of space. Competent communicators recognize that not all cultures or people view distance in the same way.

Context also influences the amount of space maintained between individuals. For example, people in line at an automated teller machine usually stand back far enough

Men in Western cultures generally tend to keep a conversational distance between each other, but in certain circumstances, such as teammates at athletic events, standing close to each other, or even touching, is not unusual.

Monika Graff / The Image Works

to give the person using the machine the feeling that a transaction is relatively private. But passengers waiting to board a bus ordinarily stand close together to avoid losing their places.

Time

chronemics

The study of how people perceive, structure, and use time as communication.

Chronemics is the study of how people perceive, structure, and use time as communication.[49] People in most Western cultures are preoccupied with time. Everything seems to have a starting and an ending time. For example, they worry about how long they have to wait for something and how long it takes to do something. They even go so far as to say that time is money. Because they place such a high value on time, it plays a significant role in nonverbal communication. They are particularly sensitive to people and events that waste their time or make exceptional demands on it. Consider your reaction, for instance, when your date keeps you waiting, when an instructor continues to lecture after the class ending time has passed, or when your supervisor gives you only one day to complete a major project. Your feelings might range from confusion to indignation to outrage, but you will almost certainly not be neutral. To some extent, your reaction depends on the identity of the other person. You will probably be more tolerant if the offending party is a friend or someone who has authority, such as your boss. For example, if a blind date keeps you waiting too long, you might decide to leave, but if your professor is late for an office appointment, you will probably suffer in silence and continue to wait for his or her arrival.

We tend to have many expectations about how time should be used, and we often judge others by their use of time. For example, workers are expected to be on time for work. Therefore, punctual workers are more likely to create a positive impression, whereas consistently late ones may be perceived as irresponsible, lazy, or uninterested. We must constantly be aware of the messages we send through our use (and misuse) of time.

Individuals can differ in their approaches to time. For example, some people always look to the future, others long for the past, and still others live for the moment. Each approach communicates something about people and the ways they use time to communicate who they are. Each culture teaches its members about time expectations, and these expectations vary. In some cultures, punctuality is expected; in others, it is not important, and, in fact, people are expected to be late. In U.S. culture, for example, you are expected to be on time for a dinner party, but being up to 20 minutes late is socially accepted and still considered "on time." In some foreign countries, such as Japan, arriving late for a dinner party is considered an insult.[50] Our use of time communicates messages about us, so it is important to adhere to the time-related norms of the culture in which we communicate.

Paralanguage/Vocalics

paralanguage or vocalics

The way we vocalize, or say, the words we speak.

Do you remember the first time you heard a recording of your own voice? If you are like most of us, you likely were a bit surprised because the voice you heard didn't sound like you. **Paralanguage or vocalics** is the way we vocalize, or say, the words we speak. Paralanguage includes speech sounds but also speech rate, accents, articulation, pronunciation, and silence. Sounds such as groans, yawns, coughs, laughter, crying, and yelping, which are nonsymbolic but can communicate very specific messages, are also included. Expressions such as "um," "uh-huh," "ya know," "like," and "OK" are referred to as vocal fillers and are considered paralanguage. Vocal fillers are often sprinkled throughout conversations without forethought or a set order. They might reflect nervousness, speech patterns of a particular subculture, or a personal habit. In any case, the use of vocal fillers can influence our image positively or damage and degrade us and others.

It's Not What You Say, but How You Say It!

"My job is really difficult."

Read the preceding statement aloud in four different ways: (1) with no expression at all, (2) as if your job is extremely difficult, (3) as if your job is anything but difficult, and (4) as if you are trying to convince someone that your job is difficult. Note how you can change the meaning without changing the words.

1. What did you do to your voice to change the meaning of the sentence?

2. Did you notice anything else about your other nonverbal behavior while using your voice to change the meaning of the sentence?

3. What did you learn about vocal expression from this exercise?

4. How can vocal expression help you to become a more competent communicator?

Paralanguage includes *pitch* (how high or low the voice is), *vocal force* (intensity or loudness of the voice), *rate* (speed), *quality* (overall impression of the voice), and pauses or silence. The way we vary our voices conveys different meanings to receivers. For example, a person who speaks quickly may communicate a different message than a person who speaks slowly. Even when the words are the same, if the rate, force, pitch, and quality differ, the receiver's interpretations will differ. Researchers estimate that approximately 38 percent of the meaning of oral communication is affected by the use of voice, by the *way* something is said rather than by *what* is said.[51]

On the basis of paralanguage, we make many judgments about words, the person saying the words, the speaking and listening roles, and the credibility of the message. Of course, judgments about people based on paralanguage can be just as unreliable as those based on body type. We must therefore recognize the effect of paralanguage on communication and adjust accordingly.

Silence

The sound of silence is a contradiction in terms; as hard as you try, it is almost impossible to have complete and absolute silence. Silence or vocal pauses are communicative, powerful messages that often speak volumes, whether intended or not. **Vocal pauses** or hesitations are usually short in duration, whereas **silence** generally refers to extended periods of time without sound. Vocal pauses can be used to emphasize a word or thought or to make a point to get others' attention. For example, a speaker stands in front of an audience and gazes at the audience in the hope of gaining the audience's attention so they will listen. A teacher pauses during a lecture to get students' attention. Sometimes, people use vocal pauses to gather their thoughts or to allow others time to think. Vocal pauses or prolonged periods of silence can also create the perception that you are unsure of yourself, unprepared, or nervous. Regardless of why vocal pauses occur, they do send messages.

Silence sometimes seems very awkward in a conversation, especially when you are talking to someone whom you do not know well and who might be of higher status than you. Most of us in this situation feel or sense the pressure to say something to get the conversation restarted. Have you ever said hello to someone you admire or respect and he or she didn't reply or acknowledge you? You likely felt slighted or less than important. It is not unusual to use silence to prevent communication with others. Silence can prevent certain topics from surfacing or stop someone from saying something he or she might later regret.

Silence is expected in certain contexts, for example, during a funeral or while listening to a speech or presentation, or it can be self-imposed as a way of thinking

vocal pauses
A hesitation, usually short in duration.

silence
An extended period of time without sound.

or doing nothing at all. Silence has many possible meanings, none of which is easily interpreted. The next time a good friend says hi, try pausing for 5 to 10 seconds before reacting. You will quickly learn the effect silence can have as a message.

Cultural differences are also related to silence. What are some negative perceptions conveyed in U.S. culture by silence at a business meeting or social gathering? In many cultures, silence is seen more positively. In Japan, for example, silence is considered more appropriate than speech in many situations.[52] Silence in Japan is also associated with credibility. In Japan, someone who is silent is more likely perceived as one of high credibility than someone who talks a lot. The Japanese also use silence to avoid both conflict and embarrassment.[53] For example, "a typical practice among many Asian peoples is to refuse to speak any further in conversation if they cannot personally accept the speaker's attitude, opinion, or way of thinking about particular issues or subjects."[54] The intercultural implications of silence are as diverse as those of other nonverbal cues. Competent communicators know they must be careful not to assume that others communicate *only* when they are talking.

Artifacts

artifacts
A personal ornament or possession that communicates information about a person.

Artifacts are personal adornments or possessions that communicate information about us. Items such as automobiles, eyeglasses, briefcases, grooming, clothing, hair color, body piercings, tattoos, and makeup communicate information about our age, gender, status, role, class, importance, group membership, personality, and relationship to others. For example, what do you tell people by the type and color of vehicle you drive? A black SUV with tinted windows conveys a different message from a green sedan, as does a sports car versus a minivan or an Escalade versus a Chevy Volt.[55]

How do you react to people who have body piercings and tattoos? Effective communicators learn to adapt their use of artifacts to a specific situation and not to judge others by appearance alone. If you want people to view you as a nonconformist, you will likely use different artifacts than those used by someone who wishes to be viewed as a conformist. For example, if you wear a suit to a job interview, you send a different message than if you wear a sweatshirt and jeans.

Environment

Environment, as discussed in Chapter 1, is the psychological and physical surroundings in which communication occurs, including the furniture, architectural design, lighting conditions, temperature, smells, colors, and sounds of the location, as well as the attitudes, feelings, perceptions, and relationships of the participants. The environment has an impact on the individuals, their backgrounds, and their perception of what is important to them at the time of interaction. The best environment allows a speaker's intended message to be delivered accurately. Thus, soft background music, dim lights, a log burning in a fireplace, a tray of hors d'oeuvres, and two candles would create the perfect environment for a romantic encounter but would not work for a pregame pep rally.

Improving Our Ability to Send and Interpret Nonverbal Communication

5.5 **Explain** why it is difficult to interpret and understand nonverbal communication and how to ensure that the message received is accurate.

We must be continuously aware of our nonverbal messages and how others receive them. Competent communicators constantly monitor their communicative behaviors to ensure that they are not misunderstood and that the intended message is received.

When you act to show you care how others perceive your behavior, you engage in self-monitoring. **Self-monitoring** involves the willingness to change behavior to fit a given situation, an awareness of how we affect others, and the ability to regulate nonverbal cues and other factors to influence others' impressions. It entails concern with both projecting the desired image and the ability to assess the effects of the image communicated to others.

Our nonverbal messages greatly influence how others perceive our communication and us. For example, an extremely bright and talented student was constantly turned down for jobs for which he was well qualified. When asked why he thought this was happening, he replied that he had no idea. To find out, friends recorded a mock interview in which another student interviewed him. Upon review of the video, he immediately noticed that he never looked at the interviewer. Instead, his gaze wandered about the room. The student's lack of direct eye contact gave the impression he lacked confidence and might not be completely candid in his communication. Once he knew why he was being rejected, he could work to change his behavior. To help him practice, his friends made a video of another interview session. This time, he was reminded to look at the interviewer each time his gaze wandered. After several such sessions, he learned to feel more comfortable with direct eye contact and consequently appeared more confident and truthful in his communication.

Although change of nonverbal behavior is not simple, it can be done with a little effort and desire. The key is to examine conscientiously how nonverbal cues may undermine your intended message. If you realize that you have distracting mannerisms, such as smirking; playing with coins; twisting your hair; shuffling your feet; or saying "you know," "like," or "OK" too much, ask others to call your attention to these behaviors. You can then make a conscious effort to change.

Nonverbal communication is complex, but you can do some things to improve your interpretation. First, be observant of and sensitive to the nonverbal messages you receive. Second, verify unclear or inconsistent nonverbal messages. For example, think about a friend who used to visit regularly but who hasn't come over in several weeks. It might seem logical to conclude that she doesn't want to see you anymore. but, then again, she might have become wrapped up in her studies, taken a part-time job, or fallen ill. To interpret her behavior accurately, consider all the possibilities and don't jump to conclusions. Because it is so tempting to make inferences based on nonverbal behavior, it is important to remember not to go beyond actual observations. When we

self-monitoring

The willingness to change behavior to fit situations, the awareness of effects on others, and the ability to regulate nonverbal cues and other factors to influence others' impressions.

MAKING CONNECTIONS FOR SUCCESS
Texting Is All Thumbs, Isn't It?

We may believe nonverbal communication such as facial expressions and tone of voice express more meaning in a spoken message than emojis in a text message or email. But is this really true?

Imagine your friend had a small fender-bender with her car to cap off an already horrible Monday. If you were to communicate the phrase "that's great" to your friend and you wanted to express this in a *sarcastic* tone:

1. What would you do to ensure that the message you sent was received as intended?

2. What are other options for sending the same message?

3. Why do you think texts and emails are often misunderstood? What are the advantages over face-to-face or phone communication?

You send an email to your instructor with your term paper project attached, and you send it in early. However, the reply from your instructor says only "received":

1. You know the instructor received your paper, how else could you interpret the instructor's message? *Should* you read anything else into his or her message? How do we learn to interpret email or text messages that lack nonverbal communication cues such as tone of voice or facial expressions? How do greetings such as *hi* or *dear* or closings such as *take care* or *best wishes* influence the overall message?

2. Without using more words, how might the instructor have communicated "nice going" or "good job"?

functional approach

Using more than one nonverbal message at a time to look for meaning.

look for meaning of more than one nonverbal message at a time, we use the **functional approach**. This approach examines nonverbal behavior not by isolated nonverbal cues but by seeing how each cue interacts and works with the others to perform various communicative functions.

At least three reasons for misinterpreting nonverbal communication are possible:

1. *Nonverbal cues have multiple meanings.* Nonverbal communication is difficult to understand because a single behavior can have many potential meanings. A frown might indicate unhappiness, sadness, anger, pain, thought, aggressiveness, disapproval, dejection, fear, fatigue, discouragement, disapproval, or a combination of these. Unlike words, nonverbal cues lack dictionary definitions.

   Interpretations are unreliable because they depend so heavily on perceptions. Suppose, for example, you just walked out of a sad movie and see a friend with tears in her eyes, talking to her sister. Her tears may reflect her reactions to the movie—or to a breakup with her boyfriend; she may be injured, or she may have just heard about a death in the family. Her tears could even result from laughing hard at something that occurred after the movie. Of course, some nonverbal behaviors, such as nodding the head for yes and shaking it for no (in U.S. society), are consistent in both their meaning and their interpretation. Unfortunately, such consistency is the exception rather than the rule.

2. *Nonverbal cues are interdependent.* The meaning of one nonverbal cue often depends on the correct interpretation of several other simultaneously occurring cues. For example, when we see someone enter a room, we begin to select certain cues about that person, such as gender, physical traits, facial expressions, voice characteristics, and clothing. Each cue intermeshes with the others and adds to the total picture. This interdependence of nonverbal behaviors and our inability to perceive all aspects of any one nonverbal communication make interpretation risky.

3. Nonverbal cues are subtle. Many nonverbal behaviors are subtle and difficult to observe. One person might overlook a cue that another person notices immediately; thus, multiple interpretations may be made in the same situation. For example, a friend tells you that a person in whom you have an interest has been looking at you, but you haven't noticed the glances or you see the eye contact as more accidental than a deliberate message of interest in you.

descriptive feedback

Describing to the sender what you perceived the message to mean.

One method to help verify the meaning of a nonverbal message when you are not certain of the sender's intention is to use **descriptive feedback**. Descriptive feedback is not always necessary, but when a message seems inconsistent with the situation or other behaviors or when you're not sure you accurately interpreted an important message, you should verify your perceptions with the other person. When you use descriptive feedback, do not express agreement or disagreement or draw conclusions; simply describe the message you believe was communicated. For example, if you think someone's behavior indicates that he is uncomfortable around you, but you're not sure, don't ask, "Why are you so nervous when I'm around?" Rather, describe the situation nonjudgmentally: "Jim, I get the impression that you may not be comfortable around me. Is that the case?" This allows the other person to explain without feeling defensive, and it enables you to avoid inaccurate interpretations.

Guidelines

SENDING AND INTERPRETING NONVERBAL COMMUNICATION

Sending

1. Be aware of how people react to you.
2. Ask friends or colleagues for their help.
3. Create and view a video to see how you appear to others.
4. Adapt to the context or situation in which you find yourself.

Interpreting

1. Nonverbal cues have multiple meanings.
2. Nonverbal cues are interdependent.
3. Nonverbal cues are subtle.
4. Use descriptive feedback to reduce misunderstandings.

〉 SUMMARY

What Is Nonverbal Communication?

 Differentiate nonverbal communication from verbal communication.

Nonverbal communication includes all behaviors, symbols, attributes, or objects, whether intended or not, that communicate messages with social meaning. It is not only what we say but also how we say it with our tone of voice; body movements; appearance; and use of space, touch, and time.

Characteristics of Nonverbal Communication

 Explain the six key characteristics of nonverbal communication.

There are many reasons to study nonverbal communication; the primary one is its pervasive effects on what we communicate to others.

- Nonverbal communication occurs constantly; it:
  - depends on context.
  - is more believable than verbal communication.
  - is a primary means of expression.
  - is related to culture
  - is ambiguous.

Functions of Nonverbal Communication

 Identify the five common functions of nonverbal communication.

Nonverbal communication adds life to our interaction because it

- *complements* what is being said.
- *repeats* verbal behavior.

- *regulates* verbal behavior.
- *substitutes* for verbal behavior.
- *deceives*.

Types of Nonverbal Communication

 Compare and contrast different types of nonverbal communication and the ways competent communicators are aware of their nonverbal communication.

Every day we perform a wide range of nonverbal behaviors without thinking about them:

- Facial expressions and body movements
  - *Eye behavior*, or *oculesics*
  - *Facial expressions*
  - *Body movements*
- Physical characteristics
- Touch (*haptics*)
- Space (*proxemics*)
- Time (*chronemics*)
- *Paralanguage* or *vocalics*
- *Silence*
- *Artifacts*
- Environment

Improving Our Ability to Send and Interpret Nonverbal Communication

 Explain why it is difficult to interpret and understand nonverbal communication and how to ensure that the message received is accurate.

To avoid misinterpretation, competent communicators are observant of, and sensitive to, the nonverbal messages they receive; consider all their possible meanings; and avoid jumping to conclusions.

⟩ DISCUSSION STARTERS

1. How have texting, emailing, and other communication technologies affected nonverbal communication?

2. In developing relationships with others, what role does nonverbal communication play?

3. "You cannot not communicate." Describe situations in which you thought you weren't communicating anything but later found out that you were.

4. Why is paralanguage so important to effective communication?

5. Explain why you think nonverbal communication is more believable than verbal communication.

6. What is the most important lesson you learned from this chapter?

CHAPTER 6

CONNECTING THROUGH SOCIAL MEDIA AND NEW TECHNOLOGIES

Social media has drastically changed how we connect with others. Now, hundreds—maybe even thousands—of possible connections are at our fingertips.

BigTunaOnline/Shutterstock

→ CHAPTER OUTLINE AND LEARNING OBJECTIVES

Connecting with Others via Social Media and New Technologies

6.1 Define computer-mediated communication and social media.

History of New Technologies

6.2 Explain the history of new technologies.

Distinguishing Social Media from Face-to-Face Communication

6.3 Differentiate social media from face-to-face communication.

Theories of Social Media and New Technologies

6.4 Summarize theories of social media and new technologies.

Managing the Dark Side of Social Media and New Technologies

6.5 Explain factors that comprise the dark side of new technologies and social media.

Improving Communication Competence via Social Media

6.6 Identify ways to improve communication competence via social media.

As Ricardo gets ready for his morning class, he scrolls through his Twitter feed to catch up on what his friends have been up to since he went to bed. He swipes over to his news app to get up to speed on the day's headlines. Then he opens Tinder to see if he has any new matches before sending a morning snap to his friends through Snapchat. In the span of just two minutes, Ricardo accessed four different apps that allowed him to get caught up on happenings with his friends, possible new friends, and the news of the day. Meanwhile, back at home, Ricardo's 80-year-old grandfather is watching the morning news, while waiting for the morning newspaper to arrive on his doorstep. Their ability to connect with others varies quite a bit.

QUESTIONS TO THINK ABOUT

1. How has social media influenced your ability to connect with others?

2. What concerns do you have about Ricardo's use of social media?

3. How often do you interact with others through social media? How has this influenced your ability to engage with others in face-to-face settings?

Pe3k/Shutterstock

People use Twitter to reach a specific group of followers and get their message out in a quick fashion.

Many of us spend a great deal of time connecting with others through new technologies, often using two or more at the same time.[1] Although we may refer to "the media" when describing a recent event, media are not actually one unified entity. Media take many different forms and have many different platforms that allow us to connect with others in various ways. From Section 1.6, you will remember that mass communication generally refers to professionals who communicate with or to a very large number of people via traditional media outlets such as radio, television, newspapers, and magazines. Television media communicate messages very broadly, whereas other media have more narrowly targeted audiences such as a special interest magazine or a Twitter account that targets a specific base of followers.

Connecting with Others via Social Media and New Technologies

6.1 **Define** computer-mediated communication and social media.

As new technologies such as Twitter and Snapchat have developed at a rapid rate, our interactions and connections with others have shifted from face-to-face communication to computer-mediated communication. **Computer-mediated communication** refers to communication that is facilitated by a wide range of new technologies, including email, social media, chat rooms, blogs, apps, and even online games. The experience of connecting with others through new technologies in a wide-ranging and, at times, anonymous environment encourages users to create online profiles, write descriptions of who they are, and construct avatars that can be used when text messaging or using social media.

Researchers have argued for many years that the integration of computers into our everyday lives would drastically alter communication and how we connect with others.[2] Their ideas from years ago are now reality. When you rely on new technologies to connect with friends, family, work colleagues, or even people you do not know, you must understand the effects that this channel has on your verbal and nonverbal communication. You must think critically about how you engage with others through new technologies.

computer-mediated communication

Communication that is facilitated by a wide range of new technologies, including email, social media, chat rooms, blogs, apps, and even online games.

Recall from Section 1.6 that communication through social media occurs when any communication is transmitted through digital devices or platforms such as smartphones, text messaging, Facebook, Twitter, Instagram, and so on. *Social media* are often considered online platforms that allow people to create a public profile and maintain and view a list of users who share a common interest. These technologies are often highly accessible and allow us to accomplish multiple objectives. For example, you use your smartphone to text with a friend, review your Facebook and Twitter feeds, tweet your followers, send and receive emails, snap a picture and post it to Instagram, and record a video and post it to Snapchat or YouTube. The use of the term *social media* means that we tend to prefer new technologies that prioritize the device's ability to foster social and relational characteristics. Through social media, you can develop new relationships, connect with others through information sharing, and connect with people who are not part of your everyday face-to-face social circle.

History of New Technologies

6.2 **Explain** the history of new technologies.

Take a look at Figure 6.1. The evolution of technology is depicted along this continuum. In the mid-1800s to mid-1900s, people likely had simple social networks made up of close friends and family they saw on a regular basis and others with whom they connected via postal mail or maybe a rare telephone call. When the first telephone call was made in the late 1800s, families and friends were likely quite excited because they were now better able to remain connected with others. Notice the large gaps between important points on the first half of the continuum. Technology was evolving but at a slow rate. Now look at the points on the right half of the continuum. Since the first communication satellite (Telstar 1) was launched in 1962 and the first cell phone call was made in 1973, technology has evolved at a rapid rate. In the span of a few short years, the first text message was sent; Google entered the Internet scene; and Facebook, MySpace, YouTube, Twitter, and Snapchat emerged as popular social media outlets.

Convergence and Multitasking

Although traditional mass communication channels such as television and radio are distinct from more interpersonal uses of media such as telephone, email, Twitter, and Instagram, the changing media environment has increasingly blurred the difference between these types of communication. For instance, when Emma tweets a video of how she feels she is being mistreated by a worker at Burger King, her tweet could potentially end up being viewed by thousands or even millions of people. This could add a "mass" element to communication that might otherwise be considered a primarily interpersonal form of communication. On the other hand, if you become angry when you watch a news anchor grill a government official during an interview on a major TV network, you might choose to interact with that news anchor via Twitter. Social media has provided this added dimension of interactivity and feedback to what was once a very linear form of mass communication.

This merging of traditional mass communication with new technologies like social media is often referred to as **media convergence**, or how the many forms of technologically mediated and face-to-face communication come together in our everyday lives. Convergence is a vital part of living in today's world, and it affects how media content is shaped and how media messages can influence audiences.[3] Face-to-face communication and communication through new technologies were once treated as separate and distinct methods of interaction, but today, they are very much interconnected. This degree of media convergence strikes to the core of who we are and how

media convergence

How the many forms of technologically mediated and face-to-face communication come together in our everyday lives.

FIGURE 6.1 The Evolution of Social Media

Notice the large gaps between the important points on the first half of the continuum. Technology was evolving but at a slow rate. As the points on the right half of the continuum illustrate, technology has rapidly evolved in recent years.

1400   **1500**   **1600**   **1700**   **1800**

1455
Johann Gutenberg
invents printing press

Morphart/Fotolia

1690
Publick Occurences,
first newspaper in
America, published

1704
First newspaper
ad appears

1741
First magazines
appear in the
Colonies

1844
Samuel Morse
invents telegraph

Avantgarde/Fotolia

1876
Alexander
Graham Bell
invents telephone

Adrio/Fotolia

we behave in the physical—or face-to-face—and digital—such as Snapchat—spaces we inhabit.

Given that media convergence has led to a massive increase in the number and types of opportunities to connect with others, we will no doubt encounter challenges. One primary challenge is **media multitasking**, or using more than one media type at the same time. In today's world, it is nearly impossible to escape media. Did you ever take a vacation from social media and completely turn off your devices? It is very hard to do given the connections we make with others through new technologies.

media multitasking

Using more than one media type at the same time.

MAKING CONNECTIONS FOR SUCCESS

Take a Vacation from Social Media

Can you tackle the impossible? Try taking a break from all forms of social media for 24 hours. Can you do it? Turn off the data function on your smartphone. Do not access Facebook or Twitter through your laptop. Use only the phone functionality of your smartphone; do not text. After you take your break, answer the following questions:

1. How would you describe your experience taking a technology break for 24 hours?

2. What does your experience tell you about the role of new technologies in your life?

3. Why do you think it is important (or not important) to take extended breaks from using technology?

Benefits and Challenges for Society

As new technologies have evolved over the years and opportunities for media convergence increase, the lines between traditional face-to-face communication and new technologies have become blurry.[4] Without a doubt, media convergence allows for increased opportunities for connecting with others and creates several benefits and challenges for society. The sheer volume of messages available through media convergence can lead to **information overload**, the difficulty in sorting through and making sense of vast amounts of information.

information overload

The difficulty in sorting through and making sense of vast amounts of information.

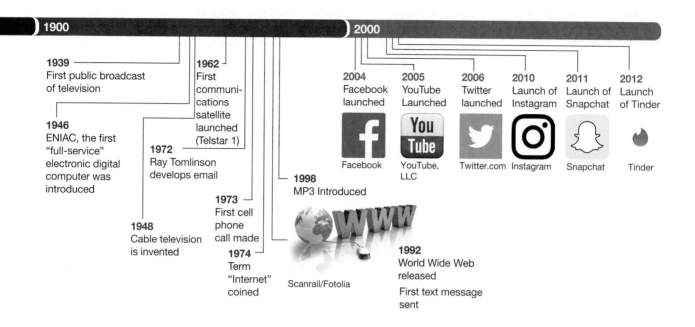

Scanrail/Fotolia

Guidelines

HANDLING MEDIA CONVERGENCE EFFECTIVELY

- **Actively participate in your democracy.** One benefit of media convergence is the great possibility for individuals and groups to participate more actively in political processes. Through new technologies, you have the opportunity to discover and provide competing voices to those of traditional media and connect with others on local, state, national, and global levels.

- **Avoid information overload.** As you think about adopting new technologies, consider tools you must have and those you can live without. With so many messages

available, it can prove challenging to critically evaluate the quality of information at your fingertips.

- **Feel empowered to contribute.** Media convergence enables individual voices to contribute to news, politics, and society in general. Social networking through Facebook or Twitter has allowed people to elevate their everyday personal lives to become more public ones. Your tweets, status updates, photos, and videos can alert everyone you know to what you are doing, how you are feeling, and what you are thinking.

Distinguishing Social Media from Face-to-Face Communication

6.3 **Differentiate** social media from face-to-face communication.

We tend to use social media because we perceive it as quick and convenient. Is one form of social media different from another type of technology? Are social media really that different from face-to-face communication? The simple answer is yes. The complete answer, though, is much more complex. For many years, communication technology scholar Nancy Baym has examined how humans create personal connections in an age of increasing reliance on social media.[5] She writes that seven concepts help us distinguish different forms of social media from one another and from face-to-face communication.

Interactivity

Interactivity refers to the ability of a communication tool to facilitate social interaction between groups or individuals. Unlike most television shows and, to a certain degree, radio, social media allow us to talk back. Because social media foster interactivity, they also lead to new possibilities to remain connected and engaged with others. Face-to-face communication, like certain forms of social media, is highly interactive. Facebook and text messaging permit us to remain linked with our local and long-distance friends and family. Many businesses use Facebook, Twitter, and other social networking tools to remain connected with and gather feedback from customers.

Temporal Structure

Face-to-face communication is instantaneous—you say something to your friend, and almost immediately he responds with verbal and nonverbal messages. Certain forms of social media may not feature this luxury. A device's **temporal structure** refers to the time it takes to send and receive messages. Face-to-face conversations, phone calls, and online instant messages occur in real time and are **synchronous** forms of communication whereby each person simultaneously serves as sender and receiver. When we use email, send a text message, or direct-message someone on Twitter, delays often occur and we must alternate being the sender and receiver of a message. These interactions are **asynchronous** methods of communication, but often they could be just as synchronous as a phone call. How quickly does it take you to respond to a text message? More than likely you feel a strong need to respond and maintain a connection with the person who texts you. In the workplace, colleagues often send and reply to messages so quickly (sometimes via collaboration tools such as Slack) that the exchange could easily be viewed as a synchronous form of communication.

Synchronous social media can make messages feel more personal[6] and even make you feel more connected with your significant other when you are far apart.[7] Unlike some synchronous social media, the asynchronous types may permit you to manage your self-presentation more strategically. You can spend considerable time crafting an email to your professor that explains your most recent absence from class. If you get into a heated argument with your romantic partner and storm out of the room, you may find it easier to compose a long email that details your frustrations, feelings, and plans for the future. We can place fewer demands on a person's time when we use asynchronous social media, but we will likely wait longer than we would like for a response.

Social Cues

Many of the challenges we experience with social media derive from a lack of **social cues**—the verbal and nonverbal features of a message that offer more information about the context, the meaning, and the identities of the involved parties. Face-to-face social cues often include facial expression, vocal tone, eye contact, and hand gestures. The absence of specific social cues with *lean* social media devices can create interpersonal challenges and misinterpretations. *Rich* forms of communication, such as Skype, FaceTime, and face-to-face communication, offer a full range of social cues, while other lean tools, such as a telephone, provide fewer.[8] Emojis help to make the meaning in our texts clearer; bitmojis bring a sender's cartoon avatar into the message, too. Bitmojis allow for messages to be personalized and communicated clearly and succinctly.

Rich social media devices provide more social cues than do lean devices. In calling your friend's smartphone when you are both on campus, what is the first thing you say after your friend answers the phone? You probably say something like, "Hey, where are you?" As is the case with many lean forms of social media, we have no idea of the physical location of our conversational partners. Yet we seek this information to develop an understood context and make the media appear richer than it really is. In face-to-face conversations, you know for sure whether your friend is busy, preoccupied, and unable to talk. If we are on a smartphone, we are unaware of these social cues unless we ask. Apps like Snapchat are rich in social cues and allow users to quickly capture and edit brief videos of their location and share it with followers on social media.

Replicability

Face-to-face conversations are difficult, if not impossible, to replicate. Stated simply, it is extremely difficult to re-create the exact words, nonverbal communication cues, and emotions felt during a particular interaction. You may find it difficult to explain to your mother what was said during a recent fight with your boyfriend. Social media's **replicability** means that communication can occur in an environment that makes it easy to record and redistribute past messages. The posts we make to an online blog or on Twitter can easily be replicated and shared with others. One thing is sure—we can never go back in time and change what message we sent; the message will always remain.

replicability
When communication occurs in an environment that makes it easy to record and redistribute past messages.

go viral
A phrase used to describe a message that reaches enormous audiences by "infecting" viewers and users with the message.

Storage

In many ways, face-to-face conversations, once they occur, are gone forever. Social media's ability for storage allows messages to be digitally saved and made accessible to other people. Facebook, Twitter, and other tools can log conversations and create a permanent storage space for our messages. Posts to a friend's Facebook page may be there to stay unless the friend deletes them. The harsh and abrasive asynchronous email that you send to a coworker can be easily forwarded to your supervisor, where it may be stored for future use. After a friend uploads pictures to Facebook following a fun weekend, how long does it take before people are tagged in those photos? Not long. In a matter of minutes, the record of your activities can be stored online. Apps like Snapchat let users take photos and videos (known as "snaps") and send them to a list of recipients, after which the snaps are automatically deleted. Although Snapchat uniquely eliminates the storage feature of social media, now, more than ever, we must remain attuned to the differences between social media and face-to-face communication—especially in light of social media's reach.

New social media platforms like Snapchat allow users to quickly send to their friends pictures and brief videos (called snaps) that are automatically deleted.

Kaspars Grinvalds/Shutterstock

Reach

Unlike face-to-face communication, social media have tremendous reach, or the ability to connect with individuals in local and long-distance places. Face-to-face communication is often limited to those individuals who can fit in a particular room. However, in one single keystroke or tap of a smartphone screen, a message can be sent to thousands or perhaps millions of people. Twitter provides a platform for messages to "**go viral**"—or reach enormous audiences by "infecting" viewers and users with the message. The incredible reach of social media has dramatically changed how we send, receive, and interpret messages. The ability to record a video, snap a picture, and send a message to thousands now rests in the palms of our hands.

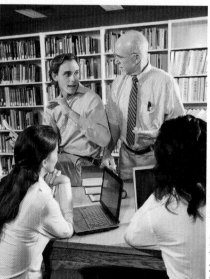

Kablonk Micro/Fotolia

Mobility

The various forms of social media feature varying degrees of mobility, or the extent to which a device is portable or stationary. Unlike social media, face-to-face communication is mobile to the extent that we are able to walk, run, or travel to a particular

Feedback is a critical component of the communication process. It allows a sender to determine whether the communication has been received and understood as intended.

Smartphone watches serve to enhance the mobility of social media. They allow us to connect with others instantly.

location to engage in conversation. Clunky desktop computers and landline telephones tie us to a specific spot. Social media users can access applications on a stationary desktop computer, a portable laptop, a tablet, or a smartphone from any location on earth—as long as cell phone service or wireless Internet access exists. The mobility of certain social media enables us to always be in touch with our friends and family. Facebook, Twitter, Instagram, and other social networks are no longer accessed only on a desktop computer; they are readily available on smartphones and other tablet devices.

Because social media keep us connected with others at all times, we are often expected to respond instantly to an email, text message, or tweet. Social media have connected us but essentially made us accountable to others at all times. And devices like the Apple Watch have further increased our ability to remain connected with others.

Theories of Social Media and New Technologies

6.4 **Summarize** theories of social media and new technologies.

The various types of new technologies assist us in conducting our relationships and connecting with others. You can use FaceTime to keep in touch with a friend who is studying abroad, you can text throughout the day with your significant other, and you use can use Snapchat to remain connected with family when you are away from home. You may have a large number of friends and acquaintances, but if you are lucky, you may also have a handful of very close friends and family—people you trust with your innermost secrets. Regardless of the number of friends and acquaintances you count as part of your social circle, you likely use social media to maintain relationships, initiate relationships online, and manage long-distance relationships. Lucky for us, popular theories of new technologies and social media can help explain how communication functions in these settings.

Social Information Processing Theory

social information processing (SIP) theory

A theory suggesting that electronically mediated relationships grow only to the extent that people gain information about each other and use that information to form impressions.

With billions upon billions of online messages and opportunities to connect with people through technology, we need to better understand how communication through social media affects our real-life relationships. **Social information processing (SIP) theory**, developed by communication scholar Joe Walther, suggests that electronically mediated relationships grow only to the extent people gain information about each other and use it to form impressions.[9] Social information processing theory is limited to an attempt to explain the nature of online interactions and how those interactions can and do lead to real-life relationships.

Walther describes two features of electronic-mediated communication that provide a justification for social information processing theory:[10]

- *Verbal cues.* When individuals are motivated to create impressions and develop relationships, they use any verbal signs available to communicate. Thus, social media users create fully formed impressions of others based solely on the content of their digital messages.

- *Extended time.* Social media used to exchange social information and form impressions of others is much slower than real-life interactions. Given sufficient time, however, there is little reason to believe electronic-mediated relationships will be weaker than any other relationships.

Social media allow people to become friends with others they have never met in real life, perhaps because the self-presentational aspects of Facebook, Twitter, and Snapchat differ from those in real life. Thus, it is likely that we have insufficient information to determine if this is someone with whom we wish to have an in-person relationship. According to Walther, people who meet online are able to make and sustain overwhelmingly positive impressions of each other. Walther goes on to say that this is because they can present their most attractive traits, accomplishments, thoughts, and actions without much contradiction regarding their physical appearance or influence from third parties who may know of their dark side. Consider Melissa and Julio, who met at a party, and Stephanie and Lorraine who met online through Tinder. According to SIP theory, even though Stephanie and Lorraine met online, over time their relationship will possess the same qualities of closeness and connection as Melissa and Julio, who met face-to-face.

Even though there are many benefits to online relationship development, those interactions come with a potential challenge. **Hyperpersonal communication** suggests that digital interactions can become exaggerated because the context affords message senders a host of communicative advantages over traditional face-to-face interactions.[11] Compared to ordinary face-to-face conversations, a hyperpersonal message sender has a greater ability to strategically develop and edit his presentation of self. If Andy seeks a romantic relationship through eHarmony.com, he may post personal pictures from a time when he was thinner and regularly working out at the gym. In other words, hyperpersonal users are able to select their messages for optimized presentation to others.

hyperpersonal communication
When the communication and context affords message senders a host of communicative advantages over traditional face-to-face interactions.

Communication through social media allows people to edit or sanitize their communication, thus creating an online image or persona, without worry of their nonverbal communication altering or contradicting their image or messages. For example, you view the Facebook profile of someone you met briefly at a community event. In her profile, the person describes herself as "quiet and reserved," lists her interests as "reading and working out," is a member of a group referred to as "volunteers to help the poor," and is active in her church. The few photos she has on her site show her with a few close friends and family members. Yet you learn by reading comments she's written on some of her Facebook friends' pages that she mocks people for shopping for clothes at secondhand stores and being too poor to afford to donate to a church fundraiser. The messages are obviously contradictory; which version are you going to believe? The answer is what Walther labels as *warranting value of personal information*, or what he suggests is "the perceived validity of information presented online with respect to illuminating someone's offline characteristics."[12]

Our real-life observations of others exert less influence and do less to shape our communication behaviors because we use social media and the cues it provides to interpret and form impressions based on those cues.

Media Multiplexity Theory

One of the most important benefits of new technologies is their ability to help us maintain our relationships. Even though we may regularly see many of our Facebook friends in face-to-face settings, we still use social media to strengthen those connections. Most relationships are characterized by *media multiplexity*—meaning that we carry out those relationships through more than one form of social media, and those in closer relationships use more forms of social media.[13] Developed by Caroline Haythornthwaite, **media multiplexity theory** explains the presence of *strong* and *weak* social ties in an individual's relational network. **Strong ties** include relationships such as those with friends, romantic partners, and family members. These relationships exhibit behavior that reflects heightened emotion, interdependence, intimacy, and high levels of closeness. In contrast, **weak ties** are casual contacts that are more loosely connected to an individual's social network

media multiplexity theory
How we carry out relationships through more than one form of social media, and those in closer relationships use more forms of social media.

strong ties
Relationships such as those with friends, romantic partners, and family members.

weak ties
Casual contacts that are more loosely connected to an individual's social network and are not characterized by intimacy.

and are not characterized by intimacy.[14] According to media multiplexity theory, the number of different social media that friends use is strongly associated with whether a tie is weak or strong. Specifically, strong ties use several forms of social media, but weak ties use only one or two social media. Think about your very best friend. You likely use many forms of social media to maintain this strong tie. You may interact on Snapchat, text regularly, talk on the phone, and maybe even Skype several times a week. Now, think about a weak tie—perhaps it is an acquaintance from a large college class. If you are Facebook friends, you may comment on a wall post every now and then, but you probably rarely—if ever—talk on the phone, text, and Skype. Social media are important devices that help us maintain our strong social ties.

Although people in close relationships use social networking sites to communicate with each other, most relationships that are maintained primarily through Facebook are actually weak. In fact, students report that, of their entire friend network on Facebook, only about one-third of those individuals are "real" friends.[15] Even though social networking sites allow users to exchange synchronous and asynchronous messages, a vast majority of friends never seem to do this. Look through your Facebook friends list. How many of these folks do you keep in contact with on a regular basis? How many would you characterize as strong social ties? Considering all of the people on your friends list, chances are you maintain very few relationships solely through Facebook.

The success of Facebook and other social networking sites as relationship maintenance tools comes from their wide but selective reach. Although you may keep in closer contact with strong ties, you can communicate with multiple weak ties simultaneously. Shelby can share the news of her engagement to all friends in a tweet or status update. Or she can choose who can receive the message in wall posts. If you are a frequent Facebook user, you probably share photos on a regular basis. Even though all of your Facebook friends may not comment on your newly posted photos, simply having access to one another's updates on Facebook may facilitate a sense of interpersonal connection.[16]

Although people use social networking sites to maintain existing relationships, they are sites of new relationship formation as well. Social networks are home to many **latent ties**—potential relationships within a social circle that are present but have not been activated.[17] Friends of friends on Facebook are a good example of latent ties and a source of new relationships. In addition, people may also explicitly seek new relational partners online through dating sites such as Tinder, eHarmony.com, and Match.com. (Ask your grandparents. Match making is not new to social media. Newspapers and magazines have always featured classified ads for people seeking romantic connections.)

latent ties
Potential relationships within a social circle that have not yet been activated.

Media Richness Theory

As we discussed earlier in this chapter, social cues characterize the communication we send and receive through new technologies. **Media richness theory** describes communication channels by the amount of verbal and nonverbal information that can be exchanged through a particular channel.[18] For instance, when you communicate with someone in a face-to-face setting, you both have a full range of social cues available. You are both part of a physical context and can utilize the same amount of verbal and nonverbal messages, such as facial expressions, gestures, eye contact, body movements, and vocal tone. Both parties are also subject to the same distractions and noise in the communication process. When the socially awkward person from your physics class (who has yet to take a communication class!) interrupts your conversation, both conversational partners may gently encourage the person to leave. All of these social cues are important to how you send, receive, and interpret messages. Face-to-face communication is probably the richest form of communication. Figure 6.2 illustrates the range of lean and rich communication channels. Note the position of face-to-face communication along the right side of the graph. As you scan further and further to the left, you can see how social media can become leaner, as the presence of rich social cues diminish.

media richness theory
A theory that describes communication channels by the amount of verbal and nonverbal information that can be exchanged through a particular channel.

FIGURE 6.2 Lean and Rich Communication Channels

Media richness theory helps classify communication channels in terms of each channel's rich or lean characteristics.

Lean ───► **Rich**

| Unaddressed documents (bulk mail, posters, billboards, advertising) | Written, addressed Documents (Letters, emails, texting) | Facebook/ Twitter/ Snapchat | Telephone | Skyping/ FaceTime | Face to face |

Some forms of social media can convey very little information about the identity of the sender. Often, this leaves people anonymous and leads to opportunities for horrible communication situations. With lean media—such as those on the left side of the continuum—it is easier for people to manipulate, expand, and distort the identity that they present to others. The absence of rich social cues can make you feel safer and give you the courage to write a nasty anonymous letter to the editor of a newspaper, post a frank comment on someone's online blog, or write a scathing complaint about a company on Yelp. Aside from FaceTime and similar services, most social media can limit communication to words and sounds, and they lack critical cues related to touch and a true sense of a shared physical space.

Managing the Dark Side of Social Media and New Technologies

6.5 **Explain** factors that comprise the dark side of new technologies and social media.

Among the most popular questions addressed in research about communication and new technologies is the extent to which Internet use fosters undesirable outcomes such as depression, loneliness, and reduced face-to-face social interaction.[19] Research suggests that individuals can compulsively use the Internet. For those who are unable to limit their Internet use, time spent online may lead to depression, loneliness, and limited face-to-face contact with others. These feelings and behaviors are symptoms associated with **problematic Internet use**—a syndrome characterized by cognitive and behavioral symptoms that can result in negative social, academic, and professional consequences.[20] People who habitually use the Internet, find themselves avoiding face-to-face interactions, and report feelings of depression and loneliness are mostly likely engaging in problematic Internet use.

problematic Internet use
A syndrome characterized by cognitive and behavioral symptoms that can result in negative social, academic, and professional consequences.

Compulsive and Excessive Internet Use

Individuals who experience problematic Internet use may be using the Internet in a compulsive or excessive manner. **Compulsive Internet use** involves a person's inability to control, reduce, or stop utilizing the Internet.[21] If Karl finds himself being woken by the alert of a new email message on his smartphone, he may feel compelled to respond to the message in the middle of the night. If he does, Karl is likely engaging in compulsive Internet use. **Excessive Internet use** is the degree to which a person feels that he or she spends an extreme amount of time online or even loses track of time while online.[22] While studying for a midterm, Suzy may become distracted by what is happening on Facebook. Determined to study for her exam, Suzy may think she can take a break to peek quickly at her newsfeed. Instead, Suzy becomes captivated by the posts and feels a need to browse Facebook, chat with her friends, and post on her and others' wall. She may tweet: "Really need to study for my midterm. Facebook is just soooo distracting." Or she may send to her friends through Snapchat a snap of her

compulsive Internet use
A person's inability to control, reduce, or stop utilizing the Internet.

excessive Internet use
The degree to which a person feels that he or she spends an extreme amount of time online or even loses track of time while online.

laying on her bed relaxing. Thinking she took a five-minute break, Suzy notices that nearly two hours have past. If this situation occurs for Suzy on a regular basis, she is most likely experiencing excessive Internet use.

If you find yourself using social media in a compulsive or excessive way, you may need to take action to improve your behavior. Consider the following guidelines.

Guidelines

AVOIDING COMPULSIVE/EXCESSIVE INTERNET USE

- **Disable your smartphone's ability to "push" notifications and email messages to you.** If you feel attached to your smartphone, chances are your phone and your various apps' features are set to automatically push notifications or download emails to your phone. That's why you're constantly alerted to an incoming message and feel compelled to react to the alert. Rather being disturbed by the constant sounds of incoming messages, turn off push notifications on your apps and change your email settings to require that you manually check for new emails. Then, when you have some free time, you can check your emails and social media if necessary.

- **Leave your social media devices behind when you plan to study.** Students report being distracted by social media when they try to study for exams. If you find yourself in this situation on a regular basis, silence your smartphone or turn it off all together. Try leaving your laptop behind when you plan to study. If your class notes are on your laptop, print them and study from the hard copy. Revise your notes with a pen or pencil. This will increase the likelihood of you remembering the information for the test, especially since research indicates that students who take notes with pen and paper increase their learning and achievement.[23]

- **Ask your friends to help you.** If your face-to-face conversations are constantly interrupted because you feel compelled to respond to a text or an email, ask your friends to help you improve your behavior. If you're having a face-to-face conversation with a friend and you inadvertently check your iPhone for new emails, your friend should quickly bring your dependence on social media to your attention. If you actively try to improve your behavior, your friends could be your best resource. If you find yourself in this situation, work to correct the behavior now. If you put a face-to-face conversation on hold, your college friend may understand. But in the workplace, your unsympathetic manager may not.

- **Seek professional help if necessary.** It may seem strange that a person's compulsive and excessive use of social media may require that he or she seek professional help. This is unfortunate, but research indicates that it is becoming the new normal. If you are tied to social media and simultaneously feel lonely, depressed, and withdrawn from face-to-face interactions, you may need to seek professional assistance. If you notice a friend in a similar situation, encourage that person to seek help. Social media offers many important benefits for communication; however, it also carries with it potential consequences.

Flaming/Trolling

We have long been able to engage in anonymous communication. Prank phone calls were once very common before Caller ID, and you can still write an anonymous letter to a newspaper editor, run a blog using an artificial persona, or create a Twitter account under a false name. However, social media provides a vast space for **flaming or trolling**—online communication that is deliberately hostile, aggressive, or insulting and usually intended to provoke anger. The anonymity of communication through new technologies has opened the door to heated and often unproductive exchanges through social media—in blogs, emails, and through Twitter and Facebook.

flaming or trolling
Online communication that is deliberately hostile, aggressive, or insulting and usually intended to provoke anger.

Flame wars erupt when friendly and productive digital discussions give way to insults and aggression. This behavior is common in online group interactions where hostility escalates and draws in more participants. Other participants may chime in and urge participants to move the discussion to another venue or ignore the aggression. Eventually people lose interest and the discussion fizzles out. But what if you find yourself as an active participant in a flame war? In an online discussion group about household pets, imagine that you come across a post (an obvious troll) that reads "All kittens on the planet should be buried up to their necks at lawn-mowing time." If you're a cat lover, you may be inclined to immediately respond and contribute to the flame war. Instead, pause, take a deep breath, and consider the following guidelines.

Guidelines

AVOIDING FLAMING/TROLLING ONLINE

- **Ignore the flame/troll entirely.** Your first impulse may be to privately or publicly respond to the poster. People who post offensive content may simply be crying out for attention. Many flamers/trolls may be experiencing online communication for the first time and/or lack basic social etiquette. A return flame may be just what the poster wants. In all likelihood, your flame won't change the person's behavior.

- **Respond privately.** Craft an email that expresses your frustration with the poster's message. Direct your words at the content of the flame, not the flamer/troll's character.

- **Ask an authority to intervene.** In cases of flagrant flaming/trolling, you may consider sending a message to the flamer/troll's system administrator. Or you may report the flamer/troll to the online group's moderator. Save this for extreme cases of repeatedly abusive flamers and trolls.

Inappropriate Self-Disclosure

Self-disclosure, or revealing information about yourself to another person, is one of the most powerful communication practices we have for strengthening a relationship (you will learn more about self-disclosure in Chapter 13). However, it can backfire if a person shares too much too soon or reveals information the other person finds inappropriate. Social media can accelerate the rate and depth at which we engage in self-disclosure. The convenience, reach, and mobility of social media have fostered inappropriate self-disclosures—particularly for those in romantic relationships that have turned sour. **Sexting** is the act of sending sexually explicit messages or photographs, primarily between smartphones via text messaging. *MTV* and *The Associated Press* partnered to provide an in-depth examination of the sexting phenomenon. Among the findings, 30 percent of teenagers reported involvement in some type of naked sexting. One in ten teenagers shared a naked image of themselves with another person. Fifty-five percent passed the sext on to more than one person.[24] In our social media age, inappropriate self-disclosures are more that just verbally spoken words. Think twice before you send a sext. If you receive a sext, delete it immediately. Don't compromise your digital identity or the identity of a friend.

Many of the inappropriate self-disclosures expressed through social media can be explained through the **Social Identity Model of Deindividuation Effects (SIDE Model)**. The SIDE Model describes the extent to which individuals identify and behave in accordance with social rather than personal identities. Their behaviors are often influenced by the characteristics of the social media device, including anonymity.[25] Fake Twitter accounts can enable people to behave in ways they otherwise would not. The SIDE Model explains that the anonymous nature of certain new technologies enable users to behave in ways that are more closely aligned with *social* identities—behaviors common through the technology—rather than *personal* identities—how the person behaves in other contexts. Although the anonymous nature of certain technologies may tempt you to behave in ways you normally would not, always remember that social media's reach and replicability can place inappropriate disclosures in the hands of many unintended recipients.

sexting
The act of sending sexually explicit messages or photographs, primarily between smartphones via text messaging.

Social Identity Model of Deindividuation Effects (SIDE) Model
A model that describes the extent to which individuals identify and behave in accordance with social rather than personal identities.

Cyberstalking and Cyberbullying

Social media has created an arena for aggressive behaviors such as cyberstalking and cyberbullying. **Cyberstalking** occurs when an individual repeatedly uses social media to stalk or harass others. The behavior may include making false

cyberstalking
When an individual repeatedly uses social media to stalk or harass others.

Handling Cyberbullying

Cyberbullying often occurs through Facebook, Twitter, email, cell phones, instant messaging, and websites. It is often done deliberately and repeatedly and is used by an individual or group with the intention of harming other people. With that in mind, answer the following questions:

1. If you have been the victim of a cyberbullying attack, how did you respond?
2. If you observed a cyberbullying attack, how did you respond?
3. What factors inluenced your ability or inclination to respond to a cyberbullying attack?

---

accusations or threats against another, habitually monitoring a person's Facebook profile, the solicitation of minors for sexual purposes, and gathering information for face-to-face harassment. Users who constantly watch what their friends are up to on Facebook are sometimes called Facebook creepers. If you frequently monitor the Facebook profiles of your friends, you are not necessarily engaging in cyberstalking because there is likely no malicious intent. You are simply using the social media device to maintain an interpersonal connection. However, if Paul regularly monitors his ex-girlfriend's Facebook page to find out when she changes her relationship status to "In a Relationship," and then attacks her with rude, hurtful, and aggressive Facebook messages, Paul is no longer just a cyberstalker; Paul has crossed the line into cyberbullying.

cyberbullying
Abusive attacks that are carried out through social media.

Cyberbullying consists of abusive attacks that are carried out through social media. Social networking sites offer an open forum for bullies who demean or threaten people without much risk of retaliation. Among teens and preteens, and even college students, the problem has serious consequences, as evidenced by the suicide of Rutgers University student Tyler Clementi. Tyler had complained to university officials that his roommate, Dharun Ravi, was spying on his sexual encounters with men. Using a webcam, Dharun covertly streamed Tyler having a sexual encounter and posted about it on Twitter, outing Tyler in the process. Days later, Dharun again attempted to videostream another sexual encounter Tyler had with a man. But this time, Dharun invited his Twitter followers to watch. Tyler found out and the next day, he posted the following status update to his Facebook page: "Jumping off the gw bridge sorry." Having told no one about his despair and leaving no clues to his decision other than the Facebook status update, Clementi is thought to have made the one-hour drive from Rutgers to the George Washington Bridge, leaving his car, his wallet, and mobile phone on a side road before leaping to his death.[26] Tyler's story highlights the unfortunate consequences of the dark side of new technologies.

Improving Communication Competence via Social Media

6.6 **Identify** ways to improve communication competence via social media.

In many ways, the use of social media as effective methods of communication challenges historic assumptions that the most important interpersonal communication occurs in face-to-face contexts.[27] Social media offer many opportunities. Social media facilitate self-disclosure and social connection; are convenient; and, at times, easy to use. Unfortunately, these media also have a dark side and can foster aggression, loneliness, and depression. As you think about how you use social media to connect with others, consider the following guidelines.

Guidelines

IMPROVING SOCIAL MEDIA COMMUNICATION COMPETENCE

- **Monitor your social media use and exposure.** Like counting steps on your Fitbit, being aware of what you consume can end up making you consume less, or at least make wiser choices about what social media you use.
- **Critically evaluate the messages you consume.** Remember that every message you receive through social media has a source, and it is your job to question its credibility. By understanding the biases, goals, and strategies of social media sources, you will be in a better position to know whether to accept or resist their messages.
- **Consider the benefits and consequences.** Social media offer many opportunities for enhancing and maintaining our connections with friends and family. Today, we have more resources to facilitate our interpersonal relationships.

Take advantage of them, but also remember that there are consequences to our use of social media. Digital messages can be replicated; stored; easily sent; and, as a result, reach hundreds (if not millions!) of people. Our lean messages can also be misinterpreted and could lead to relational conflict.

- **Remember that social media is evolving at a rapid rate.** Social media has developed quickly, especially when compared to the creation of traditional media such as television, radio, and newspapers. As a result, it is rapidly changing how we communicate with others. Remain on top of the latest changes to social media. Always consider the benefits and challenges associated with a new technology. If you keep these recommendations in mind, you will move quickly toward successful and effective communication through new technologies.

〉 SUMMARY

Connecting with Others via Social Media and New Technologies

 Define computer-mediated communication and social media.

Computer-mediated communication refers to communication that is facilitated by a wide range of new technologies, including chat rooms, email, blogs, and even online games. Social media are often considered online platforms that allow people to create a public profile and maintain and view a list of users who share a common interest.

History of New Technologies

 Explain the history of new technologies.

The rapid development of new technologies has led to *media convergence*, or how the many forms of technologically mediated and face-to-face communication come together in our every day lives, and *media multitasking*, or how we tend to use more than one media type at the same time.

Distinguishing Social Media from Face-to-Face Communication

 Differentiate social media from face-to-face communication.

Several concepts help us distinguish different forms of social media from one another and from face-to-face communication. These concepts help us understand how we make connections with others in an age in which we rely more and more on social media.

- *Interactivity* refers to the ability of a communication tool to facilitate social interaction between groups or individuals.
- A social media device's *temporal structure* refers to the time it takes to send and receive messages.
- *Social cues* are the verbal and nonverbal features of a message that offer more information about the context, the meaning, and the identities of the involved parties.
- Social media's *replicability* means that communication can occur in an environment that makes it easy to record and redistribute past messages.
- Unlike face-to-face communication, social media's storage capability allows messages to be digitally saved and made accessible to other people.
- Unlike face-to-face communication, social media have tremendous reach, or the ability to connect with individuals in both local and long-distance places.
- Social media feature varying degrees of mobility, or the extent to which a device is portable or stationary.

Theories of Social Media and New Technologies

 Summarize theories of social media and new technologies.

Lucky for us, popular theories of new technologies and social media can help explain how communication functions in various communication contexts.

- *Social information processing (SIP) theory* suggests that electronically mediated relationships grow only to the extent that people gain information about each other and use it to form impressions.

- *Media multiplexity theory* contends that we carry out relationships through more than one form of social media, and those in closer relationships use more forms of social media.

- *Media richness theory* describes communication channels by the amount of verbal and nonverbal information that can be exchanged through a particular channel.

Managing the Dark Side of Social Media and New Technologies

6.5 **Explain** factors that comprise the dark side of social media and new technologies.

Among the most popular questions addressed in research about communication and new technologies is the extent to which Internet use fosters undesirable outcomes such as depression, loneliness, and reduced face-to-face social interaction.

- These feelings and behaviors are symptoms associated with *problematic Internet use*—a syndrome characterized by cognitive and behavioral symptoms that can result in negative social, academic, and professional consequences.

- Social media provides a vast space for *flaming or trolling*—online communication that is deliberately hostile, aggressive, or insulting and usually intended to provoke anger.

- Self-disclosure, or revealing information about yourself to another person, is one of the most powerful communication practices we have for strengthening a relationship; however, it can backfire if a person shares too much too soon or reveals information the other person finds inappropriate.

- Social media has created an arena for aggressive behaviors such as *cyberstalking*—when an individual repeatedly uses social media to stalk or harass others—and *cyberbullying*—abusive attacks that are carried out through social media.

Improving Communication Competence via Social Media

6.6 **Identify** ways to improve communication competence via social media.

- It is important to monitor your social media use and exposure.

- Always critically evaluate the messages you consume.

- Consider the benefits and consequences of using certain social media platforms.

- Remember that social media is evolving at a rapid rate.

⟩ DISCUSSION STARTERS

1. As you have grown older, how has your practice of media multitasking changed?

2. What are some of the differences between face-to-face communication and communication via social media?

3. How would you characterize the ties you have created with your family versus your friends at college?

4. Do you believe you or perhaps a close friend suffers from problematic Internet use?

5. How do you critically evaluate the social media messages you consume on a daily basis?.

CHAPTER 7

CONNECTING LISTENING AND THINKING IN THE COMMUNICATION PROCESS

Oshvintsev Alexander/Shutterstock

We are often called upon to multitask, especially when listening. Some jobs require us to try to do two or more tasks at once. Listening requires focus and attention and cognitive activity. With training and practice, we can manage to multitask fairly well if some of the nonlistening activities complement listening and do not require too much thinking as we connect with others.

→ CHAPTER OUTLINE AND LEARNING OBJECTIVES

The Importance of Effective Listening

7.1 **Describe** how listening helps you make connections with others in all aspects of your life.

Effective Listening

7.2 **Explain** the complex nature of listening as a cognitive process.

The Functions of Listening

7.3 **Differentiate** among four functions of listening behavior.

Barriers to Effective Listening

7.4 **Select** specific attitudes and behaviors to help you overcome your barriers to listening.

Critical Listening and Critical Thinking: Analyzing and Evaluating Messages

7.5 **Identify** instances in which you must be a critical listener/thinker.

Improve Listening Competence

7.6 **Characterize** the speech and actions of a competent listener.

MAKING EVERYDAY CONNECTIONS

A late-night on-air personality recently talked about how confusing everything is today. He said, "It's hard to deal with alternative facts and fake news and, further, on-air news personalities and writers in social media spend more time attacking other ideas and people than they do in presenting real information."[1] His point is similar to others' views about media's messages and how, as he and his tech director said, they can "cause sound fatigue."[2] As a result, people stop listening and thinking about what is real and what is not. Many people have trouble differentiating between fact and fiction, and some even refuse to listen to or watch certain sources they believe to be unreliable, but can they really differentiate between real news and fake news? Unfortunately, in North America, we are a non-listening culture. We don't listen for a variety of reasons, including because it takes too much effort to really listen and think about issues, and because we're really not held accountable for our listening. If we don't catch the news the first time we hear it, it will be available later. If we don't pay attention to the boss or the professor, surely they will repeat it, or you or someone else will ask what they said. We have trouble listening effectively because it takes a lot of effort to really listen and think about things and because sometimes we don't like what we hear. We should listen effectively, ask discriminating questions, and weigh the information we receive to determine the truth or validity of information. You will find some guidelines for listening effectively and weighing information throughout this chapter.

QUESTIONS TO THINK ABOUT

1. Identify two to three situations where you felt fatigued by the conflicting information you received.
2. How do you differentiate between separate and conflicting pieces of information?
3. Where do you go to get additional information?
4. Describe a positive experience where you listened well and asked good questions to get at the reality of a situation.

This chapter will help you understand listening and find ways to be an effective listener. To enhance your listening competence, you need to understand the importance of effective listening, the elements of listening, the functions of listening, and the most common barriers to listening. You should analyze and evaluate what you listen to and make the connection between listening and thinking, which are separate but related cognitive processes, as well as learn the difference between listening and hearing.

Because most of us take listening for granted, we tend to think of it as a simple task. However, listening is actually quite complex. Scholars agree that listening, like communication in general, is closely linked to the thinking process. Listening scholars, including Harfield, Brownell, Janusik, Wolvin, and Coakley, state that listening is a distinct behavior, separate from other intellectual activities.[3] Listening scholars and teachers agree that hearing and listening are not the same. **Listening** is a continuous cognitive activity and is defined as the active process of receiving stimuli through the senses, constructing meaning from and responding to those stimuli.[4] **Hearing** is the passive physiological process in which sound is received by the ear. It is impossible to listen to sounds without first hearing them, but it is possible to hear sounds without listening to them. What distinguishes listening from hearing?

Communication scholars agree that the major difference between listening and hearing is that listening is an active cognitive process, while hearing is passive physical process. Either you receive the sounds or you don't. If you have normal hearing, your ears receive sounds.[5] You don't have to work at hearing; it just happens. People can have excellent hearing and be terrible listeners. Listening, on the other hand, is cognitive; is *active*; and requires energy, desire, focus, and attention.

People bring a variety of learning styles into the classroom: *visual, kinesthetic*, and *auditory* are among the most common. Some of us are *visual* learners. We need to be able to see what is discussed. Whiteboard text and drawings or PowerPoint or Prezi presentations help the visual learner. *Kinesthetic* learners need to experience: They need to move around, touch things, watch things work, and take things apart or put them back together. *Auditory* learners, by contrast, listen to messages and take in (process) that information. This kind of learner doesn't need models or hands-on experiences as much as they need to listen to and think about information.

listening

A cognitive activity that is defined as the active process of receiving, constructing meaning from information taken in through the senses, and constructing meaning from and responding to those stimuli.

hearing

The passive physiological process in which sound is received by the ear.

What kind of learner are you? What is the role of listening in your learning? What kinds of activities help you listen and learn?

Skills in listening, analyzing, processing, and recording information are often neglected during formal education. How many people do you know who have had formal training in listening? If you are a typical college student, you will complete course work in reading, writing, and speaking, but few students ever enroll in a listening course. Not only are there few opportunities for formal listening instruction, but also informal listening training is often not provided. Yet as a student, you are expected to listen approximately 50 percent of the time—listening is proportionately the most used language skill.[6] University of Northern Iowa graduate student Sarah Baker completed research to identify the basic communication skills employers seek in recent hires from among Kirkwood Community College graduates. Of the employers she surveyed, 100 percent identified listening as the number one skill.[7] Numerous surveys of national business executives suggest all college graduates need more work on communication skills; *listening* is consistently high on all lists.[8] Listening has been identified in numerous other surveys and research projects as one of the top communication skills that employers seek in entry-level hires as well as in those being promoted. Even though the research suggests that listening skills are critical, according to listening scholars Robert Bohlken, Laura Janusik, Carolyn Coakley, and Andrew Wolvin, listening receives the least instruction in school.[9] Even in the course where this text is used, it is likely that only 7 percent of class and text time is spent on listening.[10] Inefficient listening is a prevalent (and expensive) problem in our lives, in terms of time wasted, poor customer relations, and the need to redo many tasks. The International Listening Association (ILA) is a professional organization of members dedicated to the study, application, and improvement of listening in all contexts. Check out the website at listen.org to learn more facts about listening.

The Importance of Effective Listening

7.1 **Describe** how listening helps you make connections with others in all aspects of your life.

Most misunderstandings in our daily lives occur because of poor listening habits. Poor listening skills can create serious personal, professional, and financial problems. For students, poor listening can result in missed appointments, misunderstood directions, incorrect or incomplete assignments, lower grades, and lost opportunities. In relationships, poor listening can cause misunderstandings, arguments, and loss of friendships.

It might surprise you to realize how much of your waking day you spend listening: When you are not talking or reading, you are probably listening to something or someone. Many listening scholars have discovered that college students spend 50 percent or more of their time listening, almost one-fifth in speaking, and less than one-fifth in reading and writing combined (see Figure 7.1).[11] In a German study, Imhof and Weinhard found that German primary school children are expected to listen for about two-thirds of classroom time.[12] U.S. studies have similar results, stating that listening is the most common activity in the classroom.[13] These studies should help you appreciate the importance of listening.

From the time we get up in the morning until we end the day, we constantly listen to something. But most of us give little thought to the part listening plays in our everyday experiences. Parents and children both complain, "They don't listen to me." A similar refrain may be heard from relational partners, workers and bosses, as well as teachers and students. You might even have heard a friend say to you, "You really ought to listen to yourself." As simple as listening *appears* to be, many of us are not efficient listeners.

FIGURE 7.1   Proportional Time Spent by College Students in Communication Activities

The graph indicates how typical college students spend their waking time. The proportions given in this graph are averages and, of course, can vary dramatically from person to person and from situation to situation.

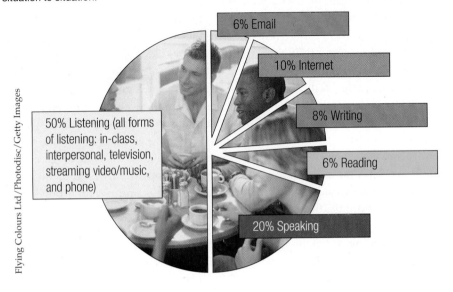

6% Email

10% Internet

8% Writing

6% Reading

50% Listening (all forms of listening: in-class, interpersonal, television, streaming video/music, and phone)

20% Speaking

Flying Colours Ltd/Photodisc/Getty Images

There can be little doubt that communication, and listening in particular, assumes a significant role in our lives. Because we spend so much time as *consumers* of communication, we need to learn as much as we can about effective listening. We live and work in a global world. Careful listening to the messages of people from other cultures and backgrounds is a successful life skill. The prevalence of all our technology and devices (tablets, iPads, and smartphones) causes interruptions and distractions and creates barriers to listening. In addition, we are surrounded by electronic messages clamoring for our attention. It is hard to shut out these distractions simply because of their almost overpowering presence. Listening scholars believe we can learn to reduce mediated as well as internal and other external distractions through cognitive, affective, and behavioral strategies.

Listening scholar Andrew D. Wolvin, author of *Listening in the Quality Organization*, indicates that the individuals who make up organizations must be effective listeners. His book identifies the role of listening in the communication process and provides suggestions for people to become more effective listeners. He concludes, "Quality listening then, is a benchmark for the quality organization of the twenty-first century. Some organizations have gotten there, while others are yet to develop a listening culture [...]. The challenge to get there is significant, but the rewards are tremendous. Indeed, our very economic, technological, political, and social lives depend on quality listening."[14]

MAKING CONNECTIONS FOR SUCCESS

Your View of Effective Listening

Think about someone you believe is a good listener and then answer the following questions:

1. What behaviors exhibited by this person do you see as characteristics of a good listener?

2. What does this person do and say that make you aware that they truly listen?

3. How can you tell whether or not this person is cognitively aware of messages?

4. How do you compare your own listening behaviors with those of the person you identified as a good listener?

5. How do you think your friends would rate you as a listener?

Effective Listening

7.2 **Explain** the complex nature of listening as a cognitive process.

A good way to understand the concept of listening is to think of it as a process. Listening is not something that just happens; it is a process that *occurs*. Because we are social beings with a strong sense of visual recognition, a good method to define a process is with a model. The model we use to define listening here is the Harfield Cognitive Listening Model© (HCLM©). The philosophy behind the HCLM maintains that cognitive processes are active and essential during the listening process.

The Harfield Cognitive Listening Model

The HCLM is both a cognitive and a relational model. From a cognitive perspective, the model works to acknowledge and advance the understanding that listening does not just happen. Listening is not simply a physical event. Listening is primarily a cognitive function. A number of synaptic or mental activities take place in the brain while we listen. The model is relational from the perspective that it demonstrates the interaction between people. It is relational from the perspective that people are more inclined to *listen to respond* rather than *listen to understand*. It is also a relational model as there are comprehensive interactions among the components of the model. The objective of the model is to demonstrate the interaction between people and direct attention to the speaker's content, not to their delivery. Listeners assign meaning to information based on their own life experience and perspective, not the sender's. Figure 7.2 illustrates the cognitive listening process.

The model identifies and defines the components and nuances of good listening. It works by breaking down listening to its foundational basics. The HCLM defines the way we listen as well as things that can affect us during the listening process. Each component of the listening process within the model is comprehensive and interconnected. The components are connected to each other much the way brain cells are connected to and interact with each other. When one step begins to break down or is nonexistent, the listening process begins to break down or becomes nonexistent.

Cognition plays a part in every component of the listening process and the HCLM. We use our thinking preferences to discern what information we consciously

FIGURE 7.2 Harfield Cognitive Listening Model[15]

Source: Depicted by Dwight R. Harfield, and used with permission.

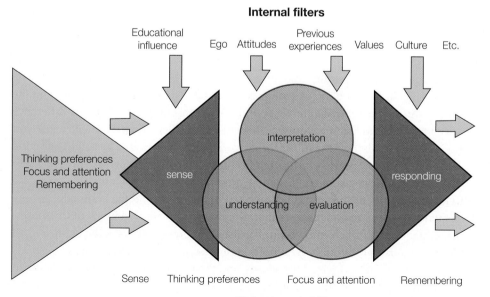

take in and how we will contextualize it. Focus and attention is used to intellectually separate important information from the unimportant at a given moment in time. Memories provide us with mental libraries of information and schema to help us recognize and understand stimuli we take in and process.

Our senses take information in through our auditory, olfactory, visual, taste, and tactile senses (even the fine hairs on our skin are included) and transmit information to our brains for processing. The brain converts those electrical impulses to information by way of our thinking preferences, ability to focus, and the brain's ability to compare the information with stored data in memory.

Interpretation, evaluation, and understanding are all cognitive functions employed to comprehend stimuli. The way we comprehend information allows us to formulate and provide a response. Our thinking preferences and our ability to focus and remember affect our comprehensive abilities, which in turn allow us to construct and deliver a response. The response creates and closes the loop on the circular interaction that is listening.

Located along the top of the model are internal filters. Internal filters are concepts such as the values, attitudes, ego, and cultural and educational influences that affect our listening. They are generated and exist based on our own life experiences and life condition. Although the list of internal filters in the model is not exhaustive, the list of internal filters each of us have can be quite extensive. Some of us might have a list of internal filters several pages long. And we each have our own personal list of internal filters. Internal filters are in good part, but not exclusively, emotionally derived and based.

Located along the bottom of the model are behavioral skills. Behavioral skills affect our listening more tangibly by establishing or recognizing our competence of the etiquette and practice of listening. Behavioral skills are the physical traits we demonstrate while we are listening. We should always practice and develop better skills to make us better listeners. We can only demonstrate the behavioral skills we are comfortable with at any given time. If our self-esteem is low on a given day or period in our lives, our behavioral skills will be affected. We could force ourselves to have better eye contact in a given situation, for example, but it will be forced on our part, and likely recognized by the speaker, potentially causing you to lose credibility. While we are on our life path of constant self-improvement, it is critical to be comfortable within ourselves while we develop the inner strength to become better listeners.[16]

We will now look at each of the concepts in the middle portion of the HCLM: sensing, information processing (understanding, interpretation, and evaluation), remembering, and responding.

Sensing

As we learned earlier, hearing is the physiological process in which sound is received by the ear. Accurate reception of sounds requires the listener to focus attention on the speaker/source, discriminate among sounds, and concentrate.[17] Given the difference between hearing and listening, answer this question: When you play music while you study, do you simply *hear* the music, or do you really *listen* to it? The sounds provide background that you hear; your hearing becomes listening only when you also carry out the remaining stages of the listening process. Note that listening is a cognitive activity. It begins in the brain and is processed in the brain, and the brain tells us how to respond. Newer[18] research shows that listening is also affected by all of the senses: hearing, smell, taste, touch, and vision. The listening process starts in the brain, and all information, taken in through the senses, is processed in the brain. Thus, the listener takes in information through all the senses, and the brain processes the information to understand it, use it, and store it for future reference.

Information Processing: Evaluation, Interpretation, and Understanding

Information processing uses *evaluation, interpretation*, and *understanding* to address comprehension when listening. In the fast pace of today's world, a premium is put on our time, energy, and attention. Each time we enter into a listening situation, we have to evaluate the message and information. (**Evaluation** is when we assess the meaning of information.) *Is the information critical? Is the information credible?* We then **interpret** the information based on tools such as our thinking preferences; the degree that we focused on the information; our existing knowledge; how we compare new information to older information; and **paralanguage**, or *how* things are said. Paralanguage—nonverbal components like intonation—and gestures or body language can also be significant factors in how we interpret a message. Upon interpreting the stimuli, we then give it meaning so we may have **understanding**. Understanding allows us to know something in our own minds, that is, in our own thoughts and language. A question at this point arises: Does the understanding we have mesh with the information the sender is transmitting?[19]

Information processing means that you weigh information and assign meaning to the stimuli you sense (hear, see, smell, taste, or touch). The ability to follow directions accurately is one of the ways we can measure whether we listen to (process) what we sense. Each of us is frequently in situations where we must process the information and find shared meaning. Past experience plays an important role in information processing; you relate and compare new sounds and ideas to those you have previously heard or otherwise sensed. To learn statistics, for example, you must first learn algebra and other mathematical principles. If you are unprepared and do not have this knowledge, you can still attend to what your statistics teacher says, but because you are unable to interpret what she is saying, you will not understand what she has presented. This inability to understand reduces your listening effectiveness.

evaluation
When we assess the meaning of information.

interpret
To explain the meaning of information.

paralanguage
The sound of words, including silence.

understanding
The part of information processing where we know something in our own minds.

information processing
Assigning meaning to the stimuli the brain selected and attended to.

Remembering

As a student, you are aware of the importance of **remembering**, or recalling something from stored memory. Most of your professors and employers expect you to recall and apply what you have heard in class or in meetings. Researchers say working memory and long-term memory are both essential processes, and different aspects are required for different situations. Listening scholar Laura Janusik found that when people were presented with a series of unrelated sentences and asked to remember the last word of each sentence, they could remember, on average, 2.805 items out of 7. In a dynamic conversational listening task in which people were asked to remember a series of related questions and respond to them, people could remember and respond to 2.946 items.[20] This finding suggests that when the topic seems more relevant, people will remember slightly more than they would if it seems irrelevant. As you'll recall, the process of perception (selective perception and selective attention) can also account for the loss of information. We tend to remember only information that supports our own views. Other information is forgotten. Remembering helps you complete assignments. Memory will also be important in your work responsibilities when an employer expects you to acquire and apply knowledge, and it is important in family and friendship situations.

remembering
Recalling something from stored memory; thinking of something again.

Thinking

Many scholars view listening as a cognitive construct. That is, the brain is the center of the listening process; listening is how we receive all kinds of information to process, store, and/or use immediately or in the future. Also, memory or "remembering" is

Monkey Business Images/Shutterstock

Effective listening is important to success in all aspects of our lives. It may surprise you to realize how much of your waking day you spend listening. When you are not talking or reading, you are probably listening to something or someone.

a critical component of the listening process. Neuroscientific research opened new avenues of understanding on both the sites of specific memories and the ways learning, listening, and memory can be enhanced. The brain has more plasticity or flexibility than previously believed. Nobel Prize–winning scientist Eric Kandel has spent his entire professional life determining how the brain works and how people can better remember the things they need to remember. Thus, the most current research in listening indicates we need to teach people how to remember as well as to listen effectively.

Dwight Harfield developed the Harfield Cognitive Listening Model (Figure 7.2) to expand and increase the emphasis on cognitive processes and listening. He also depicts two models to represent the functions of the brain; these models are shown in Figure 7.3 and Figure 7.4.[21] The idea of thinking preferences was created and popularized by researcher Ned Herrmann in 1991 when he was responsible for executive training at General Electric. Herrmann experimented with questionnaires and surveys and developed an assessment tool to measure the strength of thinking and language preferences in four distinct thinking styles. He suggested the brain could be metaphorically divided into specialized quadrants—the rational self, the safekeeping self, the feeling self, and the experimental self—each with its own characteristics and language.

Herrmann's work led him to determine a profile based on the individuals' optimal cognitive preferences.[22] The behavioral differences resulting from our mental preferences, just like handedness, are normal expressions of human dominance. Each of us has dominant preferences, mentally and physically; our mental dominances ultimately affect our behavior. Each quadrant has its own language, perception, values, gifts, and ways of knowing and being. We are all composites of those differing modes according to our particular mix of mental preferences and avoidances.

FIGURE 7.3 Whole Brain Model

This figure depicts the four quadrants of the brain and identifies the type of thinking that occurs in each quadrant. Ned Herrmann created the concept of brain dominance as a way to demonstrate how different parts of the brain work.

Source: Depicted by Dwight R. Harfield, and used with permission.

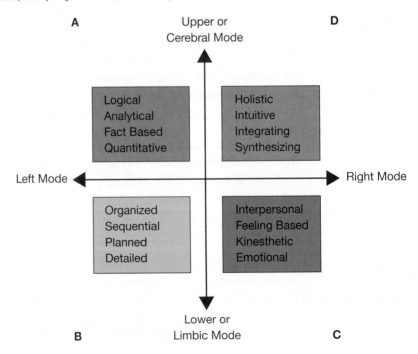

FIGURE 7.4 Our Four Different Selves

This figure identifies the specific thinking skills of each of the four quadrants of the brain. Herrmann suggests that each quadrant engages the thinker in different behaviors.

Source: Depicted by Dwight R. Harfield, and used with permission.

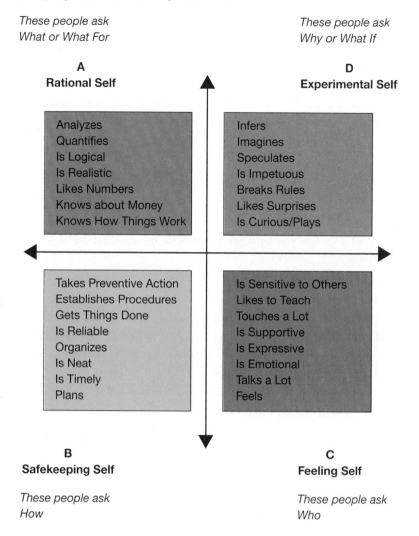

These people ask
What or What For

These people ask
Why or What If

A
Rational Self

D
Experimental Self

Analyzes
Quantifies
Is Logical
Is Realistic
Likes Numbers
Knows about Money
Knows How Things Work

Infers
Imagines
Speculates
Is Impetuous
Breaks Rules
Likes Surprises
Is Curious/Plays

Takes Preventive Action
Establishes Procedures
Gets Things Done
Is Reliable
Organizes
Is Neat
Is Timely
Plans

Is Sensitive to Others
Likes to Teach
Touches a Lot
Is Supportive
Is Expressive
Is Emotional
Talks a Lot
Feels

B
Safekeeping Self

C
Feeling Self

These people ask
How

These people ask
Who

The whole brain model in Figure 7.3 illustrates the conceptual and structural basis of the profile grid. The two left-side structures are popularly called left-brain thinking. Two right-side structures combine to represent right-brain thinking. The two upper structures are cerebral thinking, and the two lower structures are limbic thinking.[23]

The our four selves model (Figure 7.4) shows the coalition of our thinking selves in a more behavioral way:

- The left hemisphere is *verbal,* and involves speaking, reading, writing, and thinking with numbers. Analytic and sequential processing of information is carried out mostly in the left hemisphere for most people. A *left-brain* approach to problem solving is fact-based, analytic, and step-by-step, favoring words, numbers, and facts presented in a logical sequence.

- The right hemisphere is *visuospatial* and *emotional,* and involves simultaneous processing, pattern recognition, creative and holistic thinking, spatial perception, and geometry. Mental map making and our ability to rotate shapes in our mind are predominantly performed in the right hemisphere. A *right-brain* strategy seeks out insight, images, concepts, patterns, sounds, and movement, all to be built into an intuitive sense of the whole.

Each hemisphere has functions of its own, ordered processing of information, and unique "modes of knowing." The mind is composed of complementary parts, each enriching the other and each crucial to our successful functioning as human beings. Brain dominance is expressed in terms of how we prefer to learn, understand, and express or communicate something. These are called *thinking or cognitive preferences*, or *preferred modes of knowing (PMK)*.

Our thinking preference, or preferred mode of knowing, compares strongly with *what* we prefer to learn or do and *how* we go about it. It is the part of the brain we are most likely to use when we need to solve a problem, perhaps even in spite of or in addition to our training. For example, a left-brained person may prefer to learn about engineering or law. A right-brained person, in contrast, may prefer to study psychology or music. If both people were to study dance, for example, the left-brained person may learn about productions, history, facts regarding names, and so on. The right-brained person, though, would likely learn about dancing by watching and doing it.[24]

Focus and Attention Our culture currently works against people's ability to develop the skills of focus and attention in a number of ways:

- Movies and TV shows with large volumes of information are directed at us in short, stimulating, or shocking snappy scenes.
- Our society and education system are dumbed down.
- People are given information that lacks intellectual stimulation.
- We are fed an increasing amount of propaganda that asks us to believe what we are told rather than what we assemble and believe in our own minds.
- We believe we can multitask: People have so many things to do and are on the go so much that they try to do more than one thing at a time.
- Increasingly complex electronic technology in everyday living throws large masses of small bits of information at us.
- We have the growing ability to communicate with others, even when we don't want to, without ever directly seeing or hearing those people.

All these things contribute to our lack of ability to practice focus and attention. How we focus is crucial to how we learn (that is, how we acquire knowledge and skills) and remember (how we store and retrieve information). If you want to master and retain certain information, it is critical to pay close attention to it in the first place.[25] Attention is an important attribute as seen in Figure 7.5. The Chinese character "ting" ("to listen") fits the Chinese view of the listening process and reflects the complex nature of listening we describe in this chapter.

interpreting

The process of understanding the meaning of the message from the speaker's point of view and letting the speaker know that you understand.

The main difference between hearing and listening is understanding. Once we have heard, selected, and attended to sounds, we must assign meaning to them for listening to be complete. We can enhance our listening by being open and receptive to what the speaker has to say.

Interpreting

When we interpret, we simply try to make sense of the information received. The **interpreting** process has two parts: "[Y]ou take into account the total communication context so that you are better able to understand the meaning of what is said from the speaker's point of view,"[26] and you let the speaker know that you understand the message. In this stage, the specific situation and nonverbal aspects of communication come into play. An effective listener knows that facial expressions, posture, eye contact (or the lack of it), silence, and even paralanguage (the way things sound) affect messages. Good listeners work to develop greater sensitivity to these dimensions of communication.

pixelheadphoto digitalskillet/Shutterstock

FIGURE 7.5   Listening with Undivided Attention

The elements of the Chinese character "ting" for the phrase "to listen" incorporate a person's entire being: the eyes (the left character), the ears (the upper-right character), and most especially the heart (the lower-right character); the line separating the ears and heart represents undivided attention. Many Eastern cultures have similar figures and each is illustrative of the emphasis on the importance of listening in their culture (an example of the subjective nature of listening).

Evaluating

In **evaluating**, the listener analyzes evidence, sorts fact from opinion, determines the intent of the speaker, judges the accuracy of the speaker's statements and conclusions, and judges the accuracy of personal conclusions. Once we begin to assess the message we received and understood, we might no longer hear and attend to other incoming messages. Later in the chapter, we further discuss analyzing and evaluating messages.

evaluating
The listener analyzes evidence, sorts fact from opinion, determines the intent of the speaker, judges the accuracy of the speaker's statements and conclusions, and judges the accuracy of his or her own decisions.

Responding and Sending Feedback

A receiver who has listened to a message can connect with the sender by verbally or nonverbally verifying the message's reception or indicating a lack of reception. This verification is referred to as responding or feedback. **Responding** is the listener's overt behavior that indicates to the speaker what has and has not been received. Examples of such behaviors are total silence (didn't hear the message, ignored the message, or was angry about what the message said), smiling or frowning (agreeing or disagreeing with the message), and asking for clarification of what was received.

responding
Overt verbal and nonverbal behavior by the listener, indicating to the speaker what has and has not been received.

Feedback is an important part of being an effective listener. Feedback is the response to a message sent by a receiver back to a source. Feedback helps to ensure understanding and helps speakers determine communication success. Feedback should be appropriate to the situation, and it should be deliberate, thoughtful, and clear. When it is important that you grasp every detail of a message, you should paraphrase or repeat the information for the sender to verify your reception, understanding, and recall of it. This also indicates to the sender that you are actively listening and are committed to receiving the intended message.

Students provide their instructors with feedback, both consciously and unconsciously. Some students might not always be completely honest in their responses, however, or they may be guilty of **pseudolistening**. They may be mentally removed from where they are but still indicate through nodding, smiling, looking at the speaker, and so on, that they are listening to, understanding, and agreeing with everything being said—even when they were not listening. This behavior, unfortunately,

pseudolistening
When one appears to be listening by nodding, smiling, looking at the speaker, and so on, but their attention and focus is on something else.

MAKING CONNECTIONS FOR SUCCESS

Listening and Thinking

Andrew Wolvin, listening scholar, says that listening is probably one of the most complex of all human behaviors.[27] So far in this chapter, we have talked about how much listening skills are valued and used and what's involved in the listening process, as well as references to thinking. It's time to reflect on the connections between listening and thinking. Margarete Imhof, a German listening scholar, found students were able to improve their listening comprehension in difficult classes when they used active thinking prior to listening and as they listened to difficult or new material. Students were asked to use precognitive strategies, that is, to create questions to help them determine meaning in the hardest lecture course they had, prior to attending class. Imhof suggests that students ask questions of themselves prior to the communication event, and then, during the communication, work to find areas of interest and possible application.[28] With that in mind, respond to the following questions:

1. Pick a talk show or news broadcast on a television channel you don't normally watch. Create a list of questions you want to have answered before you watch the program. Tell yourself that you need to focus on the programming content. Watch the show for 30 minutes without interruptions from other sources (shut off your cell phone, put the computer to sleep, and stay in a room without other people).

2. At the end of the 30-minute period, check to see how many of your questions were answered. Did a focus on the relevance of the material make a difference?

3. Could you see how the person(s) had reasonable views, even if you did not share the views?

can lead to more unclear messages and confusion. When those who are confused admit they are not really listening, instructors are more likely to improve their presentation. Active listeners always try to get the most from the message and make sure they received it accurately and completely. And since there's a strong connection between listening and thinking, we need to think about how to use "working memory" to better facilitate effectiveness.

If you want to keep information in your working memory for future use, you have to find strategies to process and put it into long-term memory. Listening scholar Judi Brownell suggests five techniques for storing items in memory so they can be used later.[29]

- *Association.* You probably already use this in some ways to connect something new to something you already know. Situations often provide the stimulus for associations. If you remember that Tom is a tattoo artist whom you met in Toronto and use his name, these cues can help you remember Tom, where he is, and what he does.

- *Categorization.* When you organize information into categories, you can often remember better and longer. Plan your grocery shopping according to the aisles where the products are located. Remembering the categories helps you study for exams and determine what divisions to include in reports and what tasks you need to accomplish. Categorization can increase your work efficiency because the logical order facilitates retrievable memory from storage.

- *Mediation.* Meaningful information is much easier to retrieve. Unrelated pieces of data are harder to remember. *Mediation* works in the following ways. (1) Form a meaningful word out of foreign words or meaningless syllables. This author went to Denmark to find relatives. The street name meant "church on the hill" in Danish, so we looked for a church on a hill before we looked for Danish street signs and found the right place. (2) Words can be made out of the initial letters of the items presented. For example, *ALS* or *Lou Gehrig's disease* is much easier to remember than *amyotrophic lateral sclerosis*. Create "words" to enhance your ability to recall information. (3) Another mediation technique is to create a word that links two or more words and ideas. If you need to remember *cat, ball,* and *pillow,* you might link them with the word *soft*. This can help you connect the seemingly unrelated items.

- *Imagery.* Most information is processed into your memory through two sensory channels: the visual or the auditory. To tap into this, you can use *imagery* by creating visual or mental images from the information presented. If you want to remember something, you create vivid mental images of that information in order to later recall and apply it.

- *Mnemonics.* You create ways to make sense of the information presented and use visual imagery to make the impression vivid. When you combine meaningful words and vivid images, you can recall information more quickly and accurately.

Memory is only one aspect of the thinking process. The more we are able to remember, the more effectively we can analyze, evaluate, and apply concepts to the information we gain. We can use memory and thinking to be better listeners and consumers of information.

Guidelines

WORKING MEMORY

Many listening scholars suggest approaches to enhance your working memory. The following strategies from Judi Brownell will help you retain information long enough to use it.

1. **Repetition.** With this strategy, you repeat things to keep them in mind. When you have to go to the bookstore to get school supplies without a written list, you might constantly repeat your needs as you walk over: "Stapler, staples, index cards, special pen for art class, laptop case, book for listening class." Any kind of interference, however, can make you forget some or most of your list.

2. **Chunking.** When you have many things to remember, you might group them into categories so you have fewer details to remember. Have you ever thought about why telephone numbers are created as they are? Researchers suggest we can remember up to seven individual pieces of information.

If you use chunking, keep your groupings in seven or fewer categories to retain information long enough to use it immediately or help move it to long-term memory.

3. **Identification of logical patterns.** If you can identify patterns or themes in the information you hear, it is usually easier to remember, at least for a short time. Numbers in a sequence, acronyms, or mnemonics ("every good boy does fine" and "face" to remember the notes on the treble clef musical scale), are logical patterns that some of your earlier teachers may have used to help you remember their subjects.

(Adapted from Judi Brownell, *Listening: Attitudes, Principles, and Skills*, 4e. Published by Allyn and Bacon, Boston, MA, pp. 151–52. Copyright © 2010 by Pearson Education. Reprinted by permission of the publisher.)

The Functions of Listening

7.3 **Differentiate** among four functions of listening behavior.

You wake in the morning to the sound of an alarm, your roommate moving noisily around the apartment, or the blaring of the television. While you dress, a fire engine siren wails in the street. You listen to songs. At the Student Union, you join in a heated discussion about the proposed elimination of an academic program. Then you rush off to the last lecture before an upcoming exam. In the evening, you go to a concert. After the concert, you meet a good friend who is upset because they received a low grade on a test.

Throughout the day, you listened to many different people and things for a variety of purposes. You listened to the alarm to get up at the right time; you listened to your friends' opinions on the proposed removal of an academic program; you listened to your professor to acquire information about a subject; you listened to the concert for enjoyment; you listened to your troubled friend to understand their feelings. In each case, listening served a different function and involved different skills. Let's look at each of these functions in greater detail and the listening skills that each requires.

Listening to Obtain Information

You probably spend great amounts of time **listening for information**, or listening to gain comprehension. You listen as your teacher discusses process, perception, nonverbal and verbal communication, famous speakers, and similar topics to learn about speech skills. Each day, you listen for information such as news, weather forecasts, sports scores, directions, orders, assignments, names, numbers, and locations.

Listening to Evaluate

Evaluative listening is listening to judge or to analyze information. A car owner who hears a squeak coming from the front end rolls down the window and does some evaluative listening. The owner tries to pinpoint the exact location and cause of the bothersome noise. A teacher listens to students' speeches to discriminate between presentations and to assign grades. In most situations we should all listen critically: constantly judge evidence, arguments, facts, and values. We need to ask questions to be effective listeners. We are bombarded by messages asking us to believe, accept, or buy things. While we sometimes want to hear sounds in the background, when we do listen, we should evaluate everything.

Listening with Empathy

Empathy is an important skill or characteristic in all relationships and is especially important when listening because it allows you to connect with others and become both a better listener and a better friend. We define **empathy** as follows: the intellectual identification with or vicarious experiencing of the feelings, thoughts, or attitudes of another—in other words, we have the capacity to recognize and, to some extent, share feelings (e.g., happiness or sadness) that are experienced by another.[30] **Empathic listening** occurs when you listen to what someone else is experiencing and seek to understand that person's thoughts and feelings. It is not sympathy, which means that you feel sorry for the other person. Empathy means that you try to put yourself in another person's place to understand what is happening to that person. We might find it difficult to avoid making judgments when we listen to someone else's problems, but that is exactly what we must do to listen with empathy. Listening empathically can be a healing and soothing process. Empathic listening indicates that we are aware, appreciative, and understanding of another person's feelings. Empathic listeners create a supportive climate by expressing understanding of what the speaker says and means. They also reflect and clarify feelings by **perception checking** with the speaker and ask questions in order to be sure to correctly understand the points made. And empathic listeners are always genuine—they suspend judgment and let speakers share as fully as they wish.[31] Caring about someone requires a great deal of sensitivity as well as the ability to communicate that sensitivity. It is not easy to listen; it is even more difficult to listen with empathy. If we fail to empathize with others, however, we also fail to understand them.

Stockphoto Mania / Fotolia

Listening for Enjoyment

When we listen purely for pleasure, personal satisfaction, and appreciation, we **listen for enjoyment**. We usually listen to music, for example, simply because we enjoy it. The same is true for most of us when we combine listening and viewing as we watch television or a movie.

MAKING CONNECTIONS FOR SUCCESS
Listening Behaviors

A simple experiment illustrates what people tend to remember and for how long. For three minutes, read a news item or narrative to a friend, then ask the friend to repeat the key information. Do the same with several other friends. Most people will be able to report only about 50 percent of what they've heard. Then wait 24 hours and ask each person to repeat the information again. Afterwards, answer the following questions:

1. Discuss with your friends what you learned from the exercise.

2. Did some people do better than others? If so, why do you think they did?

3. Share what you learned about listening from this exercise.

Listening for enjoyment involves more than merely sitting back and letting sounds enter our ears. It also engages the thinking process. We evaluate what we sense to understand something or to learn more about it. As we listen to music, we try to find some personal value or relevance in the lyrics and instrumentation. Even if we attend an opera for the first time and do not understand the language, we can enjoy the performance as we seek to understand it. In other words, listening for enjoyment consists of the same process as other kinds of listening: We select, attend, understand, evaluate, and remember. We construct meaning from what we hear and respond to it in some way.

Barriers to Effective Listening

 Select specific attitudes and behaviors to help you overcome your barriers to listening.

Why are most people poor listeners? The answer is surprisingly complex. The quality of our listening changes from time to time and from situation to situation. We've already mentioned the impact of technology on listening—sensory overload and distractions from all forms of technology and media compete with messages from others and make it difficult to listen. A number of other barriers contribute to our ineffectiveness as listeners. The context of each communication affects how important each barrier actually is, and some of the barriers that reduce our listening effectiveness are under our control, whereas others are not. Ralph Nichols, the "father of listening research," identified barriers to effective listening.[32] Nichols and other researchers have replicated the research in subsequent studies and found similar results. Although these barriers may not be the only ones, they are the most common. And remember, listening, like communication, is a learned behavior, so we *can learn* to overcome the obstacles that interfere with our listening effectiveness.

Consider the Topic or Speaker Uninteresting

The level of interest and the amount of importance we place on a subject or a speaker usually govern how much effort we put into listening. Deciding that a subject or person is uninteresting or boring often leads us to conclude that the information being presented is not important. However, this is not necessarily true. What appears to be dull or insignificant might very well be vital for passing an exam, doing an assignment correctly, learning something, following your supervisor's instructions, making a sale, or learning a new way of doing something on the job. In other words, a competent listener keeps an open mind.

Criticize the Speaker Instead of the Message

How many times have you judged a speech by the number of *uhs* and *ums* or other filler words the speaker used? How many times has a speaker's volume, mispronunciations, or accent influenced your opinion? Have you ever missed a message because you focused on a something the speaker was wearing or on their facial expressions or nervous behaviors?

Of course, when possible, speakers should do everything in their power to eliminate personal quirks that may distract attention from their message, but listeners must also share responsibility for receiving the message. An effective listener must be able to overlook the superficial elements of a person's delivery style or appearance to concentrate on the substance of the presentation. In short, the listener must stay involved in the message, and not be distracted by the speaker or the speaker's attire or behaviors.

Concentrate on Details, Not Main Ideas

Many of us listen for specific facts, such as dates, names, definitions, figures, and locations, assuming they are the important things to know. But are they? Specific facts are needed in some situations, but we often focus too much on details. As a result, we walk away with disjointed details and no idea how they relate to each other and to the total picture.

Competent listeners focus on the main or most important ideas, not on every single word. All stages of the listening process are affected adversely when we forget that general ideas can be more significant than the details that surround them. For example, note when your communication professor says, "Be sure to write this in your notes," what follows is more important than when the information is only briefly mentioned. If your supervisor asks you to be sure to notify her when a specific person calls for an appointment, be sure to keep that name in mind, with perhaps a note on your desk as a reminder.

Avoid Difficult Listening Situations

Most of us find it difficult to keep up with the vast amount and increasing technical complexity of the information that confronts us each day. Texting, chatting, and checking Facebook, Twitter, or email are competing activities for your time. Add media messages about a variety of good and bad news and you become distracted, trying to make sense of the impact and significance of these issues while you attend to the business of life. There are times we might deal with complex listening situations by giving up and ignoring what is presented.

Concentration and energy are needed to overcome the temptation to ignore or avoid what might seem difficult and confusing. When you are faced with a difficult listening situation, the best approach is usually to ask questions. For example, physicians often use complex medical terminology when talking to patients, but patients can take the responsibility for understanding. They can ask the physician to explain terms, to review procedures, and to supply missing information. The same principles apply to the classroom or to the workplace. You should never hesitate to ask about something at the appropriate time when you don't understand it because without understanding, you cannot learn.

Sometimes, you might not listen to new and difficult information because you lack motivation, but once again, the responsibility falls on you to make the effort to listen. Try consciously and continually to listen to such communication. Each time you are successful at staying tuned in, you acquire not only some information but also improved confidence and ability.

Tolerate or Fail to Adjust to Distractions

Distractions constantly disrupt our concentration. As listeners, we have the responsibility to adjust to, compensate for, or eliminate distractions and to focus on speakers and their messages despite the competing factors from technology and the media.

We can control some distractions. If noise from another room competes with a speaker, for example, the listener can close the door, ask the person who is creating the noise to be quiet, move closer to the speaker, or ask the speaker to talk louder.

Some distractions must be overcome through mental rather than physical effort. A noise in the background can become a major distraction, or we can reduce it to a minor nuisance by forcing ourselves to listen more intently to the speaker. When distractions occur, we must consciously focus on selecting the appropriate messages and attending to them. We must filter out extraneous noise and distractions, such as people walking by, a phone's vibration, or the sound of a lawn mower outside, and concentrate on the sounds important to us. We need to forget about tomorrow's work and concentrate on what's going on at the moment. If we cannot modify internal and external noise, we must alter our internal listening behavior to understand the speaker's message.

Technology often creates distractions because it's always there. It is easy to check our phones when the professor or supervisor seems to be droning on about something that does not seem valuable (and certainly is not interesting). We need to remember that multitasking is impossible. When you're in class or in a meeting, resist the urge to text your friends or play games on your phone. Remember why you're there and don't let technology create even more sensory overload.

Fake Attention

At one time or another, everyone pretends to pay attention to something or someone. You appear to listen intently, but your mind is elsewhere. You might even smile in agreement when all you are really doing is maintaining eye contact. In class, you might pretend to take notes, although your mind might not follow what is said.

Pretending to pay attention can become a habit. Without even realizing what you are doing, you might automatically tune out a speaker and let your mind wander. If, after a speech, you cannot recall the main purpose or essential points presented by the speaker, you were probably faking attention (pseudolistening). Although it might seem harmless, such deceptive behavior can lead to misunderstandings and cause people to question your credibility and sincerity.

Table 7.1 summarizes the differences between ineffective and effective listening habits.

Competent listeners need to ask themselves, "Am I *really* paying attention?" When listeners realize they are distracted, they should make every effort to pay attention. Good listeners recognize when they are not listening well and do whatever it takes to return their attention to the speaker. You may think, "What's in it for me?" but when someone shares something that seems irrelevant to you, you can use your critical thinking and critical listening skills to try to determine how it may be helpful at some point, even if it's not right now. Competent listeners demonstrate attitudes, behaviors, and thinking that allow them to focus on others. They know that listening is an active process and requires energy and effort.

Table 7.1   INEFFECTIVE AND EFFECTIVE LISTENING HABITS

Bad Listener	Good Listener
Thinks the topic or speaker is of no interest	Finds areas of interest—keeps an open mind
Focuses on the speaker's appearance and delivery	Concentrates on the content of the presentation and overlooks speaker characteristics—stays involved
Listens only for details	Listens for ideas
Avoids difficult material	Exercises the mind—prepares to listen
Is easily distracted	Resists distractions
Fakes attention	Pays attention

Bias and Prejudice

Self-perceptions, prejudices, and personal biases can include *a barrier or anything that prevents understanding a speaker's message*. Some typical examples include egocentrism, personal interests, biases/dogmatism, defensiveness and apprehension, or a know-it-all attitude.[33] Biases and prejudices often create barriers. We have trouble listening to others when we are biased against the message or the speaker. If the speaker's views are different from our own, it is easy to tune out and think about other things; we may even decide not to listen at all. Although it takes extra effort to listen when our minds are closed, it is ultimately worthwhile to learn the views of others. If we give in to our biases, we limit ourselves in what we know and can do.

Preferred Thinking

Our preferred thinking can create barriers in the listening process from the perspective of giving or receiving information. Each quadrant of the brain has its own language, and an individual whose primary thinking is in one quadrant can grossly misinterpret an individual whose primary thinking is in the opposite quadrant. The result can be exacerbated if the listener has a very low preference in the quadrant from which the speaker is delivering the information. For example, think of an organizational (B quadrant) thinker (see Figure 7.3), a safe-keeper of information, telling a coworker how a process works. The creative (D quadrant) coworker is listening to a "this is the way we do it because this is the way we have always done it" message, while simultaneously thinking and listening in "if we do it this way, we can do it in a fraction of the time with better quality" language.[34]

Critical Listening and Critical Thinking: Analyzing and Evaluating Messages

7.5   **Identify** instances in which you must be a critical listener/thinker.

As listeners, our goal is more than simply understanding a message; we also try to become critical listeners. **Critical listening** involves analyzing and assessing the accuracy of the information presented, determining the reasonableness of its conclusions, and evaluating its presenter. In other words, we must ask ourselves questions about the message: Is the message true? Is it based on solid evidence? Is it complete? Is it logical? What motivates the speaker to present the message?

We are constantly confronted with choices and decisions. For example, we are exposed to numerous commercial messages each day in addition to the interpersonal messages we receive at school, at home, at work, and in recreational situations. We also live in a technological world. Web searches to find information for our college papers and presentations; to enhance a presentation at work; or even to learn more about a city, country, or company provide an infinite number of resources very quickly. Because we are limited in the amount of experience we can acquire on our own, we must depend on others to provide information and advice. Thus we must evaluate and assess that information to judge its value and utility. We do this through critical thinking. Critical thinking is integrally linked to critical listening because they are both part of the process of gaining an understanding of our world.

Critical thinking has many definitions. One definition of **critical thinking** suggests that critical thinkers ask and answer the right questions to determine the appropriate responses to problems and issues.[35] In an earlier work, critical thinking scholar Robert Ennis defined it as the ability to analyze and assess information.[36] From these two definitions alone, you should be able to make the connection between listening and thinking. You must listen carefully and construct meaning from ideas, messages,

critical listening

Listening that judges the accuracy of the information presented, determines the reasonableness of its conclusions, and evaluates its presenter.

critical thinking

The ability to analyze and assess information.

and actions if you are to make sense of the world around you. Critical thinking has become so important to academic institutions and to employers that more and more colleges and universities include courses or units in critical thinking in their curricula; some even provide a web page devoted to the characteristics of the critical thinker. The Foundation for Critical Thinking website provides definitions of critical thinking and characteristics of a critical thinker.[37]

Basically, you need to remember that the link between critical thinking and critical listening is this: critical thinkers have specific positive attitudes and mental habits. They are intellectually curious, flexible, objective, persistent, systematic, honest, and decisive. They use their critical listening abilities to assess information and choose the best options from among those available. Critical thinkers are aware of the ways they learn best and capitalize on opportunities to expand their learning abilities. One goal of a liberal arts education is to encourage students to think critically, to develop "habits of mind" to enable them to become effective thinkers, listeners, and communicators.

Critical thinking and critical listening are closely linked. The critical thinker knows how to analyze and assess information. The critical listener knows how to make connections between messages and issues. The critical listener also uses the ability to analyze and evaluate messages to determine whether ideas are logically presented and whether the speaker is well informed and exhibits clear thinking. Critical thinking and critical listening are closely related parts of a complex process. Listening with a critical ear involves two phases: (1) assessing the speaker's values and intent and (2) judging the accuracy of the speaker's conclusions.[38]

Assess the Speaker's Motivation

Assessing a speaker's motivation generally involves three stages of information processing: (1) make a judgment about the speaker's beliefs, (2) compare our standards with those of the speaker, and (3) evaluate the worth of the message being presented.

Values are strongly held beliefs central to the communication process and to each individual's perceptual system. They affect perception and interpretation of both the messages we send and the messages we receive. The first consideration in listening, therefore, is to determine the speaker's values by examining the message: We critically think about what the speaker is saying and how it compares to our own value system. Of course, we should not automatically dismiss a message merely because the speaker's values conflict with our own. However, anytime we are confronted with a message that differs from our own views—one that asks us to do something, buy something, or behave in a certain way—we should be aware of the purpose behind it.

The second consideration is to determine whether the message urges us to conform to or go against our principles or standards. Finally, we consider how to evaluate and respond to the messages. Critical thinking skills help us recognize and understand the motivation behind the messages we receive.

Judge the Accuracy of the Speaker's Conclusions

To make accurate judgments and to think critically about important messages, ask the following questions:

- Is the speaker qualified to draw the conclusion?
- Has the speaker actually observed the concept or issue about which he or she is talking?
- Does the speaker have a vested interest in the message?
- Does the speaker present adequate evidence to support the conclusion?
- Is the evidence relevant to the conclusion?
- Is there contrary evidence that refutes the information presented?
- Does the message contain invalid or inadequate reasoning?

Listening Self-Assessment

Let's try a metacognitive activity for a few minutes of reflection time to determine how well you think you listen in a variety of situations. Answer the following questions and follow up with a specific plan to capitalize on what you already do well and correct those areas where you are not as efficient as a listener:

1. When do you listen well?
2. What specific speaker or situation characteristics are involved when you listen well?
3. Identify four to five factors that interfere with your listening effectiveness.
4. In what behaviors do you engage to help you stay focused on the speaker/speech?
5. How do you motivate yourself to listen at work or in the classroom when you know you'll need the information later?
6. Identify three ways you will improve your listening attitudes and behaviors.

Guidelines

COMPETENT LISTENERS

1. **Be prepared to listen.** Learn to control internal and external distractions.

2. **Behave like a good listener.** Stop talking and let others have their say. Do not interrupt. Concentrate on what is being said, not on who is saying it or what the speaker is doing. Good listeners maintain eye contact with speakers, ask questions at appropriate times, and maintain flexibility as they carefully listen to the speaker's views.

3. **Take good notes.** Listen for main ideas and write down the most significant points; don't attempt to write down every word. Good note taking helps listeners remember better and longer, and provides a written indication of ideas to remember. Brevity is usually best so you can carefully listen to the speaker and analyze the speaker's intent. Write legibly and review your notes as soon after the event as possible to help you recall them later. Finally, reorganize your notes, if necessary, for clarity, before filing them for future reference. Do not get so involved in note taking that effective listening is lost. Note taking is an aid to listening, not a replacement for it. In effective listening, all seven stages of the process are brought into play. Never concentrate so hard on writing everything down that you fail to think about what is said.

4. **Ask questions to clarify information.** Make sure you know what your supervisor or teacher requires.

Improve Listening Competence

7.6 **Characterize** the speech and actions of a competent listener.

With appropriate knowledge and practice, we can become better listeners. First, we must recognize the importance of effective listening. Second, we must think of listening as an *active* behavior that requires conscious participation. Third, we must recognize that a willingness to work and a desire to improve are essential to increased listening effectiveness.

In some situations, we need not listen with full attention. For example, if we listen to music while conversing with a friend, we're not likely to create problems by attending closely to the friend and partially to the music. However, each listener must be able to identify when total energy and involvement in the listening process are crucial. Effective listening often requires both energy and concentration; listeners need to remind themselves constantly that listening is vital to communication. People call on different listening skills, depending on whether their goal is to comprehend information, critique and evaluate messages, show empathy for others, or appreciate a performance. According to the National Communication Association, competent listeners demonstrate (1) knowledge and understanding of the listening process, (2) the ability to use appropriate and effective listening skills for a given communication situation and setting, and (3) the ability to identify and manage barriers to listening (all are covered in this chapter).

Competent listeners work at listening. They are prepared to listen and know what they wish to gain from their listening experiences. Competent listeners also engage in appropriate listening behaviors. They realize that being a good listener is an active and complex process. They know they must pay attention. They do not interrupt others, they look at the speaker, they listen to ideas, and they concentrate on what is being said.

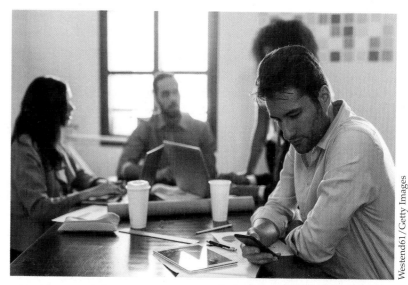

Westend61/Getty Images

Technology can both enhance and detract from effective listening; it sometimes creates sensory overload and multiple distractions. We need to focus on the ways technology can help us be effective listeners.

MAKING CONNECTIONS FOR SUCCESS
Listening and the Job Interview

Most of us spend a great deal of time on the Internet. Can we listen on the Internet? If we can, how do we do it? In today's job market, many early aspects of matching applicants and jobs are completed via some technological venue. Programs such as Zoom or GoToMeeting allow employers and potential employees to see and hear each other during the interview. Email allows both to ask and answer questions prior to or after the online interview so that everyone can see if the candidate will fit the position. Listening becomes even more critical because the technology can distract. Callie Angove, a graduate student at the University of Northern Iowa, conducted a study to determine if Skype interviews created positive or negative impressions of job candidates. The results show there were more negative impressions of a candidate interviewed via Skype than in face-to-face

settings.[39] Think about the following questions and share your answers with a classmate.

1. How do you adapt to online interviews where you can see and hear each other versus the old way of listening to and observing responses in person?

2. How do you think an employer adapts to Zoom or GoToMeeting interview information versus the traditional face-to-face interview?

3. What problems do you see when you listen to what is *not* being said during online communication?

4. Does the Internet keep us from stereotyping people, or does it make us more likely to stereotype? Why do you think as you do?

⟩ SUMMARY

The Importance of Effective Listening

7.1 **Describe** how listening helps you make connections with others in all aspects of your life.

Listening is relational; that is, it depends on two or more people interacting with each other and simultaneously being a sender and receiver. Effective listening is required in all aspects of our lives.

Effective Listening

7.2 **Explain** the complex nature of listening as a cognitive process.

The listening process is composed of five interrelated aspects, plus remembering, attention and focus, and thinking preferences; there is a listening-thinking connection that incorporates thinking and *information processing*.

- The Harfield Cognitive Listening Model (HCLM) illustrates the complex process of listening.
- The HCLM links listening and thinking to examine and understand listening as a cognitive construct.
- Accurate reception of sounds requires the listener to focus attention on the speaker, discriminate among sounds, and concentrate.
- We know that past experience plays an important role and that you relate and compare new sounds and ideas to those you have previously heard.
- If the topic seems more relevant, people will remember slightly more than if it seems irrelevant.
- Memory or *remembering* is a more critical component of the listening process than previous research suggests.
- In the *interpreting* stage, the listener simply tries to make sense of the information received.
- In the *evaluating* stage, the listener analyzes evidence, sorts fact from opinion, determines the intent of the speaker, judges the accuracy of the speaker's statements and conclusions, and judges the accuracy of personal conclusions.
- *Responding* is the listener's overt behavior that indicates to the speaker what has and has not been received.

The Functions of Listening

7.3 **Differentiate** among three functions of listening behavior.

We listen to obtain information, to evaluate, to be entertained, and to be empathic with others.

Barriers to Effective Listening

7.4 **Select** specific attitudes and behaviors to help you overcome your barriers to listening.

We can use cognitive, affective, and behavioral strategies to help us be better listeners. We need to learn ways to overcome both internal and external interference to listening.

- The listener must stay involved in the message and not be distracted by the speaker or the speaker's attire or behaviors.
- Competent listeners focus on the main or most important ideas, not on every single word.
- We need concentration and energy to overcome the temptation to ignore or avoid what seems difficult and confusing.
- As listeners, we have the responsibility to adjust to, compensate for, or eliminate distractions and to focus on speakers and their messages, despite the competing factors from technology and the media.
- Competent listeners need to ask themselves, "Am I *really* paying attention?"
- If we give in to our biases, we limit ourselves in what we know and can do.
- Our preferred thinking can create barriers in the listening process from the perspective of giving or receiving information.

Critical Listening and Critical Thinking: Analyzing and Evaluating Messages

7.5 **Identify** instances in which you must be a critical listener/thinker.

We should always listen and think about what we hear.

- We need to be good consumers of information.
- We need to differentiate between fact and opinion.

Improve Listening Competence

7.6 **Characterize** the speech and actions of a competent listener.

All of us can become better listeners. We must recognize the importance of listening effectively, think of listening as an active behavior, and be willing to work and want to improve.

〉 DISCUSSION STARTERS

1. Why do we take listening for granted?
2. How and when is effective listening important?
3. What are the characteristics of effective listening?
4. How would you describe the listening-thinking connection?
5. Explain the role of memory in the listening process.
6. Why is listening identified as a continuous cognitive activity?
7. What can you do to improve your memory?
8. Why is it important to understand the different functions of listening?
9. Explain what it means to listen with empathy.
10. What effects, both good and bad, has technology had on listening?
11. In what ways can you use technology to help you listen more effectively?
12. Provide three guidelines to help you listen to others.

CHAPTER 8

PART 2 CONNECTING IN THE PUBLIC AND RELATIONAL CONTEXTS

SELECTING A TOPIC AND CONNECTING TO THE AUDIENCE

Astrakan Images / Alamy Stock Photo

People are often faced with choosing a topic for a speech that will connect with their listeners. Effective speakers know that topics of current or future relevance will best help them make those connections.

→ CHAPTER OUTLINE AND LEARNING OBJECTIVES

Select a Speech Topic

8.1 **Apply** the requirements to choose topics for your speeches and presentations.

Determine the General Purpose, Specific Purpose, and Thesis of a Speech

8.2 **Create** general and specific purpose statements.

Audience Analysis: Connecting with the Listeners

8.3 **Evaluate** the suitability and relevance of the topics to make better connections with the audience.

MAKING EVERYDAY CONNECTIONS

A local company posted a sales assistant position. The requirements for the successful applicant include the following: effective verbal and written communication skills, the ability to work well with others (singly and with groups), critical thinking skills, and the ability to handle a number of projects during each day. Some days the sales assistant will also make presentations about the company to local groups and organizations. Successful communication is critical in all work areas.[1] A late 2014 survey discovered that "employers want new hires with technical knowledge related to the job" but indicated that's not nearly as important as good teamwork and decision-making and communication skills.[2]

Communication skills are as critical in the workplace as in the classroom. People make many presentations in their lives. Here are some examples some alums have shared:

- Lacey presented new job request formatting in her area for her coworkers in a John Deere plant.
- Kelly gave a presentation to the patients in the medical clinic where she works, on the new reporting procedures that affect them.
- Zach provided information about new stocking procedures with the new technology Kohl's implemented to save time and allow staff members to spend more time with customers.
- Josh, a Boy Scout troop leader, shared information about the new standards for badges.

These former students prepared for public communication events, even though each event was labeled as work.

The ability to give effective presentations in classes, organizations, residence hall meetings, sports team meetings, government campaigns, political demonstrations, or other events on and off campus is critical. In such instances, the speaker is the central focus of a listener's attention. The ability to communicate is one of the most important skills a person can possess. Public speaking and listening are two vital forms of communication. Beginning public communicators frequently express two concerns: fear of speaking in front of others, and fear they have nothing worthwhile to say. Both of these concerns will be discussed in detail in this part of the text.

What you learn about and apply toward making effective presentations will help for the rest of your life. The speech-making process will help you develop researching, organizing, listening, and thinking skills for both oral and written communication. In addition, these skills will help you gain self-confidence.

QUESTIONS TO THINK ABOUT

1. In school and in jobs, when have *you* made formal presentations? Informal presentations?
2. Identify topics you enjoy sharing.
3. When you have a choice about presentations or papers, where do you begin?
4. What do you know about your listeners in this class that will help you select a relevant topic *you* like?
5. What most concerns you about choosing a topic for your presentations?

Students often complain when they have to give speeches in class because they know they will never give one outside the classroom. Communication professors suggest, even though we've all been talking for a number of years, talking does not equate to effective communication. What some of these students fail to consider is public communication involves more than giving speeches and more than just talking. We frequently make many presentations of all types. As you read in the Making Everyday Connections feature above, employers prefer to hire effective communicators. This section of the text is designed to help you become a more effective and competent public communicator.

Topic selection is important in communication and English classes (and in situations at work or in the community, as well). Dr. Jesse Swan, a University of Northern Iowa professor of language and literature, talks with students about how to choose a topic for their class papers, he says, "I firmly tell them the topic comes from a very personal perspective."[3] In other words, whether you pick a topic for a speech or a paper in your classes, it must be something personal and yet important, as well as relevant to the assignment and the situation.

It is never too early to start thinking about the speech situation, the topic, and how it serves the needs of your listeners. Your task is to choose a topic of personal interest, one your listeners can connect with as well as one you'll enjoy learning more about and sharing.

Although we don't want people to make cookie-cutter speeches, established principles and guidelines of public communication help people prepare for the numerous times they *will* give speeches. Although you might never be a public speaker, you can expect to give speeches on the job, in social organizations, in your place of worship, in the courtroom, and in the classroom. At some time, almost all of us are called on to "give a presentation or a speech." We may even be called upon to create a webinar, give an online training session, or both present and evaluate online speeches or interviews.

Select a Speech Topic

8.1 **Apply** the requirements to choose topics for your speeches and presentations.

Public speaking is the art of effective oral communication with an audience.[4] Topic selection is the first step in speech preparation. In these chapters on public communication, you will read about topics presented in a variety of classroom, business, and professional situations. The choice of topics is often prompted by the situation itself, the needs of others, and the position and qualifications of the speaker. Careful selection of a topic appropriate to the situation and suitable for you requires thought and a systematic approach.

public speaking
The art of effective oral communication with an audience.

Select an Appropriate Topic

Many factors contribute to an effective speech presentation, including research, organization, wording, and delivery, but none is more important than selecting an appropriate topic. The topic and your interest and motivation as you develop and move through the process for the presentation are vital to your success as a speaker. The best topic for you, your audience, and the assignment isn't always easy to determine.

Beginning speakers are often concerned they won't be able to think of a good topic. If you read Web and print sources, get news and weather updates on your phone, receive Google alerts, or watch television, you are exposed to a variety of stimulating and interesting topics from a broad range of issues. When a topic is not assigned by the instructor, the trick is to identify a topic that matches *your* interests and qualifications, the interests and existing knowledge of your audience, and the requirements of the assignment. If you are vitally concerned about the topic and enthusiastically share it with others, your concerns can be drastically reduced.

MAKING CONNECTIONS FOR SUCCESS
Reflections on Memorable Presentations

Many of your classes require papers, and speeches or presentations. In most beginning communication classes, you are likely to make three or more formal presentations and several informal presentations. For each, you'll need to choose a topic; complete research; organize the information; and prepare, practice, and present speeches in front of your classmates and instructor. While this may seem frightening, it's a common experience for all of us, and this textbook and course are designed to help you through the process. Take a few minutes to reflect on public communication in your life by answering the following questions. If the opportunity presents itself, share your reflections with others.

1. Identify memorable speeches or presentations you've heard.
2. What made the presentation memorable, *content* or the *presentation*? Why?
3. What specific ideas do you remember?
4. What makes a topic enjoyable to you as a listener?
5. How do you respond when the speaker involves you?
6. Describe previous experiences with either a formal or an informal presentation. Explain how you chose the topic and then prepared for your presentation.

Hill Street Studios/Blend Images/Getty Images

Many factors contribute to an effective speech presentation, including research, organization, wording, and delivery, but none is more important than selecting an appropriate topic. The topic and your interest and motivation in developing and presenting it are vital to your success as a speaker.

self-inventory

A list of subjects that you know about and find interesting.

Techniques for Finding a Topic

If you have difficulty thinking of interesting subjects, some of the following techniques might help you: *self-inventory, brainstorming, reviewing the current media, engaging with social media,* and *conducting an Internet search.* All five techniques will generate a wide range of possible topics from which you can then select the most appropriate.

Self-Inventory   A **self-inventory** is a list of subjects you know about and find interesting. The list might include books and newspaper articles you've read; television shows you watch; TED Talks or YouTube clips; hobbies you enjoy; sports you participate in; and community, state, regional, national, or international issues of concern. Here are some sample topics for how to prepare your own self-inventory:

Books, Articles, Music, Web Sources, Movies You Should See

Barnes and Noble's Top 100 Books of 2017
Do video games incite violence?
How Oscar-winning movies affect our view of society

Technology/Media

iTouch, Nook, Kindle, eReaders, the iPad—What's next?
Social issues and YouTube
Social media: Facebook, LinkedIn, Twitter—Where do we go from here?

Campus/Community Issues

How to avoid staggering college debt
Why are tuition rates rising?
A student internship can enhance your hiring chances

Regional, National, International

Cyberbullying creates a toxic environment
Financial crises and their effect on the world
How strong weather patterns are formed

Hobbies/Personal

Pinterest posts can affect your behavior
Fantasy sports
Is reading dead?

Sports/Recreation

Walking is still a good way to balance work and health
What is the most effective fitness strategy?
Meditating to de-stress

Health Issues

Obesity and other medical issues and their effect on college students
Exercise and portion control can help you stay fit
Nutrition for good health
The opioid crisis

Another self-inventory technique involves listing broad categories and then narrowing them down to specific examples. If you are interested in the environment, here

Your Own Self-Inventory

We previously suggested a self-inventory as a place to start thinking about the kinds of topics you might choose for your speeches. Supply as many items as you can for each of the categories in this self-inventory. Then examine each item to determine whether it could be an appropriate speech for you, the audience, and the situation.

Media Sources/Books/Music/Movies

_____

_____

Hobbies/Interests

_____

_____

Local/State/Regional/National/International Events or Issues

_____

_____

Special Events on Campus or in the Community

_____

_____

Pet Peeves/Personal Causes

_____

_____

Health/Exercise/Nutrition Ideas

_____

_____

People We Should Know

_____

_____

Sports/Recreation/Activities

_____

_____

Notable Inventions/Products/Objects

_____

_____

Reflection

1. Which of the categories most interests you? Why?

2. Which specific topics would you avoid? Why?

3. What other categories would you pursue?

Share in class what you learned about personal topics from this exercise.

---

are some possibilities:

> **Environmental Issues**
> Climate change
> Dwindling water supplies
> Water consumption
> Water economy and you
> How you can economize on water use to save a precious resource

The category of environmental issues was narrowed to a specific area: how you can economize on water use to save a precious resource.

Brainstorming   Another useful way to select a topic is through brainstorming. **Brainstorming** is a technique used to generate as many ideas as possible within a limited amount of time. Set aside a short period (5 minutes) for intensive concentration and list all the ideas that come to mind as topics. To keep things simple, write key words or phrases only. Don't stop to think about whether the ideas are good or bad. The goal of brainstorming is to generate many ideas, so every word or phrase is appropriate. You could also search YouTube, Twitter, or other social media sources to generate possible topics. "Making Connections for Success: Social Media Research" features one approach.

brainstorming

A technique used to generate as many ideas as possible within a limited amount of time. These ideas can be used to produce topics, information, or solutions to problems.

After listing as many ideas as you can, select those that appeal to you. Then have another brainstorming session to list more ideas related to them. For example, the term *education* could serve as the springboard for an entirely new list:

- Distance learning
- Online classes
- Online classes for nontraditional, special needs, or home-schooled students
- Online degrees
- Rising rates of tuition and fees
- Mandatory community service for K–12 or college classes

MAKING CONNECTIONS FOR SUCCESS

Brainstorming

Brainstorming can be an effective tool to help you find an appropriate topic for your speeches. Use brainstorming to generate topics you might use for your next informative speech. Take 5 minutes and write down whatever ideas come to mind; do not stop to evaluate them. Then look over your list and select appealing terms. Next, brainstorm for another 5 minutes, and list topics related to your shorter list. Look at the list and follow these steps:

1. Determine the criteria to choose the *best* topic for your presentation.
2. Apply those criteria to the topics you've generated.
3. Use the criteria you established to determine the topic you will use.

Compare and contrast the criteria you listed for selecting the best topic with the criteria provided in this chapter.

With a little effort, brainstorming will help you generate a number of potential topics in a short time. And the process can be repeated until you find a suitable topic.

Review the Current Media   A third way to generate topic ideas involves the popular media. While Google made a world of information available to us, and YouTube gives us both information and entertainment, there are other sources that help you find topics. We'll look at Internet sources later. Older, but helpful media sources include newspapers, books, magazines, television, and movies. **Reviewing the current media** is an effective way to develop a list of potential topics. Consider sources such as documentaries, news specials, cable channel programs, and even regular programming. *The Readers' Guide to Periodical Literature* is a source of hundreds of up-to-date topics. For example, you can find listings of articles on technology, education, finance, government, marketing, terrorism, crime, air safety, health, television violence, technology, and entertainment.

Engage with Social Media and TED   Most of us are familiar with the popularity of Instagram, Pinterest, Twitter, Snapchat, Facebook, and blogs where users create online communities to share information, ideas, personal messages, and other content and thus turn written communication into interactive dialogue among individuals and organizations.[5] Any of the social media outlets just listed can provide possible topics and sources of information. One special website where people are invited to discuss current issues and respond to those on the site is TED (www.ted.com/talks). TED is an excellent idea generator, as well as a source for current speakers' expertise on newsworthy topics. TED is a nonprofit devoted to "ideas worth spreading." It started in 1984 as a conference bringing together people from three worlds: *t* Technology, *e* Entertainment, and *d* Design. The group holds two annual conferences in Long Beach and Palm Springs, California, each spring and the TED Global conference in Edinburgh, United Kingdom, each summer. Currently, nearly 3,000 talks are available, ranging from language to deep ocean organisms. Many colleges and schools now provide TED educational talks as well and give you an idea of interesting topics by students and professors. Browsing through the available talks might give you both a topic and a source. It is reported it takes three days to create the TED Talks presentations. Is it a surprise, then, that your instructors recommend a careful research and preparation process?

A caution should be noted about using any media to generate speech topics. Some beginning speakers have a tendency to rely on one media source for the entire speech. A summary of an interesting article or movie is not acceptable for most classroom speaking assignments. Though an excellent source for potential topics, each medium is only *one starting point* from which to build.[6] The content must be adapted to suit you and your specific audience, and most classroom assignments require a variety of sources. You should always bring something new to your topic—a fresh insight or an application suitable to the speaking situation.

reviewing the current media

A technique for developing a list of possible topics by looking at current publications, television, movies, and other forms of public communication.

MAKING CONNECTIONS FOR SUCCESS
Social Media Research

Most of us use social media. Do you want to fly somewhere for spring break? Travelocity, Orbitz, Kayak, CheapFares, Trivago, or individual airline websites allow you to find the least expensive fares. Your phone helps you plan trips and gives directions to get you there. Businesses use Facebook posts to generate sales, but Facebook can also be a source of ideas for speeches. If you're interested in food recipes and preparation, thousands of sites provide anything you want or need to know. If you want to find movie clips, try Hulu. YouTube clips provide an infinite range of possibilities, from entertainment to politics and everything in between.

We can use the web not only to find information but also to help us choose topics for our presentations. Try the following exercise:

1. Take a minute to brainstorm 10 topics in which you have some interest, already know something about, or about which you want to learn something more.
2. Choose five of the most interesting.

3. Access a search engine you have not used before or one that is relatively unfamiliar (e.g., Dogpile, http://www.dogpile.com; or DuckDuckGo, http://www.duckduckgo.com). Click on the help area or the icon that informs your effective search. Key in the words of your first topic. How many hits did you get? What does this number tell you?
4. Check the first 10 hits: scroll through the list and read those responses. Pick the most interesting one. Carefully read and evaluate that site. You want current, objective information from credible sources. How do you know if this source is trustworthy?
5. Does this topic seem like a good one? If so, pursue it further. If not, go back to the next most interesting topic and repeat the process.

This combination of personal brainstorming and web surfing helps you find topics with adequate information. This process uses the web to help you choose a topic that your web research reveals has adequate information.

Conduct An Internet Search The rapid development of technology, the ever-increasing number of websites, and the amount of new information on the web provide unique opportunities for students in a speech communication class. Use of one or more of the many available search engines provides unique topics and sources of information on any topic. Because information is often not reviewed and accepted by experts or authorities on the subject before it is placed on a web page, and because anyone who knows how to put a web page together can put data online, students need to carefully evaluate both the information presented and its source. Internet research is further discussed in the chapter on gathering and using information. (Also review Chapter 6 for social media and new technologies information.) For now, remember to look at who put the information on the website: What are their credentials? Are they trustworthy? When was it posted? Is the information objective rather than subjective? How current is it? How do you know?

How you find your topic is not the critical issue. What *is* important is that you begin your search as soon as possible. Over the years we've asked successful students about their topic search and one common factor emerges: They start looking for a topic as soon as they receive the assignment. Students who delay always have more difficulty finding an appropriate topic. Whenever you find something you think might be a good idea, write it down. The more ideas you accumulate, the easier your job of selecting a good topic will be. In addition, the earlier you choose your topic, the more time you will have to research, prepare, and practice your speech.

Assess the Appropriateness of a Topic

Once you have identified a possible topic, the next step is to determine whether it is appropriate for you, your assignment, and your audience. Ask yourself these questions:

1. Does the topic merit the listeners' attention?
2. Will the audience see a connection between you and the topic and a personal connection to the topic?

3. Will the topic meet the objectives of the assignment?
4. Does the audience have sufficient knowledge and background to understand the topic?
5. Can you make the topic understandable to everyone in the audience?
6. Is the topic of sufficient interest to you that you will be motivated to present it effectively?
7. Do you have adequate knowledge of the topic?
8. If you are not already familiar with the topic, will you be able to learn enough about it to give an informed speech?
9. Is the topic appropriate for the class assignment and situation?

If you've answered no to any of these questions, return to the search techniques to find a topic.

Narrow the Topic

Once you determine an appropriate topic, the next step is to decide whether it is narrow enough to fit the time limit and accomplish the goal of the assignment. This step can save you much time and trouble because a well-focused topic is much easier to research than one that is too general. For example, you could work for months on a speech titled "How to Create an Effective Portfolio" and still not exhaustively cover all the information. If you restrict the scope to the most important points to cover, materials to include, and the language to present strengths succinctly and effectively, you have more time to develop ideas in the speech. You could narrow the topic even further

Guidelines

SELECT AN APPROPRIATE TOPIC

1. **Choose a meaningful topic.** The more meaningful a topic, the more likely you are to put the necessary time and effort to research and develop your speech. The stronger your commitment to a topic, the more enthusiastically you will present it. A speaker's commitment to a topic usually transfers to the audience members and gets them involved. Audience involvement in a topic can be an effective gauge of your success as a speaker. The reason for giving a speech, besides completing the assignment, is to gain your listeners' attention; this is more easily accomplished if *you* consider the topic important.

2. **Choose a topic that allows you to convey an important or relevant thought to your audience.** The thought does not have to be a matter of extreme urgency, but it should at least be relevant to your listeners' interests, have some direct effect on them, or be something that you believe listeners should know. Ask yourself the following questions:

   - Will listeners want to learn more about the topic?
   - Will listeners believe the topic is relevant?
   - Will listeners be affected in some way by the topic, either now or in the future?
   - Will listeners benefit from listening to a presentation on the topic?

   - Will listeners believe you are a credible speaker on the topic?

   If you can answer yes to each of these questions, you are on your way to selecting an appropriate topic.

3. **Choose a familiar and/or interesting topic.** This will make the development and delivery of your speech easier and more enjoyable. Some knowledge of taking effective photos with your smartphone or other device might lead to a speech on how to take better photos with a camera or a smartphone. You may enjoy selecting a topic in which you are interested but about which you know little. For example, you might be intrigued by the idea of meditation as stress relief but do not know the exact procedures involved or the issues surrounding it, so your research allows you to learn and share that kind of information. Choosing an interesting topic increases the likelihood of audience attentiveness and speaker credibility. (We discuss speaker credibility in Chapter 12.)

4. **Think like a listener.** Evaluate your topic as though you were the listener. If you focus your attention on what listeners like and want to hear about this topic you know and enjoy, you are well on your way to choosing an interesting, informative, relevant, and potentially useful topic. What will listeners gain from your presentation?

by choosing how to include examples of work that demonstrate strengths for specific jobs. When you narrow your topic, you increase its potential depth, but make sure you have enough developed information to meet the requirements for your presentation.

The more abstract the topic, the more important it is to narrow it to meet the constraints of the speech situation. Let's say you have an assignment for a 10-minute speech on a concept about which you wish to gain more information for yourself and your listeners. You think holidays would be a good topic. Obviously, you cannot address all holidays in 10 minutes. So you narrow the topic to "cultural holidays." There is still an abundance of information, far too much to cover. You decide to focus on the "cultural holidays of my hometown." This is still too broad, so you narrow it to one specific holiday, "St. Patrick's Day in O'Neill, Nebraska."

This continual narrowing allows you to focus your research and content development on a more clearly defined area of the topic. This will be helpful to the speaker, as well as to listeners, because you will present more substance on an important concept. Speakers can narrow the scope of a subject according to the time limits, function, goals, location, and requirements of a specific topic. Narrowing the topic is a skill critical to your success as a communicator not only in the classroom but also in the workplace and in any organizations where you may make presentations.

Determine the General Purpose, Specific Purpose, and Thesis of a Speech

8.2 **Create** general and specific purpose statements.

Once you have chosen and narrowed your topic, you need to start thinking about how the final presentation will be structured. Speakers should begin their preparation with a clear idea of the general purpose, the specific purpose, and a focused thesis statement. In this section, we briefly discuss each of these concepts. Chapter 12 provides in-depth coverage of informative and persuasive speaking.

The General Purpose

The **general purpose**, or overall goal, of a speech is usually to perform one of three overlapping functions: *to inform, to persuade,* or *to entertain*. A speech rarely serves only one function. Even though most classroom speech assignments are intended to emphasize a single function, the speeches themselves may contain aspects of all three functions. For example, a speech about duct tape art is meant to inform, but the speech may contain some persuasive and entertaining elements as well. If you are assigned an informative or expository speech, however, you need to think carefully about how to organize and present ideas to your listeners. If the general purpose is to inform your audience, you should emphasize presentation of information about a new, interesting, and potentially useful and relevant topic.

general purpose
The overall goal of a speech, usually one of three overlapping functions: to inform, to persuade, or to entertain.

For classroom speaking assignments, your general purpose is usually specified by the instructor, but for speeches outside the classroom, the occasion, what the audience knows or doesn't know about your topic, and how you want the audience to respond will determine whether you speak primarily to inform, to persuade, or to entertain.

The speaking goal is usually designed to affect the listeners in some purposeful way. The reaction of the listeners determines whether your speech has accomplished its purpose successfully.

Informative Speeches   When the general purpose of your speech is to inform, you are expected to convey your knowledge of a particular subject. An **informative speech** enhances an audience's knowledge and understanding by explaining what something means, how something works, or how something is done. According to the

informative speech
A speech that enhances an audience's knowledge and understanding by explaining what something means, how something works, or how something is done.

"Writing Guide: Informative Speaking" at Colorado State University, "The purpose of the informative speech is to provide interesting, useful, and unique information to your audience."[7] The goal is to clearly and accurately share information and make the learning experience as enjoyable as possible for the audience.

Whether you describe how to protect yourself during an assault, discuss a proposed regulation to restrict the number of people allowed in rental houses, explain the differences among social networking sites, or report the university's proposal to honor diversity on campus, you should assume that most of your audience does not already know *all* the information you plan to present. The content of the speech depends heavily on what you think the audience knows and on how much you know or are able to learn about the topic. Your task as a speaker is to provide more information than the audience would normally get from reading an article, reading a web source, or listening to the news.

When a topic is controversial—for example, "foreign government interference in U.S. elections"—speakers whose general purpose is to inform should not take sides; instead, they might choose to provide background on what is involved in foreign government interference, what it is, and its purpose. The informative speaker might identify the pros and cons but will not take a stand. The speaker presents the information and lets the listeners draw their own conclusions.

persuasive speech

A speech that attempts to change listeners' attitudes or behaviors by advocating for or trying to gain acceptance of the speaker's point of view.

Persuasive Speeches   A **persuasive speech** attempts to change listeners' beliefs, attitudes, or behaviors by advocating or trying to gain acceptance of an idea or point of view. When speakers try to convince audience members to endorse a program to limit the damage caused by Instagram posts denigrating cultural diversity on campus, or ask citizens to petition for traffic roundabouts in high-traffic zones, or to accept that ethical behavior in the United States is on the decline, they are attempting to persuade. Speakers must present evidence and arguments to justify their positions and to win the audience over to their point of view. Be advised: Persuasion is difficult. You only have a few minutes to try to get your listeners to think about your position, and most people are not persuaded in a one-shot presentation. Choose a topic and present it so that you get your listeners to at least consider your view. You probably will not change anyone's mind too much, but if you think of your speech as the first step in getting listeners to think about your perspective on the topic, you will have succeeded.

The difference between informing and persuading is not always clear-cut. Your goal is persuasion when you try to convince your parents to loan you money for the latest iPhone. However, your message contains both informative and persuasive elements: informing them about the circumstances and your need for the latest iPhone, and convincing them that they should loan you the money to purchase it. They may accept your reasons and agree that you need it, but they still might not loan you the money. In this example, the persuasive purpose is not only to inform and convince your parents that you need the latest iPhone and the money to buy it but also to persuade them to take action—to loan you the money you need. Information is a necessary part of a persuasive speech, but the ultimate goal is action. Once your parents loan you the money, you have achieved your purpose.

While the focus of an informative speech is to convey information and understanding by explaining, reporting, or demonstrating your point of view, the purpose of a persuasive speech is to change beliefs or attitudes or motivate listeners to act in a specific manner. The action might be to think, respond, or behave in a certain way. The purpose might be to eat organic foods for better health, place greater societal emphasis on ethics, volunteer at the local food bank, or support greater campus entertainment opportunities.

The important and necessary ingredient that makes persuasion different from information is the action (to think, to respond, to behave) the speaker wants the listener to take as a result of the message presented. The informative speech provides knowledge about a topic, whereas the persuasive speech provides information *and* a direction or course of action.

Entertainment Speeches   An **entertainment speech** provides enjoyment and amusement. Speeches to entertain may be dramatic or humorous and often occur on special occasions, such as weddings, retirements, after a dinner, or at a roast. A speech to entertain generally has three key qualities: It is light, original, and appropriate to the situation. An appropriate speech does not offend the sensibilities of the audience. The speaker may use humor but not at the expense of the audience's sense of values or ethics. Effective speakers do not use offensive language or potentially offensive jokes or situations.

Entertainment is often the general purpose of special occasion speeches, including toasts given at weddings and other special events. A speech to entertain should be light, use humor, and meet the guidelines of etiquette and good sense. Wedding toasts are examples of brief speeches to entertain.

entertainment speech

A speech that provides enjoyment and amusement.

Audience members, unlike television or web viewers, are a captive audience and cannot click the mouse or remote to switch off offensive words or ideas. The speaker must use tasteful examples and stories that will not hurt anyone's feelings or violate listeners' ethical principles.

In using humor, the speaker may create imaginative illustrations and figures of speech, twist meanings, tell amusing stories, create amusing character sketches, or tell jokes—all with the willing participation of the audience and in the spirit of the occasion. This does not mean, however, that an entertaining speech cannot be both informative and persuasive or that informative and persuasive speeches cannot be entertaining. What distinguishes these three kinds of speeches is the function (informing, persuading, or entertaining) on which the speaker places the most emphasis. Therefore, the entertaining speech should leave the audience members feeling amused or entertained.

Your instructor may also require special occasion speeches, such as elevator speeches, introductions of speakers, congratulatory speeches, tributes, or eulogies. The specifics vary for each type, so listen carefully when directions are provided.

The Specific Purpose

The general purpose of a speech (to inform, to persuade, or to entertain) provides direction for its content. Once you have determined your general purpose, you are ready to determine your specific purpose. A **specific purpose** is a single phrase that defines precisely what you intend to accomplish in your speech. Jenna chose *ethnocentrism in Iowa* for her topic. Her specific purpose was "to inform my classmates of three major ways ethnocentrism is prevalent in Iowa." The clear and concise statement tells exactly what the speaker intends to do and what she wants her audience to know.

specific purpose

A single phrase that defines precisely what is to be accomplished in a speech.

An effective specific purpose identifies (1) the general purpose of the speech, (2) the audience, and (3) the exact topic to be covered. These three pieces of significant information help the speaker develop and deliver the speech. The specific purpose also identifies the audience, which is important, because different audiences may require different information. For example, if a speech is to be presented to children only, to adults only, or to both children and adults, the content will have to be adjusted to fit the particular group. Thus, even though the general and specific purposes are the same, the content of the speech will vary depending on the listeners' backgrounds, knowledge, and attitudes toward the topic.

The careful writing of a specific purpose is important to all aspects of planning and developing a successful speech. The box entitled "Guidelines: Specific Purpose" should help you write an effective specific purpose.

Formulating effective general and specific purposes makes it easier to develop your speech. They will guide your thinking and planning. You should be ready to reconsider your specific purpose, however, throughout the development stages of the speech. As you research a topic, you might find information that leads you to revise your thinking. Or you might learn something about your audience members that will convince you to adjust your specific purpose to their needs.

When speakers know the general and specific purposes of the speech, the thesis, and information about the audience to tailor the content to them, they will more likely be perceived as effective speakers and the audience will be actively involved in the speech.

The Thesis

The specific purpose of your speech states what you wish to accomplish or how you wish to affect your audience. It also serves as the foundation for the thesis of the speech. The **thesis** is a sentence that states specifically what is going to be discussed in a speech. For example, the specific purpose, "to explain to my audience the three advantages of using Prezi as a presentational aid," tells what the speaker wants to do but does not describe the content of the speech. A thesis concisely states the content: "Prezi is easier, it saves time, and it is enjoyable for both presenters and audience members." This clearly worded statement precisely identifies the three advantages of Prezi as a presentational aid. Some communication professors see the thesis as an argument they present for why the topic is important, thus, why audience members should listen and consider it.

thesis
A sentence that states specifically what is going to be discussed in a speech.

Guidelines

SPECIFIC PURPOSE

1. **The specific purpose should include a verb form that describes the general purpose of the speech.** The inclusion of the verb form clarifies the action the speaker hopes to accomplish.

   Ineffective: To inform my audience about meditation.
   Effective: To inform my audience of the three effects of meditation in reducing stress.

2. **The specific purpose should be limited to one distinct thought or idea.** The following ineffective statement is too long and contains more than one subject. An entire speech could be developed around either area. It is best to select only one idea and refine it as the purpose for the speech.

   Ineffective: To persuade my audience about the three effects of alcohol and the four ways to prevent binge drinking by college students.
   Effective: To persuade my audience to promote four ways to prevent binge drinking by college students.

3. **The specific purpose should not be a question.** Although a question may indicate the topic, it fails to specify the general purpose of the speech.

   Ineffective: What historical events have become the basis for blockbuster movies?
   Effective: To inform my audience about three blockbuster movies based on historical events.

4. **The specific purpose should be concise and carefully worded.** The ineffective statement given here tries to cover too much material, is too general, and does not state clearly what is to be achieved by the speech.

   Ineffective: Technology has enhanced every aspect of our lives.
   Effective: To inform the audience that technologies have enhanced the ability to connect with friends and family members anywhere at any time.

Phil Boorman/Cultura/Getty Images

If the specific purpose is "to persuade the audience to petition the College Hill Neighborhood Association to resist the reduced number of rental houses in the neighborhood because it harms students," the thesis might be written as follows: "The suggested restrictions for house rentals will significantly harm UNI students and their ability to find housing near the university, it will make traffic more congested, and there will be fewer open parking spots on campus due to the greater distances traveled to campus." The thesis gives the three main ideas the speaker will discuss: (1) the restrictions limit students' ability to find housing near the university, (2) the result will mean increased traffic congestion on campus, and (3) there will be even fewer parking spots on campus. In summary, the thesis should be expressed as a full sentence, should not be in the form of a question, and should be clearly and concisely worded.

Here are two examples showing the relationship of a topic to the general purpose, specific purpose, and thesis:

TOPIC:	Inexpensive, renewable energy
GENERAL PURPOSE:	To inform
SPECIFIC PURPOSE:	To inform my audience about wind as an energy source
THESIS:	Wind is an inexpensive, easily accessible, renewable energy source.
TOPIC:	Stress reduction through meditation
GENERAL PURPOSE:	To persuade
SPECIFIC PURPOSE:	To persuade my audience that meditation should be taught to help students deal with stress.
THESIS:	I will demonstrate the need to incorporate teaching meditation in wellness classes and in residence halls as a way for students to destress.

You can easily see in these examples how a broad topic area is narrowed as the speaker moves from the specific purpose to the thesis. This procedure is a crucial step in preparing a speech to meet requirements.

Audience Analysis: Connecting with the Listeners

 Evaluate the suitability and relevance of the topics to make better connections with the audience.

Selecting a topic, narrowing it, choosing a specific purpose, and creating a clear thesis statement so that you can connect your speech to the specific listeners in your audience require careful thinking as well as knowledge and understanding of your audience. The development of ideas requires similar understanding and knowledge. Therefore, the speaker needs specific information about the listeners. You have now probably spent several weeks with the people in your communication class. It is likely that each of you responded to the activities and class discussions. What people say, how they act, and their nonverbal communication have helped you form impressions of your classmates. Those impressions are important, but you might need additional information to do a good job of connecting with your audience. Because this is so critical to a speaker's success, the remainder of this chapter examines the audience's point of view, kinds of audience members, key information to gain about audiences, methods for researching audiences, and adapting your speech to an audience.

Audience analysis is the collection and interpretation of data about characteristics, attitudes, values, and beliefs of an audience. Analyzing the audience is an essential step in developing and delivering a speech. An audience becomes actively involved in a speech and reacts to the speaker, the subject, what is said, how it is said,

audience analysis

The collection and interpretation of data about characteristics, attitudes, values, and beliefs of an audience.

other audience members, and the situation. The more speakers know about the audience, the better they can adapt their speeches accordingly.

Understand the Listeners' Point of View

For our purposes, the **audience** refers to the collection of individuals who come together to watch or listen to a speech. The individuals may become part of the audience for a variety of reasons. Each individual may have several motives, and the audience members may come from many different backgrounds. Members of the hosting organization may attend only because they are loyal to and wish to support the group.

The reason individuals come together to form an audience is an important point for the speaker to consider. If people join an audience because they wish to listen to a speech, it is reasonable to assume that they also want to hear something meaningful. Most individuals ask the same basic questions about their involvement in an audience: "What's in this for me?"

This question suggests that your audience will judge what they hear on the basis of their past experiences and the relevance of the information presented. The more you know about your audience (past experiences, knowledge of the subject, relationship to the subject, and reason for being there), the easier it will be to develop a meaningful speech. For example, imagine that you are an expert on sustainability and prairie plants in agriculture and are asked to give a speech. You decide to title the speech "Assessing the Wildlife Habitat Value of Diverse Prairie Plantings." You have spent many hours getting ready for the speech and are now prepared to present it. Are you really prepared? Have you thought about the members of your audience? Who are they? What do they know about fundraising? What is their attitude toward sustainability issues? Would you present the same information to biologists, to a group of environmentalists, to students in a public relations class at your college, or to a mixed group of citizens in the community? What results would you expect if you used the same approach for all four audiences? What results would you expect if you varied your approaches? The questions and answers are essential for an effective presentation.

Captive versus Voluntary Participants

Many kinds of people listen to speeches for various reasons, but all are either captive or voluntary participants. Audience members required to listen to a particular speech are called **captive participants**. They may happen to want to hear the speech, but they have no choice but to attend. Some people may resist participation more than others.

Even though few circumstances force a person to be part of an audience, some situations demand attendance to avoid a penalty. For example, your teacher requires attendance during speech presentations, an employer requires employees to attend new product demonstrations, or a military leader orders troops to attend lectures on military maneuvers. In such situations, audience members cannot be absent and cannot leave without being noticed or penalized for doing so. To be effective, a speaker must recognize when he or she is dealing with captive participants.

In contrast to captive participants, **voluntary participants** choose to hear a particular speech because of interest or need. True volunteers attend because of the speaker, the occasion, the topic, or what they expect to hear. There is no other motivation or force behind their presence.

audience
The collection of individuals who have come together to watch or listen to someone or something, such as to listen to a speech.

captive participant
A person who is required to hear a particular speech.

voluntary participant
A person who chooses to listen to a particular speech.

Oprah Winfrey gave a eulogy for Rosa Parks. Most people in the audience already knew Ms. Parks and her contributions to the civil rights movement. What audience considerations might have influenced Oprah's speech about Rosa Parks?

Manuel Balce Ceneta / AP images

Key Audience Information

You should gather two kinds of information about your prospective audience: demographic and psychological. The more you know about your audience members, the better you will adjust to them and relate your topic to them.

Demographic Analysis   **Demographic analysis** is the collection and interpretation of basic information, such as age, gender, cultural or ethnic background, education, occupation, religion, socioeconomic status, geographical location, political affiliation, voting habits, family relationships, marital and parental status, and group memberships. The more similar the demographic characteristics of audience members, the easier it is for a speaker to adapt to listeners' needs and interests.

demographic analysis
The collection and interpretation of characteristics (age, gender, religion, occupation, and so on) of individuals, excluding values, attitudes, and beliefs.

Age   You can select a range of appropriate examples and evidence when your audience members differ in age. An age difference between the speaker and the audience can also alter what messages are presented and how they are expressed. For example, if an audience consists of only 18- to 22-year-olds, the speaker has only one age group with which to deal. If audience members range from 15 to 65 years of age, the speaker will have to take into account several age groups and make language and content choices on the basis of that wide range.

Gender   Gender, an important demographic characteristic, presents challenges. Speakers should consider the attitudes of each gender toward the other as well as the same gender attitudes. As we indicated in several places in this text, gender-based biases should be avoided. Speakers should be sensitive to potential gender-based biases—for example, referring to women as "passive" or providing examples of women only in certain careers, such as nursing or teaching. Although some topics may still be more appropriate for one gender than the other, clear-cut distinctions are becoming increasingly rare.

Cultural or Ethnic Background   Cultural or ethnic background is often not considered as thoroughly as it should be, even though a tremendous diversity of backgrounds exists in our society. Speakers should be sensitive to the different groups that may be present in their audiences. The following communication variables are culturally determined and influence the interactions of members from different ethnic and racial backgrounds:

Good of the group	Individual needs
Language usage	Rituals
Polychronic or monochronic time	Appropriate eye contact
Dealing with uncertainties	Appropriate handshakes or touch
High-context versus low-context	Traditions, cultural expectations
Use of silence	Cultural norms
Differing views of age, class, and status	

Each of these variables determines and regulates how an individual creates and interprets messages. Although the list is not exhaustive, it points out some of the important cultural and ethnic factors to consider as you plan a speech. Culture is dynamic and extremely important; culture helps define individuals in relation to the world around them. Culture is subjective. Speakers must take culture into account or they may embarrass and insult an audience and, ultimately, embarrass themselves. Speech content should not offend the values, customs, or beliefs of audience members. Learn about others' culture in order to communicate with them successfully.

Education   Although it may be impossible to find out exactly what an audience knows and understands about a specific topic, it is often possible to ascertain their general education level. Knowing whether most listeners have completed high school, college, or graduate school can help you to gauge their intellectual level and experience and to adapt your speech accordingly.

Occupation   Knowledge of audience members' occupations also tells you something about possible interest in and familiarity with some subjects. For example, professors have one view while students have another. Anyone interested in a specific topic will try to find links to her or his own interests and profession, but the speaker's knowledge of who will be listening can be helpful.

Religion   Speakers must be as sensitive to religion as they are to ethnicity. That is, they must recognize issues that touch on religious beliefs and treat them carefully. If you plan to speak on an issue that may have religious ramifications, you should evaluate how your message will affect audience members. Otherwise, you run a risk of offending or losing the attention of some or all of your audience. For example, a quotation to support your viewpoint might be more appropriately taken from the Koran than from the Bible (or, better yet, from both the Koran and the Bible) if your audience is of the Islamic faith.

Geographical Origins   Knowing your audience's geographical origins can help you adapt your speech to them. For example, people from rural communities are more likely to know and care more about agricultural topics than are those from large urban areas. People from the South might not be interested in information related to heating their homes in winter, but if they live in an oil-producing state, they might be interested in the price of a barrel of oil.

Group Membership   A group is a collection of individuals who have joined together for some common cause or purpose that may be social, professional, recreational, or charitable. When you know the special interests of individuals in your audience, you can relate your speech directly to their needs and concerns. Of course, it isn't always possible to reach every group in your audience, but by appealing to the largest group, you can create strong attention and interest. For example, a student who belonged to a sorority decided to inform her audience about sorority and fraternity functions other than social activities. Three-quarters of her student audience were not affiliated with a Greek group. Knowing this, she began her speech by talking about her thoughts on Greek organizations before she became a member. By first pointing out her reservations about such groups, she created a common understanding with her listeners. That kind of introduction would be unnecessary if three-quarters of her audience *were* affiliated with a Greek organization.

Other Demographic Factors   We earlier identified marital status, family makeup, and socioeconomic status as other possible elements of demographic analysis. This analysis provides information on listeners' priorities and interests. An awareness of socioeconomic status also supplies information about the interests of audience members and their abilities to grasp the ideas presented. More information about your listeners and what characteristics they share with you and with others promotes a better understanding of how to prepare the speech.

psychological analysis
The collection and interpretation of data about audience members' values, attitudes, and beliefs.

Psychological Analysis   **Psychological analysis** is the collection of data on audience members' values, attitudes, and beliefs. A psychological analysis seeks to determine how the audience will react to the speaker, the speaker's topic, and the surroundings in which the speech is presented. In addition to the items related to demographic analysis, a psychological analysis helps the speaker be aware of what motivates listeners to attend to the message of a particular speech. The size of the audience; the physical setting for the presentation; the knowledge level of the audience; and the attitude of the audience toward the speaker, the topic, and the situation all play vital roles in the planning, development, and delivery of a speech.

Size of Audience   The number of audience members has a considerable psychological effect on a speaking situation and strongly influences how a speech should be delivered. The larger the audience, the more difficult it is to use an informal, conversational

MAKING CONNECTIONS FOR SUCCESS
How Culture Affects the Public Speaker

Dan and Shiho discuss their upcoming assignment: a 10-minute informative speech on a topic demonstrating ethical principles. Shiho says she wants to talk about the concept of "saving face," but Dan does not understand what this expression means and how it is appropriate for the assignment. Shiho explains, "Saving face is a concept that means a person does not purposely do anything to make another lose credibility or status." Shiho says she often does not ask questions of the other students because she is aware that the questions could cause them to lose face in their own minds or in the minds of others. According to Japanese beliefs, ethical speakers and ethical listeners will not willingly cause another to lose face, nor will they willingly lose face by making a mistake.[8] Dan is fascinated and asks more questions to learn about Shiho's culture.

Each of us should be aware of cultural perspectives and how they may affect speakers and listeners in a speaking situation. Think about the cultures (or co-cultures) represented in your communication class, and then answer the following questions:

1. What values do these other cultures promote? How do you know?
2. How do the cultural values affect the way a person might respond to certain topics? Provide examples.
3. How can you increase your sensitivity and awareness of cultural perspectives?
4. What can you, as a speaker, do to adjust to different cultural values in your communication class?

speaking style. Size also affects the speaker's use of language, gestures, and visual aids. Speaking to 10 to 30 people, as in a typical classroom speech assignment, is quite different from speaking to several hundred people in an auditorium.

The size of an audience can also affect the psychological disposition of the audience members and their relationship to each other and the speaker. For example, each member of a small audience is aware of him- or herself as a unique member of the audience, and each feels a close, intimate relationship to the speaker. As the size of the audience increases, members lose their sense of identity as unique individuals and feel more distanced from the speaker. Effective speakers know this and plan their presentations to meet the requirements of each situation.

Physical Setting   In evaluating the physical setting, consider factors such as room size, ventilation, seating arrangement, lighting, speaker's platform, and potential for using visual aids. Some professional speakers require specific settings and refuse to give presentations if their conditions can't be met. Unfortunately, you do not have that choice in a classroom assignment. You can, however, assess the physical setting and take full advantage of what is available.

The seating arrangement of your audience is often predetermined, as it is in classroom settings, but sometimes a slight modification can make your presentation more effective. If you feel more comfortable out among the audience members, but have visuals or use technology, you might want to get a clicker so you can forward PowerPoint slides while you're still closer to the listeners and not standing behind the equipment. A speech communication professor was asked to address a group of 100 administrative law judges. She purposely arrived early so she could see the room and assess the speaking conditions. The seats were arranged in an immovable classroom style: The chairs were placed in uniform rows directly in front of a raised speaker's podium, on which stood a large wooden lectern with a microphone. The professor believed the setting was too formal and would inhibit her presentation, so she rearranged the area in front of the podium; thus, she moved closer to her listeners and made eye contact with everyone. These simple changes gave her presentation a more casual feeling and encouraged audience involvement.

The physical setting can also affect audience members' psychological disposition toward one another as well as toward the speaker. The more relaxed the physical setting, for example, the more open and comfortable audience members will feel in relation to

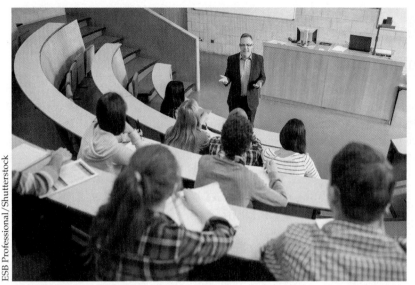

Sometimes the speaker cannot alter the physical setting, but he or she can change body position, move away from the lectern, or find other ways to better reach out to the audience, as this speaker is doing. He cannot change the seats, but he can avoid the lectern and move closer to the audience.

one another and to the speaker. The proximity of audience members to one another can also have an effect. If the audience members are scattered throughout a large meeting room, they will not have the sense of inclusion that occurs in a physical setting where the members are densely packed together. The physical closeness of other people may create a feeling of belonging to the group and help the speaker reach the audience.

Knowledge Level The extent of an audience's knowledge about a topic has a tremendous effect on the outcome of a speech. If an audience has little or no background on a topic and the speaker does not realize this, both the audience and the speaker can become frustrated. When an audience isn't ready to receive information or when the information is too technical for them to recognize, the speaker must present the material in terms everyone can understand.

A speaker must also adjust a presentation to reach a knowledgeable audience. A physician addressing a medical conference would not explain familiar medical terms. If that same physician speaks to patients and caregivers, definition of the medical terms is needed.

Even though people are apt to be more interested in subjects they know something about, an audience does not want a rehash of familiar information; they want to hear a new twist and add to their existing knowledge. For example, a student decided to present a 5-minute informative speech about the lead pencil. After interviewing his classmates, the speaker noted that they all had a similar response: "What can you

MAKING CONNECTIONS FOR SUCCESS
Connecting with the Listeners

The listeners' knowledge of the speaker strongly influences how a speech should be developed and delivered. Even people well known in their own fields or famous media personalities know they have to connect with their specific audiences. You've probably spent several weeks in this class; your instructor has provided numerous opportunities for all students to share ideas with each other, so from participation and observation, everyone in class already knows a great deal about each other. At the same time, your classmates probably do not know you extremely well. Here's how one student's first sentences helped her connect with her listeners and make a lasting impact on all who heard the speech.

> "Two years ago I was riding from the prom with my three best friends. We decided to go to Perkins before going home. None of us had been drinking, and we all enjoyed a wonderful, memorable night. Little did I know how memorable that night would be. A drunk driver, traveling at excessive speed, slammed into our car as we were turning, with the light, to go into Perkins. My friend

Lisa died upon impact. The rest of us were injured and taken by ambulance to the hospital but, luckily, had few injuries. The pain of losing Lisa will never leave me. As a result of that prom night accident, I have a new mission in life. Today, I want to share with you the reasons for the slogan, 'If you drink, don't drive.'"

The listeners were very quiet and attentive throughout the speech. As this example illustrates, sharing a personal experience helped the speaker connect with her listeners and, in turn, held their attention. Listeners will always formulate some attitude toward a speaker. Help them form one that keeps them tuned in to your presentation.

1. Identify ways other speakers have effectively connected with their listeners.
2. In what circumstances do listeners not need knowledge about the speaker as a person?
3. Create an example of an event or circumstance in your life you could use to let listeners gain more knowledge of you.

say about a lead pencil other than it is made of graphite and wood and is used for writing?" On the basis of his analysis, the student developed a creative, fascinating speech. Using a casual and entertaining style, he provided detailed information about the history of the lead pencil and its effect on society. The speech was a great success.

Attitudes and Values Related to the Topic   The audience's attitude and values as they relate to the topic are as significant as their knowledge of the speaker. If audience members do not relate to a topic, the speaker will have a difficult time getting them to listen. For instance, a student chose to speak on individual retirement accounts (IRAs) for his persuasive speech. He researched the subject thoroughly, practiced his delivery, and presented the speech in an enthusiastic manner. His audience remained cool and uninvolved. The speaker failed to consider the value the audience placed on the topic; the age of its members should have tipped him off. Saving for retirement is *not* a high priority for most college students—they're just trying to pay the bills. The speaker could have made the speech more relevant by discussing young people's indifference to retirement saving, and by convincing them to be concerned now.

Attitudes Related to the Situation   The speaker should also examine the audience's relationship to the overall situation in which the speech is presented. Why has the audience gathered? Audience members' expectations influence their attitude toward the situation, which in turn reflects on the speaker and the topic. A speaker who talks about the need to further fund Social Security to a group of 17- to 24-year-old students has chosen the wrong topic for an audience who cares little about retirement and Social Security, which is decades away for them. Listeners who believe a topic is not relevant to their own situations are less likely to listen to the speaker. If you choose such a topic, be sure to find the relevance for your listeners.

Ways to Learn about the Audience

The easiest way to find out about your audience is through observation. Your success with this method depends on the amount of experience you have with your audience and your ability to make accurate inferences. In most classroom situations, observation will yield adequate information to plan a speech, but if you seek more specific data, you may want to use a survey. A survey interview takes planning and time and is not very efficient, but it does provide an opportunity to obtain information in person and to probe for more data when necessary. If you have a large group of people, you may decide to gather information with a questionnaire. Although good questionnaires take time to write, they can be anonymous and can be administered more quickly than survey interviews, and they often yield more candid responses, especially to sensitive topics.

Observation   Probably the easiest method of audience analysis is through observation. The speaker draws on accumulated experience with a particular audience and with similar groups. Through **observation**, the speaker watches audience members and notes their behaviors and characteristics. Although this approach relies strictly on the speaker's subjective impression, it can be useful.

observation

A method of collecting information about an audience in which the speaker watches audience members and notes their behaviors and characteristics.

No doubt you have already learned a great deal about your audience from classroom assignments. You already know the number of students, the number of males and females, and their approximate ages. Through introductions, general conversations, and other interactions, you have learned about their majors, group memberships, jobs, whether they commute or live on campus, and their interests. You have learned about your classmates' attitudes, interests, values, and knowledge. You know your instructor's views and expectations for your classroom performance. You also know the size of the classroom, the location of the lectern (if there is one), the seating arrangement, the availability of audiovisual equipment, and other physical features of the environment. You have obtained all of this information by observation.

survey interview

A carefully planned and executed person-to-person question-and-answer session during which the speaker tries to discover specific information that will help in the preparation of a speech.

Survey Interviews A **survey interview** is a carefully planned and executed person-to-person, question-and-answer session during which the speaker tries to discover specific information that will help in the preparation of a speech. Such interviews can be done in person or over the phone. The purpose of the survey is to establish a solid base of fact from which to draw conclusions, make interpretations, and determine future courses of action. This method of audience research can be highly productive. To be most useful, however, surveys require a great deal of planning and organization, which takes time and energy. Many topics do not require you to survey the audience. If you wish to talk about something controversial, however, you may informally survey the audience to learn their current views; alternatively, you may set up a questionnaire, as described below, to determine what you need to know about your audience and their knowledge of your topic.

questionnaire

A set of written questions that is distributed to respondents to gather desired information.

Questionnaires A **questionnaire** is a set of written questions distributed to respondents with the aim of gathering desired information. The same questioning techniques used in survey interviews are also used in questionnaires. In some cases, questionnaires are more practical and take less time than interviews. They can be administered to relatively large groups of people at the same time. One advantage is that the respondents can remain anonymous, which often leads to greater honesty and openness in answering questions. Although learning to develop good questionnaires takes time and practice, here are some simple guidelines to help you get started:

1. Decide exactly what information you want to gather.
2. Decide on the best method for making multiple copies of your questionnaire.
3. Decide when, where, and how to distribute the questionnaire.
4. Plan the introduction to the questionnaire. Will the respondent need specific instructions on how to provide answers?
5. Make sure your questions are clear and understandable.
6. Limit the number of possible responses to each question.
7. Keep the questionnaire as brief as possible.

Figure 8.1 shows a typical questionnaire. Note that it provides simple instructions, it is brief, the questions are clear, and the number of possible responses is limited.

Use Information to Connect with Listeners

Your goal in all these types of data collection activities is to gather information so that you can relate and adapt your speech to those who make up your audience. Can you discern any patterns in the information you have gathered? What conclusions can you draw? How certain of them can you be? How can you use what you have learned to improve your speech? Let's say you want to know how students at your school feel about same-sex marriage, even though the 2015 U.S. Supreme Court decision covers the legality of the issue. You survey 50 female and 50 male students on your campus using the questionnaire in Figure 8.1. When you tally the results, you find 79 percent of the women and only 25 percent of the men believe that same-sex marriages should be legal. How will that information help you prepare a speech to convince your listeners that same-sex marriage ought to be supported?

To yield the best results, a questionnaire must be completed by a group of people who represent a sample of the entire population. You also need to make sure you have enough responses to make reliable generalizations about the group you are surveying. If your analysis is thorough and correct, you should have a fairly good picture of your audience—their relevant demographics; interests; knowledge levels; and attitudes toward the topic, the speaker, and the general situation. While your findings will rarely be uniform, you should be able to reach some general

FIGURE 8.1 Sample Questionnaire

Questionnaires contain a set of written questions and are an excellent way to quickly gather information from large groups of people. If done effectively, they can be practical, take less time than interviews, and provide anonymity for the respondent.

Check one: ____ Female ____ Male

Directions: Check the response that best indicates the strength of your agreement or disagreement with each statement.

1. Same-sex couples should be allowed to marry.
   ____ Strongly Agree
   ____ Agree
   ____ Undecided
   ____ Disagree
   ____ Strongly Disagree

2. Our society actively punishes gays, lesbians, and same-sex couples.
   ____ Strongly Agree
   ____ Agree
   ____ Undecided
   ____ Disagree
   ____ Strongly Disagree

3. Social support should be provided for same-sex couples who wish to adopt a child.
   ____ Strongly Agree
   ____ Agree
   ____ Undecided
   ____ Disagree
   ____ Strongly Disagree

4. The entire community should show more support for same-sex couples who have a child.
   ____ Strongly Agree
   ____ Agree
   ____ Undecided
   ____ Disagree
   ____ Strongly Disagree

conclusions. For example, you may find that 60 percent of your audience members strongly disagree with government restrictions on health care, 15 percent have no opinion, and 25 percent strongly agree with government health-care options. If your purpose is to persuade them that government health-care packages will provide health care for everyone, you must adjust your speech to this audience. How will you encourage those who oppose you to listen to what you have to say? What can you say to draw in those who have no opinion or who already strongly agree with you? Figure 8.1 exemplifies one way to gather audience information on same-sex marriage and related ideas.

Although it is never easy to win over people who oppose your views, you can try to do so by discussing their views first and then discussing yours. You should also make use of credible, unbiased sources—people are more likely to accept information from them. In addition, you should acknowledge that your listeners' views have as much merit as yours but assert that your views will lead to a better outcome. Remember, too: Persuasion is complex, and a 6- to 10-minute presentation is not likely to change your listeners' views drastically. The most one can probably expect is for your listeners to acknowledge your perspective as one to consider.

If your research indicates that your audience has little or no opinion about the information you are presenting, you need to *provoke their interest*. Tell them why they should listen to what you are saying and show them how the topic relates to them personally. Focus on helping them recognize the benefits and importance of your topic and remember that clearly communicating your own enthusiasm can help generate interest. Tell your listeners a memorable story, using the information you gained.

Finally, when you are dealing with an audience that concurs with your viewpoint or knows a lot about your topic, you need to acknowledge what you share with them. For example, if you and your audience agree that a new auditorium should be built, note that shared agreement and then go on to talk about what can be done to get the new facility built. In the process, you might try to strengthen their beliefs about the need for the auditorium.

No matter what the audience's position on your topic, your research will enable you to identify it in advance. You can use this information to pursue your specific purpose and to adjust your presentation. Of course, the more information you have, the better your ability to adapt your speech to your audience.

A Note about Digital Public Communication

People today seem always to be connected to something and/or someone. Technology plays such an important role in our lives that we sometimes cannot disconnect from it, even when we should. Digital public communication is also on the rise. Some of you may be taking this class as an online or distance learning class and will present your speeches to audiences you find or create in your communities, and record and upload them on the web so that your classmates may review and offer comments. At some point you may design a webinar for someone at a distance in your employer's company, or you may provide online training sessions so people can get the information on their own time and in the comfort of their homes or offices. Your professors may put their classes online through a platform such as BlackBoard or D2L, and they probably also take staff development training on a variety of issues their schools want them to understand. Most of what we talked about in this chapter (and will talk about in succeeding chapters) applies to digital public communication as well as to other forms. The difference is the kind of interactivity that can be included in online presentations. The need to know your listeners is just as essential in the digital event as in face-to-face speaking. You can be more creative, and more interactive, online, and that gives you more freedom and more creativity in presentation. It also allows you to find more digital sources to enhance the presentation. In fact, you can probably be more interactive in that format than in the regular face-to-face presentations in the classroom. You can use video to bring in examples as well as to make the presentation. You can actively engage your audience through interactive features, much as we have in this textbook. Many of you are "digital natives" who know more about technology than many of the professors who write about or teach communication classes. You can use that knowledge to your benefit when you're making digital presentations. We talked about social media and new technologies in Chapter 6. Just remember, topic selection is every bit as important for digital speaking as it is in other venues.

Stephen J. Lind suggests that "digital oratory" is "thesis-driven, vocal, embodied public address that is housed within (online) new media platforms (and that ideally takes advantage of the developing/flux-laden conventions that the online video context provides). This new form of public address lies somewhere between traditional speech-giving and media production, but it is decidedly oratorical. The public speaking component is highly valuable to a student's all-around development, in its teaching of critical thinking, meaning making, argument development, persuasion theory, general nuance and so on."[9]

⟩ SUMMARY

Select a Speech Topic

8.1 **Apply** the requirements to choose topics for your speeches and presentations.

When you choose a topic, you should begin with you and then think about the listeners, the setting, and the requirements for the speech. Some basic strategies can help you find a topic:

- *Self-inventory* allows you to think of topics for which you have a special passion for sharing.
- *Brainstorming* allows your brain to cover numerous potential topics in a short time. Deep thinking comes later. You can also use social media for brainstorming topics and approaches.
- *Review the current media*—this gives you an opportunity to see which print and nonprint sources can provide helpful information and ideas.
- Social media is increasingly more valuable and can help you find a topic and engage your listeners.
- Research can also take you to various places on the web, with an infinite number of possibilities for topics.
- Once you've found a topic, you need to assess its appropriateness for you, your listeners, the situation, and the requirements.
- Before you begin your research, you'll want to narrow the topic to fit the time limit and other guidelines.

Determine the General Purpose, Specific Purpose, and Thesis of a Speech

8.2 **Create** general and specific purpose statements.

Purpose and thesis statements allow the listeners to know what to expect and the perspective you have on the topic.

- *General purpose* statements cover the type of speech you will present, including *informative, persuasive,* and *entertainment* speeches.
- Special occasion speeches fit within the definitions of these three main types of speeches.

- *Specific purpose* statements identify which of the three types of speeches will be presented and add further information about the specific topic.
- The *thesis* statement tells the listeners what you expect them to know or do as a result of listening to your speech.

Audience Analysis: Connecting with the Listeners

8.3 **Evaluate** the suitability and relevance of the topics to make better connections with the audience.

The more you know about the *audience*, the more likely you are to gain and maintain their attention with your speech.

- Effective speakers will work to gain knowledge of the listeners and their points of view.
- *Captive* audience members are required to attend a presentation, while *voluntary participants* choose to attend the event, listen to a specific speaker, or take the opportunity to gain a perspective on the speaker's ideas.
- *Demographic analysis* can help you make better connections with your listeners as you adapt the topic and delivery to their age, gender, culture or ethnic background, education, occupation, religion, geographical origin, or group memberships.
- *Psychological analysis* helps you adapt to the audience by considering the size of the audience, the physical setting, listeners' knowledge level, and their attitudes and values toward the topic and situation.
- Common techniques to learn about the audience include *observation, survey interviews,* and *questionnaires.*
- Digital presentations require the same kind of thorough research and preparation as other forms of public communication, especially in terms of topic selection, but they allow for more creativity and interactivity in making the content come to life for the audience.

⟩ DISCUSSION STARTERS

1. Why is public communication important in today's media-saturated society?
2. In what ways can effective public communication help you connect with listeners?
3. Identify three criteria you would use to determine whether a topic is appropriate for your class and other public presentations.
4. What is the value of both a general purpose statement and a specific purpose statement?
5. How can a thesis statement present your argument about the topic and help you connect with your listeners?

6. What does demographic analysis provide to help you develop and deliver presentations?
7. Why is it important for the speaker to connect with a captive audience? How can these connections be made?
8. Why do your audience's attitudes toward you and your topic make or break a presentation?
9. What web and social media sources have you previously found useful in choosing topics?.

CHAPTER 9

RESEARCH: GATHERING AND USING INFORMATION

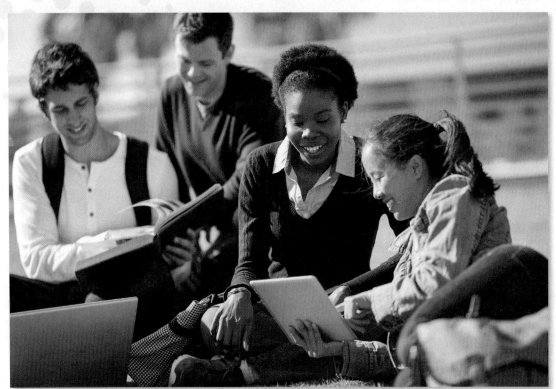

PhotoInc/E+/Getty Images

There are many information sources for your speeches. A research plan to find the best sources is critical to a successful speech. Any research you include should support and clarify your topic to make it potentially useful to your listeners.

→ CHAPTER OUTLINE AND LEARNING OBJECTIVES

Develop a Research Plan

9.1 **Develop** a research plan to gather information and find supporting materials for your speeches.

Research: Gathering Information

9.2 **Identify** five principal sources of information for your speech topic.

Use Research to Support and Clarify Ideas

9.3 **Differentiate** among the four types of materials to support and clarify your ideas.

MAKING EVERYDAY CONNECTIONS

You may think a chapter about gathering and using information sounds uninteresting or even boring. We hope you will find it helpful and that it will give you some different perspectives on research for your presentations. (As a matter of fact, we find the research part of speech preparation to be the fun part.) The ultimate goal of your research is to find compelling information and ideas you can share with your listeners about your topic. A well-researched speech brings ideas to life and satisfies your listeners' curiosity. If you are passionate about your speech, your listeners very likely will feel that passion and want to know more, so they listen better. If your research can help you find novel approaches/perspectives and teach your listeners something—make them aware this is something they need to know now or in the future—your speech will be memorable and easy to recall.

We live in an information age. There is more information available now than at any time in history and more ways to access that information than ever before. A video, "Did You Know? Shift Happens (updated for 2018)," suggests one week's worth of *The New York Times* contains more information than existed in the 18th century.[1] Then we have access to Google through our phones, and our computers allow us even more access to information. A world of information is literally at our fingertips. It is the speaker's job to find the best information from the best sources and use it to create the speeches that pique listeners' interest and transfer an idea from you to them.

QUESTIONS TO THINK ABOUT

1. Where do you usually start your search for information when you have an assignment for a paper or a presentation? Why?

2. What do you do to determine that the information you find is credible, relevant, timely, and significant?

3. What kinds of information do you usually seek from the various forms of social media? From more traditional sources?

4. Recall issues or situations where people went to great effort to get information to share with others. Identify the situation and the result.

What impresses listeners? Most will respond in a similar manner: Listeners are impressed with worthwhile, current information that is carefully constructed to tell a story in all types of speeches. If you find adequate, credible, relevant, up-to-date information, you can create an impressive speech. Gathering information can be exciting—have you ever become so caught up in seeking information on the web and been surprised to find you spent two or three hours following the information trail? The information you gather becomes the backbone of the speech and is only as good as the significance and value of that information. In this chapter, we focus on the research process and how to use the information you gather to support and clarify your message.

Develop a Research Plan

9.1 **Develop** a research plan to gather information and find supporting materials for your speeches.

You are now ready to gather information for speeches. The work and thinking you've done for the previous chapters provides the foundation for your task as you gather and develop the information you've researched to create a speech. You've already practiced topic generation through self-inventory, brainstorming, and mediated communication searches. You analyzed general information for your presentations. Now you need to think about how and where to research and what you wish to accomplish: You must strengthen your previous knowledge about the topic, find evidence to support your ideas, and make your ideas clear and relevant to your listeners. You need to consider how much background reading to do and what sources will be best to achieve this goal. You'll have to think about the types of supporting materials necessary and where you can find those materials. You must also determine how much evidence is required to make your point and convince listeners to accept your views as worthy of consideration. *In other words, you now need to think carefully about what you want to accomplish.* This is not a task for the night before your presentation is due.

Thus, you've already begun the first part of your research plan: *Start early* and *gather more information than you think you'll need* because more material may be helpful; it's always better to have more than enough information. Do not procrastinate. The longer you wait to begin your research, the more problems you're likely to have.

It takes time to create speeches. You need to find the right supporting materials and to think about what you have so you can refine, add, or delete before the presentation. Think carefully about your topic. *Where should you go to find the best information to create your speech?*

We tell our students they should *prepare a preliminary list of references* to narrow their search to the sources most likely to help them create the speech. Once the list of references is created, determine which materials to find first to provide a background and help set a direction for the speech.

You cannot read all material on the topic, so you must *be selective about materials that will enhance your own knowledge and clarify information for your listeners*. Once you have the background materials read, and complete notes, *look for the best information you can find to support your own views*.

As you read and take notes, be sure you understand *your instructor's specifications for the number and types of supporting materials required*. It's important to use a variety of types of sources, but it's also critical to have different kinds of supporting material to make your points. Variety in the mix of examples, testimony, statistics, mediated sources, and social media will help your listeners remain attentive.

Take good notes and keep complete information on the sources so you don't have to start over. In addition, be sure to identify direct quotes as well as paraphrased materials and include them with sources in the speech to avoid even a hint of plagiarism.

At some point you have to say, "Enough is enough." There's so much information available that you cannot cover everything in the time limits for classroom (and other) speeches. Once you feel you have more than enough to create the speech, stop and analyze how things fit together to make the best presentation for your listeners.

The whole point of developing and carrying out a research plan is to *think critically* about your topic and the information you will use to support the topic and grab your listeners' attention. Your task from this point on is to apply what you learned, choose good information, and use your time efficiently as you move toward speech presentations.

Research: Gathering Information

9.2 **Identify** five principal sources of information for your speech topic.

While you need to start with you and your own interests, most of us then begin our research on the web. Once you've looked at what you've already practiced, choose a topic you really like and begin with the Internet, move to social media, and then look at library and print sources to round out your research information. You'll need a variety of sources, and not all of your information can come from mediated sources. (Despite our heavy reliance on the Internet and social media, *not all information can or should derive from those sources*.) Check with your instructor or the syllabus to see specific requirements for your class. A word of caution: While few recommend Wikipedia as a source, you can often find good lists of resources on topics there and thus can begin to get ideas about *where to go to get reliable information on a topic*.

The Internet as an Information Source

Searching the Internet can be addicting, educational, entertaining, frustrating, interesting, and time-consuming. The web facilitates access to a wealth of information in a relatively short period of time. Internet information comes from a variety of sources. Some are reliable and credible, and others are not useful, credible, relevant, *or* reliable. Websites are not subject to the same evaluation and review as most print sources, so it is important that you assess not only the information on a website but also the people or organizations responsible for the site. It is no accident that when you key in the words "critical thinking," many responses will be suggested for evaluating web sources. Several of the scores of critical thinking websites are actually titled "Thinking Critically about Web Sources." Here are the basic questions you should ask and answer about your web-based information:

1. **Author.** Who wrote the material? What are their qualifications? Are the qualifications appropriate for the topic? Can you contact the author if you have questions?

2. **Publishing body.** Who publishes or sponsors the website? When you look at the web page, do you see a header or footer that shows a connection to a larger website?

Internet searches can provide a wealth of information quickly and easily from a variety of sources. Some sources are useful, reliable, and credible; others are not. It is important to check sources to ensure they are trustworthy and accurate.

Is there a link on the page that takes you to the home page? Some websites promote an organization or product; thus, the information may be biased. You can determine the credibility and objectivity of the material by checking further into the site. In addition, you can learn much from the Internet address (the uniform resource locator [URL]). Check the letters just to the left of the first backslash (/). Look beyond the backslash. If you see a tilde (~) or if the URL includes terms such as "/users/" or "/people/," you may be looking at an individual's personal page within the official pages of a larger website. If it is a personal page, you have no way of knowing whether the information on the page represents the organization. However, if you know the author's identity and qualifications (say, a librarian at an educational site), you will be able to ascertain the credibility of the personal page.

3. **Currency.** How recently was the website published, created, or updated? This information should be at the bottom of the web page or the home page. Does the document contain data recent enough to be useful? Is there a date connected to that information? (When the population of Hispanics in the United States is given with a 1990 date, for example, the information is not current.) Does the website have links to other sites that no longer work? (This is usually a hint that the site is not current.)

4. **Purpose.** Can you determine why the information is on the web? Does the site provide information, give explanations, persuade, publicize, sell products, or entertain? Sometimes the URL will give you a clue. Part of the URL contains a function indicator, such as *.gov* or *.com*, which indicates the purpose of a website:

.edu or **.gov**	Provides factual information and explanations
.com	Promotes and sells products, or provides current news and information
.org	Influences public opinion and advocates for particular organizations or issues
.net or **.com**	Entertains or provides personal information
.info	Especially used to provide truly global general information; most current registrations are in the United States
.biz	Specifically for businesses
.name	Indicates the site is for individuals
.pro	Indicates professionals; attorneys, dentists, or medical doctors, for example, register their sites for easy access (For example, Janedoe.law.pro identifies a site belonging to attorney Jane Doe.)
.museums	Accredited museums worldwide
.aero	Globally recognized suffix for airlines, airports, computer reservation systems, and related industries
.coop	Identifies business cooperatives, such as credit unions and rural electric cooperatives worldwide

Robert Kneschke/Fotolia

5. **Comparison.** How does web information compare with other available resources? If discrepancies exist among sources, check further to find the best sources of information. Remember, too, that websites change quickly. You might search a specific topic and find a large number of hits, and then return an hour later to find the number has quadrupled or even been reduced significantly. Information and websites are added rapidly and changed often. In addition, a search engine may sample more or fewer individual sites at different times. Many choices are available. Pick one search engine and look for materials on your topic, and locate specific information; then check another search engine and/or another site and determine if each has basically the same information. If so, you can probably presume they are comparable. Then choose the site that seems to work best for you. When you search, you will sometimes automatically be redirected to another site. At other times, you will need to search further or find another source. This is another good reason for writing down URLs and bookmarking websites: You can go back to the exact site to get further information or direct others to a specific site.

Social Media as an Information Source

Social media dominates much of our lives both in relationships and in the ways we gain and share art, ideas, and information. It also engages all learners. As a student you are likely active on social networks. You likely share aspects of your life and your ideas with your friends or classmates. You can find video clips, art, and graphics to help enhance your speeches. As you know, Google is more than a search engine. You can access documents, maps, artwork, videos, calendars, and information on every topic, ranging from finance to translations of books. It even catalogs endangered languages, leaving some of us to question what we did before Google.

Be sure to check your source and think about the credibility of the information. Most forms of social media can provide information, references, and examples of the material used in speeches because they are creative and innovative and thus gain and maintain listeners' attention. Wiki and Google Docs make it easier to take messages beyond the classroom walls. If you don't already use these social media tools, online tutorials can help you use social media for your own benefit. Social media can provide powerful images and help listeners respond to your speech. Technology's influence on education is both challenging and rewarding. Be sure to take time to think carefully about what you want to share with your listeners and make judicious choices of information and images from social media.

George Couros, on the Connected Principals website, identifies five impacts of social media on education. These impacts also address the use of social media in finding appropriate resources for your speeches:

1. It's free. For speakers, this means unique, accessible, free information is yours with a touch on a trackpad or smartphone screen.
2. It cuts down the isolation.
3. It builds tolerance and understanding of cultural diversity.
4. It can amplify passion.
5. The world of education is (and needs to be) more open.[2]

Oral communication teachers at the University of Northern Iowa and professional speakers suggest that every 10 minutes of speaking time requires at least 10 hours of research and preparation time. Each topic and speaking occasion need a different amount of information, but there is no question that the more information you have, the better equipped you will be to design and develop your presentation and adapt it to your audience. Of course, *quality* of information matters more than quantity, especially when your time is limited. That's why it is important to develop your research skills. When you become skilled at research, you will make better use of your time.

You as an Information Source

Most communication begins with you. You are one of the most valuable sources of available information.

Your own experiences and knowledge can contribute to the content of your speech and give you authority to speak on a subject. Abdullah is an international student from Saudi Arabia. He is active in the Saudi student organization as well as a member of the International Students Organization. When Abdullah was asked to speak to an intercultural communication class about his country and culture, he naturally thought first of his own personal experiences. He knew he had lots of good information to share with his audience, and he also knew that sources of information that would enhance his own knowledge were available. He also wanted to relate aspects of his country to what his listeners could understand. Think about the effect of Abdullah's comparisons:

> Saudi Arabia is slightly more than one-fifth the size of the United States. We have a population of 27 million, of which 8.8 million are registered as foreign expatriates and an estimated 1.5 million are undocumented immigrants. Unlike Iowa, with its vast fields of grain crops and pastures, Saudi Arabia has only 1.67 percent arable land. There is some irrigation, but not nearly as much as in Iowa. Because our underground water resources are mostly depleted and there are no rivers or lakes, my country has developed extensive seawater desalination facilities. As a result, Saudi Arabia has been a party to various international biodiversity, climate, and pollution reduction agreements.
>
> Both men and women serve in the military, and like Iowa, we have a National Guard as well as Air, Land, Marine, Naval, and Special military forces. We are not required to serve in the defense forces, but if we do, we must be between the ages of 18 and 49.
>
> Saudi Arabia is known as the birthplace of Islam and home to Islam's two holiest shrines in Mecca and Medina. The king's official title is the "Custodian of the Two Holy Mosques." One of the king's male descendants will always rule the country, as required by the country's 1992 Basic Law. Islam is the national religion. King Abdullah continued reform programs in the country and instituted interfaith dialogue initiatives to encourage religious tolerance on a global level.[3] He appointed moderates to various positions and appointed the first female to the cabinet. To promote increased political participation, the government held nationwide elections in September 2011 and announced that women will have the right to vote in future elections. A series of benefits to Saudi citizens was also instituted in 2011, so there are now funds to build affordable housing for all citizens. salary increases for government workers, and unemployment benefits. We also share the problem of undocumented immigrants.[4]
>
> From this, I hope you can see that Saudis have some of the same problems and concerns as citizens of the U.S.A. and that, as people, we are more similar than different.

Did Abdullah provide you with a new perspective of Saudi Arabia? While he talked about religion, he emphasized aspects of the geography, politics, and population, noting both similarities and differences. As a result, his classmates regarded the country a bit differently. He welcomed questions and answered them to help people learn more about his country and its similarities to Iowa and the United States.

Probe your own knowledge of a subject to organize your thoughts, develop a research plan, and eventually move more quickly through the research process.

The Interview as an Information Source

Of course, for most topics, your firsthand experience and knowledge will not be sufficient. The interview can be a valuable tool for gathering **expert opinion** (ideas, testimony, conclusions, or judgments of witnesses or recognized authorities) and the

expert opinion
Ideas, testimony, conclusions, or judgments of witnesses or recognized authorities.

most up-to-date information to support your own ideas. A good interviewer can often discover information that could never be obtained through any other sources.

An interview is a carefully planned, person-to-person, question-and-answer session aimed at gathering information. An interview requires a constant exchange of questions and answers between two individuals. Both people speak and listen, as in a social conversation. In fact, social conversations constitute the most frequent interview situation because they are often a series of questions and answers. Let's look at the steps involved and some questions you need to ask in the interview process.

1. **Establish the purpose of the interview.** What do you want to know? What information will be most helpful? How can you learn what you need to know about the topic?

2. **Choose the interviewee.** From whom will you receive the best, most up-to-date information? What are their credentials? Is the interviewee willing to provide that information openly and honestly? Is the interviewee accessible? Should other people be interviewed? How many people should be interviewed to obtain complete and accurate information?

3. **Conduct research prior to the interview.** You need to learn as much as you can before the interview, on both the interviewee and your topic, so that you can ask intelligent questions to gain the best, most important information.

4. **Record the interview.** You should either take notes or record the interview to be able to accurately retrieve information later. Be sure to ask for permission before you record someone. Choose the method that allows the best interaction. Use the guidelines in "Guidelines: Record Interviews."

5. **Prepare questions.** Carefully prepare questions in advance. Be flexible during the interview to ask additional questions, to probe further, or to follow an unexpected opportunity the interviewee might provide.

6. **Organize the interview.** An interview, like a speech, usually has three identifiable segments: an opening, a body, and a closing. Organize your interview and provide a template to record the interviewee's responses.

Guidelines

RECORD INTERVIEWS

1. **Ask permission to take notes or to record the interview.** Also let interviewees know they will have the opportunity to check the notes or that you will send a copy of the transcribed notes to them.

2. **If you are recording, be sure the recording device is working and test it prior to the interview.** Make sure you know how much time you have. Record as inconspicuously as you can during the interview.

3. **Maintain eye contact as much as possible.** The interviewee gives you a gift of time and information; honor that by attending as much as possible. (That's another reason for recording the interview.)

4. **Take notes throughout the interview.** Jot down the ideas that will help you remember and use the recorded information.

5. **Agree to follow any ground rules the interviewee establishes.** Be sure to offer the interviewee the opportunity to review the outline and at least their portion of quotations prior to presentation.

6. **Review your notes and recording as soon after the interview as possible.** You'll remember more within a short time after the interview, thus making the transcribing more beneficial.

7. **Remember to be courteous throughout the interview.** Thank the interviewee for taking time to speak with you. Let the interviewee know how to contact you and when you'll be in contact to cover your questions or theirs.

MAKING CONNECTIONS FOR SUCCESS
Think about the Interview

The most up-to-date information available is gained when you interview an expert or someone with firsthand knowledge of your topic. For the topics listed on the left in the chart, identify a person whom you could interview to obtain information about that topic. For each topic, identify at least two individuals who might give you unbiased information. Identify the person you would interview first and explain why. One example will get you started.

Topic	Interviewee
Memory and Your Brain	Psychology professor, especially one teaching cognitive psychology, or one whose research deals with memory; educational psychologist who deals with memory and learning in the classroom; or a listening scholar who looks at listening as a cognitive construct.
How Do We Separate Real News and Fake News?	_____
College Students and the First Amendment	_____
Resistance and Protest Movements	_____
Dealing with Student College Debt	_____

7. **Other considerations.** Appropriate dress, punctuality, and attentive listening contribute to a successful interview. Always give the interviewee your complete, undivided attention. If anything is unclear after you check your notes or listen to the recording, contact the interviewee for clarification as soon as possible after the interview.

8. **Use interview clips in your speech.** If your classroom has the necessary equipment, you could either include a (short) recorded interview segment, or even a live comment from your interviewee through Zoom, GotoMeeting, Adobe Connect, Skype, or your phone. Check with your instructor to determine whether this is appropriate for your classroom and if the technology is available.

The Library as an Information Source

Not all information is digitized, and some communication professors require a variety of sources, only some of which can come from the web. Library research requires some effort, but once you understand how the system works—and most libraries use essentially the same system—you will find that the library is a beneficial resource for speech preparation. Libraries are user friendly, and most libraries have invested great sums of money for computerized systems that help researchers find materials quickly and easily. Each year these systems improve and become easier to use. In addition, reference librarians are usually the most helpful people you can find.

If you do not know how to locate material, there's no time like the present to learn. A little time invested now will save a great deal later; you will find the library a convenient and pleasant place to locate information. Many academic libraries have a special area where you can drink coffee or a soda and peruse sources. Attend one of the tours or orientation sessions many libraries offer. Some provide educational packages or web-based tours with instructions on how to use the library. Principal sources of information in the library include the reference librarian, library computer-assisted search programs, and electronic catalogs.

The Library Computer Search   The library provides ample sources for your supporting materials. Many universities and colleges have network systems that allow you to enter the library indexes through home or campus computers. Once you access to the library computer, menus guide you through the steps to find what you want. You will learn where the materials are located and whether they are available at your library.

Mediated Information Sources   College libraries have access to an online database of current periodicals: newspapers, magazines, newsletters, transcripts, and wire information. Your library may also subscribe to LexisNexis, an online newspaper service that provides the most current information available. In many cases, you can access LexisNexis and read the next morning's news from another part of the world. Most libraries have an ERIC (Educational Research Information Clearinghouse) database as well. ERIC is called the world's largest digital library of education literature and provides access to reviewed convention papers. It is a source of the most up-to-date research findings, as well as opinion pieces by experts in their fields. Electronic databases for government documents and a variety of other information sources are also included. Check your library website to see what's available. The *refereed* electronic database material is a credible source for supporting material.

When searching an electronic database, you need to determine key words and phrases for your search before you begin so you can maximize your time and effort. Check the options for each; generally, the word *and* is used as a connector between key words. This allows the database to search the available materials for the information you need. Complete directions for searches are provided by your library or may be found on the screen where your search begins.

The most common Internet search is the topic-based search. When you identify a general topic (e.g., the First Amendment, communication practices in other cultures, or tips for visiting another country), you can access information about all aspects of that topic. You may receive too many responses to your query, however, and need to narrow your topic to find responses you can easily peruse. Each search engine has a tutorial to help you get started.

When you find information on the web, be sure to write down the specific bibliographic information (the URL, or address; date accessed; page number; and author or producer), print the information, and save it on a drive or bookmark it. If you create a bookmark, you also need to save that as well. As always, evaluate the value and credibility of all sources and information.

The Reference Department   Most library research begins in the reference department. Here you will find sources for specific subject areas such as dictionaries, almanacs, biographical aids, encyclopedias, yearbooks, atlases, bibliographies, indexes, and guides to periodical literature. Many are available online. If you are uncertain about what to use or how to use these materials, ask a librarian.

Specialized indexes are available for particular subjects, such as agriculture and natural resources, business and economics, statistics, biology and life sciences, computers, education, and history. A popular index is the *Readers' Guide to Periodical Literature*. This source provides information from popular periodicals. Issues of the guide are published in three paperbound issues plus a permanent annual hardbound cumulation and are also available as an electronic database.

Because magazines, research journals, and newspapers have the most recently available information on a subject, they are the most often used print resources for speech writing and research projects. If you want to know the latest opinions and trends on almost any social, political, or economic issue, newspapers and weekly magazines will usually be your best resources. Given the concern about what is and is not real, check multiple publications to ensure credibility. When you seek current research or classic studies, journals published by professional organizations (e.g., National Communication Association, American Psychological Association) will provide the best information.

If you do not know what your library has to offer, take time to learn about it. The search for knowledge is not easy, but thought and preparation will help you find ample information about almost any speech topic.

Suggestions for Research

Good research has no shortcuts, but the process can be more enjoyable and easier no matter what sources you use. Here are several suggestions:

1. **State a clear purpose before you start the research.** Your search is easier when you know what you want to find. If your speech is to persuade your audience that adequate sleep is essential to well-being, the key word is *sleep.* Begin your search with the term but also look at *healthy lifestyles, health,* and *health issues.* Consider all possible areas of research in advance to keep your research productive and efficient.

2. **Begin your research early.** It takes time to find appropriate materials; therefore, start your research as soon as possible. If you wait until the last minute, you might discover needed materials are unavailable or it takes longer to find them than you anticipated.

3. **Use computer searches when possible.** The computer is one of the simplest means of obtaining the largest number of sources on any topic. If you are unfamiliar with your library's computer system, ask for help. Librarians are there to help find what you need.

4. **Maintain a bibliography of sources.** As you find sources on the computer and in electronic catalogs, electronic databases, and periodical guides, copy them in the same form into a computer file or onto a sheet of paper or index cards (3 × 5 inch or 4 × 6 inch). Index cards are advantageous because you can sort them quickly, either alphabetically or by importance to the speech (your computer files also categorize information). In addition, current brain/memory research suggests we retain more information when we actually write it down, rather than key it into the computer.[5] List each item separately and note its importance to the presentation. This may seem tedious and time consuming, but if you fail to record something and need it later, it's much easier than starting all over because you cannot find the original. Keying and saving this information into computer files also helps you stay organized and saves time in the long run. If you cannot save your files on the library computers, type the information into an email and send it to yourself.

5. **Add appropriate mediated sources to your information base.** Refereed material examined by experts in the field is always best to have. There are many mediated sources that can add immeasurably to your data collection. We recommend viewing TED Talks, archived news programs, and documentaries as sources to at least begin to get a sense of the information available. Mediated sources also provide unique perspectives.

6. **Take notes.** Efficient and accurate note taking is a must. Once you locate information, either record it by hand or copy it for later use. Whether you quote a statement verbatim, summarize it, or paraphrase it, record the original information accurately and completely. Take ample notes and always make sure the source is fully and accurately indicated, as in the sample note cards in Figure 9.1. Nothing is more frustrating than information you cannot use because you don't know the source and cannot return to it for additional information. The more information you record, the better. You should always have more than you need to write your speech. Of course, you can also keep your notes on the computer and the same principles apply. An advantage of putting information on note cards, in addition to the memory factor mentioned above, is the ability to arrange and move cards around to find the best fit of the ideas visually.

FIGURE 9.1 Sample Note Cards

Note taking, if done accurately and completely, can save you a great deal of time and effort. It is always best to take plenty of notes and to record the sources of the notes correctly.

> Twitter
> https://www.crunchbase.com/organization/twitter#section-overview (retrieved March 30, 2018)
>
> Twitter was founded by Jack Dorsey, Biz Stone, and Evan Williams in March 2006.
>
> It was publicly launched in July 2006.
>
> Twitter is a social networking and micro-blogging service that allows users to post their latest updates.
>
> An update is limited by 280 characters and can be posted through three methods: web form, text message, or instant message.

> Google
> https://www.google.com/intl/en/about/our-company/ (retrieved March 30, 2018)
>
> Google is an American multinational Internet and software corporation specialized in Internet search, cloud computing, and advertising technologies.
>
> Google allows you to search the world's information, including web pages, images, videos, and more.
>
> Google is more popular than Facebook, Twitter, or any other form of social media.
>
> There are many special features to help you find exactly what you're looking for.

Use Research to Support and Clarify Ideas

9.3 **Differentiate** among the four types of materials to support and clarify your ideas.

More than 2,000 years ago, the famous Greek scholar Aristotle wrote that every speech has essentially two parts: a statement and its proof. Aristotle's description is still valid today, even in presentations and informal speaking situations, if we wish to be competent communicators. How a speaker clarifies and supports ideas determines the quality of the speech. The supporting material provides the *evidence* speakers need to back up or confirm their ideas. Consider the following statements:

> Today's students are much smarter than students of any earlier generation. The reason? Students have access to computer technology that gives them more available information than ever before.

On the surface, this assertion might seem valid, but is it accurate? Will an audience accept it at face value? Does the statement offer any data to help you accept the first sentence as true? What proof is provided that students who have access to computer technology have advanced more quickly than those who do not? Careful analysis shows we need to think carefully before we accept the statement as credible because no proof is offered to support the assertion.

Audiences generally accept information because of the perceived believability of the speaker or the information itself. Thus, the statement would likely be more acceptable to audiences if it were made by a well-known educator and researcher than if it were made by a student. But regardless of the source, most listeners, including your professor, require some proof or specific data before they accept a statement. Consequently, effective speakers justify each main idea in their speeches with a variety of supporting materials.

Evidence offers support and clarifies ideas; it also brings life to a speech. Evidence makes the content of a speech appealing, vivid, exciting, meaningful, acceptable, and more useful to listeners.

Consider the following statements made in a student's speech:

> Colleges and universities offer numerous free or low-cost support systems for students with disabilities, and the offices of special services should be one of the first places a student looks to get specific help for special needs.

Is this reliable information? Does the speaker explain why this information might be important? Would you accept the speaker's word that the offices of special services should be one of the first places a student looks to get help? On the surface, one may say, "Yes, that seems to be true." As the statements now read, however, the speaker does not give us enough information in this one sentence to believe the assertions. We want and need more proof. The speaker needs to present evidence before the audience will believe.

The quantity and quality of a speaker's supporting materials, plus the speaker's ability to use them correctly, make the difference between a mediocre and a good speech. In the next section, we focus on the basic kinds of supporting and clarifying materials used in speeches: testimony, examples, definitions, and statistics.

MAKING CONNECTIONS FOR SUCCESS
Find Internet Information Sources

Through her part-time job in the campus student disabilities office, Sloan learned a great deal about the services provided but felt many of her classmates were unaware of what her office does to help others. She chose to talk about the available services for her informative speech.

She found helpful support information in the pamphlets in her office, and interviewed her supervisors to get additional information, but she wanted to provide something that applied to people with disabilities everywhere in the United States. Her first step was searching the web for federal laws governing requirements in educational institutions. A Google search gave her over 6 million results in seconds. The first listing was the Disability Support Services of the Virginia Commonwealth University; much later in the list was the U.S. Department of Education Office for Civil Rights. Here Sloan obtained information about the laws and services, and subsequent results gave her insights into other colleges and universities. She was quickly certain she could find enough information for her 5- to 7-minute speech based on a variety of sources, including accurate web information.

1. How has Sloan's approach to her topic followed the suggestions offered in this chapter?

2. How reliable are her sources so far?

3. Do her sources seem to meet the criteria for good sources?

4. What other questions might Sloan ask in a Google search to get additional information?

5. What other sources might Sloan consult?

Testimony

The opinions or conclusions of witnesses or recognized authorities are referred to as **testimony**. Speakers use testimony to support or reinforce points they want their audiences to accept. The value of the testimony is related both to the listeners' opinion of its acceptability and to the speaker who presents it.

The use of testimony usually adds trustworthiness to what a speaker says—a necessity for all speakers who are not yet established as experts on their chosen speech topic. The speaker's own experience can be an excellent form of testimony, as in the previous example. When the speaker's reputation and experience are insufficient, the use of a recognized and trusted authority can be invaluable in gaining listeners' acceptance.

Testimony can either support or clarify material or both. Here is an example of testimony that does both:

> I've always admired people who give of their time as well as other resources to help those less fortunate, so I reflected on issues in my community. This year, Habitat for Humanity was building a house for a family of four who lost everything in a fire that demolished their home, garage, and vehicles. Both the Red Cross and the Salvation Army helped the family, but the biggest donors were those who assisted them with the clean-up of their destroyed property and helped build a new house on the lot. I stopped at the house-in-progress, found the project supervisor and volunteered my services.
>
> The family members were all on site doing their share. I found the experience to be truly inspirational and am glad I chose to work on this particular project. We never know when we might be in a position to need the kind of help this family did. It helped me feel that I had "paid it forward" and actually learned a few things about myself as well as some useful construction practices.

The speaker uses testimony and personal experience to help make a point about the importance of civic engagement.

Testimony can be either quoted directly or paraphrased. Paraphrasing is an effective method of condensing a long text or clarifying a technical passage. Sometimes audience members tune out speakers who use long and complex quotations. Restating long quotations in your own words helps to make the words of the source fit the tone of your speech. If you paraphrase, do not violate the meaning of the original statement.

Certain statements are so well phrased they cannot be stated any better. An example is the forceful and unforgettable statement made by John F. Kennedy in his 1961 presidential inaugural address: "Ask not what your country can do for you; ask what you can do for your country." Always quote such statements word for word. Misquoting someone can be embarrassing, but even worse, it can destroy your credibility. Double-check every quotation for accuracy and source and never use a quotation out of context.

Testimony should meet two essential tests: The person whose words are cited must be qualified by virtue of skills, training, expertise, recognition, and reputation, and the expert's opinion must be acceptable and believable to your listeners.

The person you quote should be a qualified authority on the subject. For example, an athlete's endorsement of tennis shoes and a movie star's endorsement of cosmetics are fairly believable because they use such products in their work. But when celebrities advertise products completely unrelated to their area

The value of testimony is related both to the listener's opinion of the acceptability of the message and to the speaker's credibility. Tennis star Venus Williams is a credible spokesperson for tennis-related sponsors, but she might not be a qualified authority on other subjects.

Kathy Willens/AP/Shutterstock

of expertise, their opinions become less believable. Avoid using names solely because someone is well known. The best testimony comes from a person whose knowledge and experience are related to the topic and who is recognized by your listeners.

For maximum credibility, testimony should also come from objective sources. The objectivity and neutrality of authorities are particularly important when your subject is controversial. For example, in trying to persuade an audience that today's automobiles are more fuel-efficient than those of a decade ago, it is more convincing to quote the American Automobile Association than the president of an automotive company. Listeners tend to be suspicious of opinions from a biased or self-interested source.

Examples

An **example** is a simple, representative incident or model that clarifies a point. Examples are useful when you present complex information to listeners who are unfamiliar with a topic and when your purpose is to inform or instruct. Brief examples,

example

A simple, representative incident or model that clarifies a point.

MAKING CONNECTIONS FOR SUCCESS
Oprah Winfrey's 2018 Golden Globes Speech

The Golden Globes awarded the 2018 Cecil B. DeMille Award for Lifetime Achievement to Oprah Winfrey. Honorees are expected to give an acceptance speech and have the freedom to talk about whatever moves them. Winfrey used the occasion to look at societal issues, including race and gender and the fight for equality as well as attacks on the press. She provided her story of watching Sidney Poitier make history when he was the first black man to receive an Academy Award and what an inspiration that was for her. [6] She noted that Poitier later also received the DeMille Award and how she felt honored to share her night with any girls who may have been watching her be the first black woman to receive the award.[7] She provided stories of others who were victims or who fought for the rights of others, how she attempts in her own work to say something meaningful and true about how people really behave, and ended with a note of hope for the future; that when change comes, it will come from

> ... a lot of magnificent women, many of whom are right here in this room tonight, and some pretty phenomenal men, fighting hard to make sure that they become the leaders who take us to the time when nobody ever has to say "Me too" again.[8]

The audience rose to their feet many times during the speech to applaud her words. Afterward, people commenting on the Internet reacted to Oprah's speech and some called for her to run for the presidency in 2020. Two months after the speech, people were still talking about the impact the speech had on them and for society.

You can view the speech or get a transcript of her remarks on the Internet. After viewing her speech or reading the transcript, answer the following questions:

1. Why do you think Winfrey's speech was acclaimed by so many as both powerful and inspirational?

2. Winfrey said her speech was larger than just one that involved the entertainment industry. How did she create a story that went beyond one that just affected Hollywood?

3. How did she take advantage of current events to craft a compelling story?

4. What evidential support does she provide?

5. What can we learn from Oprah about the importance of passion for the topic she chose?

Oprah Winfrey's Golden Globes acceptance speech was so powerful and inspirational, people who viewed or read it said Winfrey should run for the U.S. presidency in 2020.

Jordan Strauss/Invision/AP/Shutterstock

illustrations, and analogies are three kinds of examples that help clarify information for an audience.

brief example

A specific instance that is used to introduce a topic, drive home a point, or create a desired response.

Brief Examples   A **brief example** is a specific instance used to introduce a topic, drive home a point, or create a desired impression. A series of brief examples can also be used to create a desired impression:

> "Program change" is the label given to academic and departmental changes at many colleges and universities. In our university, these program changes usually only happen when a department hosting the program determines the program is no longer viable. However, an administrator determined program cuts based on the numbers of graduating majors in the programs and ignored the other factors such as liberal arts core requirements that certain programs met and the number of other majors that depend on those programs so students complete their degrees in a timely fashion. The administrator then looked at only one aspect of the programs, the bottom line—the small number of majors graduating each year—and used a budget crisis as the reason to close down programs and lay off faculty. Administrators used these guidelines to identify nearly 80 programs to be dropped, and approximately 50 faculty members were given notice of their "early separation" from the university because of the budget crisis, for which no factual data was presented except that these programs "had low numbers of graduates each year."

illustration

An extended example, narrative, case history, or anecdote that is striking and memorable.

factual illustration

A report of something that exists or actually happened.

hypothetical illustration

A report of something that could happen, given a specific set of circumstances.

Illustrations   An **illustration**, or extended example, is a narrative, case history, or anecdote that is striking and memorable. Illustrations often exemplify concepts, conditions, or circumstances, or they demonstrate findings. If an example refers to a single item or event, it is an illustration. Because illustrations offer more detail than brief examples, they are useful in establishing proof.

An illustration lends depth to and explains the point a speaker is trying to make. It also gives the information more meaning. An illustration may be either factual or hypothetical. A **factual illustration** tells what actually happened; a **hypothetical illustration** tells what *could* happen, given a specific set of circumstances.

A hypothetical illustration, because it is speculative, asks listeners to use their imaginations. Such examples are often short stories that relate to a general principle or concept. The following hypothetical example helped students envision the impact of sleep deprivation on their physical and emotional status:

> Rosmiza is a typical college student. She carries a 12-hour course load and works 10 hours each week at the campus library. She is conscientious and feels she needs to study long hours preparing for her speeches. Even though she plans for her assignments, she often feels the pressure of not enough time to get everything completed and she stays up late. She pulled all-nighters several times in the last two weeks and now feels as if she can't make it through the day. In addition to her fatigue, she feels she's coming down with a cold and knows she doesn't have the time to be sick. Rosmiza makes it through the week, but over the weekend she must work her ten hours at the library, finish her speech for class, write a research report for another class, and get reading assignments completed. She was surprised when she nearly passed out in the library and had to have friends help her get back to the residence hall. Rosmiza's real problem was *sleep deprivation*, a common malady among college students, especially at mid-term. Sleep deprivation is the physical and emotional state where lack of sleep emphasizes the stress factors and causes one's body to shut down. She quickly learned that it takes more than one day to catch up on her sleep so she can finish the semester.

This hypothetical illustration demonstrates the effects of sleep deprivation on both body and mind. While many students (and others) recognize that their lack of sleep puts increased pressure on them, they often keep going even when time out for some sleep would be better for them in the long term.

Guidelines

USE EXAMPLES

1. **Use factual examples to add authenticity to your presentation.** Factual examples build on the basic information presented and add credibility to both you and your speech.

2. **Use realistic examples that relate directly to your discussion.** If you try to generalize from unusual or rare situations, you risk undermining credibility.

3. **Use authentic, accurate, and verifiable examples.** Always give credit to the source so your listeners can verify it.

The use of a hypothetical illustration can be particularly effective when it involves the listeners. The illustration should create a vivid picture in listeners' minds. The more realistic the situation, the more likely it is that the listeners will become involved. A speaker should always specify whether an illustration is factual or hypothetical.

Analogies   An **analogy** is a comparison of two things that are similar in certain essential characteristics. Analogies explain or prove the unknown by comparing it to the known.

Analogies are of two kinds. A **figurative analogy** draws comparisons between things in different categories. For example, in her description of the immigration experience in Postville, Iowa, a student related that the people she surveyed indicated in the past that they felt Postville was a "melting pot," an immigration pattern in which new cultures blend with the dominant culture. More recent interviewees said their immigration experience was a "tossed salad," in which newcomers keep their own cultural practices and do not try to blend in.[9]

A **literal analogy** is a comparison of members of the same category and makes a simple comparison—for example, two majors (communication and English), two search engines (GoodSearch and Google), or two genres of music (classical and country).

Most topics offer opportunities to use analogies. Figurative analogies make ideas vivid and clear, whereas literal analogies supply evidence to support points. Analogies are effective, efficient, and creative means of supporting and clarifying information.

analogy
A comparison of two things that are similar in certain essential characteristics.

figurative analogy
A comparison of things in different categories.

literal analogy
A comparison of members of the same category.

Definitions

Be sure you define all unfamiliar words and concepts, especially technical terms, if you want listeners to understand and accept your speech. Nothing is more frustrating to listeners than a speaker who uses terminology they do not understand. In most cases, it is better to offer too much explanation than too little. Do not, however, patronize your audience by explaining the obvious. You can use several different kinds of definitions to keep the attention of your audience. For example, "Axiology is defined as a branch of philosophical study dealing with values and value orientations. Theorists cite axiology when they want to make sure readers understand that their own personal values influence the way they conduct research to build theories."[10] This information explains what axiology is and what it does.

A **logical definition**, the most common form, usually contains two parts, a term's dictionary definition and the characteristics that distinguish the term from other items in the same category.

An **operational definition** explains how an object or concept works, gives the steps that make up a process, or states how conceptual terms are measured. Here's an

logical definition
A definition consisting of a term's dictionary definition and the characteristics that distinguish the term from other members of the same category.

operational definition
A definition that explains how an object or concept works or lists the steps in a process.

example:

> A student who has 30 or more hours of credit with a grade point average of 2.80 (on a 4.0 scale) in the major prerequisites will be admitted as a student in good standing in most campus majors.

definition by example

Clarifying a term, not by describing it or giving its meaning but by mentioning or showing an example of it.

A **definition by example** clarifies a term not by describing it or giving its meaning but by mentioning or showing an example of it.

> Business people talk about "lean strategies" in the workplace. By this, they mean anything we can do to make the workplace a better place for everyone without making it a worse place for anyone.

statistics

Numerical data that show relationships or summarize or interpret many instances.

Statistics

Numerical data that show relationships or summarize or interpret many instances are known as **statistics**. Every day we are confronted with numerical analyses. "UNICEF reports there are more than 210 million orphans in the world today with 86 million in India, 44 million in Africa, 10 million in Mexico. Further, UNICEF says 35,000 children die every day from hunger and malnutrition."[11] Although statistics can be interesting or even compelling, they can also be confusing and difficult to interpret.

Movie and theatre celebrity Hugh Jackman uses his name and fame for various causes and charities. He is a spokesperson for World Vision and World Wide Orphans, and he regularly travels to specific locations and makes speeches to draw attention to the world's problems. He often speaks about adoption, global poverty, hunger, saving the planet, or promoting fair trade.

Statistics enable speakers to summarize a large number of data rapidly, to analyze specific occurrences or instances, to isolate trends, and to calculate probabilities of future events. They are used to clarify and support a speaker's position. For example, consider these two statements:

> Many children around the world will be orphaned by AIDS.[12]

> UNICEF estimates that a child is orphaned by AIDS at the rate of one every 14 seconds. This disease weakens whole nations. We risk losing the next generation.[13]

The first statement is broad and possibly misleading. The second cites a specific cause and numbers and gives listeners a clearer view of the effect of AIDS on children and on nations. The second statement also refers to a current source to add credence to the data. Statistics can be used to emphasize the magnitude of a problem, as seen in the following example:

> By the year 2000, the HIV/AIDS crisis created more than 13 million orphans worldwide. More than 90 percent live in sub-Saharan Africa.[14]

Statistics can also be informative:

> AIDS also impacts the economic progress of developing countries as it claims teachers, doctors, and other specialist human resources. In 1999 alone, an estimated 860,000 children lost their teachers to AIDS in sub-Saharan Africa.[15]

Four guidelines will help make the most of the statistics you've gathered:

1. **Make sure the statistics you present in your speech are from neutral and trustworthy and credible sources.** The motives of the source of any statistics must be carefully assessed. For example, if you heard two sets of data on fuel economy per gallon of gasoline—one prepared by Ford Motor Company and the other by *Consumer Reports*—which would you expect to be more reliable? Although Ford's data may be accurate, listeners would tend to believe the data are biased. It is to a speaker's advantage, therefore, to use the more neutral source.

   It can be difficult to identify the most neutral source. For example, whose statistics would you use if you wished to inform your audience about the number of orphans in Africa? Mission One Million is a faith-based organization established in October 2003 to meet the needs of orphaned and abandoned children; to expand Christianity by supporting and raising up missions; and to plan churches in the least evangelized, most populated, and poorest third world countries.[16]

   UNICEF estimates there are over 132 million orphans in sub-Saharan Africa, Asia, Latin America, and the Caribbean. UNICEF is the driving force that helps build a world in which the rights of every child are realized. This organization has the global authority to influence decision makers and a variety of partners at the grassroots level to turn most innovations into reality to help children.[17]

   Numbers may differ from these two sources but their goals are similar; thus, the choice is debatable unless you intend to take a position on the issue. Remember, statistics can be used in many different ways and can thus influence interpretations and outcomes.

2. **Take time to explain the statistics you use.** Interpret and relate your statistics to your listeners. Numbers, by themselves, have little meaning until you explain them. Consider the following use of statistics:

   > It is estimated that more than 20 million children under the age of 15 living in the sub-Saharan African desert have been robbed of one or both parents by HIV/AIDS. The number of orphans will grow exponentially due to the large number of HIV/AIDS cases already diagnosed. Nearly one-fourth (25 percent) of the population of children under 15 in 11 sub-Saharan African countries will be orphaned by HIV/AIDS.[18]

   This explanation provides meaningful statistics by clearly identifying specific numbers and percentages.

   When using data that listeners may have difficulty understanding or visualizing, try to provide appropriate comparisons to make the data more meaningful.

3. **Use statistics sparingly.** Statistics are difficult to comprehend. If you use too many, you run the risk of boring or confusing your audience. Use statistics only when necessary and make sure they are easy to understand. The following example would be difficult for even the most attentive listener to comprehend:

   > The most immediate needs households with orphans cannot meet in the Mwanza region of the United Republic of Tanzania include the following: school materials, 41 percent; health-care expenses, 23 percent; food, 21 percent; clothes, 11 percent; and other, 4 percent.

It would be much easier to understand if the data were presented in pie charts, or verbally, as follows:

> Of the most immediate needs that households with orphans cannot meet in the Mwanza region of the United Republic of Tanzania are three major needs: More than 40 percent cannot supply school materials, almost one-quarter of the homes cannot provide health-care expenses, and just over one-fifth of the homes cannot provide adequate food for these orphans.[19]

Guidelines

TIPS FOR USING STATISTICS

1. **Make sure your statistics come from reliable, neutral sources.** Avoid biased sources such as those selling a product or promoting their own services.

2. **Use statistics sparingly.** Numbers can be compelling but they can also create a loss of interest unless used well.

3. **Take the time to explain the statistics to your listeners.** What do the numbers mean? Numbers or statistics, in and of themselves, have no meaning until you give them meaning in the context of your speech.

4. **Display statistics visually whenever possible.** This saves explanation time. And it helps you remember specifics.

4. **Round off large numbers when possible.** Listeners more readily understand and remember uncomplicated figures. It's easier to recall that Warren Buffett pledged approximately 10 million Berkshire Hathaway shares, spread over multiple years with annual contributions, to the Bill and Melinda Gates Foundation. The Gates Foundation received 5 percent of the shares, worth about $500,000 in 2006, and comparable amounts in succeeding years. The minute details are difficult to remember, but it's easier to remember the rounded number of shares and their approximate worth.[20]

Figure 9.2 shows how complex data can be summarized and presented in an interesting way. Note how the graphics make it easier to understand the statistics presented.

UNICEF and other caregiving organizations provide food, water, clothing, school materials, and other necessary supplies to the world's children who are most in need. According to UNICEF, in the Mwanza region of the Republic of Tanzania alone, the most immediate needs that households with orphans cannot meet include the following: 41 percent cannot provide school materials; 23 percent cannot provide health-care expenses, thus causing greater numbers of children to be ill; 21 percent cannot provide adequate food; 11 percent cannot provide clothing; and 4 percent cannot provide other needs.[21]

FIGURE 9.2 Visualizing Statistical Data

A chart with statistics can help summarize complex data and make ideas interesting to your audience.
Source: Based on *Africa's Orphaned Generations*, Ch. 2, UNICEF, accessed March 31, 2012, from http://www.unicef.org/sowc06/pdfs/africas_orphans.pdf.

The Most Immediate Needs That Households with Orphans Cannot Meet

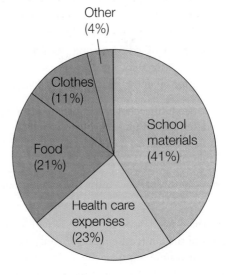

⟩ SUMMARY

Develop a Research Plan

9.1 **Develop** a research plan to gather information and find supporting materials for your speeches.

You now will be able to build on the knowledge gained in the previous chapters when you practiced topic generation and the creation of general and specific purpose statements and a thesis for speeches.

- Begin early.
- Gather more information than you'll need.
- Think carefully about your topic: Where should you go to find the best information to help you create the speech?
- Prepare a preliminary list of references.
- Be selective in choosing materials to enhance your knowledge.
- Meet your instructor's requirements for numbers and types of supporting materials.
- Take good notes and keep complete information on the sources.
- Know when to say, "Enough is enough."

Research: Gathering Information

9.2 **Identify** five principal sources of information for your speech topic.

Many excellent sources of information can help you develop your speeches:

- The Internet provides good information but be sure to evaluate carefully what you find on the web.
- Social media can be a good source of information because it provides a starting point and possible examples.
- You should be your first source of information. Choose topics you like and/or that are important to you.
- The interview gives you up-to-date information about a topic from an expert on the topic.
- Mediated information databases can help you find current, relevant topics.
- The library provides great amounts of information both in hard copy and through electronic databases.
- All sources should give you reliable, current, consistent information from believable, credible persons.

Use Research to Support and Clarify Ideas

9.3 **Differentiate** among the four types of materials to support and clarify your ideas.

Once you've selected a topic, developed a research plan, and started gathering materials to support your ideas, you need to determine carefully which of the four types of materials you can use to support your main points.

- *Testimony* provides current, relevant information from an expert or reliable source. You gain credibility when your testimony is from trusted sources.
- *Examples*, *definitions*, and *statistics* provide tangible clarification of your topic.

⟩ DISCUSSION STARTERS

1. Why is it important to have a research plan? What is yours?

2. What do you need to know about a topic before you begin your research?

3. Provide three sources you might consult to clarify and enhance speeches.

4. What unique perspectives can electronic sources provide?

5. When is an interview a particularly appropriate method?

6. Your speech topic is "sexual harassment." When you choose library research, where should you begin?

7. When and why is the reference section a good place to gather materials for a speech?

8. Identify three good supporting and clarifying materials you've heard others use.

9. On what basis should you judge the effectiveness of a source of information to support a particular point of view?

10. As a listener, how do you feel when you hear someone using statistics in a speech?

11. Why should you evaluate a web source?

CHAPTER 10

ORGANIZING AND OUTLINING YOUR SPEECH

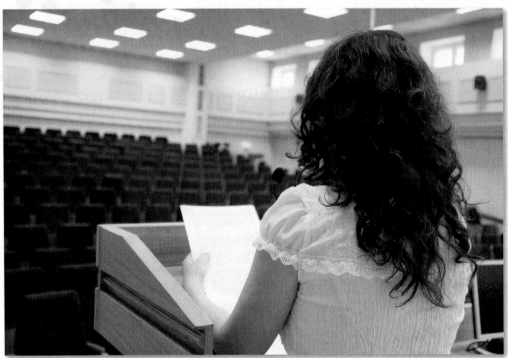

Cimmerian/E+/Getty Images

A well-organized speech is key to your success as a presenter. Listeners want to hear an introduction that captures their interest, an organized speech that makes sense and has current or future relevance for them, and a conclusion that ties things together well.

→ CHAPTER OUTLINE AND LEARNING OBJECTIVES

Organize the Body of Your Speech

10.1 **Identify** ways to organize the body of your speeches.

Organize the Introduction of Your Speech

10.2 **Organize** the introduction of your speech.

Organize the Conclusion of Your Speech

10.3 **Compose** an effective conclusion to your speech.

Outline Your Speech

10.4 **Construct** outlines to help you stay organized in your presentations.

MAKING EVERYDAY CONNECTIONS

One of the questions communication professors often hear is this: "Why do we have to use specific organizational patterns? We never hear those patterns in speeches we hear in the news or in any place other than the classroom." In many ways, those questions are true: The organizational patterns you learn and use in this class are very specific and demonstrate how to organize your speeches. They are not the only ways, of course. While you may not use these exact organizational patterns, you do need to present organized speeches, and at least some of the patterns can be used for any speeches or presentations you make. Once you learn to carefully structure speeches, you can better create an organized speech for your listeners. Think of these activities as training to develop the skills and tools necessary to be an effective presenter. The organizational patterns you'll use in this class provide practice in organizing and outlining your speeches; once you've learned and used a variety of patterns, you can easily adapt what you

know to different topics and venues. Remember, your goal is to practice effective communication through organized presentations. There are many ways to accomplish organized speeches, and your practice in class helps you know what is needed and how you can effectively say what is needed so your listeners can easily follow you. Learning and using specific organizational patterns in class provides a foundation for using other forms outside class.

QUESTIONS TO THINK ABOUT

1. Identify five ways speakers appear to be organized.
2. List five things you do to help *your* listeners follow *your* thoughts.
3. What recommendations would you offer speakers to help you *really* listen?
4. How do you feel when you're listening to a speaker who seems disorganized?

You now have two of the toughest of the speaker's jobs completed: You've chosen a topic and gathered information. The next task is to organize the information into a sequence or pattern of organization. Organization is a skill and one of the best ways to learn and apply organizational skills is in speech preparation. Although there are no *prescriptions* for success, established organizational patterns can help you learn to present material in understandable ways. The point in using specific organizational patterns for class assignments is that once you have successfully used one these organizational patterns, you can move on to other ways to construct speeches.

Organizing your speech involves arranging its parts into a systematic and meaningful whole. Speeches are usually organized into three main parts: *introduction, body,* and *conclusion.* By this point, you have determined general and specific purposes and formulated a draft of your thesis statement. This work should help guide you to organize your speech. Because the body is the main part of any speech and contains most of its content, we recommend that students begin by working on it first and then prepare the introduction and conclusion; thus, we examine the body first. Some instructors may want you to take each part of the speech in order, so be sure to follow their advice.

organizing
Arranging ideas and elements into a systematic and meaningful whole.

Organize the Body of Your Speech

10.1   **Identify** ways to organize the body of your speeches.

The **body** of a speech presents the main content, and organizing the speech will help you formulate your thesis statement. To ensure a well-organized body of your speech, your content must be divided into a limited number of thoughtfully selected, connected, ordered, supported, and stated main points.

body
The main content of a speech that develops the speaker's general and specific purposes.

Develop the Main Points

Well-developed **main points**, the principal subdivisions of a speech, are critical to an effective thesis statement (and speech). Let's assume your purpose is to inform your audience about social media and you want to discuss its uses and effects. Your

main points
The principal subdivisions of a speech.

research guided you to choose a specific perspective on the topic. To determine your specific purpose and main points and to finalize the thesis for your informative speech on social media, you decide to ask and answer three questions:

1. What are social media?
2. How have social media changed the world?
3. What do I need to know to use social media effectively?

Since you have thoroughly researched your subject, you can easily determine the main points. The following is an example of an organization with three main points:

I. Social media include web-based and mobile-based technologies that create user-generated content and interactive communication between individuals, organizations, or businesses.
II. Social media have changed every aspect of our lives, including business, education, relationships, political campaigns, and a degree of awareness of global issues.
III. Social media need to be monitored so we can be effective creators and consumers.

The body of the speech will take shape around these three main points. These points are derived from communication, media studies, sociology, and educational research. While communication professors usually recommend no more than three main points in a 5- to 7-minute speech, some topics lend themselves to four or five main points and some to only two, depending on the topic and assigned time restraints for your speech.

Not every piece of information you gathered constitutes a main point. Main points are broad, overarching statements that help to organize the many particulars you found through your research. In this example, "Facebook" or "Snapchat" may well be two of the subpoints of the first point, but neither probably would be a complete main point in a short speech.

Relate Main Points, Specific Purpose, and Thesis   The main points serve as the basis for the thesis statement. Together, the specific purpose and the thesis will determine the direction of the speech. Here is a persuasive thesis structured from the main points noted earlier:

SPECIFIC PURPOSE: To persuade my audience about the impact of social media on our lives, both as creators and consumers.

THESIS: Social media significantly affect our lives; thus, we need to be effective creators and consumers.

Here is another example of developing purpose, thesis, and main points. Let's say your purpose is to inform your listeners about cyber bullying. Your thesis statement might then be something such as:

We need to understand that social media has a downside; we need to understand cyber bullying and recognize its strong link to suicide in young people.

This thesis statement establishes three main points: the downside of social media, an explanation of cyber bullying, and the links of social media to youth suicides. Or perhaps you are assigned to present a speech that will persuade your audience to act in some specific way. From your research on social media, you know that it has both costs and benefits, and you want your listeners to monitor children's and young adolescents' use of Facebook and other forms of social media.

You can take numerous approaches, but remember that you ultimately want your listeners to know the benefits as well as the dangers of various forms of social media. In this speech, you are not just reporting facts; you want your listeners to *do* something. You must make a compelling argument to make them listen *and* act.

As you begin to apply your research, think about the general purpose: to persuade my listeners to understand social media. Then ask yourself, "What should my listeners know about social media?" As you generate answers, the main points of your speech will emerge. Eventually, you might determine that blogs, chat rooms, Facebook, LinkedIn, Twitter, and YouTube provide communication and connection, but they also have disadvantages. You are now ready to refine your specific purpose and state your thesis and main points:

SPECIFIC PURPOSE: To persuade my audience that Facebook, Twitter, and other social media need to be monitored when children and adolescents are connected.

THESIS: Facebook, Twitter, and other forms of social media keep us connected with others, but they can be used negatively and must be carefully monitored to ensure safe use.

Main Points:

I. Facebook and Twitter are two popular forms of social media used by youth and adolescents.
II. Social media can create harmful situations for any of us, but especially for young people.
III. Social media should be monitored for content and connections for young people.

Present the Main Points   Main points, like the specific purpose and thesis, should be carefully developed and written. They should also be specific, vivid, relevant, and parallel in structure. (We use Roman numerals to designate main points because, as you will see later, they eventually become the main elements in the speech outline.)

Be Specific   The more specific your main points, the less confusion they will create and the more meaning they will have for your audience. It can be easy to misunderstand a speaker who makes vague, overgeneralized statements. Each main point in a speech should be independent of the others and simple to understand. Compare the following:

Ineffective Main Point:

I. Widespread use of social media has changed the world, is always available, and is used differently by different generations of users.

Effective Main Points:

I. Social media have changed communication in every facet of life.
II. Generational differences exist in the use of social media.
III. Social media, with their "always available" features, create risks of distraction and anxiety.

MAKING CONNECTIONS FOR SUCCESS
Creating Purpose and Thesis Statements

Your assignment is to create and present a 6- to 8-minute informative speech. Your instructors say the topic should be one you find important and relevant. They also suggest you choose a topic on something personal or that has had an effect on your family and friends. As a practice activity, choose one of the following topics and write a general purpose, a specific purpose, and a thesis statement. Be prepared to share and justify your statements with your instructor and classmates.

1. What we should know about boutique drugs
2. You, too, can create an educational TED Talk
3. Listening is a much-needed skill everywhere in today's world
4. The March for Our Lives Movement demands safety
5. Your own choice

As you can see, the first example contains three ideas in one point, which makes it too complicated. The second example divides the three ideas into three separate points, thus making each one easier to understand.

Use Vivid Language   We cannot overemphasize the importance of language choice. When you listen to or present speeches, you become aware of words and their effects. You're already aware that the language we use for conversation and speeches (oral language) is more interesting and vital than written language. Now you need to consider how to make the best choices to help you reach your listeners. The more vivid your main points, the more likely they are to create interest. Main points should be thought-provoking, attention-grabbing ideas that stand out from the supporting materials.

> VIVID LANGUAGE: Apple's iBeacon may cause you to spend more on impulse purchases as retailers tempt you with digital coupons and special offers.
>
> LESS VIVID LANGUAGE: Apps already on your phone such as Apple's iBeacon can determine where you are in a store and provide you with special offers and digital coupons just as you approach specific products and tempt you to buy things not on your list.

Vivid phrasing may be shorter or longer than less vivid language, but it should not be exaggerated. Anything less than vivid, natural words may hurt the speaker's credibility. The limits of good taste and ethical considerations should be observed.

Show Relevance   Main points relevant to the audience's immediate interests encourage greater involvement and empathy. For instance, instead of saying, "Obesity among the young has reached high levels," say, "Obesity in the young is dangerously high." Using direct references to the audience, whenever possible increases the connections between you, what you are saying, and your audience. Audience members like to know how the speaker's subject relates to them and why they should listen.

Create Parallel Structure   Main points should be expressed in parallel structure—that is, using similar grammatical patterns and wording—when possible.

Not Parallel:

I. The world's number one health risk is hunger.
II. Tuberculosis, malaria, and AIDS combined do not match the number of deaths from hunger.
III. Over 15,000 men, women, and children will die of hunger today.

Parallel:

I. Hunger is the world's number one health risk.
II. Hunger results in more deaths than tuberculosis, malaria, and AIDS combined.
III. Hunger causes the deaths of 15,000 men, women, and children each day.[1]

Parallel structure of the main points makes material easier to develop and remember. Listeners usually have only one opportunity to hear a speech; therefore, anything you can do to make the main points stand out from the rest of the content works to your benefit. In the above example, the speaker strengthens the bond with the audience by consistently focusing on the effects of hunger and beginning each main point with the word *hunger*.

Limit the Number of Main Points   The number of main points in your speech will depend on at least three considerations. First, the time available for most classroom speeches is limited by practical considerations. As a result, most classroom speeches have two or three points and no more than five points.

Second, the content to be covered in the speech, especially the amount and complexity of the supporting materials required for each point, affects the number of points. Try to balance the amount of time you devote to each main point. For example, if you are assigned a 5- to 7-minute speech, plan to allow no more than 2 minutes for the introduction and conclusion, distributing the remaining time equally among the main points. Of course, this is a *guideline*. It isn't always possible to balance the main points exactly and you don't want to do so. The nature of some speech topics requires that some main points be emphasized more than others or that the introduction or conclusion be longer.

Third, an audience should be able to sort out and recall each main point. This recall is impossible if too many points are presented. Common sense tells us three points are easier to remember than five. Therefore, as a speaker, you must set reasonable expectations for both you and your listeners. If you have too many main points and a limited amount of time, you will be unable to develop each point thoroughly enough to make it clear, convincing, and memorable.

Order the Main Points Once you identify your main points, you must decide presentation order. This decision takes serious analysis because the order determines the structure and strategy of your speech. The most effective order of presentation depends on the topic, purpose, and audience. Several basic patterns of presentation have been recommended and used over the years: *time sequence (chronological), spatial, topical, problem–solution, cause–effect (or effect–cause)*, and *Monroe's motivated sequence*.

The Time-Sequence Pattern In the **time-sequence (or chronological) pattern**, the presentation begins at a particular point in time and continues either forward or backward. The key is to follow a natural time sequence and avoid jumping haphazardly from one time period to another. This pattern is especially useful for tracing the steps in a process, the relationships within a series of events, or the development of ideas. Certain topics lend themselves to the time sequence, such as how to create a readable blog; how to reduce, reuse, and recycle; ways to create an indoor garden in your residence hall room; tips to create an effective website. Here is an example of a time sequence that moves forward from a specific time point:

time-sequence (or chronological) pattern
An order of presentation that begins at a particular point in time and continues either forward or backward.

    Main Points:

      I. The first step in establishing an effective website is to acquire a domain name.
     II. The second step is to choose a web host.
    III. The third step is to create an attractive website.

A reverse-order sequence begins at a specific time period and works chronologically backward. For example, a speech discussing citizens' concerns about world hunger, organized in reverse-order time sequence, could be as follows:

  I. The number of the world's hungry people continues to rise.
 II. During the first decade of the 21st century, humanitarians and activists began serious efforts to eliminate world hunger.
III. Hunger and malnutrition were recognized as a major global issue from the 1930s forward.[2]
 IV. U.S. president Herbert Hoover and Norman Borlaug began massive efforts to find solutions to provide food for the world's hungry people in the 1930s.

The time-sequence or chronological pattern can also be used to explain a process as well as move forward or backward to explain how historically significant issues are addressed.

The Spatial Pattern In a **spatial pattern** of presentation, the content of a speech is organized according to relationships in space—where we can find things. This method is especially appropriate for presentations describing distances, directions, or physical surroundings. For example, a spatial pattern might be used to explain how to create a

spatial pattern
An order of presentation in which the content of a speech is organized according to relationships in space.

wildflower space in your yard, strategies to improve your recall of information, or how to make your dorm room more comfortable. A spatial pattern connects the relationships among all the main points. Here is an example of main points organized according to a spatial pattern:

Main Points:

I. The Smithsonian has so many attractions you won't be able to see everything in one trip, therefore you must pick and choose the best areas for you.

II. Make your first stop the Smithsonian Castle, which houses the Smithsonian Visitors Center, for an orientation and free guides and maps.

III. To make the best use of the day, make your way from the Castle via public transportation to the National Mall in downtown Washington, DC, where 10 of its 19 museums are found.[3]

IV. Choose your favorites, consult the map, and create a route that allows you to move from one museum choice to the next in a minimum amount of time.

topical pattern

An order of presentation in which the main topic is divided into a series of related subtopics.

The Topical Pattern   According to the **topical pattern**, the main topic is divided into a series of related subtopics. Each subtopic becomes a main point in the speech, and all main points are joined to form a coherent whole. In this way, the topical pattern is a unifying structure.

We use the topical pattern when no other patterns of organization apply to the topic or purpose of a speech. The topical pattern works well for topics such as the health benefits of marijuana, what you gain from a study skills class, or the differences between language usage in papers and speeches. Here's how the topical pattern could be used to organize the main points of a speech on Earth Day:

Main Points:

I. Earth Day was created on April 22, 1970, by Wisconsin senator Gaylord Nelson to bring attention to environmental issues.

II. Earth Day has always capitalized on placing environmental concerns at the forefront of political and public consciousness.

III. Earth Day 2015 events were attended by billions of people from around the globe who spoke out on fighting climate change, planted trees, and cleaned up parks and streams.[4]

When the topical pattern is used correctly, each main point is parallel in structure and related to the others. Because the topical pattern is versatile, it can be adapted to most speech purposes and effectively present material on a variety of topics.

Four other patterns (problem–solution, cause–effect, effect–cause, and Monroe's motivated sequence) are primarily used in persuasive speaking and will be discussed in Chapter 12, which concentrates on informative and persuasive speaking.

Choosing the Best Pattern   We emphasized the importance of matching the pattern of organization to your topic, specific purpose, and thesis. You must also consider another key factor: your listeners. The savvy speaker anticipates audience responses. Therefore, if your audience analysis indicates that important questions or objections are likely to be raised, you should arrange your main points to meet those objections. For example, if you advocate mandatory community service and are certain someone in your audience will object to mandates of any kind, you might structure your presentation as follows:

Main Points:

I. Community service allows us to create a more caring world.

II. Community service gives us a feeling of satisfaction.

III. Community service today helps establish a pattern for paying it forward.

Listeners generally find a speaker easier to follow when a strong organizational pattern is provided in the speech. Visuals can also enhance the organization and clarity of the speech. A coherent speech is more interesting and is easier to understand.

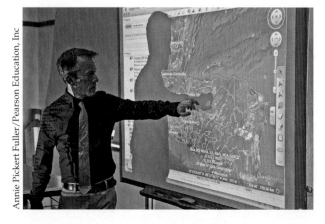

Annie Pickert Fuller/Pearson Education, Inc

FIGURE 10.1 Mind Mapping

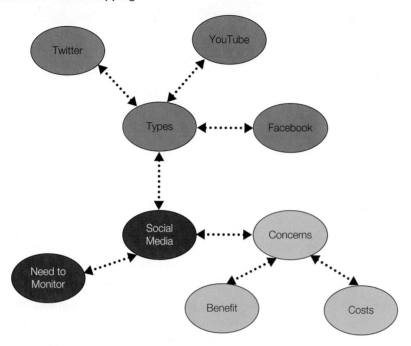

Culture may influence the way you prefer to organize a speech. Some cultures and co-cultures use alternative, but effective, organizational patterns. Mind mapping and narratives or storytelling, for example, are used for organizing presentations. The narrative form is now recognized by communication teachers as especially effective for social issues. Some speakers effectively use a combination of one or more organizational patterns in a given speech. *Until you're confident* in your ability to organize your thoughts, you may wish to use one primary organizational pattern in any given speech and then branch out to other patterns when you are comfortable about speaking.

Whatever organizational pattern you choose, you can make that pattern work for you when you make the speech compelling. For example, **mind mapping**[5] is an organizational strategy where you visually "map out" how various ideas connect. In a mind map, one starts in the center with a word or symbol and then writes down all the things that come to mind about that word or topic (see Figure 10.1). If you were mind mapping a social media speech, you might begin with a circle labeled "social media" and then identify the aspects of social media that should be considered all around that circle.

Another strategy identified above is **narrative or storytelling**. A story in a speech doesn't have to be long and involved and need not follow the guidelines for traditional stories. Instead, it is an account that brings more enthusiasm, realism, or even passion to the topic. Think about a speech or class lecture you found enjoyable. What did the speaker do? Why was it enjoyable? For example, one of the authors remembers a class on the religions of the world where note taking was easy, the content was memorable, and the professor's presentations were spellbinding. His lectures may have been written on yellowed paper, but the content was anything but dry and boring. (The professor opened the notebook at the beginning of class and never looked at it again until he picked up the notebook to leave the room.)

Connect the Main Points

A conversation can move from one unrelated topic to another without losing meaning or impact. For a speaker to communicate effectively with an audience who hears the message only once and who is not able to stop the speaker to ask questions, however,

mind mapping
A visual organizational strategy that uses words or symbols to identify the concepts and their connections to each other.

narrative or storytelling
An organizational strategy using a reporting of ideas and situations, as in a "story," but without the traditional components of a story.

Learn More about Organizing

Your instructor gives a homework assignment: Learn more about patterns of organizing and outlining by using web information.

Open your browser and type in "social media and the right to privacy," "what is Yammer," "medical marijuana," or a topic of your choice and determine what issues might work as main ideas for a speech. You might watch the YouTube video of mind mapping's creator, Tony Buzan, who explains mind mapping,[6] to see if this organizational pattern would work for you and your topic. You can also search "Monroe's motivated sequence" (or read Chapter 12)

to learn more about this organizational method. Finally, do an on-line search on "organizational speech patterns":

1. Read one or more of the options, find a pattern you like, and create an outline of a speech for either mind mapping, Monroe's motivated sequence, or narrative/storytelling.

2. Discuss your outline and the strengths and weaknesses of the organization pattern you chose, and then share with your classmates.

---

the thoughts in the speech must be systematically connected. The four most common connecting devices speakers use, singly or in combination, are transitions, signposts, internal previews, and internal summaries.

transition

A phrase or word used to link ideas.

Transitions   Phrases and words used to link ideas are called **transitions**. They form a bridge between what has already been presented and what will be presented next. Transitions are typically used between the introduction and the body of a speech, between main ideas, between supporting materials and visual aids, and between the body and the conclusion. A transition can review previous information, preview information to come, or summarize key thoughts. Here are some typical transition statements one could make:

> Moving from Facebook to Twitter, …
> Now that I have discussed the history of the Internet, I will talk about its uses.
> Turning now to…
> The final point is…
> Another example is…
> Keep these four items I discussed in mind, as we move to this conclusion.

signpost

A word, phrase, or short statement that indicates to an audience the direction a speaker will take next.

Signposts   Just as a traffic sign informs drivers about travel conditions, **signposts** are words, phrases, and short statements intended to let the audience know what is ahead. Here are some typical signposts:

> The next point…   First, let me explain…
> To recap this idea…   As you look at this figure…
> My second point is…   Finally…

Questions can also be used as signposts:

> How many people are affected by the tax cut program passed in 2017?
> What are differences between spoken and written language?
> How can we respond responsibly to the large number of orphans in the world?

Such questions draw the audience's attention to a forthcoming answer.

A signpost not only prepares an audience for what to expect next but also alerts the audience that the upcoming information is important. Some examples are as follows:

> The bottom line is…
> Solutions we could try are…
> One thing you need to recognize is…

internal preview

Short statements that give advance warning, or a preview, of the point(s) to be covered.

Internal Previews   Short statements called **internal previews** give advance warning, or a preview, of the point(s) to be covered. Here is an example: "Next we'll look at possible solutions to the problem of flawed budget priorities."

Internal Summaries An **internal summary** is a short review statement given at the end of a main point. Here is an example:

> Let's summarize what we've learned. Eating disorders have the highest mortality rate of any mental illness. Eating disorders affect 8 million Americans—7 million women and 1 million men—and eating disorders are often untreated.[7]

internal summary

A short review statement given at the end of a main point.

Support the Main Points

Main points by themselves are nothing more than assertions. It is crucial that each main point be supported and the support be relevant and logically organized. The body of a speech expands to outline form, where the main points are followed by subpoints, which in turn may be broken into further supporting points:

  I. There are more than 1 billion orphans in the world.
  - A. Children over the age of 10 are *unlikely* to be adopted.
    1. Prospective parents want babies or toddlers.
    2. Children with disabilities are viewed by some as high-risk, high-maintenance children.
  - B. All children need a loving home.
  II. The total number of orphans in sub-Saharan Africa is greater than the total number of children in Denmark, Ireland, Norway, Canada, and Sweden.
  - A. There are currently an estimated 53.1 million orphans in sub-Saharan Africa.
  - B. An estimated 12 percent of all children in sub-Saharan Africa are orphans.[8]

Supporting materials should be clearly related to the specific purpose, thesis, and main points of the speech.

Organize the Introduction of Your Speech

10.2 **Organize** the introduction of your speech.

Experienced speakers often develop their introductions after, not before, they finish the body of the speech (because they now know exactly what will be covered). An **introduction** includes opening statements that serve two important functions: *motivating* the audience to listen and *orienting* them to the subject. Therefore, your introduction should prepare the audience for the main ideas of your speech by setting the stage for the topic.

introduction

Opening statement that orients the audience to the subject and motivates them to listen.

Your introduction should be based on the information you gathered in your audience analysis. If your analysis was accurate and thorough, you should have a pretty good understanding of your audience's frame of reference and how it might differ from your own. Your introduction should meet three goals: orient the audience to the topic, motivate the audience to listen, and forecast (preview) the main points.

Orient the Audience to the Topic

Decide how much background information to provide on the basis of what your audience knows or does not know about your subject. This is the appropriate time to gain attention, state your specific purpose and thesis statement, and define terms that are essential to understanding the speech.

Several approaches can be used to gain attention and arouse the interest of your audience, such as referring to the subject or occasion, using personal references or narratives, asking rhetorical questions, presenting a startling statement, using humor, or incorporating quotations. You should choose these devices carefully to fit the audience, occasion, and context. None is *always* effective, and each has limitations. For example, using humor to focus your listeners' attention on a serious topic such as disease would not be effective. Consider the overall speech as you choose your approach because all parts of the speech must fit together well to achieve your desired purpose.

Refer to the Subject or Occasion   You may be asked to speak on a special occasion, such as a holiday, founders' day, graduation, or an anniversary. Here is a sample attention-getter related to an occasion:

> Dr. Galvin has always been my role model for her teaching, research, and service. When asked for information, she readily gives it. When someone needs a helping hand, she's one of the first volunteers. When you look in the dictionary for "service to the discipline of communication," you'll see her picture. It gives me great pleasure to present this distinguished service award to Dr. Kathleen Galvin.

Use Personal References or Narratives   Whenever you can relate your own experience to a speech, do so. Personal experiences make your speech more meaningful to your audience and show them that you know your subject. Here's how a speaker used a personal experience to introduce a speech on why she didn't eat chocolate.

> I never wanted to eat chocolate. My friends would always ask for chocolate and offer to share with me, but I wasn't interested. I was taught to eat what was put before me, so when I went to a birthday party and was served chocolate cake with chocolate ice cream, I ate it and immediately became violently ill. I was allergic to chocolate. No wonder it never had any appeal for me.

Ask Rhetorical Questions   A rhetorical question is a question for which no answer is expected. Asking rhetorical questions in an introduction usually encourages an audience to become intellectually involved. (Asking real questions is also an effective way to get your audience interested and involved in the speech, but it is important to let the audience know that you expect answers from them when asking this type of question.) Such questions can also be used to create suspense. Here's one example of a rhetorical question used to involve the audience:

> Have you ever wished you could just eat anything you like, whenever you like? If so, you're in the majority of citizens in the United States.

Present A Startling Statement   A startling statement can be used when you want to shock or surprise your audience. Startling statements are extremely effective at getting attention, as shown by this example: "The harsh reality is this: Party time is over!" Startling stories can also be used to grab your audience's attention:

Nobel Prize–winning author Toni Morrison is a world-renowned novelist who has many resources she can call on to arouse the interest of an audience. She often refers to the subject or occasion, tells stories, uses personal and biographical information, and reads passages from her work to get her audience's attention.

> There may be a time bomb within your body. Really. It may be ticking away unmercifully, and unless you recognize the symptoms and change your lifestyle, that time bomb may cause you to have serious health problems and even affect the length of your life. The time bomb within is stress. "We're all under stress," according to Drs. Bruce McEwen and George Chrousos. And, when we're stressed, our bodies react with a "fight-or-flight" response. The body pumps out adrenaline, increasing heart rate and blood pressure (and readying us to fight), and sending more blood to our muscles (so we can flee).[9]

Use Humor   A funny story, a relevant joke, or a humorous approach not only gains the attention of your audience but also relaxes them. Stories and jokes must be tied to the content of the speech and not offered simply for the sake of humor. One speaker began her talk as follows:

> An airline pilot wrote that on this particular flight he had hammered his plane into the runway really hard. The airline had a policy that required the first officer to stand at the door while the passengers exited, give a smile, and a "Thanks for flying XYZ airline."
>
> He said that in light of his bad landing, he had a hard time looking the passengers in the eye, thinking that someone would have a smart comment, but no one seemed annoyed.
>
> Finally, everyone had gotten off except for one [elderly] woman walking with a cane. She approached and asked, conspiratorially, "Sonny, mind if I ask you a question?"
>
> "Why no Ma'am, what is it?"
>
> "Did we land or were we shot down?"[10]
>
> You may wonder why I'm beginning my speech with a joke, but the answer is easy. My mother and grandmother always told me, "Laughter is the best medicine. It will cure whatever ails you." And, the longer I live, the wiser those words seem to be. Laughter is strong medicine for the mind and body. Research shows that laughter is a powerful antidote to stress, pain, and conflict. Nothing works faster or more dependably to bring your mind and body back into balance than a good laugh.
>
> Let me share four reasons why laughter is good for your health.
>
> 1. Laughter relaxes the whole body.
> 2. Laughter boosts the immune system.
> 3. Laughter triggers the release of endorphins.
> 4. Laughter protects the heart.[11]

Incorporate Quotations Sometimes a quotation can grab your audience's attention and, if cited accurately, also adds to the credibility of your speech. A student talking about language started her speech as follows:

> Lee Iacocca once said, "It's important to talk to people in their own language. If you do it well, they'll say, 'God, he said exactly what I was thinking.' And when they begin to respect you, they'll follow you to the death."[12] Today I want to talk with you about the power of language and how you can use it to help you be a competent communicator.

Whatever you choose to gain attention and maintain interest in your introduction, it should be relevant and should orient the audience to the topic.

State the Specific Purpose and Thesis Once you have your audience's attention, you need to state the specific purpose and thesis statement of your speech. Both the specific purpose and thesis statement were discussed in detail earlier in this chapter. Sometimes the specific purpose and thesis statement are best stated together; sometimes it is appropriate to state the specific purpose at the beginning and the thesis toward the end of the introduction, where it serves as a preview of the speech. When you state the specific purpose and thesis, you orient listeners to your topic and give them a clear indication of where you are headed with your speech. This preview is also essential in helping listeners recall what you said because they have only one opportunity to hear your message.

Ellen DeGeneres uses her fame to support causes. Her use of quotations, personal experiences, and humor gets her listeners involved and helps them pay attention to the message.

Lisa O'Connor/ZUMAPRESS.inc/Alamy Stock Photo

Motivate the Audience to Listen

Design your introductory comments to "hook" your listeners. You must hold their interest and attention throughout the entire presentation, but that task will be easier if you can capture them by making the topic significant to them and by establishing your credibility.

A standard way of making your topic relevant is simply to point out the reasons for presenting your speech. The audience must find a reason to listen as early in the speech as possible. You should also consider whether it is necessary to establish your credibility in speaking on the topic you have selected.

credibility
A speaker's believability, based on the audience's evaluation of the speaker's competence, experience, character, and charisma.

Credibility refers to a speaker's believability based on the audience's evaluation of the speaker's competence, experience, and character. For example, if Lady Gaga, singer and entertainer, were to speak on immigration policies or climate change needs, she would have to establish her credibility on the subject by relating to the subject and indicating how she became an expert on the topic.

Forecast the Main Points

Before you finish introducing your speech, let the audience know what you will cover in the speech itself. This is known as *forecasting*, and it affords listeners a road map so they know where you will take them in the remainder of your speech. Forecasting helps your audience be better listeners.

Let's look at some sample introductions. The following examples show how to orient and motivate your listeners and forecast the main points of your speech:

> Laughter is a powerful antidote to stress, pain, and conflict. Nothing works faster or more dependably to bring your mind and body back into balance than a good laugh. Humor lightens your burdens, inspires hopes, connects you to others, and keeps you grounded, focused, and alert.
>
> With so much power to heal and renew, the ability to laugh easily and frequently is a tremendous resource for surmounting problems, enhancing your relationships, and supporting both physical and emotional health. Laughter relaxes you, it boosts your immune system, it triggers the release of endorphins that promote an overall sense of well-being, *and* it protects your heart.[13]

Can you label the specific parts of the previous introduction? Now look at the following example to see if you can identify the specific parts:

> Grandma used to tell me, "The day is wasted if I have not laughed." She was a wise woman who was able to laugh every day, despite extenuating circumstances and poor health. And, she made sure all of her grandchildren knew how to laugh and laugh frequently. Laughing with others is more powerful than laughing alone. Furthermore, shared laughter is one of the most effective tools for keeping relationships exciting. Humor improves the quality of your connections with coworkers, family members, and friends. Humor allows you to be more spontaneous, let go of defensiveness, release inhibitions, and express your true feeling.[14]

This introduction accomplishes several functions at one time: It gets attention, it relates the topic directly to the audience and to the speaker, it establishes the speaker's credibility on the topic, and it also notes the main points of the speech.

The following sample introduction incorporates background and an attention-getter; it provides listeners with a reason to listen, points out the significance of the topic, lets the listener know "what's in it for me," and states the specific purpose and thesis:

Three years ago my sister and brother-in-law decided to add to their family by adopting. Because there are so many orphans worldwide, they decided to adopt an international child who might not otherwise be adopted because of age or disabilities. They started their information search on the Internet and found so much information they had to quickly think about what they wanted to know. They learned that the things they should first consider were age, gender, race, and medical needs. My whole family was involved in their decision-making process, so it made sense for us to do our own research, too.

The things we discovered might be helpful to you now or sometime in the future, since the number of orphans waiting to be adopted has risen sharply in the last few years, and you, or someone you know, may find international adoption a possibility. At the very least, you can be knowledgeable about the process if it ever comes up for discussion. I'll share some ideas about where to start, finding your child, and legal considerations when you, family members, and friends are adopting.[15]

MAKING CONNECTIONS FOR SUCCESS
Introducing Your Speech

First impressions are very important. Think back to your first day of this class. You made some instantaneous judgments about the class, the professor, and your classmates. Have those first impressions changed? Researchers and business people tell us that speakers, interviewees, and salespersons must get the listeners' attention in the first 15 seconds or risk losing them. Communication scholar David Zarefsky says, "The introduction to a speech powerfully affects the audience's first impressions of a speaker."[16]

Analyze this introduction and answer the following questions:

Men aboard Captain Cook's ship first used the surfboard in March 1779. Surfing is a difficult sport to learn. Today I'd like to share my experience in surfing, the history of surfing, and how to surf.

1. Which of the guidelines for the introduction are not covered?

2. What could be done to make this introduction lively and attention-getting?

Guidelines

DEVELOP YOUR INTRODUCTION

1. **Keep the introduction relatively brief.** Your introduction should make up only 5 to 10 percent of the total content (30 to 50 seconds).

2. **Allow plenty of time to prepare the introduction carefully.** Because it is critical to the success of your speech, it should not be rushed or written at the last minute.

3. **Make the introduction creative and interesting.** To accomplish this, think of several possible introductions, and choose the most effective one.

4. **As you research your speech, watch for material to use in the introduction.** Keep a notebook or file of interesting quotations, stories, humorous statements, and other items that might give your opening some dazzle. But

remember: A successful introduction *must* be relevant to the speech topic.

5. **Develop the introduction after you have completed the main part of your speech.** Relevant introductions are easier to create after you determine the content and direction of the body.

6. **Write out the introduction, word for word.** This section of the speech is too important to improvise or leave to chance. When you know exactly what you will say at the beginning of your speech, you are more confident and will get off to a strong start. Then practice delivering the introduction until you can present it conversationally but flawlessly. If you follow this guideline, you won't need to have the word-for-word introduction on your notecards or outline.

Organize the Conclusion of Your Speech

10.3   **Compose** an effective conclusion to your speech.

conclusion

Closing statements that focus the audience's thoughts on the specific purpose of a speech and bring the most important points together in a condensed and uniform way.

Your **conclusion** should focus your audience's thoughts on the specific purpose of your speech and bring your most important points together in a condensed and uniform way. Your conclusion should relate to your introduction and help your audience make the connections between the various parts and points of the message. In persuasive speeches, you may also use your conclusion to spell out the action or policies you recommend to solve a problem. In every case, your conclusion should reinforce what you want your listeners to remember.

Because your conclusion is as important as any other part of your presentation, you should give it the same amount of attention. Be especially careful to avoid adding new information in this part of the speech. In addition, remember that you, as a speaker, have only one chance to get your message across to your audience. Repetition is an important strategy to help listeners recall the important information you presented.

Show That You Are Finishing the Speech

You need to prepare your listeners for the end of your speech; otherwise, they are left hanging and feeling uncomfortable, sensing that something is missing. Do not bluntly state that you are finishing or even say, "In conclusion…" and especially do *not* say, "That's it." Instead, you should carefully and creatively indicate that the speech is winding down. An example might be, "As we've discussed, there are five ways we can become better listeners."

Make Your Thesis Clear

Repetition is important when you have only one chance for the listeners to hear your message. Be sure you creatively remind your listeners of your central idea: "You've already heard me tell you earlier that effective listening is a highly valued skill you can learn."

Review the Main Points

Repeating the main points of a speech is particularly helpful anytime you want your audience to remember them. For example, the speaker who informed her audience about barriers to effective listening concluded her speech as follows:

> Let me review the barriers that have the most impact on our listening. They are factual, mental, language, and physical distractions. If you remember these and how they affect listening, you will be a more effective listener.

In addition to helping the audience remember your content, reviewing the speech reinforces both your purpose and the thesis statement.

End with a Memorable Thought

A memorable thought may include referring back to an attention-getting device, citing a quotation, or issuing a challenge or appeal. A memorable quotation is a good way to leave a lasting impression on your audience. When it is relevant and reinforces your thesis statement, a quotation can give your speech additional authority and help increase your credibility. It is crucial that you always cite the source of all quoted information or any information that is not your own. Ethical communicators understand the importance of citing sources as part of the responsibilities of the speaker.

If your purpose is to persuade, the conclusion may also include a challenge or appeal to action. The following conclusion recaps the main points and asks the listeners to take action:

> Sleep researchers are just beginning to understand what we have lost when we lose sleep. Our bodies change drastically when we're sleep deprived and there are many health risks. Hormone levels change to the point that our energy levels are very low when we awaken and are actually comparable to the low morning levels usually associated with the elderly. Furthermore, sleep deprivation may lead to obesity, a decline in immune function, fuzzy thinking, and even to cancer risks. You need to change your schedules! You need at least 8 hours of sleep. Plan your work so that you can always get a good night's rest. If you do get behind, take a nap! A short nap works best—about 45 minutes can improve your health, your attitude, and your thinking. I urge you to take charge of your life. Get some sleep![17]

Signal the audience that your speech is nearing its end by using phrases such as, "Today, we have examined…," "In the past minutes, we have considered…," or "Finally, let me share…." Each prepares the audience for your concluding remarks. The following conclusion lets listeners know the speech is nearly finished, and it summarizes and synthesizes the major points covered. An appeal for action is made, and listeners are left with a memorable thought.

> Eating disorders are pervasive in our society. Yet many insurance firms don't offer coverage for treatment. They filter out what they believe to be "legitimate" mental illness—and many don't believe eating disorders fall into that category.

President John F. Kennedy's memorable inaugural address concludes: "And so, my fellow Americans, ask not what your country can do for you; ask what you can do for your country." President Barack Obama concluded his inaugural speech in a similar way: "My fellow citizens of the world, ask not what America will do for you, but what together we can do for the freedom of man." Do you find each memorable? Why or why not?

MAKING CONNECTIONS FOR SUCCESS
Effective Conclusions

One of this writer's colleagues was laughing as she came into the office. "I swear, the next time a student says, 'That's about it' or, 'That's all' I'm going to do a Porky Pig imitation—buhdee, buhdee, buhdee!" Communication professors are not the only ones who get frustrated with speakers who just stop and don't really conclude their speeches. A conclusion should provide a summary and a synthesis and, metaphorically speaking, should "put a bow on the package."

Jeremy Rifkin, author, consultant, economist, and technology guru, gave a speech titled "The BioTech Century" in May 1998 at the City Club in Cleveland, Ohio. Here's his conclusion:

> So I am hoping the public can come up into this debate. We are very far behind…. I work with business leaders and CEOs all over the world, and I can tell you the developments going on in the Life Science industries are so fast; they're moving so quick; they're so far advanced from what the public understands that we have a great gap here. The public needs to be informed in discussions like the one we're having today, and then you and I need to be engaged.
>
> We cannot leave these decisions only up to the scientists in the laboratory or the executives in the corporate boardrooms of the Life Science industry, because these technologies should not just be arbitrated in the marketplace. They affect all future generations. If this isn't the technology revolution that we discussed broadly and intimately, which one will we ever? So my hope is that beginning in the next few years, we can begin to engage this great question about the future of our evolution. How do we move into this century of genetic commerce and how do we begin to engage this daunting new science in a way that'll benefit our children and create a renaissance rather than great upheaval for future generations?[19]

You can view the entire speech on the American Rhetoric website. Answer the following questions as you reflect on Rifkin's speech and how well it meets the criteria established in this section:

1. We say that effective conclusions leave the listener with something to think about and remember. Did Rifkin do that?
2. What is his final message?
3. What is the effect of the way the words are arranged?
4. Does the conclusion seem to fit the title "The BioTech Century"?

Guidelines

DEVELOP YOUR CONCLUSION

1. **The conclusion should be brief and should end with a definite summarizing statement.** The conclusion should account for between 5 and 15 percent of the content of the speech (30 to 60 seconds).

2. **The conclusion should contain no new information.** If it was not mentioned in either the introduction or the body of your speech, it should not be in the conclusion.

3. **The preparation of the conclusion should not be rushed.** Allow plenty of time to develop it, and craft it carefully, but deliver it extemporaneously.

4. **Leave your audience with something memorable.** Think of several possible endings and choose the best one (i.e., the one that best serves the purpose of your speech).

5. **Write out the conclusion word for word.** Then learn it so well you can end your speech smoothly, conversationally, and confidently.

This means that countless eating disorder sufferers who are not employed by large companies with a group health plan may not be able to receive adequate psychological attention.

Mental health coverage is necessary for treating these diseases, as the cost of eating disorder therapy can reach hundreds of thousands of dollars. Remember the example of the 65-pound young woman I earlier cited who spent five weeks in the intensive care unit.

Please talk with your employers and legislators to change policies for all members—not just those who are part of large corporations—so everyone can receive the psychological care he or she needs.[18]

Synthesize and Summarize

Your conclusion should let listeners know you are about to finish the speech. It should also clearly remind them of your thesis and the main points you've covered. Essentially, your conclusion leaves your listeners with a summary and synthesis—something memorable that ties your ideas together.

Outline Your Speech

10.4 **Construct** outlines to help you stay organized in your presentations.

Outlining is one of the most difficult steps in preparing a speech. The outline demonstrates the organization of your speech. **Outlining** involves arranging the entire contents of a speech in a logical sequence and writing that sequence in a standardized form. The outline is often referred to as the blueprint or skeleton of a speech. Organizing is arranging ideas or elements in a systematic and meaningful way. To organize your speech, select one of the patterns of organization discussed earlier in the chapter. Both organizing and outlining involve arranging information to form a meaningful sequence, but outlining is a more rigorous writing process. David Zarefsky, communication scholar and public speaking textbook author, says, "Speakers depend on outlines at two stages: when they put the speech together and when they deliver it. Each stage requires a different kind of outline."[20]

Outlining is more detailed than organizing and helps to unify and clarify thinking, to make relationships clear, and to provide the proper balance and emphasis for each point as it relates to the specific purpose of a speech or written paper. Outlining also helps ensure that information is both accurate and relevant.

As you prepare your outline, you gain an overview of your entire presentation. Developing an outline should help you gauge the amount of support you have for each

outlining
Arranging materials in a logical sequence, often referred to as the blueprint or skeleton of a speech, and writing out that sequence in a standardized form.

of your main points and identify any points that need further development. The actual process of outlining usually requires three steps: creating a preliminary outline that identifies the topic and the main points to be covered in the speech, expanding the preliminary outline into a full-sentence outline that clearly and fully develops the speech content, and condensing the full-sentence outline into a presentational outline to aid delivery.

Principles of Outlining

You should keep in mind three principles as you prepare your outlines: subordination, coordination, and parallelism. **Subordination** clearly identifies the hierarchy of ideas. The most important ideas are main points and are supported by subpoints (that is, they are subordinate to the main points), and the outline uses specific rules for format. **Coordination** suggests that ideas with the same level of importance use the same kinds of numbers (Roman and Arabic) and letters (capitalized and not capitalized) to visually indicate the relationships between ideas. **Parallelism** is the term for using similar grammatical forms and language patterns for all ideas, main points, subpoints, and sub-subpoints. If you have a I, you must have a II; if you have a 1, you must have a 2; if you have an A, you must have a B; and each entry must be key words, a complete sentence, or a phrase. You should not mix phrases and complete sentences. Furthermore, your language should be parallel, as demonstrated in earlier examples. The format looks something like this:

I. Listening is learned [main point].
   A. Listening can be taught [subpoint].
   B. Listening skills must be developed [subpoint].
      1. You can change your listening behaviors [evidence].
      2. You can change your attitude about listening [evidence].
   C. Effective listeners learn to avoid common barriers [subpoint].
      1. Ralph Nichols identified ways to overcome barriers to effective listening [evidence].
         a. Find areas of interest [backing for the evidence].
         b. Listen for main ideas, not details.
      2. Listening is an active process; it doesn't just happen [evidence].
   D. Listening is connected with thinking [supporting idea, or subpoint].
II. Listening is a cognitive construct [main point].

The following sections on preliminary outlines, full-sentence outlines, and presentation outlines follow these rules of outlining and can serve as examples as you prepare your own outlines.

The Preliminary Outline

A **preliminary outline** is a list of all the points that *may* be used in a speech. Suppose you are preparing an 8- to 10-minute persuasive speech on bullying. Because of the limited amount of time, you know you cannot possibly cover everything related to the topic. And because your general purpose is to persuade, you need to focus the content of your speech on that goal. Thus, you recall what you have already read about topic selection, audience analysis, gathering information, and using supporting and clarifying materials. Then you determine your specific purpose: to persuade my audience to take action against all forms of bullying. On the basis of this specific purpose, you can prepare a preliminary outline of possible main points, as shown in the following sample. Once your possible main points are arranged in this way, you will find it easier to analyze your thoughts. You can then decide exactly which main thoughts to include in your speech and choose the best order for presenting them. Here is what your preliminary outline might look like:

subordination
Clearly identifies the hierarchy of ideas: The most important points are main points and are supported by subpoints (that is, they are subordinate to the main points); the outline uses specific rules for format.

coordination
Ideas with the same level of importance use the same kind of numbers (Roman and Arabic) and letters (capitalized and noncapitalized) to indicate visually the relationships between ideas.

parallelism
Style in which all ideas, main points, subpoints, and sub-subpoints use similar grammatical forms and language patterns.

preliminary outline
A list of all the main points that may be used in a speech.

SAMPLE PRELIMINARY OUTLINE FOR A PERSUASIVE SPEECH

TITLE: Take Action against Bullying

GENERAL PURPOSE: To persuade

SPECIFIC PURPOSE: To persuade my audience to take actions against all forms of bullying

POSSIBLE MAIN POINTS

I. What is bullying?

    A. Definition of "bullying"

    B. The forms of bullying

II. Reasons for bullying

    A. Being the "new kid" in the school

    B. Being different from other students

III. The solutions to bullying

    A. Adults look for signs and educate young people about bullying.

    B. Help kids take action against bullying.

    C. What each of us can do to stop bullying

The Full-Sentence Outline

full-sentence outline

An outline that expands on the ideas you have decided to include in your speech. It identifies the main points and subpoints you will cover, written as full sentences.

A **full-sentence outline** expands on the preliminary outline and includes all the ideas you have decided to include in your speech. The full-sentence outline identifies the main points and subpoints you will cover, written as full sentences. Although a full-sentence outline will not include every single word you'll utter, you will have a detailed view of the speech. Some professors require a full-sentence outline as a final outline, turned in with an evaluation sheet prior to speaking. (Other

MAKING CONNECTIONS FOR SUCCESS

Ordering Ideas in an Outline

For a speech titled "Make Reading Your Hobby," rearrange the following sentences in proper outline form for the body. Think about the principles of outlining as you look over the entries. Make sure to arrange the content in a logical sequence. Place the number of each sentence in the proper place in the outline. (See page 228 to verify your answers.)

1. Low-cost rental libraries are numerous.

2. Reading is enjoyable.

3. It may lead to advancement in one's job.

4. Books contain exciting tales of love and adventure.

5. Many paperback books range in cost from $7.95 to $19.95.

6. People who read books are most successful socially.

7. Reading is profitable.

8. One meets many interesting characters in books.

9. Reading is inexpensive.

I. _____

    A. _____

    B. _____

II. _____

    A. _____

    B. _____

III. _____

    A. _____

    B. _____

Guidelines

OUTLINING

1. **The preliminary outline should include a list** of the topics that you might cover in the speech.

2. **A good outline should identify the importance of the ideas you will present.** The consistent format, with subordination, coordination, and parallelism, provides a visual of the hierarchy of ideas.

3. **The outline should provide** an overview of your content.

4. **The outline should help you clarify your thinking.** It gives the ordering of ideas and the amount of supporting material you have for those ideas.

5. **It is sometimes helpful to write out the entire introduction and conclusion in your outline so that you can make sure you have included everything you need.** Check with your instructor to see if that is what he or she requires. Some instructors do not want the introduction and conclusion written out because this may make the speaker dependent on the written word and thus less conversational. Other instructors require both introduction and conclusion to be outlined so speakers can remember what they want to say.

teachers want only a preliminary outline prior to presentation and a presentational outline turned in with the evaluation sheet and list of references.) Be sure to ask or listen for any specifics required by your instructor. The full-sentence outline should conclude with a bibliography or list of references identifying all sources you used in your speech; it helps you create a presentational outline, which we'll discuss in succeeding pages.

As we stated in Chapter 8, you can choose one topic that can be prepared and delivered either as an informative or persuasive speech. The following full-sentence outlines illustrate this very well. Sarah Johansen's speech on the charity Helen Keller International is first outlined as an informative speech, then as a persuasive speech. Note that the introduction to the informative speech contains more than one sentence, as is the usual custom. Because Sarah begins with a visualization and asks her listeners to close their eyes and imagine, it would not make sense to the reader if it were only one sentence.

SAMPLE FULL-SENTENCE INFORMATIVE SPEECH OUTLINE

"Helen Keller International," informative speech by Sarah Johansen, Fundamentals of Communication student, University of Nebraska–Lincoln, used with permission.

Topic	**TOPIC:** Helen Keller International
Title	**TITLE:** A Charity with Vision: Helen Keller International
General Purpose	**GENERAL PURPOSE:** To inform
Specific Purpose	**SPECIFIC PURPOSE:** To inform my audience about the charity organization Helen Keller International and raise awareness for its cause
Thesis	**THESIS:** To inform my audience about the mission and history of Helen Keller International, how it acts to prevent blindness, and its actions to reduce malnutrition worldwide

INTRODUCTION

Attention-getter relates topic to the listeners

I. Close your eyes for just a moment. Without sight, you must depend on other senses to remain aware of everything going on around you. Now imagine losing your sense of hearing as well. How would you communicate with others and stay aware of your surroundings? [Note: Because the speaker uses visualization, *this introduction is longer than one might have for another type of introduction. It won't make sense with just one sentence.*]

Orientation

    A. Helen Keller was both blind and deaf and still managed to have an incredibly successful and inspirational life and was known for her intelligence and ambition.

Forecasts a main point of the speech

    B. One of her many accomplishments was cofounding the organization Helen Keller International (HKI) in 1915 with George Kessler.

Forecasts a main point

    C. The organization is a legacy Helen Keller left for us to continue, with her spirit and enthusiasm at its heart, in order to better the world.

BODY

II. Helen Keller International's Mission and History

Background

    A. Helen Keller was blinded at the age of 2 after a terrible fever and soon after lost her sense of hearing.

Supporting material

    B. George Kessler was a New Yorker who survived the sinking of the *Lusitania* in 1915 and committed his life to helping soldiers who had lost vision in combat.

Supporting material

    C. George and his wife asked Helen Keller for her support and formed the Permanent Blind Relief War Fund for Soldiers & Sailors of the Allies in 1915, which helped blinded veterans learn how to read Braille, make chairs, and knit.

        1. The Fund expanded and incorporated civilians as well as veterans, and by 1970 the focus shifted to preventing blindness by distributing vitamin A capsules in Central America and in the Asia-Pacific region.

Further evidence to support the first main point.

        2. The name Helen Keller International was adopted in 1977 and serves not only the blind but also those who are underprivileged and at risk for blindness.

    D. HKI's mission statement emphasizes their dedication to improving health outcomes and saving the eyesight of the world's poor and underprivileged, and their work establishing programs to mitigate the causes and effects of blindness and malnutrition.

    E. HKI now serves in 22 countries around the globe in Africa, the Asia-Pacific region, and the Americas.

Second main point: the work of the organization

III. Helen Keller International and Preventing Blindness

    A. The number one treatable cause of blindness in the world is cataracts.

        1. According to the book *Principles of Human Anatomy*, a cataract is the loss of transparency of the lens of the eye, which has a number of causes, including age and sun exposure.

        2. HKI trains nurses and surgeons and provides medical equipment in underdeveloped countries so cataract surgeries can be performed for as little as $12 a patient.

    B. Vitamin A deficiency is the leading cause of childhood blindness.

        1. According to *Africa News*, "an estimated 250,000 to 500,000 vitamin A–deficient children become blind every year, and half of them die within 12 months of losing their sight."

        2. HKI provides vitamin A supplementation to children twice a year in order to prevent blindness.

        3. Gary Heiting states that vitamin A helps keep the cornea of the eye healthy and helps prevent macular degeneration.

Second main point is supported by specific evidence on the utility of Helen Keller International.

    C. In the United States, a program called ChildSight, a branch of HKI, has been instated that screens the eyesight of, and delivers glasses to, underprivileged children.

Third main point: other benefits of the work of the organization

IV. Helen Keller International and Reducing Malnutrition

    A. Vitamin A supplementation, according to www.HKI.org, "not only can prevent a lifetime of darkness, but can also result in a 25% reduction in child mortality."

B. HKI provides low-cost vitamin and mineral supplements to severely malnourished populations.

C. The Homestead Food Production program created self-sufficient gardens in Cambodia, the Philippines, Bangladesh, and Nepal.

D. Food fortification program provides more nutritious foods for families and communities around the world.

> Four subpoints to support the additional features and work of Helen Keller International

CONCLUSION

V. Helen Keller International is an exceptional charity that is solely focused on the betterment of lives all around the world.

> Summary and synthesis of the speech—leaves the listeners with something to remember

A. The treatment of blindness in both children and adults has improved the quality of life for many individuals in underprivileged countries.

B. Food production and sustainability provided by HKI will drastically affect the world's hunger and malnutrition problems.

C. Helen Keller's legacy lives on through this organization and will continue to help people all over the world.

> Subpoints reinforce the important work of the organization

REFERENCES

Heiting, Gary. "Vitamin A and Beta Carotene: Eye Benefits." *All About Vision*. N.p., June 2011 Web. Retrieved May 19, 2012, from www.allaboutvision.com/nutrition/vitamin_a.htm.

Helen Keller International 2012. Web. Retrieved May 19, 2012, from www.hki.org.

"Nutrition; A Sweet Potato a Day." *Africa News,* Nov. 29, 2011. LexisNexis. Web. Retrieved May 19, 2012, from https://www.lexisnexis.com.

Tortora, Gerard J., and Mark T. Nielsen. *Principles of Human Anatomy*, 12th ed. Print. New York: John Wiley & Sons, Inc., 2012. 728.

A SAMPLE FULL-SENTENCE OUTLINE
FOR A PERSUASIVE SPEECH

Sarah Johansen, University of Nebraska–Lincoln (modified slightly; used with permission)

TOPIC: Helen Keller International: Worthy Charitable Organization

TITLE: A Charity with Vision: Helen Keller International

> General Purpose: To persuade

SPECIFIC PURPOSE: To persuade my audience that they should donate to Helen Keller International

THESIS: Helen Keller International is a trustworthy charity that is worthy of your donations.

INTRODUCTION

> Attention-getter lets listeners know the work and value of this charitable organization

Horrific events affect millions of children and adults all over the world and are reasons why Helen Keller International (HKI) is working diligently to help improve eyesight, nutrition, and lives of people much less fortunate than those of us here in this room.

BODY

> This is both the Thesis and First main point

I. Helen Keller International Is Worthy of Donation

A. ChildSight is a HKI program in the U.S. that "brings education into focus" by screening vision and providing eyeglasses to underprivileged children.

1. Improved vision increases confidence and drastically improves scholastic performance.

Evidence of worthiness

      2. TOMS has partnered with HKI to provide prescription glasses from their eyewear line to qualified children.

   B. Another HKI program, Vitamin A Supplementation, saves vision as well as lives in other countries.

      1. This program costs only $1 for a child to receive supplements for a year.

      2. According to hki.org, "Vitamin A supplementation is considered to be the most cost effective, high-priority public health treatment in the world."

More evidence

      3. Over 85 million capsules were delivered to children last year.

   C. In order to reduce malnutrition worldwide, HKI is creating programs that help to grow and sustain food production in developing countries.

      1. According to Emily Hillenbrand's article "Transforming Gender in Homestead Food Production," the Homestead Food Production program instituted by HKI, "promotes small-scale agriculture among women, specifically to improve women's and children's nutrition outcomes."

      2. Homestead Food Production program also helps to create jobs by growing gardens and crops.

Internal summary before moving to second main point

   D. To sum it up: "Helen Keller International gets more bang for the buck than almost any group I can think of." Nicholas D. Kristof

Second main point

II. Helen Keller International Is a Trustworthy Organization

   A. How donor funds are used are clearly explained on hki.org. Eighty-five percent of profit goes directly to programs, 2 percent goes to fundraising, and 13 percent goes toward administrative expenses.

   B. HKI's current audited financial statements are available to the public on its website.

   C. According to Better Business Bureau records, HKI meets all 20 Standards for Charity Accountability.

All subpoints provide evidence of worthiness

   D. It has received a four-star rating from Charity Navigator, the highest rating an organization can receive.

Third main point

III. What You Can Do to Help

   A. Twenty-five dollars supplies a student in the U.S. with a pair of glasses, $50 plants a Homestead garden for about 40 people, $100 provides 100 children with Vitamin A supplementation for a year, and $250 pays for five individuals to have cataract surgery.

   B. Online donations are the easiest way to contribute to the organization.

   C. There are other ways to help HKI through other businesses.

      1. Aframes eyewear donates 5 percent of their profits to HKI's Vitamin A Supplementation program.

      2. Baking for Good is on online bake sale that provides 15 percent of each purchase to a charity of the consumer's choice.

Evidence provides support for how donations can help others

      3. There is also a list of other small businesses that help out HKI and can be found at www.hki.org.

CONCLUSION

Conclusion summarizes the main points, reinforces the specific purpose (to persuade the listeners to donate to HKI) and leaves listeners with a thought about the value of their contributions

   A. You cannot deny that it is hard for us to imagine a life where losing sight is a major concern, but we must try to put ourselves in someone else's shoes.

   B. Helen Keller International is working to bring light where there is darkness, bring food where there is famine, and bring the vision of a better world to all of humanity.

   C. A quote by Helen Keller accurately describes the miracles HKI performs: "Alone we can do so little, together we can do so much."

REFERENCES

"Charity Review of Helen Keller International." *Better Business Bureau*. N.p., 2012. Web. 23 May 2012. http://www.bbb.org/charity-reviews/national/blind-and-visually-impaired/helen-keller-international-in-new-york-ny-2499.

Helen Keller International. Helen Keller International, 2012. Web. 19 May 2012. www.hki.org.

Hillenbrand, Emily. "Transforming Gender in Homestead Food Production." Print. *Gender & Development* 18.3 (November 2010): 401-425.

Sight and Survival. Helen Keller International, 2007. Web. 23 May 2012. http://www .youtube.com/user/HKI1915?feature=watch.

The Presentational Outline

A **presentational outline** is a concise, condensed outline with notations, usually a combination of full sentences and key words and phrases. This is the outline you will work from when you present your speech. The advantages of the presentational outline as a delivery aid are that it is concise, requires little space, and is comprehensible at a glance.

Your presentational outline should include your main points and sufficient clarifying and supporting material to aid you in the presentation. The outline *may* also include your complete introduction and conclusion, although the choice is up to you (and your instructor). Key words and phrases are important in a presentational outline because they remind you of the points you want to make. Some speakers use codes, symbols, or even colors to remind them of key points, vocal pauses, changes in speaking rate, and so on. But remember, if your presentational outline is too long, complex, or detailed, you can easily get too involved in your notes and lose contact with your audience. The example of the informative speech on the charity Helen Keller International shows a concise, condensed presentational outline with notations to help the speaker deliver the speech.

The presentational outline can be easily transferred onto note cards. Some speakers prefer to use note cards, and in some classroom situations students are *required* to use them. The number of note cards and their use should be kept to a minimum. Classroom assignments sometimes specify that you use only one side of two or three cards. When this is the case, you need to adjust the amount and type of information you include to aid you in remembering key information. Note cards are easier to handle than a full sheet of paper, and usually require only one hand, so you can gesture. The sample presentational outline below meets requirements for our classes.

presentational outline

A concise, condensed outline with notations, usually a combination of full sentences and key words and phrases.

MAKING CONNECTIONS FOR SUCCESS
Citing Sources

The Internet has excellent sources to help you create reference pages. (Some instructors will ask for a bibliography; others, a notes page; and some may want a "sources cited" page. All are acceptable, but be sure to ask your instructor for her or his preference.) The *Modern Language Association Handbook for Writers of Research Papers*, 8th edition; the *Publication Manual of the American Psychological Association*, 6th edition; and the *Chicago Manual of Style*, 17th edition, are all excellent sources to help you put your reference page together. Most can be found online through your own institution's library website. Several universities have complete websites for guidelines to citation. One such website is that of the Duke University libraries.

Complete the following activity to help prepare you for the specific outline and reference page required by your instructor:

A. Go online to find guidelines for citing sources.
B. Determine how to cite two different kinds of print sources.
C. Next, determine how to cite web sources.
D. Look again to see whether you can find examples of how to cite an email interview. If that site does not include personal or email interviews or conversations, search for another site to determine how to cite interviews.
E. Bookmark or print these sites so you have a handy reference for citing sources. (This will be useful when you create the reference page to turn in.)

With that in mind, answer the following questions:

1. What were the best sources you found?
2. What guidelines seemed most helpful to you?

Guidelines

USING PRESENTATIONAL NOTE CARDS

1. **Use only a few note cards (they are a help but cannot capture the whole speech).** The object is to serve as an aid or guide.

2. **Always number the note cards so that, if they get out of order, you can reorder them quickly.** Numbers in the upper left-hand corner will help you stay organized.

3. **Write on only one side of the card.** Remember, the cards are to help you and should not have complete details.

4. **Use abbreviations as much as possible.** Just be sure you remember how you use abbreviations.

5. **Do not write out your speech—use an outline format.** Outlining helps you remain conversational and thus more interesting.

6. **If you prefer, write out the introduction and conclusion in their entirety.** That does not mean you should read either one word-for-word, but writing them out helps you remember better.

7. **List only the main points and subpoints on the cards.** Too much information is distracting and may mean you spend too much time looking at the card.

8. **If necessary, write out quotations, statistical data, and other information that must be cited accurately.** When you want to be totally accurate, this kind of data should be exact when you discuss it in the speech.

SAMPLE PRESENTATIONAL OUTLINE FOR AN INFORMATIVE SPEECH

Sarah Johansen, University of Nebraska–Lincoln (modified slightly; used with permission)

Topic	**TOPIC:** Helen Keller International
Title	**TITLE:** A charity with vision: Helen Keller International
General Purpose	**GENERAL PURPOSE:** To inform
Specific Purpose	**SPECIFIC PURPOSE:** To inform my audience about the charity organization Helen Keller International and raise awareness for its cause
Thesis	**THESIS:** To inform my audience about the mission and history of Helen Keller International, how it is acting to prevent blindness, and its actions to reduce malnutrition worldwide.

INTRODUCTION

Sarah might annotate her presentational outline in this way (boldface, red italic type) to help her remember to cover everything in her speech.

Look at audience.

I. Close your eyes for just a moment. Without sight, you must depend on other senses to remain aware of everything going on around you.

   A. Helen Keller was both blind and deaf and still managed to have an incredibly successful and inspirational life.

   B. One of her many accomplishments was cofounding the organization Helen Keller International (HKI) in 1915 with George Kessler.

Show the website.

   C. The organization is a legacy Helen Keller left for us to continue.

Pause briefly, move, look at audience.

BODY

First main point

II. Helen Keller International's Mission and History

   A. Helen Keller was blinded at the age of 2 after a terrible fever and then lost her hearing.

Present picture of Helen Keller as a child.

   B. George Kessler, a New Yorker, committed his life to helping soldiers who had lost vision in combat.

     1. George and his wife asked Helen Keller for her support and formed the Permanent Blind Relief War Fund for Soldiers & Sailors of the Allies.

     2. The Fund expanded and incorporated civilians as well as veterans; by 1970, the focus shifted to preventing blindness.

     3. The name Helen Keller International was adopted in 1977.

   C. HKI's mission statement emphasizes their dedication to improving health outcomes and saving the eyesight of the world's poor and underprivileged, and their work establishing programs to mitigate the causes and effects of blindness and malnutrition.

Show world map, pointing out general areas and specific locations.

III. HKI and Blindness Prevention   Second main point

   A. Cataracts are the number one treatable cause of blindness.

     1. *The Principles of Human Anatomy* identifies a cataract as the loss of transparency of the lens of the eye.

Project picture of eyes.

     2. HKI trains medical teams and provides medical equipment in underdeveloped countries.

   B. Vitamin A deficiency is the leading cause of childhood blindness.

     1. According to *Africa News*, "an estimated one-quarter to one-half of the vitamin A–deficient children become blind every year, and half of them die within 12 months of losing their sight."

     2. HKI provides vitamin A supplementation twice a year.

     3. Gary Heiting states that vitamin A helps keep the eye healthy.

   C. In the United States, ChildSight, a branch of HKI, screens the eyesight of, and delivers glasses to, underprivileged children.

Show PowerPoint slide of workers delivering glasses.
Pause.

IV. HKI Reduces Malnutrition   Third main point

   A. Vitamin A supplementation "not only can prevent a lifetime of darkness, but can also result in a 25 percent reduction in child mortality."

   B. HKI provides supplements to severely malnourished populations.

   C. The Homestead Food Production program created self-sufficient gardens in impoverished areas.

   D. Food fortification programs provide more nutritious foods around the world.

Show additional scenes of the work of HKI.
Pause.

CONCLUSION

V. HKI is an exceptional charity solely focused on the betterment of lives.

   A. The treatment of blindness has improved the quality of life for many in underprivileged countries.

   B. HKI drastically affects the world's hunger and malnutrition problems.

   C. Helen Keller's legacy will continue to help people all over the world.

Pause, smile, gather notes, remove visuals, move to sit down (or wait to answer questions if appropriate).

❭ SUMMARY

Organize the Body of Your Speech

10.1   **Identify** ways to organize the body of your speeches.

- You can now use your research to develop *main points* that help you present the most important aspects of your topic. Your general and specific purpose statements guide your listeners so they can recognize what you expect of them.

- Order the *main points* of a speech to help your listeners interpret your content.

- Assess the organizational patterns described and choose the best for your own speeches.

- Use *transitions, signposts, internal previews*, and *internal summaries* in your own speeches.

Organize the Introduction of Your Speech

10.2   **Organize** the introduction of your speech.

Introductions should orient listeners to the topic, motivate them to listen, and provide the direction of your speech. You should be able to complete preliminary and presentational outlines for your speeches.

Organize the Conclusion of Your Speech

10.3   **Compose** an effective conclusion to your speech.

The *conclusion* lets your listeners know you are finishing the speech and provides a summary and synthesis of the ideas presented so they leave knowing why you made the speech and what you hoped they would gain from it. The conclusion reinforces your thesis.

Outline Your Speech

10.4   **Construct** outlines to help you stay organized in your presentations.

- *Outlines* are created to help you remain organized. They also help your listeners tune in to your messages.

- To make sure that listeners know your intent, outlines should follow three principles: *subordination, coordination*, and *parallelism*.

- *Preliminary outlines* are often words or phrases you create to help determine how things fit together.

- *Full-sentence outlines* provide a clear overview, but not the entire speech, to ensure that you stay on track and help your audience listen.

- *Presentational outlines* help you remember to look at your audience, smile, use your visuals, cover up your visuals, and move in a way that emphasizes the important aspects of your content.

❭ DISCUSSION STARTERS

1. How do you respond when you listen to a speaker who seems disorganized? To one who seems easy to follow and organized?

2. Discuss the times when you heard speakers and had no idea where they were going or why they chose the topic they did. How did you respond to the speech? To the speaker?

3. Identify three specific ideas or strategies you will consider as you work on your own speeches for this class.

4. If you will use different organizational strategies outside the classroom, why do your authors and instructors require the organizational patterns identified in this chapter and in class?

5. Think about a somewhat controversial topic you could use in this class. Identify three ways you might introduce the speech to get your classmates to listen to your ideas on the subject.

6. Why should we *not* end the speech with, "That's it"?

Answers and Explanations

Making Connections: Ordering Ideas in an Outline (page 220)

One set of possible answers: I. (2), A. (4), B. (8), II. (9), A. (1), B. (5), III. (7), A. (3), B. (6).

CHAPTER 11

MANAGING ANXIETY AND APPREHENSION WHEN DELIVERING YOUR SPEECH

Paul Bradbury/Caiaimage/OJO+/Getty Images

Most of us have some anxiety before giving a speech. The important thing to remember is this: Careful preparation and practice of your delivery can help you manage anxiety so you can speak effectively. Competent communicators are well prepared; thus they don't have to worry unnecessarily about the presentation.

→ CHAPTER OUTLINE AND LEARNING OBJECTIVES

Manage Speech Anxiety

11.1 **Identify** ways you can manage your speech anxiety/communication apprehension.

Methods of Delivery

11.2 **Demonstrate** appropriate use of the four methods of delivery.

Vocal and Physical Aspects of Delivery

11.3 **Analyze** your own vocal and physical aspects of delivery and find ways to improve both.

Presentational Aids

11.4 **Construct** presentational aids that enhance your speeches and help your listeners attend to the presentation.

Presentation Software

11.5 **Explore** how integrating software programs can aid your presentation.

Practice Your Delivery

11.6 **Perform** your speech delivery in practice sessions to help you gain confidence.

MAKING EVERYDAY CONNECTIONS

If you're a typical student, no matter what your age or geographical area, the mere thought of giving a speech creates some degree of anxiety or apprehension. In fact, many people identify fear of speaking as their number one fear. Anxiety is a normal response to being alone in front of a group of people—as one is when giving a speech. Most of us have some degree of anxiety; others have *communication apprehension*, that is, more anxiety that causes greater problems. Both can *usually* be managed with preparation, practice, and strategies to reduce their effects.

When students come to our offices and explain how nervous they get when giving speeches, your authors usually ask some questions and then explain that most people have some anxiety when preparing and delivering a speech. We also suggest some degree of anxiety is helpful as long as speakers use it in a positive way. We advise students to think about anxiety or apprehension as a behavior they can manage.

Before you read the chapter to find suggestions that will help you *manage* your apprehension and deliver effective speeches, take a few minutes to think about and answer the following questions.

QUESTIONS TO THINK ABOUT

1. How do you feel about giving speeches and making presentations?
2. When you experienced anxiety before or during a presentation, what specific reactions did you have?
3. Identify four or five thoughts and behaviors you normally employ to manage your anxiety.
4. Describe what you did in the past to manage your apprehension when speaking.

Presenting speeches can be fun. You might not believe that now, but if you have carefully completed all your work up to this point, you, too, may enjoy sharing your thoughts with the class. You have researched, organized, and arranged your ideas. Now you can focus on the delivery.

You should diligently prepare for your speech presentations. If you can, rehearse in the classroom. If not, find a room comparable to the one where you'll give your speech and practice out loud. If possible, get someone to listen to you and provide feedback about both content and delivery. Why? First, it allows you to know how the speech sounds. The written word and the spoken word are not the same and do not have the same effect. Practice helps you hear the difference. Second, practicing in front of someone provides you with listener response; you need that to help you make the right choices and to feel more confident about your speech. Do you still feel anxious about your presentation? The following information may help you find ways to alter your thinking and view anxiety as beneficial. You may also find behavioral strategies to help you manage your anxiety.

Manage Speech Anxiety

11.1   **Identify** ways you can manage your speech anxiety/communication apprehension.

speech anxiety
Fear of speaking before an audience.

communication apprehension
The most severe form of speech anxiety; an anxiety syndrome associated with either real or anticipated communication with another person or persons.

Communication researchers differentiate between **speech anxiety**, a multisystem response that creates a combination of biochemical changes in the body in a communication situation,[1] and **communication apprehension**, the most severe form, defined as an anxiety syndrome associated with either real or anticipated communication with another person or persons.[2] It is commonly accepted that the more we know about stage fright and communication apprehension and how to cope with either, the better able we are to *manage* the resulting behaviors.

Communication apprehension and speech anxiety are two of the most researched areas in communication. One of the reasons is that speaking in front of others is identified as people's greatest fear.[3] Most of us have some degree of anxiety when we speak in front of others. Your authors, based on their experiences, find that anxiety and apprehension can give speakers the motivation to do well. Anxiety is a problem only when we cannot manage it or when we choose *not* to communicate because of it.

Communication Apprehension

Communication apprehension can be seen in individuals who either consciously or subconsciously decide to remain silent. They perceive that their silence offers them greater advantages than speaking out or that the disadvantages of communicating outweigh any potential gains. Among the fears of those with communication apprehension is that of speaking before (or even thinking about speaking before) a group. However, not everyone who fears speaking before a group necessarily suffers from communication apprehension. That term refers to the much deeper problem of cutting oneself off from most, if not all, communication with others.

Communication apprehension often begins at an early age as a result of negative feedback. Children who are not encouraged to communicate or who are punished for doing so are likely to learn that communicating is undesirable and that silence is beneficial. As these children avoid communicating, others may unknowingly contribute further to their fear by asking questions such as "Cat got your tongue?" or "Are you afraid to talk?" Such words can make already anxious people feel inadequate and thus perpetuate the fear and anxiety associated with communicating. Communication-apprehensive individuals fear speaking (or even thinking about speaking) in all contexts, including one-on-one communication and small-group discussions. Because many of us have either some anxiety or communication apprehension, the focus of this chapter is to help you learn to manage those anxieties that keep you from being an effective communicator.

Symptoms of Speech Anxiety

Speech anxiety refers more specifically to the fear of speaking before an audience or group. Anxiety is a chemical reactive condition during which our bodies secrete hormones and adrenaline that eventually overload our physical and emotional responses. These chemical reactions are the same as those you might experience when you are waiting to see a friend you haven't seen in years or going to your first job interview. Your heart begins to beat faster, and your blood pressure starts to rise. More sugar is pumped into your system, and your stomach churns. When you experience these reactions, you may feel as if your body is operating in high gear and that little or nothing can be done about it. You should realize that some of these feelings are normal and, for most us, will not interfere with our speech performance.

Speakers often experience the behavioral signs of speech anxiety listed in Table 11.1. These behaviors can occur separately or in any combination, depending on the degree of apprehension experienced by the speaker. Speakers who feel apprehension may also make telling statements. For example, they may offer self-critical excuses or apologies such as, "I'm not any good at this anyway," "I didn't really prepare for this because I didn't have enough time," or "I never was able to say this correctly." These comments tend to draw more attention to speakers' nervousness and thus magnify the problem and usually do not improve the situation.

Speakers who have speech anxiety often overestimate how much the audience notices their behavior, and the audience often tends to underestimate a speaker's anxiety.

Table 11.1   BEHAVIORS ASSOCIATED WITH SPEECH ANXIETY

Voice	Quivering, too soft, monotonous, too fast, nonemphatic
Fluency	Stammering, halting, awkward pauses, hunting for words, speech blocks
Mouth and throat	Breathing heavily, clearing throat often, swallowing repeatedly
Facial expressions	No eye contact, rolling eyes, tense facial muscles, grimaces, twitches
Arms and hands	Rigid and tense, fidgeting, waving hands
Body movement	Swaying, pacing, shuffling feet, weight shifts
Nonvisible symptoms	Feeling too warm, too much saliva, dry mouth, butterflies in the stomach

Many communication professors have lists of behaviors such as the ones here. One of the first lists was published more than 40 years ago but is still viable. [Based on A. Mulac and A. R. Sherman, "Behavior Assessment of Speech Anxiety," *Quarterly Journal of Speech* 60, 2 (April 1974): 138.]

For example, audiences cannot detect a speaker who is experiencing butterflies unless the butterflies cause an observable reaction or the speaker's voice sounds nervous.

Causes of Speech Anxiety

Just as physicians can better treat an illness if they know its cause, people can better control apprehension/anxiety if they can determine the underlying problem. Many people treat only the symptoms and tend to ignore the causes; when you try to remove the symptoms without understanding the causes, it is usually a losing battle.

People may develop speech anxiety if they constantly hear that speaking in front of others can be a terrible experience. If speakers believe something can go wrong and they might make fools of themselves, they are apt to lose confidence and develop speech anxiety.

In our society, success, winning, and "being number one" are too often considered all-important. When we can't be the most successful, we sometimes consider ourselves failures. No one likes to fail; therefore, we are likely to believe that success brings rewards and failure brings punishment. If you are a winner, you are praised; if you are a loser, you are ridiculed. Consequently, we are under tremendous pressure to succeed.

When we are not successful at something, we are often told to try again. But if the consequences of the failure are dramatic and the payoff for success doesn't seem worth the effort, we may prefer to avoid the situation. Avoidance may result in punishment, but we may perceive that as better than failure. Sometimes society is more lenient. For example, in a competition we assume that there will be a winner and a loser. No one likes to lose, but playing your best and losing is usually acceptable. When someone makes a mistake in a speech, however, we may be more critical. Rather than acknowledge that the person is making an honest effort, we might perceive him or her as inadequate or unskilled. Consequently, the stress created by fear of making mistakes in front of others can be so great that it produces high anxiety and sometimes complete avoidance of speaking situations. We learn to respond in specific ways when facing something that creates anxiety because we have become conditioned to do so. Our reactions to a speech-making situation are *learned*. Because speech anxiety is a learned behavior, the only solution for its sufferers is to examine potential reasons for the anxiety and then use this knowledge to learn how to manage it.

Communication Apprehension, Anxiety, and Cultural Concerns

Increasing numbers of international students and Americans whose first language is not English enter our classrooms each year. Because of language and cultural differences, these students have some anxieties that go beyond those of native speakers. In interviews with international students and their professors, Xiaofan Liao learned that most international students were concerned about talking in class: "I don't know your language as well as I should. I'm nervous about responding in class." They were afraid they would not fully understand the assignment, that others would not understand them, and that they would "lose face" with their American professors and classmates.[4]

Some international students were concerned about translating from English to their own language and back again, and they were worried that the translation process would be slow and perhaps inaccurate. They also felt that they didn't really fit in; their foreign status often precluded their U.S. classmates from interacting with them. Some of them stated the classroom situation was so different from what they were accustomed to that it made them even more nervous. In each case, they felt that their differences translated to being perceived as in some way inferior to the native-speaking students and called undue negative attention to them. Giving a speech in front of a group is difficult for most of us. Those from different language and cultural backgrounds have additional stresses.

How Technology Can Help Manage Anxiety and Apprehension

What happens when you get anxious about speaking? Does your mouth feel as if it were filled with cotton? Or do you have too much saliva? Some people get cold and have clammy hands, while others flush, and every bit of visible skin, especially the neck and face, gets bright red. Communication scholar James McCroskey and his colleagues researched communication apprehension extensively, and while it may be of some comfort to know that most of us experience some degree of anxiety or fear when faced with real or imagined public speaking situations, apprehension causes some of us major problems. There are some strategies, however, to help us work through those states.

We can use technology to help manage communication apprehension or speech anxiety. Those who teach special anxiety sections suggest the first step in learning to manage your anxiety is to *recognize* it. And you can use various forms of technology to help you manage your fears. Here are some specific steps to help you:

1. List the physical symptoms of your anxiety when you think about giving a speech or when you're actually making a presentation (e.g., dry mouth, getting red in the face, and the like).

2. Compare your symptoms with the list in Table 11.1.

3. Once you have your speech in good presentational order (and well before the assigned due date), complete the following:

    a. Record yourself as you extemporaneously deliver the speech.

    b. Play back your recording and reflect on what you did well, where you had problems, and how you can improve the presentation.

    c. Adjust your speech and make any refinements or changes you think will help you reduce the difficulties.

    d. Record yourself again and follow the same procedure as above, and record a second or third time.

    e. View the recording and once again reflect on any changes needed. Practice the new version of your speech.

    f. Create a YouTube presentation and send the link to five of your family members and/or friends; ask them to send their feedback. (If you don't have the necessary equipment or knowledge to create a YouTube presentation, just record your presentation and share that with others.)

    g. Use their feedback to reflect on how you can improve your presentation.

    h. Make any changes in your presentation and create a new YouTube or video recording of your presentation. Share this new recording with one of the initial viewers and with one new viewer (e.g., a roommate, coworker, or classmate) and ask for their feedback.

    i. Use their feedback to improve your speech and delivery.

    j. At this point, you will have made the presentation at least five times and reflected on your presentation, and you will have feedback from several other people well in advance of your class presentation.

4. This preparation and practice should help you manage at least some anxiety because you received feedback from others and refined your speech and presentation.

After following the steps above, answer the following questions:

1. Describe the specific steps you took to manage your speech anxiety.

2. Did the feedback from others help to identify symptoms that you may have missed? If so, how did you address those symptoms in subsequent presentations?

Treating Speech Anxiety and Apprehension

Although speaking before a group can produce stress and anxiety, few people allow their nervousness to prevent them from attempts at success. Even well-known speakers and entertainers feel some nervousness before giving a speech, but they have learned to *control* it. Hugh Jackman, internationally acclaimed actor, hosted the 2009 Academy Awards; in a prebroadcast session, he acknowledged he was nervous because of the number of people in the profession and in the television audience who would judge him for a long time if he didn't "do well."[5]

Many classroom teachers admit to some degree of anxiety prior to meeting their classes for the first time. Even elected officials and those seeking elected offices admit they experience some nervousness prior to giving a speech, but they learn to manage it. The key to managing anxiety is the desire to do so. To cope with speech anxiety, we must realize the potential for failure always exists, but we cannot let it stop us from trying. If we allowed the possibility of failure to overwhelm us, we probably would never do or learn anything. A child beginning to walk is a prime example of how most of our learning occurs. At first, the child wobbles, takes a small step, and falls. But when the child falls, someone is usually there to offer help, support, and encouragement to

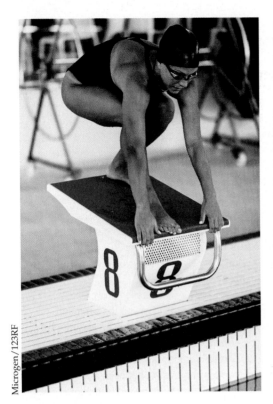

Microgen/123RF

Speech anxiety has no cures—only ways to reduce, manage, or control it so it does not interfere with your presentation just as athletes learn to manage their performance anxiety.

systematic desensitization
A relaxation technique designed to reduce the tenseness associated with anxiety.

continue. In addition, the child usually is determined to walk regardless of the difficulties. Speech making, like learning to walk, involves many of the same processes. Help, support, and encouragement are important, but the essential ingredient is determination to succeed.

Most successful people will tell you that before they were successful, they had some failures and moments of embarrassment. Their drive and self-confidence pushed them to try again. Some of our first speeches were not very good, and we were quite nervous about speaking in front of our classmates. However, it didn't take us long to realize even the best speakers in the class felt the same way. The only difference was they weren't afraid to make a mistake. Many of us expect perfection and are often too hard on ourselves. Some students, after giving a speech, said they were extremely nervous, although the audience detected no signs of their nervousness. Competitive athletes know that doing well requires the same kind of behavior recommended for reducing your speech anxiety: preparation; positive thinking; visualizing success; and practice, practice, practice.

Giving a speech and completing a pass play in a football game are not the same, but both require similar preparation. The successful pass play requires research, organization, learning, observation, practice, willingness to work hard, ability to perform, confidence, knowing your opponent's defense (or knowing your audience), and timing. A successful speech/presentation requires all of the aforementioned factors in addition to selecting an appropriate topic.

If none of the strategies in "Guidelines: Managing Your Speech Anxiety" helps to reduce your anxiety, you should probably seek professional help. Individuals who suffer from abnormal levels of speech anxiety should know that the negative feelings associated with speaking in front of others do not simply occur; they develop over a long time. Therefore, these negative feelings do not always disappear easily. With help, though, we can do something about apprehension and anxiety. Most colleges and universities have counselors or psychologists who are trained to reduce the fear of speaking in public. Some offer special sections of the beginning communication course for those who are anxious about speaking in front of others. If your fears cause problems, check with your instructor for strategies or referral to a specialist.

Systematic desensitization is a relaxation technique designed to reduce the tenseness associated with anxiety.[6] The goal is to help develop a new, relaxed response to the anxiety-provoking event. Try this: Imagine yourself standing in front of this class, ready to give your speech. Visualize the wonderful speech you will give. You confidently place your notes on the lectern, look at the audience, smile, take a deep breath, and begin speaking. Your audience smiles and nods throughout the speech, and you become more and more relaxed as you speak. When you finish, they applaud loudly.

Guidelines

MANAGE YOUR SPEECH ANXIETY

1. **You are not alone.** Almost everyone has some anxiety about giving a speech or making a presentation.

2. **Be prepared.** The more knowledge of and passion for the topic you have, the easier it is to concentrate on what you want to share rather than the fact that you are speaking.

3. **Be informed.** Know your audience and the surroundings in which your presentation will take place.

4. **Think positively.** Prepare yourself mentally for success. Believe you are going to be successful, and you probably will be.

5. **Practice,** Practice, practice, practice, and then practice more.

6. **Be informed.** Ask your instructor for additional advice and other possible available treatment programs.

7. **Don't give up.** Others want you to succeed, and you can if you want to do so.

Someone says, "That was a wonderful speech!" Remember how it felt to be so relaxed. Go through this visualization process and think about how relaxed you are. This kind of mental rehearsal helps you change negative thoughts to positive ones.

Meditation is another practice used by many to help them relax and focus on the tasks at hand. Meditation is defined as the process of spending time in quiet thought.[7] Meditation is popular; activists, actors, athletes, listeners, politicians, speakers, and people in the public eye as well as in everyday life have learned the benefits of meditation. Neuroscientists have found meditation is a helpful way to reduce all stress. A number of studies found that the brain and the body both work better and more efficiently in those who use mediation to center themselves and put their concerns to rest. Try this: Find a quiet spot. Stand tall. Close your eyes. Take a deep breath from the abdomen and hold it for a count of 10. Concentrate on holding your breath and counting. Then, slowly release the air by blowing through pursed lips, as if you were blowing a bubble, to the count of five. Wait quietly with your eyes closed for a count of 10 and repeat the process. Repeat 10 times with your eyes closed. The 10 repetitions will slow your breathing, your heart rate, and the brain activity. Next, sit down in a comfortable position and repeat the process another 10 times. Use a modified version of this every time you feel anxious or apprehensive about speaking. On the day of your scheduled presentation, try two or more repetitions before you go to class, and, just prior to your turn to speak, use a modified meditation routine to help you calm yourself.

Meditation may be done sitting in a chair or sitting lotus style on your legs. Whatever you try, remember that it's the deep breathing and cleansing of one's thoughts that provides the benefits.[8]

It is not easy to overcome anxiety in public speaking situations, but remember that some anxiety can be helpful and is a normal reaction to speaking in public. When we asked students for specific ways they dealt with their anxieties, they suggested the following:

1. Practice and have your introduction, main points, and conclusion clear in your mind. Students believe that once they know their introductions, main points, and conclusions, it is a lot easier to remember the details.

2. Walk confidently to the speaking area. Students believe this helps create confidence. If you're confident, it is likely you will feel relaxed. In other words, positive behavior results in positive outcomes.

3. Do not start your speech until you are ready. Students and instructors suggest that having everything under control before starting to speak makes it easier to relax and concentrate on the speech rather than on you.

4. Look at your audience and focus most of the time on friendly faces. Students believe that concentrating on those who are likely to give positive feedback helps promote a good feeling about speaking.

These suggestions are probably not new or surprising, but they will help in your quest to become a successful speaker. The best thing you can do is continue to give speeches in class and take more classes that will afford opportunities to speak under the supervision of a trained instructor. You can reduce and control your fear of speaking, but you need to continue to work at doing so, as well as follow the guidelines and suggestions offered here.

meditation
The process of spending time in quiet thought.

Methods of Delivery

11.2 **Demonstrate** appropriate use of the four methods of delivery.

Effective delivery conveys the speaker's purpose and ideas in a clear and interesting manner so the audience attends to and retains what was said as the speaker intended it. The effectiveness of a speech therefore depends both on what is said and on how it is conveyed. No two speakers are alike. For example, it is unlikely anyone could deliver the "I Have a Dream" speech as effectively as did Martin Luther King Jr. This speech, by one of the greatest speakers of the 20th century and widely regarded as a masterpiece, was delivered on August 28, 1963, to more than 200,000 people gathered in Washington, DC, to participate in a peaceful demonstration furthering the cause of equal rights for African Americans. If you have heard a recording of this speech, you know how King's delivery affected his audience. He had a rich baritone voice modulated by the cadences of a Southern Baptist preacher and the fervor of a crusader. Although the words of the speech can be repeated and King's style can be imitated, the setting, timing, and circumstances cannot be reconstructed. Therefore, the effect King had on that day can never be repeated. You can view/hear the speech at the American Rhetoric website (www.americanrhetoric.com).

A poorly developed speech can be improved by effective delivery, and a well-written speech can be ruined by ineffective delivery. No set of rules guarantees an effective delivery in every situation. The only consistent rule is that you must be yourself! Of course, as a beginning speaker, you probably have many questions about how to deliver a speech: How many notes should I use? Will I have or need a microphone? Where and how should I stand? Where or at whom should I look? How many and what kinds of gestures should I use? How and when should I use my visual aids? How loudly should I speak? How fast or slow should I speak?

Such questions are valid, but the answers will vary from person to person and from situation to situation. In the end, effective delivery is achieved by practice under the direction of a competent instructor. An awareness of self and knowledge of effective delivery also help to improve delivery. Although a speech may be delivered in many different ways, the four most common methods of delivery are impromptu, manuscript, memorized, and extemporaneous (see Table 11.2).

Impromptu Delivery

impromptu delivery
A delivery style in which a speaker delivers a speech with little or no planning or preparation.

The delivery of a speech with little or no formal planning or preparation (no research, no organization) is called **impromptu delivery**. You have used this method many times, perhaps without even realizing it. Whenever you speak without prior preparation, whether in response to a question in class, to a sudden request at a business meeting, or to a comment made by a friend, you use the impromptu method of delivery. The more formal or demanding the situation, the more most speakers prefer to avoid this approach. At times, however, you have no choice. In such cases, muster your self-control, relax, and concentrate on what you wish to say. The lack of preparation time distinguishes the impromptu method from other methods of delivery and forces speakers to depend solely on their ability to think on their feet.

Table 11.2   METHODS OF DELIVERY: ADVANTAGES AND DISADVANTAGES

	Advantages	Disadvantages
Impromptu	Spontaneous; flexible; conversational	No time for preparation; can be inaccurate; difficult to organize; can be stressful
Manuscript	Good for material that is technical or detailed or that requires complete preciseness and high accuracy; can be timed to the second; prepared	No flexibility; great amount of preparation time; difficult to adapt to audience response; may sound mechanical; lack of eye contact
Memorized	Good for short speeches; speaker can concentrate on delivery; easier to maintain eye contact; prepared	Inflexible; requires practice and repetition; speaker can forget or lose place; difficult to adapt to audience response
Extemporaneous	Organized; conversational; prepared	May sound mechanical; may be intimidating to inexperienced speakers; great amount of eye contact required

Manuscript Delivery

Reading the speech word for word is known as **manuscript delivery**. Speakers who use this method are never at a loss for words. A speaker should use a manuscript for situations in which every word, phrase, and sentence must be stated precisely. Using a manuscript is not uncommon for politicians, clergy, teachers, and others who need to present information completely and accurately or who are likely to be quoted after their presentations. But for beginners, manuscript delivery is often discouraged because it invites the speaker to concentrate more on the script than the audience and reduces eye contact with the audience. Furthermore, speakers who work from manuscripts are less able to adapt to the reactions of the audience and thus may sound mechanical. They are so busy concentrating on reading the speech they may be unable to respond to their listeners.

manuscript delivery
A delivery style in which a speaker writes the speech in its entirety and then reads it word for word.

Memorized Delivery

Memorized delivery requires you to memorize your speech in its entirety, usually from a word-for-word script. This kind of delivery is suited to short presentations, such as toasts, acceptance speeches, and introductions, and is also commonly used by speakers in contests and on lecture circuits. Speakers frequently memorize certain parts of their speeches, including examples, short stories, statistics, quotations, and other materials they can call up at the appropriate time. Politicians, salespeople, tour guides, and others often have a memorized pitch, or speech, to fit their needs.

Memorization has one advantage: You can concentrate less on what you have to say and focus more on your delivery. Of course, this is true only if you are extremely confident and have memorized your speech so completely you don't need to think about each word. One disadvantage of memorized delivery is its lack of flexibility; it doesn't allow for much, if any, adaptation to your audience. Beginning speakers face another disadvantage: They might forget what they want to say and become embarrassed. In addition, it is difficult to deliver a memorized speech without sounding mechanical. Effective presentation of a memorized address requires a great deal of practice and confidence.

memorized delivery
A delivery style in which a speaker memorizes a speech in its entirety from a word-for-word script.

extemporaneous delivery
A delivery style in which the speaker carefully prepares the speech in advance but delivers it using only a few notes and with a high degree of spontaneity.

Extemporaneous Delivery

In **extemporaneous delivery**, the speaker uses a carefully prepared and researched speech but delivers it from notes, with a high degree of spontaneity. Extemporaneous delivery is the method most commonly used in speech classrooms and in other public communication situations. When you give a report at work, for example, you will probably be expected to present your remarks extemporaneously. If you are a member of a problem-solving group at your place of worship and you have been selected to present the group's deliberations, you will also be expected to deliver your remarks in an extemporaneous manner. Instructors often require extemporaneous delivery in the communication classroom because it is the best style for most instances of public speaking.

Extemporaneous delivery is situated somewhere between memorized or manuscript delivery and impromptu delivery. Speakers depend on a brief presentational outline or notes and choose the actual wording of the speech at the time of delivery. They sometimes prefer to use a keyword outline, which simply outlines the points and subpoints of the speech, using keywords. This helps keep the speaker organized and on track but does not allow the speaker to become too reliant on the outline or notes.

An extemporaneous speech might at first seem as difficult as an impromptu speech; in fact it is much easier because it eliminates memorization

Extemporaneous delivery allows this young woman to appear relaxed and conversational. Her smile and natural gestures along with her eye contact help her appear confident and allow her to personally address her listeners.

Cleve Bryant/Photoedit

and manuscript writing, and leaves more time for preparation and practice. Thus once you have prepared your outline, you can practice your delivery. The goal of the extemporaneous method is a conversational and spontaneous quality. Conversationality and spontaneity are two hallmarks of speech delivery listeners find appealing. It is much easier to listen to and attend to conversational, lively, and spontaneous speakers. Each time you practice your speech, the wording may be somewhat different, although the content remains the same. Your objective should always be to use delivery to help you share meaningful ideas with your audience.

The advantages of extemporaneous delivery include the following: It gives you better control of your presentation than the impromptu method, it allows more spontaneity and directness than the memorized and manuscript methods of delivery, and it is more adaptable to a variety of speaking situations than the other methods. Most teachers, as well as professional speakers, prefer to use the extemporaneous method because it allows them to adjust to the situation moment by moment—listeners seem puzzled, so the supervisor stops to ask questions; listeners seem to be losing attention, so the teacher skips ahead. Extemporaneous delivery also allows audience members to become more involved in listening to the message.

Vocal and Physical Aspects of Delivery

11.3 **Analyze** your own vocal and physical aspects of delivery and find ways to improve both.

Without solid content and valid sources, nothing is worth communicating; but without effective delivery, even the most compelling information cannot be clearly and vividly presented. Because the audience is the ultimate judge of effectiveness, you must deliver your speech well to involve them in it. Audience members like to feel as if they are being personally addressed. Try to think of your presentation as a conversation and your audience as your partners in dialogue. Then use your voice and body to create this impression.

Vocal Aspects

Many beginning speakers overlook the important role of voice in delivery. Your voice should be pleasant to listen to, relate easily and clearly to your thoughts, and express a range of emotions. Your voice should convey the meaning you intend. The more natural, spontaneous, and effortless you appear to be, regardless of how hard you work, the more your listener can focus on what you say rather than on how you say it. Three aspects of voice that determine the effectiveness of delivery are *vocal quality*, *intelligibility*, and *vocal variety*.

vocal quality
The overall impression a speaker's voice makes on his or her listeners.

Vocal Quality   The overall impression a speaker's voice makes on listeners is referred to as **vocal quality**. Voices may be harsh, nasal, thin, mellow, resonant, or full bodied. Attitude can affect the quality of the voice and reveal to listeners whether the speaker is happy, confident, angry, fearful, or sad. Think about those times when you were extremely tired: How did your voice sound? Did you hide your tiredness from people listening to you? Probably not. Think about times when you were really excited about a topic. How do you think you sounded to your listeners? Generally, when we're really involved and interested in something, the voice carries energy and excitement and draws others into the conversation. Vocal quality is a highly accurate indicator of the presenter's sincerity. In addition, listeners tend to believe that speakers whose vocal delivery is interesting and easy to listen to are more credible and will probably be more willing to listen to those who use their voices effectively.

Intelligibility A speaker's **intelligibility**, the degree to which an audience can hear and understand words, is determined by vocal volume; distinctiveness of sound; accuracy of pronunciation; articulation; and stress placed on syllables, words, and phrases. The keys to high intelligibility are self-awareness and consideration for listeners.

intelligibility
Speaker's vocal volume, distinctiveness of sound, clarity of pronunciation, articulation, and stress placed on syllables, words, and phrases.

- **Volume.** To determine the proper volume, consider the size of the room and observe listeners' reactions. Do listeners look as if they're straining to hear you? Or is your voice too loud or booming for the size of the room?

- **Pronunciation.** We have all been known to mispronounce words. For example, a common word like *February* is often mispronounced as *Feb-u-ary* instead of *Feb-ru-ary*. Sometimes we mispronounce words out of habit, incorrect learning, or a regionalism. When we mispronounce words, we lower our intelligibility and also run the risk of lowering our credibility. Speakers often drop off word endings, which makes it difficult to understand what is being said: The dropping of the *g* from words ending in *ing*, for example, makes it difficult for persons from other cultures to understand the words. Saying, "I'm askin' ya…" instead of "I'm asking you…" also may result in a loss of credibility. Effective speakers in formal settings need to make sure the words they use are clearly spoken, correctly used, and understandable. Always check a pronunciation dictionary for the most accurate pronunciations.

- **Grammar.** Grammatical correctness is an important consideration. Not only is the classroom teacher bothered by incorrect grammar and inappropriate use of words, but we are also judged in the world outside the classroom by the way we present our ideas. This suggests that, before we present a speech, we should practice it before others who might detect our errors, dropped sounds, grammatically incorrect words, and mispronunciations.

  Mispronounced words are different from regional and ethnic dialects that affect pronunciation. The effect of dialect on an audience depends a great deal on the makeup of the audience and whether or not audience members understand the difference between dialect usage and standard pronunciation of words. Speakers should always strive to learn similarities and differences between their own dialects and those of others and adapt their messages to the situation.

- **Articulation.** Good articulation involves producing and saying words clearly and distinctly. Physical problems, such as cleft palate, difficulty in controlling the tongue, or a misaligned jaw, can create articulation problems that require specialized help, but most articulation problems result from laziness. We sometimes chop, slur, or mumble words because we do not take the time to learn the words correctly. People say "gonna" instead of "going to," "didja" instead of "did you," or "dunno" instead of "don't know." These articulation errors can lead your listeners to believe you are less credible and can reduce clarity. Unfortunately, many people don't realize their articulation is sloppy or incorrect unless someone tells

MAKING CONNECTIONS FOR SUCCESS
Effective Use of Your Voice

Have you ever really stopped to listen to broadcast journalists? Take a few minutes to watch the local newscast and also one of the national or international broadcasts (e.g., ABC, BBC, CBC, CBS, CNN, FOX, ESPN, NBC, Al-Jazeera). Television personalities and nationally syndicated radio announcers often have very clear vocal delivery. They don't drop word endings; they have naturally animated vocal patterns; and they rarely use fillers and vocalized pauses such as "um," "uh," "and uh," or "like."

1. Now, listen to your instructors and classmates. How many have "easy to listen to" voices? What is the big difference between those who use their voices effectively and those who do not?

2. What effect do fillers, such as those identified here, have on you?

3. What other vocal characteristics distract you?

4. What vocal characteristics help you attend to the speaker?

them. Listen to what you say and how you sound. Concentrate on identifying and eliminating your most common articulation errors. Correcting articulation errors can be well worth the effort; you will sound more intelligent and more professional, and you will further establish your credibility as an educated person.

- **Vocal fillers.** Fillers such as "um," "uh," "ah," "and uh," "like," and "you know" can become both distracting and irritating to your listeners. Most communication instructors will note (and probably reduce your grade) when your speech has too many vocal fillers.

vocal variety

Variations in rate, force, and pitch.

Vocal Variety   The combination of rate, force, and pitch variations that add to a speaker's overall vocal quality is called **vocal variety**. Such variety gives feeling to your delivery and adds emphasis to what you say. Your voice allows listeners to perceive subtle differences in the intent of your messages by altering rate, force, and pitch, promoting a genuine understanding between you and your audience.

rate

Speed at which a speaker speaks, normally between 120 and 175 words per minute.

- **Rate.** The speed at which a speaker speaks—usually between 120 and 175 words per minute—is known as **rate**. Speaking at the appropriate rate requires self-awareness. If your rate is too fast or too slow or never changes, it can detract from the impact of your message. Sometimes when we're nervous, our speaking rate increases so much we are practically unintelligible to our listeners. We must learn to control this rapid rate by breathing deeply before we begin speaking and by purposely using pauses to help us slow down and concentrate on the message.

pause

A brief stop in speaking to gain attention, add emphasis, separate, or otherwise punctuate ideas.

- **Pauses.** A **pause** can be an effective means of gaining attention, adding emphasis to an important point, and enabling listeners to follow shifts in ideas. Pauses punctuate and emphasize thoughts. Beginning speakers need to realize the important contribution of both rate and pauses to the overall effect of their presentations. Listen carefully to accomplished speakers. Notice how an effective speaker varies rate and uses pauses to set off ideas, prepare for the next point, and provide silent emphasis for ideas. Again, accomplished speakers tend to do this within the context of a conversational style.

force

The intensity and volume level of the voice.

- **Force.** The intensity and volume of the voice is called **force**. You must choose a volume level that is comfortable for your audience. However, you can use force to communicate your ideas with confidence and vigor, emphasize an important point, and regain lagging interest. When you learn how to use force, you can greatly increase your effectiveness as a speaker.

pitch

How low or high the voice is on a tonal scale.

- **Pitch. Pitch** refers to how low or high the voice is on a tonal scale. Variety in pitch can eliminate monotony and add emphasis to keywords. Variety in pitch contributes to greater conversationality and thus makes it easy for the listener to maintain interest in and attention to the speaker and message.

MAKING CONNECTIONS FOR SUCCESS

Use of Pauses

Read the following (aloud) without a pause.

Aidan said that he had a fear of public speaking and he said getting up in front of people is much more frightening than the thought of death or even taxes and he hoped he would be able to avoid giving speeches even though he had to take an oral communication class.

Now read the same sentence and pause appropriately with periods and commas.

Aidan expressed his fear of public speaking. He said, "Getting up in front of people is much more frightening than the thought of death or even taxes." He hoped he could avoid giving speeches, even though he had to take an oral communication class.

1. What difference do the pauses make in what you hear?
2. How did the use of verbal punctuation—your pauses—help convey the meaning?

Obviously, any change in rate, force, or pitch makes a word, phrase, or sentence stand out. The greater the amount of change or the more sudden the change, the more emphatic the word or statement. You can use such contrasts to make selected ideas seem more important than material delivered without such variations.

Physical Aspects

An awareness of effective nonverbal communication is essential when you present a speech. Among the physical factors that can affect delivery are personal appearance, body movement, gestures, facial expressions, and eye contact. Each of these must be well coordinated and relevant to the purpose of your speech.

When presenting your speech, you should be very cognizant of your personal appearance because it can affect your credibility and how your listeners perceive you.

Personal Appearance   Personal appearance—what speakers look like and the way they dress, groom, and present themselves to others—is an extremely important consideration. Typical "student attire" is not always acceptable. As a general rule, you should use common sense in dressing for the occasion. For example, caps, any large pieces of jewelry, and loud/colorful clothing may distract your audience from what you are saying (and have a negative effect on the people evaluating your presentation). Most instructors frown on the wearing of caps for another reason as well: Caps hide your facial expressions. Exceptions to this include head coverings worn for religious reasons. First impressions are based mainly on appearance. Your audience members may form instant, hard-to-change opinions about your attitude toward them and yourself. In this way, appearance can affect your credibility.

Research in nonverbal and relational communication suggests that personal appearance has a function in communication. Appearance can have an impact on a speaker's self-image and thus can affect how the speaker communicates with others.[9] You should dress for a special occasion when you present your speech. When you look good, you feel good, and that has a positive effect on your performance.

Body Movement   Body movement is closely related to personal appearance. It includes posture, which should be relaxed and natural; avoid slouching. Because listeners' attention instinctively follows moving objects, your motions should be easy and purposeful. The use of movement—stepping to the side, forward, or backward—can hold attention and help to communicate ideas. Movement can also serve as a nonverbal transition between points. Purposeful movement, along with posture, can indicate confidence and convey a positive self-image. Too much movement or unmotivated, nervous movement, however, can distract your listeners, make them think you are not poised and confident, and detract from your credibility.

Gestures   You can use **gestures**—movements of the head, arms, and hands—to help illustrate, emphasize, or clarify a point. Gestures should be spontaneous, not forced. For example, when you talk to acquaintances about something you have strong feelings about, your gestures come naturally. If you are sad, angry, or happy, you automatically make gestures that express your emotions. To obtain equally natural gestures when giving a speech, you need to be equally involved in what you are saying. If you concentrate on getting your message across rather than on your gestures, you will find you move more freely and naturally.

gesture
A movement of the head, arms, or hands that helps to illustrate, emphasize, or clarify an idea.

When you first learn how to give a speech, gestures might seem a bit uncomfortable, but no gestures might also seem awkward. To overcome this problem, practice the use of gestures in front of others who are willing to offer positive suggestions for improvement. Be assured that, as you give more and more speeches, you will find gestures become more natural and easier. Soon, without even thinking, your strong and smooth-flowing gestures will help hold your listeners' attention and add meaning to your message.

MAKING CONNECTIONS FOR SUCCESS
Nonverbal Behavior and Effective Presentation of Information

Physical and vocal factors can play an important part in the effect of your presentation on listeners. Your messages and delivery can be enhanced or damaged by the way you present ideas. In an effort to analyze the behaviors of others in presenting information, take the next few days to observe professors, classmates, and others as they present information. Consider the messages (words, ideas) and the manner of presentation (physical and vocal factors of delivery). Take notes about the presenter and the presentation, and then answer these questions:

1. How did speakers use their voices to communicate ideas?
2. When did speakers vary their rates? What was the effect?

3. What positive factors of physical and vocal delivery did you observe? What effect did these positive aspects have on you, the listener?
4. What negative factors of physical and vocal delivery did you observe? What effect did these negatives have on you, the listener?
5. What aspects of delivery made a particularly positive impression on you?
6. What will you remember about presentations from this activity?

Facial Expressions Facial expressions are configurations of the face that can reflect, augment, contradict, or be unrelated to a speaker's vocal delivery. They account for much of the emotional impact of a speaker's message. Your face is a highly expressive part of your body. Facial expressions quickly and accurately tell your audience a lot about you. For example, whether you are serious, happy, worried, or angry, the audience will be able to "read" your face. Because your audience will infer a great deal from your facial expression, it is important to look warm and friendly. Such an expression will inform your listeners that you are interested in them and in what you are saying. Of course, your topic, your purpose, the situation, and your audience will all determine exactly what facial expressions are appropriate as you progress through your speech.

eye contact

The extent to which a speaker looks directly at audience members.

Eye Contact The extent to which a speaker looks *directly* at audience members, making **eye contact**, is associated with facial expression. Facial expressions indicate a speaker's feelings about the message, while eye contact seems more related to a speaker's feelings about the listeners. Eye contact is the most important physical aspect of delivery because it indicates interest and concern for others and implies self-confidence. Most speech communication teachers recommend that you look at your audience while you are speaking, not over their heads or at a spot on the wall.

When you look at members of your audience, you establish a communicative bond between them and you. Speakers who ignore their audiences are often perceived as tentative, ill at ease, insincere, or dishonest.

This speaker appears confident and natural as she speaks to her audience. Her gestures are expressive and she has moved closer to the audience to help communicate her interest in them and in the topic.

Eye contact with your audience should be pleasant and personal. Give your listeners the feeling you are talking to them as individuals in a casual conversation. When speaking to a small audience (5 to 30 people), try to look at each individual for a few seconds at a time. To avoid looking shifty, move your eyes gradually and smoothly from one person to another. For larger groups, it is best to scan the audience and occasionally talk to a specific member or members. Do not look over people's heads, and avoid

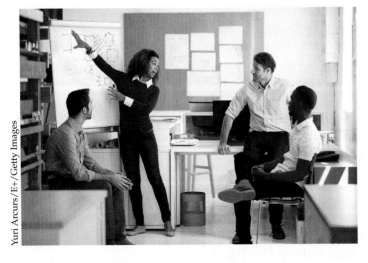

Yuri Arcurs/E+/Getty Images

MAKING CONNECTIONS FOR SUCCESS
Speech Delivery

Technology has influenced every aspect of our lives, including the way teachers teach, students learn, candidates campaign for office and win support for their priorities, and businesspeople make presentations. Use your browser and go to AmericanRhetoric.com and choose one of the speeches from either the Online Speech Bank or the Top 100 Speeches. View the speech and analyze the speaker as you watch by answering the following questions.

1. What do you notice about eye contact, gestures, and body movement? How effective was the physical delivery?
2. View the clip for vocal delivery. What do you notice about vocal variety, rate, pitch, force, and volume?
3. Evaluate the overall delivery of the speech. What worked? What needed improvement?

---

staring, which can give the impression that you're angry or hostile. Try not to make your listeners uncomfortable. We have students serve as peer listeners and evaluate speakers. They often comment on the failure to establish eye contact and note when a speaker looks at a few listeners and not the entire audience. If you look at only one or two people, others will feel left out, and those whom you "stared at" will feel uncomfortable.

Your eyes should convey that you are confident, sincere, and speaking with conviction. The message listeners should receive from your eye contact is that you care about them and about what you are saying. At first, establishing eye contact with an audience may make you uncomfortable, but as you gain experience, you will feel more at ease. You will soon find that eye contact puts you in control of the situation and helps you to answer these questions: Can they hear me? Do they understand? Are they listening?

When you work to strengthen your use of positive vocal and physical behaviors and to reduce negative ones, you will greatly improve your delivery. Table 11.3 lists several behaviors that can detract from the effectiveness of a speech. Observe yourself in front of a mirror or ask a supportive friend for feedback during a practice session to avoid these problems.

Table 11.3 DISTRACTING SPEAKER BEHAVIORS

General Delivery	Eyes	Body
Rapid speech	Rolling eyes	Tense, rigid
Speaking too slowly	Looking at the floor or ceiling	Sloppy posture
Sighing	Staring	Swaying
Nervous laughter or smiles	Lack of sustained eye contact	Dancing
Choppiness	**Voice**	Hunched shoulders
Awkward pauses	Monotone	Leaning on lectern
Face	Singsong patterns	**Feet/Legs**
Scowls	Nasal voice	Shuffling
Listless look	Mumbling	Weight shifts
Hands	Too soft	Crossing legs
Waving	Too loud	Leg or foot shakes
Playing with hair or object (such as note cards or a pen)		
Hands in pocket		

Presentational Aids

11.4 **Construct** presentational aids that enhance your speeches and help your listeners attend to the presentation.

Speakers face multiple challenges. Among them are determining how to grab listeners' attention and making information clear to them. Your topic and your delivery (including verbal and nonverbal communication) are extremely important in gaining and keeping listeners' attention. Of course, your listeners' need to know or desire to listen is also important in gaining and maintaining attention and interest. Some speeches, because of the complexity of their content, require presentational aids. Presentational aids should be used only when they reinforce, engage, support, and clarify a speaker's message.

Benefits of Presentational Aids

The question you should ask before using presentational aids is: Will this presentational aid enhance, improve, and make my presentation more interesting as well as more understandable to my audience? If the answer is yes, then using the presentational aid makes sense. If a presentational aid is included for no other reason than to use one, however, it can become a distraction as well as interfere with the message conveyed. Many instructors require students to use presentational aids in at least one of their speeches because of the benefit gained from experience. **Presentational aids**, also referred to as visual aids or audiovisual aids, are materials and equipment—such as diagrams, models, real objects, photographs, tables, charts, graphs, and computer-generated materials—that speakers may use to enhance content as well as delivery. All presentational aids must serve a meaningful purpose to enhance the speech. In today's media-saturated society, so much of what is communicated has a sound or visual component to help get a message across to an audience. Thus, when a presentational aid can be used, it can be quite effective in helping speakers drive home their point.

presentational aids
Materials and equipment, such as diagrams, models, real objects, photographs, tables, charts, and graphs, that speakers may use to enhance the speech's content and delivery.

Every speaker should consider five conditions before using presentational aids:

1. Will they help make your speech more understandable to the audience?
2. Will they help accomplish your purpose?
3. Will the audience regard you as unprepared if you don't use them?
4. Will they hold the audience's attention?
5. Will they enhance your credibility?

If any of these conditions are not met, then using presentational aids will likely not benefit your presentation.

The use of presentational aids has several advantages, which are examined in the following paragraphs.

Make a Speech Understandable and Memorable Presentational aids can make it easier for listeners to understand and remember the content of a speech.[10] Of course, a great deal depends on the aids themselves and how they are used. Words, as we all know, are abstract, and listeners have to translate them into mental images. The problem arises when different listeners and especially culturally diverse listeners conjure up different mental images for the same word or words speakers use. Presentational aids can produce a more concrete image or, at the very least, provide a connection with the messages that speakers wish to convey.

Speakers can better control the images audience members receive when they use both verbal and visual components in their speech. In general, people remember information better when they both hear and see something. Researchers have found that presentations using visuals improve retention of speech content. Listeners who heard a presentation that included visuals remembered approximately 85 percent of what they heard and saw after 3 hours, and they remembered 65 percent after 3 days.[11] Listeners who heard the same presentation without visuals recalled approximately 70 percent after 3 hours and only 10 percent of the information after 3 days. It's clear from the research that visuals, if appropriate and used correctly, have a significant impact on retention of information.

Enhance Speaker Credibility   A well-done visual presentation tells your listeners you put additional effort into preparing your speech. Audiences see speakers who use presentational aids, according to the research, as more professional, better prepared, more interesting, more persuasive, and more concrete. In some situations, especially business and professional settings, visuals are the norm and are expected. If they are not used, an audience may have the impression you did not prepare and that you weren't taking the audience seriously. We recommend you know your audience's expectations and the context of the presentation to ensure that you make a successful connection with your audience.

When you use appropriate presentational aids, you show your audience you are believable and thus trustworthy. You let them see for themselves what you are talking about, and you show them you want them to understand rather than rely solely on words. When you show presentational aids from reliable and credible sources, you tell your audience you are open to their scrutiny and are determined to be truthful and fair minded, which ultimately enhances your credibility.

Create Audience Attention and Interest   Gaining and keeping an audience's attention and interest is not an easy process and usually requires a lot of preparation and effort on the speaker's part. We have already indicated that a speech is often more successful when speakers use variety in their voices, gestures, and movements. It is also true that presentational aids enhance a speech by adding variety and interest. When speakers use pictures, charts, graphs, video clips, slides, or objects, they alter their presentation and thus increase an audience's attention, even if only momentarily. If the presentational aid is done well and is meaningful to the audience, it will likely not only gain your listeners' attention but will also make the speech more interesting, which should be the goal of every speaker. Thus, if presentational aids are carefully developed and add to an understanding of the speech content, they will gain the attention of your listeners and actually enhance their interest.

Provide Support   Presentational aids can serve as an excellent form of evidence and help bolster speakers' points of view. Suppose you claim that today's television shows have become more violent than just two years ago. You could support this claim by providing a graph that clearly illustrates the increase in the number of violent episodes and you could show some short video clips on how the violence has escalated over the years.

Presentational aids provide another form of support, especially when the aids are from reputable sources: You will, in effect, improve your credibility. For example, when you show a picture of a homeless family living in a car, you illustrate how poverty affects people and provide evidence to support your words. Presentational aids allow your audience to literally see for themselves the real-world representations of concepts in your speech. This makes your message more immediate and believable.

Help With Delivery   Often, speakers have trouble with their delivery or with remembering part of what they want to say. Thus, many speakers tend to become overly reliant on notes; this reduces their eye contact with the audience and can make them sound mechanical. When overused, notes can give the impression the speaker is unprepared and unrehearsed. The perception of being unprepared reduces credibility or at the very least makes the audience less desirous of listening to the speaker.

There is no substitute, of course, for practicing your delivery, but the use of presentational aids can also help guide your delivery. Correctly used presentational aids can become an outline for parts of your speech. Each year your authors facilitate many workshops for a variety of audiences, and all use technology to project ideas or keywords. These visual presentational aids not only help the participants' comprehension but also function as an outline, reminding speakers and listeners of what is to be addressed and what is coming next. Many beginning speakers have also found that the prompts of presentational aids do help to alleviate speaking anxiety.

Even more than reducing speaking anxiety, presentational aids can actually help make you seem more dynamic. When used correctly, presentational aids allow speakers to move more easily from point to point and to become more physically active during their presentations. Clearly, presentational aids can increase speakers' confidence.

Research has shown that listeners remember information longer when it is accompanied by audio, visual, or presentational aids.[12] Many businesses require employees to make presentations and to use the computer to enhance their presentations. Some company managers believe speakers are not really performing well unless they use the computer for audio, visual, or audiovisual aids. Although classroom teachers do not always require the use of computer-generated or computer-assisted presentational materials, it is important to know they are common in the workplace. More and more, organizations require computer-aided presentations. Medical doctors and dentists, for instance, create multimedia presentational aids to help explain procedures, illnesses, and treatments to their patients. We'll next look at types of presentational aids and the methods of presenting them in speeches.

Choose and Use Effective Presentational Aids

If you plan to use presentational aids, keep the following guidelines in mind:

1. **Presentational aids should serve a need.** They should never be used just for the sake of using them. In some cases, visual aids are not appropriate, but in others they can get a point across better than words alone. For example, it is easier to show an audience how to create PowerPoint slides than it is to tell them. Furthermore, it is easier yet to tell *and* to show them.

2. **Presentational aids should be planned and adapted to the audience and the situation.** The size of the visual aid and the distance between you and your audience should be considered. The visual material should be kept simple and free from too much detail.

3. **Presentational aids should not dominate or take over a speaker's job.** They should supplement, but never replace, the speaker. Do not rely too heavily on visual aids; instead, use them to help elaborate or explain a point or idea or to create interest. In a speech, visual aids *always* require explanation by the speaker in order to make them meaningful.

4. **Presentational aids should look as professionally prepared as possible.** Accurate and neat materials create a positive impression on the audience and reflect favorably on the competence of the speaker. Aids should be free from factual and spelling errors. They should also be bright, attractive, and easy to read from any spot in the audience. Audience members ought to be able to see, read, and understand the presentational aid once the speaker has carefully explained it.

5. **Presentational aids should be practical—easy to prepare, use, and transport.** Aids should not interfere with the speaker and presentation, and they should not call undue attention to themselves.

6. **Presentational aids that are not original or that contain information that is not the speaker's require documentation.** Cite the source either directly on the aid where the audience can see it or in the context of the speech.

7. **Visuals should contain only one idea—one graph per poster, and so on.** Remember, presentational aids are meant to clarify and strengthen the speaker's message. Limit yourself to one idea per poster, slide, chart, graph, or computer-generated screen so listeners can focus on one idea at the time you are talking about the corresponding idea or concept. Too much information distracts listeners.

Using aids during a presentation requires planning and coordination. They should not distract the audience or interrupt the flow of the speech. See "Guidelines: Using Presentational Aids" near the end of the chapter for ideas on using presentational aids.

Types of Presentational Aids

A variety of different presentational aids and the methods for presenting them to audiences are available. The most frequently used types of presentational aids are computer-generated images, video and digitized video clips, and, when these images and video or video clips are not available or practical, then real objects, models, photographs and prints, diagrams, tables, and graphs.

Computer-Generated Images   Millions of images that could be used as presentational aids are found on the Internet. All you must do is search for a specific type of visual image, and you are likely to find what you are looking for in just a few seconds. Let's say you are interested in "college sports mascots" and want to show some pictures and talk about their meaning, history, or impact. Enter the keywords "college sports mascots," and you will find not only pictures of each mascot but the history of each as well. Almost any image, graph, or chart you want is accessible on the Internet. If you know how to do a search on a computer, there is no limit to the images you can find on any subject. Of course, it is always prudent to check out the source of the visual aid and to credit any visuals used in your presentation: Cite the sources as oral footnotes in the speech to ensure credibility.

Video and Digitized Video Clips   The Internet is a rich source for video clips on thousands of subjects, and you can also create and place your own digitized video clips for your presentations. When using video in your presentation, it is important that it is relevant to your presentation. In addition, it should not dominate or distract; an appropriate short video clip can enhance your presentation. For example, a student used a 30-second video clip in her informative speech to illustrate how personal information on the Internet can affect getting into college or getting a job. The clip clearly demonstrated what is reasonable and what may be inappropriate to place on a website.

You can also use short video clips to demonstrate a process or to show part of a famous political speech to make a point more realistic. However, it is still important to maintain eye contact with your audience while the clip is playing. And the video clip should occupy only a very brief portion of your speech; for example, in a 5- to 7-minute speech, a video clip should be no more than 30 seconds. For longer speeches (10 or more minutes), a video clip could last up to a minute or more. Ideally, the video clip is used to illustrate an idea or point you make. It does not replace the speech itself. Video can be extremely interesting and a powerful way to express an idea, but it can also create problems if its use is not well rehearsed. For example, when equipment malfunctions or the clip cannot be located, it is difficult for most speakers to recover from such events and achieve their purpose. If at all possible, download clips you will use and have them ready to access at the appropriate time, or include a link in your PowerPoint or Prezi slides so you can easily access the clip.

We next discuss those presentational aids that could be used in a speech when computer-generated images or video clips are either not available or not practical.

Real Objects   A real object is any three-dimensional representation that illustrates or brings to life an idea, concept, or activity you wish to communicate to your audience. Objects can make excellent presentational aids if they are (1) large enough to be seen by everyone in the audience and (2) small enough to be effectively used in a speech. To make sure the object is beneficial to your speech, prepare and practice in advance with your object. For example, a musical instrument, a piece of sporting equipment, or a kind of food might be appropriate objects to use in a speech. Using a real object can make your topic come alive, but it can also create problems if the object is too large, too small, or too difficult to show.

Use of any object or prop should help your audience focus on your speech purpose, not serve as a distraction. Pets, for example, are often unpredictable and can be distracting before, during, and after a speech. Thus, we recommend not using anything that you cannot control or that risks becoming a distraction.

Models   You should consider a model when it is not practical to display the actual object because of size or cost. A model—or representation of a real object—allows a speaker to enlarge or shrink an object to a convenient size for use in a speech. For example, it may be impractical to show the actual circuitry of a computer microchip, which is no larger than a pinhead, or the inside of a biofuel engine, which is too large (not to mention too expensive). Models of these objects would be appropriate and accomplish the same purpose as the actual objects. Some of these items and some of the models can be displayed on a digital display presenter

Models can be life size. For example, a premed student who wants to inform classmates about the parts of the brain affected when a football player or boxer takes serious blows to the head can do so by showing one or more models of the brain to illustrate the point. Constructing a three-dimensional model requires skill and effort, and can be expensive. When students used models in our classes, they were often able to borrow them from other academic departments or private businesses or organizations.

Photographs, Drawings, and Diagrams   When models, objects, or computer-generated images are not available or practical, a photograph, drawing, or diagram might be the solution. Deciding which to use depends on what you wish to illustrate and what is available. A photograph is an excellent tool for explaining details and surroundings. One student, speaking on artistic style, brought in several prints to illustrate the differences. Another student who spoke on poverty in third-world countries brought in a powerful set of photos showing people living in extremely poor conditions. A student who spoke about the effects of global climate change on Alaska's glaciers brought in two enlarged photos from two different personal trips to Alaska. The photos were of the same glacier and clearly illustrated how much the glacier had shrunk in just a five-year period. Thus, the photos helped reinforce her point.

When photographs or prints are unavailable, are too small, or lack adequate detail, a drawing or diagram may be used. Most of us are not very artistic, but that should not be a concern because most drawings or diagrams used in the classroom that are not computer generated or created by a professional artist can be relatively simple. Figure 11.1 illustrates a simple line drawing showing the location of work areas in a workroom-remodeling project.

A speaker could use an architect's blueprint, a table or graph illustrating statistics, a chart illustrating a company's organizational hierarchy, a drawing of basic football plays, or a map of various regions within a country. Almost anything can be diagramed and drawn. For example, a table is an orderly arrangement of data in columns to highlight similarities and differences, as shown in Figure 11.2.

FIGURE 11.1   Example of a Simple Line Drawing

Line drawings need not be complex or elaborate; they can, in fact, be rather simple.

Tables conveniently display large amounts of information or data in a relatively small space, but they can be too complex or lengthy (and perhaps boring) and may even require complex and lengthy explanations. As with any presentational aid, a table must be concise, simple, and clear so that the important information is easy to comprehend by your audience.

Graphs are sometimes better because they can help make statistical data more vivid and they can illustrate relationships in ways that are easy for an audience to grasp. A line graph, as illustrated in Figure 11.3, can be particularly helpful for clarifying comparative data over time. Graphs can help show trends over a span of days, months, or years.

Bar graphs are another simple way to illustrate comparisons. Figure 11.4 demonstrates how a bar graph clearly illustrates the comparison of popular literary genres and the number of men and women who prefer each type.

Pie graphs illustrate proportional divisions of a whole set of data. Each wedge of the pie represents a percentage of the whole. Pie graphs are often used to show distribution patterns and financial distributions. The pie graph in Figure 11.5 clearly illustrates the percentages of those with and without health insurance. Notice, too, the pie graph starts with a radius drawn vertically from the center to the 12 o'clock position. Each segment is then drawn in clockwise, from the largest down to the smallest.

FIGURE 11.2   Example of Data Presented as a Table

Tables display large amounts of data in a relatively small space. The more complex the data, the more explanation is required to make the table meaningful to your listeners. Be sure the table accurately reflects content, and keep it simple and brief.

Popular Pharmaceuticals, Uses, Costs, and Effects			
Drug	**Uses**	**Cost**	**Effects**
Tylenol™ Over-the-counter	Aches, pains	$19.95 per 200 tabs	General pain relief; some side effects (minor)
Omeprazole™ Prescription only	Heartburn, stomach ulcers	$145.29 per 90 tabs, 40 mg	Used for treating acid-induced inflammation and ulcer; few side effects
Celebrex™ Prescription only	Joint pain	$124.17 per 180 tabs, 100 mg	Acute pain relief; some side effects, some major side effects

FIGURE 11.3 Example of a Simple Line Graph

Line graphs provide all kinds of data. This example illustrates the comparison of population and automobile registrations over a 90-year period.

FIGURE 11.4 Example of a Simple Bar Graph

This bar graph demonstrates favorite book types for men and women. Comparisons are helpful ways to illustrate various kinds of information.

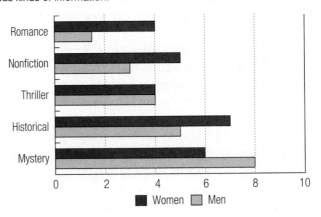

FIGURE 11.5 Example of a Simple Pie Graph

This pie graph shows how many people have and do not have insurance. It begins with the larger number at the top in the 12 o'clock position and moves clockwise to the smaller.

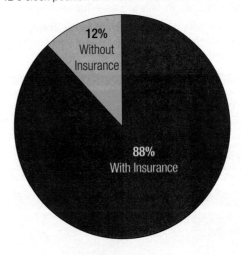

Presentation Software

11.5   **Explore** how integrating software programs can aid your presentation.

PowerPoint and Prezi can be either an effective tool or something your intended listeners just tune out. We've all seen some really good and some really bad uses of these formats. What's the difference? As you know, good presentations emphasize content, not technology. An effective speaker knows that all presentational aids are supposed to *enhance* the presentation, not *become* (or replace) the presentation.

Decide When and Whether to Use PowerPoint or Prezi in Your Presentations

Contrary to popular belief, neither PowerPoint nor Prezi is *always* the best presentational software. When was the last time you were impressed by a PowerPoint or a Prezi presentation? Most public speaking instructors place some limitations on its use for classroom presentations. And when instructors allow or require PowerPoint or Prezi, they have specific criteria for its use. While we should all be prepared to take advantage of whatever presentational technology is available to us, we also should make careful choices about its use. You don't have to use this software just because it's available, unless it is *required* in your job or in a classroom assignment. Whatever you decide, be sure the presentational aid enhances the speech. If you have more than four slides in a 7- to 10-minute speech, you have too many. Many Internet sources from the business sector suggest a maximum of 10 slides in a 20-minute business presentation. If you decide to, or are required to, use PowerPoint or Prezi, keep the following in mind:

1. Your own perspective—what are you trying to accomplish?
2. Will PowerPoint or Prezi augment your speech?
3. Is the topic appropriate?
4. Does the room or environment support its use?
5. Will it help you make your points?
6. Have you used enough but not too many slides?

Create Effective PowerPoint or Prezi Presentations

It's important to make the right choices. The use of color, the type and size of the font, and the use of graphics and pictures are all important factors in effective PowerPoint and Prezi presentations.

Color   If you want your presentations to connect with your audience and make your content memorable, choose clear, clean, and not too busy background colors and designs. For the classroom, we encourage students to select neutral, blue, or green backgrounds with little or no movement or sound. Blues and greens are calming, but also readable. Keep the material uncluttered. Use contrasting colors. Text colors should be black or white, and they can sometimes be yellow on darker backgrounds in order to connect with the viewers. Red text may pixilate (dance and waver) and is very hard to read on dark backgrounds. Yellow is an attention-getting color, but too much can make words and images dance on the screen. In classrooms where one cannot adjust the lighting, it's often preferable to have a neutral (beige, gray, or plain white) background with dark bold headings and subheads. Some color can be used in bulleted points or graphics. Be sure to check out the slides in the classroom prior to your presentation to make sure that the size is appropriate and the colors work.

Type and Size of Font   Times New Roman, Times, Helvetica, and Courier are good fonts for your computer-generated presentations. These fonts are clean and easy to read. Avoid fonts with too many curves and extras, which distract and are hard to

Visual presentational aids can greatly enhance a speech if properly used. The visual should enhance but not *become* the speech. Carefully used presentational aids can help the listener stay involved in the speech.

read. You can create an interest factor by using a sans serif font such as Helvetica for headings and Times New Roman (serif) for bulleted points. (Serif typeface letters have "feet," or small flourish strokes, at the upper and lower end of each letter.) Since you want everyone to see and read this part of your presentation, keep these elements big enough for easy readability.

Displaying the Slide Show   Display your presentation only when you are referring to it. You can also include blank slides for those times when the material might distract or isn't being talked about. Practice any special effects in advance if you plan to use them.

Use of Graphics and Pictures   Graphics and pictures help create and maintain interest. They should be used sparingly, however, to keep your listeners connected to your topic. A good rule of thumb is that no more than 25 percent of your slides should have pictures or graphics on them. If you don't know how to import pictures or graphics, use the help function of your computer's program, or check with the technology department or division of your college. Many schools offer both free and course credit workshops in PowerPoint, Word, Excel, and other software packages. If you don't feel comfortable using the computer, one of these free workshops would be beneficial.

The Internet is filled with good examples of video clips, movie clips, illustrations, and examples. Carefully search and make judicious use of materials readily available to anyone who has a computer and Internet access. Make sure your clips are in good taste and truly illustrate what you want them to. Check the credibility of these sources (and cite them appropriately) as well. If there's a question on some of the material, either don't use it or explain why or how it's applicable. Of course, you can create your own YouTube clips as well as take your own pictures, and you can create computer-generated aids. Just remember to make sure that the presentation aids don't take the place of the presentation itself.

The presentational outline with PowerPoint slides for a speech on typefaces and fonts provides an example for your analysis. Notes that the speaker makes to her- or himself are indicated in red italic text.

SAMPLE PRESENTATIONAL OUTLINE FOR A SPEECH WITH POWERPOINT SLIDES

This presentational outline is for a speech given in a class on message design and delivery. It emphasizes how PowerPoint should *enhance*, not *become*, the presentation.

Notes the speaker makes to him- or herself are in *red italics*.

Using Typeface and Fonts in Your PowerPoint Presentations

(slide 1)

TITLE: Using Typefaces and Fonts in Your PowerPoint Presentations

PURPOSE: To inform the audience about the requirements of typefaces, fonts, designs, and colors in PowerPoint in your speeches.

THESIS: Use of PowerPoint requires careful choice in font type, size, amount of text, and background design and colors.

Get the PowerPoint presentation up on the computer.

Do not display slides until needed.

Look at audience and smile.

INTRODUCTION: I want you to think about presentations in and out of the classroom. Briefly jot down your answers to these questions. How many times have you seen a PowerPoint presentation this semester? When was the last time you were impressed by such a presentation?

Pause.

We are often required to create a PowerPoint, and we sometimes think that's the *best* way to get our ideas across. Today we'll look at some of the choices we can make for font size and typefaces as well as background design and colors to create more compelling PowerPoints that actually augment the speech.

BODY

I. What are typefaces and font sizes, and what do they have to do with making a PowerPoint presentation?

Show title slide (slide 1) while talking and move to slide 2, which explains typeface differences.

A. Typeface refers to a family of type (examples)

1. Serif

2. Sans serif

3. In between

4. Where used and why?

Pause; move to slide 3, which deals with font size.

B. Font size

1. Guidelines

2. 44 points for headings

3. 36 or 40 points text

4. 28 smallest

5. Auditorium requires larger

Switch to blank screen (slide 4).

II. How much text do I use on slides?

Show slide 5.

A. How should text be used?

B. How much is enough?

Switch to blank screen (slide 6).

III. Background design display

Slide 7

A. Choice of background color or no color?

B. Best colors

C. How much design on background?

Switch to blank screen (slide 8).

D. Should I import graphics?

IV. General guidelines

Show final slide (slide 9) with general guidelines, then show final blank slide (slide 10).

Typeface is a family of font types

- Serif—have structural details on the ends of some strokes
- Sans Serif—no structural details or flourishes
- In Between— combination, smaller flourishes
- Where used and why?

(slide 2)

Only 10 slides were used in the 12-minute presentation: six slides with text (including the title slide) and four blank slides. The amount of information on each slide is minimal. An Americans with Disabilities Act (ADA)-compliant blue background was used so anyone would be able to read the slides easily.

Font Sizes

- Guidelines
- 44 points for headings
- 35–40 points text
- 28 smallest
- Auditorium requires larger

(slide 3)

The slides reinforce the points made in the speech and illustrate the font sizes and types.

Blank slides draw the listeners' attention to the speaker and not the slide.

How much text do I use on slides?

How much is enough?

(slide 5)

Background Design/Display

- Color or no color?
- Best colors
- How much design on background?
- Should I import graphics?

(slide 7)

General Guidelines

(slide 9)

CONCLUSION

Now that we've covered some of the basics of design for PowerPoint presentations, I hope you will know what typefaces might work best and what font sizes to use in specific situations. The decision to use a background color or one of the available templates in PowerPoint and whether or not to include graphics depends on you, your topic, and especially the conditions in the room where you present. Good luck! May your next PowerPoint presentation be impressive!

Smile, ask for questions, answer, remove USB drive, and move to sit down.

Microsoft® PowerPoint, Microsoft Corporation.

Using Presentational Aids: Who's Really in Control?

Remember that any technology is a tool and should not be allowed to replace the speaker or the message. William Germano, in an article in *The Chronicle of Higher Education*, reminds us, "... A tool is not a friend and is often a rival."[13] We must learn to use technology, and indeed any other presentational aid, so it serves us and does not take our place as speakers or become the message. Too often the presentation becomes the content, not the means to enhance or illustrate the content. Remember that you are in control and need to be so. Your audience should remember your points because *you* made the points and your aids reinforced those points.

Murphy's Law tells us we can expect the worst to happen. But well-prepared speeches with carefully constructed presentational aids need not fail. The speaker should be prepared for any eventuality. If you have done your research, organized your materials, made careful choices about the aids you use, and have practiced faithfully, you can overcome whatever difficulties may arise. Your authors always have a plan B or even a plan C when they make presentations in the classroom and in the

MAKING CONNECTIONS FOR SUCCESS

The Gettysburg Address

Imagine what President Lincoln might have done with PowerPoint when he delivered the Gettysburg Address. Peter Norvig created a six-slide parody of Lincoln's Gettysburg Address to demonstrate how PowerPoint can become hopelessly irrelevant and boring. Search the Internet to view Norvig's PowerPoint Gettysburg Address (https://norvig.com/Gettysburg). Compare those six slides to the actual speech:

Fourscore and seven years ago our fathers brought forth on this continent a new nation, conceived in liberty and dedicated to the proposition that all men are created equal.

Now we are engaged in a great civil war, testing whether that nation or any nation so conceived and so dedicated can long endure. We are met on a great battlefield of that war. We have come to dedicate a portion of that field as a final resting-place for those who here gave their lives that that nation might live. It is altogether fitting and proper that we should do this.

But, in a larger sense, we cannot dedicate, we cannot consecrate, we cannot hallow this ground. The brave men, living and dead, who struggled here have consecrated it far above our poor power to add or detract. The world will little note nor long remember what we say here, but it can

never forget what they did here. It is for us the living rather to be dedicated here to the unfinished work which they who fought here have thus far so nobly advanced. It is rather for us to be here dedicated to the great task remaining before us—that from these honored dead we take increased devotion to that cause for which they gave the last full measure of devotion—that we here highly resolve that these dead shall not have died in vain, that this nation under God shall have a new birth of freedom, and that government of the people, by the people, for the people shall not perish from the earth.

Now compare the PowerPoint version and Lincoln's original version, and answer the following:

1. Which version is the most effective?
2. What distractions does the PowerPoint create?
3. How does PowerPoint take away the meaning?
4. What nonessential items become parts of the presentation?
5. How does the comparison of these two versions affect your thinking about PowerPoint in your own presentations?

The implications seem obvious. Keep this example in mind as you decide whether to use PowerPoint or some other presentational aid.

workforce. We generally have a flash drive or CD with our PowerPoint presentations on them. In case the files are not readable, however, we also bring hard copies of the PowerPoints (generally, we print the four slides per handout in color and bring them along) so we can use the projector function in the room, even if the computer won't read the files. That way, even if we don't have a visual, we can explain what's on the PowerPoint slides and use a chalkboard or whiteboard to illustrate. If the lamp on the projector burns out, you won't be able to project your aids. That means you have to find another way to show your audience what you want. If it's a small enough group and we know how many will be there, we bring hard copies of the most important slides (figures, charts, guidelines).

The important thing to remember is that none of us is perfect and an equipment failure is not the end of the world. Prepare for the best and the worst, and you'll be able to pull off your presentation successfully.

Poise   If you've done all that we've recommended in this text, you will be prepared and should feel poised and confident. It's far easier to feel good about a presentation when you're thoroughly prepared for any eventuality.

Recovery   Everyone makes mistakes, and sometimes Murphy's Law works its way into our presentations. The only thing you can do is to be ready for anything. If you know your topic, have prepared well, and have practiced carefully, your chances of recovering from the little mishaps increases significantly. Don't make a big deal of things you cannot help. One of our colleagues teaches a distance learning class with 25 students in the classroom in the United States, and 10 students in St. Petersburg and 10 in Moscow in Russia; all are connected by two-way interactive technology. The classroom is a "smart classroom" with current technology and the ability to see students and teachers simultaneously in all three classrooms. Our colleague says that she always worries about the technical aspects and how they interfere with presentations. One day her students told her, "Hey, don't worry about the technical stuff! We know it, we recognize it's no one's fault. Just go with it and don't call undue attention

Guidelines

USING PRESENTATIONAL AIDS

1. **Display visual materials only while you are using them.** Do not distract your audience by showing your presentation aids too early or by leaving them on display after you've finished talking about them. Even with a PowerPoint or Prezi presentation, you can create a black, blank, or white screen to avoid distracting your listeners.

2. **Keep your presentational aids on display long enough to give everyone ample opportunity to absorb the information.** Find the happy medium between "too long" and "not long enough."

3. **Ensure that everyone can see your aids by making them neat, simple, large, bright, and readable.** If you use computer-generated text, the same guidelines apply. Depending on the size of the room, however, your font size should rarely be less than 36 points. For larger rooms, a 48-point or up to a 60-point font is desirable. The same thing applies to the television screen if you're in a distance learning classroom. The size, background for, and color of the text all become critical issues. For televised presentations, a blue background with either a white or yellow text color is preferable. The opposite is true for yellow or white on paper displayed on an ELMO or other projection device, and many posters, charts, or graphs. Light colors fade and are virtually invisible on paper products. Red and black text work better for noncomputer presentational aids.

4. **Practice in the room with the equipment you'll use.** This should be done well ahead of time.

5. **Do not talk to your displayed objects or to the chalkboard.** Discuss the content while maintaining eye contact with your audience.

6. **Do not stand in front of your presentational aids.** Determine where you will place or show your aids and use a pointer or a laser to avoid blocking your audience's view.

7. **Practice using your presentational aids until you feel comfortable with them.** It becomes quite obvious to your listeners if you're uncomfortable and unfamiliar with the aids you've selected.

to it and don't apologize for something you cannot help."[14] We echo their advice: Don't worry about what you have no control over. Know that things happen and be prepared to deal with whatever comes up in the situation.

Practice Your Delivery

11.6 **Perform** your speech delivery in practice sessions to help you gain confidence.

The best way to ensure effective delivery is to practice, practice, and practice. Practice early and often until you feel comfortable with your speech content. Exactly how much practice you will need depends on a number of considerations, including how much experience you have speaking before audiences, how familiar you are with your subject, and how long your speech is. There is no magic amount of time that will make your delivery perfect.

If your speech is not to be memorized, make sure to use slightly different wording in each run-through. When you memorize a speech, it is possible to master the words without mastering the content. Your goal should be to learn your content, which will mean you have mastered its ideas.

In practicing your delivery, it is important to start with small segments. For example, practice the introduction, then one main point at a time, and then the conclusion. After you have rehearsed each small segment several times in isolation, practice the entire speech until you have mastered the content and the ideas flow smoothly.

If possible, practice in the same room where you will speak or, at least, under similar conditions. This helps you see how things look from the front of the class and plan where you should place your visual aids. Your last practice session should leave you with a sense of confidence and a desire to present your speech.

Finally, concentrate on what you are saying and to whom you are saying it. Above all, be yourself.

› SUMMARY

Manage Speech Anxiety

11.1 **Identify** ways you can manage your speech anxiety/communication apprehension.

- Anxiety can be managed through behavioral and cognitive means.
- *Communication apprehension* is a more serious form of *speech anxiety*, but it, too, can usually be managed through work and practice, as well as adopting a positive attitude toward change.
- The symptoms of speech anxiety can also be controlled through behavioral and cognitive strategies.
- Speech anxiety has many causes, but through analysis and practice, you can reduce the impact of past experiences.
- Not all cultures can deal with speech anxiety in the same ways. For some, trying to adapt to the majority culture is, in itself, stressful. In such cases, students and instructors should work out some kind of compromise about specific actions.

- Speech anxiety can generally be controlled. This chapter provided specific strategies to help you do so.

Methods of Delivery

11.2 **Demonstrate** appropriate use of the four methods of delivery.

- *Impromptu delivery* is used when it's okay to "wing it," but it should usually not be used for formal classroom presentations. Sometimes in the workplace or in community groups, you will be called upon to make a speech without prior notice. Practice in this method of delivery can help prepare you for these occasions.
- *Manuscript delivery* is often mechanical but is also necessary in certain situations in which the exact wording can influence policies or put the speaker in a better light.
- *Memorized delivery* allows the speaker to move around and get away from the lectern, but it may cause an uncomfortable situation if memory fails.

- *Extemporaneous delivery* is usually recommended for most situations and allows speakers to be fully prepared yet conversational in their delivery.

Vocal and Physical Aspects of Delivery

11.3 **Analyze** your own vocal and physical aspects of delivery and find ways to improve both.

- Speakers need to use *vocal variety*—changes in *pitch*, volume, *force*, and *rate*—to make their voices interesting and compelling for the listeners.

- The physical aspects of delivery can greatly increase your listeners' ability to be interested in your ideas. Facial expressions, *eye contact*, movement, and *gestures* also help focus the listeners' attention on specific ideas or let them know when you are moving from one topic to another.

Presentational Aids

11.4 **Construct** presentational aids that enhance your speeches and help your listeners attend to the presentation.

- *Presentational aids* provide many benefits. They give you the opportunity to make ideas memorable and provide some variety for listeners. Research shows that speeches with presentational aids are remembered better than those without them.

- Speakers should always remember their purpose for speaking and what they want listeners to know about the topic. Presentational aids can help them focus on the ideas and use the information later.

- While we often think of PowerPoint or Prezi as the best presentational aids, others are equally effective in certain situations. In fact, some of the more "traditional" aids can add variety and interest as well as explanations that can get lost in the PowerPoint or Prezi presentation.

Presentation Software

11.5 **Explore** how integrating software programs can aid your presentation.

- If you use PowerPoint or Prezi, make good choices: Don't put too much information on any one slide; don't have too many slides; find ways to cover the slides when they are not in use; and note color, font, and size, and what's most effective for the room in which you are presenting.

- Assess your presentational aids to ensure that they clarify and support your speeches.

- Produce effective presentational software aids for your speeches.

Practice Your Delivery

11.6 **Perform** your speech delivery in practice sessions to help you gain confidence.

- If at all possible, practice in the room where you'll present, with the equipment you'll be using.

- Ask a friend to listen and observe and then offer comments about your speech and delivery.

- Practice helps you find the areas that need improvement or in which you don't seem as confident.

- Practice sessions help you see what might go wrong and find alternatives or allow you to adjust to things that might go wrong.

⟩ DISCUSSION STARTERS

1. Explain your physical and cognitive behaviors when you speak before others.

2. Describe what listeners have done in previous presentations to help you, as a speaker, overcome anxiety.

3. Of the delivery methods discussed in this chapter, which ones seem best for you? Why?

4. Discuss two or three reasons you think communication instructors recommend or even require extemporaneous delivery for your classroom speeches.

5. Think about an effective presentation. What vocal and physical factors helped make the presentation effective?

6. When and why would you use presentational aids in your speeches?

7. Are there topics or situations where you should or should not use PowerPoint or Prezi in a speech?

8. Now that you have read this chapter, identify two topics and situations where you and your classmates might use presentational aids and not let them overpower the content.

9. Why should speakers be listener oriented?

CHAPTER 12

INFORMATIVE AND PERSUASIVE SPEAKING

Monkey Business Images/Shutterstock

Many careers require that people have a strong ability to present vast amounts of information. If you lack the skills to explain carefully, both you and your audience may be frustrated.

→ CHAPTER OUTLINE AND LEARNING OBJECTIVES

Distinctions between Informative and Persuasive Speaking

12.1 **Explain** the distinctions between informative and persuasive speeches.

The Goals of Persuasive Speaking

12.2 **Identify** the goals of persuasion.

Topics for Informative and Persuasive Speeches

12.3 **Choose** appropriate topics for your informative and persuasive speeches.

Preparing and Developing an Informative Speech

12.4 **Prepare and develop** an informative speech to meet your professor's specific criteria.

Evaluating the Informative Speech

12.5 **Evaluate and assess** your own informative speeches prior to classroom presentation and **apply** evaluation criteria to the speeches of others.

Persuasive Claims

12.6 **Construct and support** a persuasive claim.

Establishing Credibility (Ethos)

12.7 **Explain** how Aristotle's modes of presentation—ethos, logos, and pathos—increase your credibility.

Preparing and Developing a Persuasive Speech

12.8 **Develop** your persuasive speech by carefully researching your topic; organizing the content; providing appropriate supporting materials; and making strong, logical arguments.

Fallacies in Argument Development

12.9 **Recognize** errors in your own thinking so you can correct them and present logical claims and evidence.

Evaluating the Persuasive Speech

12.10 **Evaluate and assess** your own persuasive speeches and those of others.

MAKING EVERYDAY CONNECTIONS

"Professor Lee, how do I present an interesting informative speech? I don't want to sound like a college instructor. I want my listeners to listen to me. What should I do?" Each semester, students tell their instructors they're unable to think of interesting topics. Some seem to believe that an informative speech is boring. Nothing could be further from the truth. The goal of the informative speech is to provide potentially useful information that may offer a different perspective from what one normally thinks. It leaves the receivers with new information that is beneficial to them. It explains and leads to a better understanding of the information than what was understood prior to the presentation.

Often when presenting information to others, we are actually persuading them, although we are often unaware of this. The difference between informing and persuading is not always clear. In order for us to persuade, we must use information, but we use it to help us convince others about a particular viewpoint or to change their behaviors in some way. When working on a group project with others, we might persuade another to choose a certain topic or to take on a specific role in the group. We are constantly persuading others, whether at school or in our personal lives.

For example, we might try to convince a roommate to go to a movie instead of doing homework, a family member to watch a particular TV series, or your professor that you really didn't skip class but that you overslept. While these examples are persuasive in nature, whether intended or not, persuasion requires a specific goal that you wish to accomplish. Persuasion requires evidence that is believable and credible.

QUESTIONS TO THINK ABOUT

1. Explain why you think the concerns described above are or are not accurate?

2. What other concerns do you have about *your* speeches?

3. What differences lie in the types of information you receive and share in the classroom as opposed to other areas of your life?

4. How many times a day do you receive information you need to use immediately or at some time in the future?

5. What do you think are some of the key differences between informative and persuasive speaking?

We've talked about the preparation process in Chapters 8–11. Now it's time to focus on informative and persuasive speeches. We'll start with the informative speech. Is there a reason the informative speech is among the first formal speeches assigned in most communication classes? Yes, there is! Much of what we do in our lives involves information—someone asks for information and you provide it, or you ask another person for information and then use what you learned. **Information** is knowledge obtained from investigation, study, or instruction.[1] (By permission, From Merriam-Webster.com © 2018 by Merriam-Webster, Inc. https://www.merriam-webster.com/dictionary/information)

information
Knowledge obtained from investigation, study, or instruction.

Even if this sounds simple, think about explaining how to create a Snapchat account to a friend when you're speaking by smartphone, about giving someone directions to create an Instagram account when you're not sitting next to each other and neither is at a computer, or describing how to set up a WiFi network when you're not side-by-side to show the questioner. If you've ever tried to explain something detailed and relatively complex to someone who knows little about it, you know it takes time and careful choice of language, as well as organization, to accomplish your goal.

Teachers inform on a daily basis. People in many jobs are required to present vast amounts of information. If you lack the skills to explain carefully, both you and your listeners may be frustrated. To help with this process, this section of the chapter discusses the informative speech, from choosing a topic to delivering a speech about it. Learning what you need to know and do when presenting information will help you both in your personal and professional life. The informative speech provides a foundation for every speaking situation you face, including persuasive speaking situations.

Stockfour/Shutterstock

We send and receive vast amounts of information every day, in every kind of situation. It's no wonder, then, that informative speech is often one of the first assigned in communication classes such as this one.

Distinctions between Informative and Persuasive Speaking

12.1 **Explain** the distinctions between informative and persuasive speeches.

The general goal of informative speakers is to increase their listeners' knowledge. The distinction between informing and persuading is slight. The informative speech is meant to increase knowledge, whereas the persuasive speech is meant to alter attitudes and behavior. Information can be presented without any attempt to persuade, but persuasion cannot be accomplished without information.

Two examples illustrates the difference between information and persuasion. You go into an Apple store to look at the latest MacBook. The salesperson wants to sell you one, so she does her best to persuade you to buy one. She shares all kinds of information about the computer: its speed, its storage, its flexibility, the ease of maintenance, its security, an explanation of all features, the warranty, and the available technical support. Is she informing or persuading? She provided you with ample information and then makes comparisons to other computers or, at the very least, gives you compelling reasons to buy that MacBook. She may give you knowledge and understanding (information) about the computer, but her goal is to persuade you to buy, even though you do not purchase the MacBook. She still made a persuasive speech—even though you did not ultimately buy the MacBook—because her *goal* was persuasive: She wanted you to buy the computer. Your boss explains how to use a piece of equipment safely. He wants you to understand how it operates and what safety mechanisms are in place. His intention is not to persuade you but to inform you how to use the equipment safely. Is he informing you or persuading you? His goal is to inform you on how to be safe using the equipment. He would be persuading you only if he tries to convince you if one safety method is better than another for solving problems.

The key to understanding the difference between information and persuasion lies in recognizing that, *although information may contain some elements of persuasion, all persuasion must provide information.* What separates an informative speech from a persuasive one is the goal of the speaker.

The Goals of Persuasive Speaking

12.2 **Identify** the goals of persuasion.

persuasion

A communication process, involving both verbal and nonverbal messages, that attempts to reinforce or change listeners' attitudes, beliefs, values, or behavior.

Persuasion is a communication process, involving both verbal and nonverbal messages, that attempts to reinforce or change listeners' attitudes, beliefs, values, or behaviors. Communication scholar David Zarefsky says, "[P]ersuasive strategies aim not only to provide information but also to affect audience members' attitudes and behavior. They ask for a greater degree of commitment from listeners than informative strategies do."[2] Is it possible to change people's attitudes, beliefs, or values without changing their behaviors? The answer is yes. For example, you might present your friend with reasons for attending a home football game. Your friend might agree and still not go. Were you persuasive? You might have been able to convince your friend that your ideas are valid, but you were not able to alter her behavior. Which is more important?

The ultimate goal of all persuasion is action or change. Successful persuasion may accomplish one or more of the following: *reinforce* existing beliefs, attitudes, or behaviors; *change* existing beliefs, attitudes, or behaviors; or *lead to* new beliefs, attitudes, or behaviors. When you want to convince someone *not* to change, you try to reinforce the existing belief, attitude, or behavior. At other times, you may want a person to do something different. When a speaker's main goal is to achieve change or action, the speaker will pursue one of four subgoals: *adoption, discontinuance, deterrence,* or *continuance* of a particular behavior.[3]

Persuasion is usually not a one-time event; often, persuasion occurs over time, and the effect of a persuasive message on a listener may not be apparent until sometime after the message is received. In other words, the listener might think about the message for days or even weeks and, with additional experiences, messages, and information, then decide to follow through on the speaker's request for action or change.

Speakers whose topic is the environment face some stiff competition from listeners who believe the environment is a nonissue.

Adoption is an action subgoal asking listeners to demonstrate their acceptance of an attitude, belief, or value by performing the behavior suggested by the speaker. One of your classmates might give a speech on volunteering at the nearby nature reserve. If you had not previously even considered spending time at a nature reserve or had not known what is done in such a place, but you decide to go after the speech, you have displayed adoption. Your classmate persuaded you. This adoption of the persuasive message might be only temporary, and you might not stay with the program throughout your college career or after, but you have responded positively to your classmate's initial persuasive message: to adopt a behavior.

Discontinuance is the opposite of adoption. **Discontinuance** is an action subgoal that asks listeners to demonstrate their alteration of an attitude, belief, or value by *stopping* certain behaviors. If your action is discontinuance, you want your listeners to stop doing something—for instance, smoking, littering, eating too many sugary foods, or illegally streaming movies. In these instances, you try to get your listeners to discontinue a negative behavior.

Deterrence is an action that asks listeners to demonstrate their acceptance of an attitude, belief, or value by avoiding certain behaviors. Sample deterrence messages are as follows: If you already eat a good breakfast, don't stop now; if you don't use illegal drugs, don't start now; if you are registered to vote, continue going to the polls. This action is similar to discontinuance in that you do not want a negative behavior to occur, but in deterrence, you are trying to *prevent* its occurrence rather than *end* its occurrence.

Continuance is an action asking listeners to demonstrate their acceptance of an attitude, belief, or value by continuing to perform the behavior suggested by the speaker. For example, continue to volunteer in the community; continue to purchase and consume more organic foods. This action is similar to adoption because you want a positive behavior to occur; with continuance, however, you are trying to *keep* an existing behavior rather than *begin* a new behavior.

Note that the first two actions, adoption and discontinuance, ask people to *change* their behavior, whereas the last two, deterrence and continuance, ask people *not to change* but to continue doing what they are already doing *or not change to something different*. Can you think of times when someone tried to persuade you to take action on one of these goals? They frequently occur in our interactions with others.

Getting others to change or not to change their behaviors is not always easy. A speaker might have to accept that a change in attitudes, beliefs, or values, such as adopting the idea of eating healthier foods, is part of the persuasive process and almost always occurs before a change in behavior can take place. Not all persuasive speaking leads to action, nor should persuasive speakers consider themselves failures if they do not obtain behavior change. Persuasion usually occurs over time; therefore, the speaker might not always be aware of whether the message was truly persuasive. Often, listeners are persuaded only after they have heard similar messages from a

adoption
An action that asks listeners to demonstrate their acceptance of attitudes, beliefs, or values by performing the behavior suggested by the speaker.

discontinuance
An action that asks listeners to demonstrate their alteration of an attitude, belief, or value by stopping certain behaviors.

deterrence
An action that asks listeners to demonstrate their acceptance of an attitude, belief, or value by avoiding certain behavior.

continuance
An action goal that asks listeners to demonstrate their acceptance of an attitude, belief, or value by continuing to perform the behavior suggested by the speaker.

variety of people, over a period of time. Especially as a beginner at persuasive speaking, you should not always expect to obtain a change in attitude, action, or behavior, but you should be able to compel others to listen to what you have to say and to consider your point of view.

Topics for Informative and Persuasive Speeches

12.3 **Choose** appropriate topics for your informative and persuasive speeches.

Are you concerned that you don't know what informative or persuasive speeches would be interesting to your listeners? Most of us have a wealth of information and a vast list of potential topics based on what we have learned from classes, readings, and other experiences. Think about topics mentioned or covered in other classes, such as social media in the workplace, the Internet, biological discoveries to create better and healthier lives, computers and agriculture, computers and mechanics, computers and art, changes in education, medical advances, alternative health care, global terrorism, gender issues in the 21st century, the impact of an elderly population on our governmental agencies, civic engagement, spirituality and religion, and multiculturalism. The list is endless, and the potential for informative or persuasive topics is almost limitless.

Connecting with others through communication is easier when they see the value in and the uses for the information you share with them. Most of us want the information we receive to be important and useful. We often think, "What's in it for me?" (WIIFM?) You first select a topic you like and know something about, then you need to think about your audience: Is the topic potentially useful to my listeners? Some topics are givens—"preparing for the job interview," "classes to help in the job search," or "getting along with others." These are topics most college students might find useful, if not right now at least at some point in the future. Topics with less evident personal value, such as "revising construction standards" or "the best cities to visit while on vacation," might seem less interesting, so you will have to clearly answer the question, WIIFM? If you are passionately interested in something, your passion alone can likely help generate interest. Although you may doubt your topic is worthwhile, if you think about your particular interests, past experiences, and special knowledge, you will no doubt discover that you, too, have a great deal to share.

Successful speakers next consider their audiences as they decide whether to inform or persuade. They communicate information accurately and clearly but, most important, they make the information meaningful and interesting to their audience by providing new information or correcting misinformation, especially when they are persuading. We will first discuss informative speech topics and then discuss persuasive speech topics.

The Informative Speech

Informative speech topics can be classified in many ways. One scheme divides topics into *objects*, *processes*, *events*, and *concepts*.

Objects Speeches about *objects* examine concrete subjects: people, animals, things, structures, and places. Here are some possibilities:

> Airline travel laws
> Beyoncé
> First ladies and their accomplishments
> One World Trade Center
> Gay–straight student alliance groups

These topics are general and must be narrowed to meet the guidelines of most class-room speaking situations.

Here are some specific purpose statements for informative speeches about concrete subjects, following the guidelines suggested earlier:

- To inform my audience about the history of the role of the First Lady and their policy accomplishments.
- To share with my audience the zoning approval processes needed during the construction of One World Trade Center.
- To share with my listeners the laws concerning airline travel around the world.

Each of these purpose statements is appropriate for an informative speech.

Processes   A *process* topic usually focuses on a demonstration in which the speaker explains how something is done or how it takes place. Here are a few sample specific purpose statements for informative speeches about processes:

- To inform my audience how the brain processes and stores visual information.
- To explain how sugar causes the number one health crisis in North America today.
- To inform my listeners about how an ordinary citizen can affect the legislative process.

Speeches about processes generally serve two purposes: to increase understanding and to teach someone *how to do something*. This could involve anything from knowing cardiopulmonary resuscitation (CPR) and its lifesaving effects to how to buy the right car.

Process speeches are usually organized in time-sequence (chronological) order, meaning that they proceed step-by-step from the beginning of the process to its end. For example, let's say your speech is on saving lives through an automated external defibrillator. You would walk your listeners through all the necessary steps and procedures so they would know exactly what to do if the occasion were to arise.

Description of a process usually benefits from the use of a visual aid. Some processes may require an actual demonstration to be fully understood. For example, to inform listeners about how to fold fancy napkin shapes, you might have to do the folding during the speech and ask your audience to follow along.

Events   Informative speeches about *events* discuss happenings or occasions. The many possible topics include the following:

The college football playoff
Global financial chaos and reform
The Pope Francis effect
Mardi Gras
The popularity of National Association for Stock Car Auto Racing (NASCAR) events
Student protests about tuition
Student protests against administrative actions
The Supreme Court ruling in *United States v. Windsor*

Appropriate specific purposes for some of these topics might include the following:

- To share the effects of global financial chaos and reform on the United States.
- To inform the audience about how decisions are made as part of the college football playoff.
- To explain the popularity of NASCAR events.

The Dalai Lama is the spiritual leader of the Tibetan people, a world religious figure, and a possible topic for your informative speech. He says he's guided by three major commitments: the promotion of basic human values in the interest of human happiness; the fostering of inter-religious harmony; and the welfare of the Tibetan people, focusing on the survival of their identity, culture, and religion.

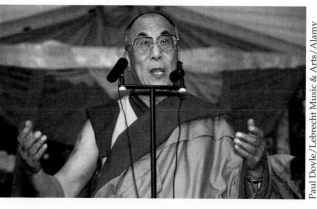

Paul Doyle/Lebrecht Music & Arts/Alamy Stock Photo

MAKING CONNECTIONS FOR SUCCESS
Experimenting with Informative Speech Topics

The speech process entails time and effort as you plan, research, organize, create, and practice the speech. Answering the following questions will give you some practical application for the actual speech:

1. Select one of the purpose statements from each category in the previous sections.

2. Indicate the organizational pattern you think will work for each statement.

3. Identify two useful presentational aids and be prepared to provide a rationale for why you think they would be beneficial.

4. Identify three forms of support to help your listeners attend to and remember this information.

Concepts Speeches about *concepts* deal with abstract topics such as beliefs, theories, ideas, and principles. The challenge is to make the subject matter concrete so the audience can easily understand it. Concept-based topics include the following:

Immigration controversies
Increase in all forms of bullying
The cost of opiod addiction
Social media addiction
Law enforcement and racial profiling
Global warming or climate change?
Suicide

These topics are too vague or broad to be meaningful. If you were to ask a dozen people what each term or phrase means, you would probably receive a dozen different answers. The speaker is responsible for narrowing and focusing the subject so the audience understands the intended meaning. Here are specific purpose statements based on some of the general, abstract topics:

- To inform my audience about teens' vulnerability to cyberbullying.
- To share ways we can reduce our social media use.
- To share the effects of excessive social media use on depression and loneliness.

Speeches about concepts take extra time and effort to develop because of their abstract nature. These topics require the use of concrete examples, definitions, and clear language.

Whether a speech is about an object, a process, an event, or a concept is not always clear because a subject may overlap these categories. Often, the specific purpose the speaker chooses to emphasize determines the category. It is important to decide on your approach to the subject and then develop your speech accordingly. Review any previous information and class discussion and handouts for more specific information about topic selection and how to determine which topics may be best suited for you and your audience (see Appendix 12 at the end of this chapter for more topics).

Guidelines
CHOOSING A TOPIC FOR AN INFORMATIVE SPEECH

1. **When you prepare an informative speech, you should begin with yourself.** What are your interests? About what topics are you passionately concerned?

2. **Informative speeches should appeal to the audience and provide knowledge of something potentially useful or beneficial.** What are some examples of potentially useful informative speech topics?

3. **Your audience will listen to you if you make the speech compelling.** What can you do to make a speech resonate with your listeners?

The Persuasive Speech

Some topics and themes lend themselves more readily to persuasive speaking than others. Current and controversial subjects are especially adaptable. The list of topics in Appendix 12 at the end of this chapter illustrates the variety of possibilities. You will increase your likelihood of success if you follow these suggestions:

1. Whenever possible, select a topic in which you are interested or about which you know something, want to speak, need to speak, or are personally concerned. Remember, it is not always possible to choose your own topic; sometimes someone else chooses it for you. For example, a nursing supervisor might tell one of the nurses that he has to speak to a group of visitors about the importance of using sun protection factor (SPF) 30 or higher sunblock to prevent skin cancer. Certainly, that might not be the nurse's first choice of topic, but he does meet some of the other criteria for speaking on the subject: knowledge of the topic, awareness of the need, and a personal and professional concern about the topic.

2. Select a worthwhile subject of potential concern to your audience.

3. Select a topic with a goal for influence or action. For example, the notion that exercise and eating well are good for your health might be a good persuasive theme, but if everyone in your audience is already healthy and physically in good shape, could you find a strong persuasive strategy?

Persuasive speeches often, but not always, deal with topics for which two or more opposing viewpoints exist and occur in situations in which the speaker's point of view differs from that of the audience. For example, the speaker might want the audience to support higher tuition because it will lead to higher-quality instruction, but most of the audience members may believe tuition is already too high. Especially when a speaker's goal is adoption or discontinuance, some difference must exist between the speaker's view and that of the audience, or persuasion is not needed. However, when the speaker's goal is deterrence or avoidance, the points of view of both speaker and audience might be more closely aligned. In

MAKING CONNECTIONS FOR SUCCESS

Everyday Acts of Persuasion

People often believe persuasion refers to situations only in which you change someone's mind and reverse a listener's beliefs. Actually, persuasion is broader. Our views have more substance than a simple, "Yes, I believe that," or "No, I disagree." Most of us have a range of commitment to many given ideas. Persuasive speakers want to move their listeners in one way or the other along a continuum. Both Presidents George W. Bush and Barack Obama as well as Congress addressed the economic problems leading to the recession of 2008–2009. Major economists believed that the only way to "save the nation" from greater problems and a bona fide depression was to provide a stimulus package to shore up financial institutions and automobile manufacturers. As soon as President Obama stated that he would increase the financial stimulus package, some journalists and members of the public began to complain that he was turning the United States into a socialist state. Some newspapers touted the headline, "Obama's First 100 Days a Failure." Others praised his initiative as daring.

1. Identify one example in your own life of each of the above (strengthening, weakening, converting, or inducing an action). How did the speakers attempt to do each? What was the effect on you? Be prepared to talk about this effect.

2. What types of action subgoals have you experienced in the last day or two?

3. How did the persuader attempt to persuade you? How successful was this persuader?

4. Select an issue that is current but avoid one that is common knowledge or that has been discussed widely, unless you plan to add a *new* perspective to it (see Appendix 12 at the end of this chapter for a list of possible persuasive topics).

such cases, the speaker's goal is to *reinforce* beliefs, attitudes, or behaviors that are similar to those proposed in the speech.

Speakers may want their listeners to think about something from a new perspective and may try to influence the listeners to accept a specific point of view. The speaker's goal is to persuade the listeners that one viewpoint is sound, valid, or worthwhile, and the speaker wants to influence the listeners to accept that specific perspective. Such speeches typically address *questions of fact, questions of value, questions of policy*, or any combination of these three types of questions.

question of fact

A question that asks what is true and what is false.

Questions of Fact   A **question of fact** asks what is true and what is false. Consider these questions: What is an advantage to being on LinkedIn? Who created Facebook? Where is the headquarters for Google? These questions can be answered with a fact that can be verified in reference books or on websites. Because they are so cut and dried, there can be little debate about them, thus making them weak topics for a persuasive speech.

In contrast, persuasive speeches may be built on predictions of future events that will eventually become matters of fact. Consider these: Is the textbook a relic of the past? When will science find cures for the most deadly diseases of humankind? Neither of these questions can be answered with certainty, but a persuasive speaker could build an effective case predicting the answer to each.

Persuasive speeches can also be based on complicated answers to questions of fact or justifications for answers that are unclear. Why has wind energy not become more popular? Are the costs too great? Is it inefficient? Does the wind charger break down? Are hazards to the environment too great? Although no single answer covers the entire situation, a speaker could build a strong argument to show that one of these factors is the primary cause for decreased adoption of wind energy use.

Finally, some persuasive speeches may attempt to answer questions of fact that are not completely verifiable: Is Eastern medicine a rival to or superior to Western medicine? Does astrology provide us with real answers for our lives? Can acupuncture reduce pain more effectively than medicine? A speech on why we should reduce our consumption of sugar might be planned this way:

Specific Purpose

Thesis

SPECIFIC PURPOSE: To persuade my listeners that sugar is harmful to our health.

THESIS: It is in our best interest to reduce consumption of sugar to lower the possibility of numerous health problems.

MAIN POINT

I. Seventy-nine million American adults have blood sugar levels that are too high.

SUBPOINTS

A. The normal range of blood sugar levels is...

B. High blood sugar levels are warning signs for further health problems.

MAIN POINT

II. Common ways we consume too much sugar.

SUBPOINTS

A. Junk food

B. Carbonated beverages

C. Eating fast food because we're in a hurry

D. Grabbing a sugary treat because we need energy to make it through the day[4]

On the surface, questions of fact may appear more appropriate for an informative speech than for a persuasive one, but if you consider the difficulty of persuading an audience that college athletics are big business, that a major fire will destroy much of Southern California, or that the pyramids of Egypt were designed by an intelligence far superior to ours today, you can see that questions of fact offer rich possibilities for persuasion.

Questions of Value   A **question of value** asks whether something is good or bad, desirable or undesirable. Value is defined as a general, relatively long-lasting ideal that guides behavior. A value requires a more judgmental response than a fact. Here are some typical questions of value: Who is the most likable celebrity in Australia? Who were the 10 best (or worst) U.S. presidents? Is a vegan diet really superior? The answers to these questions are not based solely on fact but on what each individual considers right or wrong, ethical or unethical, acceptable or unacceptable, or a good or a bad choice. People regularly make value-laden comments through social media. When was the last time you saw a Twitter follower weigh in with his or her opinion on the latest controversy playing out in the media?

The answers to questions of value may seem based solely on personal opinion and subjectivity, rather than on objective evidence, but this is not the case. Effective persuasive speakers use evidence to support their positions and are able to justify their opinions.

Values vary dramatically from one person to the next. Person *A* might think social media is bad for society, and Person *B* might think it is good; Person *A* might think alcohol should be illegal on campus, and Person *B* might think it should be legal. When it comes to questions of value, one person's judgment is no better or worse than another's. People's values are usually complicated because they are rooted in emotion rather than reason. It is often extremely difficult to convince people to change their values. A speaker's position on a question of value might be difficult to defend. You will need to gather a great deal of research and evidence and build a strong case to support one value over another—even though you know your values are right—because your listeners also believe their values are right.

question of value

A question that asks whether something is good or bad, desirable or undesirable.

Specific Purpose	**SPECIFIC PURPOSE:** To persuade my listeners that reducing clutter makes you more productive.
Thesis	**THESIS:** Reducing clutter can make you more productive, mentally healthier, and save you time.

MAIN POINT

I. Unresolved emotional issues are often the cause of a cluttered lifestyle.

SUBPOINTS

A. Clutter undermines real productivity.

B. The reality show *Hoarders* demonstrates the internal conflict about what is important in life.

C. "I know where everything is in that stack. Don't mess me up!" is a common refrain of those who clutter and hoard.

MAIN POINT

II. Organization experts and psychologists say that clutter is a sign that some portion of our lives is out of control.

SUBPOINTS

A. They say those who struggle with clutter are simply avoiding the need to make decisions about other things in life.

B. Anxiety, depression, and grief are some of the reasons we let clutter take over our lives.[5]

question of policy
A question that asks what actions should be taken.

Questions of Policy   A **question of policy** goes beyond seeking a judgmental response or a course of action. Whereas a question of value asks whether something is right or wrong, a question of policy asks whether something should or should not be done: Should college health centers provide birth control to students? Should all plastic water bottles be banned? Should Facebook allow pictures with graphic scenes, such as violent assaults? Questions of policy involve both facts and values and are never simple.

Persuasive speakers can defend an existing policy, suggest modifications of an existing policy, offer a new policy to replace an old one, or create a policy where none exists. If you defend an existing policy, you must persuade your listeners that what exists is best for the situation. If you want to modify or replace an existing policy, you must persuade your listeners that the old policy does not work and that your new one will. If you hope to create a new policy, you must persuade your audience that a policy is needed and yours is the right one for the situation.

When discussing questions of policy, persuasive speakers usually focus on three considerations: need, plan, and suitability. If you believe things are not working as some think, you must argue there is a *need* for change. When you advocate change, you must provide a *plan*, or a solution. The plan tells the audience what you think should be done. Finally, you must defend your plan by explaining its *suitability* for the situation. Study the use of need, plan, and suitability in the following:

Specific Purpose	**SPECIFIC PURPOSE:** To persuade my listeners that each of us can make a difference in another's life.
Thesis	**THESIS:** Each of us can have a tremendous impact on others, even people suffering from depression, by just taking a few moments to offer a kind comment or do something nice for them.
Need	I. One of every five young people and one of every four college students or adults suffer from some form of diagnosable mental illness. A. Suicide is the third leading cause of death among people ages 15–24, and the second leading cause of death in college students ages 20–24. B. About 19 percent of young people contemplate or attempt suicide each year. C. Forty-four percent of American college students reported feeling symptoms of depression.[6]

Plan	II. Seventeen-year-old Graeme Carlson, a twelfth-grade student in Selkirk, Manitoba, created PingPongPositive.org to help others feel better about themselves and the world.
	
	A. Graeme tells about a new friend who gave him a book to read because she thought he would really enjoy it.
	
	B. Graeme felt much better because of the act of friendship and the gift of the book.
	
	C. He decided to create ping-pong balls with uplifting messages and gave away 500 ping-pong balls after giving someone a compliment.
	
	   1. He created a website to promote this unique way of paying it forward.
	
	   2. Graeme also set up a Facebook page, a Twitter account, and YouTube clips.
	
	   3. He received messages from all over Canada, the United States, Europe, and Asia.
	
	   4. Canadian Broadcasting System (CBC) offices in Winnipeg ordered 250 specially designed ping-pong balls to help further the cause.

Suitability	III. Graeme says that he feels good when he reads about what others have done with their ping-pong balls, and while he still suffers from depression, he knows that people really do care and that helps him feel better. A. You, too, can find a unique way to make others feel better, or you can add to the ping-pong balls going around the world. B. If each of us would compliment even one person and give him or her a ping-pong ball as a reminder of how much others mean to us, the world would be a healthier, happier place.[7]

Preparing and Developing an Informative Speech

12.4 **Prepare and develop** an informative speech to meet your professor's specific criteria.

The previous chapters on public communication relate directly to the principles and skills of informative speaking. All aspects of topic selection; audience analysis; information gathering; preparation of supporting and clarifying materials; and organizing, outlining, and delivering a speech are crucial to the effectiveness and eventual success of your informative presentation. In addition, you should be familiar with strategies for competing with distractions and noises, such as students arriving late, a maintenance crew working in the next classroom, a lawn mower outside the window, and whispering in the audience. Such interferences cannot be ignored if you want to be successful in transmitting information to others. To achieve your main goal to enhance the audience's knowledge, you must attain two subgoals: to gain audience members' attention and to increase their understanding.

Gain and Maintain Audience Attention

Motivating the audience to pay attention is critical to the success of any speech. (See Chapter 7 on listening for more on motivating your audience to listen.) To accomplish this, you should follow a strategy that will work well for your audience. Gaining and maintaining the attention of the audience is extremely important when you present information. Audience members must believe they will benefit from the information, perceive it as relevant to their lives, and find it interesting enough to want to listen. This task is quite challenging to the beginning speaker, but if you make your audience the central focus of the speech and use a little creativity, you can easily gain and hold their attention.

Generate a Need for the Information   A student gave a speech on the benefits of seat belt use. After reading his peer evaluations and reflecting on the video of his speech, he emailed to ask why no one liked the speech. When he was asked whether he had determined how many in his class do not use seat belts, he did not have an answer. When asked if he knew the average seat belt use in his state, he did not have those statistics either. When we told him that the latest statistics from the highway patrol and the department of transportation suggest that 82 percent of people in his state use seat belts, he was surprised. This should give you two reasons his listeners did not seem to like his speech: Most of them already knew the benefits of seat belt use and use them regularly, and he had not done enough research to go beyond what his listeners already knew. As a result, his audience did not feel motivated to listen. How could he have engaged his audience better? He might have done a survey to find out what they knew, or he might have looked carefully at statistics. Or he could have found a way to make the speech more relevant to his listeners in this way:

> I realize that most of you already wear seat belts when you drive or ride in a vehicle, but did you know that even in Iowa, where seat belt usage is said to be at 82 percent, injuries resulting because a seat belt was not in use account for more than 25 percent of all traffic deaths? That means that six of us in this class could have life-threatening injuries if we were involved in an automobile accident and were not wearing a seat belt.

This opening acknowledges the high percentage of people in the state who use seat belts, and it also piques interest because it asks a rhetorical question to make the listener aware of the consequences of failure to wear a seat belt. Notice that the speaker also makes the percentages memorable by identifying the number of class members who could be affected.

Let's look at other examples of rhetorical questions used to begin a speech:

- Some medical doctors believe that the high blood sugar epidemic is North America's number one health crisis. Are you aware that around 29 million American adults have diabetes, and of that 29 million, over 8 million are undiagnosed?[8]

- Here in North America we have many blessings, but all countries do not have even the basic necessities, such as food, clean water, and education. For instance, did you know a child dies of hunger every 15 seconds?[9]

- Eating disorders are pervasive in our society. Would you be surprised to learn that eating disorders have the highest mortality rate of any mental illness in the Western world?[10]

Speakers can also use questions meant to generate responses from the audience as a strategy to gain and maintain audience interest and attention.

Create Information Relevance   People are much more likely to pay attention when they believe a speech relates directly to them. A speaker who gives an audience a reason to listen by relating the topic to their needs and interests creates **information relevance**. Ask yourself whether the information you intend to present is relevant to your listeners. If it is not, think about how you might make it so. In one of our classes, a student wanted to talk about the Amish community that lived in her area, so she chose to learn more about and share information on the Amish culture with the class. Her speech was well received because she used facts the students already knew and then added new information.

Another student spent his spring break volunteering for Habitat for Humanity. The group built a home for those who might not otherwise have a stable, safe residence. He talked about the work involved but also gave fascinating information about how many houses have been built and families provided for in this way, and he touched on the value of volunteering and the good feeling he had because he had done something for someone else.

Provide a Fresh Perspective   Information perceived as *new* also attracts the attention of an audience. But whenever this statement is mentioned in class, someone responds, "But there isn't anything new to present." Actually, discussing something new does not necessarily mean you have to present something the audience has never heard. It does mean you need to devise a *new view or angle*. AIDS, safe sex, pollution, use of seat belts, smoking, drugs, and recycling are subjects that communication professors and other listeners have heard discussed too many times. A speaker who provides a fresh perspective on a familiar topic makes it more interesting and thus increases the chances of holding the audience's attention. One speaker informed the audience about illegal drugs that are medically helpful in treating certain diseases. She began her speech in the following manner:

> You have read and heard so much about cocaine, crack, heroin, and other illegal drugs you are probably sick of the subject, but these drugs are not all bad. You might at first think that I am too liberal, but my mother is on drugs, and I am glad. You see, my mother is suffering from cancer, and the only relief she can get is from the small doses of heroin she receives each day to ease the pain. Today, I am going to inform you about illegal drugs that actually aid our sick and dying.

This approach is not new, but it is *different*. Rather than taking a stand either for or against illegal drugs, the speaker

information relevance

Making information relevant to an audience to give them a reason to listen.

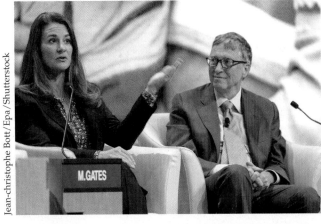

Melinda and Bill Gates, and Bill Gates Sr., oversee the Gates Foundation, a philanthropy benefitting scores of institutions and individuals around the world. Melinda Gates is also in demand as a speaker because of her unique global perspective.

Jean-christophe Bott/Epa/Shutterstock

focused on certain instances in which the use of illegal drugs can be beneficial. This also helped her to stay within the guidelines of the informative speech.

Focus on the Unusual   Sometimes a focus on an unusual aspect of a topic helps a speaker maintain the attention of the audience. A speaker might begin the speech like this:

> In an age when equality between the sexes seems closer to reality, there are some occupations in which there are still more men than women. One occupational area is pilots and flight instructors. It may surprise you to know that the flight instructor who has the world record for training the most pilots is Evelyn Johnson of Morristown, Tennessee. Ms. Johnson logged nearly 58,000 flight hours, trained more than 5,000 pilots, and covered 5.5 million miles. The woman known as "Mama Bird" quit flying in 2006 only after a car accident led to an amputation of her leg. Even then she managed the local airport until shortly before her death on May 10, 2012.[11]

Increase Understanding of the Topic

Once you have gained your listeners' attention, you've created the opportunity to increase their understanding. Understanding is the ability to interpret, grasp, or assign meaning to an idea. You can enhance your audience's understanding by organizing your presentation systematically, choosing appropriate language, and providing clear definitions.

Organize Your Presentation   In a well-organized speech, ideas are managed in a clear and orderly sequence that makes the material easy to follow and understand. The most commonly used organizational patterns in informative speeches are chronological or time-sequence, topical, and spatial. Effective organization helps increase the speaker's credibility and improves the listeners' comprehension and retention of information. Two organizational techniques that aid understanding in both informative and persuasive speeches are *planned repetition* and *advance organizers*.

Plan for Repetition   **Planned repetition** is the deliberate restatement of a thought to increase the likelihood the audience will understand and remember it. The repetition of information generally helps us remember things more completely. For example, if you ask someone for another's cell phone number and have nothing to write the number on until you call, you probably say the number over and over so you can remember it long enough to add it to your contact list or dial the number.

The guiding principle behind most television commercials is repetition. Although we might find it bothersome, constant repetition of the same commercial reminds us of the product and thus increases the chances we will purchase it. You can use this

planned repetition
The deliberate restating of a thought to increase the likelihood the audience will understand and remember it.

MAKING CONNECTIONS FOR SUCCESS
Make It Lively, Please!

Words can be dry and uninteresting, or they can grab our attention and compel us to listen to someone. Read the six sentences or phrases below:

- Wall Street caused the economic mess.
- Foreign automobile manufacturers produce better cars.
- iPhones are useful.
- Sugar causes many health problems.
- Community volunteerism is important.
- What kinds of jobs will I find when I graduate?

Now answer the following questions to see if you can bring the sentences above to life:

1. Use definitions, concrete words, or descriptors to make the phrases livelier.
2. Compare your words with the original. What are the differences?
3. Was it easy to change the phrases so they were lively?
4. Compare your changes with those of your classmates. What were the similarities and differences?

same principle in an informative speech to help your audience remember key ideas. For example, you might say:

> Medical doctors have successfully developed a "smart bomb" on breast cancer that delivers the treatment to tumor cells but leaves healthy cells alone. This experimental "smart bomb" treatment successfully extended the time women lived without progression of their cancers. The treatment appears to improve survival: 65 percent of women who received the "smart bomb" treatment were still alive after 2 years, while only 47 percent of those medicated with standard drugs were still alive after 2 years.[12]

You could also put critical information in a computer slide presentation or on a poster. Or you could write it on the board for additional repetition and emphasis. Internal summaries and previews may also include repetition of the points made and help the audience focus on what is yet to come in the speech.

advance organizer
A statement that warns the listener that significant information is coming.

Use Advance Organizers   **Advance organizers** are similar to signposts in that they signal what is coming, but they also warn that what is about to be said is significant. They signal the listener to pay attention.

> It's important for all of us to be a part of this movement. If you understand this next step in the process, you will also understand the need to act quickly.

These warnings grab the attention of your audience and emphasize that forthcoming information is both necessary and important. Teachers use advance organizers to make sure students know what is essential. Examples include the following:

> Here's a big hint. What I next tell you will form the background for your involvement in the group projects.
>
> The following concepts will be critical for you to understand to complete the project.

Advance organizers also serve as previews of main points. Use of advance organizers in introductions helps your audience concentrate on what is coming in the speech. For example, one speaker used the following statements in her introduction to alert her audience and to indicate what was important to meet her specific purpose:

> Anorexia, bulimia, and binge eating disorders often surface during adolescence or the early years of college, but both men and women may show signs of trouble much earlier. There are six signs that can alert you to an eating disorder in another person. Knowing these signs can help you spot potential problems early.[13]

Choose Language Carefully   It is extremely important to match your level of language to the knowledge your audience already has about your topic. If you are speaking with experts or with people who are familiar with your topic, feel free to use technical terms without explaining them, but if your audience is unfamiliar with your subject, you will need to choose your words carefully and define any special terms. In some cases, you should avoid technical terms altogether. This may be necessary when such terms would confuse your listeners or when your audience lacks the ability or background to understand them. Sometimes a speaker's use of too many technical terms turns an audience off or even creates hostility. Choose language carefully to avoid creating unnecessary problems. When possible, select concrete rather than abstract words and use descriptions to make your points clearer.

Use Concrete Words   To increase understanding, try to use as many concrete words as possible. Concrete words are symbols for specific things one can experience through the senses. In addition, concrete words stand for specific people, places, things, or acts; for instance, Winnipeg, Manitoba, Canada, is more concrete than a Canadian city. Familiar, concrete language allows your listeners to form mental images similar to yours.

If you say something is comparable in size to a grapefruit, your listeners should form a fairly accurate picture of what you have in mind. Concrete words leave less room for misinterpretation and misunderstanding.

Abstract words refer to ideas, qualities, or relationships: justice, equality, joy, freedom, or classmates. The meaning of these words relies on the experiences and intentions of the people who express them. If a speaker says, "The travel security system is good," we don't know whether he means air traffic, highway traffic, rail traffic, or bus traffic. We also don't know what is *good*. Abstract language is imprecise and often leaves listeners confused about the speaker's intent.

Use Description   To make something more concrete, a speaker might describe its size, quantity, shape, weight, composition, texture, color, age, strength, or fit. These descriptive words are called **descriptors**. The more descriptors a speaker uses that relate to the listeners' experiences, the greater is the likelihood that the message will be understood. One speaker used these descriptors in talking about the threat of cyber warfare:

descriptors
Words used to describe something.

> According to PBS, "Eligible Receiver" is the code name of a government simulation where a team of hackers was organized to infiltrate Pentagon systems. The team was allowed to use only publicly available computer equipment and hacking software. While the information is still classified, we know that the hackers were able to infiltrate and take control of the Pacific command center computers as well as power grids and 911 systems in nine major U.S. cities. This simulation demonstrated the real lack of consciousness about cyber warfare. During the first three days of the exercise, nobody believed we were under cyber attack. This whole exercise underscores America's reliance on information technology systems and their vulnerabilities to attack.[14]

The speaker's explanations provide one specific example of what the team was able to accomplish with information technology at the Pentagon, without being detected. The descriptors are a chilling reminder that, in modern warfare, the things we take for granted can be used against us.

Use Definitions   One way to ensure your audience's understanding is to define all potentially unfamiliar and complex words. The most common form of definition used by speakers, the logical definition, usually contains two parts: the dictionary definition and the characteristics that distinguish the term from other members of the same category. An operational definition explains how an object or concept works, and a definition by example explains a term or a concept by using examples, either verbal or actual, to illustrate a point. In addition, four other methods can clearly define a term for your listeners: using *contrast definitions, synonyms, antonyms,* and *etymologies.*

Show Contrasts   A **contrast definition** is used to show or emphasize differences. This type of definition is helpful when you want to distinguish between similar terms. For example, a speaker discussing communication apprehension and speech anxiety

contrast definition
A definition that shows or emphasizes differences.

MAKING CONNECTIONS FOR SUCCESS

Specific Word Choice

Concrete words are more easily understandable. If our words are too abstract, we might confuse the listeners or make them tune out. Rewrite the following sentences to make them more concrete:

1. Street violence has increased.

2. The flu is dangerous.

3. Lots of food service programs promote healthier eating.

4. Cyberbullying is a real problem in our schools.

5. Be prepared to share your changes with the class.

differentiated one term from the other by stating that communication apprehension is a trait or global anxiety, whereas speech anxiety is a state or situational anxiety. A person suffering from communication apprehension might also have speech anxiety, but a person with speech anxiety will not necessarily have communication apprehension. A contrast definition might also point out differences in causes and effects. Thus the speaker might point out that people with communication apprehension actively avoid all interaction with others, whereas people with speech anxiety merely feel a bit of controllable discomfort when addressing an audience.

Use Synonyms   The use of synonyms can also help clarify the meaning of a word. A **synonym** is a word, phrase, or concept with exactly the same or nearly the same meaning as another word, term, or concept. In describing a communicative extrovert, a speaker used the phrases "willingness to talk openly" and "ability to speak in any situation without reservation." Each phrase describes the behavior exhibited by a person who is a communicative extrovert.

Use Antonyms   In contrast, an **antonym** is a word, phrase, or concept that has the opposite meaning of another word, phrase, or concept. For example, a communicative extrovert is the opposite of someone with communication apprehension. Such a person is not shy, reserved, unwilling to talk, or afraid to speak. The person greatly enjoys talking with others. Using an antonym helps the audience to compare differences and leaves the listener with a memorable definition of an unfamiliar term.

Use Etymologies   An **etymology** is a form of definition that traces the origin and development of a word. One student used etymology to explain how the Olympic Games got their name. In the Greek system of telling time, an Olympiad was the period of four years that elapsed between two successive celebrations of the Olympian. This method of figuring time became common in about 300 BC, and all events were dated from 776 BC, the beginning of the first known Olympic Games. Such a definition provides the audience with a novel way to remember key information. Excellent sources of word etymologies are the *Oxford English Dictionary* and the *Etymological Dictionary of Modern English.*

Whenever any possibility exists that your audience may not understand a term or concept, select the kind of definition that provides the clearest explanation. In some instances, more than one kind might be necessary. To err by overdefining is better than an inadequate definition so your audience wonders what you're talking about.

synonym

A word, term, or concept that is the same or nearly the same in meaning as another word, term, or concept.

antonym

A word, phrase, or concept that is opposite in meaning to another word, phrase, or concept.

etymology

A form of definition that traces the origin and development of a word.

Guidelines

AVOIDING MAKING ASSUMPTIONS

1. **Ask yourself whether your listeners already know what you are talking about. Audience analysis may be appropriate.** If you are addressing your class, randomly select some of your classmates and ask them what they know about your topic and its related terminology.

2. **If you believe that even one audience member might not understand, take the time to briefly define and explain your topic.**

3. **If you believe a majority of your listeners already know what you mean, say something such as, "Many of you probably know what euthanasia is, but for those who don't..."** In this way, you acknowledge those who already know and help those who do not.

4. **Do not assume your audience knows the introductory information, especially if you have any doubts about what they know.** You can always move through your basic definitions and explanations quickly if your audience seems to understand, but it is difficult to regain their interest and attention once you start talking over their heads.

Hints for Effective Informative Speaking

Adhering to the following two additional guidelines should be particularly helpful to ensure success: Avoid assumptions and personalize information.

Avoid Assumptions   A student began speaking about CPR by emphasizing its importance in saving lives. However, she failed to explain that the acronym CPR stands for *cardiovascular pulmonary resuscitation;* she assumed that everyone already knew what it meant. Most of the audience did understand, but a number of people did not. In addition, some knew what the acronym meant but did not know how the technique worked. Because at least half of her classmates were unfamiliar with the technique, they found the speaker's presentation confusing and frustrating. One mistaken assumption undercut all the work she had put into her speech. Use the guidelines on the previous page to avoid assumptions.

Teaching others the fine art of surfboarding requires an understanding of the listeners, careful organization, and planning. When the instructor shares personal stories, the listeners are likely to remember more.

Personalize Information   When you relate your topic to your listeners so they can see its relevance, you are personalizing information. Carson presented a speech about the dreaded "freshman 15" and the changed eating and activity habits of first-year college students.

> I am one of those students who gained weight and realized I didn't feel good about myself. I'm going to share with you my own ways of moving back to a healthier lifestyle.

Personalized information not only holds attention but also attracts interest. For example, think of your most effective instructors. Chances are they take ordinary material and personalize it into meaningful, interesting knowledge. Listening to a string of facts can be frustrating, but a speech comes to life when it contains personal illustrations.

Most of us are interested in others. If we were not, there would be no *People* magazine, no *National Enquirer*, no *Late Show with Stephen Colbert*, no *Survivor*, no *The Ellen DeGeneres Show*, and no *Dr. Phil*. Stories are much more likely to affect listeners than are statistics. Whenever possible, personalize your information and dramatize it in human terms.

One student began an informative speech about the Heimlich maneuver, a technique used to clear the throat of someone who is choking, by relating the story of a 4-year-old boy who saved his 3-year-old friend. The boy had watched a television show in which the maneuver was used to save the life of one of the main characters, and simply reenacted what he saw. The use of this dramatic, real-life episode grabbed the listeners' attention and prepared them for his discussion of who developed the technique, how it works, and how many lives it has saved.

Guidelines

PERSONALIZE INFORMATION IN YOUR SPEECHES

1. **Use examples and information that specifically relate to your audience.** This will help you make a stronger connection with your listeners.

2. **Draw conclusions that your audience members can identify with and explain what those conclusions may mean for them.** This will go a long way in building strong rapport with them.

3. **Refer to people who are similar to your audience members**—for example, single parents, nontraditional students, students of color, international students, computer science majors, commuters who must drive to campus.

4. **Refer to topics and events that affect your listeners,** such as campus activities, elections, state and local laws, social events, tax cuts or increases, cultural programs, and career decisions.

Evaluating the Informative Speech

12.5 **Evaluate and assess** your own informative speeches prior to classroom presentation and **apply** evaluation criteria to the speeches of others.

Every instructor uses specific criteria to evaluate a speaker's competence in content and delivery of a speech. The following are some common criteria used by instructors around the world. Keep them in mind as you prepare your speech.

We include samples of a speaker's self-evaluation form and a listener's evaluation form (Figures 12.1 and 12.2) so both speakers and audience members will be aware of their responsibilities to each other.

Topic

The selection of a topic should meet the following criteria:

- The topic should merit your audience's attention.
- The focus of the topic should take into account the audience's level of knowledge.

FIGURE 12.1 Speaker's Self-Evaluation Form

After you have completed an informative speech, take a few moments to think about your preparation and presentation. Complete the phrases on this form by stating what you would do similarly or differently, and why, if you were to give this same speech again.

Title of speech: _____.

Date and place given: _____.

My topic was _____.

I liked the topic because _____.

My research could be improved by _____.

The organizational pattern I chose was _____.

The introduction was _____.

The body of the speech needed _____.

My conclusion seemed to be _____.

My explanation of ideas should _____.

The support I provided for my ideas was _____.

My use of language might _____.

My visual delivery was _____.

My vocal delivery needed _____.

The ways I adapted my topic, ideas, and language to this audience were _____

_____.

Things I would change are _____,

because _____.

Things I would retain are _____,

because _____.

If I were to grade myself, the grade would be _____ , because _____

_____.

- Listeners should be able to see the relationship between the topic and the speaker and between the topic and themselves.
- The topic of the speech should be adequately covered in the time available. The topic should be narrow enough to be fully developed.

General Requirements

These general requirements hold for all informative speech presentations:

- The purpose of the speech should be clearly to inform and should be stated as such.
- The speech should meet the time requirements set by the assignment.
- The speaker should cite sources of information other than the speaker's own knowledge.
- The speech purpose should be relevant to the assignment and relate to the audience.
- The speech should show evidence of careful preparation.

FIGURE 12.2 Listener's Evaluation Form

This form can be used to evaluate speeches given by your classmates. Follow your instructor's directions for providing such feedback.

Speaker _____ Topic _____

Date _____ Listener _____

The speaker considered this topic for this class, assignment, and context by

_____ .

A new or different perspective I gained was _____ .

The organization of the speech was _____ .

The reasons for my comments on organization are _____ .

Four things the speaker did to keep me listening were: _____

_____ .

The speaker's purpose was _____ .

The types of supporting materials used included _____ .

Presentational aids, if used, enhanced/did not enhance the speech because

_____ .

The speaker's language helped/hindered me in the following ways: _____

_____ .

The speaker could improve the physical aspects of delivery by _____ .

The one comment I wish to make about vocal delivery is _____ .

The speaker needed to explain _____ .

One aspect I especially liked was _____ .

One area that needs improvement in the future is _____ .

Audience Analysis

The speaker must shape the speech to suit the audience, which often requires research (for example, determining the listeners' past experiences, beliefs, attitudes, values). The choices made by the speaker regarding content and the development of ideas should be customized for the listeners' benefit.

- The speech should reflect appropriate audience analysis.
- The speech should show listeners why the topic is important to them.
- At several points the speaker should connect with the listeners through familiar examples or identify listeners' preferences or experiences.

Supporting Materials

Supporting materials supply documented evidence that the information conveyed in the speech is accurate and credible.

- The speech should be well documented.
- The sources should be cited completely and accurately.
- The research should be up to date as much as possible.
- The speaker should use adequate and sufficient clarifying materials.
- Visual aids, if used, should be appropriate, add to the audience's understanding of the speech content, and follow the guidelines established by the assignment.

Organization

When judging the speech organization, the evaluator looks for a carefully planned, well-developed informative speech that takes a unified approach to the material being presented.

- The introduction should be properly developed.
  - It should orient the audience to the topic, gain attention, and arouse interest.
  - It should include a specific purpose and thesis statement.
  - It should define terms (if necessary).
  - It should be relevant.
  - It should establish credibility.
- The organization of the body should be clear and easy to follow.
  - The main points should be clear and parallel in structure.
  - The main points should relate to the purpose of the speech.
  - Transitions should provide appropriate links between ideas.
  - The organizational pattern should be appropriate.
- The conclusion should be properly developed.
  - It should reinforce the purpose by reviewing the main points.
  - It should end with a memorable thought.

Delivery

Delivery techniques provide evidence that the speaker is aware of audience interests, is involved in and enthusiastic about the topic, and truly wants to share the material with the listeners.

- The speaker's stance and posture should be suitable.
- The speaker's eye contact with the audience should be appropriate.
- The speaker should follow the assignment in method of delivery (use of notes and number of note cards).

- The speaker's facial expressions should convey and clarify thoughts.
- The speaker's body movements should be appropriate and effective.
- The speaker's vocal delivery should enhance the speech with appropriate volume and rate, conversational quality, enthusiastic tone, clear enunciation, appropriate pauses, and appropriate vocal variety.

Language Choice

Language choice can enhance and clarify ideas considerably.

- Language choice should be appropriate to the assignment and audience.
- Word choice should be appropriate for college-level students.
- Grammar should be appropriate and show college-level competence.
- Word pronunciations should be correct.

Speakers should always analyze their presentations. We are often called on to make reports or provide information in the workplace, in the groups of which we are members, and in classrooms. Because speaking is so prevalent, it is important for the speaker to step back and carefully and critically reflect on the speech, the situation, the audience, and the performance. If we hope to become effective communicators in public settings, we need to use reflective thinking to objectively analyze our performance and how successful we were. Figure 12.1 (earlier in this section) shows a sample speaker's self-evaluation form to facilitate this reflection process.

We spend much more time listening to speeches than we do making speeches, and though this section may seem to focus on making effective speeches, it is also important to be a critical consumer of speeches and other presentations. Figure 12.2 (earlier in this section) provides a sample listener's evaluation form for listeners to respond to the speaker directly in writing. It is useful for the speaker to obtain listeners' perspectives on a speech. Honest and tactful feedback can be invaluable. But it is also a good idea to self-evaluate presentations, even when you will not be passing your comments on to the speaker. Listeners are encouraged to use Figure 12.2 as a basis for creating their own evaluations and applying their own criteria to presentations.

The following informative speech outline provides full content. The speech was used in Chapter 10 to provide examples of the full sentence and presentational outlines.

A SAMPLE INFORMATIVE SPEECH WITH COMMENTARY

Sarah Johansen, University of Nebraska–Lincoln. Used with permission.

TOPIC: Helen Keller International

TITLE: A Charity with Vision: Helen Keller International

GENERAL PURPOSE: To inform

SPECIFIC PURPOSE: To inform my audience about the charity organization Helen Keller International and raise awareness for its cause

THESIS: To inform my audience about the mission and history of Helen Keller International, how it acts to prevent blindness, and its actions to reduce malnutrition worldwide

INTRODUCTION

In her introduction, Sarah uses her listeners' senses to help them focus on what it would be like to lose one's sight and then makes the loss more relevant to them. This material helps to motivate and orient her listeners to the topic.

I. Close your eyes for just a moment. Without sight, you must depend on other senses to remain aware of everything going on around you. Now imagine losing your sense of hearing as well. How would you communicate with others and stay aware of your surroundings?

    A. Helen Keller was both blind and deaf and still managed to have an incredibly successful and inspirational life and was known for her intelligence and ambition.

    B. One of her many accomplishments was cofounding the organization Helen Keller International (HKI) in 1915 with George Kessler.

    C. The organization is a legacy Helen Keller left for us to continue, with her spirit and enthusiasm at its heart, in order to better the world.

BODY

II. Helen Keller International's Mission and History

    A. Helen Keller was blinded at the age of 2 after a terrible fever and soon after lost her sense of hearing.

    B. George Kessler was a New Yorker who survived the sinking of the *Lusitania* in 1915 and committed his life to helping soldiers who had lost vision in combat.

    C. George and his wife asked Helen Keller for her support and formed the Permanent Blind Relief War Fund for Soldiers & Sailors of the Allies in 1915, which helped blinded veterans learn how to read Braille, make chairs, and knit.

        1. The fund expanded and incorporated civilians as well as veterans, and by 1970 the focus shifted to preventing blindness by distributing vitamin A capsules in Central America and in the Asia-Pacific region.

        2. The name Helen Keller International was adopted in 1977, and it serves not only the blind but also those who are underprivileged and at risk for blindness.

    D. HKI's mission statement emphasizes their dedication to improving health outcomes and saving the eyesight of the world's poor and underprivileged, and their work establishing programs to mitigate the causes and effects of blindness and malnutrition.

    E. HKI now serves in 22 countries around the globe: in Africa, the Asia-Pacific region, and the Americas.

III. Helen Keller International and Preventing Blindness

    A. The number one treatable cause of blindness in the world is cataracts.

        1. According to the book *Principles of Human Anatomy*, a cataract is the loss of transparency of the lens of the eye, which has a number of causes, including age and sun exposure.

        2. HKI trains nurses and surgeons and provides medical equipment in underdeveloped countries so that cataract surgeries can be performed for as little as $12 a patient.

    B. Vitamin A deficiency is the leading cause of childhood blindness.

        1. According to *Africa News*, "an estimated 250,000 to 500,000 vitamin A–deficient children become blind every year, and half of them die within 12 months of losing their sight."

        2. HKI provides vitamin A supplementation to children twice a year in order to prevent blindness.

        3. Gary Heiting states that vitamin A helps keep the cornea of the eye healthy and helps prevent macular degeneration.

    C. In the United States, a program called ChildSight, a branch of HKI, has been established that screens the eyesight of, and delivers glasses to, underprivileged children.

IV. Helen Keller International and Reducing Malnutrition

    A. Vitamin A supplementation, according to www.hki.org, "not only can prevent a lifetime of darkness, but can also result in a 25% reduction in child mortality."

In each of her subpoints, Sarah reinforces Helen Keller's accomplishments, despite the loss of both sight and hearing.

Note how Sarah adds specific information to provide the listeners with more detail throughout her speech.

In the first main point of the body, Sarah talks about Keller's background and that of George Kessler, who helped establish the charity that became Helen Keller International.

Sarah expands on the historical information about Helen Keller International as well as the specific strategies it uses to help the most vulnerable and disadvantaged people in the world.

Sarah's subpoints and sub-subpoints in her first main point provide a view of the organization and what it does to help people around the globe.

The second main point elaborates on the specific diseases and causes of vision loss and identifies ChildSight, the branch of Helen Keller International that works to help save the eyesight of underprivileged children.

Sarah provides information on the maladies treated and also shows how Helen Keller International trains medical teams as well as provides equipment and supplies to eradicate the problems.

The third main point describes what the organization does to reduce malnutrition and provide the needed vitamin and mineral supplements to save eyesight throughout the world. In this main point, Sarah shows us how Helen Keller International finds solutions to health problems that may be taken for granted in developed countries. Helen Keller International provides health care answers that are beyond the means of people and even governments in these vulnerable populations.

B. HKI provides low-cost vitamin and mineral supplements to severely malnourished populations.

C. The Homestead Food Production program created self-sufficient gardens in Cambodia, the Philippines, Bangladesh, and Nepal.

D. Food fortification program provides more nutritious foods for families and communities around the world.

CONCLUSION

V. Helen Keller International is an exceptional charity solely focused on the betterment of lives all around the world.

A. The treatment of blindness in both children and adults has improved the quality of life for many individuals in underprivileged countries.

B. Food production and sustainability provided by HKI will drastically affect the world's hunger and malnutrition problems.

C. Helen Keller's legacy lives on through this organization and will continue to help people all over the world.[9]

REFERENCES

Heiting, Gary. "Vitamin A and Beta Carotene: Eye Benefits." *All About Vision*. N.p., June 2011 (web). Retrieved May 19, 2012, from www.allaboutvision.com/nutrition/vitamin_a.htm.

Helen Keller International 2012 (web). Retrieved May 19, 2012, from www.hki.org.

"Nutrition; A Sweet Potato a Day." *Africa News*, Nov. 29, 2011. LexisNexis. (web). Retrieved May 19, 2012, from https://www.lexisnexis.com.

Tortora, Gerard J., and Mark T. Nielsen. *Principles of Human Anatomy*, 12th ed. New York: John Wiley & Sons, Inc., 2012. P. 728 (print).

In her conclusion, Sarah summarizes and synthesizes the main points of the speech and reinforces the remarkable work of the Helen Keller International charity.

Sarah makes her listeners aware of the beneficial effects of Helen Keller International's actions in areas of the world with high hunger, malnutrition, and mortality rates.

Sarah has references from a variety of sources. One has information about vitamins and the benefits for eyes and comes from a website. The Helen Keller International website provides unique insights into the organization and its work. One newspaper article came from Africa News *and was accessed through LexisNexis, and the fourth source came from a textbook. The sources are varied and provide differing pieces of information for the speech.*

Now it's time for you to think about Sarah's speech: How would you evaluate the evidence Sarah provided? In much of her speech, she uses Helen Keller International website facts and statistics. Does she provide enough oral footnotes to identify where other information was gained? Are the sources reliable? Does she help you to consider this a viable charity? Does this speech make you think about the statement "the sky is the limit" when it comes to choices for the informative speech?

Persuasive Claims

12.6 **Construct and support** a persuasive claim.

When attempting to answer questions of fact, value, and policy in the persuasive speech process, we cannot always develop a formal logical answer that will irrefutably counter the objections of others. Formal rules of argument do not always determine who is right and who is wrong. Even when you supply compelling evidence to support your view, most evidence is not 100 percent clear-cut and may be interpreted in different ways. These factors make persuasive speaking especially challenging.

Aristotle, an ancient Greek philosopher, claimed that speakers had three modes of persuasion available to them: *ethos, logos,* and *pathos.* The speaker's actions and demeanor create each of these appeals during the speech. Aristotle believed one could appeal through **ethos**, or a speaker's ethical character. Speakers gain character or reputation through their ethical acts. Ethos is perceived in a speaker when the speaker identifies sources, is careful to give credit, does not offend the listeners, and generally establishes her- or himself as ethical. We often refer to the credibility of a speaker; perceived ethos leads to listeners' belief that a speaker is credible. **Logos** refers to the substance of the speech or the speaker's logical appeals. A speaker who is perceived

ethos
The speaker's character as perceived by the listeners.

logos
The substance of the speech or the logical appeals the speaker makes.

MAKING CONNECTIONS FOR SUCCESS
Persuasive Speech Ideas on the Web

Have you ever thought about how famous people from the past sounded or how memorable speeches were constructed? Reading or listening to historically famous speeches or looking at lists of persuasive topics can be a motivation for your topic choices. Here are some ideas to help you find good examples as well as topics of interest.

1. Search "top 100 speeches" to access a list compiled by 137 of the leading scholars of American public address. Listen to one and try to determine why these scholars chose it as one of the most influential.

2. Search "speeches of influential women from around the world," listen to or read one of them, and evaluate the content.

3. Search "the top 10 greatest speeches of the 20th century" and listen to one to determine why it was included in such a prestigious list.

4. Are you interested in government, politics, or political debates? You can find the televised presidential debates on the web by searching "presidential debates." Choose one and see if you can determine why the ultimately successful candidate resonated with voters.

5. To get an idea about what other students have chosen for their persuasive topics, go to YouTube and search "persuasive speeches + topic (e.g., organ donation)." View two of the speeches. Do not copy these speeches but reflect on what each speaker did well and what he or she needed to improve.

6. A web search can help you find all kinds of persuasive topics. A number of communication professors include lists of possible topics (similar to Appendix 12 at the end of this chapter). Search "persuasive speech topics" and see what suggestions you find. Write them down and be prepared to share them with your instructor and classmates.

---

pathos

The speaker's evoking of appropriate emotion from the listeners.

to have logos provides sensible reasons to support his or her arguments or to support substantial points made in the speech. **Pathos** is the emotional appeal that can have a powerful effect on an audience, but it must be carefully handled. Emotional appeals can get in the way, appear too artificial, or just simply obstruct the speaker's message. Thus, a speaker must carefully evoke appropriate emotions from listeners. All three of Aristotle's modes of persuasion are helpful in establishing oneself as a carefully prepared speaker creating a well-thought-out speech.

Stephen Toulmin, a British philosopher, developed a model to help present everyday persuasive arguments.[15] Although not everyone uses Toulmin's model for understanding and presenting arguments, a brief discussion of the model may be helpful to both listeners and speakers as a means of evaluating arguments. Toulmin's approach to supporting a persuasive position or argument involves three basic parts: claim, data, and warrant. The *claim* is what the persuader wants or hopes will be believed, accepted, or done (or, in terms of what we discussed in the previous section, whether it is a fact, a value, or a policy). Claims, however, require evidence, or what Toulmin refers to as *data*. Data are the supporting materials or evidence that should influence the listener to accept the claim as stated. Unfortunately, a clear or irrefutable relationship between the claim and the data does not always exist. Thus, the persuader must explain the relationship between the claim and the data. Toulmin refers to this as the *warrant*. Here is a possible application of Toulmin's model:

CLAIM:	Despite the fact that wind energy is an achievable, totally safe, renewable form of energy and is good for the environment and the economy, the U.S. Congress seems to prefer to research and otherwise spend billions on oil rather than wind energy.
DATA:	Currently, the United States gives a production tax credit of 2.2-cents-per-kilowatt-hour benefit to encourage the use of wind-generated energy. That tax credit may soon end, and Congress is unlikely to renew it. Even though wind energy is beneficial, its use will slow down. "In the United States, the market this year is very, very busy..." Thomson Reuters quoted Vestas CEO Ditlev Engel, who spoke with a gathering of European ministers and senior officials. "But because of the potential lapse of the regulatory framework in the U.S., this market will probably go down 80 percent next year."[16]
WARRANT:	Wind is an inexpensive source of energy. Committing to a standard of 25 percent renewable electricity in the next 10 years would create much-needed new jobs, maintain current jobs, and substantially reduce our carbon footprint.

According to Toulmin's model, listeners can usually respond to the claims in three ways.

1. **They can accept the claim at face value.** This usually occurs when common knowledge holds that the claim is probably true. For example, a statement that U.S. educational programs need improvement is generally acceptable at face value.

2. **They can reject the claim outright at face value.** This usually happens when the claim is clearly false, such as the claim that U.S. lakes and streams have no pollution. It also occurs when listeners are biased against the claim or see no relationship between the claim and themselves. For example, if a claim that U.S. forests are not being depleted is made to a group trying to preserve the environment, it is unlikely they would accept this claim because of their biased views.

3. **They can accept or reject the claim according to their evaluation of data and warrant.** The person making the claim must provide evidence to support the claim or demonstrate that it is true.

Competent speakers must develop arguments strong enough to make the claim and supporting evidence stand on their own merits. They realize not everyone interprets the evidence in the same way they do, nor will everyone be convinced, even though the evidence they present may be, in their opinion, the best available. Because credibility is so important in the persuasive process, we'll discuss further how to establish it.

Establishing Credibility (Ethos)

12.7 **Explain** how Aristotle's modes of presentation—ethos, logos, and pathos—increase your credibility.

The most valuable tool you, as a persuasive speaker, can possess is credibility or believability based on the audience's evaluation of you as a person. Of course, you still need to have sound arguments and present them so that you connect with the listeners, but unless you're perceived as credible, there's a chance your logic and appeal will not help you. Credibility is granted when you establish yourself as worthy of the listeners' attention from the beginning of your speech. At various points in this text, we have referred to ethos and to the speaker's credibility. Listeners assess your competence, knowledge, and experience; your charisma and energy; as well as your character. The audience is the ultimate judge of credibility, but you can do much to influence their opinion.

Competence

An audience judges your competence by the amount of knowledge, degree of involvement, and extent of experience you display. The more expertise you show in your subject, the more likely your audience will accept what you have to say. You can establish your expertise in several ways:

1. **Demonstrate involvement.** When Michael was a 16-year-old high school student, he spent a week on a mission trip to Guatemala. While there, the volunteers built 10 homes and helped provide food, clothing, and medical supplies to the villagers. Although his visit and subsequent volunteer efforts do not, in themselves, make him an expert on volunteerism, they establish his credibility as a speaker because of his firsthand involvement.

2. **Relate experience.** One young man volunteered at the Red Cross and talked about the ever-increasing need for blood donors because of illness and world calamities. He cited specific statistics about the amount of blood and supplies sent to Haiti, California, Japan, and Indonesia after the earthquakes. His own experience in helping get supplies ready to send made his listeners accept him as a knowledgeable person.

Actor Michael J. Fox has been public with his struggles with Parkinson's disease and shared personal experiences, which make him a credible and persuasive advocate for research to find a cure.

trustworthiness

The audience's perception of a speaker's reliability and dependability.

oral footnote

Providing, within the speech, the source that particular information comes from, such as, "According to Newsweek magazine of July 27, 2018..."

3. **Cite research.** Quoting information from written sources and interviews with experts can add weight and objectivity to your arguments. Mentioning respected sources adds to your credibility and indicates you are well read. Let's say you want to persuade your listeners they can overcome communication apprehension. The following research may enhance your credibility on this topic:

> According to James McCroskey, the communication professor who created the concept of communication apprehension, thousands of people in the United States alone suffer from some degree of communication apprehension. He has published hundreds of articles on the symptoms and effects of communication apprehension. McCroskey's website identifies him as the author, coauthor, or editor of 44 books and 200 journal articles. *The Quiet Ones: Communication Apprehension and Shyness* deals with communication apprehension.[17]

Character

An audience's judgment of your character is based on their perceptions of your trustworthiness and ethics. The best way to establish your character is to be honest and fair.

Trustworthiness   A speaker's **trustworthiness** is the audience's perception of the speaker's reliability and dependability. Others attribute trustworthiness on the basis of their past experiences with us. For example, instructors may judge our reliability according to whether we come to class every time it meets. Friends may evaluate our dependability according to how well we follow through on our promises. People who have had positive experiences with us are more apt to believe we are trustworthy.

Ethics   In Chapter 1, we defined *ethics* as an individual's system of moral principles and stated that ethics plays a key role in communication. Though this is certainly true in communication in general, it is especially so in persuasion. Persuasive speakers who are known to be unethical or dishonest are less likely to achieve their persuasive purpose than are people recognized as ethical and honest. You must earn your reputation as an ethical person through your actions, like using **oral footnotes** in your speech. You can establish yourself as an ethical speaker when you:

1. **Cite sources when information is not your own and cite them accurately.** As you develop your speech, be sure you give credit to sources of information and to others' ideas. If you do not mention the sources of your information, you are guilty of plagiarism. Provide the audience with an **oral footnote**, such as "the following was taken from..." or "this quotation is from...and cited in the *New York Times*." Be specific about from whom and from where your information came.

2. **Do not falsify or distort information to make your point.** Never make up information, attribute information to a source not responsible for it, take quotations out of context, or distort information to meet your purpose.

3. **Show respect for your audience.** When audience members perceive you are respectful, even though they may not agree with your point of view, they are more likely to listen. And when they listen, you at least have a chance of persuading them. Do not trick audience members into accepting your point of view or ridicule them if they disagree with you.

Charisma

As we stated earlier, other factors influence the way the audience perceives you. Among those is **charisma**, or the appeal or attractiveness the audience perceives in the speaker, which contributes to the speaker's credibility. We often associate charisma with leaders who have special appeal for large numbers of people. Charismatic speakers seem to be sincerely interested in their listeners, speak with energy and enthusiasm, and generally seem attractive and likable. A credible speaker will take command of the speaking situation and engage the listeners so that they know the message is honest, well prepared, and relevant. Charismatic speakers are able to involve the audience in their messages.

Your listeners' evaluation of your credibility ultimately determines whether they accept or reject your persuasive goals. You should remember: Credibility is earned, it depends on others' perceptions, and it is not permanent. Credibility changes from topic to topic, from situation to situation, and from audience to audience; thus, you must establish your credibility each time you speak.

charisma
The appeal or attractiveness that the audience perceives in the speaker, contributing to the speaker's credibility.

Preparing and Developing a Persuasive Speech

 Develop your persuasive speech by carefully researching your topic; organizing the content; providing appropriate supporting materials; and making strong, logical arguments.

In a classroom situation, you typically have only one opportunity to coax your audience to accept your persuasive purpose. Therefore, it is important to set realistic persuasive goals and to give some special thought to what is covered in previous chapters about researching, organizing, and gathering support for your speech.

Researching the Topic

Research for a persuasive speech must be especially thorough. You will need to gather as much information as possible about your topic because the more you know, the better equipped you will be to support your position. When doing your research, look primarily for evidence that supports and clarifies your views. If, in the process, you discover information that contradicts your stand, make note of it and look for material you can use to refute such information. Anticipating possible objections is especially helpful when your position is controversial and when your listeners' opinions are likely to be split. If you know the arguments that could be used against you, you will be better able to support and defend your position.

Organizing the Speech

A persuasive speech requires making several special decisions that will affect its organization. Here are decisions especially related to persuasive speaking:

1. **Should you present one side or both sides of an issue?** The answer to this question depends on your audience. If your listeners basically support your position, then presenting one side may be sufficient. If their views are divided or opposed to your position, it may be more effective to present both sides. This decision also depends on your listeners' knowledge of the topic and their evaluation of your credibility. If audience members are well informed and educated, presenting both sides of an argument helps minimize the effect counterarguments can have on your audience.

2. **When should you present your strongest arguments?** Presenting your strongest arguments at either the beginning or the end of your speech is more effective than presenting them in the middle. A good strategy is to state your strongest arguments early and then repeat them toward the end. Because audience attention is most likely to wander in the middle of a speech, this is a good time to present personal examples supporting your position.

3. **What is the best way to organize your persuasive speech?** The most effective sequence of presentation depends on your topic, specific purpose, and audience. Among the patterns of organization that work well for persuasive speeches are *problem–solution, cause–effect*, and *Monroe's motivated sequence*.

problem–solution pattern

Order of presentation that first discusses a problem and then suggests solutions.

The Problem–Solution Pattern   A speech that follows the **problem–solution pattern** usually has two main points: the problem and the suggested solution. The problem is defined as a need, doubt, uncertainty, or difficulty, and the suggested solution remedies or eliminates the problem without creating other problems. A problem–solution approach could be used to address topics such as too few volunteers at the local food bank, the need for people to donate their time at a local museum, the increase in bullying, or an increase in the number of youth suicides because of bullying or cyberbullying.

The problem–solution pattern, correctly used, should do more than state a problem and a solution; it should help the audience understand both the problem and the solution and why the solution will work. For example, a speech advocating legal consequences for bullying might follow this problem–solution pattern:

PROBLEM:

   I. In recent months there has been a dramatic increase in the number of youth suicides.

SOLUTION:

   II. Everyone, especially students, must learn the consequences of bullying people because of their sexuality, their abilities, their disabilities, or the mere fact they are different may lead to suicides, and ultimately may find the bully facing legal issues.

The problem–solution pattern usually includes three to five of the following:

1. A *definition and description* of the problem, including its symptoms and size
2. A *critical analysis of the problem*, including causes, current actions, and requirements for a solution
3. *Suggestions of possible solutions*, including a description of each solution's strengths and weaknesses
4. A *recommendation of the best solution*, including a thorough justification of its superiority over other proposed solutions
5. A *discussion of the best solution put into operation*, including a description of how the plan can be implemented

cause–effect pattern

An order of presentation in which the speaker first explains the causes of an event, problem, or issue and then discusses its consequences.

The Cause–Effect Pattern   In the **cause–effect pattern**, the speaker explains the causes of an event, problem, or issue and discusses its consequences. Causes and effects may be presented in two different sequences. A speaker may both describe certain forces or factors and then show the effects that follow from them or describe conditions or events and then point out the forces or factors that caused them.

Using the cause–effect pattern, a speaker might arrange a speech on the health risks of hunger in either of the following ways:

CAUSE:

   I. Hunger is the world's number one health risk.

EFFECT:

   II. Today alone, over 15,000 men, women, and children will die of hunger.

OR

EFFECT:

I. Hunger results in more deaths than tuberculosis, malaria, and AIDS combined.

CAUSE:

II. Hunger, malnutrition, and poverty cause senseless deaths.[18]

Because the cause–effect pattern can be used in a variety of ways, it is a useful format for either informative or persuasive speeches. As long as the cause can be directly related to the effect you are trying to prove, this pattern is an excellent choice for many different topics and a beneficial means of reaching your listeners.

Consider the following example of using the cause–effect pattern to discuss the effects of senseless deaths due to eating disorders. A speaker might begin by discussing eating disorders as having the highest mortality rate of all mental illnesses. Over 8 million Americans experience eating disorders today. In fact, as many as two of every 100 students suffer from some type of eating disorder. Or the speaker might reverse the process and first point out that many insurance firms don't offer coverage for treatment for these pervasive disorders, despite the fact that millions of affected men and women in the United States require intensive treatment.[19]

Regardless of the exact sequence, a speech organized by cause and effect has two main points: a description of the factors that are the *cause* and a prediction or identification of the subsequent *effect*, or vice versa. Topics such as eating disorders in young adults, television violence, gaining the "freshman 15," and new approaches to improving memory all lend themselves to the cause–effect pattern.

Monroe's Motivated Sequence Pattern A widely used pattern of organization for the persuasive speech is **Monroe's motivated sequence**, developed by Professor Alan H. Monroe of Purdue University in the 1930s.[20] This pattern is specifically designed to help the speaker combine sound logic and practical psychology and is useful in persuasive speaking as well as in sales and marketing. The motivated sequence is particularly effective because it follows the human thinking process and motivates listeners to take action. The sequence has five steps: *attention, need, satisfaction, visualization,* and *action*.

> **Monroe's motivated sequence**
> A pattern of organization specifically developed for persuasive speaking that combines logic and practical psychology. Five steps are involved: attention, need, satisfaction, visualization, and action.

1. **Attention.** In the first step, the persuader attempts to create an interest in the topic so the audience wants to listen. This step takes place in the introduction and follows the guidelines for an effective presentation. The speaker is subtly saying, "Please pay attention. This is important to you."

2. **Need.** In the second step, the persuader focuses on the problem by analyzing the things that are wrong and relating them to the audience's interests, wants, or desires. At this point the speaker is saying, "This is wrong, and we must do something about it."

3. **Satisfaction.** In the third step, the persuader provides a solution or plan of action that will eliminate the problem and thus satisfy the audience's interests, wants, and desires. The speaker is saying, "What I have to offer is the way to solve the problem."

4. **Visualization.** In the fourth step, the persuader explains in detail how the solution will meet the audience's need. The speaker's message now becomes, "This is how my plan will work to solve the problem, and if you accept my solution, things will be much better."

5. **Action.** In the fifth and final step, the persuader asks the audience for a commitment to put the proposed solution to work. The speaker basically concludes by saying, "Take action!"

The following brief speech outline is used for the persuasive speech example later in the chapter. Michael Schwabe uses Monroe's motivated sequence to try to persuade his listeners to donate time and/or money to a specific mission.

Specific Purpose	**SPECIFIC PURPOSE:** To persuade my audience to donate time and/or money to missions in developing countries
Attention	**INTRODUCTION** Have you ever seen a disabled child abandoned by family because he or she couldn't work? I have. Have you ever seen a husband and father unable to provide for his family after losing both his arms in a work accident? I have. Have you ever heard the cries of help from a family living in a cardboard home with only three walls and half a roof? I have. Last week, you heard about how problems such as these are common among citizens of Guatemala. Last week, you heard about how a family of missionaries called Bethel Ministries is trying to help these citizens. What you *didn't* hear last week was *why this matters to you.* What you *didn't* hear was, "Why should I spend time or money to help these people?" Well, *today*, that's exactly what I'd like to tell you. I want to tell you why Bethel Ministries is worthy of your acknowledgment. To do this, I'd like to remind you of some of the problems facing Guatemalans, and explain how your time or money can directly solve many of these problems. I. My experience when on a mission trip to Guatemala

Need	**BODY**
	
	   II. Fifty-one percent of Guatemalans live below the international poverty line.
	      A. Health care is extremely limited.
	      B. There are only six hospital beds for every 10,000 citizens.
	      C. Guatemalans are categorized as being at "high" risk of catching infectious diseases.
	      D. The problems won't go away on their own.

Satisfaction	III. A small amount of money can work wonders for the citizens of Guatemala.
	      A. Donations can directly benefit the people.
	      B. Mission trips allow you to help with such things as wheelchair distribution, home construction, and medical care.

Visualization	IV. Imagine this scenario: A new house is built to protect families from the harsh weather, decreasing their exposure to the elements and illness; people are provided with medical care that allows them to work and support their families; and families can rebuild.
Action	**CONCLUSION** I encourage you, I implore you, I beg you—donate as much time or money to help missions in Guatemala as you can spare. If people like us don't or won't help, who will?[21]

M. Schwabe, "Volunteering with Bethel Missions in Guatemala." Persuasive speech given at the University of Nebraska–Lincoln. Used with permission.

The motivated sequence is most often used in persuasion. Advertisers also commonly use it because it sells ideas.

Supporting Materials

In persuasive speeches, speakers try to influence audience members through their impressive supporting materials. They choose these materials carefully to build the kind of appeal most likely to sway their listeners. On the basis of the topic and their audience analysis, persuasive speakers try to connect to their listeners' needs, to logic, or to emotions.

appeal to needs
An attempt to move people to action by calling on their physical and psychological requirements and desires.

Appeals to Needs An **appeal to needs** attempts to move people to action by calling on physical and psychological requirements and desires. Of course, different people have different needs, but most of us want to protect or enhance factors that affect our physical, safety, social, and self-esteem needs, according to psychologist Abraham Maslow. According to Maslow's hierarchy of individual needs, our lower-order needs must be satisfied before higher-order needs can be met.

Physical needs are our most basic physiological requirements, such as food, water, sleep, sex, and other physical comforts. *Safety needs* pertain to our desires for stability, order, and protection from violence; freedom from stress and disease; security; and structure. *Social needs* relate to our hopes to be loved and to belong and our needs for affection from family and friends, for membership in groups, and for the acceptance and approval of others. *Self-esteem needs* reflect our desires for recognition, respect from others, and self-respect.

Speakers can appeal to any of these needs to motivate listeners to take action. A speaker trying to sell individual retirement accounts would aim his appeal at our requirements for security and stability; a speaker who hoped to persuade us to lose weight would call on our needs for physical comfort, acceptance by others, and self-esteem. Our readiness to accept ideas or to take action depends heavily on the speaker's ability to relate a message to what we need.

Logical Appeals (Logos) Attempts to move people to action through the use of evidence and proof are called **logical appeals**. When speakers lead their listeners to think, "Yes, that's logical" or "That makes sense," they are building a case by calling on their audience's ability to reason. To accomplish this, competent persuasive speakers use evidence such as statistics, examples, testimony, and any other supporting materials that will sway their listeners.

logical appeal
An attempt to move people to action through the use of evidence and proof.

A logical appeal requires an ability to argue for your point of view. When you argue in persuasive speaking, you usually make a claim or state an argument or *proposition*, something you want your listeners to believe after you complete your speech. A claim or proposition usually assumes things can be done more than one way. For example, abortion should be illegal or it should be legal; the electoral process should or should not be changed. Speakers usually try to justify such a position with reason and evidence. The *justification*, or data, involves the use of all the supporting materials you can find to support your claim or proposition, including statistics, facts, examples, testimony, pictures, objects, and so on.

In presenting their evidence, persuasive speakers guide their listeners through a carefully planned sequence of thought that clearly leads to the desired conclusion. This train of logic may fall into one of four categories: *deductive reasoning, inductive reasoning, causal reasoning*, or *reasoning by analogy*.

Deductive reasoning is a sequence of thought that moves from general information to a specific conclusion. It presents a general premise (a generalization) and a minor premise (a specific instance) that lead to a precise deduction (a conclusion about the instance). One student set up his argument as follows:

deductive reasoning
A sequence of thought that moves from general information to a specific conclusion; it consists of a general premise, a minor premise, and a conclusion.

GENERAL PREMISE: People in developed countries consume too much sugar.
MINOR PREMISE: Sugar causes health problems.
CONCLUSION: Anyone who consumes too much sugar will have health problems.

Great care must be taken to ensure that the premises are accurate because faulty premises can lead only to a faulty conclusion. For example:

FAULTY GENERAL PREMISE: Democrats are radical in all their views.
MINOR PREMISE: Tomás is a Democrat.
FAULTY CONCLUSION: Tomás is radical in all his views.

The general premise must be both accurate and defensible before deductive reasoning can be used effectively as evidence to support a position.

Inductive reasoning is the opposite of deductive reasoning; it is a sequence of thought that moves from the specific to the general. An argument based on inductive

inductive reasoning
A sequence of thought that moves from specific facts to a general conclusion.

reasoning usually progresses from a series of related facts or situations to a general conclusion. A student discussing the need to protect oneself from identity theft might lead her listeners through the following sequence of inductive reasoning:

FACTS:
1. Identity theft is a growing problem.
2. Identity theft can produce devastating results.
3. It's a hassle to get your identity and your good credit back.
4. Identity theft claims a new victim every 4.5 seconds.
5. You can protect yourself against identity theft.

CONCLUSION: You could be the next victim of identity theft unless you take steps to protect yourself.

When your facts can be verified, when the number of facts is sufficient, and when links between the facts and the conclusion are solid, inductive reasoning can be an excellent way to persuade an audience of the validity of your argument.

Inductive reasoning can also be misused. How often have you heard general statements such as the following: All college professors are radical liberals; all car salespeople are dishonest; religiously devout people of all kinds are ethical; all accounting majors are brilliant. Each of these generalizations is based on someone's past experience. The reality, however, is that limited past experience does not support the conclusion.

To avoid problems when using inductive reasoning, make sure your facts are accurate and that they support your conclusion. Furthermore, make sure your conclusion does not extend beyond the facts you have presented. You will undermine your own case if your conclusion is so general that someone can easily point out exceptions to it.

causal reasoning
A sequence of thought that links causes with effects; it either implies or explicitly states the word *because*.

Causal reasoning is a sequence of thought that links causes with effects. Thus, it always implies or includes the word *because*: Earth's temperature is rising *because* of greenhouse gases. As in any form of reasoning, it is necessary to support the conclusion with evidence. In the example in this paragraph, the speaker would go on to cite scientific evidence linking increase in carbon dioxide production to rising temperatures. The more verifiable and valid the evidence, the more defensible is the conclusion about the cause-and-effect relationship between greenhouse gases and temperature. Even though other factors may also cause Earth's warming, the speaker's argument can be considered reasonable if it is based on scientific evidence that supports the speaker's point of view.

reasoning by analogy
A sequence of thought that compares similar things or circumstances to draw a conclusion.

Reasoning by analogy is a sequence of thought that compares similar things or circumstances to draw a conclusion. It says, in effect, what holds true in one case will also hold true in a similar one. If you were to argue that we should make every effort to use energy from renewable sources, you might use the following reasoning:

GENERAL PREMISE: The majority of energy used in the United States comes from nonrenewable sources, and our carbon footprint is harming the environment.

MINOR PREMISE: People in developing countries that use energy from mostly renewable sources do not have such a large carbon footprint.

CONCLUSION: U.S. citizens can use energy from renewable sources to reduce the carbon footprint of this nation.

Analogies are effective reasoning tools when used wisely and if there is appropriate support for the conclusion. The relationship in the analogy must be valid, and the conclusion should be based on the assumption that all other factors are equal. For instance, our example is based on the assumption that people in developing nations are careful with the use of energy—a positive action—and Americans would do well to emulate the conservation of a diminishing natural resource. If the argument implied that there were reasons for alternative energy other than that nonrenewable energy is a diminishing natural resource, the argument would fail. To avoid problems when using analogies, it is crucial to consider any dissimilarity that might refute your point.

You might wish to base your speech on a single form of reasoning, or you might prefer a combination of types of reasoning. Whatever your choice, remember: Your argument is only as good as the evidence you use to support it.

Emotional Appeals   Attempts to move people to action by playing on their feelings—for example, by making them feel guilty, unhappy, afraid, happy, proud, sympathetic, or nostalgic—are known as **emotional appeals**. Because emotions are extremely strong motivators, this form of appeal can be highly effective. Note how the following introduction to a persuasive speech appeals to the emotions:

> My grandfather is a wonderful, caring person. He was always the person who would listen to me and lend me a shoulder to cry on. He is also one of the most intelligent people I've ever known. When I was growing up, Grandpa gave me suggestions to help me solve all kinds of problems, everything from completing my homework, to discussing why my friends were not friendly, to helping me find a summer job. Today, however, my grandfather doesn't know who I am, let alone my name, and he often doesn't even realize that I'm in the room with him. You see, Grandpa suffers from Alzheimer's disease. There is no cure, and we still don't know very much about it. What we do know, however, is that it takes the real person and his mind and leaves a hollow shell.

Emotional appeals can be so powerful that they sway people to do illogical things. When a student cheats on an exam, for example, there is no logical justification, but the student may believe she is justified from an emotional viewpoint because of parental pressure to get good grades. In fact, persuasive speakers often mix both logical and emotional appeals to achieve the strongest effect. Persuasive speakers need to be aware of the issue of ethics discussed throughout this text. A speaker must present valid, reliable information in a way that will appeal to listeners but will not violate their rights or responsibilities. The speaker should be fair, accurate in voicing views, careful in presenting information, and attentive to the strategies used. An ethical speaker uses emotional appeals carefully and truthfully.

emotional appeal
An attempt to move people to action by playing on their feelings.

Fallacies in Argument Development

12.9 **Recognize** errors in your own thinking so you can correct them and present logical claims and evidence.

As both creators and consumers of persuasive messages, all of us must be able to analyze and evaluate others' as well as our own use of reasoning to support these messages. It is especially important to avoid presenting flawed arguments, thereby causing listeners to question your credibility. Arguments that are flawed because they do not follow the rules of logic—and, therefore, are not believable—are called **fallacies**. Flawed reasoning occurs all the time, and often people do not realize they used flawed arguments. As a critical thinker, however, you must understand what fallacies are, how to recognize them, and why you should not use them or let others use them in their communication.

fallacy
An argument that is flawed because it does not follow the rules of logic.

Many different types of fallacies are used in communication, but only the major errors are presented here. Let's look at basic fallacies in reasoning and evidence.

Fallacies of Reason

Questionable Cause   **Questionable cause** is a common fallacy and occurs when a speaker asserts something that does not relate to or produce the outcome claimed in the argument. It is part of our nature to want to know what caused certain events to occur. If tuition increases, people want to know why; if the national deficit increases, we want to know why; if parking space on campus or at the shopping center is eliminated, we want

questionable cause
A fallacy that occurs when a speaker alleges something that does not relate to or produce the outcome claimed in the argument.

answers! In a desire to know the cause of certain behaviors or events, we sometimes attribute what has happened to something unrelated to the situation. For example, if you claim attendance at home athletic events has increased because there's nothing else to do on campus, you've used a questionable cause, especially if the number of activities on campus and in the community is the same as in previous years.

Ad Hominem   When someone attacks a person rather than the person's argument, he or she resorts to an **ad hominem** fallacy. This is also referred to as *name-calling*. If you call someone a jerk in response to an argument to diminish the relevance or significance of the argument, you are using name-calling as a refutation of the argument. This is merely a smoke screen; it shows an inability to provide good counterarguments or evidence to challenge what the other person claims. Name-calling, ridiculing, or personal attacks on another person can diffuse an argument, but it usually results in a bad argument and sidesteps the issue.

Fallacies of Evidence

Fact Versus Opinion   A major misuse of information involves the presentation of facts and opinions. Speakers who state opinions as if they are facts can mislead and may present a fallacious argument. For example, "our university's policy on drinking is too stringent" and "our university is short 250 parking spaces" are both statements of information. Which is fact, and which is opinion? The first statement is opinion, and the second is fact. How can you tell which is which? Facts can be verified; the lack of parking spaces can be verified, whereas the university's policy on drinking may or may not be stringent, which is a matter of opinion.

Giving opinions can be helpful in persuasive speeches or arguments, but to treat an opinion as though it were fact or a fact as though it were an opinion is an error in critical thinking. In either case, you will appear to claim too little or too much and raise questions about your competence and ethics.

Red Herring   Another misuse or avoidance of facts arises when one includes irrelevant information to divert attention from the real issue. This occurs when a speaker wishes to draw attention away from an issue being questioned or challenged. Have you ever questioned someone about something he or she did wrong, and the response didn't relate to the event to which you were referring? In fact, the person may change the subject or even attack your credibility to avoid a discussion of the issue. Irrelevant information used to divert attention from the real issue is referred to as a **red herring** fallacy.

Hasty Generalization   As a common critical thinking fallacy, the **hasty generalization** occurs when a speaker doesn't have sufficient data and therefore argues or reasons from a specific example. Conclusions are drawn from insufficient data or cases. It is not uncommon to find people make generalizations based on only one or a few examples. For instance, to argue that male students think date rape is not a problem on their campus, a speaker might cite the opinions of two or three close friends. The speaker then states the following conclusion: "In surveying people I know, I've found most students do not believe date rape is a problem on our campus." The argument that date rape is not a problem might sound impressive, but the survey does not represent a large or representative sample of students; therefore, the claim is unjustified. The argument can be refuted as a hasty generalization.

ad hominem
A fallacy that attacks a person rather than the argument itself. This is also referred to as *name-calling*.

red herring
A fallacy that uses irrelevant information to divert attention away from the real issue.

hasty generalization
A fallacy that occurs when a speaker does not have sufficient data and therefore argues or reasons from a specific example.

To persuade the jury, an attorney in a courtroom must use facts and evidence, not opinions, and must avoid logical fallacies.

Sirtravelalot/Shutterstock

MAKING CONNECTIONS FOR SUCCESS
Recognizing Fallacies in Persuasion

We are constantly bombarded by attempts to persuade us to do something. Telemarketers ask us to take advantage of a credit card to solve our financial problems (and likely create new ones); four or five direct-mail advertisers send offers for better cable and Internet services; another set of calls and mailings wants us to donate to a worthy cause; a speaker pleads with us to donate blood to the local chapter of the Red Cross. Advertisers often use fallacious reasoning to make their products seem better. They rely on our need to know to get us to attend to their messages. They provide only enough data to pique curiosity but then fail to give us enough information to make a judgment on the product. They give us either–or situations and predict dire consequences if we don't buy their product or service.

Keep track of persuasive attempts for a two-day period. Identify and create a list of the number of times someone tries to persuade you and then analyze the content so you can share it with your class.

1. How many different persuasive attempts were made in that two-day period?
2. What kinds of reasoning did the persuaders use?
3. What strategies appealed to you? Which ones did not?
4. If any were successful, what made the persuasion a success?
5. Were the persuaders ethical? If so, how? If not, why?

Post Hoc Fallacy   Another kind of faulty reasoning about what comes after something is the *post hoc ergo propter hoc* **fallacy**—from the Latin for "after that, therefore because of that." For example, you get an email message warning that if you delete the message and don't send it to four or nine friends you will have bad luck; then you get a flat tire on the way to work. Faulty reasoning may lead you to believe that your failure to send the message caused the bad luck.

post hoc ergo propter hoc **fallacy**
A fallacy of reasoning in which one attributes something as a cause simply because it followed (came after) another incident.

Either–Or Reasoning   The kind of faulty reasoning found when someone claims that either something is right or it's wrong—there's no in-between—is called **either–or reasoning**. Former President George W. Bush claimed "Every nation, in every region, now has a decision to make. Either you are with us, or you are with the terrorists."[22]

either–or reasoning
A fallacy of reasoning in which only two options exist: There is black or white, right or wrong, but nothing in between.

When you develop or encounter reasoning or arguments that do not fit any of the fallacies described in the text, but you doubt the argument's validity, put the argument to the following test: Can the argument be outlined? Do the data support the claim? Does a solid relationship exist between the data and the claim? It is not important to know the name of a specific type of fallacy but rather to analyze how arguments are developed and used to determine whether they are valid.

Evaluating the Persuasive Speech

12.10   **Evaluate and assess** your own persuasive speeches and those of others.

Here are some of the criteria used to evaluate the competence of speakers and the effectiveness of their persuasive speeches. Your instructor may consider these areas when assessing your speech. You should be aware of them while preparing a persuasive speech. Many of the criteria used to evaluate an informative speech also apply to the persuasive speech. The criteria below are unique to the evaluation of a persuasive speech:

- The purpose of the speech should clearly be to persuade and be stated as such.
- The speech should include a goal; that is, the audience should be asked to think something, believe something, or take action.
- Supporting materials should appeal to the audience's needs, logic, and emotions.
- Supporting materials should include a variety of factual statements, statistical data, personal experiences, analogies, contrasts, examples and illustrations, expert testimony, value appeals, and eyewitness accounts.

- The organizational pattern should be appropriate.
- The speaker should convey a persuasive attitude through focus, energy, and appropriate vocal variety.

Speakers should evaluate their own speeches and those of others. The forms in Figures 12.3 and 12.4 can help you analyze and reflect on the speeches you give and those to which you listen.

FIGURE 12.3 Speaker's Self-Reflection Evaluation Form

On completing your persuasive speech, take a few moments to reflect on what you presented. This form can help you organize your thinking about the speech. Put yourself in the place of your listeners and be specific in your comments on each aspect of the speech. Whenever there's a choice, circle the appropriate response and provide explanations. Always provide an explanation.

Name _____ Title of Speech _____

Topic   *I would stay with this topic because*

   OR, *I would change the perspective I present because* _____

_____.

Research   *How would you change the way you researched your speech?*
_____

Appropriateness   *In what ways was this speech appropriate to you, the classroom, the situation, the audience, the time limits?* _____

Organization   *My organization could be improved by* _____

_____

The introduction   *What would you change and/or retain from the introduction you used?* _____.

_____

The body of the speech needed _____ to make it complete.

The conclusion was effective/ineffective in the following ways: _____.

I would change the conclusion as follows:

Explanation and clarity of ideas was effective/ineffective because _____

_____.

The claims or arguments presented worked well/need change _____.

Analyze each of the following and provide a complete response *(at least one full sentence)*:

Support for ideas   *(valid, worthwhile, ethical, sufficient number, clear?)* _____

Use of language _____

Visual delivery   *(movement, gestures, eye contact, posture)* _____

Vocal delivery   *(conversationality, sincerity, variety, ease of listening)*_____

The ways I adapted this speech to this audience:_____
_____

If I were to give this speech again, I would change the following:

_____,

because_____.

What would you retain? Why?_____
_____

What have you learned from this presentation?_____

FIGURE 12.4 Sample Listener Evaluation Form for Persuasive Speeches

Listeners are often called on to evaluate speakers. Some instructors have listeners complete an evaluation similar to this one. It provides the speaker with invaluable information. It is also a good critical thinking exercise for the listener.

Speaker _____ Topic _____ Date _____

1. How well did this speech meet the criteria for a persuasive speech?_____

2. What was the speaker's specific purpose?_____

3. What was the speaker's thesis?_____

4. Which arguments did you believe?_____

5. Which arguments did you have difficulty believing?_____

6. Were you convinced about the claim or argument the speaker presented?
   Why or why not?_____
   _____

7. What would it take to make you change your beliefs, attitudes, or behaviors
   about this topic?_____

8. How did this speaker and the stand taken in this speech influence you? _____
   _____

9. Did you hear any faulty reasoning in this speech? What kind? How could the
   reasoning be improved?_____
   _____

10. What types of evidence and support were provided for arguments, statements,
    and claims?_____
    _____

11. Was the speaker believable? Why or why not? What could the speaker do to
    be more believable?_____

12. Was the speaker ethical? Fair? Accurate?_____

13. What kinds of appeals were used?_____

14. Was the speaker easy to follow? Was the organization clear?_____
    _____

Guidelines

FOR PERSUASIVE SPEAKERS

1. **Establish yourself as an ethical communicator.** Employ good research, oral footnotes, and careful use of language and information. This will increase your credibility as a speaker.

2. **Use repetition and restatement to help your listeners remember your speech.** This will significantly add to the clarity of your presentation.

3. **Use appropriate organizational patterns.** This will make your speech easy to follow.

4. **Select appropriate supporting materials.** This will bolster the arguments that you make in your speech.

5. **Use sound reasoning.** Think about Toulmin's model and make your claim, support your claim with evidence (data), and show how the claim and data connect (warrant). This will strengthen your argument.

A SAMPLE PERSUASIVE SPEECH WITH COMMENTARY

Sarah Johansen, University of Nebraska–Lincoln. Used with permission.

SPECIFIC PURPOSE: To persuade my audience that they should donate to Helen Keller International

THESIS: Helen Keller International is a trustworthy charity that is worthy of your donations.

INTRODUCTION

According to the 2007 short film *Sight and Survival*, a child goes blind every minute, an adult every five seconds, and 6 million children under the age of five die from malnutrition every year. Horrific events affect millions of children and adults all over the world and are reasons why Helen Keller International is working diligently to help improve eyesight, nutrition, and lives of people much less fortunate than those of us here in this room. Without monetary generosity provided by individuals just like us, blindness and malnutrition will only continue to plague underprivileged countries. I have personally donated to Helen Keller International because I believe strongly in its mission.

I. Helen Keller International is Worthy of Donation

    A. ChildSight is a HKI program in the United States that "brings education into focus" by screening vision and providing eyeglasses to underprivileged children.

        1. Improved vision increases confidence and drastically improves scholastic performance.

        2. TOMS has partnered with HKI to provide prescription glasses from their eyewear line to qualified children.

    B. Another HKI program, Vitamin A Supplementation, saves vision as well as lives in other countries.

        1. This program costs only $1 for a child to receive supplements for a year.

        2. According to hki.org, "Vitamin A supplementation is considered to be the most cost effective, high-priority public health treatment in the world."

        3. Over 85 million capsules were delivered to children last year.

    C. In order to reduce malnutrition worldwide, HKI is creating programs that help to grow and sustain food production in developing countries.

Sarah's introduction captures the listeners' attention and conveys how passionately she feels about Helen Keller International. She orients the listeners to her topic, motivates them to pay attention, and establishes her own credibility because she has personally donated to this charity.

In her first main point in the body of the speech, Sarah explains how Helen Keller International is worthy of your donation. She highlights several programs Helen Keller International has developed to provide vision screening, eyeglasses, and vitamin A supplementation, and to combat malnutrition. She provides statistics and presents the findings from relevant research studies. Her information is compelling and makes the listener stop to think about the good things this charity is doing.

1. According to Emily Hillenbrad's 2010 article "Transforming Gender in Homestead Food Production," the Homestead Food Production program instated by HKI, "promotes small-scale agriculture among women, specifically to improve women's and children's nutrition outcomes."

2. Homestead Food Production program also helps to create jobs by growing gardens and crops.

D. There are so many different ways HKI helps with vision and malnutrition that it is impossible to touch upon all of them in this speech. To sum it up: "Helen Keller International gets more bang for the buck than almost any group I can think of." Nicholas D. Kristof

II. Helen Keller International Is a Trustworthy Organization

A. How donor funds are used are clearly explained on hki.org. Eighty-five percent of profit goes directly to programs, 2% goes to fundraising, and 13% goes to administrative expenses.

B. HKI's current audited financial statements are available to the public on its website.

C. According to the 2009 Better Business Bureau records, HKI meets all 20 Standards for Charity Accountability.

D. It has received a four-star rating from Charity Navigator, the highest rating an organization can receive.

III. What You Can Do to Help

A. Twenty-five dollars supplies a student in the United States with a pair of glasses, $50 plants a Homestead garden for about 40 people, $100 provides 100 children with vitamin A supplementation for a year, and $250 pays for five individuals to have cataract surgery.

B. Donations online are the easiest way to contribute to the organization.

C. There are other ways to help HKI as well through other businesses.

1. Aframes eyewear donates 5% of its profits to HKI's Vitamin A Supplementation program.

2. Baking for Good is on online bake sale that provides 15% of each purchase to a charity of the consumer's choice.

3. There is also a list of other small businesses that help HKI and can be found at hki.org

In her second main point, Sarah shows us how Helen Keller International manages the money we donate. She provides specific information and explains how donations are divided and funneled to certain areas of the organization. She makes the point that the organization regularly undergoes financial audits, which are publicly available on the charity's website.

Sarah does a good job of explaining what we could do to help. She shares how donations of various sizes benefit people who need it most. Sarah explains how we can make a donation and how other organizations contribute to Helen Keller International.

In her conclusion, Sarah asks us to put ourselves in someone else's shoes and take action—donate money so that Helen Keller International can help others. She makes us believe that our contributions are important and that Helen Keller International is worthy of our support.

CONCLUSION

- You cannot deny that it is hard for us to imagine a life where losing sight is a major concern, but we must try to put ourselves in someone else's shoes. A mother not being able to see her newborn baby due to a cataract, a child who is both blind and dying from a *preventable* vitamin A deficiency, a man who farms rice for a living crippled from malnutrition and can no longer stand on his own.

- Helen Keller International is working to bring light where there is darkness, bring food where there is famine, and bring the vision of a better world to all of humanity.

- A quote by Helen Keller accurately describes the miracles HKI performs: "Alone we can do so little, together we can do so much."

REFERENCES

"Charity Review of Helen Keller International." *Better Business Bureau*. N.p., 2012. Web. 23 May 2012. http://www.bbb.org/charity-reviews/national/blind-and-visually-impaired/helen-keller-international-in-new-york-ny-2499.

Helen Keller International. Helen Keller International, 2012. Web. 19 May 2012. www.hki.org.

Hillenbrand, Emily. "Transforming gender in homestead food production." *Gender & Development* 18.3 Nov. (2010).

Sight and Survival. Helen Keller International, 2007. Web. 23 May 2012. http://www.youtube.com/user/HKI1915?feature=watch.

⟩ SUMMARY

Distinctions between Informative and Persuasive Speaking

12.1 **Explain** the distinctions between informative and persuasive speeches.

- We live in an information-oriented society in which the ability to present and receive *information* is vital. Now, as in the past, people who possess information and communicate it effectively are the ones who possess power and command respect.

- Informative speeches are one of the most common we're asked or required to present. The goal of an informative speech is to increase understanding, while the goal of persuasive speaking is to change (alter) attitudes and/or behaviors. Information can be presented without attempting to persuade, but *persuasion* cannot be attempted without information.

- You must gain listeners' attention, motivate them to listen, and increase their understanding of the topic.

The Goals of Persuasive Speaking

12.2 **Identify** the goals of persuasion.

- Persuasion is always about change—either in attitude or behaviors.

- The subgoals of persuasion (*adoption, discontinuance, deterrence,* or *continuance*) allow you to choose how you want the listeners to change.

- Be realistic in setting your persuasive goal and determining what you expect to achieve.

Topics for Informative and Persuasive Speeches

12.3 **Choose** appropriate topics for your informative and persuasive speeches.

- Topics for informative and persuasive speeches are almost limitless. Choose something interesting, about which you already have some knowledge, and that you can find additional information on through your research.

- Your informative speech topic should also be of interest and potentially useful for your listeners. Your specific purpose and the type of topic you choose will determine how you present the speech.

- Persuasive speech topics may begin with *questions of fact, value,* or *policy.*

- Your choice of one of these questions helps you determine what to include in the persuasive speech.

- While you start with yourself, you need to keep your listeners and their knowledge and interests in mind as you choose a topic.

Preparing and Developing an Informative Speech

12.4 **Prepare and develop** an informative speech to meet your professor's specific criteria.

- Each instructor has specific criteria she or he wants you to follow. Check your syllabus or check with the instructor, if necessary, to determine all requirements, for both content and delivery.

- Your speech needs to gain and maintain attention.

- The more meaningful the topic and perspective, the more listeners pay attention to the speaker's message.

- Listeners want novel ideas and want to know "What's in it for me?"

- The audience will listen if you give them reasons to listen.

- The speech should be well organized so the listeners know where you're going and why.

- Your language should be clear, direct, and understandable. It should give the listener a view of the topic at hand.

- Personalize the information to make it relevant, both for you and for your listeners.

Evaluating the Informative Speech

12.5 **Evaluate and assess** your own speeches prior to classroom presentation and **apply** evaluation criteria to the speeches of others.

- The sample evaluation criteria should make you aware of the characteristics of an effective informative speech and speaker.

- Competent communicators analyze their listeners so they know their choices will work. They find ample sources from a variety of references, and they work to show their listeners the importance of the topic.

Persuasive Claims

12.6 **Construct and support** a persuasive claim.

- Credibility is something the listeners attribute to you when you are seen as competent, with good character and a degree of *charisma.*

- Your speech should identify the sources of your information in *oral footnotes* and in the notes or bibliography section.

Establishing Credibility (Ethos)

12.7 **Explain** how Aristotle's modes of presentation— *ethos, logos,* and *pathos*—increase your credibility.

- The speaker's actions and demeanor create each of these appeals during the speech.
- *Ethos* refers to the speaker's ethical character.
- *Logos* refers to the substance of the speech or the speaker's logical appeals.
- *Pathos* is the emotional appeal that can move an audience.

Preparing and Developing a Persuasive Speech

12.8 **Develop** your persuasive speech by carefully researching your topic; organizing the content; providing appropriate supporting materials; and making strong, logical arguments.

- Present a persuasive speech that demonstrates your ability to construct and support your persuasive goals.
- Careful research and organization will help you reach your listeners and help you meet the criteria for the assignment.
- Be sure to include enough supporting materials to provide sufficient evidence for the topic.

- Check your analysis to make sure that you make strong, logical arguments.

Fallacies in Argument Development

12.9 **Recognize** errors in your own thinking so you can correct them and present logical claims and evidence.

- *Fallacies* in argument development should be avoided.
- Carefully analyze your arguments to make sure they are logical and free of wrongful attribution and *hasty generalizations.*
- Criticize ideas, not the people who hold them.
- Don't mislead yourself or your listeners by reaching the wrong conclusion about your arguments.

Evaluating the Persuasive Speech

12.10 **Evaluate and assess** your own persuasive speeches and those of others.

- Look at the evaluation criteria provided by your instructor to make sure you have addressed and fulfilled those requirements.
- Apply evaluation criteria to your speech well before your class presentation so you can use those criteria to improve your speech.

⟩ DISCUSSION STARTERS ——————————

1. What factors influence your view of an effective informative message? An effective persuasive message?

2. What advice would you give someone about selecting a topic for an informative speech? A persuasive speech?

3. Identify three topics that will work for an informative speech and explain how you can make them interesting and relevant for your audience. Do the same for a persuasive speech.

4. What characteristics enhance your own evaluation of a speaker?

5. Are supporting materials used differently in a persuasive speech than in an informative speech? Explain your views.

Appendix 12

Possible Speech Topics

Here are some possible topics for informative speeches. The items listed are not titles of specific speeches and need to be narrowed to fit specific purposes, time limits, or other requirements set by your instructor. Almost any topic can be used to create informative or persuasive speeches. The key is in how you develop the ideas. If you're presenting information as information *only*, it becomes an informative speech. If you present an argument and evidence as supporting material, and you want your listeners to change something in some way, you're giving a persuasive speech.

Informative Speech Topics

The European experiment and its effect on the world's economy

The "sanitizing" of news

How Puerto Rico has dealt with the aftermath of Hurricane Maria

What does it mean when foods are labeled "organic"?

What it means to be a vegan

The high blood sugar epidemic

Eating disorders

Caffeine can harm your health

Caffeine can benefit you

The effects of energy drinks

World hunger

How "grandma's kitchen cures" can really help you

Learning financial literacy

Going green

Latest social media trends

The Green Movement

Mental health issues

Virtual schools

Social media have changed etiquette

Why are people divided by politics and religion?

Islamic State of Iraq and Syria (ISIS) and terrorist activities

Title IX and Sports

The Violence against Women Act

The watchdogs of student loans

Xenophobia and intercultural competence

Listening is linked to thinking

What are the areas of the brain?

Are the world's religions all that different?

Space exploration and private enterprise

How to safeguard yourself from identity theft

The appropriate way to use Skype in interview situations

Leadership skills and you

Have libraries become a thing of the past?

Is ethical conduct an outdated practice?

Why do so many news anchors alter reality in their reporting?

Eating disorders are pervasive in our society

How to sponsor a child from developing countries

Why are pharmaceuticals so expensive?

What is autism?

How we can make the world a happier place for our animal friends?

Persuasive Speech Topics

News in the United States is sanitized—how do we learn the truth?

Cyberbullying must be stopped

Facebook is a tool to eradicate social injustices

Twitter is more than just a way to link with others

The monitoring of Facebook helps control the masses

Sexting: crime or indiscretion?

The failure of the European experiment—or has it failed?

Reality shows are popular because…

Citizens are required to be socially responsible

How volunteerism can change both society and you

Society's views on marriage for same-sex couples

The overmedication of people in developed countries

Children must be taught about money

There should be a tax on high-sugar drinks

Is marital infidelity a matter for the courts?

How we can reduce our blood sugar levels to achieve better health?

Nearly 8 million children around the world are without life's necessities

Eating disorders are pervasive in our society

Why podcasts are better than broadcasts

The false-positive tests: screening for terrorists

Homeland security takes our freedoms away

The controversy surrounding women's health

Why the Violence Against Women Act can help all of us

Student loans—the next financial debacle

Neighborhood watch—vigilantes in action?

Why arguments of politics and religion are best left inside the home

Ways we can personally help improve the economy

International adoptions should be promoted

How we can stop bullying?

Take the first step in going green

How do we solve the lingering problem with multitasking and air traffic control?

Are the airways really safer than highway traffic?

What should be done to improve public education?

How can we improve the barter system to take power away from Wall Street?

Chinese medicine and acupuncture cure many diseases

How leadership skills can help groups communicate

Why you should not rely on energy drinks for the long term

Wind energy, bane or benefit?

Combating hunger, the world's number one health risk

World hunger and your contribution to solving the problem

E-books and learning: Are the two mutually exclusive?

CONNECTING THROUGH INTERPERSONAL COMMUNICATION: DEVELOPING, MAINTAINING, AND DISSOLVING RELATIONSHIPS

Maridav/Shutterstock

Interpersonal communication occurs between two or more people; it can be casual or formal, public or private; and some personal information is shared.

→ CHAPTER OUTLINE AND LEARNING OBJECTIVES

Connecting with Others via Interpersonal Communication

13.1 Explain what it means to connect with others through interpersonal communication.

Interpersonal Communication Competence

13.2 Characterize the importance of interpersonal communication competence.

Theories of Interpersonal Communication

13.3 Compare and contrast six theories related to relationships and interpersonal communication.

Self-Disclosure in Relationships

13.4 Outline the roles of self-disclosure, privacy, gender, culture, and rhetorical sensitivity in interpersonal relationships.

Relationship Formation

13.5 **Identify** the stages of relationship development and growth.

Relationship Dissolution

13.6 **Identify** the stages of relationship deterioration and dissolution.

Interpersonal Conflict

13.7 **Explain** what interpersonal conflict is, what causes it, why it can be beneficial, and strategies to manage and resolve it.

Improving Communication Competence in Relationships

13.8 **Apply** effective interpersonal communication skills and competencies in personal and professional relationships.

MAKING EVERYDAY CONNECTIONS

"Unplugged for 40 Days" is the headline of a newspaper article that speaks to how reliant on and, in some cases, addicted to social media we have become.[1] The article discusses Hillary Umland, a 31-year-old Catholic who decided to give up her 2- to 3-hour daily routine with Facebook, Twitter, and texting for Lent (a Christian period of 40 days of prayer, penance, fasting, and denial). According to the reporter, she had all of the withdrawal symptoms of any addiction, including a restless feeling and an extremely strong desire to use social media. Umland says that days of staring aimlessly at her computer are over for at least a few more weeks. She admits that it's almost been a month now that she hasn't checked Facebook or Twitter and according to her "it really sucks." Research indicates that Facebook has, on average, nearly 2 billion monthly active users worldwide, with over 1 billion people using Facebook on their mobile device each day.[2] It is interesting that this is not the first time Umland has tried to give up social media—last year she says she lasted about two weeks but claims this time she has more resolve.

When asked what she is doing since she is not glued to her computer and cell phone, she said she was reading the same book on a consistent basis, something she had not done in a long time.[3] Jim Jansen, a team leader and associate campus religious worker with the Office of Student Affairs at the University of Nebraska–Lincoln, says:

> There's nothing wrong with Facebook, but if you talk to them [students], I think many of them will say it's kind of like a quick sugar high for relationships. Somewhere on that intuitive level, we can just feel the difference between the electronic connection and the real personal connection.[4]

Umland found herself agreeing with the above statement, and hoped that the time away from Facebook and the like allowed her to reconnect in person with others in her life.But that it's hard to do so when everyone else hasn't pulled the plug on their social media as well.

QUESTIONS TO THINK ABOUT

1. How can technology help or hurt personal relationships?

2. If all social media were turned off for a week, how would you react?

3. Which do you find more satisfying: communication via social media, including online and texting, or face-to-face communication? Why?

4. What are some of your most embarrassing social media gaffes and what did you do to explain them?

It is evident that more and more of our time is spent communicating with others using one form or another of social media, such as Facebook, Twitter, Pinterest, Instagram, YouTube, Snapchat, and LinkedIn. Snapchat recently hit 10 billion daily video views while raking in nearly $1 billion in revenue. Twitter surpassed 310 million users, while Instagram added 100 million users in six months.[5] The Pew Research Center found that 18- to 24-year-olds send and receive, on average, approximately 4,000 text messages per month—or about 130 per day.[6] The Pew Research Center's Internet & American Life Project survey of people 18 and older who use social networking sites (SNS) found that respondents tend to rate SNS as "very positive" in terms of personal rewards and overall satisfaction. Further, they found 61 percent of their sample of SNS users experienced feeling closer to another person, while 68 percent said they experienced feeling good about themselves.[7] There is no question that social media is changing how we meet, interact, and form relationships with others.

Whether in a coffee shop, workplace, library, student union, dorm, athletic event, or meeting; on an airplane, train, website; or in any online or face-to-face setting where we interact verbally and nonverbally, the success or effectiveness of our interactions depends on our interpersonal communication skills. What does it mean to be a competent communicator in interpersonal situations? This chapter provides answers to this question.

Connecting with Others via Interpersonal Communication

13.1 **Explain** what it means to connect with others through interpersonal communication.

Connecting with others and forming relationships are what interpersonal communication is all about. We often think of it as interaction that occurs only among those with whom we have close relationships. While it is true interpersonal communication is used in our close relationships, it also occurs in a variety of contexts and situations and can be impersonal and superficial or personal and intimate, private or public, and unstructured or highly structured. Our interpersonal competencies likely differ not only from each other but also from situation to situation and from one person to another. Competent interpersonal communicators know how to adjust and communicate effectively with a variety of people from diverse backgrounds to establish short- or long-term relationships, whether in person or via social media.

Relationships

A **relationship** is an association between at least two people. It can be new or old, momentary or long-lasting, superficial or involved, casual or intimate, friendly or unfriendly, relaxed or tense, hateful or loving, important or unimportant, good or bad, happy or unhappy, and so on. Relationships can also be described in terms of the level of intimacy or kinship—girlfriend, boyfriend, lover, partner, wife, husband, mother, father, child, uncle, cousin, stepparent, or stepchild. Sometimes relationships

relationship
An association between at least two people, which may be described in terms of intimacy or kinship.

MAKING CONNECTIONS FOR SUCCESS

Proper Email and Email Etiquette

To: professorsmith@unl.edu
From: grantpartyallnight@gmail.com
Re: i have some questions about class

Hey, I am in your 2:30 class and I don't know what is expected of me on your next assignment—is it do on Tuesday or Thursday; your directions wasn't clear. I THINK THIS CLASS REQUIRES TOO MUCH WORK AND I DON'T HAVE THE TIME THIS WEEK TO GET IT DONE. I also need to be out of town next week so I am going to have to miss class. Will I miss anything when I am gone? I really enjoy having u as a techer.

With the above in mind, answer the following questions:

1. How would you react if you were the professor receiving the email?

2. What email etiquette rules did Grant violate, if any? Explain.

3. Rewrite the email as you think it should be written.

4. Develop a set of etiquette guidelines you believe should be followed when sending email or text messages. Would your rules be the same for every audience? Explain.

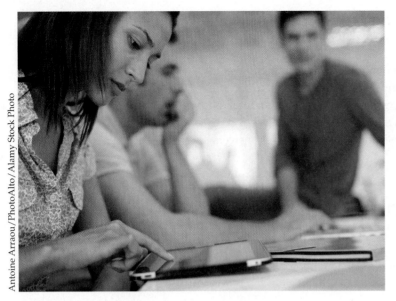

More and more time is spent on social media rather than in face-to-face interactions. Which do you find more satisfying: social media and texting or face-to-face communication?

can be described on the basis of the roles people have in the relationship—roommates, Facebook friends, neighbors, boss and employee, coworkers, classmates, doctor and patient, ex-spouses, and so on.

Relationships can be described in terms of time spent together, such as, "I knew her in high school" or "They just met him the other day." Relationships may be based on shared activities or participation in events—"We play volleyball together," "We go to the same yoga classes," "He's in my class," "She works with me," or "We are from the same hometown."[8] Relationships are sometimes described in terms of situation or happenstance—"We met online," "We met on the plane," or "I sit behind you in our communication class." However we describe them, we all have relationships with others.

Interpersonal Communication

In Chapter 1, we defined interpersonal communication as creating and sharing meaning between persons who are in a relationship. This definition implies that interpersonal communication occurs between two or more people; it can be casual or formal, public or private; and some personal information is shared.

As noted above, interpersonal communication is often thought of as interaction only among those having close relationships. This, of course, is not always true; some individuals disclose the most personal information about themselves or others to complete strangers via social media or to someone they are sitting next to on an airplane, but they may not communicate the same information to a loved one they see every day. Thus, interpersonal communication occurs in a variety of contexts and situations. It is also characterized in different ways. Our interpersonal competencies also differ from person to person, as well as from situation to situation. Those who are competent know how to tailor their interpersonal communication to suit people from diverse backgrounds and establish short- or long-term relationships.

Interpersonal Communication Competence

13.2 **Characterize** the importance of interpersonal communication competence.

Whether we get to know others might have little or nothing to do with their specific characteristics or ours. Usually, the likelihood that two people will become acquainted has to do with contact through physical proximity and a positive rather than a negative experience at the time of the face-to-face or social media contact. After you encounter a person several times and easily recognize him or her, you will likely become comfortable interacting with the person or at least making casual conversation. The relationship development and your reception often depend on how well you and the other person interact. Of course, we know that sometimes we interact better than at other times.

Competent communicators recognize it is unlikely they will always communicate perfectly, but they usually continue to try to do so. Competence implies appropriateness. What this means is that competent communicators can adapt to particular situations and individuals. They know how to use language appropriately no matter the situation, whether a friend's wedding, an intimate moment, or a job interview.

What are the skills associated with competence in interpersonal communication situations? According to communication scholars, the following five skills lead to competence in interpersonal communication:[9]

1. The ability to adapt and know how to communicate in specific situations, for example, when to be empathic and comforting or when to talk and when to listen.

2. The ability to adapt and appropriately communicate in specific interactions, for example, know when to speak out aggressively and when to be reserved and more deferential.

3. The ability to understand your own and the other person's values, beliefs, attitudes, or feelings. In other words, how does the other person view him- or herself or what does he or she think about various people, issues, or events?

4. The ability to self-monitor. Self-monitoring is the ability to regulate your communication both before and during an interaction. It is a form of rhetorical sensitivity (see discussion later in this chapter on rhetorical sensitivity). In other words, a person who self-monitors can attend to the feedback of others and recognize the impact of what they say.

5. The ability to be fair and ethical. This means treating people as unique human beings. It is a commitment to self-respect and respect for others as well. Interpersonally competent communicators are sensitive to all ideas and perspectives discussed. They know everyone sees the world differently; thus they are considerate of those who disagree with them.

The "Guidelines: Suggestions for Effective Interpersonal Interactions" box offers concrete ways these competencies can result in more satisfying interpersonal relationships.

We are influenced by first impressions on a daily basis, whether observing people in a store or coffee shop, or meeting people for the first time, such as new roommates, study partners, classmates, or friends of someone you know.

Guidelines

SUGGESTIONS FOR EFFECTIVE INTERPERSONAL INTERACTIONS

Conversation with others is a two-way responsibility; you can't rely on the other person to carry the conversation for you—a monologue is not a conversation. To become effective at interacting, you must be fully connected and work to ensure that the other person feels connected and comfortable. Here are some suggestions:

1. **Use the other person's name as much as possible as you talk with him or her.** Some ways you can remember are: Say the name at least three times when first interacting with someone you just met. Have the person restate it or spell it for you if necessary. Knowing and recalling a person's name creates the impression that the person matters to you and helps make small talk a bit more comfortable.

2. **Look at the other person, but strive for balance and comfort in eye contact.** When you look at the other person, you indicate you are paying attention and are interested in him or her. It also shows you are confident in yourself.

3. **Be careful in your use of eye contact with people from cultural or ethnic backgrounds different than**

your own. For example, some cultures believe staring at someone or looking into someone's eyes is disrespectful. When communicating with people from these cultures, you might focus on the face in general, but not directly on a person's eyes.

4. **Encourage the other person to talk about him- or herself.** People generally like to talk about themselves. It can be a strong motivator for continuing the conversation. Listen carefully and ask questions such as, "What are you planning to do after graduation?" "What did you like most about _____ (the play, the movie, the book, the game, and so on)?" "What does your work involve?" "What do you like to do in your spare time?" "What do you enjoy most about your work?" and "Tell me about yourself." Use follow-up questions to keep the person talking, if necessary.

5. **Keep the conversation casual, light, and positive.** Moving too quickly to disclose personal information can be threatening and a real conversation stopper. In addition, no one likes negative people or whiners. If you come across

as one, your likelihood of future interaction is dramatically reduced.

6. **Be confident and listen carefully to what is being said.** It is critical to have confidence to make small talk. Confidence doesn't mean arrogance; it does mean you are not afraid to enter into conversation with others. It is likely the other person may have similar reservations about chatting with you as you might have about them. Your interest will also motivate the others to continue the conversation rather than end it abruptly.

7. **Keep abreast of current events.** Know what is going on around you: Watch the news; use the Internet; read current magazines and newspapers on a regular basis. This knowledge can help because current events are often the topics of small talk. Your awareness of current events makes small talk easier; plus, it shows others you are concerned about what is going on around you.

8. **Use casual talk to help reduce the uncertainty between you and others.** This will increase your chances of initiating and developing a more lasting relationship.

9. **Know when and how to end the conversation.** It is important to know when the conversation should end. Initial conversations are not usually intended to last very long. If they run too long you run the risk of boredom and discomfort. Even if the conversation is going well and you both are enjoying yourselves, you might end it before it becomes uncomfortable. Ending a conversation can be awkward or difficult, but your best strategy is to have a few well-rehearsed exit lines. Make sure you use the person's name when exiting—for example, "Debra, I'd better move on to other guests. I enjoyed visiting with you" or "Jim, I would like to get some food before it's gone."

Theories of Interpersonal Communication

13.3 **Compare and contrast** six theories related to relationships and interpersonal communication.

Most of us want relationships to give our lives meaning and to fulfill a variety of social and psychological needs. Our motivations for staying in relationships are certainly varied and not always completely understood, as when people who have choices remain in abusive, codependent, or obsessive relationships. In this section, we discuss six theories that help explain why we have such a strong desire to interact with and form and keep relationships with others: *uncertainty reduction theory, uncertainty management theory, social penetration theory, social exchange theory, interpersonal needs theory,* and *dialectical theory.*

Uncertainty Reduction Theory

Our desire to know about others and to understand how and why they behave as they do can be partially explained by uncertainty reduction theory.[10] The core assumption of **uncertainty reduction theory**, developed by communication scholars Charles Berger and Richard Calabrese, is that, when people meet, they seek to reduce the unknowns about each other. The more attracted they are to others, the stronger the desire to know more about them. A desire to reduce uncertainty about those individuals motivates people to have further communication with them.

The theory, according to Berger, suggests the drive to reduce uncertainty regarding those we meet is motivated by three prior conditions:

1. **Anticipation of future contact:** We will likely see them again.

2. **Incentive value or reward:** They can give us something we need.

3. **Deviance:** They act in a strange or unusual way.[11]

Berger believes these three factors are part of our natural curiosity because we really want to know more about the person. No matter how close we become to another, we always begin a relationship as strangers.

According to the theory, reducing uncertainty is necessary for a relationship to develop; as we increase our desire to enter a relationship with someone, we use more uncertainty reduction behavior. Berger describes three strategies used to learn about others. The first is referred to as "passive," when we unobtrusively observe others

uncertainty reduction theory
A theory suggesting that when we meet others, our need to know about them tends to make us draw inferences from observable physical data.

from a distance, or what some might refer to as "scoping out"; the second is referred to as "active," in which we ask a third party for information; and the third is referred to as "interactive," when we talk directly with the other person and request specific information by asking questions.[12]

To illustrate the three strategies, consider the following example: Olivia sees Sam across a crowded room at a party and is interested in meeting him. She observes that he is standing by himself and thus assumes he came to the party by himself, but she isn't sure (passive strategy). She knows nothing about Sam and doesn't know if he is dating anyone or if he is serious about someone, for that matter. Olivia's uncertainty is high, but so is her desire to find out more about him. She texts a friend who knows Sam and learns he is not dating anyone, but the friend doesn't know whether he came with anyone to the party (active strategy). Olivia's uncertainty has been somewhat reduced but certainly not eliminated. She decides that the only way to learn more about Sam is to be direct and talk with him (interactive strategy). She asks him if he is with anyone and finds out that he came by himself and that he is not dating anyone at the present time. The party ends; Olivia and Sam are still talking with each other and have enjoyed their time visiting, but now they must decide what will happen next with their relationship. After almost an hour of conversation, they decide to share cell numbers and email addresses with the idea they might continue the relationship. Sam texts Olivia about 10 minutes after they depart: "had a good time 2nite, c u soon."

Of course at times our need to know about someone isn't a consideration or possible to pursue because we have no interest in the person or he or she is not available to us.

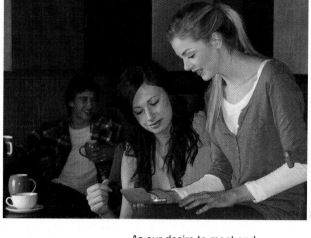

As our desire to meet and learn about others increases, so does our desire to reduce our uncertainty about them. This motivates us to communicate with them.

Uncertainty Management Theory

Dale Brashers, a communication scholar who is interested in health communication, especially as it relates to those living with HIV or AIDS, developed uncertainty management theory to further refine uncertainty reduction theory. Brashers believes uncertainty is more complex than previously thought. His research found that patients with HIV sometimes preferred uncertainty to certainty.[13]

Uncertainty management theory takes into account the different ways people respond both psychologically and communicatively to uncertainty, especially in health decisions. The theory has three main features: (1) the interpretation and experience of uncertainty, (2) the effect of emotion related to uncertainty, and (3) the ways communication and emotion are managed when uncertainty exists.[14] While Brashers was specifically interested in health, this theory can be applied to many other situations. For example, a person going through a breakup after a long-term relationship suspects his or her spouse cheated but stops short of confirming it because confirmation might be too painful. Uncertainty reduction theory suggests that seeking and gaining information is the best way to reduce uncertainty, but sometimes reduction is not the goal. Uncertainty management theory makes us aware that we can communicate in different ways, depending on whether our goal is to increase, decrease, or maintain uncertainty. In serious illness situations, for example, we will often seek out a second opinion that may offer a less certain outcome because we hope the illness may not be as bad as first diagnosed.[15]

In addition to seeking or avoiding information, people use four other ways to manage their uncertainty, according to Brashers. First, those who live with lots of uncertainty learn to adapt to it. For example, Brashers and his colleagues found those

uncertainty management theory
A theory that takes into account different ways people react psychologically and communicatively to uncertainty.

with serious illness might focus on short-term diagnoses, which provide more certainty, rather than on the long-range outlook, which may be significantly more uncertain. The second way to manage uncertainty is to rely on the social support of others in order to cope. The positive or reassuring outlook of others can lead to feelings of hope or some relief from the uncertainty. The third way is to balance the need to know with the desire *not* to know. Finally, the fourth is learning to know which information to trust and which information to ignore.[16]

Social Penetration Theory

social penetration theory
A theory suggesting that disclosures in a relationship become increasingly intimate as the relationship develops.

Going beyond information gathering, **social penetration theory**, developed by social psychologists Irwin Altman and Dalmas Taylor, provides a view of how people connect with each other and how their communication moves from small talk to more intimate and self-revealing talk. Social penetration is the process of increasing disclosure and intimacy in a relationship.[17] Figure 13.1 illustrates the progression of our interactions as a relationship becomes more friendly or intimate.

According to the theory, as the relationship evolves, the interaction becomes more personal and intimate. The model resembles an onion or dartboard and looks at both the depth and the breadth of penetration. The **depth of penetration** is represented as penetration from external factual information (the outer ring) to inner feelings (the center of the circle or bull's-eye) revealing more private information about the self. The outer ring represents superficial communication, such as small talk, "Hi, I'm Joe from Clemson, South Carolina." The innermost circle, or bull's-eye, represents intimacy and close personal disclosures, such as "I love you with all my heart and soul." As the relationship becomes more intimate, it will involve more personal information and intimacy about one's self. **Breadth of penetration** is the range or spread of what an individual discloses to another about him- or herself. Thus, to have lasting relationships, what is disclosed must have both depth and breadth.

depth of penetration
The deepness or intimacy of the disclosure to others.

breadth of penetration
The range or spread of areas that are disclosed to others.

Social Exchange Theory

Social exchange theory is an interpersonal communication theory that explains why we form relationships. Have you ever entered a relationship and thought about the benefits that might be gained from it? Of course you have. For example, right after meeting someone, we are likely to sort out the pluses and minuses of forming a friendship. In other words, we try to determine whether the benefits of the relationship will

FIGURE 13.1 Social Penetration Model

Social penetration theory portrays relationship development as starting with factual information and small talk. As the relationship develops, conversations become more personal, including feelings about self and values. (From *Social Penetration: The Development of Interpersonal Relationships.* Copyright © 1973 by Irwin Altman and Dalmas Taylor.)

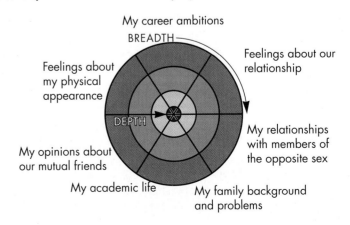

outweigh the cost. Whether we do this subconsciously or consciously, we do it. Social psychologists John Thibaut and Harold Kelley originated **social exchange theory**, which is based on the assumption that people weigh the costs and benefits associated with entering a relationship and seek out relationships that benefit them while avoiding those that don't.[18]

Thibaut and Kelley believe that most of us are motivated to enter and maintain relationships in terms of the exchange of benefits and costs. A **benefit** is anything we perceive to improve our self-interest. It refers to things or relationships that bring us pleasure, satisfaction, or gratification. For example, outcomes such as good feelings, status, prestige, economic gain, or fulfillment of emotional needs are considered benefits of a relationship. **Costs** are negative things or behaviors we perceive to be not beneficial to our self-interest. For example, to enter or maintain a relationship takes time and physical and emotional energy, which are considered costs of the relationship.

The theory suggests that when we first meet someone, we mentally weigh the potential rewards and costs of creating a relationship with that person. For example, you are not very good at math but you are required to take calculus. You go to class and sit next to Jim. You briefly discuss the class and a little about the professor. You learn Jim has taken at least one other course from the professor and did exceptionally well. Because of this brief interaction, you perceive a number of potential benefits of becoming friends with Jim. You know he can help you with calculus, he is easy to talk with, and he appears to know his way around campus. Jim also weighs the benefits and costs of beginning a relationship with you. He thinks you are easy to talk with and likes your openness about seeking help from him.

Jim also knows there may be a potential downside to getting to know you better and creating a relationship. This is especially true if all you want from him is his time and help to learn calculus. Jim is a very active student and also holds a part-time job, so his free time is extremely valuable. He also knows you are an easy person to talk with and that by helping you he will learn more and be better prepared for the exams. In addition, he likes helping others. After factoring in all the pluses and minuses, Jim suggests that you get together to study for the first exam.

Social exchange theory implies that if the benefits gained in a relationship are greater than any potential costs, then we likely would regard the relationship positively. But if the benefit gain (benefits minus costs) falls below a certain level, we

social exchange theory
A theory based on the assumption that people consciously and deliberately weigh the costs and rewards associated with a relationship or interaction.

benefit
Anything that is perceived to improve our self-interest.

costs
Negative things or behaviors that we perceive to be not beneficial to our self-interest.

MAKING CONNECTIONS FOR SUCCESS

Online Relationships

Social media has indeed changed our ways of interacting and connecting with others. Lori and Jerome met for the first time through an online dating website. They viewed each other's posted pictures and information. They exchanged emails for a few days, regularly chatted on the phone and texted each other for about a week, and then agreed to meet for their first date. Everything just clicked between them. After six months of dating, Jerome proposed to Lori. Six months later, nearly one year after they first met online, Lori and Jerome got married. Lori and Jerome both agreed that they faced some challenges with meeting people online. Some people feed you exaggerations and lies and expect you to believe it. Many people think meeting someone online is odd, while others believe it paves the way for the future of dating.

You have read about uncertainty reduction theory, uncertainty management theory, and social exchange theory, all of which have given you insights into online relationships. With that in mind, answer the following questions:

1. Which of the theories best describes your most recent interpersonal communication with others?

2. In what ways does social exchange theory help you understand relationship development?

3. What risks, if any, did Lori take in assuming that Jerome was honest in his communication?

4. What role does communication via social media have in your life and how do you see it differing from face-to-face interactions?

might find a relationship or interaction not worth the potential cost. The ratio between benefits and costs varies from person to person and from situation to situation. Thus, a desirable ratio of benefits to costs for one person may be quite different for another person. If a relationship is healthy and satisfying, the benefits and costs for both parties are probably equal, thereby leading to a lasting relationship.

Interpersonal Needs Theory

Interpersonal communication literature consistently discusses the premise that each of us needs to include others in our activities and to be included in theirs, to exert control over others and have them control us, and to give affection to others as well as receive it from others. Will Schutz, a psychologist and one of the most respected leaders in the field of human relations, provides insight into our communication behaviors in his **interpersonal needs theory**. Schutz's theory consists of three needs: affection, inclusion, and control.[19] Although many other needs exist, according to Schutz, most interpersonal behavior and motivation can be directly related to the need for affection, inclusion, and control. Although needs differ from person to person, from situation to situation, and from culture to culture, knowing and understanding our interpersonal needs should help us see how they influence and motivate our interactions with others.

> **interpersonal needs theory**
> A theory that provides insight into our motivation to communicate. This theory consists of three needs: affection, inclusion, and control.

For most of us, our interpersonal needs do not remain static; desire and importance vary with circumstances. For instance, giving and receiving affection might be far more important in a relationship, especially as the relationship intensifies and moves toward bonding, whereas inclusion might be more significant when a relationship is coming apart. Awareness of personal needs and the needs of others also varies, depending on the depth of a relationship, the timing, the context, and so forth. Each need motivates us to interact with others in specific ways.

The Need for Affection The need for affection is the need to feel likable or lovable. The bottom line is that we need to belong and be loved. Every day we see people striving to fulfill this need; for example, people who join social groups or dating services are seeking to fulfill their need for belonging and love. According to Schutz's theory, a person who seems to be liked by many and therefore has adequately fulfilled this need is referred to as *personal*. Kory Floyd, a communication scholar, in his review of research related to communicating affection, found that people who give and receive affection are generally healthier and happier than those who receive or give little affection.[20]

The Need for Inclusion The interpersonal need for inclusion encompasses our needs to feel significant and worthwhile. Schutz describes individuals in terms of this need as *social*, *undersocial*, or *oversocial*. Undersocial people do not like being around other people; they find communicating with others threatening. They tend to be shy and find initiating conversations with others difficult.

Oversocial people cannot stop themselves from getting involved and communicating with others. They attempt to dominate conversations, often speak out of turn, and find it hard to keep quiet. They prefer situations in which they can take over relationships by dominating the flow of communication. The oversocial person fears being ignored by others. Perhaps you know people like this. How do you react to them?

Social people have satisfied their needs for inclusion. They are capable of handling situations with or without others, and few, if any, situations make them feel uncomfortable. They have confidence in themselves and are assertive enough to speak when they feel it is necessary to do so. The research suggests most of us feel mental and physical distress when our need for inclusion is not met, and thus we are motivated to engage others in order to belong.[21]

The Need for Control The third need is our motivation for power or influence in our relationships. As we mature, our need to have control or influence increases, which determines how a relationship will evolve. In relationships we find satisfying,

MAKING CONNECTIONS FOR SUCCESS
It's Me That Counts

Brad and Paige have been dating for more than six months. They agree that they have a very close relationship. After a romantic dinner at their favorite restaurant, Brad and Paige go back to Paige's apartment and are in the middle of some serious kissing when Paige says, "Brad, I want you to stop. I don't want to go any further." Brad says, "Are you kidding me? Don't you love me? I mean, it's not like we haven't been going out for six months." Paige does not respond immediately; she seems to have been caught off guard. Finally, she says, "Brad, I do know how you feel about me, and I trust you, but having sex right now just isn't right for me. I also don't want to end up having a kid before we are married." Brad quickly says, "But

I thought you really cared about me. You know, Paige, I love you!" Paige replies, "I know, but I'm not ready for sex, and I really don't want to until I'm married—you have to understand that."

Consider the above scenario and answer the following questions:

1. Is Brad's communication motivated more out of self-interest than interest in Paige? Explain.

2. How would you describe Brad and Paige's relationship based on their interaction with each other?

3. Describe the relationship in terms of social exchange theory.

---

control is shared, and each person has some say in what happens. These relationships foster mutual respect and shared responsibility. Relationships in which we have little or no say are generally much less satisfying and often are one-sided.[22]

Of course, there are times when we wish to give up or relinquish control because we may not feel competent or we don't want to feel responsible for what happens. At times, too, we may feel overwhelmed by having too much control and responsibility, especially if we are not confident in our ability to make the right decisions. Finally, most of us are happiest and most satisfied when we have moderate amounts of control.

Schutz's theory of needs clearly illustrates the reasons that motivate us to communicate with others. We develop relationships with others for many reasons. The social needs we've discussed explain a great deal about our motivation to form relationships, but relationships are developed for other reasons: to avoid or lessen feelings of loneliness, to learn more about ourselves, and to share our lives with others.

Dialectical Theory

Dialectical theory suggests relationships, as well as individuals, confront many tensions that push and pull in many different directions at the same time. For example, you might want to be out with your friends for the evening, but you have an important paper due in a few days and you haven't started it yet. Thus, you have to decide between being with your friends or beginning your paper. Or you might want your best friend to spend more time with you; then, when your friend does, you decide you want more time to yourself. This might lead to your friend saying, "I thought you wanted to spend more time together, and now that we can, you're never around. So what do you want?" These examples illustrate the contradictory impulses or tensions resulting from the push and pull in different directions. Each person has opposing yet intersecting

dialectical theory

An interpersonal communication theory that suggests that contradictory impulses push and pull us in conflicting directions with others.

The need for affection and inclusion for most of us is a motivator to interact with others. However, many isolate themselves from others for fear they will not be accepted or liked for who they are, or because they find interacting with others threatening.

Stephen Oliver / Alamy Stock Photo

desires, which tug at the relationship in various ways. Three dialectical tensions are commonly identified in the research: connected–autonomy, openness–closedness, and novelty–predictability.[23]

Connection–Autonomy Relationships require both the desire to connect to another person and the desire to retain autonomy as an individual. We want to connect to others, such as partners, friends, parents, siblings, or coworkers, but we also want to retain some control and independence or autonomy over our lives. We desire our close relationships to be defined as "us," but this does not mean we want to sacrifice our individuality or control over who we are.

When connection or integration is overly emphasized in a relationship, it can lead to the feeling of being smothered or consumed by a partner, friend, parent, or coworker, so we feel entrapped and controlled by the relationship, thus leaving us with no life of our own. Intimacy at its highest level requires a bonding that connects us with another person emotionally, intellectually, and physically, but it does not mean or require a complete loss of self. In healthy relationships, a reasonable balance of being connected and maintaining autonomy is sustained. Relationships that move too far in one direction or the other in terms of control versus autonomy are usually extremely unstable and potentially destructive.

Openness–Closedness The second dialectic tension is the desire to be open and expressive on the one hand and closed and private on the other. But even at the beginning of new relationships, when we seek as much information as we can about the other person, a counterforce cautions against revealing too much too soon about ourselves. This tension between self-disclosing and keeping our privacy continues throughout the various stages of relationship development. We know that open expression is a necessary prerequisite for us to reach intimacy and bond with another person. We also know that when we reveal ourselves to another individual, both we and our relationship are more vulnerable. All of us therefore face the dilemma of how much self-disclosure or honesty we should allow with friends, relatives, and romantic partners and how much will be too much. Too much self-disclosure, as you will read later in this chapter, can lead to strains on a relationship and is a sign of not being a competent or, at the very least, not a thoughtful communicator. Relationships grow on the strength of the trust established between partners. When the trust between partners is violated by revealing private information or by telling a partner something he or she is not prepared to hear, the relationship is at risk for deterioration or termination.

Novelty–Predictability To develop and build healthy relationships, a certain amount of predictability is needed. Without some stability or constancy, the potential for uncertainty and ambivalence is too great for a long-term relationship to survive. Therefore, we need relationships that accommodate a certain amount of predictability. Families are a central stabilizing force in most people's lives and provide an anchor for security in a very unpredictable world. Predictability is a comfort to most of us because we know what to expect. Too much predictability in some aspects of a relationship, however, may make the relationship routine and boring, thus requiring a call for something unique or different. The dialectical tension created by the desire for predictability and consistency versus novelty and uncertainty in a relationship requires communication competence to relieve the tension and to prevent destructive conflict from occurring. For example, your roommate wants to stay in and rent a movie, but you want to go out dancing with friends. You could solve the problem by telling your roommate that you would like her to join you and that you would be more than happy to rent a movie tomorrow night instead. Pushes and pulls, or dialectic tensions, will always be part of every relationship, and how we communicate will likely determine whether the relationship grows, stagnates, or terminates.

Managing Relational Tensions   How we deal with the tensions in our lives creates some interesting communication challenges. It is also important to understand that relationships have both private and public dimensions and do not exist in a vacuum. Many tensions or pushes and pulls from outside a relationship, as well as inside, can directly or indirectly affect how the parties in a relationship deal with or manage their dialectical tensions. Communication scholars Leslie Baxter and Barbara Montgomery suggest a number of approaches for managing dialectical tensions.[24] The least helpful in dealing with tensions is *denial* that tension exists. How many times have you heard someone who faces stress or tension say, "Everything is fine—there's no problem." The denial strategy is avoidance or cover-up, which often leads to lying or deception, if not to you, then most certainly to others. The dialectical tension does not disappear by denying its existence; it must be dealt with through open communication. If a friend is really struggling with school and seems down, you must continue to talk with him or her to uncover the problem. You might start out by saying, "I know you're having a tough time with your classes. How can I help you?" You hope the friend will open up and talk about the issue. You need to listen and be supportive.

Baxter suggests that most people use a variety of strategies to manage their dialectical tension.[25] The most often chosen are selection, segmentation, reframing, moderation, and reaffirmation. The strategy of *selection* is one in which one end of the dialectical tension is chosen over the other. For example, a married couple who wants to be by themselves over the Thanksgiving holiday find themselves in a dilemma with their in-laws, who want to spend the holiday with them. They might choose to go along with the in-laws to avoid tension.

The strategy of *segmentation* is a tactic in which a couple compartmentalizes different aspects of their relationship. For example, a couple might manage the tension between being open and being closed with each other by deciding to share information about their mutual friends but not to discuss their past romantic encounters because that might be too hurtful or too insensitive. Thus, by agreement, some things are open for discussion and others are closed.

Reframing is a strategy that allows tensions to be redefined so that tension is diluted, is made less obvious, or is even made to disappear. Couples who have long-distance relationships might say being apart has brought more intimacy and closeness to their relationship. Even though the relationship has a great deal of stress due to their physical separation, the couple have reframed it by suggesting that distance allows for greater intimacy and closeness.

The strategy of *moderation* is characterized by compromises in which deals are struck to help reduce tensions. For example, a parent wants to know everything about your private life and constantly asks questions about personal things you really do not want to share. You choose to answer some of the less private questions but ignore the most personal ones, thus reducing some of the tension created by the questions.

Reaffirmation is the strategy in which individuals recognize that dialectical tensions will always be present, and therefore they should accept them and even embrace the challenges such tensions produce. For example, you know a good friend has extremely liberal views on social issues that are totally contrary to your views. You know you will never agree on whether to use and/or legalize marijuana, but you might have some interesting discussions about the subject and perhaps even educate each other. You should not ignore your friend's opinion or deny dialectical tension, but you should consider it part of being human. Relationships always experience pushes and pulls, and to grow a lasting relationship, the parties must manage and control the tensions through communication. The result of not managing and controlling tensions will likely be conflict.

Self-Disclosure in Relationships

13.4 **Outline** the roles of self-disclosure, privacy, gender, culture, and rhetorical sensitivity in interpersonal relationships.

Relationships are built on interaction. The more sincere, honest, and open the interactions, the stronger and more lasting the relationship is likely to be. Much of our interpersonal communication, however, is small talk. Such light conversation might not provide a means for us to learn who we are, to fulfill our interpersonal needs, or to grow in our relationships. Nonetheless, it does maintain an important opening to further interaction. Self-disclosure is one type of interaction that changes as a relationship becomes closer.

To reduce uncertainty, as suggested by uncertainty reduction theory, and to meet our physical and emotional needs, we must communicate who we are; we must disclose information about ourselves, as suggested by social penetration theory. **Self-disclosure**, or the voluntary sharing of information about ourselves that another person is not likely to know, can be as simple and nonthreatening as telling our name or as complex and threatening as revealing deep feelings.

When self-disclosure occurs in caring relationships, it usually results in greater self-understanding and self-improvement. In addition, our self-disclosure to others encourages them to reciprocate and creates an atmosphere that fosters interpersonal communication and meaningful relationships.

self-disclosure
Voluntary sharing of information about the self that another person is not likely to know.

Why Do We Self-Disclose?

Many abilities differentiate human beings from other animals, one of which is to keep and share information about ourselves. We self-disclose for a variety of reasons: for others to better understand who we are, to gain sympathy, to see what others think, to gain trust, or to connect with others and establish relationships. Self-disclosure is essential if we are to form and maintain relationships. Here we will discuss three reasons why we self-disclose: self-presentation, relationship building, and catharsis.

self-presentation
An intentional self-disclosure tactic used to reveal certain aspects about ourselves for specific reasons.

Self-presentation **Self-presentation** is an intentional self-disclosure tactic used to reveal certain aspects about ourselves for specific reasons. When asked in an employment interview, for example, to talk about yourself, you are often requested to discuss your background, experiences, and accomplishments. When you disclose information about yourself that may not be known to the interviewer, you are engaged in

---

MAKING CONNECTIONS FOR SUCCESS

The Importance of Small Talk

The ability to connect with others through small talk can lead to big things, according to Debra Fine, author of *The Fine Art of Small Talk*.[26] A former engineer, Fine recalls being so uncomfortable at networking events she would hide in the restroom. Now a professional speaker, Fine says the ability to connect with people through small talk is an acquired skill. Successful people know how to use small talk effectively and know its importance in entering and maintaining relationships. With that in mind, answer the following questions:

1. Do you find making small talk easy or difficult? Why?

2. Develop a set of tips for general social icebreakers and business or professional icebreakers that might improve your small talk and share them with others in your class.

3. Do you think communication via social media affects small talk? In what ways? Is communicating on Facebook or Twitter a form of small talk? Why or why not?

4. What are some different ways you would use to move beyond small talk?

5. When is it appropriate to move beyond small talk?

self-presentation. The purpose of providing information about yourself is to emphasize that you are the person best suited for the job. For example, you tell the interviewer you are a highly organized person with excellent communication skills or that you are a team player and you enjoy meeting and working with people from a variety of backgrounds. You might disclose, for example, that you come from a relatively poor background and you have worked to help pay your tuition—you imply by your statements you are self-sufficient in the hope the interviewer will judge you positively.

Denkou Images/Alamy Stock Photo

Thus, when appealing to others, we tend to describe ourselves in more favorable terms (more favorable than we really deserve) to impress others with whom we want to have a relationship. In short, we sometimes bend the truth to enhance our own appeal to establish relationships. Many good examples of this can be found in online dating services (Tinder, Match.com, and the like). The self-descriptions some of us give are, to say the least, not very accurate. In fact, some of us describe ourselves in very flattering terms because we realize this is a good way to gain more contacts and establish relationships. Clearly, impression management now occurs both online and in face-to-face meetings.

Relationship Building   We self-disclose to start or maintain relationships. Self-disclosure via small talk or social conversation is one way we enter into relationships with others. The level of self-disclosure at some point can move to more intimate and self-revealing talk as the relationship develops. There are exceptions to this progression, of course, and the depth and number of interactions can vary dramatically from one relationship to another. In addition, moving from light social talk to more intimate and revealing talk does not necessarily imply the relationship will automatically be a quality relationship.[27]

A relationship's location on the continuum between casual acquaintance and intimate confidant is determined by how people interact with each other and by their specific communication behaviors. The way we communicate with another person reflects the nature and type of relationship.

Catharsis   Self-disclosing communication can be a form of communicative release or catharsis. This is especially true when we want to rid ourselves of information causing tension, guilt, or sadness.[28] It is a way of getting something off our mind to reduce stress. For you as a student, examples include telling your parents you are in debt because you've been gambling or that you aren't doing as well in school as they think because you've been oversleeping. The benefit of this type of disclosure is that it rids us of dealing with an issue or problem by ourselves and invites sympathy or help.

The rapid development of social media has led to new ways to help others cope with the loss of a dear friend or loved one. Increasingly, one or more family members may honor their loved one by preparing a commemorative Facebook page that memorializes the life of the deceased. These pages have become a "place" where mourners can "visit" with their departed loved one and connect with other mourners, leave messages of condolence, share stories about the deceased, and leave messages directed to the deceased. These cathartic messages function as part of **transcorporeal communication**—a process through which a living person sends a digital message to a deceased person through a website or social networking site. *Trans* indicates that communication occurs beyond the state of human life, and *corporeal* indicates a relationship to a physical material body.[29] Deceased individuals no longer maintain a physical presence. Therefore, we direct our digital messages toward a person who

To reduce uncertainty and to meet our physical and emotional needs, we must communicate who we are; we must disclose information about ourselves. When self-disclosure occurs in caring relationships, it usually results in greater self-understanding and self-improvement.

transcorporeal communication
A process through which a living person sends a digital message to a deceased person through a website or social networking site.

is in a different state rather being physically present. Communicating in this manner, which is often exhibited in Facebook memorial walls and groups, reconnects the living with the deceased and helps us make cathartic sense of our lives without our friends and loved ones.

When Shouldn't We Self-Disclose Too Much?

Although full disclosure can be cleansing, it can also be harmful, risky, unwise, or insensitive, as well as detrimental to a relationship. At one time or another, most of us have chosen not to say what was on our minds or not to tell others something about ourselves, themselves, or others because it might be hurtful. There are many reasons for withholding information, but it is usually to protect others, to avoid a potentially negative reaction, or to avoid hurting others or ourselves. Self-disclosure, therefore, is not always wise or appropriate.

The open and honest sharing of our feelings, thoughts, concerns, and secrets with others is at the heart of self-disclosure. This openness and honesty would be ideal, but it is not always practical or wise. Ultimately, self-disclosure must be based on personal judgment rather than rigid rules. The key should always be concern for both self and others.

Self-Disclosure and Privacy

privacy
The claim of individuals, groups, or institutions to determine for themselves when, how, and to what extent information about themselves is communicated to others.

How much is too much self-disclosure and when does it begin to invade or affect our privacy? **Privacy** is "the claim of individuals, groups, or institutions to determine for themselves when, how, and to what extent information about themselves is communicated to others."[30] These are not easy questions to answer because what might be appropriate for one situation may not be for another. Thus, an important task for people in relationships is the negotiation of privacy boundaries.[31] Privacy boundaries work in a way very similar to personal space boundaries. Just as we control and protect access to our physical self—for example, how close we allow others to come to us—in the same way we control and protect our privacy boundaries. Sandra Petronio, a communication scholar and expert in the area of privacy and how we manage our privacy boundaries, states:

> Revealing private information is risky because there is a potential vulnerability when revealing aspects of the self. Receiving private information from another may also result in the need for protecting oneself. In order to manage disclosing and receiving privacy information, individuals erect a metaphoric boundary to reduce the possibility of losing face and as a means of protection. Also, people use a set of rules or criteria to control the boundary and regulate the flow of private information to and from others.[32]

The process of sharing more and more personal information about one's self with another person encourages further intrusion into one's privacy, whether wanted or unwanted. Privacy boundaries would seem to be common sense, but they are not always clear to either party in a relationship. For example, a man and a woman have been dating for several years and have been sexually intimate, but they are not married. The couple might try to control the privacy of their relationship because revealing past relational secrets could be embarrassing, or they could be fully open about their relationships with others. The determination of what should be kept private from each other and what should be kept private from others is usually negotiated by the mutual consent of the parties involved in the relationship.

When or if the boundaries of a relationship are violated or crossed, tensions may result, creating an imbalance. Thus, negotiations between relationship partners often involve what can and should be shared and what is or should be off limits. Boundaries are erected to protect, control the flow of information, and regulate vulnerability. When one partner violates the privacy of the other, for example, attempts are made to reconstruct the privacy boundary by changing the topic or by avoiding the situation.

Self-Disclosure and Gender

Using the terms *women* and *men* as identifiers to describe or distinguish communication between the sexes is troublesome. The terms imply sameness across all women and all men that might or might not be true. For example, to say, "Women disclose their feelings more often than men do" may not be true for all women or all men. Some men disclose more feelings than some women do, and vice versa. Thus, we must be careful to avoid stereotyping solely based on biological sex differences.[33]

Some research and some authors support the idea that men and women do communicate using different sets of rules and meanings. Deborah Tannen, in her book *You Just Don't Understand: Women and Men in Conversation*, reviewed many research studies and takes the position that women's verbal and nonverbal behaviors are different from men's. For example, she found that men talk less personally or inclusively when compared to women, and that women tend to make more validating and confirming statements than men do.[34] Women are more likely to talk about their relationships and disclose a deeper level of intimacy, but men often do not center their talk on relational closeness.[35]

Women seem to disclose more to those with whom they are close, whereas men seem to disclose more to those whom they trust. It also appears that men and women differ in the defensive and protective strategies used to reduce embarrassment and maintain privacy boundaries. Men's defensive strategies include blaming the incident on something else, laughing at their own behavior, or retreating from the situation, whereas women's defensive strategies often include blaming others and criticizing themselves. No matter how privacy is defined or explained, the means by which people regulate the release of private information is through disclosure.[36]

All of us should have someone with whom we can share our feelings and thoughts because it is generally good for our well-being and personal satisfaction. Self-disclosure is the most sensitive and beautiful form of communication we can engage in, but it must be done with care.

MAKING CONNECTIONS FOR SUCCESS

The Dark Side of Technology: Freedom and Temptation

Facebook, Twitter, Snapchat, texting—all offer myriad communication possibilities to help us stay connected, broaden our social networks, and communicate more frequently and efficiently with friends, family, or work colleagues. But there is a dark side to these communication options and the freedom to share whatever personal information, opinions, or photos one chooses. With new and emerging communication tools come increased risks and temptations—from the mildly irritating tendency to waste time to potentially harmful and dangerous behaviors, such as cyber bullying or sexting, which is "sending, receiving, or forwarding" inappropriate photos via a cell phone.[37]

A recent survey found that one in five teens had sent or posted a naked picture of her- or himself, and a third had received a picture or video of this type via text message or email.[38] The criminal justice system is now involved, and teens are being prosecuted and labeled as sex offenders. Although these teens may evade the law, the online trail is harder to escape.

The labels and youthful indiscretions may follow them for years, creating problems when applying to college or for a job or running for public office. With that in mind, answer the following questions:

1. What cautions can be applied to other forms of online communication?

2. What responsibilities come with the freedom to communicate via social media?

3. Do you think sexting should be considered a felony, or is it simply bad judgment? Should the law be involved in regulating online behavior? If so, what types of behavior?

4. Teens and technology can be a volatile combination. Why do you think this is so?

5. With access to the Internet and other technology occurring at increasingly younger ages, what safeguards, if any, can or should be put in place?

Self-Disclosure and Culture

In general, people from different cultural backgrounds tend to follow similar patterns of self-disclosure. For example, people from various cultures are likely to begin relationships with small talk and progress to more intimate levels of interaction as the relationship continues. Of course, differences do exist, especially in the initial contact stage, in some cultures; but, in general, as people become friends, those differences seem to diminish.

Think about some of the characteristics that describe your cultural background, however, and how they might or might not influence your communication. Do you see yourself simply as an American, or do you identify with some other ethnic or racial group? Do others view you the same way? How does your ethnicity affect your communication and with whom you choose to communicate? Do you use certain expressions understood only by members of your ethnic group? When you interact with people from a different ethnic group, how difficult is it for you to communicate? The answers to these questions will help you understand cultural differences and why interacting with people from diverse backgrounds is much more complex than simply exchanging information. It requires thought, recognition of differences, and some adjustments for communication to be meaningful to both parties. Not everyone thinks and communicates in exactly the same way. This may be especially important to remember when we interact with people from cultures different from our own. Disclosure is culturally regulated by norms of appropriateness, so we must understand cultural differences.

Self-Disclosure and Rhetorical Sensitivity

rhetorical sensitivity

A cautious approach to self-disclosure in which the situation and factors about the other person are considered before communication begins.

According to communication scholars Roderick Hart and Don Burks, **rhetorical sensitivity** is an alternative form of communication that can be applied to situations in which wide-open self-disclosure could be harmful. For example, you want to tell your friend that he needs to get more sleep, as he's out every night and falling asleep in class. Instead of telling him what you really think, you mention a story you read online about a car crash that resulted from a sleep-deprived driver, in the hope your friend will get the message. It represents a cautious approach to exchanging information while developing a relationship.[39] Rhetorically sensitive people can balance their self-interest with the interests of others. They can adjust their communication to take into account the beliefs, values, and mood of the other person. Considering the other person's views or feelings does not mean changing your own, but it does mean finding an effective way to communicate your thoughts without offending or hurting the other person.

Honest self-disclosure can be harmful if it is stated in a way that damages the relationship. Rhetorically sensitive people understand self-disclosure and know how to adapt their messages to a particular audience and situation. Rhetorically sensitive individuals generally display the following attributes:

- They accept personal complexity; they understand that every person is made up of many selves. For example, one person may be a mother, a daughter, a Republican, an Asian American, an abuse victim, a student, and a consumer.
- They are flexible and avoid rigidity in communicating with others.
- They do not change their own values but can communicate them in a variety of ways to avoid offending others.
- They sense when it is appropriate to communicate something and when it is not.[40] Rhetorically sensitive people understand self-disclosure and know how to adapt their messages to a particular audience and situation.
- They are aware of the language they choose, such as gender-inclusive nonsexist language; they do not use homophobic or racist language or inappropriate jokes that offend others.

Guidelines

SUGGESTIONS FOR APPROPRIATE SELF-DISCLOSURE

There are no hard-and-fast rules when it comes to self-disclosure, but self-disclosing to others should be based on common sense and good judgment. Here are some suggestions that might help you use self-disclosure appropriately and competently:

1. **Use reasoned self-disclosure.** Although open and honest relationships are desirable, it is important to recognize situational constraints. For example, as a youngster, you might have been caught shoplifting from a local store. You shoplifted only that one time and were required to do some community service. However, you are now running for public office, and you must decide whether to disclose the fact that you stole from a local store. To do so would more than likely hurt your chances of winning the election. However, if you know that something you did is going to come out, mentioning it before it does come out illustrates that you are not hiding anything.

2. **Make self-disclosure a two-way process.** One-sided self-disclosure generally leads to relationships that are not very enduring, meaningful, or healthy. For example, once a mutual give-and-take is established, if one person self-discloses, the other person will usually follow suit. As trust increases between individuals, self-disclosure will likely expand, and with continued self-disclosure, relationships become stronger.

3. **Make self-disclosure appropriate to the situation and the person.** When we disclose personal information about ourselves, we run the risk of being hurt or rejected. We can minimize the risk somewhat if we carefully match the disclosure to the person and the situation. Self-disclosure should be a slow process; rushing it, as some have done on the Internet, can unnecessarily increase vulnerability.

4. **Consider diversity.** The appropriateness and the level of self-disclosure vary by culture, group, and individual. Not all cultures foster self-expression in the same way that you might. Even within the United States, culture differences can be found among groups, such as between men and women. Consider these differences as you decide how much, to whom, and when to disclose personal information.

5. **Be open and honest.** The goal of self-disclosing is to match the amount and kind of self-disclosure to the situation. Thus, open and honest sharing of our feelings, concerns, and secrets with others is at the heart of self-disclosure. This does not mean, however, that we must disclose everything or that we cannot withhold information if it is likely to hurt us or someone else.

6. **Base self-disclosure on personal judgment.** Ultimately, self-disclosure must be based on personal judgment rather than rigid rules. Self-disclosure should, if used properly, be the most sensitive and meaningful form of communication we engage in as we enter and maintain relationships. For many reasons, we sometimes find it difficult to disclose to others. However, when relationships are based on mutual feelings and genuine communication, they cannot help but grow and mature.

Relationship Formation

13.5 **Identify** the stages of relationship development and growth.

Whether or not two specific individuals ever come in contact with each other may depend on circumstance and situation. We are influenced daily by others we meet and by their first impressions. How and why a relationship develops may depend on *interpersonal attraction* and how the relationship manages the stages of coming together or growth.

Interpersonal Attraction

Most of us develop relationships quite routinely, although the process is easier for some people than for others. **Interpersonal attraction** is the desire to interact with someone based on a variety of factors, including physical attractiveness, personality, rewards, proximity, or similarities. Although these are perhaps obvious referents, interpersonal attraction is a complex phenomenon. Communication scholars James McCroskey and Thomas McCain identified three types of attraction: (1) social attraction ("He would fit into my circle of friends"), (2) physical attraction ("I think she's or he's hot"), and (3) task attraction ("My confidence in her ability to get the job done

interpersonal attraction

The desire to interact with someone based on a variety of factors, including physical attractiveness, personality, rewards, proximity, or similarities.

makes me want to work with her").[41] In other words, interpersonal attraction has a lot to do with evaluating others.

Any given person (including you) is liked by some people, disliked by some, and seen as neutral by many others. Why? This question is not easily answered, but, to some extent, differences in attraction depend on the person making the evaluation. Attraction also depends, in part, on the similarities and differences between the evaluator and the person being evaluated. As acquaintances evolve from first encounters to more engaged relationships, two additional factors come into play: the need to associate with someone and reactions to observable physical attributes.

What leads to attraction and eventual friendship? More than 7 billion people inhabit our planet, and several thousand of them could conceivably become your friends. That is exceedingly unlikely to happen, however. Any one of us is likely to become aware of, interact with, and personally know only a small fraction of these individuals. However, social media now allow us to have hundreds of acquaintances all over the world. Most online acquaintances remain online acquaintances or friends with whom we may share personal information, but they seldom become intimate friends.

When two people come into contact and experience a relatively positive effect, either in person or online, they begin a transition to the initiating stages of a possible relationship. They may simply remain superficial acquaintances who exchange friendly greetings whenever they happen to encounter one another but never interact otherwise. Or they may begin to talk in person or text each other, learn each other's names, and exchange bits and pieces of personal information. At this point, they might be described as close acquaintances or online friends. Which of these two outcomes depends on the extent to which each person is motivated by the need to associate or the need for inclusion (discussed later in this chapter) and the way each person reacts to the observable attributes of the other or the perceived attributes based on the messages they exchange online.

"Love at first sight," or being wowed, is a phenomenon expressed in various ways by different cultures. No matter the expression, the underlying idea is the same: that sometimes seeing someone for the first time can bring a powerful feeling of attraction toward that person. We all have heard the phrase, "Beauty is only skin deep." It is a warning about giving too much weight to outward appearance. But research seems to indicate that even if we want to follow this advice, we can't, because physical appearance is such a powerful factor in our attraction to others.[42] So, even when we want to, it is difficult to ignore or avoid physical attraction as a motivator to establishing a relationship.

Physical Attributes   When we like—or dislike—some people at first sight, it is an indication we have observed something about them that provides positive or negative information. For example, if a stranger reminds you of someone you know and like, association extends your response to the person.[43]

You tend to like the stranger simply on the basis of a superficial resemblance to someone else. In other instances, the cue might not be related to a specific person in your past but to a subgroup of people to whom you respond positively—the stranger has a Wisconsin accent and you have a fondness for people from your home state. In a similar way, resemblance to a specific person you dislike or to a subgroup of people you dislike can cause you to instantly dislike or avoid a stranger. As we discussed in Chapters 2 and 5, stereotypes are poor predictors of behavior; nevertheless, we find we do react to other people on the basis of superficial characteristics.

Most of us know that reacting to stereotypes on the basis of appearance is meaningless. However, people do, in fact, respond positively to those who are extremely attractive and negatively to those who are very unattractive.[44] This is especially true in the early stages of interpersonal contact with strangers. We commonly accept or reject people on the basis of observable characteristics, such as skin color, sexual orientation, height, weight, accent, and hair color. Physical attractiveness is a very powerful message and influences many types of interpersonal evaluations.

Communication and Attraction   How does attractiveness affect relationships and interpersonal communication? Most people, according to one study, fear rejection by those who are more attractive than they are. Many people tend to reject others who are far less attractive than they believe themselves to be; in other words, they say, "I can do better than that." In general, most of us move toward those who are similar to us in attractiveness.

The idea that "opposites attract" is as old as the adage "birds of a feather flock together" and appears to have little truth to it. In plays, movies, and television series, a familiar story line is one where two quite different people are attracted to each other, in part because they are so different. Think, for example, of Marge and Homer Simpson or a movie such as *Shrek*. In contrast, such real-life pairings are relatively rare.[45]

Why do these exceptions occur, and what explains them? If one person in a relationship is more attractive than another, for example, people tend to infer that the less attractive person in the relationship has an attribute that "balances" the mismatch, such as wealth, power, intelligence, sex appeal, or fame. For example, in the classic 1991 animated movie *Beauty and the Beast*, the Beast's appearance is unattractive, but his kindness, gentleness, and bravery make Belle (who was extremely beautiful) fall in love with him and make it believable. However, the overall conclusion of most research is that similarity is a much stronger basis for attraction than are differences.[46]

Chemistry or Physical Attraction   Whether we wish to accept it or not, physical appearance does play a role in determining relationships. Although this attractiveness might not always predict the outcome of a relationship, research suggests that physical attractiveness is important as an attention getter.[47] Most of us are aware that sometimes our first impressions and reasons for being attracted to another are not completely rational. Sudden lust, love at first sight, or the intense dislike of someone with whom we have had no previous contact can seem inexplicable. Many social psychologists suggest relationship development has a lot to do with the "chemistry" between the individuals in the relationship. Either the chemistry is right and the relationship develops, or it's a mismatch and the relationship never seems to move beyond the initial stages. The chemistry explanation probably holds some truth, but many other variables influence the development of a relationship.

We are most often attracted to individuals who support us and have similar interests, attitudes, likes, and dislikes. In fact, when asked to characterize the ideal friend, people often describe someone who is similar to their perceptions of themselves. Those who are religious tend to seek other religious people; those who like sports, other sports fans; and those who like children, others who like children. Opposites do sometimes attract, as described above, but relationships in which important attitudes or behaviors differ significantly are often strained and more likely to deteriorate than are those where there are no major disparities.

Meeting Online   According to communication scholars Malcolm Parks and Kory Floyd, conflicting theories on interpersonal communication and relationship development exist. Because online interaction is limited by fewer social cues (i.e., nonverbal communication) and potential feedback delays can lead to uncertainty (and difficulty in reducing uncertainty about the other person), the development of personal relationships might be prevented, or at least restrained.[48]

Usually, opposites don't attract, but when they do, underlying similarities are present because similarity is usually a much better predictor of attraction. When seemingly opposite people are attracted to each other, they typically find they have a great deal in common—though this similarity may not be visible to casual, outside observers.

Gareth Boden/Pearson Education Ltd

Online interactions are generally assumed to lack many typical characteristics of face-to-face discussions that can aid in relationship development. An important question researchers ask is, "Are the conditions that exist in face-to-face interactions necessary for a relationship to develop into something that is ongoing or lasting?" Although the interactions between people who communicate through social media rather than face-to-face communication indicate what people want in a lasting relationship, evidence is not conclusive that their mediated communication will lead to one. In research studies of personal online ads placed by heterosexual and homosexual men and women, several trends emerged: (1) Heterosexual men wanted what heterosexual women offered—physical attractiveness, (2) heterosexual women sought what heterosexual men offered—financial security, (3) homosexual men emphasized physical attractiveness in their ads even more than did heterosexual men, and (4) homosexual women tended to play down the importance of physical attractiveness.[49] Online ads placed by people ages 50 or above tend to place much less emphasis on physical appearance and instead focus on less sexual relational goals.[50] Of course, with our ability to use Skype and FaceTime, the differences between face-to-face and online interactions are dramatically reduced. Although these encounters can be very similar, they also can be more carefully controlled and choreographed than face-to-face interactions.

Parks and Floyd found women are more likely to form online relationships than men and also found age and marital status were not related to the likelihood of developing a personal online relationship. People who were married and divorced, according to their survey results, were equally likely to form personal relationships over the Internet. In fact, of the 176 people Parks and Floyd surveyed, about 30 percent developed personal relationships. The more in-depth and personal an online relationship becomes, the more likely it is that communication will move beyond the computer or social media device to more private and direct channels, such as the telephone, letters, or face-to-face communication.[51] As with all relationships, online relationships go through stages of initiation, maintenance, and sometimes deterioration and termination.

Relationships: Initiation or Coming Together

Communication scholars such as Mark Knapp and Anita Vangelisti believe that for relationships to move beyond a brief encounter, they must go through various stages of growth and patterns of communication.[52] Although the relationship stages in Knapp

---

MAKING CONNECTIONS FOR SUCCESS
Soul Mate Online—Finding the Right One

Go online and type in any of the following search terms—"finding a date," "finding a relationship," or "finding a mate"—and you will discover over a million different sites. Here are some of their slogans:

"When you are ready to find the love of your life."

"A marriage a day, a match every 17 minutes."

"Genuine People, Real Love."

"Over 100,000 current members searching for meaningful relationships."

"Ever wish there was an easy way to find the person you were meant to be with?"

"To create a deep and meaningful connection."

Online sites such as Tinder, eHarmony.com, Match.com, and hundreds more offer ways to meet others, find a date, get married, be friends, or connect. With that in mind, answer the following questions:

1. Why do you think websites such as those listed above are so popular?

2. How would you describe the perfect mate?

3. How can you be sure you have found the perfect mate?

4. If you were to go online to look for a relationship, what criteria would you use to determine whether you would make a face-to-face connection with someone?

5. What, if any, problems might you encounter with these types of services? What problems do you see if you provide personal online information for others to read?

and Vangelisti's model are generally romantic in nature, they do not suggest that only romantic relationships or mixed-gender relationships are included. In fact, Knapp and Vangelisti suggest any and all kinds of relationships can reach the highest level of commitment. David McWhirter and Andrew Mattison, research psychologists, found that when same-sex intimate relationships form, the same patterns or stages of development occur as with mixed-sex pairs.[53]

Knapp and Vangelisti strongly emphasize that the model simplifies a complex process. For example, in their model they show each stage adjacent to the next, seeming to suggest that when a communicating couple left one stage, they entered the next. This is not their intention. Each stage actually contains behaviors from other stages, so stage identification is a matter of emphasis.[54]

Knapp and Vangelisti further explain that not all relationships go through the stages at the same rate, in the same way, or necessarily sequentially, and many relationships move in and out of the stages as they progress or regress. They note we should resist the temptation to perceive stages of coming together as only "good" and those of coming apart as only "bad." In fact, sometimes the termination of a relationship may be a good thing or, conversely, becoming more intimate with someone may not necessarily be a good thing. The coming-together sequence, however, often progresses from initiating to experimenting, intensifying, integrating, and ultimately bonding.[55]

Initiating   Initiating is the stage during which individuals meet and interact for the first time. The initial interaction might consist of a brief exchange of words, either online or in person. If conversation does not begin, the initiating stage may end, and the potential relationship might not progress any further. Whether the interaction continues depends on various assessments the individuals make—for example, whether the other person is attractive or unattractive, approachable or unapproachable. A connection must be made to motivate one or both of the individuals to continue the interaction if a relationship is to develop.

During the initiating stage, we mentally process many impressions that lead to a key decision: "Yes, I do want to meet you" or "No, I am not interested in you." It might take less than 15 seconds to determine whether a relationship will progress. At this stage, most of us feel extremely vulnerable and cautious. Social media plays a larger and larger role in how people from all over the world meet and interact and, ironically, seems to encourage less caution despite the potential dangers of getting to know someone online and the need to assess whether the information others share is truthful and accurate.

Experimenting   Experimenting is the stage of coming together that requires risk taking because little is known about the other person. You attempt to answer the question, "Who is this person?" This stage can be extremely awkward, consisting mainly of small talk: "What's your name?" "Where are you from?" "What's your major?" "Do you know so-and-so?" Such conversation serves several important functions in the development of a relationship: (1) It uncovers similarities and interests that might lead to deeper conversation, (2) it serves as an audition for the potential friend, (3) it lets the other person know who you are and provides clues to how he or she can get to know you better, and (4) it establishes the common ground you share with the other person.

Relationships in the experimenting stage are "generally pleasant, relaxed, overtly uncritical, and casual."[56] Most relationships, according to Knapp and Vangelisti, do not progress very far beyond the experimenting stage. However, relationships that remain at the experimental level can become satisfying friendships or acquaintances.

Intensifying   The intensifying stage marks an increase in the participants' commitment and involvement in the relationship. Simply put, the two people become close friends. The commitment is typified by an increased sharing of more personal and private information, or self-disclosure, about self and family. At this stage it would not be unusual to share confidences such as "My mother and father are affectionate people," "I love you," "I am a sensitive person," "I once cheated on an exam," "My father is having another relationship," "I was promoted," "I drink too heavily," and "I don't use drugs."

Although the relationship deepens at this stage, there is still a sense of caution and testing to gain approval before continuing. In typical romantic relationships, we see much testing of commitment—sitting close, for instance, may occur before holding hands, hugging, or kissing. As the relationship matures, the participants become more sensitive to each other's needs. During this phase, verbal communication changes, depending on how the individuals interact with each other. For example:

1. **Forms of address become informal**—a first name, nickname, or a term of endearment is used.

2. **Use of the first-person plural becomes more common**—"We should do this," or "Let's do this."

3. **Private symbols begin to develop**—special slang, nicknames, or jargon or conventional language forms with mutually understood, private meanings.

4. **Verbal shortcuts occur because of familiarity with each other**—for example, washing dishes might become "dishes," or "let's go to sleep" might become "bedtime."

5. **More direct expressions of commitment may appear**—"We really have a good thing going" or "I don't know who I'd talk to if you weren't around." Sometimes such expressions receive an echo—"I really like you a lot" or "I really like you, too, Taylor."

6. **Each partner acts increasingly as a helper in the other's daily process of understanding what he or she is all about**—"In other words, you mean you're . . ." or "But yesterday you said you were . . .".[57]

Integrating   When integrating occurs, the relationship has a sense of togetherness. Others expect to see the individuals together, and when they do not, they often ask about the other person. The two people have established a deep commitment, and the relationship has become extremely important to them. Many assumptions take place between the individuals. For example, sharing is expected, and borrowing from the other person usually needs no formal request because it is assumed to be all right.

Although a strong mutual commitment characterizes this stage of a relationship, it does not mean a total giving of oneself to the other. The verbal and nonverbal expressions of the integrating stage take many forms. For example, some individuals believe their relationship is something special or unique. Some share rings, pins, pictures, and other artifacts to illustrate to themselves and others their commitment to each other. The two may begin to behave in similar ways. Still others indicate their sense of togetherness through word choice—*our* account, *our* apartment, *our* car.

Bonding   The final stage in a relationship's development and growth is bonding, the public announcement of the commitment—as when a couple announces that they are engaged or getting married. Bonding involves the understanding that the commitment has progressed from private knowledge to public knowledge, thus making a breakup of the relationship more difficult.

The integrating stage of relationship development conveys a sense of togetherness. The two people have established a deep commitment, and the relationship has become extremely important to them.

Sergey Ryzhov/Shutterstock

Getting to Know Others: How Relationships Begin

The following is taken from an essay titled "The Donut Shop Experiment," written by Jonathan Butler, a high school history teacher in Riverside, California. According to Butler, he and a group of his friends and relatives wanted to do something crazy on a Saturday night. They were tired of board games and television. So about 10 of them, some under 30 and some over—brothers, a sister, a friend, in-laws, and parents—struck on an idea that the group of them would infiltrate a little café in twos and threes, at differing times, until all were seated around the counter. They would arrange themselves as couples chatting, an old man sitting alone, or three friends in a row. Their plan was to interrelate—"get acquainted"—as total strangers appearing to get to know one another. Their plan was to see how the others in the café would react.

They chose a donut shop with a truck-stop atmosphere that lacked promise socially. Then one of them asked the cashier, "Say, do you use bleached flour in these donuts?" From that one question, conversation flowed and relationships began to form.

Butler writes, "The conversation ranged from food to politics to music to how strangers never talk in strange places like a café."

The people in the café, according to Butler, reflected on what they were doing and laughed, realizing that an improbable conglomerate of people had formed some kind of community.

The group of 10 left the café and arrived back at Butler's home, dazed by the experience. Butler ends the story with these words: "How thin the walls that divide us from one another at ballparks and grocery stores and restaurants. How paper-thin."[58]

Think about Butler's experience and answer the following questions:

1. What do you think Butler means by his last statement?
2. Why is it so easy to communicate with those we don't know via social media but not as easy when we are in face-to-face situations?
3. What does Butler's café experiment tell us about communication and relationships?
4. What does it mean to have "people skills"?
5. How would you explain the above story using Knapp and Vangelisti's stages of coming together?

The relationship at this stage is contractual in nature, even though a formal contract, such as a marriage license, is not required. Both parties must understand, however, that a relationship exists, which entails explicit and implicit agreements to hold it together. The commitment implies the relationship is "for better or for worse" and is defined according to established norms, policies, or laws of the culture and society in which it exists.

It takes time and energy to maintain a relationship. Most people in relationships, no matter how good they are, know and accept that some conflict is inevitable. They also know that conflict, if handled appropriately, can lead to a stronger and lasting relationship.

Relationship Maintenance Strategies

Earlier in this chapter, we explained, through the various interpersonal communication theories, why we seek relationships and their importance to our well-being as humans. Our focus, for the most part, was on creating relationships and positive interactions; however, we also believe that at times maintaining healthy relationships includes some unpleasant interactions and conflicts.

Relational maintenance behaviors help us understand how we sustain a relationship so it continues to grow and thrive. Earlier in this chapter, we discussed social exchange theory in terms of costs and benefits. Let's say you recently met someone with whom you have become friends. Both you and your new friend are satisfied with the costs and benefits of the relationship. Laura Stafford and Dan Canary, two communication researchers, determined five primary relational maintenance behaviors couples can use to build and maintain relationships: *positivity, openness, assurances, blending social networks,* and *sharing tasks*.[59]

Positivity   Communicative behaviors make others feel good or comfortable around us. For example, communicative behaviors include acting friendly or cheerful; being patient and forgiving; being optimistic, courteous, cooperative, complementary, and polite; and avoiding criticism. Individuals who typically communicate in this way are fun and pleasant to be around. Couple partners who engage in these types of behaviors often show affection for each other, seldom complain, and keep their relationship strong.

Openness   Openness occurs when a person is willing to interact with a friend or relational partner about their relationship. Those who use this relational maintenance strategy are willing to self-disclose their thoughts and feelings, and ask how the other person feels about the relationship. People who use the openness strategy like to have talks about how the relationship is going and like to share their needs and wants in regard to the relationship.

Assurances   Assurances, according to Stafford and Canary, are the verbal and nonverbal behaviors one or both partners in a relationship use to demonstrate their commitment or faithfulness to the other. When someone expresses assurances, he or she shows commitment to the relationship and implies it has a future.

Blending Social Networks

Social networks include common friends, coworkers, and family relationships. For example, close friends are likely to know each other's families and share social friends and other associates. Common friends help a couple bond the relationship.

Sharing Tasks

Each person in the relationship does his or her fair share of the work that needs to be done and takes equal responsibility for what faces both of them. For example, if a friend lets you borrow her computer when yours is not working, you might let her use your car to run an errand. If your partner cooks a meal, then you might offer to clean up afterward. Sharing tasks requires effort and energy to make the relationship work. Thus, both individuals contribute to the relationship, which makes it more stable. At times, however, a couple struggles to keep the relationship together and signs arise that it is in trouble.

Relationship Dissolution

13.6   **Identify** the stages of relationship deterioration and dissolution.

Not every relationship is destined to last. The way both parties handle a relationship's dissolution can affect the well-being of both.

Signs That Show a Relationship Is in Trouble

Before we concede a relationship is over, certain warning signs, as well as some possible repair strategies, might help to prevent its breakup. At least three signs point to problems: aggressive behavior, lies, and betrayal.

Aggressive Behavior   A preliminary warning sign a relationship is heading toward trouble occurs when one of the parties becomes a little too aggressive by aiming hurtful communication at the other. At some time we all say something we wished we hadn't said to someone about whom we care. However, whether intentional or not, when people communicate hurtful statements to one another with increasing frequency, it is a sign that their relationship may be in trouble.

Lies   Another warning sign of trouble in a relationship is when one deceives another with lies. Whether the lie is significant or trivial, it weakens the relationship's foundation, which is trust. Recent research findings indicate when people find themselves on the receiving end of lies they react with mistrust of, and dislike toward, the liar.[60]

We are all more or less adept at the art of deception. As you already know, online dating is extremely popular for creating relationships, but not everyone provides completely truthful information. Researchers report that online dating profiles are full of misinformation and deception. A survey of users of online dating services report that 86 percent of those participating believed that others misrepresented their physical appearance.[61]

The research objective was to compare online profile information with actual observed characteristics. They found that when describing height, weight, and age online as part of a personal profile, 48 percent lied about their height, 60 percent lied about their weight, and 19 percent lied about their age. It was also found that males lied slightly more than females regarding height and weight, but when it came to age women lied more than men.[62] According to the researchers, men tended to overestimate their height, while women mainly underestimated their weight.

Another study by the same researchers found several patterns in those who used deception that were missing from those who were more truthful. For example, those who were more likely to be less than truthful would not use "I" to reference themselves; they would also use indirect adjectives, such as "not boring" instead of "exciting," as well as provide shorter descriptions of themselves.[63]

Given the fact most of us engage in deception at some time, how can it be recognized? The answer seems to involve careful attention to both verbal and nonverbal cues. In addition to nonverbal cues, such as blinking more when a lie is being told or exaggerated facial expressions, other signs of lying sometimes are present in the tone of voice or in the words chosen.[64] When people lie, their pitch often rises, especially if they are highly motivated to lie. Another sign is taking longer than expected to answer a question or describe events. Detection of lying is far from certain; some people are very skillful liars.

Betrayal Another warning sign of a relationship in trouble is betrayal. For example, if you tell a friend a personal secret and especially ask for complete confidentiality, and the friend then spreads the story to others, you have been betrayed. Some common examples of betrayal include extramarital affairs, gossip, and harmful criticism behind someone's back. Deception and betrayal are similar; in fact, they are almost synonymous. The difference is that betrayal violates a confidence and an agreed-on expectation.

Relationships injured by deception and betrayals are often not repairable because of the amount of hurt caused by such breaches of trust. However, situations such as out-of-hand arguments or simple misunderstandings can often be corrected or resolved. In these cases, competent communication can repair and possibly save the relationship.

MAKING CONNECTIONS FOR SUCCESS

Deception in a Relationship

I (Darin) have always been a little concerned about Olivia—she is such a charmer. She told me she was through with Aaron, her old boyfriend. We began sleeping together, spending a couple of nights plus weekends together at each other's places. Then a friend of mine told me that she saw Olivia with her "ex," and it didn't look as if they had parted ways. My friend also said that Olivia and her "ex" appeared to be intensely involved with each other. I saw Olivia today, and she didn't act differently. In fact, she acted as if everything was the same.

Consider the scenario presented above and answer the following questions:

1. What would you do in this situation?

2. What would you tell Darin to do?

3. What does a situation like this do to a relationship?

4. Is there anything that Olivia can do to explain her behavior to Darin?

5. Are there any considerations that Darin should take into account before he jumps to conclusions?

Relationships: Coming Apart or Breaking Up

Most people in relationships at one time or another have their differences or declines as a result of disclosures, lies, or betrayal. Couples can use relationship maintenance behaviors to help them deal with these issues. How partners in the relationship interact with each other during periods of disagreement will lead to a strengthening or deterioration of the relationship. There are no guarantees that a commitment to a relationship at one point in time will result in a lasting relationship at another point in time. When a relationship stops growing and differences begin to emerge, the coming-apart process begins. Some relationships go through some or all of the stages in this process and emerge stronger than before, but when the forces that pull a relationship apart are stronger than the forces that hold it together, the relationship will end.

As they did for the coming-together process, Knapp and Vangelisti described the stages that a relationship goes through when it is coming apart. Similar to the coming-together stages, those of coming apart, according to Knapp and Vangelisti, do not flow necessarily in a sequential order, and it is likely that relationships often move into and out of the different stages. The coming-apart process has five stages: *differentiating, circumscribing, stagnating, avoiding,* and *terminating.*[65]

Differentiating In differentiating, the first stage of coming apart, the differences between the individuals are highlighted and become forces that slow or limit the growth of the relationship. The pair's communication tends to focus on how each differs from the other, and tolerance of these differences decreases. Indeed, differences that were once overlooked or negotiated now become the center of attention, putting stress on the relationship and its existence. Typically, things once described as "ours" now become "mine:" "This is my apartment," "These are my books," and "They are my friends."

Conversations often move from mild disagreement to heated anger: "Do I have to do all the work around here? You don't do a thing." "Why is it that your so-called friends never clean up after themselves?" "I pay the water bill, but you're the one who takes long

When one or both partners become aggressive and/or use hurtful messages, it is a warning sign that the relationship is in trouble. As the frequency of hurtful messages increases, it becomes less likely the relationship can be repaired.

Monkey Business Images/Shutterstock

showers." Conflict begins to overshadow the more positive aspects of the relationship and might lead to abuse of one or both parties in the relationship.

Circumscribing   In the circumscribing stage, information exchange is reduced, and some areas of difference are completely avoided because conversation would only lead to a deepening of the conflict. Comments during this stage might include the following: "I don't want to talk about it." "Can't you see I'm busy?" "Why do you keep bringing up the past?" "Let's just be friends and forget it." Communication loses some of its personal qualities, is less spontaneous, and becomes increasingly superficial as the relationship becomes more strained. Interactions, in their amount and depth of disclosure, resemble those of the initiating and experimenting stages of coming together: "Have you eaten?" "Did I get any calls today?" "I saw Joe, and he said to say hi."

People in the circumscribing stage often conceal their faltering relationship in public. A couple might sit in cold silence and stare stonily into space on their drive to a party. But once they arrive at their destination, they put on their party personalities—they smile, tell jokes, and do not disagree with one another. When they return to the privacy of their car, they resume their cold behavior.

Stagnating   The relationship reaches a standstill at the stagnating stage. The participants avoid interaction and take care to sidestep controversy. Some people believe this is the "boring" stage of a relationship, but they don't do anything about it. Little hope remains for the relationship once it has deteriorated to this stage, yet one of the participants might still want it to be revived.

During stagnation, both verbal and nonverbal communication tend to be thoroughly thought out, and the partners plan what to say, the interactions are stylized and cold. Both parties are apt to reflect unhappiness and act as if each is a stranger to the other.

Often the stagnation stage is relatively brief, but sometimes it is extended because of complications. For example, some people are seriously distressed by the loss of their relationship, even though they know a split is the right decision. Children or others may count on the survival of the relationship, thus the breakup is more difficult. Others may prolong the situation out of fear of additional pain and in hope of getting the relationship back on track, or even in an attempt to punish the other person.

MAKING CONNECTIONS FOR SUCCESS
The Dark Side of Interpersonal Relationships

Most of what we have discussed to this point about entering and maintaining relationships has been more or less positive. Our goal is to discuss the positive aspects of relationships and how to be a successful communicator in interpersonal situations. However, we all know that relationships can at times have a painful and negative side. Consider the following scenario.

Elissa and Josh met in a history course. He was athletic, good looking, and sensitive, and had a great personality. They began dating and appeared to be the perfect couple. Elissa began spending more and more time with Josh and less and less time with her college girlfriends. Elissa felt that was a lot easier than responding to Josh's endless questions about her whereabouts and what she was doing every moment of the day. Elissa's friends noticed a dramatic change in her personality. She seemed to lose interest in the things she loved to do before she met Josh. She became distant and moody—just not herself. Elissa doesn't understand Josh's behavior because she has asked him a thousand times if he loves her and trusts her and he always answers, "Of course I do."

With the scenario above in mind, answer the following questions:

1. What do you think is going on?

2. What do you think happens to communication in an abusive relationship?

3. What are the warning signs someone is in an abusive relationship?

4. Provide examples of verbal abuse.

5. Why is the phrase "If you loved me, you would . . ." a red flag and sign of potential abuse?

6. How has technology increased the opportunities for abuse in relationships?

7. What can you do if you find yourself in an abusive relationship?

Avoiding   Up to this point, participants in the relationship still see each other or share the same living quarters. But physical or emotional distancing and eventual separation mark the fourth stage, the avoiding stage. The basic message is, "I'm not interested in being with you anymore." As far as the participants are concerned, the relationship is over, and they have no interest in reestablishing it.

At times, the interaction in this stage is brief, direct, unfriendly, and even antagonistic: "I really don't care to see you." "Don't call me—we have nothing to discuss." "I'm busy tonight. For that matter, I'm going to be busy for quite some time."

Terminating   The last stage in the breaking up of a relationship occurs when the individuals take the necessary steps to end it. Termination can be early—that is, when the relationship has barely begun—or it can occur after many years. For relationships that break up in the early stages of development, such as initiating or experimenting, the feelings of parting are usually not complex or lasting.

The interaction during this stage is self-centered and seeks to justify the termination: "I need to do something for myself—I've always put more into the relationship than I've gotten out of it." "We just have too many differences that I didn't know existed until now." "I found out we just weren't meant for each other." When both individuals know the relationship is ending, they say good-bye to each other in three ways: in a summary statement; in behaviors signaling the termination or limited contact; and in comments about what the relationship will be like in the future, if there is to be any relationship at all.[66]

Summary statements review the relationship and provide a rationale for its termination: "Although our love used to be very special, we both have changed over the years. We are not the same couple we were when we first met." Ending behaviors reflect new rules of contact: "It would be good for both of us not to see so much of each other." "I wish you would stop coming over all the time." Finally, when the relationship is over, the participants state their preferences for dealing with each other in the future: "I don't want to see you anymore." "We can get together once in a while, but I only want us to be friends and nothing more."

The stages of coming together and coming apart are complex and continuous as we move into, through, and out of relationships. Knapp and Vangelisti acknowledge that not all relationships move through each of the escalating and deescalating stages at the same pace or always in sequential order, but they state most relationships go through the interaction stages systematically and sequentially. They also suggest it is possible for people to skip steps during both the growth process and the deterioration of a relationship. You might have had or heard of relationships that go from the initiating stage—"Hi, my name is . . ."—to "Let's go to your place so that we can get to know each other better." These relationships move from the initiating step right to the intensifying step. Termination may also occur suddenly and without warning in this situation, thus violating or skipping all the steps of coming apart. For example, in *Runaway Bride*, a popular movie in the late 1990s, Julia Roberts portrays a character who falls in love with several different men, but in each case, she leaves them standing at the altar because she does not believe the relationship is right.

Interpersonal Conflict

13.7   **Explain** what interpersonal conflict is, what causes it, why it can be beneficial, and strategies to manage and resolve it.

Conflict, like dialectic tensions in relationships, occurs for a variety of reasons. Most conflicts are actions to block or interfere with others' interests because of incompatibility perceptions.

Conflict, according to communication scholars William Wilmot and Joyce Hocker, "is an expressed struggle between at least two interdependent parties who perceive incompatible goals, scarce resources, and interference from others in achieving their goals."[67] The key terms in the definition are *expressed struggle, interdependent parties, incompatible goals, scarce resources,* and *interference from others.* Suppose you want to go to a dance on Friday evening with several of your friends, but your best friend wants to go to a movie. Both of you explain what you want to do (expressed struggle): You want to go to the dance, neither of you wants to go out without including the other on Friday evening (interdependent parties), you cannot go to both the dance and the movie in the same evening (incompatible goals), neither of you can afford to do both because of time and money (scarce resources), and your other friends will not consider going to the movie (interference). You have incompatible goals, and it seems one person must lose for the other to win.

The word *conflict* almost automatically brings to mind word such as *fight, abuse, aggressiveness, violence, mistreatment, argument, disagreement, quarrel, clash,* and *differences*. None of these words has a positive tone or gives us any reason to believe anything good can come from conflict. Wilmot and Hocker suggest that terms such as *exciting, strengthening, helpful, clarifying, growth producing, creative, courageous, enriching, intimate, opportune,* and *energizing* could also be associated with conflict.[68]

We often exert much energy to avoid conflict, when in fact disagreements and differences of opinion can ultimately lead to compromise and far better solutions for everyone. Conflict plays such a major role in our lives that we need to understand its causes, why it is often destructive, and how we can better manage it or at least control it.

What Causes Conflict?

Conflict occurs on many different levels, in all aspects of our lives, whether in our classes, our university, our communities, our organizations, or our country. Conflict is a natural and normal part of any relationship. Suppose you asked a large number of people to describe the major factor that contributes to conflict in interpersonal relationships. How do you think they would answer? The number one answer you would likely receive is poor or inadequate communication. However, if you asked the same people for the best way to resolve or eliminate conflict, they would more than likely also say communication. Isn't it interesting that communication is cited as both a cause and a solution for resolving conflict? We often attribute the causes for and the resolution of conflict to "communication" and not to us. In other words, we don't take responsibility for conflict but rather blame it on our communication. If we use communication effectively and carefully, we can reduce or at least manage conflict more readily.

Faulty communication is a social factor that can lead to conflict. Individuals communicate in ways that anger or annoy others, even though it might not be the communicator's intention to do so. Have you ever been harshly criticized in a way you believed was unjustified, insensitive, unfair, and not the least bit helpful? If you have, you know this type of perceived criticism leaves you feeling upset, angry, and ready to attack, thus setting the stage for conflict, even though the criticism might not have been a result of incompatible goals.

A faulty attribution, such as errors concerning the causes of others' behaviors, is another social factor that may lead to conflict.[69] When individuals believe their goals or interests have been thwarted, they generally try to determine reasons. Was it poor planning on their part? Was it simply a case of bad luck? Was it a lack of the appropriate resources to reach the goal? Or was it because of someone's intentional interference? If it is concluded that the last-mentioned is the reason, the seeds for

conflict

An expressed struggle between at least two interdependent parties who perceive incompatible goals, scarce resources, and interference from others in achieving their goals.

conflict may be planted, even if the other person actually had nothing to do with the situation.

Another cause of conflict is faulty perceptions and our tendency to perceive our own views as objective and reflective of reality but to perceive others' views as biased or not based in reality. As a result, stereotyping or prejudices create conflicting views by magnifying differences between our views and those of others, especially others whom we believe are different from us. Differences may be magnified for many of us when we confront cultures different from our own.

Finally, personality traits or characteristics can lead to conflict. This is especially true of type A individuals: those who are highly competitive, like to win, are always in a hurry, and are relatively irritable when others interfere with attaining goals. Type A individuals, because of their nature, are more likely to get into conflicts than type B individuals, who are calmer and less irritable about events around them.

What causes conflict? Conflict does not stem solely from incompatible goals. On the contrary, conflict often results from social factors such as long-standing grudges or resentment, the desire for revenge, inaccurate social perceptions, ineffective communication, and similar factors. Although the major cause of conflict may be incompatible goals, the social causes of conflict are also factors to consider.

Does Conflict Have to Be Destructive?

Conflict does *not* have to be destructive. It becomes so when the involved parties are unwilling to negotiate their differences and instead engage in harmful and hurtful tactics—a win-at-any-cost approach. Here are some ways in which conflict can or may be destructive:

- When the resolution of a conflict ends with a winner and a loser
- When individuals act too aggressively, when they withdraw from each other, when they withhold their feelings from each other, or when they accuse each other of causing their problems
- When it prevents people from doing their work or feeling good about themselves
- When it forces people to do things that they do not want to do
- When the outcome is more important than the relationship
- When conflict is a form of bullying and there is a power difference between parties—"the winner takes all"[70]

Of course, not all relationship breakups result from conflict, nor are they all necessarily destructive or harmful. However, when conflict results in the termination of relationships and leaves one or both of the parties feeling foolish, inadequate, or angry, it is usually destructive and hurtful.

MAKING CONNECTIONS FOR SUCCESS

Conflict Online

Conflict can occur just as easily online as it does in face-to-face communication. Some people believe there is a tendency to communicate more forcefully and directly online than in face-to-face interactions. For example, a colleague emails you a political cartoon that belittles your preferred candidate in an election. Your colleague tells you your candidate is an idiot. You send back a political cartoon poking fun at his or her political candidate. Thus, rather than resolving conflicts or differences, the conflicts tend to escalate more readily online. With that in mind, answer the following questions:

1. Why does online conflict occur so easily?
2. What can you do to reduce online conflicts?
3. Create a guide for improving online communication etiquette. What advice would you give others to reduce or prevent online conflicts?

When Is Conflict Beneficial?

Most of us very likely see more disadvantages than benefits in conflict. However, not all conflict is destructive. For example, it is fine to have conflicts over ideas, but it is not acceptable or appropriate to attack someone personally for his or her ideas. It can be beneficial to have disagreements or conflicting views about ideas because of the potential to exchange valuable information or to gain a better understanding of an issue. Here are other potential benefits of conflict:

- It can bring out problems that need to be solved.
- It can bring people together to clarify their goals and look for new ways to do things.
- It can eliminate resentments and help people understand each other.
- It can bring out creativity in solving our differences.
- It can produce acceptable solutions that allow people to live more in harmony with each other.
- It can help people pay attention to other points of view.
- It can bring new life into a relationship and strengthen it.

Constructive conflict is characterized by a we-orientation, cooperation, and flexibility.[71] If possible, it is good to reach a solution agreeable to all. This does not mean we have to feel warm and fuzzy while the differences are worked out, but it does mean that conflicting parties must be willing to negotiate, respect the other party's differences, and cooperate to resolve differences.

Constructive conflict can be frustrating and difficult as well as contentious; it requires competent communicators who are knowledgeable, skillful, sensitive, committed, and ethical in resolving their differences. Many people believe the more they discuss their differences, the more likely they will be to resolve them. Of course, that is possible, but most of the time more communication leads to further difference and disagreements. If the parties who try to resolve differences understand and use conflict management strategies in their communication rather than just more of the same communication, however, they are more likely to reach some agreement and resolution.

What Are Useful Strategies for Conflict Management or Resolution in Interpersonal Relationships?

Because most interpersonal conflicts can be costly in terms of time, stress, energy, and other resources, people experiencing conflict generally choose to resolve their differences as quickly as possible if they can. Of course, in some situations, conflicts are not confronted, and sometimes conflicts go on for an indefinite time; generally speaking, however, these conflicts are not beneficial to a relationship's growth. We need to learn how to deal with conflict in beneficial ways. How we deal with disagreements or conflict can either strengthen a relationship or split it apart. In other words, conflict can be managed well, or it can be managed poorly.

The research literature refers mainly to five options to resolve conflict: *withdrawing, accommodating, forcing, negotiating,* and *collaboration.*[72] Each strategy involves a different outcome, which can be positive, negative, or both in its effect on relationships involved in conflict.

Withdrawing When we choose to avoid further conflict by either psychologically or physically removing ourselves from the situation, we are withdrawing. This can be done by changing the topic, cracking jokes, ignoring, or leaving the situation altogether. Usually, when a withdrawal strategy is used, the conflict is temporarily avoided, but it really doesn't go away. Withdrawal is a temporary escape from the conflict, but both parties know it has not been resolved.

Stonewalling is a powerful form of avoiding conflict.[73] When people exhibit stony silence, refuse to discuss problems, or physically remove themselves from another person who is complaining, disagreeing, or attacking, they are said to be stonewalling. Consider the following discussion between a mother and daughter:

MELISSA: We need to discuss your unwillingness to set a budget. Your use of the credit card is going to bankrupt your father and me.

TIFF: It isn't a problem, and there is nothing to talk about.

MELISSA: We have to talk about it because you are ruining our credit.

TIFF: Get a life; I am not ruining anything. I'll pay you back. [leaves the house]

Tiff is stonewalling by withdrawing from the conflict and claims she has everything under control. She believes discussing her use of the credit card will only intensify the conflict between her and her mother. Her mother is likely becoming frustrated with Tiff's stonewalling, which can also communicate Tiff's disapproval, self-righteousness, indifference, and defensiveness toward her mother.

Research indicates avoidance is frequently used to manage conflict.[74] Many of us want to avoid conflict whenever we can. One research study found that 50 percent of the time, college students used avoiding or withdrawing strategies to keep conflict from escalating.[75] Other research studies found that men use stonewalling more often than women do because of their fear they won't be able to control themselves.[76]

An advantage to withdrawal is that it gives time for one or both of the involved individuals to think about it and to calm down before again trying to deal with the conflict. The disadvantage is that it can create more hostility and ultimately make dealing with the conflict more difficult in the long run. So withdrawal can be a useful strategy, but it is also limited in its ability to truly resolve the conflict.

Accommodating   A person who uses accommodating as a means for managing or resolving conflicts does not assert his or her own needs but rather prefers to go along to get along. This form of conflict management requires one person to yield or give in to another person's needs and desires.[77] The accommodator sets aside his or her concerns in favor of pleasing the other person because holding the relationship together is more important than continuing the conflict. In some situations, when someone accommodates another to resolve a conflict, the accommodating person gives up because the conflict just isn't worth the stress and destruction of the relationship, so in a sense it is a win–win situation. Of course, if one person always accommodates another in a committed relationship, one person is always winning and the other is always losing, and that imbalance can eventually lead to future conflicts.

Accommodation tactics, according to communication scholars Alan Sillars and Bill Wilmot, include giving up or giving in, disengagement, denial of needs, or a desire to get along.[78] When a person *gives up* or *gives in* to the other person, he or she basically says, "Have it your way," "I don't want to fight about this," or "Whatever." If the person *disengages*, he or she says, "I don't care," "I don't want any part of it," or "I don't have the time to fight about this." If the person *denies* his or her own needs, the person says, "I am OK; you go without me" or "I can take care of it, even if I have to stay longer." Finally, if the person is motivated by *desire to get along*, he or she says, "It's more important to work together than it is for me to get what I want" or "I am unhappy and miserable when we fight. Let's let this go and start over again. I don't even know why we are fighting."

Forcing   Forcing is a strategy where one person has power and dominance over another. It can result in aggression and could include threats, criticisms, hostile remarks, jokes, ridicule, sarcasm, intimidation, fault finding, coercion, or manipulation. Extreme cases of forcing include date rape, child abuse, battering, bullying,[79] and sexual harassment. This is a lose–lose situation. The person with the power claims victory, and the other person loses. However, in this situation, the competition is unfair because one individual has more control and power over the other, which ensures a victory regardless of the virtue of the other person's position.

Of course, on occasion the dominance of one person could serve the relationship, as in an emergency situation when a decision must be quickly made. However, the essence of force is to pressure others to agree with something so we get what we want. The more force we use to get others to do what we want or to agree with us, the more likely it is that resentment will increase, leading to more destructive types of conflicts.

Negotiating Negotiating usually involves a give-and-take process and leads to each party having some satisfaction and some dissatisfaction with the outcome. In other words, "Give a little and get a little." Some people interpret this to be a lose–lose style of conflict management. Compromise only truly works if there is shared power because if one of the parties is perceived as powerless, there is no compelling need to compromise.[80]

Many of us are led to believe compromise or negotiation is a good way for both parties in a conflict to resolve their differences. We are told it is fair because it means both parties win something and both lose something. Thus compromise appears on the surface to be a reasonable approach to conflict, although it has potential problems. The most obvious problem is that the quality of the solution might be reduced. This is especially true if one of the parties in the conflict actually had a better solution that had to be compromised to reach agreement. Compromise can become an easy way out and might prevent creative new solutions from emerging. In addition, the compromise approach is often not the first choice in personal relationships because it frequently requires one or both parties to give in or give up on what they want.

Despite the negative aspects of negotiating or compromising, it might be the only possible way to approach a conflict. This is most likely true when the parties involved have equal power, if no other alternative is available, if the outcome is not critical, if essential values are not undermined, or if the settlement is only temporary until a better one can be found.

Collaboration Collaboration is a strategy of conflict management that requires cooperation and mutual respect. It usually involves a problem-solving approach and addresses all concerns of both parties to arrive at a mutually satisfying solution. It is a "we" rather than a "me" approach to negotiation. It might require extra effort by both parties because more resources and considerations of new options that meet the approval of both parties might be needed.

For collaboration to work as a strategy, both parties must recognize a conflict exists, and they must want to find creative ways to resolve their differences. When both parties recognize a conflict, they usually engage in some sort of confrontation, which is the opposite of avoidance. Degrees of confrontation range from the very violent (often depicted in the media) to the respectful. For collaboration to be successful, both parties must be willing to resolve their differences, treat each other as equals, be honest and open in their differences, be empathetic toward each other, and be willing to listen to each other's points of view.

The collaboration strategy is usually considered a win–win situation for both sides in the conflict. Both sides believe they have accomplished or gained something from the solution because of their willingness to listen to each other concerning the issues. In addition, when both parties believe they have the opportunity to voice their opinions and they have agreed in good faith to settle the dispute, it truly is a win–win situation. The collaboration strategy to manage conflict is the best strategy for a relationship because it shows that each party cares about the other's well-being and interests. According to Wilmot and Hocker, collaborating, as a conflict management style, produces consistently positive outcomes that leave the participants satisfied with their decisions, the process, and the growth in their interpersonal relationship.[81]

Many scholars agree conflict is inevitable in all relationships and it need not be destructive. It often produces stronger and more durable relationships. Conflict in itself should be considered neither negative nor destructive, but a natural part of any relationship.

Relational Repair Strategies

For situations when both parties want to preserve the relationship, Steve Duck, a communication scholar, suggests the following tactics for repairing a damaged relationship between couples:

- Engage in more open and honest communication and exhibit a willingness to listen to the other person with an open mind.
- Be willing to bring out the other person's positive side.
- Evaluate the potential rewards and costs for keeping the relationship together versus the rewards and costs for changing or ending it.
- Seek out the support of others to help keep the relationship together.
- Both parties must be willing to focus on the positive aspects of their relationship.
- Both parties must be willing to reinterpret the other's behaviors as positive and well intentioned.
- Both parties have to be willing to reduce negativity and keep a balanced perspective.[82]

Repairing relationships requires cooperation and mutual agreement; both parties must want to preserve the relationship. Relationship repair also requires effective interpersonal communication.

Improving Communication Competence in Relationships

13.8 **Apply** effective interpersonal communication skills and competencies in personal and professional relationships.

The goal of this text is to encourage readers to become competent communicators who can connect with others and develop relationships, whether personal or professional. Communication scholars Brant Burleson and Wendy Samter consider the following interpersonal skills important in developing and maintaining relationships: *conversational skill* (the ability to initiate, maintain, and terminate enjoyable casual conversations), *referential skill* (the ability to convey information clearly and unambiguously), *ego supportive skill* (the ability to make another person feel good about him- or herself), *comforting skill* (the ability to make others feel better when depressed, sad, or upset), *persuasive skill* (the ability to sway people to modify their thoughts and behaviors), *narrative skill* (the ability to entertain through jokes, gossip, stories, and the like), and *regulations* (the ability to help someone who has violated a social custom to fix the mistake effectively).[83] How would you rate yourself on each of the above communication skills? Most of us would likely rate ourselves as fairly good at most with room for improvement in each of them.

In the remainder of this chapter, we will provide suggestions to help you become a more competent communicator. Effective communicators:

1. Address issues clearly and try to avoid ambiguous or abstract statements.
2. Are likely to treat others with respect and therefore would not deliberately yell abuses or throw temper tantrums.
3. Know that praise, making the other person feel special, and telling that person what he or she wants to hear will most likely produce desired responses.[84]

At first glance, these characteristics make a lot of sense. However, they are characterized by shades of gray. Each of us can probably think of times when being a little abstract or ambiguous was better than being too clear or direct in our communication. In certain situations, getting angry or throwing a tantrum might be appropriate to get across a point. You can probably also think of situations in which too much praise or too much agreement can lead to mistrust. Interpersonal situations often require a variety of communication strategies, some of which may violate expected norms. Although we do not endorse unethical behaviors, disrespect, or rudeness, some situations demand unusual strategies.

The following section offers a variety of behaviors and actions to improve interpersonal communication.

Establish Supportive and Caring Relationships

Establishing supportive and caring relationships is important to our well-being, and this process is generally easier when communication is both positive and supportive.[85] Eric Simon and Leslie Baxter, communication scholars, describe the following positive strategies for romantic exchanges:

1. **Act** cheerful and positive when talking to the other.
2. **Do** favors for the other or help with tasks.
3. **Initiate** celebrations of special events from your shared past, such as the first time you met.
4. **Do** things to surprise the other person.
5. **Suggest** that you go out to eat together at a favorite or special restaurant.
6. **Create** a romantic environment, perhaps with candlelight and flowers.
7. **Give** the other person items of sentimental value, such as gifts or cards.
8. **Suggest** ways to spend time doing things together.[86]

Assurances include the following verbal and nonverbal actions:

1. **Physically** display affection through kisses and hugs.
2. **Express** aloud to the other person what it would be like without him or her.
3. **Reminisce** aloud with the other about good times you had together in the past.
4. **Say** "I love you."
5. **Express** long-term commitment to the relationship.
6. **Act** playfully toward the other person.[87]

Research findings suggest that engaging in behaviors such as these increases relationship commitment and satisfaction. However, Simon and Baxter found females were more likely than males to report use of assurance and romance strategies, which suggests that females tend to undertake more relationship maintenance activity than do their male partners.[88]

Nurture a Supportive Environment

Positive and supportive communication occurs in caring, open, flexible, warm, animated, and receptive environments. In such environments, communication is constructive and centers on the individuals and their relationship. Following are

Positive and supportive communication environments are caring, open, flexible, warm, animated, and receptive.

Blend Images/Shutterstock

some descriptions of how people feel when constructive communication is at the center of the relationship.[89] One of the most effective and constructive means of demonstrating care and support for someone is to invite more communication.

Invite More Communication

Many of us listen to others express their feelings and then immediately express our own. This gives the impression we don't even acknowledge the other's existence, let alone what he or she has said. In contrast, skilled and caring communicators do not usually respond immediately with ideas, judgments, or feelings or express their own views. Instead, they invite others to express more of their thoughts by responding with noncommittal responses such as these:

> Interesting.
> Uh-huh.
> You did, huh?
> I see.
> Oh.
> Really?

Or they might be more direct in asking the other person to continue, saying, for example,

> That's interesting. Go on.
> Tell me about it.
> Let's discuss it.
> Tell me everything.
> I understand. What else happened?

Such invitations to talk can contribute much to the development of a meaningful relationship. The willingness to listen and reserve judgment creates a positive and supportive environment that, in effect, tells people they are valuable, they are loved, and they have control over their own behavior.

> SUMMARY

Connecting with Others via Interpersonal Communication

13.1 **Explain** what it means to connect with others through interpersonal communication.

- Connecting with others and forming relationships are what interpersonal communication is all about.
- Interpersonal communication is creating and sharing meaning between persons who are in a relationship.
- Interpersonal communication allows relationships to become established and to grow, satisfying our social needs.

Interpersonal Communication Competence

13.2 **Characterize** the importance of interpersonal communication competence.

Competent communicators recognize they will not always communicate perfectly in every situation. They adapt and know when to be empathic and comforting; know when to speak out aggressively and when to be reserved and more deferential; understand values, beliefs, attitudes, and feelings; know how to self-monitor; and recognize it is a two-way responsibility for effective interactions.

Theories of Interpersonal Communication

13.3 **Compare and contrast** six theories related to relationships and interpersonal communication.

- *Uncertainty reduction theory* asserts that when people meet, they often seek to reduce uncertainty about each other.
- *Uncertainty management theory* takes into account the different ways people respond both psychologically and communicatively to uncertainty.
- *Social penetration theory* provides a view of how people connect with each other and how their communication moves from small talk to more intimate and self-revealing talk.

- *Social exchange theory* suggests that if the *benefits* gained in a relationship are greater than any potential *costs*, then we likely would regard the relationship positively.
- *Interpersonal needs theory* consists of three needs: affection, inclusion, and control.
- *Dialectical theory* suggests that relationships, as well as individuals, confront many tensions that push and pull them in many different directions at the same time.

Self-Disclosure in Relationships

13.4 **Outline** the roles of self-disclosure, privacy, gender, culture, and rhetorical sensitivity in interpersonal relationships.

- Relationships are built on interaction. The more sincere, honest, and open the interactions, the stronger and more lasting the relationship is likely to be.
- We self-disclose for a variety of different reasons: for others to better understand who we are, to gain sympathy, to see what others think, to gain trust, or to connect with others and establish relationships.
- There are many reasons for withholding information, but it is usually to protect others, to avoid a potentially negative reaction, or to avoid hurting others or ourselves.
- Just as we control and protect access to our physical self—for example, how close we allow others to come to us—we also control and protect our privacy boundaries.
- Women are more likely to talk about their relationships and disclose a deeper level of intimacy, but men often do not center their talk on relational closeness.
- In general, people from any cultural background tend to follow similar patterns of self-disclosure.
- *Rhetorical sensitivity* is an alternative form of communication that can be applied to situations in which wide-open self-disclosure could be harmful.

Relationship Formation

13.5 **Identify** the stages of relationship development and growth.

How and why a relationship develops may depend on interpersonal attraction and how the people manage the stages of coming together or growth of the relationship.

- Interpersonal relationships depend on interpersonal attraction.
- *Interpersonal attraction* is the desire to interact with someone and is based on physical attraction, personality, rewards, proximity, or similarities.

- Coming together includes the following stages: initiating, experimenting, intensifying, integrating, and bonding.
- Relational maintenance behaviors or strategies help to sustain relationships so they grow and thrive. These behaviors include positivity, openness, assurances, blending social networks, and sharing tasks.

Relationship Dissolution

13.6 **Identify** the stages of relationship deterioration and dissolution.

Not every relationship is destined to last a lifetime. The way both parties handle a relationship's dissolution can affect the well-being of both.

- Warning signs that a relationship is in trouble include aggressive behavior, lies, and betrayal.
- The coming-apart process has five stages—differentiating, circumscribing, stagnating, avoiding, and terminating—according to Mark Knapp and Anita Vangelisti.

Interpersonal Conflict

13.7 **Explain** what interpersonal conflict is, what causes it, why it can be beneficial, and strategies to manage and resolve it.

Conflict is an expressed struggle between at least two interdependent parties who perceive incompatible goals, scarce resources, and interference from others. Conflict can occur on many different levels in a variety of situations and contexts.

- The number one cause of most conflicts is inadequate communication.
- Conflict does not have to be destructive.
- Conflict can be beneficial and lead to stronger and better relationships.
- Each conflict resolution strategy involves different outcomes, which can be either positive or negative in their effects on relationships. In the withdrawal strategy, we choose to avoid further conflict. In the accommodating strategy, we do not assert our own needs but prefer to go along. In the forcing strategy, one person has power and dominance over another person. Negotiating is a give-and-take process and can lead to each party's having some satisfaction and some dissatisfaction with the outcome. Collaboration requires cooperation and mutual respect.
- To help restore or possibly save a relationship, competent communicators know how to use repair strategies and effective interpersonal communication.

Improving Communication Competence in Relationships

13.8 **Apply** effective interpersonal communication skills and competencies in personal and professional relationships.

Interpersonal skills are important in developing and maintaining relationships. They include: *conversational skill* (the ability to initiate, maintain, and terminate enjoyable casual conversations), *referential skill* (the ability to convey information clearly and unambiguously), *ego supportive skill* (the ability to make another person feel good about him- or herself), *comforting skill* (the ability to make others feel better when depressed, sad, or upset), *persuasive skill* (the ability to sway people to modify their thoughts and behaviors), *narrative skill* (the ability to entertain through jokes, gossip, stories, and the like), and *regulations* (the ability to help someone who has violated a social custom to fix the mistake effectively).

- A supportive and caring relationship is important to our well-being; the process is generally easier when communication is both positive and supportive.

- In a supportive environment, communication between individuals usually reflects caring, openness, flexibility, warmth, animation, and receptivity.

- The best way to develop and maintain relationships is to invite more effective communication.

⟩ DISCUSSION STARTERS ────────────

1. Discuss the six interpersonal communication theories and decide which best explains our need to know others and to form relationships.

2. What are some inappropriate communicative behaviors you have observed in interpersonal situations? Why do you think these behaviors occur? Why did these behaviors bother you?

3. Explain the difference between being rhetorically sensitive and being honest in self-disclosure.

4. Develop a set of rules you think should be applied when self-disclosing personal information to others through social media.

5. In your opinion, what communication behaviors play the strongest role in the development of relationships? Explain.

6. In relationship breakups you have had, were there coming-apart stages similar to what Knapp and Vangelisti presented? How were they similar and how were they different?

7. What advice would you give someone who wanted to improve his or her interpersonal communication?

CONNECTING THROUGH PARTICIPATING IN GROUPS AND TEAMS

Robert Kneschke/Fotolia

Working in groups requires effective communication, organization, and leadership as well as cooperation among members to reach the group's goals.

→ CHAPTER OUTLINE AND LEARNING OBJECTIVES

Small-Group Communication: Making the Connection to Our Everyday Lives

14.1 **Understand** the differences between a group and a team, and their roles in our everyday lives.

Purposes and Types of Groups

14.2 **Distinguish** among different types of groups—both face-to-face and on social media.

Characteristics of Small Groups

14.3 **Describe** the characteristics of small groups.

Establishing a Group Culture

14.4 **Explain** how a group's culture, size, and norms affect group communication.

Leadership

14.5 **Understand** the difference between leadership and leaders and the various leadership styles and behaviors they exhibit.

Ethical Behavior in Group Communication

14.6 **Describe** the role of ethics in small-group communication.

Member Participation

14.7 **Differentiate** among the roles of group members and explain their various contributions.

Managing Group Conflict

14.8 **Describe** conflict, its impacts, and the conflict management strategies that can manage it.

Problem Solving and Decision Making

14.9 **Explain** the reflective thinking process and functional communication theory.

Working in Groups or Teams: Advantages and Disadvantages

14.10 **Explain** the advantages and disadvantages of participating in groups and how to overcome the disadvantages.

Evaluating Small-Group Performance

14.11 **Describe** the role of evaluation in small-group performance.

MAKING EVERYDAY CONNECTIONS

Amy and her classmates Mark, Sally, and Bethany are spending an evening in the library, working on a group project for their management class. Another group member, Susan, commutes to campus and has a young child at home. Since the group is meeting late at night, Susan joins the group meeting via Skype. Amy prepared an agenda and attempts to keep the group focused. Bethany is drifting in and out of paying attention, checking her texts with her boyfriend. About 10 minutes into the meeting, Susan begins to have trouble hearing what the other group members are saying because of her connection via Skype. Whenever Susan tries to say something, only half of what she says comes through clearly. Mark becomes very frustrated because he has to repeat himself. Annoyed, Sally opens her Facebook page and begins instant messaging with a few friends about other topics. Amy struggles to keep the group on task. Because of the problems with Skype, Amy tells Susan she will fill her in on what the group has accomplished tomorrow in class. Amy continues the meeting. She asks specific questions of Bethany and Sally to gauge their opinions and pull them into the conversation. Bethany puts her phone away and Sally closes her Facebook page. The group works together for the next hour. After they finish, Amy, Bethany, Mark, and Sally head toward home but decide to stop for a late-night snack. They really enjoy each other's company and find that they have many things in common.

When she was a student, Dana hated meetings because she always found them to be such a waste of time. She now works as an account executive for DST, a large international financial and healthcare company, in Kansas City. A typical day for her begins at 7:30 a.m. taking her two boys to school and then arriving at work around 8:00 a.m. Most days for Dana start with a web conference with her counterparts in Tokyo, Milan, New York, and Chicago to discuss the implementation and development of a survey for a major international client. At 9:30 a.m., she meets with her team to discuss the design of the survey. At 11:00, she is off to meet with the production staff of a local client to discuss the results of another survey; at noon, she has a luncheon meeting with members of the Kansas City Community Foundation to plan a fundraiser for a new soccer field for kids. After dinner, at 7:30 p.m., she will join the neighborhood association, which is meeting to discuss the neighborhood summer picnic. Meetings, meetings, meetings....

QUESTIONS TO THINK ABOUT

1. What are some of Amy's strengths and weaknesses as a leader?

2. Aside from the obvious problems with Skype detailed above, what other challenges might social media pose when a group tries to accomplish its task?

3. Describe the outcomes, whether positive or negative, regarding meetings that you participated in during the past year.

4. What did you learn about group interaction and groups in general from the above scenario?

Employment and hiring data clearly indicate that teamwork and working in groups are hiring prerequisites and necessary abilities for a successful career with most organizations. Many variables contribute to a group's success or failure. Prior success cannot guarantee a group will produce similarly successful results. Nonetheless, understanding key principles and factors, along with improving your competencies as a group member or group leader, can increase the chances for achieving personal satisfaction and group success.

This chapter explains how group members communicate, the difference between a small group and work team, the purposes and types of groups, their defining characteristics, the difference between leadership and a leader of a group or team, the importance of ethical behavior in groups, member participation roles, conflict management for groups, problem-solving and decision-making stategies, the advantages and disadvantages of groups, and group performance evaluation.

Small-Group Communication: Making the Connection to Our Everyday Lives

14.1 **Understand** the differences between a group and a team, and their roles in our everyday lives.

Small-group communication requires a variety of communication competencies, including the ability to ask effective questions, listen, deal with interpersonal relationships, resolve conflicts, and present ideas clearly. In addition, constructive group communication requires that group members respect one another, provide credible information, support each other, foster a positive climate, challenge each other's ideas and positions, persuade each other, and hold high ethical standards.

What a Group Is

For our purposes, we define a **group** as a collection of individuals who influence one another, have a common purpose, take on roles, are interdependent, and interact. If any element is missing, what exists is a collection of independent people, not a group. A group of students standing at a corner waiting for a bus, for example, meets only some criteria of a group. They have a common purpose (transportation), they may interact, and they may make an impression on one another. Nevertheless, they do not constitute a group according to our definition because they are not interdependent and they do not take on roles. They do share certain basic goals, such as getting to a destination safely. They don't expect to interact in the future, however, and usually don't perceive themselves as part of a group—unless some type of emergency occurs, which will change their status radically.

Small-group communication involves the exchange of information among a relatively small number of people, ideally five to seven, who have a common purpose, such as solving a problem, making a decision, or sharing information. Effective group communication requires an honest, flexible, assertive, enthusiastic, and tolerant communication style. Effective group members recognize the importance of all group members' input and ensure the opportunity for everyone to participate. They are willing not only to listen to others but also to discuss ideas and issues, whether they agree or disagree with them.

group
A collection of individuals who influence one another, have a common purpose, take on roles, are interdependent, and interact together.

(left) Elena Rostunova/Shutterstock;
(right) Wavebreakmedia/Shutterstock

The photo on the left shows a collection of people who happen to be in the same place at the same time; they do not make up a group. The photo on the right shows a group in which the members interact with one another and share common goals and outcomes. Moreover, they feel they are, in fact, part of a group or team.

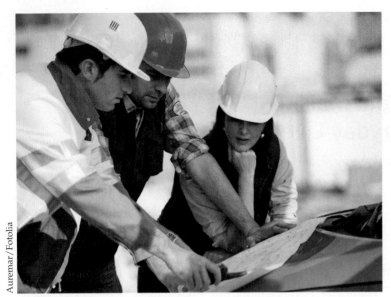

The work team is ideally suited for solving workplace problems. Each person brings his or her own special expertise to the project or goal and coordinates efforts with others on a common solution.

work team

A special form of group characterized by a close-knit relationship among people with different and complementary abilities and by a strong sense of identity.

What a Work Team Is

Because groups known as work teams are so common in our society and in the classroom, we focus on them here. Many scholars who study groups believe a distinction exists between group involvement and team involvement.[1] A **work team** is a special form of group, characterized by close-knit relationships among people with different and complementary abilities and by a strong sense of identity. Similar to groups, work teams involve interaction, interdependence, common goals, personality, commitment, cohesiveness, and rules. Work teams do differ from groups, however, in three ways:

1. Work teams are more likely to consist of people with diverse abilities. For example, a surgical team might include several surgeons, an anesthesiologist, and a number of nurses, each contributing a different skill or perspective to the operation. Both a group and a work team consist of several people, each working toward the common goal of the group, whereas work teams also have individuals with a specialization in, or a different perspective on, a common situation. For example, players on a football team usually have specific specialties or roles that help contribute to the team's overall effectiveness.

2. Work teams usually develop more interdependence. A sports team, for example, usually cannot succeed unless all the players believe they are part of a unit, whereas in a problem-solving group, members might work independently, only coming together to present and discuss each other's solutions. They might eventually see themselves as a unit, or not, depending on the group's communication and cohesiveness, but this wouldn't be necessary to the group's overall success.

3. Members of work teams have a high degree of group identity and are more likely to identify themselves as team members than as individuals who happen to be on a team.[2]

Thus, all teams consist of groups, but not all groups are teams.

MAKING CONNECTIONS FOR SUCCESS

Team Building a YouTube Video

Whether you are a group of students or a group of employees, team building and work teams are going to be part of your life. Teams are built in many ways, but what we do know is that to have a successful work team, *everyone* on the team must have a role and participate, and the team must have some structure to function effectively.

Your instructor will assign students in your class to small groups of five to seven students to make a creative and innovative YouTube video about a communication concept. The task of your group is to create a video that illustrates the concept in an innovative and creative way. It is important for everyone in the group to participate both in the creation of the video and its presentation to the class. With that in mind, answer the following questions:

1. What would be your initial reaction to this assignment?
2. How would you organize the group so that it can complete the assigned task?
3. What skills do you think are needed for the group to complete the assigned task successfully?
4. What would an outside observer see as the strengths and weaknesses of the group?
5. Should the group become a work team and, if so, what would make it a work team rather than a group?

Purposes and Types of Groups

 14.2 **Distinguish** among different types of groups—both face-to-face and on social media.

It is important to understand the types of groups and why they are formed. Small groups fall into one of two major categories: *primary* and *secondary*. Each serves different human needs, but characteristics of each are found in almost every group in which we participate.

Primary Groups

Primary groups focus on social or interpersonal relationships among members and exist primarily to satisfy what are labeled primary needs, such as those we discussed in terms of interpersonal communication: the need for inclusion (belonging) and affection (esteem, likeability, love). Primary groups are usually long term and include family; roommates; friends who meet to socialize; coworkers sharing time off together; and other groups of friends who might share vacations, multiplayer video games, and so on. The groups might at times make decisions, solve problems, or take on a particular task, but their main purpose is to socialize, support one another, chat about a variety of topics, let off steam, and enjoy each other's company.

Primary groups are at the heart of interpersonal communication and are important to understanding small-group communication in general.[3] The main purposes of the primary group are member enjoyment and companionship and support among members. Primary groups are not the main focus of this chapter; typically, primary groups are studied in sociology, psychology, and interpersonal communication courses.

primary group
A group that focuses on social and interpersonal relationships.

Secondary Groups

Secondary groups are the main focus of this chapter and exist to accomplish tasks or achieve goals. They are formed for the purpose of doing work, such as completing a class assignment, solving a problem, or making a decision. Members join together to exert power over their situation and others. The main reason for secondary groups is to get something done, but they can also help members achieve their primary needs for socialization and affection. Secondary groups include a variety of types of groups: decision making, problem solving, committees, learning and information sharing, and therapy or personal growth.[4]

secondary group
A group that exists to accomplish tasks or achieve goals.

People come together in groups to *make decisions* on issues such as deciding what to do for homecoming decorations, where to hold a dance, which play to stage, or which computer is the most practical for a department's needs. It is not unusual for groups to vote on such issues to determine the decision. Voting is done especially when no clear agreement is reached about which is the most acceptable option. When voting, groups usually accept the majority's position. Discussing alternatives with others helps people decide which choice is the best not only for them but for the group as a whole. In addition, when everyone in the group participates in the decision-making process, all are more likely to accept the final outcome and help carry it out. Most of us resent being told what to do; we are more tolerant of a decision if we help to shape it.

Small groups can also excel at *solving problems*. People form problem-solving groups in almost every imaginable context: in the workplace, in government, in school, and sometimes at home. The problems they attempt to solve include how to improve health care, how to make a better product, how to perform a task more effectively or efficiently, how to stop violence, how to resolve the crime problem on campus, how to improve the image of fraternities on campus, and how to share computer time with siblings.

As you can see, groups serve a variety of purposes and often multiple purposes at the same time. For example, a group can solve problems while simultaneously functioning as a learning, social, cathartic, or therapeutic outlet for its members. It was customary in the early and middle years of the 20th century for most people to work relatively independently of one another. Even in large organizations, people had individual responsibilities and coordinated with others only when necessary.

Social Media Groups

Social media are changing the way we share information and work in groups, so face-to-face interactions are not always necessary. With the introduction of Skype, FaceTime, and a variety of other social media, it is possible to carry on group communication as if you were face-to-face with others who may be in a variety of different locations. As you know, both text and voice communication can take place online in groups. Such methods or approaches can be effective when something has to be decided quickly and it is not possible to gather everyone together at the same time. This form of communication is referred to as *asynchronous* communication, which means that message responses have slight or prolonged time delays and participants must alternate sending and receiving messages. Another drawback is that nonverbal communication, such as facial and body expressions—and, in the case of texting, vocal expression—is limited.

The number of nonverbal and verbal cues allowed by a medium determines its richness. For example, face-to-face interactions would be the richest because they provide for a wide range of both verbal and nonverbal cues to convey meaning and make interpretation of the received messages easier. This does not mean that online group interactions will necessarily lead to misunderstandings, but it does mean that misunderstandings are more likely to occur during online texting interactions than during teleconferencing, videoconferencing, or face-to-face interactions.

Synchronous communication occurs when the interaction is face-to-face or when the interaction is in real time, and messages are sent and received at once. Even though some online interactions, such as Skype and FaceTime, are close to real time, they may contain some delay, and participants may take turns being sender and receiver.

While asynchronous online interaction can be beneficial, it can also create some distinct challenges, especially when instant messaging is used. One study found that instant messages can provide social support similar to that of face-to-face or phone interactions, but the feeling of disconnect from each other seems more predominant.[5] The disconnected feeling, according to the researchers, isn't so much the lack of nonverbal communication but rather the result of multitasking. That is, those who are interacting are also doing a variety of other activities, such as having multiple instant messaging windows open or browsing the Internet.

As technologies continue to improve, the notion that face-to-face interaction is the richest in terms of quality and influence may not hold true. Research that compares various forms of interaction finds "face-to-face conversations may not always be the rich, deep, and inherently superior means of communication."[6]

Whenever technology is used, it increases the chances for misunderstanding; thus, we need to carefully consider the messages we craft and carefully interpret the ones we receive to keep misunderstandings to a minimum. Several factors must be considered when comparing online communication to other forms of group interaction. Each form has its distinct advantages and disadvantages; no one form is necessarily better than any other. Many differences in online versus face-to-face communication are attributed to the comfort level of those who use it. Those who have grown up with social media are generally more able to adapt to online communication than are those who haven't.[7]

Today more and more group interaction occurs via social media, where a group in one location can easily interact with other groups in multiple locations throughout the world.

Entering and Participating in an Online Group

It's your turn to either join or create your own online group, if you haven't already done so. Those of you who already participate in an international online group may skip the following and proceed to the questions listed. For those of you who aren't in an online group, one possible place to start is www.groups.yahoo.com. Groups can be found for almost everything and anything, or you can create your own group. You will need to participate in an online group to answer the questions that follow. It is easy to connect with people who share your interests to discuss sports, health, relationships, school, and news and to communicate with a variety of individuals.

1. How do interactions differ when communicating online versus communicating in face-to-face groups?
2. How many and in what types of online groups do you participate?
3. What are the interesting and exciting aspects of the online group? How are they more interesting and exciting than face-to-face groups?
4. How can group members help to establish and uphold online group rules?
5. What are some problems you have encountered in online groups, and how have you dealt with them?

Characteristics of Small Groups

14.3 **Describe** the characteristics of small groups.

Small-group characteristics include *interdependence, commitment, cohesiveness*, and the *gender makeup* that give each group its uniqueness. These characteristics also help to determine who will join a group, how well the group functions and achieves its goals, and how members interact.

Interdependence

Probably the most essential characteristic of a small group is **interdependence**—the fact that group members are mutually dependent. Interdependence is reflected in all the other group characteristics; without it there would be no group. Interdependence is built on each member's willingness to subordinate his or her individual desires and goals to accomplish the group's goal.

interdependence
Mutual dependence of group members on one another.

Groups function best and are most satisfying for their members when each individual recognizes and respects the crucial role interdependence plays in group processes. A group's success depends on each member's cooperation, accountability, and willingness to work toward a common goal.

Commitment

Another important characteristic of a group is commitment—to the task, to the group, and to the other individuals in the group. **Commitment** is the desire of group members to work together to complete their task to the satisfaction of the entire group. Members' commitment often stems from interpersonal attraction to others who seem to have similar interests; commonality of attitudes, beliefs, and values; the fulfillment of interpersonal needs; and the rewards the group can offer. A massive study by the Gallup Organization of over 1.4 million workers in 66 countries found that "trusting that one's coworkers share a commitment to quality is a key to great...performance."[8] Commitment is essential to group success. It is also essential because, without it, groups perform as individuals, but with it, they become a powerful unit of collective performance.[9]

commitment
The desire of group members to work together to complete a task to the satisfaction of the entire group.

Commitment is important to a group's effectiveness and ultimate success. How often have you been involved with other students doing a group assignment in which one or two members did most, if not all, of the work and the others did little or nothing? Those who do little or nothing not only lack commitment; they also make group work frustrating for those who are committed to doing the work. For a group to be truly effective, all members must be committed to each other and to the successful completion of the assigned task.

Cohesiveness

cohesiveness

The attraction that group members feel for each other and their willingness to stick together; a form of loyalty.

As an extension of commitment, **cohesiveness** refers to the attraction group members feel for one another and their willingness to stick together. Consider two groups. In the first, members truly like one another; strongly desire to achieve the goals that the group seeks; and believe they could not find another better, more satisfactory group. In the second, the opposite is true: Members don't care for one another; they do not share common goals; and actively seek other, more rewarding groups. Which group would exert a stronger pull on its members? The answer should be obvious: the first. The rewards for being in the first group outweigh those of leaving the group. Cohesiveness is based on each member's need to remain in the group and the group's ability to provide members with rewards, making it worthwhile to give time and energy to the group. In a sense, cohesiveness is a form of loyalty or commitment.

Cohesiveness in a group does not automatically ensure success, and when loyalty is too strong, it can create problems. It can lead to conformity or unwillingness to change an unsuccessful decision or policy. Cohesiveness is a positive force when it attracts members of the group toward one another and increases effective group interaction, but it becomes a negative influence if group members "go along simply to get along" or lose the ability to question group decisions. For example, you may be a member of a club, sorority, fraternity, or team where some members cheated or used illegal drugs, but no one calls them out because of loyalty to the organization, even though members' actions could ultimately destroy the organization's reputation.

Gender Differences in Group Behavior

The differences between the way individuals display masculine behaviors and feminine behaviors in groups are not always clear, and the results of research are not always accurate or fair to one gender or the other. Much of the research examining feminine and masculine traits compares averages. Thus, specific individual behaviors are usually not accounted for, leaving only averages for our consideration.

Research related to biological sex shows that groups consisting of both males and females are more likely to be dominated by males talking than by females talking. Males on average tend to demonstrate more task-related behavior than do females; that is, males tend to be more goal oriented than females and males can be more impatient about moving on to the next issue or problem. Females tend to offer positive responses to others' comments and, in general, express their personal opinions more readily than males. Males are more likely to have greater objectivity in their comments than are females.[10]

Because of stereotypical beliefs, females are sometimes perceived as less competent than males in solving problems or making decisions. However, researchers have found little, if any, difference between the problem-solving abilities of males and females. The research does suggest that men appear to be better than women at certain kinds of problem-solving tasks, such as technical or mechanical issues, but that difference is reduced or eliminated when males and females work together and when all are highly motivated to solve the problem.[11]

When groups compete, it appears that, on average, females cooperate with their opponents more than males do. Females are more likely to share resources with their opponents and are interested in fairness more than in winning. Males, on average, are more willing than females to engage in aggressive behavior and gain advantage through deception and deceit. In addition, males are more likely to be antisocial, using revenge and verbal aggression, whereas females tend to choose socially acceptable behavior, such as reasoning and understanding, to resolve conflict.[12]

MAKING CONNECTIONS FOR SUCCESS
Gender and Groups

Do males and females really live in two separate worlds? John Gray discussed gender differences in his two books *Men Are from Mars, Women Are from Venus* and *Why Mars and Venus Collide*. Gray's popular books claimed that males and females differ not only in what they think but also in how they communicate. In mixed-sex groups, Gray claimed, males' speech is mainly task oriented or instrumental, such as giving information, opinions, and suggestions. They tend to talk more, tell more jokes, and offer more solutions. Conversely, females are generally more supportive and facilitative in their communication. They agree, express interest in what others say, and encourage others' participation. Females also share feelings, display interest in other group members, and listen intently to them.

1. On the basis of your experiences in groups, do you find the above generalization to be an accurate description of how males and females communicate in groups? Explain.

2. Why is Gray's analysis of males and females participating in groups too simplistic?

3. How can males and females adjust their communication styles to be more effective within groups?

When groups are small, females prefer to work with other females, whereas most males don't seem to have a preference. When comparing the research on males and females based on gender rather than biological sex, we are beginning to find that differences are based less on biological sex than on traits that have traditionally been considered "masculine" and "feminine." That is, individuals who have "masculine" traits, whether they are male or female, are more likely to be competitive and attempt to dominate and control interactions. While these traits lead to obtaining the group's goal, they can also lead to dissatisfaction among group members and reduce the amount of interaction by some members who are intimidated by the controlling members. Those with "feminine" traits—of either sex—are less likely to display those behaviors of their "masculine" counterparts and may be seen as weak, lacking in control, and trying to satisfy everyone while accomplishing little.[13] It is important that both "masculine" and "feminine" traits be balanced in order to reach the group's objectives, and to do so while maintaining a cohesive group. The research reviewed helps to explain some of the differences in how males and females interact in groups and teams. We must emphasize again, however, that much of the research reflects generalizations rather than specifics; thus, not all males and females exhibit these behaviors.

Establishing a Group Culture

14.4 **Explain** how a group's culture, size, and norms affect group communication.

Just like societies, organizations, and other large groups, small groups develop unique cultures. **Group culture** "is the pattern of values, beliefs, norms, and behaviors shared by group members that shape a group's individual 'personality.'"[14] Group culture is created by many factors, including the interaction patterns of group members, the roles members are assigned, the purpose for the group, the mixture of people included in the group, members' behaviors, and norms and rules followed by the group.

The group's culture underlies all of its actions and behaviors. Group culture is not static; it constantly changes and develops as it adapts to each new situation or event it confronts as well as to the needs of the group and its members. A group's culture is expressed in behaviors such as how its members organize, who begins the interactions, how much interaction is allowed by any one member, who interacts with whom, how formally or informally people behave, how much or how little conflict is permitted, how much or how little socializing takes place, and how much or how little tolerance for ambiguity the group allows.

group culture

The pattern of values, beliefs, norms, and behaviors that is shared by group members and that shapes a group's individual "personality."

Group Size

Group size refers to the number of participants and has important ramifications for the group's effectiveness. Although a group has no perfect number of members, groups of certain sizes seem appropriate for certain kinds of tasks. For example, five-member groups are the most effective for dealing with intellectual tasks; coordinating, analyzing, and evaluating information; and making administrative decisions. Many small-group experts recommend that groups have no fewer than three and no more than nine members. They also advise an odd number of participants (five, seven, or nine) for some decision-making and problem-solving groups. An odd number of members helps to ensure fewer stalemates and thus a lower likelihood that voting will end in a tie.

A group that is too small can limit the information and ideas generated, whereas a group that is too large can limit the contribution each person can make. When deciding on the most effective size for a group, consider the following points:

1. Large groups reduce the time and amount of individual interaction.

2. Large groups provide a greater opportunity for aggressive members to assert their dominance. As a result, less assertive members might feel isolated and might withdraw from the group altogether.

3. Large groups make it difficult to follow a set agenda. It is easy for someone in a large group to switch topics or introduce subjects that are not related to the group's original priorities.

Group Norms

norms

Expected and shared ways in which group members behave.

The expected and shared ways group members behave are called **norms**. Both informal and formal guidelines determine which behaviors are acceptable and which are not. In most group situations, the norms are informal and unwritten. In some social groups, such as a book club or cooking group, certain behaviors are expected. At a minimum, it is assumed members will respect each other, show up on time for meetings, attend the majority of gatherings, allow others time to communicate, and support other members' contributions and opinions.

For a group to function effectively, its members must agree on how things are to be done. Therefore, no matter what their size or task, groups establish norms. This is done for a variety of reasons; the strongest one is that shared ways of behaving enable members to attain group goals and to satisfy interpersonal needs. Without guidelines for behavior, most groups would be ineffective and disorganized.

In formal situations, to increase efficiency and order, many groups use preestablished rules to guide their interaction. *Robert's Rules of Order* is the most widely used authority on conducting social, business, and government meetings.[15] Such formal rules specify the roles of members; how meetings are conducted; and how topics for discussion are introduced, discussed, and accepted or rejected by the group's members. When it is important to maintain formal order, a group may appoint a parliamentarian to ensure the rules are correctly interpreted and followed.

Group culture is created by many factors, including the interaction patterns of the group's members, the roles members are assigned, the group's purpose, the mixture of people included in the group, members' behaviors, and norms and rules followed by the group.

Norms also develop in online groups. For example, group members develop ways of communicating with each other both formally and informally and devise their own ways of communicating via email, Skype, or other online means.[16] Groups tend to use emails to chat and coordinate meeting times or use doodle.com, a meeting-planning website, to schedule times and to communicate with those who were not present or available to meet. As online groups mature over time, so does conformity to the norms of the group.

Leadership

14.5 **Understand** the difference between leadership and leaders and the various leadership styles and behaviors they exhibit.

Try the following with your friends. Ask them to rate themselves on a ten-point scale ranging from 1 (very low) to 10 (very high) on their leadership potential. Unless they are unusual, here's what you'll likely find: Most will rate themselves as average or above average.[17] This indicates they view themselves and leadership potential favorably. What is leadership? In a sense it is a lot like love: easy to recognize but hard to define. **Leadership** is *an influence process* that includes any behavior that helps to clarify a group's purpose or guide a group to achieve its goals. A **leader** is a person who is assigned, selected, or emerges to take the leadership role. In most cases, only one person has the title of leader, although at times the assigned or appointed leader, should there be one, does not show leadership. It is also possible that when no leader is appointed or assigned, someone emerges as the leader or two or more people emerge and share the leader responsibilities via their leadership behaviors. In other words, a leader is a role or title held, whereas leadership is the behavior that influences or facilitates to achieve a goal or goals.

Leading a Group or Team

A leader is the person usually at the center of a group's attention or the person to whom the group members address their messages. A leader is identified by his or her position or title, such as police chief, mayor, council president, chairperson of a committee, boss, teacher, coach, captain, father, mother, and so on. However, this method of identification requires caution. Even though a title signifies a person is the stated leader, it does not mean the person has leadership skills.

Another way to identify a leader is by the behaviors he or she displays in guiding others. If a person communicates a direction and others follow that direction to reach a goal, that person is demonstrating leadership as well as the power and ability to get others to accomplish the goal.

In most cases, a leader's ability to lead determines the success or failure of a group or team. Granted, not all successes or failures directly relate to the person in charge because the participants, the nature of the task, and the information available for completing the task also contribute to the outcome. The role of the leader is to ensure the accomplishment of the assigned task. To do this, the leader must be objective enough to determine how the group is functioning and whether it is progressing toward its goal. This requires, at times, the ability to step back and examine the group objectively.

Leaders must help address at least two sets of needs found in all groups. **Task needs** are related to the content of the task and all behaviors that lead to the completion of the task, including defining and assessing the task, gathering information, studying the problem, and solving the problem. **Maintenance needs** are related to organizing and developing a group so that members realize personal satisfaction from working together. Maintenance needs pertain to intangibles such as atmosphere, structure, role responsibility, praise, and social–emotional control. To meet both task and maintenance needs, leaders in small groups must perform a number of functions:

Initiating—preparing members for discussion
Organizing—keeping members on track
Maintaining effective interaction—encouraging participation
Ensuring member satisfaction—promoting interpersonal relationships
Facilitating understanding—encouraging effective listening
Stimulating creativity and critical thinking—encouraging evaluation and improvement

leadership
An influence process that includes any behavior that helps clarify a purpose or guides to achieve a goal or goals.

leader
A person who is assigned, selected or emerges to take the leadership role.

task needs
Needs related to the content of the task to be done and all behaviors that lead to the completion of it.

maintenance needs
Needs related to organizing and developing a group so that members can realize personal satisfaction from working together.

Leadership Styles and Behavior

Not all leaders are alike. They may share certain characteristics or qualities to a degree, but more than likely, they differ in personal, behavioral, or leadership style. Research has identified two useful dimensions by which to classify leaders: as task-oriented or relationship-oriented leaders or by the amount of power they yield to group members.

Leadership and Task or Relationship Orientation   Although there are as many different leadership styles as leaders, research on leader behavior suggests that most leaders can be described as **initiating structure** (or task-oriented) leaders or **consideration** (or relationship-oriented) leaders.[18] Leaders who initiate structure tend to focus on getting the job done. They engage in actions such as organizing work, making sure rules are followed, setting goals, and ensuring that everyone knows who is in charge. For example, the vice president at Google in charge of finding talented workers thrives in her position by being extremely particular in hiring, a fanatical user of social networking, and apolitical when analyzing new ideas.[19] You may have experienced leaders like this and, in some group situations, this style can get the job done or the problem solved. However, leaders who adopt this style tend to sacrifice relationship development unless it helps get the task done more quickly.

Leaders who lead by consideration tend to focus on interpersonal relationships and the need for group members to like them. They engage in actions such as doing favors for group members, taking time to explain things to them, and watching out for their well-being. Leaders who do not focus on consideration usually don't care about the group members or whether the group members like them or not. (See Figure 14.1 for an overview of the two styles.)

Is either of these styles superior? Probably not. Both offer a mix of advantages and disadvantages. Leaders who show concern for others generally foster stronger morale, but such leaders often avoid telling others what to do or offering critical feedback to improve the contribution of group members. This could result in inefficiency and failure to accomplish tasks in a timely manner. In contrast, when leaders focus solely on attaining goals, efficiency may be high, but group members feel no commitment to the outcome or to the leader. Superior leaders are more likely to balance the two styles.

Leadership and Power Distribution   Leadership is classified at times according to how much or how little power the leader assigns to group members. Researchers have identified three primary styles of leadership: autocratic, democratic, and laissez-faire,[20] each having a distinctive approach to group communication.

initiating structure

A dimension of leadership that focuses on getting the job done.

consideration

A dimension of leadership that focuses on establishing good interpersonal relationships and on being liked by group members.

FIGURE 14.1   Leadership Styles: Task and Relationship Orientation

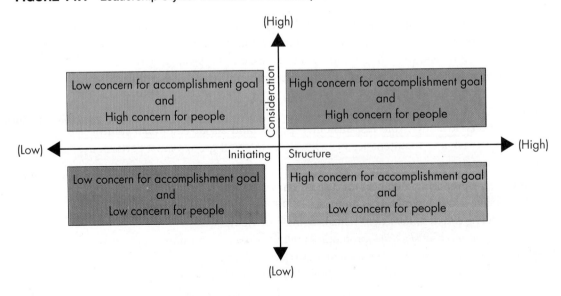

Table 14.1 LEADERSHIP STYLES: A COMPARISON

Autocratic	Democratic	Laissez-Faire
Keeps complete control	Shares control	Gives up control
Sets policy and makes all decisions for the group	Involves members in setting policy and making decisions; does not make any decisions without consulting group members	Gives total freedom to group members to make policies and decisions; gets involved only when called on
Defines tasks and assigns them to members	May guide task assignment to be sure work is accomplished, but allows members to divide work	Completely avoids participation

In theory, the differences among the three styles of leadership are clear. The **autocratic leader** has complete control, the **democratic leader** shares control, and the **laissez-faire leader** gives up control (see Table 14.1). In practice, though, the three styles are not always so clear-cut. Most effective leaders do not use the same style all the time but vary their style to match each situation. Certain circumstances, group members, or group purposes call for direct control, whereas others require little or no control. For example, a military leader in combat and a doctor in a medical emergency will undoubtedly be autocratic leaders. Such situations require immediate action, and putting decisions to a vote could create problems. Autocratic leaders can have a negative impact on a group—for example, a jury foreperson who imposes her opinion or rushes the decision so that other jurists agree with her.

Researchers have concluded skilled leaders have the ability to understand a situation and adapt their behaviors to meet its particular constraints.[21] Leadership entails the capacity to determine the most appropriate style and behaviors for given situations.

Research, although not conclusive, suggests the democratic leadership style is superior to the autocratic style in getting a task done and at the same time satisfies group members.[22] Autocratic leaders are likely to get more done, but member satisfaction is considerably lower. Probably the most significant research finding is that autocratic leaders generate more hostility and aggression among group members, whereas democratic leaders produce more originality, individuality, and independence.[23]

autocratic leader

A leader who has control and makes decisions with little or no consultation with others.

democratic leader

A leader who shares control and makes decisions in consultation with others.

laissez-faire leader

A leader who gives up control, is passive, and usually requires that others take over if the group is to succeed.

Leadership and Gender Differences

Women have made great strides in assuming leadership roles in elected offices (e.g., governors, mayors, and legislators). They have also been appointed to the Supreme Court and cabinet positions, hold high rank in the military, and head major corporations. Women are also the leaders in creating and building a culture of creativity in

MAKING CONNECTIONS FOR SUCCESS

What Makes a Leader?

Imagine two different groups of college students that meet to discuss how they would implement the new regulations for their dorm's common room. In one of the groups, you are the only member who comes to the meeting prepared. None of the other members are aware of the rules or are prepared to discuss them and their implementation. In the second group, all of the group members have knowledge of the rules and are fully prepared to focus on implementation.

1. If you were asked to lead the two groups, what leadership style do you think you would use in each, and why?

2. What problems might you encounter in each group, if any?

3. Explain the characteristics or skills needed to be an effective leader in each group.

4. Of the qualities or skills you have identified, which do you think is the most important for each group and why?

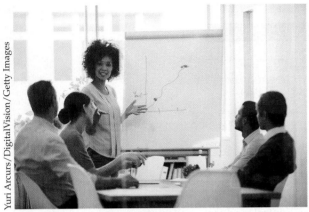

Leadership style can be classified by how much or how little power the leader assigns to group members. Democratic leaders, for example, guide and direct the group, and though committed to being open to all points of view, they represent only a majority or plurality of points of view of the group.

organizations. They are the ones stimulating people's minds by constantly pushing and creating new trends and ideas.[24] There are 32 women CEOs in Fortune 500 companies. This is a new record.[25] Thus, while there has been improvement, the gender gap between men and women still exists not only in leadership positions but in equal pay as well.

Early research on small-group leadership found that men usually emerged as leaders. Today it seems that biological sex is irrelevant, although psychological gender is not. It now appears that task-oriented women emerge as leaders as often as men who are task-oriented. A study of groups of women found that those who emerged as leaders combined intelligence with "masculinity" or androgyny (exhibiting both "masculine" and "feminine" characteristics).[26] A study examining groups consisting of both males and females found that, regardless of sex, "masculine" and androgynous members stood out as leaders more often than "feminine" members.[27] The research related to gender and leadership shows that men and women lead equally well, and group members are equally satisfied with both.[28] It is clear that women have made great strides in recent years and as in the past have proven to be effective leaders in a variety of settings and situations.

Do male leaders and female leaders differ in their style or approach to leadership? What do you think? This debate has gone on for well over 30 years. Marilyn Loden, in her book *Feminine Leadership or How to Succeed in Business without Being One of the Boys*, contends that the sexes do indeed differ in terms of leadership style.[29] Loden believes female leaders often adopt a style that emphasizes cooperation and indirect means of management, whereas males tend to exhibit an "I'm in charge" directive strategy. However, recent research on male and female leadership done by social scientists has generally found no consistent or significant difference between the sexes in terms of leadership style. In fact, if you want to find differences between leadership styles in men and women, you would have to first ask, "Which woman and which man?"[30] The question is, "Who is right?"

Because of the complexity of the subject, finding the answer to this question is not simple. In a review of 150 research studies, Alice Eagly and Blair Johnson found potential differences between male and female leadership styles on two dimensions: (1) task accomplishment versus maintenance of interpersonal relationships and (2) participative (democratic) versus directive (autocratic) leadership style.[31]

MAKING CONNECTIONS FOR SUCCESS
Are Women Better Leaders?

According to a special report "As Leaders, Women Rule,"[32] more women are taking on leadership roles in government and business. The report stated that gender differences in leadership abilities were often small but that women, when rated by their peers, underlings, and bosses, scored higher than their male counterparts on a wide variety of measures—from producing high-quality work to goal setting to mentoring employees. Using elaborate performance evaluations of women executives, researchers found that women overall received higher ratings than men on almost

every leadership skill measured. With that in mind, answer the following questions:

1. On the basis of what this report suggests—that women are better leaders—why don't women hold more leadership positions?

2. Defend or refute the report's contention that women are better leaders.

3. When considering the traits we generally associate with leadership, are those traits likely to be more "masculine" or "feminine"? Explain.

Sex-role stereotypes suggest that female leaders might show more concern for interpersonal relations and tend to be more democratic in their leadership style than male leaders are. Results of Eagly and Johnson's study, however, did not support these stereotypes. Their results suggest that no evidence supports any substantial difference between men and women regarding the first dimension (task accomplishment versus maintenance of interpersonal relationships). There is, however, a significant difference between males and females regarding the second dimension (participative versus directive leadership style). Eagly and Johnson found women were more democratic, or participative, in style than men were. What do you think accounts for this difference?

The difference in leadership style might exist because, as evidence suggests, women generally possess better interpersonal skills than men do. In addition to the remaining hurdles for women, emerging evidence suggests gender stereotyping in the workplace is weakening. However, this cause-and-effect connection is only speculative. Thus, generalizing about male and female leadership behaviors can be misleading for a variety of reasons. It is when men and woman are treated as if socialized in different cultures that we tend to stereotype—for example, that men are task-oriented and powerful, while woman are emotional and powerless.[33] Unfortunately, when women violate expectations of being warm and nurturing and act in more "masculine" ways, they are more likely to be treated with hostility and rejection.[34] Further research must be done before a definitive conclusion can be drawn about gender differences in leadership style and whether (and in what situations) those differences might be to a leader's advantage or disadvantage.[35]

Ethical Behavior in Group Communication

14.6 **Describe** the role of ethics in small-group communication.

For groups to perform effectively, leaders and members must be ethical. All people in civilized societies are expected to follow certain behavioral assumptions—laws, rules, standards, or agreed-on norms. It is important to realize that groups, by their

Guidelines

ETHICAL GROUP BEHAVIOR

1. **All group members should have the right to state an opinion or a unique perspective.** No one should be prevented from speaking openly, even when expressing unpopular views. Disagreeing with another person's ideas is in no way wrong; it is wrong, however, to attack the person instead of the idea.

2. **Group members should be willing to share all legitimate information that might benefit the group in reaching its goal.** Deliberately withholding information that might benefit the group is a violation of the group's trust and is unethical. Times might arise when withholding information to protect the group or specific group members may be appropriate. For example, not divulging something a group member says about another member avoids creating bad or hurt feelings.

3. **All group members should conduct themselves with honesty and integrity.** Members of a group should

not deliberately deceive or present false or untruthful information. It is unacceptable to present inaccurate information in an attempt to persuade others to accept a particular viewpoint. The same principle holds for the group itself: It is wrong for the group to present results based on misrepresentation of facts. It is deceitful to persuade others to accept conclusions supported by misinformation.

4. **Confidential information shared in the group should remain confidential.** It is extremely unethical to share private information outside the group.

5. **Group members must use information ethically.** Members should give credit to the source of the information, should not falsify data or information, and should present all relevant information and all points of view to prevent bias.[36]

William Perugin/123RF

Groups that share a common bond and are ethical in supporting each other consider the group's well-being before their own.

very nature, take on a collectivistic orientation in that the successful group must be more important than any one individual. This perspective can raise ethical considerations about the commitment one has toward other group members and the group goal. This does not mean individuals should condone unethical behaviors, such as intentionally deceiving one another or manufacturing information or evidence to persuade others in the group to accept a particular point of view.

The expectations that people will be respectful of each other's opinions apply especially to behaviors within groups and raise some special ethical concerns all groups and group members should consider when participating in group-related activities. The bottom line is that every group member, as well as the group as a whole, must be ethical, honest, respectful, fair, flexible, and responsible in actions and communication.

Member Participation

14.7 **Differentiate** among the roles of group members and explain their various contributions.

A group's success requires actively involved and committed members. Just like leaders, members of groups have certain responsibilities and roles.

Roles of Group Members

Group scholars Kenneth Benne and Paul Sheats developed a comprehensive list of roles that group members can assume.[37] Benne and Sheats classified the roles into three categories: group task, group building and maintenance, and self-centered roles. The most successful groups include members who fill the task and building/maintenance roles, and who avoid the self-centered roles.

Group task roles help the group accomplish its task or objective. They include behaviors that provide direction, propose ideas, and make suggestions to solve problems—these roles are referred to as *initiators* or *contributors*. Group members may also take on *information seeker* or *information giver* roles. The information seeker looks for more information or clarification of ideas, while the information giver provides information that in-

Every group member must be willing to contribute to, and take responsibility for, the success of the group. Successful group outcomes depend on group members' assuming various roles that are productive and beneficial to the group's outcome.

Phovoir/Shutterstock

cludes facts and examples. Members may also become an *evaluator/critic*, one who evaluates the information and conclusions regarding their usefulness and accuracy; an *energizer*, a motivator who keeps the group moving toward its goal; an *orienter*, a member who periodically summarizes what has been discussed; or a *coordinator*, a member who clarifies and shows relationships among ideas, viewpoints, and suggestions.

Group building and maintenance roles help define a group's social atmosphere. The *encouragers* offer praise and recognize the contributions of others. *Harmonizers* are the mediators for disagreements and always try to ensure a positive climate. *Compromisers* attempt to avoid and solve conflicts and find acceptable solutions. *Gatekeepers* manage the flow of interaction in the group. *Standard setters* remind the group

Guidelines

THINGS TO CONSIDER WHEN PLANNING AND MANAGING A MEETING

1. Avoid holding unnecessary meetings.

2. Invite only people who need to be there (*not* everyone who might have an opinion on the topic).

3. Identify a purpose, plan an agenda, and distribute the agenda in advance.

4. Assign a leader, if one hasn't already been determined, to keep the discussion on track.

5. Establish start, break, and stop times, and stick to them.

6. Don't let people drone on, dominate, or avoid participation during discussions.

7. Don't allow conversations to wander off the subject.

8. Decide what follow-up actions are needed after the meeting and set deadlines for their completion.

9. Follow up to make sure that members act on decisions made at the meeting.

Source: From Harrison Conference Services, Business Schools at the University of Georgia and Georgia State University.

of its goals. *Followers* cooperate to work together with other group members. Finally, *feeling expressers* articulate the group's feelings and attitudes.

Some individuals may adopt *self-centered roles*, which are generally counterproductive or destructive to a group and tend to hinder group progress. Among them are the *aggressors*, who deflate others to make themselves look better. *Blockers* resist others' ideas and in general disagree with everything. The *recognition seekers* are similar to aggressors in that they want to be the center of the group's attention. Jokers or people who engage in horseplay are referred to as *buffoons*. *Dominators* are autocrats, who want to be in charge. *Help seekers* are in the group only to satisfy their own needs. *Withdrawers* just don't say or do anything.

In most groups, members are eager to make constructive contributions. From time to time, however, you will encounter individuals whose attitudes are not so positive. For the good of the group, it is important to recognize such people and learn how to cope with them.

Contributions of Group Members

Both the leader and all group members must recognize and handle counterproductive contributions. Sometimes the best approach to these situations is to discuss them openly: "John, you've been been quiet about this problem. What do you think?" "Sally, your jokes seem to indicate that you don't believe the issue is very serious. Why?" Sometimes conflict needs to be resolved with a vote by the group. This lets members know the position of the majority so that discussion can continue.

Each group participant should study the agenda in advance in order to be ready to discuss. Probably one of the biggest weaknesses of beginning group participants is being unprepared to discuss; thus valuable time, effort, and input are lost. Successful group outcomes depend on open-mindedness, a positive attitude, the ability to listen, a willingness to contribute, and preparation.

Reaching Group Members' Consensus

The goal of most groups is to arrive at decisions or solutions that are agreed on and acceptable to at least most, if not all, of the group members. The process of reaching consensus assumes that all group members have been able to express how they feel and think about the alternatives and have been given equitable opportunities to influence the outcome. However, it is important that consensus not come too quickly; if it does, the group may be a victim of *groupthink* (see Learning Objective 14.10 for more information and a definition of groupthink). Consensus on controversial issues usually is not arrived at easily. It requires a certain amount of patience and a willingness to look for areas of agreement. This process, of course, can be very time consuming.

Is the time taken to reach consensus worth the effort? It has been proven again and again that groups using effective group discussion methods, such as communicating openly, coming prepared to discuss, and willing to challenge ideas and evidence, almost always arrive at better-quality decisions than individuals alone.[38] It has also been shown that groups reaching agreement, regardless of the time it takes, are more likely to take ownership of their decisions and maintain their agreement longer.[39]

Communication scholars Steven Beebe and John Masterson provide three recommendations for reaching consensus in groups:

1. Groups have a tendency to change topics and to get off track, so members should try to keep themselves oriented toward the group's goal. Groups often don't reach consensus because they engage in discussing issues irrelevant to their goal.

2. Members should be other oriented and sensitive to all ideas. Listen and do not constantly interrupt one another. Make a good-faith effort to set aside your views and seek to understand others.

3. Promote group member interaction and dialogue. It is important that everyone feels that his or her voice is heard and that no one withholds his or her views, even when those views are contrary to those held by others.[40]

Managing Group Conflict

14.8 **Describe** conflict, its impacts, and the conflict management strategies that can manage it.

When you hear the word *conflict*, what comes to mind? For most people, it conjures up terms such as *argument, dislike, fight, stress, hate, competition, disagreement, hostility, discord, friction, disunity,* and so on. All of these words do relate to conflict. However, they illustrate only the negative side of the concept. After all, in U.S. society, most people value and stress the importance of agreement and getting along with others. However, our society also loves competition. Sayings such as "All's fair in love and war" or "Stick to your guns" are often cited as representative of the American way. But the desire to get along with others and the desire to best them in competition contradict each other. The idea that "if one person wins, another must lose" is implanted in almost every American's mind early in life.

On the one hand, we would like to avoid conflict and preserve unity. On the other hand, we cannot experience the thrill of winning unless we enter into conflict. Is there any middle ground between these two polarities? Can conflict be resolved only by forcing someone to lose? Must conflict always hurt someone?

Whenever people come together to communicate, conflict is nearly inevitable. But conflict does not always have to be harmful. In fact, it can be productive and, if properly managed, it can result in better decisions and solutions to problems.

Conflict and Group Communication

Communication scholars William Wilmot and Joyce Hocker assert that communication and conflict are related in the following ways: Communication behavior often *creates* conflict, communication behavior *reflects* conflict, and communication is the *vehicle* for the productive or destructive management of conflict.[41] *Conflict* was defined in Chapter 13 as "an expressed struggle between at least two interdependent parties who perceive incompatible goals, scarce resources, and interference from others in achieving their goals."[42]

Effective group decision making and problem solving often depend on conflict and open disagreement. The benefits of group conflict, when it is understood and controlled, include a deeper understanding of group members and issues, greater involvement and increased motivation, better decisions, and enhanced group cohesiveness. These benefits are more likely when groups accept collaboration and compromise.

Of course, too much conflict can create unmanageable tension and heighten disagreement, resulting in personal attacks on individual group members. If personal attacks come to dominate meetings, they produce no benefits and usually lead to hurt feelings, withdrawal, and eventually the disbanding of the group.

In collaboration, negotiating and problem solving are used to find a solution that fully meets the needs of all parties involved in a group conflict. In other words, each party achieves its desired results. **Principled negotiation** is a procedure that helps group members negotiate consensus by collaboration through the expression of each different need and a search for alternatives to meet those needs. For example, suppose you are serving on a committee to select the commencement speaker, and some committee members want to bring in a controversial speaker. Some of the more radical members want to select Bill Ayers, an elementary education theorist who was a 1960s antiwar activist; who cofounded the violent left-wing organization the Weather Underground, which conducted a campaign to bomb public buildings during the 1960s and 1970s; and who now is a retired professor in the College of Education at the University of Illinois at Chicago, where he held the titles of Distinguished Professor of Education and Senior University Scholar. Other members are recommending Ann Coulter, an American social and political commentator who is well known for her conservative political opinions and the controversial way she defends them; Bill Maher, a former stand-up comedian and host of *Politically Incorrect* and now host of *Real Time* on HBO, in which he uses a lot of profane language and has been extremely controversial regarding Muslims and conservative women; and Rick Warren, an American evangelical minister and author who holds traditional evangelical views on social issues such as same-sex marriage and stem cell research. Much discussion ensues, but both sides eventually see the benefits of each view and agree a controversial speaker would be good, but not one as controversial as Ayers, Coulter, Maher, or Warren. Ultimately, they decide to invite Tim D. Cook, an American business executive and the CEO of Apple Inc. Cook joined Apple in March 1998 as Senior Vice President of Worldwide Operations—he also served as Executive Vice President of Worldwide Sales and Operations—and was Chief Operating Officer until he was named the CEO of Apple on August 24, 2011, when he succeeded Steve Jobs. Cook's net worth is estamated at $400 million. The collaboration between the committee members generated by the initial conflict has resulted in a speaker they could all agree on. The result is an ideal solution in which both sides win.

The positive outcomes of conflict, according to Gloria Galanes and Katherine Adams, are as follows:

1. Conflict can produce better understanding of both issues and people.
2. Conflict can increase member motivation.
3. Conflict can produce better decisions.
4. Conflict can produce greater cohesiveness among group members.[43]

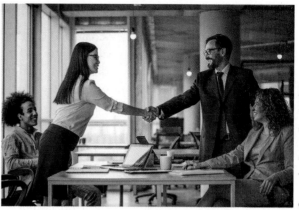

Svyatoslav Lypynskyy/123RF

A committee consisting of management and labor discusses a benefit issue in a conference setting To gain consensus, members who are not in agreement negotiate until agreement is reached. They do this by identifying different needs and searching for alternatives to meet those needs.

principled negotiation
A procedure that helps group members negotiate consensus by collaboration through the expression of each differing need and a search for alternatives to meet those needs.

Ethical Behavior and Conflict

Adam and Galanes assert that using ethical behaviors during a conflict situation creates a better understanding of the issues and increases cohesiveness while minimizing destructive outcomes, such as hurt feelings and personal attacks.[44] They list a number of suggestions to help individuals behave ethically during conflicts:

1. Express disagreements openly and honestly. It is important to put disagreements on the table for discussion.

2. Stick to the issues. Be direct and get to the point.

3. Use rhetorical sensitivity when presenting your disagreements. Don't simply put down others' ideas or views.

4. Criticize the idea and not the person.

5. Base disagreements on solid evidence and good reasoning, not on rumor, emotions, or unsubstantiated information.

6. Be receptive to disagreements. Don't become defensive simply because someone disagrees with you. Keep an open mind and listen carefully.

7. Always remain calm even if someone attacks you. Take a reasoned approach and do not take the attack personally.

8. Look for ways to integrate ideas and to negotiate differences whenever possible.

Problem Solving and Decision Making

14.9 **Explain** the reflective thinking process and functional communication theory.

Although the goal of most classroom discussions is to share information, the goal of most other discussions is to solve problems and make decisions—for example, How can we raise more money for new computers? How can we prevent date rape? What can be done to eliminate unethical behavior in our organization?

When solving problems and making decisions, groups must consider the alternatives and arrive at a consensus for the solution. To do this most effectively, they must first take an organized and thorough approach to determining the exact nature of the problem.

Determining and Stating the Problem

Unless an instructor or situation determines a topic to be discussed, the initial step of a classroom group is to select a topic. This is not always easy; after all, the topic has to be both important and interesting to everyone in the group to ensure a good discussion. A starting place might be areas that need improvement on your campus: What should be the role of athletics on the campus? Should better protection be provided for students who attend evening classes? The surrounding community is also a source for discussion topics: What can be done about public parking in the downtown area? What can the business community do to help college students get better jobs? State, regional, and national issues can provide a broader base for topics: Can the state provide sufficient funding to the university? What should be the role of the federal government in providing loans to students? Selecting from thousands of topics and problems takes time. However, if the group does its homework, picking a topic that is agreeable to all members should not be difficult.

After a topic or problem is selected or provided, it should be stated in the form of a question. When phrasing discussion questions, whether for a classroom learning experience or another context, keep the following in mind:[45]

1. The wording should reflect the discussion purpose or task at hand; for example, what should be done to make our campus a green campus?

2. The wording should focus attention on the real problem; for example, what can be done to establish a recycling program on campus?

3. The wording should specify whose behavior is subject to change; for example, how can we encourage students to recycle?

Discuss the Problem and Its Solution

In group situations, whether in the classroom or another context, it is important to determine a plan or procedure for discussing and solving a problem.

Dewey's Reflective Thinking   John Dewey, a philosopher during the 1900s, described the mental steps taken by individuals when solving problems. The steps developed by Dewey are referred to as "reflective thinking" steps because they provide a logical, rational way of generating solutions to a problem and deciding on a solution.[46] Groups often use the Dewey reflective thinking steps as an effective and efficient way to solve problems and make decisions. Here are Dewey's five steps to help solve problems and make decisions:

1. Clearly identify or define the problem you are trying to solve.
2. Analyze the problem: What are its causes, or the conditions underlying the problem?
3. Suggest possible solutions.
4. Select the best solution, then discuss why it is the best and how it will solve the problem.
5. Once the best solution is decided upon, the group now must decide how it will be put into operation.[47]

Gouran and Hirokawa's Functional Theory   Dewey's classic work focuses on the group problem-solving and decision-making process. Communication researchers Dennis Gouran and Randy Hirokawa built on Dewey's work with their functional theory, which describes how communication can help or hinder group problem solving and decision making.[48] Functional theory assumes that groups want to make good decisions and focuses on ways to improve a group's functional communication. It also assumes the group has all the necessary information and resources needed, as well as the communicative and thinking ability to do the best job. Further, Gouran and Hirokawa indicate that if those conditions are present, group success depends on three additional factors.

1. **The task.** Functional theory asserts that five task requirements must be met for a group to complete its goal successfully:
   - Members fully understand the problem or issue being discussed.
   - They know the minimum criteria for a successful solution.
   - They identify all reasonable solutions from which to choose.
   - They evaluate the advantages and disadvantages of all the reasonable solutions against the agreed-upon criteria for selecting the best solution.
   - They select the best solution.
2. **How group members use communication to overcome any obstacles they may confront.** A group's success may face many obstacles, for example:
   - Group members may fail to find all of the pertinent information or to share all of the relevant information with one another.

- Instead of making the determination of the best solution the first priority, some group members may put relationships first in order to avoid disagreements or to pressure others to conform and get along.
- Some group members may be more interested in their own interests instead of what is best for the group.

As suggested earlier in this chapter, it is important for group members and leaders to deal with members who directly affect the quality of a group's decision.

3. **The participants' willingness to review and reconsider their decisions.** The issue is one of commitment to their decision.
   - If any potential flaws arise, the group must be willing to take a second look even if it means starting over. The group should review the process and decision to ensure that the best possible choice is being made.

In solving problems and making decisions, it is always wise to incorporate a process that follows a plan such as the one suggested by Dewey or by Gouran and Hirokawa. The reflective thinking steps should be used as a guide to decision making, not as an exact formula in approaching every problem. According to researchers and group scholars, group members prefer to have direction and a process to follow during group work. Having a plan helps groups generate ideas and come to better decisions, and it essentially saves time and energy as well as reducing frustrations.[49]

Brainstorming

Sometimes groups find themselves unable to formulate new ideas or be creative in solving a particular aspect of a problem. In such cases, they may find brainstorming helpful. Brainstorming (defined in Chapter 8 on page 163) can be used during any phase of the group discussion process to produce topics, information, or solutions. During the brainstorming session, group members suggest as many topic-related ideas as they can think of, no matter how farfetched they might seem. One person records the ideas for later analysis. The leader lets the comments flow freely and may prompt the group by suggesting extensions of new ideas that have been voiced.

The leader of a brainstorming group should create an open atmosphere that encourages creativity and spontaneity. Therefore, it is important that the leader be a person of high energy who responds enthusiastically to new ideas. The leader should provide reinforcement and support to all members and encourage the members to contribute even if they hit a dry spell. For example, the leader can use prompts such as these: "Let's generate at least two more ideas." "We've done great up to now—let's try one more time to generate some really innovative ideas."

Group members, as well as the leader, must not express disapproval (communicated by comments or looks) of any items until all ideas have been generated. Once the group has run out of ideas or time, the results should be evaluated. During this stage, members should work together to appraise each and every idea. The goal is to determine which idea or ideas merit more attention. It is appropriate to discard unfeasible or weak ideas, to improve undeveloped ideas, to consolidate related ideas, and to discuss further the most promising ones.

Groups are usually formed because a task must be accomplished or a problem must be solved. The problem illustrated in this photo is obvious, but how to address it requires the group to find a solution.

Matauw/Fotolia

Working in Groups or Teams: Advantages and Disadvantages

14.10 **Explain** the advantages and disadvantages of participating in groups and how to overcome the disadvantages.

As you know, with many activities you have participated in, whether it be in academics, athletics, recreation, or your personal life, there are advantages and disadvantages. Knowledge of the advantages and potential disadvantages of working in groups helps you set more realistic expectations and capitalize on the values of the groups while minimizing the potential downsides.

Advantages

Take a moment to think about all the groups to which you belong: student organizations, clubs, religious groups, social groups, work groups, and informal groups of friends. Why did you join them in the first place? It doesn't take a scholar to tell you that people join groups for many reasons, and your reasons are probably similar to those that motivate others to join groups. Paul Paulus, a social psychologist, suggests people join groups for at least five common reasons:

1. *Groups help satisfy important psychological and social needs,* such as the need for attention and affection or the need to belong. Imagine what it would be like to be absolutely alone, in total isolation from others. Very few of us find such a prospect appealing.

2. *Group membership helps people achieve goals that otherwise might not be accomplished.* Groups make it easier to perform certain tasks, solve difficult problems, and make complex decisions that might overwhelm one individual.

3. *Group membership provides multiple sources of information and knowledge that might not be available to one individual.*

4. *Groups help meet the need for security.* The old saying that there is safety in numbers rings true in many situations; belonging to groups can provide protection and security against common enemies. For example, people join neighborhood watch groups to protect themselves from criminal activity.

5. *Group membership also contributes to an individual's positive social identity.* It becomes part of a person's self-concept. The more prestigious and restrictive the groups to which a person is admitted, the more that person's self-concept is bolstered.[50]

Other advantages to participating in groups or teams include innovation and creativity, as supported by the maxim "two heads are better than one," especially when it comes to working on difficult tasks or solving complex problems.[51] You are more likely to remember what you discussed because you actively engaged in a discussion with others rather than passively thought about it. According to Beebe and Masterson, working in groups and teams helps to improve learning and comprehension; for example, if you are scheduled to take an exam, they indicate studying by yourself doesn't allow for the asking and answering of questions. Beebe and Masterson also suggest discussion helps you learn and comprehend more of what you learn better than if you did it by yourself.[52]

The Disadvantages of Working in Small Groups

Most of what we have said so far about groups has been positive, and it is true that groups have many advantages over individuals working alone. But limitations related to groups can also lead to less effective and less satisfying outcomes.

groupthink

A dysfunction in which group members value the harmony of the group more than new ideas, fail to critically examine ideas, hesitate to change flawed decisions, or lack willingness to allow new members to participate.

Going Along to Get Along Too much cohesiveness can lead to conformity and blind loyalty to a group even when it is not in the individual group member's best interest to conform. Groups can become too cohesive or committed, resulting in **groupthink**—a dysfunction in which group members see the harmony of the group as more important than considering new ideas, critically examining their own assumptions, changing their own flawed decisions, or allowing new members to participate.[53]

The following situation illustrates groupthink. Students are asked to choose one of three solutions to a certain social problem and join with other students who selected the same solution. Usually, all three solutions are chosen and each group's task is to defend its solution and to persuade the instructor that its solution is the best of the three. As an incentive for preparing a sound argument, students are told the instructor will accept only one group solution as the best.

As the groups begin to work, their members make a modest effort to pull together and define their argument. Each group selects a representative to present its argument. After hearing each representative, the instructor announces he or she is undecided regarding which group offered the best solution. Therefore, all groups have one more chance to develop their arguments. The instructor also announces that students who did not like their group's solution are welcome to join another group. No one switches groups, even though some are tempted to do so after hearing presentations by other group representatives.

To raise the stakes, the instructor states the groups with the second- and third-best solutions will be assigned a homework project over the weekend, whereas the winning group will be exempt. In response, the intensity within each group builds. Members pull their chairs closer together and talk more forcefully about their solution. They support one another's views more openly. The common objective has become clear and compelling: To avoid the research project, the students are motivated to persuade their instructor. Oddly enough, this particular type of motivation can be hazardous. Groupthink is more likely to occur when a group's cohesiveness and commitment are too high and when the group is under pressure to achieve consensus at the expense of doing the best possible work. Once this collective state of mind develops, it seems groups become unwilling and perhaps unable to change a decision, even if they realize it is a poor one.

Research on groupthink indicates it is a real and pervasive phenomenon and explains some of the disastrous group decisions.[54] According to Irving Janis, a specialist in organizational behavior, eight symptoms lead to groupthink. They fall into three categories:

1. **Overestimation of the group's power and morality**
   - An illusion that the group is invulnerable creates excessive optimism and encourages taking extreme risks.
   - A belief the group will not be judged on the basis of the ethical or moral consequences of its decisions.

2. **Closed-mindedness**
   - A tendency to rationalize or discount negative information that might lead members to reconsider their assumptions before making a decision.
   - Stereotypical views of other groups as too weak and stupid to warrant genuine attempts to negotiate differences.

3. **Pressures toward uniformity**
   - Individual self-censorship of differences that deviate from the group (that is, members are inclined to minimize their uniqueness and doubt the importance of their individual contributions).
   - A shared illusion of unanimity that pushes members to conform to the majority view as a result of self-censorship and the assumption that silence means consent.

- Pressure on group members who express arguments that differ from the majority to conform by making it clear dissent is contrary to what is expected of all loyal members.
- The setting of "mindguards" against threatening information to protect the group members from adverse information that might shatter their shared complacency regarding their decisions.[55]

Procedures can be used to minimize the possibility of groupthink. Here are some examples:

- Assign one group member to be a devil's advocate who intentionally questions and criticizes the group's actions.
- Encourage members to "kick the problem around."
- Ensure that every group member has an opportunity to voice an opinion.
- Encourage individuals to express disagreement without being chastised by the group for doing so.
- Set a guideline that prevents leaders from stating their conclusion or opinions first.
- Invite outside experts to participate in the group or review conclusions to ensure all views have been considered.[56]

Time-Consuming Nature of Group Work   A second disadvantage of groups is that the decision-making or problem-solving process can be time consuming. It almost always takes longer to accomplish something when a group does it. The more members in a group, the more time it takes to achieve the group's objectives. Individuals can almost always complete a task in a shorter amount of time than a group. For example, if you were to take a math problem-solving test, you would probably read each problem silently to yourself, write notes to yourself on scratch paper, and then attempt to solve the problems. If you were in a group, you would first have to discuss each problem, decide how the problem should be solved, and then work out the solution to the problem. In other words, group work is different from individual work because interaction must take place between and among the members.

Varying Interaction   A third disadvantage is unequal contribution. One reason for varying interactions is because each member has a different communication style and comfort level with the group. Some members might dominate and overwhelm conversations, whereas other members might not contribute at all. Furthermore, the most verbally aggressive and dominant person in the group might not always have the best ideas.

Unfair Workloads   A fourth disadvantage of groups is that often members believe the workload is unfair. The most frequent complaint we hear from students is that they believe some group members lack motivation and do not do their fair share of the work. This is referred to as social loafing. **Social loafing** is the tendency for individuals to lower their work effort after they join a group.[57] For example, suppose you and several other communication majors are forming a communication club. Your first task is to develop bylaws and gain approval of the university to have the club on campus. Everyone in the group knows the task and agrees to help. A meeting is scheduled to discuss these matters. Will all the group members put forth equal effort? Probably not. Some will do as much as they can, whereas others will simply do little or nothing; they may show up with a few ideas but do not take the task seriously because they were too busy doing other things. Social loafers can also be irresponsible by not showing up on time or not showing up at all because they believe others will do the work for them. Lack of motivation seems to be the central reason for social loafing.

social loafing
Tendency for individuals to lower their work effort after they join a group.

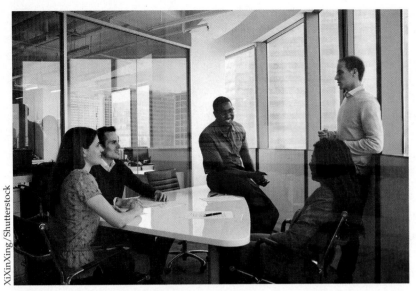

A disadvantage of groups is that not all members are committed to do their fair share of the work.

Although there is no magical list of procedures or behaviors to reduce social loafing, here are a few suggestions: Make outputs individually identifiable, increase commitment to the task and the sense of task importance, make sure each person's contribution is unique—not identical—to those of others, and build group cohesiveness. If these suggestions do not work, and if it is possible or reasonable, eliminate non-contributors from the group.

Pressure to Fail A fifth disadvantage is that the weaker group members control the outcome and therefore require others who might want to excel to do only the minimum necessary to get the job done and no more. In fact, members who do not cooperate and do excel beyond other group members might find themselves teased, chastised, or worse for breaking the group's norm. For example, Sam has 2 weeks of school left before she is to graduate and begin her new job as sales representative for a national distributor. In her organizational behavior class, she was assigned a major group project. She knows no matter what she does on the group project she will pass and therefore doesn't need to do very much. Thus, when meeting with her group, she says, "Hey guys, we don't have to take this assignment so seriously. All we have to do is to get it done." By encouraging the group to do the minimum, Sam pressures the group to fail, or at the very least to do a below-average job.

grouphate phenomenon
Dislike for groups.

Grouphate Phenomenon A final disadvantage results from negative experiences some have had in previous groups in which members lacked effective communication skills or disliked group work. This dislike for groups has been termed the **grouphate phenomenon**.[58] For some people, group work is so distasteful they avoid group situations whenever possible. In our experience, those who hate participating in groups the most are those who have little or no skill or lack training in how to communicate in groups.

MAKING CONNECTIONS FOR SUCCESS

Effective Groups

Imagine you are part of a campus group that the dean of student affairs has assigned to determine ways to make your campus greener. The group is made up of a variety of students, all selected by the dean. Everything seems perfect except for one member who recently had a personal crisis: He is very distracted and constantly looks at his text messages. His behavior affects the group's ability to focus on

the problem at hand. With that in mind, answer the following questions:

1. How would you deal with the situation?
2. What would you say to the group member who is going through the crisis?
3. What would you say to other group members?

Evaluating Small-Group Performance

14.11 **Describe** the role of evaluation in small-group performance.

It is important for groups and group members to understand they are responsible for their successes and failures. It is the responsibility of the group to fix its own problems or at least attempt to do so. Of course, when a group cannot resolve a problem, or if a split occurs in the group, sometimes an outside negotiator is necessary, but that should occur only after all other efforts have failed.

To ensure success, every group must evaluate its effectiveness periodically. The evaluation can take place at any time, but it is especially effective at the end of one task and before another begins.

Evaluation is also important in classroom exercises. As students learn about group communication, they need their instructor's feedback to evaluate themselves. Such self-evaluation should consider the following questions:

1. Are we using our time efficiently? If not, why not?
2. Does everyone have an opportunity to participate?
3. Do some people dominate the discussion?
4. Do people listen to what others are saying?
5. Does each person bring adequate information and research to the discussion?
6. Is the atmosphere free from personal conflict?
7. Does the group communication stay within the agenda?
8. Are members happy with the direction of the discussion? If not, why?
9. Do we set realistic goals for our meetings?
10. Do we get things accomplished? If not, why?

For an evaluation to produce results, its findings must be made known to all members of the group. A crucial requirement for such sharing is a nonthreatening atmosphere. The leader and all members must be willing to examine the situation without becoming defensive. If the group is not getting its job done or if its members are unhappy, corrective steps must be taken.

〉 SUMMARY

Small-Group Communication: Making the Connection to Our Everyday Lives

14.1 **Understand** the differences between a group and a team, and their roles in our everyday lives.

- Small-group communication involves the exchange of information among a relatively small number of people, ideally five to seven.
- In small-group communication, a small number of people share a common purpose, influence one another, take on roles, are interdependent, and interact with one another.

Purposes and Types of Groups

14.2 **Distinguish** among different types of groups—both face-to-face and on social media.

- *Primary groups* focus on social or interpersonal relationships and include family, close friends, Facebook friends, coworkers, and neighbors.
- *Secondary groups*, which exist to accomplish tasks or achieve goals, include decision-making, problem-solving, committee, learning, and therapy groups.
- Social media change how and when groups can meet and enable groups with members in different locations to make decisions quickly if necessary.

Characteristics of Small Groups

14.3　**Describe** the characteristics of small groups.

- The most essential characteristic of a group is its *interdependence*, or the mutual dependence among members.
- The members' *commitment* to the group is key to the group's success.
- *Cohesiveness*, the attraction among the group members, is important, but when it becomes too strong, it can interfere with good decision making.
- The differences between the way men and women communicate in groups are not clear, and the results of research are not always accurate or fair to one gender or the other.

Establishing a Group Culture

14.4　**Explain** how a group's culture, size, and norms affect group communication.

- *Group culture* is the pattern of values, beliefs, norms, and behaviors shared by group members that shape a group's individual personality.
- The group size has important ramifications for a group's effectiveness; a group that is too small can limit information and ideas; a group that is too large can limit individual contributions.
- Group *norms*, the informal and formal guidelines or rules of expected behaviors that are established by group members, guide the group's interaction.

Leadership

14.5　**Understand** the difference between leadership and leaders and the various leadership styles and behaviors they exhibit.

- *Leadership* is an influence process that includes specific behaviors, while a leader is assigned or emerges from the group.
- Leadership is a behavior that helps clarify a group's purpose or guides a group to achieve its goals.
- Leadership style can be measured in two ways: by orientation to either task (concern for accomplishment) and relationship (concern for people) or by the amount of power the *leader* yields to the members (autocratic, democratic, or laissez-faire styles).
- Sex-role stereotypes suggest that female leaders show more concern for interpersonal relations and tend to be more democratic in their leadership style than male leaders.

Ethical Behavior in Group Communication

14.6　**Describe** the role of ethics in small-group communication.

- For groups to perform at a high level, both leaders and members must be ethical. Group members should have a right to speak openly, share information with the group, be honest and act with integrity, keep shared information confidential if asked to do so, and use information ethically.

Member Participation

14.7　**Differentiate** among the roles of group members and explain their various contributions.

- Successful groups depend on group members' performing a variety of roles, such as group task and building and maintenance roles. Self-centered roles also come into play, and they can be counterproductive and destructive.
- Group task roles help accomplish the group's task or objective; group building and maintenance roles define the social atmosphere of the group.
- Self-centered group contributions are generally counterproductive and destructive to the group; the best approach to handling counterproductive and destructive behaviors is to discuss them openly.

Managing Group Conflict

14.8　**Describe** conflict, its impacts, and the conflict management strategies that can manage it.

- Groups can experience conflicts, as is true anytime two or more people come together. However, competently trained groups know how to use principled negotiation, a procedure that helps group members negotiate consensus by collaborating to find alternatives to meet differing needs.
- Effective group decision making and problem solving often depend on conflict and open disagreement.
- Online interactions may be more likely to display relational and task conflict than face-to-face interactions.
- *Principled negotiation*, a procedure that helps groups negotiate consensus, takes into account the other party's views.
- Ethical behavior can help groups increase their understanding of issues and enhance group cohesiveness while minimizing destructive outcomes.

Problem Solving and Decision Making

14.9 **Explain** the reflective thinking process and functional communication theory.

- The goal of most small-group communication is to solve problems or make decisions.
- To do this effectively, groups must be able to state the problem clearly.
- Reflective thinking focuses on the decision-making process and includes becoming aware of the problem, defining and describing it, arriving at possible solutions, evaluating advantages and disadvantages, and then choosing the best solution. Functional theory focuses on the communication process and assumes groups make the best decisions when they have all of the information and resources available to them.
- Groups sometimes find themselves unable to generate new ideas or think of decisions; thus, brainstorming can be the answer.
- The goal of most groups is to arrive at consensus in their decisions.

Working in Groups or Teams: Advantages and Disadvantages

14.10 **Explain** the advantages and disadvantages of participating in groups and how to overcome the disadvantages.

- Group membership helps satisfy psychological and social needs, achieve goals that otherwise might not be accomplished, provide multiple sources of information, meet the need for security, and contribute to an individual's social identity.
- The following are disadvantages of groups: Members can become too cohesive or committed, *groupthink* may result, groups are time consuming, not all members contribute equally, the *social loafer* can affect the outcome, pressure to fail can occur, and *grouphate* can occur.

Evaluating Small-Group Performance

14.11 **Describe** the role of evaluation in small-group performance.

- To ensure continuous success and progress, groups should undertake a self-analysis periodically and look for areas in which to improve.

〉 DISCUSSION STARTERS

1. Describe why it is important to know how to work in a group or on a work team.

2. Suggest behaviors that would make group work more efficient.

3. Which group characteristic (interdependence, commitment, cohesiveness, group size, or group culture) do you think is the most important for a group to succeed? Why?

4. Discuss two norms in your class that apply to a group.

5. Describe a recent event in which groupthink occurred and why it occurred.

6. Explain what you think are the differences, if any, that females and males brought to a group discussion in which you have participated.

7. In what ways has social media changed the way we enter and work in groups?

8. Describe what it means to be an ethical group member.

9. From your experiences, how can a social loafer affect a group's climate, motivation, and productivity?

10. Describe a competent leader of a group or team.

11. How would you get withdrawn group members back into a discussion without embarrassing them?

12. Determine the criteria that you think would effectively evaluate a group.

CHAPTER 15

CONNECTING THROUGH WORKPLACE COMMUNICATION: PREPARING FOR YOUR FUTURE

Connecting via open communication in the workplace with colleagues leads to a successful career and happier life.

Nick White and Fiona Jackson-Downes/Cultura/Getty Images

→ CHAPTER OUTLINE AND LEARNING OBJECTIVES

Communication and a Successful Career

15.1 Describe what it takes to have a successful career and the qualities employers seek in applicants.

Conducting the Job Search

15.2 Explain how to conduct an effective job search.

Preparing for an Interview

15.3 Explain the steps in preparing for a job interview.

The Interview

15.4 Describe yourself to potential employers in an effective and competent way to give them information and reasons to hire you.

Getting the Job Offer

15.5 Explain why employers may accept or reject an applicant.

MAKING EVERYDAY CONNECTIONS

Rachelle, a mother of two children, started college before having children, but she and her husband decided that she should put her college education on hold in order to raise their children. The children are now in middle and high school. They are old enough to be on their own and thus Rachelle and her husband have decided it is a good time for her to complete her degree in communication. Because she has been out of the job market and is unaware of potential job opportunities for communication majors, she turns to her advisor, career services office, and the Internet for help.

Markaus, who is graduating in May, is pursuing a public relations position with a major corporation in his hometown of Omaha, Nebraska. Through a friend of a friend, Markaus is able to contact the personnel director of S & S Shipping Enterprises to discuss an opening in the company's public relations department.

Edden, a junior, is looking for an internship in marketing in order to get some experience before she begins a real job. She has contacted several marketing firms through her university internship office and is about to interview for an assistant's position.

Dionne needs to earn some money in order to make her rent payment while attending college. She decides to get a part-time job and is scheduled to interview with a local clothing store.

QUESTIONS TO THINK ABOUT

1. Which of the individuals above comes closest to representing you and your future? Explain.

2. When and how should you start preparing for your career?

3. Describe the value of doing an internship.

It is never too early to prepare for your future, whether you are a first-year student or a senior who is about to graduate. The important part of preparation is getting started, and those who do this early will likely be the best prepared and have successful careers. In this chapter we examine communication in the workplace and what you should do to prepare for the internship and the employment search interview—what you can expect to encounter and how you can make the best impression in a job interview.[1]

Communication and a Successful Career

15.1 **Describe** what it takes to have a successful career and the qualities employers seek in applicants.

Besides obtaining a college degree in your chosen field, your ability to communicate effectively in a variety of contexts is essential to almost every career and your success whichever career you choose. It is stated in almost every textbook related to business communication and in a significant numbers of research studies that the ability to communicate effectively in the workplace is essential.[2] For example, one study of over 1,000 employers at Fortune 1000 companies indicated that most workers send and receive an average of 178 messages each day.[3] People in various leadership roles in organizations often spend 80 to 90 percent of their average workweek communicating. Communication is pervasive in every career, and its effectiveness is essential for businesses and the individuals in them to be successful. This is evident in the number of research studies and textbooks written on the subject. However, what truly matters to the success of every business or organization is the overall quality of its communication.

It is difficult to name a career field or specific job that does not require some proficiency in communication, either written or oral or both. Over the past several years, employers who have been asked if college graduates are adequately prepared to enter the world of work have answered with either no or somewhat. This concern is expressed not only by employers but also by politicians and higher education professionals. The reason for their response is that they believe higher education has failed at closing what they refer to as the skill gap. The difference between the skills new graduates have and the skills that employers are demanding of those they want to employ has gotten wider. The question that needs answering is, "Which specific skills, knowledge, and abilities should students be acquiring so that they can thrive in an unpredictable and competitive 21st-century economy?"[4]

The National Association of Colleges and Employers (NACE) surveyed 1,000 employers (receiving 201 completed surveys, a 20.5 percent rate of return) between August and October 2017 regarding the skills and qualities they look for when hiring new employees. The results of the survey are summarized in Table 15.1. The bottom line is that employers are looking for talented people who are flexible and able to adapt to all kinds of situations.

In the same survey, NACE asked employers how ready recent graduates were to perform the competencies they were looking for in hiring employees. It is interesting to note that employers who were surveyed found very few graduates of four-year universities, on average, were extremely proficient in the skills they were seeking in future employees. What they did find is that most employees were "very proficient" related to the skills they were seeking. However, this also means half were not "very proficient" related to the skills they were seeking in graduates whom they were hiring.

In the same survey, NACE asked employers to rate employees on readiness of needed proficiencies or career readiness of the essential competencies employers want in an employee. There appears to be a substantial gap between competencies proficiency considered essential by employers compared to those they rated as proficient except for digital technology. The largest gaps were related to critical thinking/problem solving, professionalism/work ethic, oral/written communications, and leadership, all of which are core competencies employers considered essential skills. See Table 15.2 for the complete data of need versus proficiency of career readiness competencies.

Once you graduate from college, you will find yourself continuing the learning process on the job. The difference will be from sitting in a classroom to attending training sessions or on the job learning. You will learn quickly that communication and developing relationships are not very different in life after college than it is in college. The preceding chapters of this text, you will learn quickly, are essential to your future success. It should be clear to you that the more you know about communication and its role in your everyday lives and in your future career, the more likely you will be successful and more satisfied in both.

Table 15.1 EMPLOYERS RATE THE ESSENTIAL NEED OF THE CAREER READINESS COMPETENCIES

Career Readiness Competencies	Weighted Average Rating*
Critical thinking/problem solving	4.62
Teamwork/collaboration	4.56
Professionalism/work ethic	4.46
Oral/written communications	4.30
Leadership	3.82
Digital technology	3.73
Career management	3.46
Global/multicultural fluency	3.01

* 5-point scale, where 1 = Not essential, 2 = Not very essential, 3 = Somewhat essential, 4 = Essential, 5 = Absolutely essential.

SOURCE: Data from Job Outlook 2018, National Association of Colleges and Employers. This report can be found at https://www.naceweb.org/career-readiness/competencies/employers-rate-career-competencies-new-hire-proficiency/. Last retrieved on March 14, 2018.

Table 15.2 **NEED VERSUS PROFICIENCY OF CAREER READINESS COMPETENCIES, BY PERCENTAGE OF RESPONDENTS**

Career Readiness Competencies	Considered Essential*	Rated Proficient[†]
Teamwork/collaboration	97.5%	77.0%
Digital technology	64.2%	65.8%
Critical thinking/problem solving	99.2%	55.8%
Professionalism/work ethic	100%	42.5%
Oral/written communications	95.9%	41.6%
Leadership	68.6%	33.0%
Global/multicultural fluency	31.1%	20.7%
Career Management	47.1%	17.3%

Source: Data from Job Outlook 2018, National Association of Colleges and Employers. This report can be found at https://www.naceweb.org/career-readiness/competencies/employers-rate-career-competencies-new-hire-proficiency/. Last retrieved on March 14, 2018.

* The percentages corresponding to "considered essential" represent, among all responding employers, the percentage who, on a 5-point scale, indicated that the respective competency was either "essential" (4) or "absolutely essential" (5) for college graduates to enter their workforce.

[†]The percentages corresponding to "rated proficient" represent, among all responding employers, the percentage who, on a 5-point scale, rated recent graduates either "very" (4) or "extremely" (5) proficient in the respective competency.

Dr. Kelli Smith, former assistant director of career services at the University of Nebraska–Lincoln, suggests that students get as much experience in team building and working in teams as possible.[5] According to Smith, companies are looking for individuals who can work with others. One company recruiter asks students the following question: "When you work as a part of a team, what unique role do you play?" Smith said, "Hiring people who are team players is important to many organizations that have downsized and have fewer management positions because they are much more team-oriented." What is your role when working with others? Is it leading, organizing, brainstorming, or something else?

Dr. Smith also said internships are important to gain work experience. Smith suggests that students get involved in internships related to the jobs they will seek after graduation. She says students who have had internships can say they have done the job or similar work, thus giving them a better chance at getting a job than those with no experience. "Such experiences [internships] are also key for networking and helping students decide whether or not a certain career is the right fit for them," Smith said.

Almost every career requires skills such as writing, speaking, reading, listening, decision making, researching, and reasoning. In addition most organizations want to hire individuals who show leadership abilities and possess interpersonal communication, organization, and persuasive skills. A number of characteristics are important for high-level professional positions, including ambition, assertiveness, competitiveness, dependability, initiative, motivation, responsibility, and responsiveness.[6] The way you acquire these skills and behaviors described above is largely up to you. No matter how bright and knowledgeable you might be, landing a high-level or professional job will be extremely difficult, if not impossible, wthout them.

Employers in many professional fields also look for creativity. Is the applicant spontaneous? Some recruiters will ask off-the-wall questions just to see if this "throws" an applicant. How does an applicant respond in these tough situations? Can the applicant be creative with his or her answers? This is important to most employers because in business situations with customers, employees often have to respond to sudden changes and unfamiliar problems. What employers look for most in applicants and employees are personal qualities such as assertiveness, self-motivation, ambition, and a competitive instinct. Employers say they can usually learn whether applicants have these qualities by how they present themselves and by the types of activities or jobs they have held while in school. Next, we discuss the steps you must consider in order to obtain your first job after graduation.

Thinking about Your Future

Think about what each person must be able to demonstrate in order to land a job. Skills! That one word means a lot to your future. The recurring theme among the experts we surveyed is an emphasis on skills and competencies rather than on completing specific studies.

Some exceptional sources you might consider to help you answer the questions below and prepare for your job interview are the following: P. Klaus, *Brag: The Art of Tooting Your Own Horn without Blowing It* (New York: Warner Books, 2004); D. Bolles, *What Color Is Your Parachute?* (Berkeley, CA: Ten Speed Press, 2010) (Bolles also has a website you should consider: www.jobhuntersbible.com); M. Carole, *Perfect Phrases for the Perfect Interview* (New York: McGraw-Hill, 2005); J. E. Wall, *Jobseekers* *Online Goldmine* (Indianapolis, IN: JIST Works, 2006); and M. Yates, *Knock 'Em Dead: The Ultimate Job Seekers Guide* (Cincinnati, OH: Adam Media Corp, 2006). *U.S. News & World Report* describes "best careers" annually. This can be a helpful resource for college students.

1. You know the most important skills employers are looking for, but how would you prove that *you* have them?

2. What courses have you taken that have allowed you to develop the various skills or competencies listed in this chapter that you will need to be successful in your future career? Explain how you obtained those skills or why you didn't obtain them.

Conducting the Job Search

15.2 **Explain** how to conduct an effective job search.

In today's reasonably good economic times, it is not unusual for applicants with superb qualifications to face tremendous competition for the best jobs. According to placement service data, the average applicant should spend 15 to 25 hours per week searching for employment. Highly motivated people will treat the search as if it were a job itself. The more time a person spends searching, the sooner and more likely he or she receive job offers.[7] One way to begin your job search is networking, which is discussed next.

Networking

networking

The systematic contacting of people who can provide information about available jobs or who can offer jobs.

Newspaper and online ads, professional magazines, placement services, former teachers, and people working in jobs you are interested in can all be good sources of job leads. However, the most productive approach to locating jobs is networking. **Networking** is the systematic contacting of people who can provide information about available jobs or who can offer jobs. Relatives, friends, classmates, colleagues, alumni, and people at social and professional gatherings are all potential sources of information. If one of your contacts does not personally know of any job openings, ask if he or she knows of anyone who might. Then contact that person. In this way, your network expands from one person to another, and you gain information from each new contact. Many social networking sites such as Facebook, LinkedIn, and Twitter can be helpful when seeking job opportunities. LinkedIn, the best-known site to connect those with jobs to those looking for work, has over 500 million users and continues to grow.[8] Many employers search networks and websites to find qualified candidates. LinkedIn allows the user to list past experiences, awards, and skills as well as presentations, portfolios, and other documents. However, LinkedIn should not be a passive resource where one hopes an organization finds the profile and reaches out for employment opportunities. Users should use LinkedIn to research industries, employers, and key people at organizations of interest. Connecting to professional groups or alumni associations expands the potential number of contacts. LinkedIn allows users (both employees and employers) to create profiles and connections to each other in an online network similar to real-world professional relationships.[9]

MAKING CONNECTIONS FOR SUCCESS
Networking via Social Media

Many online networks will help you with your job search and with preparing you for the job interview. LinkedIn is one professional network to which many professionals are turning; it provides a variety of support for professionals and potential employees. It currently has more than 500 million registered users in over 200 countries.[10] It offers an excellent way to connect with others via social media, and it's not uncommon to have professional contacts on Facebook and Twitter as well.

Go to LinkedIn and determine how it can help you in your search and preparation for a job. Visit the LinkedIn Learning Center online for information and specific resources available. Take time to review Learning Webinars to learn about developing an online presence and engaging with your network. Plan to complete your profile fully, including a professional summary, work history, and education.

1. Have you or someone you know ever networked via social media? What were the positives and negatives of your or the other person's experience?

2. Explain how traditional networking strategies can be beneficial when searching for a job.

Why should you network? The answer is simple: It is the best strategic approach you can take for finding a job and/or opportunities and to help you develop as professional. Many employers depend on others, both inside and outside their organizations, to recommend individuals for various positions. Often, therefore, there are many good jobs not listed or advertised—it is referred to as the *hidden job market*. Thus, it is important to build relationships with those you already know in the workforce as well as those you meet at career fairs; through faculty contacts; or by discussing your career plans with family, friends, or others. It is also a good idea to post messages of your job interests on social media.

Career Fairs

Most college campuses hold career fairs, which are useful for networking as well as for making contacts with organizations for internships or jobs. Contact the career services office at your college or university and ask when the next career fair will take place in your area. You should attend as many career fairs as time permits. You don't have to wait until your senior year to attend a career fair. By making contact with an organization early in your education, you can establish a relationship with that company as well as be in the best position for getting an internship or a job after graduation.

Some career centers, private employment organizations, or even employers may host "virtual" career fairs where job seekers connect via some form of chat (email, video, phone) during set online meeting times. These types of events usually include job postings and an opportunity for job seekers to post a résumé.

If you do plan to attend a career fair at your university or community, you should prepare for it as professionally as possible. If you are early in your college career, that is, a first- or second-year student, you might want to go to a career fair to see what it is like. Your intent is to observe what takes place and what others do at the fair. When you are a junior or senior, it is time to make contacts with employers in your chosen career field. You can do the following to prepare yourself for a good experience at a job fair:

- Check your profile to ensure it is up-to-date on all websites where you have posted your information.
- Know which employers are attending the career fair and research them.
- Update your résumé and if possible tailor it to specific careers.
- Dress to impress—you want to make a good impression.
- Know what you are going to say (plan an *elevator pitch*—a one- to two-minute introduction of yourself).[11]

The day of the fair arrives and you are ready to make an impression. Here are some recommendations:

- Prioritize which employers you definitely want to meet.
- Place a number of hard copies of your résumé in folder and carry them with you.
- When greeting a recruiter, give a firm handshake, make eye contact, and show enthusiasm and interest.
- Ask recruiters if they have any tips for applying online, especially if the recruiter doesn't or can't take a copy of your résumé.
- Always ask for contact information or a business card.[12]

The Internet

One of the most valuable tools available in preparing for the employment interview is the Internet. For example, you can learn how to prepare for the interview, write a résumé, research organizations, find job opportunities, find out what questions are commonly asked in interviews, and even get advice on what to wear to an interview. Most colleges and universities have a career services office you can visit in person or contact through a home page. The career services' home page can be an extremely valuable source of information. The University of Nebraska–Lincoln's (UNL's) Career Services, for example, provides information pertaining to almost every aspect of careers and the employment interview. For example, the "job search preparation" area leads to information on networking, job search strategies, résumé tips and a sample résumé, tips for writing cover letters and sample cover letters, whom to give as references, and interviewing tips.

Here are some sample websites for job searches and career information. Conduct an Internet search to find additional sources:

- LinkedIn.com (business- and employment-oriented service that operates via websites and mobile apps)
- Monster.com (an American-based global employment website owned and operated by Monster Worldwide, Inc.)
- CareerBuilder.com (search by job type, industry, or field of interest)
- Indeed.com (American worldwide employment-related search engine for job listings—it was launched in November 2004 and has become the most widely used job search engine in the world)

In addition, consult targeted websites appropriate to your needs. Such websites may have a geographic focus, for example, to help you learn about opportunities in the community in which you want to work; an industry focus such as government, nonprofit, or education; or types of positions such as internship listing sites.

It is increasingly common for job applicants to connect with potential employers electronically. If you fill out an online application, here are some suggestions:

- Proofread your information as carefully and as thoroughly as you can—ask someone who is competent in editing to read it to ensure it is error free.
- Follow instructions on the website. However, you should be careful when providing personal information such as a Social Security number. Unless the site is secure, it is recommended that you do not provide your Social Security number.
- Look at the entire application site before filling out anything to plan what and how you will respond. Make sure you understand how the "submit" options work so that your application information is received.
- Submit separate applications for each individual position in which you have an interest. Update or change your profile as appropriate to fit each position.
- Cover letters may not be requested or allowed on the site, but often there are open text boxes where parts of your cover letter could be included, if appropriate.

- Contact the employer directly about specific openings after submitting electronically to ensure your materials were received.[13]

Here are some additional suggestions for applying via email:

- Make sure your email account name will add to your credibility.
- Use a meaningful and short subject line and include your name (for example, "Application from Mary Smith regarding your sales representative position").
- Use the format the employer requests and include your résumé in the text or as an attachment. Write the email as a formal business letter, using an appropriate greeting.
- If you attach your résumé and cover letter via email, use a standard font such as Times New Roman or Arial. You may want to save your documents in PDF form so they may be easily viewed on a variety of email and web browsers.[14]

Preparing for an Interview

15.3 **Explain** the steps in preparing for a job interview.

Although it may seem years away for some of you to begin thinking about a career, it is never too early to begin preparing. Preparing for a job interview takes planning and some thought about what will be expected of you as an applicant. Initial job interviews typically average only 20 to 30 minutes—a short time in comparison to the time you spend earning a college degree. *Yet these are probably the most important minutes you will spend in determining your future.* You may be surprised to learn how many applicants fail to plan adequately. Instead, they enter the interview saying essentially, "Here I am, now what?" This gives the impression they are indifferent, an impression that is seldom dispelled in the course of the interview. It is up to you to ensure that you do not leave an impression of indifference and that you present a positive picture of yourself. The first item for you to consider is a list of your accomplishments to date and how you will present them to others. This is usually done via a résumé.

Writing a Résumé

It is important that you build your skills both in and outside the classroom with internships or part-time jobs. You should also consider joining or being elected to student organizations, volunteering for community organizations, or helping a faculty member with research projects. Most of us are unable to remember what we have accomplished over time; thus it is important to begin by keeping a list of experiences and skills that can be used as documentation of accomplishments.

A **résumé** is a written document that briefly and accurately describes an individual's personal, educational, and professional qualifications and experiences. A well-written résumé increases a person's chances of making a good impression. A poorly written résumé can seriously jeopardize a person's chances, even though he or she may be well qualified. The résumé is your personal marketing tool showing you are qualified or that you are an ideal candidate for specific jobs. If the résumé is done well and illustrates your strengths effectively, it will likely generate interviews or at least follow-up interaction with employers. Here is a list of details to consider when writing an effective and well-organized résumé:

résumé

A written document that briefly and accurately describes an individual's personal, educational, and professional qualifications and experiences

1. All margins should be set to 1 inch.
2. The font should be one that is easy to read and either 10 or 12 points in font size.
3. Bold face, underlining, and italics should be used purposely to highlight and separate sections.
4. Limit the length of your résumé to one page unless more than one page is typical in the area in which you are applying.

5. You should also develop a separate unformatted version of your résumé for an online application if required.

6. Always list experiences in chronological order, with the most recent first.

7. If you include your GPA, it should be accurate. Do not round it up.[15]

What should you include on your résumé? Here's a list:

1. Contact information, that is, name, address, city, state, zip code, phone, email, LinkedIn address, professional website, or other.

2. Educational background, that is, the name of the institution, location, degree (fully spelled out), date of graduation, and major(s).

3. It is highly recommended to include your work experience, skills, activities, honors/awards and other relevant experiences.

4. A career or professional objective, or related coursework, is optional.

5. Do not include references. Create a list but place them on a separate page—provide your references only if requested.[16]

A résumé is an extremely powerful form of communication. Because it represents an applicant, it must be accurate, complete, and neat. The contents and layouts of résumés vary as widely as the number of individuals who apply for jobs. A general rule, and the safest, is to keep it simple; limit it to one or two pages; and list items within each section, beginning with the most current one. Employers are busy and do not have time to read lengthy, overly involved résumés.

As an applicant, you are not required to provide information that might be used in a discriminatory way. This includes your age, sex, marital status, race, religion, and other data as set forth by Title VII of the Equal Employment Opportunity Act of 1972 and other affirmative action laws. The inclusion of such facts in a résumé is up to the applicant, but it is generally advised that they be omitted.

When writing your résumé, you should use bullet statements that describe and show what you have accomplished. Effective bullet statements are ones that answer "what," "how," and "why." You already know what employers are looking for in an employee; now you have to show the employers that you have what they are seeking. This can only be done if you can describe what you have accomplished or will be able to accomplish through actions that you have taken and the results of those actions.

Start each listed bullet point with an action verb. "Your Ultimate Job Search Guide" provides examples of action verbs for you to consider. The following list includes action verbs as they relate to specific applicant characteristics:

- *Leadership or Initiative*: accomplished, achieved, influenced, managed, motivated, coordinated, trained.
- *Teamwork or Interpersonal*: helped, encouraged, consulted, supported, interacted, engaged.
- *Problem Solving*: solved, improved, enhanced, identified, adjusted, mediated, concluded.
- *Written Communication*: authored, documented, drafted, wrote, critiqued, edited.
- *Verbal Communication*: negotiated, sold, discussed, advocated, convinced, facilitated, presented
- *Analytical*: analyzed, evaluated, validated, estimated, compared, projected, researched.
- *Technical*: audited, designed, modified, tested, built, calculated, demonstrated, installed.
- *Organized or Detailed*: revised, arranged, consolidated, prioritized, executed, planned, organized.
- *Creativity*: displayed, created, designed, launched, marketed, produced, developed.

Examples of Résumés

A "getting involved" type of résumé is designed to obtain a scholarship, a study broad program, or a part-time job (see Figure 15.1). A chronological résumé presents students wanting to gain experience (see Figure 15.2). A résumé designed for starting or continuing a full-time career is shown in Figure 15.3.

Many employment counselors recommend that college students include a brief career objective on the résumé immediately following the introductory information. The objective should be as specific as possible. Two examples:

> To become a public relations director in either a major corporation or an agency.
> To obtain experience in sales, advertising, or marketing.

In the educational section of the résumé, the applicant should list colleges and universities attended, degrees conferred, majors, minors, special major subjects, and scholarships. A statement about grade achievement may be included, but is not required.

The experience section should include paid and unpaid jobs held, the dates held, and their locations. If the applicant has held numerous part-time jobs, list only a few of the most important, most recent, and most relevant jobs. Discuss other job experiences during the interview if it is appropriate to do so. Within this experience section, describe your responsibilities. Start each phrase with an action verb followed by details about the responsibility. You may want to use numbers, dollars, or keywords to give the reader a better idea of the scope of your skills.

In the extracurricular activities section, the applicant should list all offices held, social and professional organizations he or she was involved in, and any athletic participation. This section demonstrates the applicant's outside interests; well roundedness; and social, leadership, and organizational skills. Such information is less important for experienced or older applicants who have demonstrated similar skills in other areas.

List your references on a separate page and provide them only if requested. Even though you might not plan to apply for a job now, it is wise to get to know your professors and to make sure they get to know you. Find appropriate times (office hours, perhaps) and reasons (discussion of a paper or an assignment) to visit with your professors so they become acquainted with you. Professors will find it easier to be contacted as a reference or write a letter of recommendation for you if they know who you are, and the reference will be more personal and believable.

Never put a person's name on a reference list unless you have his or her permission to do so. When asking individuals to serve as a reference for you, give them a copy of your résumé and tell them what kind of job you are seeking. While some employers may ask for written letters of recommendation, most will just request contact information so they can directly communicate with your references. You should always ask if the person would be able to provide a positive reference. If he or she says no or seems hesitant, then move on to someone else. See Figure 15.4 for an example separate reference page and its format.

After you write your résumé, proofread it carefully for errors and omissions. Then ask a counselor or career advisor in the career services office or a professor to suggest improvements.

If you follow the steps above, your completed résumé should be acceptable.

Creating Your Website or Blog

Many of today's job applicants successfully use social media or create websites as a way to get their résumé or portfolio out to others. By doing this, and if you are careful and follow the guidelines already suggested in this chapter, you create another avenue and effective means of selling yourself and what you have to offer. You should develop these sites with professionalism to showcase your creative, design, technical, and writing skills.

FIGURE 15.1   Getting Involved

The transition résumé is helpful when converting a high school résumé to a college résumé. The academic résumé is useful when applying for academic scholarships, awards, honors, or graduate or professional school.

From page 22 of "Your Ultimate Job Search Guide 2017-2018" Career Services, 225 Nebraska Union. Reprinted with permission of University of Nebraska-Lincoln Career Service, www.unl.edu/careers.

Résumé Example 1: Getting Involved

Targeted toward students applying for scholarships, study abroad, or part-time jobs.

RILEY GREENE

860 North 17th Street #304 | Abel Residence Hall | Lincoln, NE 68508
402-555-5555 | riley.greene16@gmail.com

OBJECTIVE
To obtain a scholarship based on academics and financial need for study abroad in New Zealand

EDUCATION
University of Nebraska–Lincoln, Lincoln, NE
Bachelor of Arts
Major: Undeclared
Graduation: May 20XX (anticipated)
GPA: #.##/4.00

Lincoln North Star High School, Lincoln, NE
High School Diploma
Graduation: May 20XX

WORK EXPERIENCE
Subway, Lincoln, NE
Sandwich Artist, June 20XX – Present
- Perform informal oral satisfaction survey at checkout to show care for customers' experience
- Complete financial transactions with attention to detail and accuracy
- Communicate with customers to determine their needs and create custom sandwiches to specifications

Private Families, Lincoln, NE
Babysitter, October 20XX – May 20XX
- Supervised the safety of three elementary school age children twice-weekly
- Created age-appropriate educational opportunities to support creative and academic growth

LEADERSHIP/VOLUNTEER EXPERIENCE
Center for People in Need, Lincoln, NE
Volunteer, June 20XX – Present
- Prepare food for events of up to 100 people, emphasizing attention to known food allergens
- Coordinate "Teen for a Day" events in which young women in grades 6-12 may shop for new clothes for the upcoming school year for free to start the year off successfully

Orchestra & Marching Band, Lincoln North Star High School, Lincoln, NE
First Chair Trumpet, September 20XX – May 20XX; *Member*, October 20XX – May 20XX
- Earned first chair position out of 20 other students based on performance ability and leadership skills
- Practiced 2 hours daily while balancing academics and other activities

HONORS
James Canfield Scholarship, University of Nebraska–Lincoln, Lincoln, NE, August 20XX – Present

SKILLS
Computer: Microsoft Word and PowerPoint
Languages: Basic written and conversational Spanish

TIP: If you are still deciding on your major, list it as "Undeclared" with a degree in Bachelor of Arts or Bachelor of Science. Remember to change this to the correct degree and major once you declare your major.

TIP: Include your GPA or major GPA if it is 3.0 or above.

TIP: You may include your high school education and experiences on your résumé initially but this information should be removed by your junior year.

TIP: Start with a strong action verb in present tense if you are still working in the role.

TIP: Start with a strong action verb in past tense if you are no longer working in the role.

TIP: If you have held more than one position at an organization, show the progression and save space by listing the organization first.

TIP: In the "Skills" section, focus on "hard" or "technical" skills relevant to your field. Integrate into bullet statements if possible.

MAKING CONNECTIONS FOR SUCCESS

The Dark Side of the Web

Some employers now require applicants to provide passwords for their social media sites along with their résumés and references. Companies not asking for passwords have taken other steps—asking potential employees to friend their HR managers or to log on to a company computer while interviewing. Other employers ask hired employees to sign no disparagement agreements that essentially prevent the employee from saying or writing anything negative about an employer on social media.[17]

1. How will you respond to such requests should you be asked?

2. What can you do to avoid having your social media pages become a negative influence on whether or not you are hired?

FIGURE 15.2 Chronological Résumé

An internship résumé highlights course work and areas of internship to potential employers. The cover letter of inquiry is used when an applicant is uncertain about what jobs or positions are available with a particular employer.

From page 23 of "Your Ultimate Job Search Guide 2017-2018" Career Services, 225 Nebraska Union. Reprinted with permission of University of Nebraska-Lincoln Career Service, www.unl.edu/careers.

Résumé Example 2: Gaining Experience

Targeted toward students applying for internships, research opportunities, or major-related experiences.

RILEY GREENE
1234 Kennedy Drive | Lincoln, NE 68512 | 402-555-5555 | riley.greene16@gmail.com
www.linkedin.com/in/rileygreene

OBJECTIVE
To obtain the Executive Store Intern position at Target utilizing analytical, communication, and teamwork skills

EDUCATION
University of Nebraska–Lincoln, Lincoln, NE
Bachelor of Arts, May 20XX (anticipated)
Major: Psychology; GPA: #.##/4.00
Scholarships: James Canfield Scholarship and Global Gateway Scholarship

Lincoln University, Christ Church, New Zealand
New Zealand Study Tour (6 credits of history), Summer 20XX

WORK EXPERIENCE
University of Nebraska Foundation, Lincoln, NE
Phonathon Caller, September 20XX – Present
- Persuade alumni and friends of the University to make financial contributions totaling more than $200,000 in pledges within first three months
- Analyze potential donor information prior to call to identify specific resources for targeted sales approach

Subway, Lincoln, NE
Sandwich Artist, June 20XX – August 20XX
- Completed financial transactions with attention to detail and accuracy ensuring positive customer experience

ACTIVITIES
Undergraduate Psychology Organization, University of Nebraska–Lincoln, Lincoln, NE
Member, October 20XX – Present
- Learn more about the field of psychology from peers and faculty

University Program Council (UPC), University of Nebraska–Lincoln, Lincoln, NE
Member, January 20XX – Present
- Collaborate in a team to coordinate and promote entertaining educational events to the campus community

VOLUNTEER EXPERIENCE
Alternative Service Break, Pine Ridge, SD
Participant, March 20XX
- Volunteered in the Pine Ridge Indian Reservation, tribal headquarters of the Oglala Sioux Tribe
- Tutored elementary school students to provide mentorship toward higher education goals

Center for People in Need, Lincoln, NE
Volunteer, June 20XX – October 20XX
- Coordinated events to support families and individuals in need with donations from the community
- Provided supplemental nutrition assistance to approximately 100 individuals monthly

SKILLS
Computer: Microsoft Word, PowerPoint, Excel
Language: Basic written and conversational Spanish

TIP: Include a URL to your LinkedIn profile, professional website, or blog for networking purposes and to share additional information with employers.

TIP: If including an "Objective" section when applying to a specific position, include the job title and organization name.

TIP: Make sure your degree, major, and GPA (if included) are listed accurately.

TIP: At the internship level, employers do not expect a significant amount of related experience. For positions that seem unrelated to your career goals, highlight duties and responsibilities that are transferable.

TIP: Along with duties and responsibilities, focus on specific achievements or results.

TIP: Use quantities in your experience descriptions to communicate results and your level of responsibility.

TIP: Alter the format and structure of your résumé to highlight different activities and experiences.

Researching the Organization via the Web

Before arriving for an interview, you should know the full name of the company and background information on the company's history; where its headquarters, plants, offices, or stores are located; what products or services it offers; and what its economic growth has been as well as its future prospects. Such knowledge demonstrates your initiative and interest to the interviewer and can serve as a springboard for discussion. This also shows you have an interest in the company rather than giving the impression you're settling for whatever job you can find.

Begin by conducting an online search for the organization. Pursue the sites fully; often there is an "about" or "organization information" tab that describes the organization—its history, locations, services, products, subsidiaries, and so on. You will likely find

FIGURE 15.3 Getting the Job

The résumé layout may vary, depending on the experiences and skills of the individual applicant.

From page 24 of "Your Ultimate Job Search Guide 2017-2018" Career Services, 225 Nebraska Union. Reprinted with permission of University of Nebraska-Lincoln Career Service, www.unl.edu/careers.

Résumé Example 3: Getting the Job

Targeted toward candidates seeking full-time career opportunities.

RILEY GREENE
1234 Kennedy Drive | Lincoln, NE 68512 | 402-555-5555 | riley.greene16@gmail.com
www.linkedin.com/in/rileygreene

EDUCATION
University of Nebraska–Lincoln, Lincoln, NE
Bachelor of Arts, May 20XX (anticipated)
Major: Psychology; GPA: #.##/4.00

Lincoln University, Christ Church, New Zealand
New Zealand Study Tour (6 credits of history), Summer 20XX

RELEVANT EXPERIENCE
University of Nebraska Foundation, Lincoln, NE
Phonathon Caller, September 20XX – Present
- Persuade alumni and others to make financial contributions using acute speaking and listening skills
- Earned top 10% fundraiser status within first three months by generating more than $200,000 in pledges

Target, Kansas City, MO
Executive Store Intern, May 20XX – August 20XX
- Interacted with 50+ customers daily using effective customer service, organization, and multi-tasking abilities to ensure a positive experience and resolve any problems
- Cross-trained in all departments, including electronics, to appropriately support customers' individual needs

Department of Psychology, University of Nebraska–Lincoln, Lincoln, NE
Research Methods and Data Analysis Research Project Participant, August 20XX – December 20XX
- Analyzed complex statistical data using Microsoft Excel and SPSS to test research project hypotheses
- Used critical thinking skills to evaluate appropriateness of research conclusions based on data
- Demonstrated technical writing ability by presenting research project in a concise yet detailed poster format

ACTIVITIES
Undergraduate Psychology Organization, University of Nebraska–Lincoln, Lincoln, NE
Vice-President, January 20XX – Present
- Recruit potential new members through social media announcements, classroom visits, and flyers increasing overall membership by 5%
Member, January 20XX-Present
- Build relationships with peers and faculty while learning more about the psychology field

University Program Council (UPC), University of Nebraska–Lincoln, Lincoln, NE
Member, January 20XX – December 20XX
- Researched and conducted outreach to entertainment speakers and groups following up as needed
- Coordinated and promoted entertaining educational speakers to the campus community in a 5-person team

VOLUNTEER EXPERIENCE
Alternative Service Break, Pine Ridge, SD
Participant, March 20XX
- Tutored elementary school students on the Pine Ridge Reservation and encouraged participation in extracurricular activities

SELECTED HONORS
Psi Chi (academic honorary in psychology), October 20XX-Present
James Canfield Scholarship (based on academic achievement), August 20XX-May 20XX

ADDITIONAL EXPERIENCE
Subway, *Sandwich Artist*, Lincoln, NE, June 20XX-August 20XX

TIP: Incorporate words or phrases directly from the job description that pertain to your skills and experience (shown in red for demonstration purposes only—do not use red in your résumé or cover letter).

TIP: Emphasize significant experience, paid or unpaid, by creating a "Relevant Experience" section.

TIP: Related coursework can highlight achievement, knowledge, or skills in areas of interest to the employer.

TIP: If you have held more than one position at an organization, show the progression and save space by listing the organization first.

TIP: See the red words as they relate to the sample job description on p. 384.

TIP: Additional, nonrelated experience may be listed simply to show work longevity and ability to manage time, handle money, work with the public, etc.

additional sites that provide information about organizations in the news, competitors' information, and other tidbits that will clearly indicate you have been thorough in doing your homework and are truly interested in the organization. You can also visit your campus or career service's library if you are unable to find the desired information online.

Writing the Cover Letter

A cover letter is often necessary to supplement your résumé by providing an overview of your reasons for applying for a particular job or position. It also provides an overview of your qualifications, experiences, or background to help the employer determine your fit for a particular job. Cover letters should provide a clear connection between your résumé and the job description provided by the employer. If the letter connects well to the job description, it will give the reader a reason to read your résumé.

FIGURE 15.4 Reference Page

The reference page should be neat and provide enough information about the person and his or her credibility. The contact information should be up-to-date, complete, and accurate.

From page 25 of "Your Ultimate Job Search Guide 2017-2018" Career Services, 225 Nebraska Union. Reprinted with permission of University of Nebraska-Lincoln Career Service, www.unl.edu/careers.

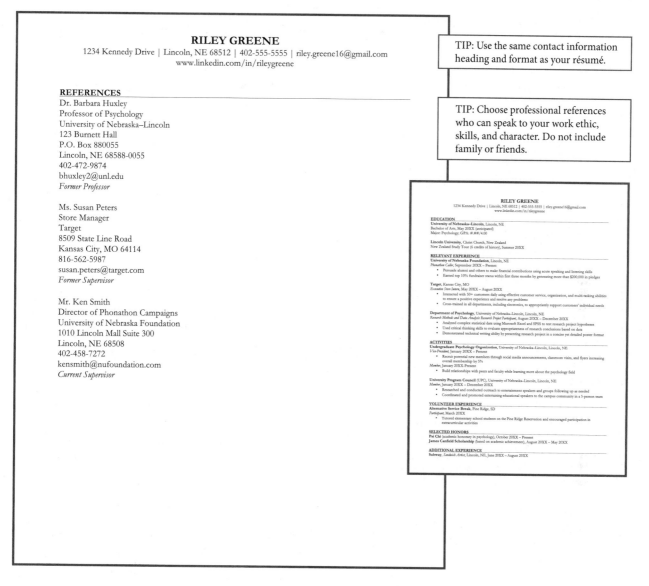

It is recommended, if possible, to tailor cover letters to each position or job. An effective cover letter requires time, thought, and effort. Before you begin to write your cover letter, you should:

- Research the organization
- Review the job description, especially key requirements of the job
- Focus on the skills and experiences you have that fit the job

When drafting your cover letter, you should:

- Indicate a tone of professionalism and confidence
- Make sure you proofread your letter carefully to ensure there are no spelling or grammar errors
- Include with your cover letter a copy of your résumé when you send it via snail or email.[18]

See Figure 15.5 for a sample cover letter and job description.

FIGURE 15.5   Sample Cover Letter That Incorporates the Job Description

From page 28 of "Your Ultimate Job Search Guide 2017-2018" Career Services, 225 Nebraska Union. Reprinted with permission of University of Nebraska-Lincoln Career Service, www.unl.edu/careers.

Sample Job Description

Technical Sales Representative

YYY Company, named a "Best Place to Work" five years in a row, is seeking ambitious candidates for our technical sales representative position. At YYY Company, we embrace working as a team to meet our clients' needs and driving industry leading results. Our goal is to make a positive impact for our clients and on the world.

This entry level sales role will build relationships with internal and external clients managing the entire sales process including regular outreach and follow-up, maintain a deep understanding of the product, and ability to identify the unique needs of the client to provide appropriate products. When our clients win, we win.

Preferred Qualifications:
- Bachelor's degree in related field.
- Written and verbal communication skills to appropriately explain complex concepts to peers/clients.
- Ability to work independently and as part of a team.
- Strong problem-solving and critical thinking skills.
- A self-motivated individual who is able to get results.
- Knowledge of Microsoft Office programs.

Sample Cover Letter

RILEY GREENE
1234 Kennedy Drive | Lincoln, NE 68512 | 402-555-5555 | riley.greene16@gmail.com
www.linkedin.com/in/rileygreene

October 7, 20XX

Ms. Kathy Beck
Human Resources Director
YYY Company
4444 Old Cheney Road
Lincoln, NE 68516

Dear Ms. Beck:

My psychology major combined with my sales experience and interest in technology has prepared me for the Technical Sales Representative position at YYY Company. I found this opportunity on Husker Hire Link. YYY's strong reputation in the industry, earning a Best Places to Work award based on your staff development and customer service focus, fits my work style. I am eager to apply the skills I developed from my relevant academic and work experiences to the role to make a positive impact on your organization.

I gained strong sales and customer service experience this past summer when I worked as an Executive Store Intern at Target and in my current role as a Phonathon Caller with the University of Nebraska Foundation. From these experiences I gained a good understanding of how to build relationships with a diverse clientele. Therefore, I will be comfortable creating an individualized sales approach when working with YYY's various clients to provide technical options that meet their unique needs. In addition, both positions required me to work independently and in a team daily, so I can apply the necessary organizational, communication, and prioritization skills needed to achieve the best possible results for YYY Company and your clients.

Problem-solving and critical thinking are skills I gained and used in every psychology class. Specifically, in my Research Methods and Data Analysis course, I regularly reviewed research reports to evaluate the validity of their methods and conclusions based on data and explained complex concepts in both verbal and written form to peers and the professor. In addition, I learned SPSS and taught myself Microsoft Excel in order to conduct detailed analysis of complex issues, which also sparked my interest in technology. Therefore, I am eager to learn more about YYY's products and am confident in my ability to communicate them in a simple and effective way to your clients in the Technical Sales Representative position. I understand what might be motivating people's thoughts and actions which will allow me to find a sales approach that will resonate with the individual. In short, I want to help your clients win.

Thank you for your time and consideration of my qualifications for the Technical Sales Representative position at YYY Company. As you can see from my attached résumé, the communication, problem solving, and critical thinking skills I gained from my sales and academic experience will help me succeed in this role. I will contact you in two weeks regarding my application and the possibility of meeting to further discuss the position. My contact information can be found in the letterhead above. I am excited for this opportunity.

Sincerely,

Riley Greene

Riley Greene

Attachment

> TIP: Instead of your contact information in standard business format, you could use your résumé contact information heading.

> TIP: Incorporate words and phrases directly from the job description that pertain to your skills and experience (shown in red for demonstration purposes only—do not use red in your résumé or cover letter).

Today, it is common to send an email as your cover letter. If sending your cover letter via an email, it is recommended that it be a shortened version. In addition, you should attach a copy of your résumé. Again, make sure your email is professional and does not have any spelling and grammar errors. You should also send your email to a specific person. Doing so shows that you have done your homework, and it is more personal. See Figure 15.6 for a sample email cover letter.

FIGURE 15.6 Email Cover Letter That Is Shortened and Addressed to a Specific Person

From page 29 of "Your Ultimate Job Search Guide 2017-2018" Career Services, 225 Nebraska Union. Reprinted with permission of University of Nebraska-Lincoln Career Service, www.unl.edu/careers.

Tailored Cover Letter Email Sample

In some cases, you may be asked to apply via email. In this case, use a condensed version of your cover letter as the body of the email.

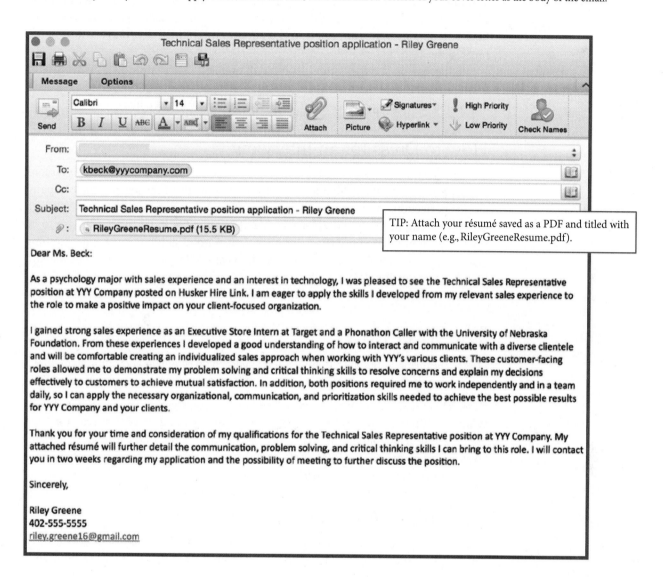

Technical Sales Representative position application - Riley Greene

To: kbeck@yyycompany.com

Cc:

Subject: Technical Sales Representative position application - Riley Greene

📎: RileyGreeneResume.pdf (15.5 KB)

TIP: Attach your résumé saved as a PDF and titled with your name (e.g., RileyGreeneResume.pdf).

Dear Ms. Beck:

As a psychology major with sales experience and an interest in technology, I was pleased to see the Technical Sales Representative position at YYY Company posted on Husker Hire Link. I am eager to apply the skills I developed from my relevant sales experience to the role to make a positive impact on your client-focused organization.

I gained strong sales experience as an Executive Store Intern at Target and a Phonathon Caller with the University of Nebraska Foundation. From these experiences I developed a good understanding of how to interact and communicate with a diverse clientele and will be comfortable creating an individualized sales approach when working with YYY's various clients. These customer-facing roles allowed me to demonstrate my problem solving and critical thinking skills to resolve concerns and explain my decisions effectively to customers to achieve mutual satisfaction. In addition, both positions required me to work independently and in a team daily, so I can apply the necessary organizational, communication, and prioritization skills needed to achieve the best possible results for YYY Company and your clients.

Thank you for your time and consideration of my qualifications for the Technical Sales Representative position at YYY Company. My attached résumé will further detail the communication, problem solving, and critical thinking skills I can bring to this role. I will contact you in two weeks regarding my application and the possibility of meeting to further discuss the position.

Sincerely,

Riley Greene
402-555-5555
riley.greene16@gmail.com

Developing Questions to Ask the Interviewer

In preparation for the interview, make a list of possible questions to ask the interviewer. Sometimes an interviewer might choose to say little or to stop talking altogether, in which case it becomes your responsibility to carry the conversation by asking questions and continuing to emphasize your qualifications for the job. How you ask the question is important; for example, if you know some travel is involved, and you want to travel, instead of asking, "How much traveling is involved in the job?" you might ask, "What kinds of opportunities for travel are there?" The latter question conveys more enthusiasm than the former. Sample questions you might ask include "Are there training programs for new employees?" "What's the next step up from the starting position?" "Will I be able to continue my education?" "Why do you work for the organization or company?" "What do you like most about working for the organization or company?"

The Mock Interview

It is highly recommended you prepare by participating in several mock interviews prior to interviewing with potential employers. Most university and college career services offer mock interviews. These help prepare you for the questions you are likely to be asked and give you advice on how to present yourself more effectively. These mock interviews may also be video-recorded so you can see just how you appear in the interview and what you might need to do to create a better impression.

If the career services center doesn't offer mock interviews, ask an advisor, a friend, or a classmate to rehearse with you. The mock interview should be as realistic as possible so you experience what the actual interview may be like.

How to Dress for an Interview

Your primary goal in dressing for an interview is to feel great about the way you look while projecting an image that matches the requirements of the job and the company. Go for perfection. Wear professionally pressed clothing in natural fabrics. Although casual clothing in many workplace settings is acceptable today, it is still wise to be conservative in what you wear to an interview. A good guide for interview clothing is to dress "one step above" what you would wear on the job. You want to be remembered as a professional with skills, not for inappropriate attire.

The Interview

15.4 **Describe** yourself to potential employers in an effective and competent way to give them information and reasons to hire you.

Research suggests most interviewers develop a strong opinion about a job applicant within the first 30 seconds. If you do poorly at the opening, your chances of getting the job are slim, no matter how brilliantly you handle the rest of the interview. It might seem unfair or superficial, but people do judge others based on first impressions, and such impressions can be long lasting.

Creating a Favorable First Impression

Think of the employment or internship interview for what it is—a sale. You must sell yourself, and the best way to do that is to know yourself thoroughly, both your strengths and weaknesses. If you create a positive first impression with recruiters, they will more likely show a positive regard toward you, provide more detailed information about the job, sell their organization to you, and ultimately spend less time asking questions.[19]

As a job applicant, show good judgment and common sense about appearance, assertiveness, being on time, and being at the right place. Always maintain eye contact with the interviewer; it shows that you are confident. Most interviewers greet the applicant with a handshake. Make sure your clasp is firm.

Before leaving, try to find out exactly what action will follow the interview and when it will happen. Shake hands as you say goodbye and thank the interviewer for spending time with you.

If you plan and follow the simple suggestions listed above, you should be able to avoid any serious problems.

Frequently Asked Questions

Successful applicants listen carefully to the entire question and think before responding. They are honest and, while rehearsed and prepared, do not give canned answers. They are enthusiastic, speak positively about themselves and their experiences, and ask questions of the interviewer. Here are some common questions interviewers ask and some possible responses to them:

1. **"What can you tell me about yourself?"** This is not an invitation to give your life history. The interviewer is looking for clues about your character, qualifications, ambitions, and motivations. The following is a good example of a positive response. "In high school, I was involved in competitive sports, and I always tried to improve in each sport in which I participated. As a college student, I worked part-time in a clothing store and found I could sell things easily. The sale was important, but for me, it was even more important to make sure the customer was satisfied. It wasn't long before customers came back to the store and specifically asked for me to help them. I'm very competitive, and it means a lot to me to be the best."

2. **"Why do you want to work for us?"** This is an obvious question, and if you have done research on the company, you should be able to give a good answer. Organize your reasons into several short sentences that clearly spell out your interest. "You are a leader in the field of electronics. Your company is a Fortune 500 company. Your management is very progressive."

3. **"Why should I hire you?"** Once again, you should not be long winded, but you should provide a summary of your qualifications. Be positive and show that you are capable of doing the job. "Based on the internships I have participated in and the related part-time experiences I have had, I can do the job."

4. **"How do you feel about your progress to date?"** Never apologize for what you have done. "I think I did well in school. In fact, in a number of courses I received the highest exam scores in the class." "As an intern for X Company, I received some of the highest evaluations given in years." "Considering that I played on the university's volleyball team and worked part-time, I think you'll agree that I accomplished quite a bit during my four years in school."

5. **"What would you like to be doing five years from now?"** Know what you can realistically accomplish. You can find out by talking to others about what they accomplished in their first five years with a particular company. "I hope to be the best I can be at my job, and because many in this line of work are promoted to area manager, I am planning on that also."

6. **"What is your greatest weakness?"** You cannot avoid this question by saying that you do not have any; everyone has weaknesses. The best approach is to admit your weakness but show that you are working on it and have a plan to overcome it. If possible, cite a weakness that will work to the company's advantage. "I'm not very good at detail work, but I have been working on it, and I've improved dramatically over the past several years." "I'm such a perfectionist that I won't stop until a report is written just right."

7. **"What is your greatest strength?"** Do not brag or become too egotistical, but let the employer know that you believe in yourself and that you know your strengths. "I believe my strongest asset is my ability to persist in getting things done. I feel a real sense of accomplishment when I finish a job and it turns out just as I'd planned. I've set some high goals for myself. For example, I want to graduate with highest distinction. And even though I had a slow start in my first year, I made up for it by doing an honors thesis."

8. **"What goals have you set, and how did you meet them?"** This question examines your ability to plan and meet your plan with specific actions. "Last year, during a magazine drive to raise money for our band trip, I set my goal at raising

20 percent more than I had the year before. I asked each of my customers from last year to give me the name of one or two new people who might also buy a magazine. I not only met my goal but was the top salesperson on the drive."

Here are a few other questions commonly asked in the employment interview:

What is your dream job?
Under what type of supervision do you think you would do your best work?
What kind of legacy did you leave in college?
What are the differences between a leader and a manager?
What motivates you to get up in the morning?
Do you consider yourself a risk taker?
What was the last risk you took?
What five characteristics would make you a great salesperson?

No matter what question you are asked, answer it honestly and succinctly. Most interviewers are looking for positive statements, well-expressed ideas, persuasiveness, and clear thinking under pressure.

If you are asked a question that violates the affirmative action laws, you can decline to answer. You might say, "Can you explain how that question is relevant to the position being offered?" You might simply ask the interviewer why he or she is asking you that question. Make sure that you are tactful, but be firm in letting the interviewer know he or she is doing something illegal.

Many employers use a behavioral interviewing style. Rather than ask if you have a specific skill or trait, the employer asks you to provide a specific example of a time when you demonstrated the skill or trait. For these questions, tell a brief but descriptive story with a clear:

- Beginning (the situation or challenge being faced)
- Middle (the action that you specifically took)
- End (the results)

If you do not have the direct experience requested, provide examples of similar situations. Use stories with positive outcomes whenever possible, but if the story does not have a positive outcome, add what you learned from the experience.

Interviewing and Technology

Over 150 million employment interviews are conducted in the United States each year, resulting in hundreds of thousands of jobs filled. Surveys have indicated that 82 percent of all companies are using or will be using videoconference technology such as Skype to conduct recruiting interviews.[20] Although the technology allows the mediated interview to be comparable to face-to-face interviews, there are significant differences. Some find it more difficult to interact freely and naturally while on screen. Because visual cues are limited by seeing only the upper bodies or faces of participants, nonverbal cues are fewer. One study found employers had trouble "reading nonverbal behaviors such as facial expression, eye contact, and fidgeting" and determining "whether a pause was due to the technology, or the applicant being stumped."[21] If you are asked to interview via video, make sure you test the technology prior to the interview. Maintain an uncluttered, professional background and dress professionally. Look at the camera rather than the screen or keyboard to maintain eye contact.

Many employers use telephone interviews as a way to identify and recruit candidates for employment. Phone interviews are often used to screen candidates and narrow the pool of applicants who will be invited for in-person interviews. They are also used as a way to minimize the expenses involved in interviewing out-of-town candidates. With the increase in cell phone usage, the phone interview has its own challenges. Make sure the phone is fully charged and you have a strong signal. You may want to purchase a headset to increase the sound quality as well as keep your hands free during the interview.

Writing a Thank-You Note

You should always follow up every interview with a brief but professional note, thanking the interviewer for his or her time. The thank-you note should follow as soon as possible, but promptness is not as important as what you say. A thank-you note should be sent regardless of whether or not you think you will get an offer. A handwritten note is a very personal way of saying thank you and will likely make the best impression on the interviewer. If much of the correspondence with the employer was via email, a formal thank-you note may be sent through email, which also helps provide a more timely response to the employer.

Getting the Job Offer

15.5 **Explain** why employers may accept or reject an applicant.

You have worked hard to prepare yourself to launch your career. Some final considerations may help you present yourself in the best possible light.

Factors Leading to Job Offers

A well-rounded applicant with good grades, some relevant work experience, a variety of extracurricular activities, an all-around pleasant personality, and effective written and oral communication skills is more likely to get job offers than are those who do not possess these qualities, according to Jason Meyers of *Collegiate Employment Institute Newsletter*.[22] Meyers says, "Sounds too good to be true? Perhaps it is, but a candidate who strives to attain these qualities and who comes across as a hard-working, mature individual should have a promising career outlook."[23]

A research study cited by Meyers in his article asked recruiters to describe what they believed to be the qualities of a well-rounded individual. They listed maturity, ability to be part of a team, good work ethic, good decision-making skills, superior work habits, and good judgment. Another study cited by Meyers found the most popular characteristics recruiters sought in job applicants fit two categories: (1) quantifiable characteristics, such as grade point average, education, and work experience, and (2) interpersonal characteristics, such as communication skills, personality, and career and management skills. The study suggests that a balance of the quantifiable characteristics and interpersonal characteristics is what makes an ideal job candidate.[24]

It seems that those who are well prepared; have effective communication skills; are mature, motivated, hard-working, team players; and can make good decisions will always be in demand. You must ask yourself how you match these qualities now and try to improve in those areas in which you are not as strong. You must also be able to demonstrate that you actually possess these qualities through the actions you have taken.

Factors Leading to Rejection

Employers from numerous companies were asked, "What negative factors most often lead to the rejection of an applicant?" Here are their responses:

1. Negative personality or poor impression; more specifically, lack of motivation, ambition, maturity, aggressiveness, or enthusiasm, or lack of respect—not knowing the interviewer's name or using his or her first name shows disrespect.
2. Inability to communicate; poor communication skills.

3. Lack of competence; inadequate training.

4. Exaggerated skills and experience on the résumé.

5. Lack of specific goals,

6. Sloppy appearance,

7. Failure to clean social media sites; digital junk—pictures that might be either good or bad or seem scandalous.

8. Lack of interest in type of work, showing a bad attitude, or exhibiting a slight arrogance during the interview.

9. Unwillingness to travel or relocate.

10. Poor preparation for the interview and/or showing up late.

11. Lack of experience.

12. Demonstrating emotional distress.[25]

Remember that a rejection or not receiving a job offer has a lot to do with the number of people seeking jobs and the number of jobs available. You can, of course, enhance your chances of getting job offers by being prepared and presenting yourself in a positive and energetic way.

〉 SUMMARY

Communiction and a Successful Career

15.1 **Describe** what it takes to have a successful career and the qualities employers seek in applicants.

To have a successful career requires the ability to communicate effectively.

- Communication effectiveness is essential in every business organization and for individuals in them to be successful.
- Developing relationships at work are not very different from forming relationships in college.
- Internships are important for gaining experience and for establishing networks.
- Almost every career requires certain skills such as writing, speaking, reading, listening, decision making, problem solving, researching, and reasoning.

Conducting the Job Search

15.2 **Explain** how to conduct an effective job search.

Even during good economic times there is always a good amount of competition for the best jobs. It requires a good deal of effort to obtain the best jobs available.

- One of the most productive ways of locating jobs is networking.
- Attending career fairs allows for person-to-person interactions with employees of various different organizations.
- When attending career fairs prepare and arrive as a professional to ensure that you give a good impression.

- Another valuable tool to use when preparing for the interview and to search for jobs is the Internet.

Preparing for an Interview

15.3 **Explain** the steps in preparing for a job interview.

Preparing for a job interview should begin early because it requires lots of planning and thought to be ready for what might be one of the most important communications in your life.

- Developing a résumé requires documentation of skills and activities both inside and outside the classroom.
- The résumé is an extremely powerful form of communication. It requires brevity and accuracy of one's qualifications and experiences.
- Applicants should prepare questions to ask the interviewer and dress appropriately.

The Interview

15.4 **Describe** yourself to potential employers in an effective and competent way to give them information and reasons to hire you.

- The employment or internship interview is "a sale."
- Successful applicants listen carefully to each question asked of them before responding.
- Create a favorable impression: Be prepared and research the organization or company.
- Write a thank-you note, preferably handwritten and addressed to the interviewer.

Getting the Job Offer

15.5 **Explain** why employers may accept or reject an applicant.

You have worked hard to prepare yourself to launch your career. Some final considerations may help you present yourself in the best possible light.

- To ensure getting an offer, be prepared and be able to describe why you are the best candidate for the job.

- A well-prepared applicant asks themselves how well they are matched to the job description and the qualities the employer is seeking in an applicant.

- Be aware and avoid the factors leading to rejection. The inability to communicate effectively is one of the main reasons for being rejected. Other reasons include a negative personality, lack of competence, over-exaggerated skills, inadequate training, lack of specific goals, and failure to clean social media sites.

⟩ DISCUSSION STARTERS

1. Describe the qualities that you think employers are seeking in an employee.

2. What steps or considerations would you recommend to someone who is beginning a job search? What do you think is the most important first step in the process?

3. Explain what a person should consider before going into an employment interview.

4. How does knowing your strengths and weaknesses help you succeed in an employment interview?

5. What should a résumé include and what shouldn't it include?

6. Why is attending career fairs a good idea?

7. Explain why an applicant might be rejected for a job.

Glossary

A

abstract word   The symbol for an idea, quality, or relationship.

accommodation   A process through which people adjust their language and style of speaking toward the people with whom they are communicating.

achievement culture   A culture that values assertiveness, achievement, ambition, and competitiveness.

ad hominem   A fallacy that attacks a person rather than the argument itself. This is also referred to as *name-calling*.

adoption   An action that asks listeners to demonstrate their acceptance of attitudes, beliefs, or values by performing the behavior suggested by the speaker.

advance organizer   A statement that warns the listener that significant information is coming.

analogy   A comparison of two things that are similar in certain essential characteristics.

androgyny   A socially constructed concept related to having both masculine and feminine traits.

antonym   A word, phrase, or concept that is opposite in meaning to another word, phrase, or concept.

anxiety   A feeling of worry, nervousness, or unease.

appeal to needs   An attempt to move people to action by calling on their physical and psychological requirements and desires.

artifacts   A personal ornament or possession that communicates information about a person.

asynchronous   Channels of communication that allow participants to take turns serving as sender and receiver.

attitude   An evaluative feeling or way of thinking about oneself, others, events, ideas, or objects.

attribution   The complex process through which we attempt to understand the reasons behind others' behaviors.

audience analysis   The collection and interpretation of data about characteristics, attitudes, values, and beliefs of an audience.

audience   The collection of individuals who have come together to watch or listen to someone or something, such as to listen to a speech.

autocratic leader   A leader who has control and makes decisions with little or no consultation with others.

B

behavioral affirmation   Seeing or hearing what we want to see or hear.

behavioral confirmation   When we act in a way that makes our expectations about a group come true.

belief   A conviction or confidence in the truth of something that is not based on absolute proof.

benefit   Anything that is perceived to improve our self-interest.

body   The main content of a speech that develops the speaker's general and specific purposes.

brainstorming   A technique used to generate as many ideas as possible within a limited amount of time. These ideas can be used to produce topics, information, or solutions to problems.

breadth of penetration   The range or spread of areas that are disclosed to others.

brief example   A specific instance that is used to introduce a topic, drive home a point, or create a desired response.

bypassing   A misunderstanding that occurs between a sender and a receiver because of the symbolic nature of language.

C

captive participant   A person who is required to hear a particular speech.

causal reasoning   A sequence of thought that links causes with effects; it either implies or explicitly states the word *because*.

cause–effect pattern   An order of presentation in which the speaker first explains the causes of an event, problem, or issue and then discusses its consequences.

channel   The means by which messages flow between sources and receivers.

charisma   The appeal or attractiveness that the audience perceives in the speaker, contributing to the speaker's credibility.

chronemics   The study of how people perceive, structure, and use time as communication.

closure   Filling in of details so a partially perceived entity or message is complete.

co-culture   A group that exists within a larger, dominant culture but differs from the dominant culture.

code-switch or style-switch   For people from co-cultures, to speak the language of their own culture but switch to that of the dominant culture when needed and appropriate.

cognitive complexity   A measure of our ability to process and store simple to complicated information.

cohesiveness   The attraction that group members feel for each other and their willingness to stick together; a form of loyalty.

collectivistic orientation   Tendency to put aside individual goals for the well-being of the group.

commitment   The desire of group members to work together to complete a task to the satisfaction of the entire group.

communication apprehension   The most severe form of speech anxiety; an anxiety syndrome associated with either real or anticipated communication with another person or persons.

communication competence   The ability to communicate effectively, characterized by skills and understandings that enable communicators to exchange messages accurately and successfully.

communication via social media   Any communication transmitted through digital devices or platforms (smartphones, text messaging, Facebook, Twitter, Snapchat, etc.).

communication   The simultaneous sharing and creating of meaning through human symbolic interaction.

communications   Generally used to denote the delivery systems for mediated and mass communication.

complementing   The use of nonverbal cues to complete, describe, or accent verbal cues.

compulsive Internet use   A person's inability to control, reduce, or stop utilizing the Internet.

computer-mediated communication   Communication that is facilitated by a wide range of new technologies, including email, social media, chat rooms, blogs, apps, and even online games.

conclusion   Closing statements that focus the audience's thoughts on the specific purpose of a speech and bring the most important points together in a condensed and uniform way.

concrete word   A symbol for a specific thing that can be pointed to or physically experienced.

conflict   An expressed struggle between at least two interdependent parties who perceive incompatible goals, scarce resources, and interference from others in achieving their goals.

connotation   The subjective meaning of a word; what a word suggests because of feelings or associations it evokes.

consideration   A dimension of leadership that focuses on establishing good interpersonal relationships and on being liked by group members.

context   The broad circumstances or situation in which communication occurs.

continuance   An action goal that asks listeners to demonstrate their acceptance of an attitude, belief, or value by continuing to perform the behavior suggested by the speaker.

contrast definition   A definition that shows or emphasizes differences.

convenience   The ease with which people connect with others through social media.

convergence   When speakers shift their language or nonverbal behaviors toward each other's way of communicating.

coordination   Ideas with the same level of importance use the same kind of numbers (Roman and Arabic) and letters (capitalized and noncapitalized) to indicate visually the relationships between ideas.

costs   Negative things or behaviors that we perceive to be not beneficial to our self-interest.

credibility   A speaker's believability, based on the audience's evaluation of the speaker's competence, experience, character, and charisma.

critical listening   Listening that judges the accuracy of the information presented, determines the reasonableness of its conclusions, and evaluates its presenter.

critical thinking   The ability to analyze and assess information.

cultural rituals   Practices, behaviors, celebrations, and traditions common to people, organizations, and institutions.

culture shock   The psychological discomfort experienced when interaction occurs in a different culture or when one's current cultural experiences are contradicted or disrupted.

culture   A set of interpretations about beliefs, values, norms, and social practices that affect behaviors of a relatively large group of people.

cyberbullying   Abusive attacks that are carried out through social media.

cyberstalking   When an individual repeatedly uses social media to stalk or harass others.

D

dating   A form of indexing that sorts people, events, ideas, and objects according to time.

deceiving   Purposely misleading others by using nonverbal cues to create false impressions or to convey incorrect information.

decoding   The process of translating a message into the thoughts or feelings that were communicated.

deductive reasoning   A sequence of thought that moves from general information to a specific conclusion; it consists of a general premise, a minor premise, and a conclusion.

definition by example   Clarifying a term, not by describing it or giving its meaning but by mentioning or showing an example of it.

democratic leader   A leader who shares control and makes decisions in consultation with others.

demographic analysis   The collection and interpretation of characteristics (age, gender, religion, occupation, and so on) of individuals, excluding values, attitudes, and beliefs.

denotation   The objective meaning of a word; the standard dictionary definition.

depth of penetration   The deepness or intimacy of the disclosure to others.

descriptive feedback   Describing to the sender what you perceived the message to mean.

descriptors   Words used to describe something.

deterrence   An action that asks listeners to demonstrate their acceptance of an attitude, belief, or value by avoiding certain behavior.

dialectical theory   An interpersonal communication theory that suggests that contradictory impulses push and pull us in conflicting directions with others.

discontinuance   An action that asks listeners to demonstrate their alteration of an attitude, belief, or value by stopping certain behaviors.

discrimination   The verbal or nonverbal communication behaviors that foster prejudiced attitudes including the act of excluding or denying people access to products, rights, and services based on their race, gender, sexual orientation, disability, and so on.

dominant culture   The learned system of values, beliefs, attitudes, and orientations held by people who are in power in a society.

doublespeak   The deliberate misuse of language to distort meaning.

dyadic communication   An exchange of information between two people.

E

either–or reasoning   A fallacy of reasoning in which only two options exist: There is black or white, right or wrong, but nothing in between.

emotional appeal   An attempt to move people to action by playing on their feelings.

empathic listening   Listening to understand what another person is thinking and feeling.

empathy   The intellectual identification with or vicarious experiencing of the feelings, thoughts, or attitudes of another.

encoding   Process by which the source translates thoughts or feelings into words, sounds, and physical expressions, which together make up the actual message that is to be sent.

entertainment speech   A speech that provides enjoyment and amusement.

environment   The psychological and physical surroundings in which communication occurs.

ethics   An individual's system of moral principles.

ethnocentrism   A learned belief that our own culture is superior to all others.

ethos   The speaker's character as perceived by the listeners.

etymology   A form of definition that traces the origin and development of a word.

euphemism   The use of an inoffensive or mild expression in place of one that might offend, cause embarrassment, or suggest something unpleasant.

evaluating   The listener analyzes evidence, sorts fact from opinion, determines the intent of the speaker, judges the accuracy of the speaker's statements and conclusions, and judges the accuracy of his or her own decisions.

evaluation   When we assess the meaning of information.

evaluative listening   Listening to judge or analyze information.

example   A simple, representative incident or model that clarifies a point.

excessive Internet use   The degree to which a person feels that he or she spends an extreme amount of time online or even loses track of time while online.

expert opinion   Ideas, testimony, conclusions, or judgments of witnesses or recognized authorities.

extemporaneous delivery   A delivery style in which the speaker carefully prepares the speech in advance but delivers it using only a few notes and with a high degree of spontaneity.

eye behavior   A category of kinesics and a subcategory of facial expressions that includes any movement or behavior of the eyes.

eye contact   The extent to which a speaker looks directly at audience members.

F

facework   A term used to describe the verbal and nonverbal ways we act to maintain our own presenting image.

facial expressions   Configuration of the face that can reflect, augment, contradict, or appear unrelated to a speaker's vocal delivery.

facial management techniques   Control of facial muscles to conceal inappropriate or unacceptable responses.

factual illustration   A report of something that exists or actually happened.

fallacy   An argument that is flawed because it does not follow the rules of logic.

feedback   The response to a message that a receiver sends back to a source.

figurative analogy   A comparison of things in different categories.

flaming or trolling   Online communication that is deliberately hostile, aggressive, or insulting and usually intended to provoke anger.

force   The intensity and volume level of the voice.

full-sentence outline   An outline that expands on the ideas you have decided to include in your speech. It identifies the main points and subpoints you will cover, written as full sentences.

functional approach   Using more than one nonverbal message at a time to look for meaning.

fundamental attribution error   Perceiving others as acting as they do because they are "that kind of person" rather than because of any external factors that may have influenced their behavior.

G

gender-inclusive language   Language that does not discriminate against males or females.

gender   A socially constructed concept related to masculine and feminine behaviors that are learned.

general purpose   The overall goal of a speech, usually one of three overlapping functions: to inform, to persuade, or to entertain.

gesture   A movement of the head, arms, or hands that helps to illustrate, emphasize, or clarify an idea.

go viral   A phrase used to describe a message that reaches enormous audiences by "infecting" viewers and users with the message.

grammar   Rules that govern how words are put together to form phrases and sentences.

group culture   The pattern of values, beliefs, norms, and behaviors that is shared by group members and that shapes a group's individual "personality."

group   A collection of individuals who influence one another, have a common purpose, take on roles, are interdependent, and interact together.

grouphate phenomenon Dislike for groups.

groupthink A dysfunction in which group members value the harmony of the group more than new ideas, fail to critically examine ideas, hesitate to change flawed decisions, or lack willingness to allow new members to participate.

H

haptics Tactile, or touch, communication; one of the most basic forms of communication.

hasty generalization A fallacy that occurs when a speaker does not have sufficient data and therefore argues or reasons from a specific example.

hearing The passive physiological process in which sound is received by the ear.

high-context culture A culture in which the meaning of the communication act is inferred from the situation or location.

homophobic language Language that denigrates or places lesser value on someone from the lesbian, gay, bisexual, or transgender community.

hyperpersonal communication When the communication and context affords message senders a host of communicative advantages over traditional face-to-face interactions.

hypothetical illustration A report of something that could happen, given a specific set of circumstances.

I

idioms Words whose meanings cannot be understood according to ordinary usage.

illustration An extended example, narrative, case history, or anecdote that is striking and memorable.

impression management Creating a positive image of oneself to influence the perceptions of others.

impromptu delivery A delivery style in which a speaker delivers a speech with little or no planning or preparation.

indexing A technique to reduce indiscrimination by identifying the specific persons, ideas, events, or objects a statement refers to.

indiscrimination The neglect of individual differences and overemphasis of similarities.

individualistic orientation Tendency to stress self or personal goals and achievements over group goals and achievements.

inductive reasoning A sequence of thought that moves from specific facts to a general conclusion.

information overload The difficulty in sorting through and making sense of vast amounts of information.

information processing Assigning meaning to the stimuli the brain selected and attended to.

information relevance Making information relevant to an audience to give them a reason to listen.

information Knowledge obtained from investigation, study, or instruction.

informative speech A speech that enhances an audience's knowledge and understanding by explaining what something means, how something works, or how something is done.

initiating structure A dimension of leadership that focuses on getting the job done.

intelligibility Speaker's vocal volume, distinctiveness of sound, clarity of pronunciation, articulation, and stress placed on syllables, words, and phrases.

intentional communication A message purposely sent to a specific receiver.

interactivity The ability of a communication tool to facilitate social interaction between groups or individuals.

intercultural communication Communication between people who are unlike culturally and have different views of the world.

intercultural sensitivity Awareness of behaviors that may offend others.

interdependence Mutual dependence of group members on one another.

interference Anything that changes the meaning of an intended message.

internal preview Short statements that give advance warning, or a preview, of the point(s) to be covered.

internal summary A short review statement given at the end of a main point.

interpersonal attraction The desire to interact with someone based on a variety of factors, including physical attractiveness, personality, rewards, proximity, or similarities.

interpersonal communication The creating and sharing of meaning between people who are in a relationship.

interpersonal needs theory A theory that provides insight into our motivation to communicate. This theory consists of three needs: affection, inclusion, and control.

interpret To explain the meaning of information.

interpretation Assigning of meaning to stimuli.

interpreting The process of understanding the meaning of the message from the speaker's point of view and letting the speaker know that you understand.

interview A carefully planned and executed question-and-answer session designed to exchange desired information between two parties.

intrapersonal communication The process of understanding information within oneself.

introduction Opening statement that orients the audience to the subject and motivates them to listen.

J

jargon Language used by certain groups or specific disciplines that may be technical or too specialized to be understood by the general population.

K

kinesics Sometimes referred to as "body language"; any movement of the face or body that communicates a message.

L

laissez-faire leader A leader who gives up control, is passive, and usually requires that others take over if the group is to succeed.

language A structured system of signs, sounds, gestures, or marks used and understood to express ideas and feelings among people within a community, nation, geographic area, or cultural tradition.

latent ties   Potential relationships within a social circle that have not yet been activated.

leader   A person who is assigned, selected or emerges to take the leadership role.

leadership   An influence process that includes any behavior that helps clarify a purpose or guides to achieve a goal or goals.

listen for enjoyment   To listen for pleasure, personal satisfaction, or appreciation.

listening for information   Listening to gain comprehension.

listening   A cognitive activity that is defined as the active process of receiving, constructing meaning from information taken in through the senses, and constructing meaning from and responding to those stimuli.

literal analogy   A comparison of members of the same category.

logical appeal   An attempt to move people to action through the use of evidence and proof.

logical definition   A definition consisting of a term's dictionary definition and the characteristics that distinguish the term from other members of the same category.

logos   The substance of the speech or the logical appeals the speaker makes.

low-context culture   A culture in which the meaning of the communication act is inferred from the messages being sent and not the location where the communication occurs.

M

main points   The principal subdivisions of a speech.

maintenance needs   Needs related to organizing and developing a group so that members can realize personal satisfaction from working together.

manuscript delivery   A delivery style in which a speaker writes the speech in its entirety and then reads it word for word.

mass communication   When professionals communicate with or to a large number of people via radio, television, newspapers, magazines, books, or movies.

media convergence   How the many forms of technologically mediated and face-to-face communication come together in our every day lives.

media multiplexity theory   How we carry out relationships through more than one form of social media, and those in closer relationships use more forms of social media.

media multitasking   Using more than one media type at the same time.

media richness theory   A theory that describes communication channels by the amount of verbal and nonverbal information that can be exchanged through a particular channel.

meditation   The process of spending time in quiet thought.

memorized delivery   A delivery style in which a speaker memorizes a speech in its entirety from a word-for-word script.

message   The communication produced by the source.

metaphor   A figure of speech that associates two things or ideas, not commonly linked, as a means of description.

mind mapping   A visual organizational strategy that uses words or symbols to identify the concepts and their connections to each other.

miscommunication   The understanding that social media may naturally inhibit the clarity of communication.

monochronic culture   A culture that sticks to a schedule and values punctuality, uninterrupted task completion, meeting deadlines, and following plans.

Monroe's motivated sequence   A pattern of organization specifically developed for persuasive speaking that combines logic and practical psychology. Five steps are involved: attention, need, satisfaction, visualization, and action.

muted group theory   A theory suggesting that underrepresented groups (women, the poor, people with disabilities, seniors, gays, blacks, Latinos, etc.) often are not as free or as able to say what they mean, when and where they wish.

N

narrative or storytelling   An organizational strategy using a reporting of ideas and situations, as in a "story," but without the traditional components of a story.

networking   The systematic contacting of people who can provide information about available jobs or who can offer jobs.

nonverbal communication   Behaviors, symbols, attributes, or objects—whether intended or not—that communicate messages with social meaning.

norms   Expected and shared ways in which group members behave.

nurturing culture   A culture that places value on relationships and quality of life.

O

observation   A method of collecting information about an audience in which the speaker watches audience members and notes their behaviors and characteristics.

oculesics   Study of eye movement or eye behavior.

online communication attitude   An attitude that shapes how we interact with other people and how we present ourselves through social media.

online communication apprehension   Anxiety and nervousness associated with communicating through social media.

online self-disclosure   The degree to which individuals self-regulate what they reveal about themselves using social media.

online social connection   The belief that online communication enables social contact.

operational definition   A definition that explains how an object or concept works or lists the steps in a process.

oral footnote   Providing, within the speech, the source that particular information comes from, such as, "According to Newsweek magazine of July 27, 2018 …"

organization   Sorting, organizing, or categorizing.

organizing   Arranging ideas and elements into a systematic and meaningful whole.

other-enhancement   When someone compliments individuals in order to make them feel good about themselves.

outlining   Arranging materials in a logical sequence, often referred to as the blueprint or skeleton of a speech, and writing out that sequence in a standardized form.

overaccommodate   Going too far in changing your language based on an incorrect or stereotypical notion of another group.

P

paralanguage   The sound of words, including silence.

paralanguage or vocalics   The way we vocalize, or say, the words we speak.

parallelism   Style in which all ideas, main points, subpoints, and sub-subpoints use similar grammatical forms and language patterns.

pathos   The speaker's evoking of appropriate emotion from the listeners.

pause   A brief stop in speaking to gain attention, add emphasis, separate, or otherwise punctuate ideas.

pendulum effect   Escalating conflict between two individuals or groups that results from their use of polar terms to describe and defend their perceptions of reality.

perception checking   Asking questions to see if your interpretation is correct.

perception   The process of selecting, organizing, and interpreting information to give personal meaning to the communication we receive.

perceptual set   A fixed, previously determined view of events, objects, or people.

personal-social identity continuum   The two ways the self can be categorized: at a personal level, in which the uniqueness of the individual is emphasized; and at the social identity level, in which the self is thought of as a member of a group.

persuasion   A communication process, involving both verbal and nonverbal messages, that attempts to reinforce or change listeners' attitudes, beliefs, values, or behavior.

persuasive speech   A speech that attempts to change listeners' attitudes or behaviors by advocating or trying to gain acceptance of listeners' point of view.

pitch   How low or high the voice is on a tonal scale.

plagiarism   The use of another person's information, language, or ideas without citing the originator and making it appear that the user is the originator.

planned repetition   The deliberate restating of a thought to increase the likelihood the audience will understand and remember it.

polarization   The tendency to view things in terms of extremes.

polychronic culture   A culture that is comfortable dealing with multiple people and tasks at the same time.

post hoc ergo propter hoc **fallacy**   A fallacy of reasoning in which one attributes something as a cause simply because it followed (came after) another incident.

power distance   The extent to which members of a culture expect and accept that power will be unequally shared.

preliminary outline   A list of all the main points that may be used in a speech.

presentational aids   Materials and equipment, such as diagrams, models, real objects, photographs, tables, charts, and graphs, that speakers may use to enhance the speech's content and delivery.

presentational outline   A concise, condensed outline with notations, usually a combination of full sentences and key words and phrases.

primary group   A group that focuses on social and interpersonal relationships.

principled negotiation   A procedure that helps group members negotiate consensus by collaboration through the expression of each differing need and a search for alternatives to meet those needs.

privacy   The claim of individuals, groups, or institutions to determine for themselves when, how, and to what extent information about themselves is communicated to others.

problematic Internet use   A syndrome characterized by cognitive and behavioral symptoms that can result in negative social, academic, and professional consequences.

problem–solution pattern   Order of presentation that first discusses a problem and then suggests solutions.

process   A series of actions having no beginning or end and is constantly changing.

proxemics   The study of the use of space and of distance between individuals when they are communicating.

proximity   The grouping of two or more stimuli that are close to one another.

pseudolistening   When one appears to be listening by nodding, smiling, looking at the speaker, and so on, but their attention and focus is on something else.

psychological analysis   The collection and interpretation of data about audience members' values, attitudes, and beliefs.

public communication   Transmission of a message from a person who speaks to a number of individuals who listen.

public speaking   The art of effective oral communication with an audience.

Q

question of fact   A question that asks what is true and what is false.

question of policy   A question that asks what actions should be taken.

question of value   A question that asks whether something is good or bad, desirable or undesirable.

questionable cause   A fallacy that occurs when a speaker alleges something that does not relate to or produce the outcome claimed in the argument.

questionnaire   A set of written questions that is distributed to respondents to gather desired information.

R

rate   Speed at which a speaker speaks, normally between 120 and 175 words per minute.

reasoning by analogy   A sequence of thought that compares similar things or circumstances to draw a conclusion.

receiver   The individual who analyzes and interprets the message.

red herring   A fallacy that uses irrelevant information to divert attention away from the real issue.

regulating   The use of nonverbal cues to control the flow of communication.

relationship An association between at least two people, which may be described in terms of intimacy or kinship.

remembering Recalling something from stored memory; thinking of something again.

repeating The use of nonverbal cues to convey the same meaning as the verbal message.

repertoire Wide range of communication behaviors from which effective communicators make choices.

replicability When communication occurs in an environment that makes it easy to record and redistribute past messages.

responding Overt verbal and nonverbal behavior by the listener, indicating to the speaker what has and has not been received.

reviewing the current media A technique for developing a list of possible topics by looking at current publications, television, movies, and other forms of public communication.

rhetorical sensitivity A cautious approach to self-disclosure in which the situation and factors about the other person are considered before communication begins.

résumé A written document that briefly and accurately describes an individual's personal, educational, and professional qualifications and experiences

S

secondary group A group that exists to accomplish tasks or achieve goals.

selection Sorting of one stimulus from another.

selective attention Attending to a specific message while ignoring or downplaying another.

selective exposure Making deliberate choices to experience or to avoid particular stimuli.

selective retention The processing, storing, and retrieving of information that we have already selected, organized, and interpreted.

self-concept A person's perceived self, which consists of an organized collection of beliefs and attitudes about self.

self-disclosure Voluntary sharing of information about the self that another person is not likely to know.

self-enhancement A type of motivation to make people feel good about themselves in order to maintain self-esteem.

self-esteem A person's feelings and attitudes toward him- or herself.

self-fulfilling prophecy Expectations we have of ourselves or that others have of us that help to create the conditions that lead us to act in predictable ways.

self-image A person's mental picture of him- or herself.

self-inventory A list of subjects that you know about and find interesting.

self-monitoring The willingness to change behavior to fit situations, the awareness of effects on others, and the ability to regulate nonverbal cues and other factors to influence others' impressions.

self-presentation An intentional self-disclosure tactic used to reveal certain aspects about ourselves for specific reasons.

semantics The study of meaning, or the association of words with ideas, feelings, and contexts.

sex The anatomical and physiological differences between males and females that are genetically determined.

sexist language Language that creates sexual stereotypes or implies that one gender is superior to another.

sexting The act of sending sexually explicit messages or photographs, primarily between smartphones via text messaging.

signpost A word, phrase, or short statement that indicates to an audience the direction a speaker will take next.

silence An extended period of time without sound.

similarity The grouping of stimuli that resemble one another in size, shape, color, or other traits.

slang Language used by groups to keep the meaning of the communication within the group. Slang words change frequently and are specific to regions and/or groups.

small-group communication An exchange of information among a relatively small number of people, ideally five to seven, who share a common purpose, such as completing a task, solving a problem, making a decision, or sharing information.

social cues The verbal and nonverbal features of a message that offer more information about the context, the meaning, and the identities of the involved parties.

social exchange theory A theory based on the assumption that people consciously and deliberately weigh the costs and rewards associated with a relationship or interaction.

social identity theory Specifies that we have a *personal identity*, which is our sense of our unique individual personalities, and a *social identity*, the part of our self-concept that comes from our group memberships.

social information processing (SIP) theory A theory suggesting that electronically mediated relationships grow only to the extent that people gain information about each other and use that information to form impressions.

social loafing Tendency for individuals to lower their work effort after they join a group.

social media Highly accessible technologies that facilitate communication, interaction, and connection with others.

social network A group of individuals who are connected by friendship, family, common interests, beliefs, or knowledge.

social penetration theory A theory suggesting that disclosures in a relationship become increasingly intimate as the relationship develops.

Social Identity Model of Deindividuation Effects (SIDE) Model A model that describes the extent to which individuals identify and behave in accordance with social rather than personal identities.

source The creator of the message.

spatial pattern An order of presentation in which the content of a speech is organized according to relationships in space.

specific purpose A single phrase that defines precisely what is to be accomplished in a speech.

speech anxiety Fear of speaking before an audience.

statistics Numerical data that show relationships or summarize or interpret many instances.

stereotyping The categorizing of events, objects, and people without regard to unique individual characteristics and qualities.

strong ties Relationships such as those with friends, romantic partners, and family members.

subordination Clearly identifies the hierarchy of ideas: The most important points are main points and are supported by subpoints (that is, they are subordinate to the main points); the outline uses specific rules for format.

substituting The use of nonverbal cues in place of oral messages when speaking is impossible, undesirable, or inappropriate.

survey interview A carefully planned and executed person-to-person question-and-answer session during which the speaker tries to discover specific information that will help in the preparation of a speech.

synchronous Channels of communication that allow participants to serve simultaneously as sender and receiver.

synonym A word, term, or concept that is the same or nearly the same in meaning as another word, term, or concept.

system Combination of parts acting interdependently to form a whole.

systematic desensitization A relaxation technique designed to reduce the tenseness associated with anxiety.

T

task needs Needs related to the content of the task to be done and all behaviors that lead to the completion of it.

temporal structure The time it takes to send and receive messages.

territoriality The need to identify certain areas of space as one's own.

testimony Opinions or conclusions of witnesses or recognized authorities.

thesis A sentence that states specifically what is going to be discussed in a speech.

time-sequence (or chronological) pattern An order of presentation that begins at a particular point in time and continues either forward or backward.

topical pattern An order of presentation in which the main topic is divided into a series of related subtopics.

transactional Exchange of communication in which the communicators act simultaneously; that is, encoding and decoding occur at the same time.

transcorporeal communication A process through which a living person sends a digital message to a deceased person through a website or social networking site.

transition A phrase or word used to link ideas.

trustworthiness The audience's perception of a speaker's reliability and dependability.

U

uncertainty avoidance The process through which cultures adapt their behaviors to reduce uncertainty.

uncertainty management theory A theory that takes into account different ways people react psychologically and communicatively to uncertainty.

uncertainty reduction theory A theory suggesting that when we meet others, our need to know about them tends to make us draw inferences from observable physical data.

understanding The part of information processing where we know something in our own minds.

unintentional communication A message not intended to be sent or was not intended for the individual who received it.

V

values Relatively long-lasting principles or standards that guide our behavior or judgment of what is important.

verbal immediacy Identifies and projects the speaker's feelings and makes the message more relevant to the listener.

vividness Active, direct, and fresh language that brings a sense of excitement, urgency, and forcefulness to a message.

vocal pauses A hesitation, usually short in duration.

vocal quality The overall impression a speaker's voice makes on his or her listeners.

vocal variety Variations in rate, force, and pitch.

voluntary participant A person who chooses to listen to a particular speech.

W

weak ties Casual contacts that are more loosely connected to an individual's social network and are not characterized by intimacy.

word A symbol that stands for the object or concept it names.

work team A special form of group characterized by a close-knit relationship among people with different and complementary abilities and by a strong sense of identity.

Endnotes

Chapter 1

1. "Tinder Rape Suspect Had Prior Arrest," *The Daily Reveille*, July 29, 2014.

2. "Pope Francis Urges Young People Not to Waste Time on Internet," *NBC News*, August 5, 2014.

3. "Number of photo messages created by Snapchat users every day during 3rd quarter 2016 and 1st quarter 2017 (in billions)," retrieved November 26, 2017, from https://www.statista.com/statistics/257128/number-of-photo-messages-sent-by-snapchat-users-every-day/.

4. "Snapchat by the numbers: Stats, demographics and fun facts," retrieved July 31, 2017, from https://www.omnicoreagency.com/snapchat-statistics/.

5. Zephoria Digital Marketing, retrieved July 31, 2017, from https://zephoria.com/top-15-valuable-facebook-statistics/.

6. "18-24-Year-Old Smartphone Owners Send and Receive Almost 4K Texts per Month," retrieved November 3, 2014, from http://www.marketingcharts.com/online/18-24-year-old-smartphone-owners-send-and-receive-almost-4k-texts-per-month-27993/.

7. L. A. Samovar, R. E. Porter, E. R. McDaniel, and C. S. Roy, *Communication between Cultures*, 9th ed. (Belmont, CA: Cengage, 2017).

8. A. Doyle, "Communication Skills for Workplace Success: Employers Look for These Communication Skills," *The Balance*, retrieved October 27, 2017, from https://www.thebalance.com/communication-skills-list-2063779, updated August 24, 2017.

9. Personal conversations with business executives, personnel managers, and recruiters, October 2017.

10. J. Walther, "Interpersonal Effects in Computer-Mediated Interaction: A Relational Perspective," *Communication Research* 19 (1992): 52–90.

11. A. G. Walton, "6 Ways Social Media Affects Our Mental Health," *Forbes*, from https://www.forbes.com/sites/alicegwalton/2017/06/30/a-run-down-of-social-medias-effects-on-our-mental-health/#116e42d72e5a.

12. M. D. Shear, G. Thrush, and M. Haberman, "John Kelly, Asserting Authority, Fires Anthony Scaramucci," *The New York Times*, July 31, 2017.

13. Aristotle, *The Rhetoric and Poetics of Aristotle*, trans. W. R. Roberts and I. Bywater (New York: The Modern Library, 1954), 24–25.

14. W. M. Smail, *Quintilian on Education*, Book XII, Chapter 1 (Oxford, UK: Clarendon Press, 1938), 108.

15. U.S. Census Bureau, "2010 Census Data," released March 2011, retrieved November 26, 2017, from https://www.census.gov/2010census/data/.

16. U.S. Census Bureau, Population Division "Annual Estimates of the Resident Population: April 1, 2010 to July 1, 2016," released December 2016, retrieved November 26, 2017, from https://factfinder.census.gov/faces/nav/jsf/pages/community_facts.xhtml?src=bkmk.

17. D. K. Berlo, *The Process of Communication* (New York: Holt, Rinehart, & Winston, 1960), 23.

18. L. Forsdale, *Perspectives on Communication* (Reading, MA: Addison-Wesley, 1981).

19. H. J. Leavitt and R. Mueller, "Some Effects of Feedback on Communication," *Human Relations* 4 (1951): 401–10.

20. B. S. Wood, ed., *Development of Functional Communication Competencies: Grades 7–12* (Urbana, IL: ERIC Clearinghouse on Reading and Communication Skills and Speech Communication Association, 1977), 5.

Chapter 2

1. R. L. Scott, "On Viewing Rhetoric as Epistemic: Ten Years Later," *The Central States Speech Journal* (Winter 1976): 261.

2. T. Harnden, "Caroline Kennedy Repeats 'You Know' 142 Times in Interview," Telegraph.co.uk, January 25, 2009, 1.

3. W. V. Haney, *Communication and Organizational-Behavior: Text and Cases*, 3rd ed. (Homewood, IL: Irwin, 1973), 289–408. The term *perceptual set* is similar to what W. V. Haney refers to as "programming" or "frozen evaluation" in his book *Communication and Interpersonal Relations: Text and Cases*, 5th ed. (Homewood, IL: Irwin, 1986), 205–06, 408–38.

4. C. Stewart and W. Cash Jr., *Interviewing: Principles and Practices*, 13th ed. (New York: McGraw-Hill, 2011), 32.

5. S. Kassin, *Psychology* (Upper Saddle River, NJ: Prentice Hall, 1998); D. T. Gilbert and P. S. Malone, "The Correspondence Bias," *Psychological Bulletin* 117 (1995): 21–28; F. Van Overwalle, "Dispositional Attributions Require the Joint Application of the Methods of Difference and Agreement," *Personality and Social Psychology Bulletin* 23 (1997): 974–80; E. E. Jones, "The Rocky Road from Acts to Dispositions," *American Psychologist* 34 (1979): 107–17; and R. A. Baron and N. R. Branscombe, *Social Psychology*, 13th ed. (Boston: Pearson, 2012), 86.

6. H. M. Cheverton and D. Byrne, "Development and Validation of the Primary Choice Clothing Questionnaire." Presented at the meeting of the Eastern Psychological Association, Boston, February 1998, 9-1–9-2. D. Mack and D. Rainey, "Female Applicants, Grooming and Personnel Selection," *Journal of Social Behavior and Personality* 5 (1990): 399–407; and B. P. Meier, M. D. Robinson, and G. L. Clore, "Why Good Guys Wear White: Automatic Inferences about Stimulus Valence Based on Brightness," *Psychological Science* 15 (2004): 82–87.

7. C. S. Fichten and R. Amsel, "Trait Attribution about College Students with a Physical Disability: Circumplex Analysis and Methodological Issues," *Journal of Applied Social Psychology* 16 (1986): 410–27; S. J. McKelvie, "Stereotyping in Perception of Attractiveness, Age, and Gender in Schematic Faces," *Social Behavior and Personality* 9 (1994): 753–60; and M. L. Shannon and C. P. Stark, "The Influence of Physical Appearance on Personnel Selection," *Social Behavior and Personality* 31 (2003): 613–24.

8. The definition is based on work found in J. N. Martin and T. K. Nakayama, *Intercultural Communication in Contexts*, 5th ed. (New York: McGraw Hill, 2010), 84–93; L. A. Samovar and R. E. Porter, *Communication between Cultures*, 7th ed. (Belmont, CA: Wadsworth, 2010), 19–33; E. R. McDaniel, L. A. Samovar, and R. E. Porter, "Understanding Intercultural Communication: An Overview," in *Intercultural Communication: A Reader*, 13th ed., eds. L. A. Samovar, R. E. Porter, and E. R. McDaniel (Boston: Wadsworth, 2012), 10–13; D. W. Klopf and J. C. McCroskey, *Intercultural Communication Encounters* (Boston: Allyn and Bacon, 2007), 6–7.

9. K. L. Floyd and G. B. Ray, "Mapping the Affectionate Voice: Vocalic Predictors of Perceived Affection in Initial Interactions," *Western Journal of Communication* 67 (Winter 2003): 56–73.

10. Ibid., 68.

11. J. T. Wood, *Interpersonal Communication: Everyday Encounter*, 8th ed. (Boston: Wadsworth, 2016), 92.

12. B. Corcoran, "My Favorite Mistake," *Newsweek*, January 23, 2012: 60.

13. A. Gerike, *Old Is Not a Four-Letter Word: A Midlife Guide* (Watsonville, CA: Papier Mâchè Press, 1997).

14. D. J. Bem, "Self-Perception Theory," in *Advances in Experimental Social Psychology*, vol. 6, ed. L. Berkowitz (New York: Academic Press, 1972).

15. J. W. Kinch, "A Formalized Theory of Self-Concept," *American Journal of Sociology* 68 (January 1963): 481–86.

16. Ibid., 481.

17. Ibid., 482–83.

18. H. Tajfel and J. C. Turner, "The Social Identity Theory of Intergroup Behavior," in *The Social Psychology of Intergroup Relations*, 2nd ed., eds. S. Worchel and W. G. Austin (Monterey, CA: Brooks-Cole, 1986), 7–24.

19. K. J. Reynolds, J. C. Turner, N. R. Branscombe, K. I. Mavor, B. Bizumic, and E. Subasic, "Interactionism in Personality and Social Psychology: An Integrated Approach to Understanding the Mind of Behavior," *European Journal of Personality* 24 (2010); 458–82.

20. K. Neff, "Don't Fall into the Self-Esteem Trap:: Try a Little Self-Kindness," *New Yorker Magazine* (December 2014): 75–80.

21. P. J. Oaks and K. J. Reynolds, "Asking the Accuracy Question: Is Measurement the Answer?," in *The Social Psychology of Stereotyping and Group Life*, eds. R. Spears, P. J. Oaks, N. Ellemers, and S. A. Haslam (Oxford: Blackwell, 1997), 51–71.

22. A. M. Ledbetter, "Measuring Online Communication Attitude: Instrument Development and Validation," *Communication Monographs* 76 (2014): 463–86.

23. Ibid., 463–86.

24. S. Lau and L. K. Kwok, "Relationships of Family Environment to Adolescent's Depression and Self-Concept," *Social Behavior and Personality* 27 (2000): 41–50.

25. Ibid., 41–50.

26. H. Giles, S. Davis, J. Gasiorek, and J. Giles, *Successful Aging: A Communication Guide to Empowerment* (Barcelona: Aresta, 2013), 22.

27. Ibid., 25–36.

28. D. T. Miller, "The Norm of Self-Interest," *American Psychologist* 54 (1999): 1053–60.

29. C. Kanagawa, S. E. Cross, and H. R. Markus, "Who Am I? The Cultural Psychology of the Conceptual Self," *Journal of Personality and Social Psychology Bulletin* 27 (2001): 90–103.

30. Ibid., 90–103.

31. S. A. Ribeau, J. R. Baldwin, and M. L. Hecht, "An African-American Communication Perspective," in *Intercultural Communication: A Reader*, eds. L. A. Samovar and R. E. Porter (Belmont, CA: Wadsworth, 1994), 143; J. R. Baldwin and M. Hecht, "Unpacking Group-Based Intolerance: A Holographic Look at Identity and Intolerance," in *Intercultural Communication: A Reader*, 10th ed., eds. L. A. Samovar and R. E. Porter (Belmont, CA: Wadsworth, 2003), 358.

32. J. B. Beckwith, "Terminology and Social Relevance in Psychological Research on Gender," *Social Behavior and Personality* 22 (1994): 329–36;

J. T. Wood, *Gendered Lives: Communication, Gender and Culture*, 11th ed. (Belmont, CA: Wadsworth, 2013), 19.

33. J. T. Wood, *Gender Lives: Communication, Gender, and Culture*, 12th ed. (Belmont, CA: Thomson Wadsworth, 2017), 36–38.

34. Ibid., 43–44.

35. Ibid., 43–44.

36. N. Grieve, "Beyond Sexual Stereotypes. Androgyny: A Model or an Ideal?" in *Australian Women: Feminist Perspectives*, eds. N. Grieve and P. Grimshaw (Melbourne, Australia: Oxford University Press, 1980), 247–57.

37. J. T. Wood, 109–120.

38. D. A. Vogel, M. A. Lake, S. Evans, and K. H. Karraker, "Children's and Adults Sex-Stereotyped Perceptions of Infants," *Sex Roles* 24 (1991): 601–16.

39. M. E. Heilman, R. F. Martell, and M. C. Simon, "The Vagaries of Sex Bias: Conditions Regulating the Underevaluation, Equivaluation, and Overevaluation of Female Job Applicants," *Organizational Behavior and Human Decision Processes* 41 (1988): 98–110.

40. M. Chen and J. A. Bargh, "Nonconscious Behavioral Confirmation Processes: The Self-Fulfilling Consequences of Automatic Stereotype Activation," *Journal of Experimental Social Psychology* 33 (1997): 541–60; T. Claire and S. T. Fiske, "A Systematic View of Behavioral Confirmation: Counterpoint to the Individualist View," in *Intergroup Cognition and Intergroup Behavior*, eds. C. Sedikides, J. Schopler, and C. A. Insko (Mahwah, NJ: Erlbaum, 1998), 205–31.

41. B. A. Bettencourt and N. Miller, "Gender Differences in Aggression as a Function of Provocation: A Meta-Analysis," *Psychological Bulletin* 119 (1996): 422–47.

42. Adapted from D. Tannen, *You Just Don't Understand: Women and Men in Conversation* (New York: Morrow, 1990), 24.

43. Ibid., 25.

44. C. E. Epstein, *Deceptive Distinctions: Sex, Gender, and the Social Order* (New Haven, CT: Yale University Press, 1988), 25.

45. M. R. Gunnar-Von Gnechten, "Changing a Frightening Toy into a Pleasant Toy by Allowing the Infant to Control Its Actions," *Developmental Psychology* 14 (1978): 157–62; J. H. Block, "Differential Premises Arising from Differential Socialization of the Sexes: Some Conjectures," *Child Development* 54 (1983): 1335–54; J. T. Spence and R. L. Helmreich, *Masculinity and Femininity: Their Psychological Dimension and Antecedents* (Austin: University of Texas Press, 1978).

46. R. Rosenthal and L. Jacobson, *Pygmalion in the Classroom: Teacher Expectation and Pupils' Intellectual Development* (New York: Holt, Rinehart, & Winston, 1968), vii; T. Good and J. Brophy, *Looking in Classrooms*, 4th ed. (New York: Harper & Row, 1987).

47. C. S. Carver, L. A. Kus, and M. F. Scheier, "Effects of Good versus Bad Mood and Optimistic versus Pessimistic Outlook on Social Accep-

tance versus Rejection," *Journal of Social and Clinical Psychology* 13 (1994): 138–51.

48. M. D. Alicke, D. S. Vredenburg, M. Hiatt, and O. Govorun, "The Better Than Myself Effect," *Motivation and Emotion* 25 (2001): 7–22; Y. Klar, "Way beyond Compare: The Nonselective Superiority and Inferiority Bias in Judging Randomly Assigned Group Members Relative to Their Peers," *Journal of Experimental Social Psychology* 38 (2002): 331–51.

49. R. B. Sanitioso and R. Wlodarski, "In Search of Information That Confirms a Desired Self-Perception: Motivation Processing of Social Feedback and Choice of Interactions," *Personality and Social Psychology Bulletin* 30 (2004): 412–22.

50. B. R. Schlenker, M. F. Weigold, and J. R. Hallam, "Self-Serving Attribution in Social Context," *Journal of Personality and Social Psychology* 58 (1990): 855–63.

51. M. H. Bond, "Chinese Values," in *The Handbook of Chinese Psychology*, ed. M. H. Bond (Oxford, UK: Oxford University Press, 1996), 208–26.

52. R. Kurzban and J. Weeden, "Hurry Date: Mate Preferences in Action," *Evolution and Human Behavior* 26 (2005): 227–44.

53. C. M. Shaw and R. Edwards, "Self-Concepts and Self-Presentations of Males and Females: Similarities and Differences," *Communication Reports* 10 (1997): 55–62.

54. Ibid., 55–62.

55. A. L. Gonzales and J. T. Hancock, "Mirror, Mirror on My Facebook Wall: Effects of Exposure to Facebook on Self-Esteem," *Cyberpsychology, Behavior and Social Networks* 14 (2011): 79–83.

56. Ibid., 79–80.

57. Ibid., 79.

58. E. Goffman, *The Presentation of Self in Everyday Life* (Garden City, NY: Doubleday, 1959).

59. M. R. Barrick, J. A. Shaffer, and S. W. DeGrassi, "What You See May Not Be What You Get: Relationships among Self-Presentation Tactics and Ratings of Interview and Job Performance," *Journal of Applied Psychology* 94 (2009): 1394–411.

60. S. J. Wayne, R. C. Liden, I. K. Graft, and G. R. Ferris, "The Role of Upward Influence Tactics in Human Resource Decisions," *Personnel Psychology* 50 (1997): 979–1006; L. A. Witt and G. B. Ferris, "Social Skill as Moderator of the Conscientiousness-Performance Relationship: Convergent Results across Four Studies," *Journal of Applied Psychology* 84 (2003): 808–20; R. Vonk, "The Slime Effect: Suspicion and Dislike of Likeable Behavior toward Superiors," *Journal of Personality and Social Psychology* 74 (1998): 849–64; and R. A. Baron, "Self-Presentation in Job Interviews: When There Can Be 'Too Much of a Good Thing,'" *Journal of Applied Social Psychology* 16 (1986): 16–28.

Chapter 3

1. N. L. Gage and D. C. Berliner, *Educational Psychology*, 6th ed. (Boston: Houghton Mifflin, 1998), 152–53.

2. E. R. McDaniel, L. A. Samovar, and R. E. Porter, "Under-standing Intercultural Communication: An Overview," in *Intercultural Communication: A Reader*, 13th ed., eds. L. A. Samovar, R. E. Porter, and E. R. McDaniel (Boston: Wads-worth, 2012), 13–16.

3. N. Dresser, *Multicultural Manners* (New York: Wiley, 1996), 89–90.

4. M. W. Lustig and J. Koester, *Intercultural Competence: Interpersonal Communication across Cultures* (New York: HarperCollins, 1993).

5. E. T. Hall, *Beyond Culture* (New York: Anchor/Doubleday, 1976).

6. S. Nicholas, "'I live Hopi, I just don't speak it.': The Critical Intersection of Language, Culture, and Identity in the Lives of Contemporary Hopi Youth," *Journal of Language, Identity & Education, 8* (2009): 321–334.

7. L. R. France, "Lady Gaga Responds to Super Bowl Body Shaming," *CNN*. Retrieved December 18, 2017, from http://www.cnn.com/2017/02/08/entertainment/lady-gaga-body-shamed/index.html.

8. "The Fattening Rooms of Calabar," 19 July 2007, *BBC News*. Retrieved March 1, 2018 from http://news.bbc.co.uk/2/hi/6904640.stm.

9. G. Hofstede, *Culture's Consequences* (Beverly Hills, CA: Sage, 1980).

10. E. M. Rogers, W. B. Hart, and Y. Miike, "Edward T. Hall and the History of Intercultural Communication: The United States and Japan," *Keio Communication Review, 24* (2002): 3-26.

11. W. B. Gudykunst, "Toward a Theory of Effective Interpersonal and Intergroup Communication: An Anxiety/Uncertainty Management (AUM) Perspective," in R. L. Wiseman and J. Koester (eds.), *Intercultural Communication Competence* (Newbury Park, CA: Sage, 1993) 33–71.

12. G. Hofstede, G. J. Hofstede, and M. Minkov, *Cultures and Organizations: Software of the Mind,* 3rd ed. (New York: McGraw Hill, 2010).

13. H. Hoeken, C. Van den Brandt, R. Crijns, N. Dominguez, B. Hendriks, B. Planken, and M. Starren, "International Advertising in Western Europe: Should Differences in Uncertainty Avoidance Be Considered When Advertising in Belgium, France, the Netherlands, and Spain?", *Journal of Business Communication, 40* (2003): 195–218.

14. G. Hofstede, G. J. Hofstede, and M. Minkov, *Cultures and Organizations: Software of the Mind,* 3rd ed. (New York: McGraw-Hill, 2010).

15. K. Nishiyama, *Doing Business in Japan: Successful Strategies for Intercultural Communication* (Honolulu: University of Hawaii Press, 2000), 28.

16. N. Postman, *Technopoly* (New York: Alfred A. Knopf, 1992), 4.

17. H. Tajfel, and J. C. Turner, "An Integrative Theory of Intergroup Conflict," in S. Worchel and W. Austin (eds.), *Psychology of Intergroup Relations* (Chicago: Nelson-Hall, 1986), 2–24.

18. J. Luckmann, *Transcultural Communication in Nursing* (New York: Delmar, 1999).

19. Martin and Nakayama, 5; and E. R. McDaniel, L. A. Samovar, and R. E. Porter, "Understanding Intercultural Communication: An Overview," in *Intercultural Communication: A Reader*, 13th ed., eds. L. A. Samovar, R. E. Porter, and E. R. McDaniel (Boston: Wadsworth, 2012), 13.

20. H. Giles, S. Reid, and J. Harwood, J. (eds.), *The Dynamics of Intergroup Communication* (New York: Peter Lang, 2010).

21. J. M. Bennett and M. J. Bennett, "Developing Intercultural Sensitivity: An Integrative Approach to Global and Domestic Diversity," in D. Landis, J. M. Bennett, and M. J. Bennett (eds.), *Handbook of Intercultural Training*, 3rd ed. (Thousand Oaks, CA: Sage, 2004), 147–165.

22. M. Snyder and O. Klein, "Construing and Constructing Others: On the Reality and the Generality of the Behavioral Confirmation Scenario," *Interaction Studies 6* (2005): 53–67.

23. F. Jandt, *An Introduction to Intercultural Communication* (Los Angeles: Sage, 2010).

24. C. Gallois, A. Franklyn-Stokes, H. Giles, and N. Coupland, "Communication Accommodation in Intercultural Encounters," in Y. Y. Kim and W. B. Gudykunst (eds.), *Theories in Intercultural Communication* (Newbury Park, CA: Sage, 1988), 157–185.

25. J. Harwood and H. Giles (eds.), *Intergroup Communication: Multiple Perspectives* (New York: Peter Lang, 2005).

26. L. Arasaratnam, "Research in Intercultural Communication Competence," *Journal of Intercultural Communication, 13,* (2007): 66–73.

Chapter 4

1. K. Tracy and J. S. Robles, *Everyday Talk: Building and Reflecting Identities,* 2nd ed. (New York: Guilford Publications, 2013).

2. *New York Times* Top Stories for December 31, 2017, "President Trump has brought a reality-show accessibility to a once-aloof office, invigorating voters who felt alienated by the establishment." NYTimes.com News Alert, email, December 31, 2017, nytdirect@nytimes.

3. United States, Office of the Press Secretary, "Press Briefing by Press Secretary Sean Spicer," *The White House*, no. 01, January 22, 2017, www.whitehouse.gov/the-press-office/2017/01/22/press-briefing-press-secretary-sean-spicer-1222017-01.

4. "On NBC's 'Meet The Press,' Trump advisor Kellyanne Conway challenges Chuck Todd for saying that White House press secretary Sean Spicer has told multiple "falsehoods…,"KellyAnne Conway, interview with Chuck Todd on NBC's *Meet the Press,* January 22, 2017, accessed December 5, 2017, from https://www.realclearpolitics.com/video/2017/01/22/chuck_todd_to_kellyanne_conway_alternative_facts_are_not_facts.html.

5. D. R. Harfield, CLP, personal communication, March 25, 2015.

6. "The Power of Words," YouTube, accessed March 1, 2012, from www.youtube.com/watch?v=Hzgzim5m7oU.

7. P. H. Collins, *Fighting Words: Black Women and the Search for Justice,* synopsis on University of Minnesota Press website, accessed May 10, 2012, from www.upress.umn.edu/book-division/books/fighting-words.

8. D. R. Harfield, CLP, language and the way we think, personal communication, March 25, 2015.

9. L. A. Samovar and R. E. Porter, eds., *Intercultural Communication: A Reader* (Belmont, CA: Wadsworth, 2003), 358.

10. C. Ogbondah (UNI faculty member from Africa), personal communication, March 1, 2018.

11. Helpful African Proverbs, compiled by Kane Mathis, retrieved January 29, 2012, from www.kairarecords.com/kane/proverbs.htm.

12. W. Abrego (student from El Salvador), personal communication, November 15, 2017.

13. G. A. Miller, *The Psychology of Communication* (Baltimore: Penguin, 1967).

14. L. Carroll, *Alice's Adventures in Wonderland, Through the Looking Glass, and The Hunting of the Snark* (New York: Modern Library, 1925), 246–47.

15. A. Korzybski, *Science and Sanity: An Introduction to Non-Aristotelian Systems and General Semantics* (Lancaster, PA: Science Press Printing, 1933).

16. P. Dickson, *Slang!* (New York: Pocket Books, 1990).

17. Ibid.

18. W. Lutz, *Doublespeak: From "Revenue Enhancement" to "Terminal Living": How Government, Business, Advertisers, and Others Use Language to Deceive You* (New York: Harper & Row, 1987), 3–4.

19. Ibid.

20. K. Cushner, A. McClelland, and P. Safford, *Human Diversity in Education: An Integrative Approach*, 3rd ed. (New York: McGraw-Hill, 2010).

21. Adapted from W. V. Haney, *Communication and Organizational Behavior,* 3rd ed. (Homewood, IL: Irwin, 1973), 211–330

22. *Communication and Interpersonal Relations,* 5th ed. (Homewood, IL: Irwin, 1986), 213–405.

23. News bulletins from W. R. Espy, "Say When," *This Week,* July 13, 1952, quoted in W. V. Haney, *Communication and Organizational Behavior,* 3rd ed. (Homewood, IL: Irwin, 1973), 396.

24. D. Tannen, *You Just Don't Understand* (New York: Morrow, 1990).

25. C. Miller and K. Swift, *The Handbook on Nonsexist Writing,* 2nd ed. (New York: Harper & Row, 1988).

26. Guidelines may be found in a variety of places. One interesting website is the Coe College, Cedar Rapids, Iowa, speaking center and writing center, found at www.public.coe.edu/~wcenter/handouts_nonsexist.php. Another source is B. D. Sorrels, *Nonsexist Communicator: Solving the Problem of Gender and Awkwardness in Modern English* (Englewood Cliffs, NJ: Prentice Hall, 1983).

27. E. T. Hall, *The Hidden Dimension* (Garden City, NY: Doubleday, 1966).

28. G. Deutscher, "Does Your Language Shape How You Think?" *New York Times* online, August 26, 2010, retrieved January 14, 2015, from www.nytimes.com/2010/08/29/magazine/29language-t.html?_r=0&page wanted=print.

29. Ibid.

30. Ibid.

31. Ibid.

32. J. Neuliep, *Intercultural Communication: A Contextual Approach*, 2nd ed. (Thousand Oaks, CA: Sage Publications, 2018), 252.

33. B. L. Whorf, *Language, Thought, and Reality: Selected Writings of Benjamin Lee Whorf*, ed. J. B. Carroll (Cambridge, UK: Cambridge University Press, 1956).

34. K. Tracy, and J. S. Robles, *Everyday Talk: Building and Reflecting Identities*, 2nd ed. (New York: Guilford Publications, 2013), 71.

35. C. Kramerae, *Women and Men Speaking* (Rowley, MA: Newbury, 1981).

36. M. Houston, "Multiple Perspectives: African merican Women Conceive Their Talk," *Women and Language* 23 (2002): 11–23.

37. N. Postman, *Technopoly* (New York: Alfred A. Knopf, 1992), 4.

38. Ibid.

39. United States Supreme Court. *New York Times Co. v. United States. United States Reports*, vol. 403, 30 June 1971, pp. 713–763. Library of Congress, https://cdn.loc.gov/service/ll/usrep/usrep403/usrep403713/usrep403713.pdf.

40. S. Wyche, "Colin Kaepernick Explains Why He Sat during National Anthem," *Nfl.com*, National Football League, August 28 2016, accessed March 25, 2018, from www.nfl.com/news/story/0ap3000000691077/article/colin-kaepernick-explains-why-he-sat-during-national-anthem.

41. "Message from John Sargent: Fire and Fury," January 8, 2018, accessed January 15, 2018, from macus.supadu.com/wp-content/uploads/2018/01/Message-From-John-Sargent-Fire-and-Fury.png.

42. J. J. Bradac, J. W. Bowers, and J. A. Courtright, "Three Language Variables in Communication Research: Intensity, Immediacy, and Diversity," *Human Communication Research* 5 (1979): 257–69.

43. Lord Chesterfield (1694-1773), Philip Stanhope quotations, accessed January 25, 2015, from http://www.brainyquote.com/quotes/authors/p/philip_stanhope.html#J6eWL2lQdOoJx95H.99.

Chapter 5

1. M. L. Knapp and J. Hall, *Nonverbal Communication in Human Interaction*, 7th ed. (Belmont, CA: Wadsworth/Cengage Learning, 2010), 5.

2. Ibid., 12–21.

3. M. Argyle, F. Alkema, and R. Gilmour, "The Communication of Friendly and Hostile Attitudes by Verbal and Nonverbal Signals," *European Journal of Social Psychology* 1 (1971): 385–402.

4. B. M. DePaulo, J. J. Lindsay, B. E. Malone, L. Muhlenbruck, K. Chandler, and H. Cooper, "Cues to Deception," *Psychological Bulletin* 129 (2003): 74–118.

5. D. Matsumoto, B. Franklin, J. Choi, D. Rogers, and H. Tatani. "Cultural Influences on the Expression and Perception of Emotion," in W. Gudykunst and B. Mody, eds., *The Handbook of International and Intercultural Communication* (Thousand Oaks, CA: Sage, 2002), 107–26; and M. S. Remland, *Nonverbal Communication in Everyday Life*, 3rd ed. (Boston: Pearson, 2009), 152.

6. T. Novinger, *Intercultural Communication: A Practical Guide* (Austin: University of Texas Press, 2001), 64.

7. M. S. Remland, 211.

8. D. Matsumoto et al., 107–206.

9. B. Mesquita and J. Leu, "The Cultural Psychology of Emotion," in S. Kitayama and D. Cohen, eds., *Handbook of Cultural Psychology* (New York: Guildford Press, 2007), 734–59.

10. D. E. Madell and S. J. Muncer, "Control over Social Interactions: An Important Reason for Young People's Use of the Internet and Mobile Phones for Communication?" *Cyber Psychology and Behavior* 10 (2007): 137–40.

11. B. M. DePaul and D. A. Kashy, "Everyday Lies in Close and Casual Relationship," *Journal of Personality and Social Psychology* 74 (1998): 63–79.

12. P. Eckman, *Telling Lies: Clues to Deceit in the Marketplace, Politics, and Marriage*, 3rd ed. (New York: Norton, 2001); and B. E. Malone and B. M. DePaulo, "Measuring Sensitivity to Deception," in J. A. Hall and F. Bernieri, eds., *Interpersonal Sensitivity: Theory, Measurement, and Application* (Mahwah, NJ: Erlbaum, 2001): 103–24.

13. N. L. Etcoff, P. Ekman, J. J. Magee, and M. G. Frank, "Lie Detection and Language Comprehension, *Nature* 40 (2000): 139.

14. M. O'Sullivan, "The Fundamental Attribution Error in Detecting Deception: The Boy-Who-Cried-Wolf Effect," *Personality and Social Psychology Bulletin* 29 (2003): 1316–27.

15. T. H. Feeley and M. A. Turck, "The Behavioral Correlates of Sanctioned and Unsanctioned Deceptive Communication," *Journal of Nonverbal Behavior* 22 (1998): 189–204; and A. Vrij, L. Akehurst, and P. Morris, "Individual Differences in Hand Movements during Deception," *Journal of Nonverbal Behavior* 21 (1997): 87–102.

16. L. Anolli and R. Ciceri, "The Voice of Deception: Vocal Strategies of Naïve and Able Liars," *Journal of Nonverbal Behavior* 21 (1997): 259–85.

17. J. M. Tyler, R. S. Feldman, and A. Reichert, "The Price of Deceptive Behavior: Disliking and Lying to People Who Lie to Us," *Journal of Experimental Social Psychology* 42 (2006): 69–77.

18. Ibid., 69–77.

19. J. A. Hall and D. Matsumoto, "Gender Differences in Judgments of Multiple Emotions from Facial Expressions," *Emotion* 3 (2004): 201–206.

20. C. Mayo and N. M. Henley, eds., *Gender and Nonverbal Behavior* (Secaucus, NJ: Springer-Verlag, 1981).

21. R. Rosenthal and B. M. DePaul, "Sex Differences in Accommodation in *Nonverbal Communication*," in R. Rosenthal, ed., *Skill in Nonverbal Communication* (Cambridge, MA: Oelgeschlager, Gunn & Hain, 1979): 68–103.

22. S. W. Janik, A. R. Wellens, J. L. Goldberg, and L. F. Dell'osso, "Eyes as the Center of Focus in the Visual Examination of Human Faces," *Perceptual and Motor Skills* 4 (1978): 857–58.

23. D. Leathers, *Successful Nonverbal Communication: Principles and Applications* (New York: Macmillan, 1986).

24. P. Andersen, *Nonverbal Communication: Forms and Functions* (Long Grove, IL: Waveland Press, 2008).

25. C. L. Kleinke, "Gaze and Eye Contact: A Research Review," *Psychological Review* 100 (1986): 78–100.

26. P. G. Zimbardo, *Shyness: What It Is, What to Do about It* (Reading, MA: Addison-Wesley, 1977).

27. P. Greenbaum and H. W. Rosenfield, "Patterns of Avoidance in Responses to Interpersonal Staring and Proximity: Effects of Bystanders on Drivers at a Traffic Intersection," *Journal of Personality and Social Psychology* 36 (1978): 575–87.

28. P. C. Ellsworth and J. M. Carlsmith, "Eye Contact and Gaze Aversion in Aggressive Encounter," *Journal of Personality and Social Psychology* 33 (1973): 117–22.

29. Ibid.

30. C. Izard, *The Psychology of Emotions* (New York: Plenum, 1991); and P. Rozin, L. Lowery, and R. Ebert, "Varieties of Disgust Faces and the Structure of Disgust," *Journal of Personality and Social Psychology* 66 (1994): 870–81.

31. P. Ekman and K. Heider, "The Universality of a Contempt Expression: A Replication," *Motivation and Emotion* 12 (1988): 303–08; and P. Ekman, "Are There Basic Emotions?" *Psychology Review* 99 (1992): 550–53.

32. B. Knutson, "Facial Expression of Emotions Influence Interpersonal Trait Inferences," *Journal of Nonverbal Behavior* 20 (1996): 165–82.

33. H. Aguinis, M. Simonsen, and C. Pierce, "Effects of Nonverbal Behavior on Perceptions of Power Bases," *Journal of Social Psychology* 138 (1998): 455–70.

34. M. T. Motley, "Facial Affect and Verbal Context in Conversation: Facial Expression as Interjection," *Human Communication Research* 20 (1993): 3–40.

35. M. Zukerman, D. T. Larrance, N. H. Spiegel, and R. Klorman, "Controlling Nonverbal Displays: Facial Expressions and Tone of Voice," *Journal of Experimental Social Psychology* 17 (1981): 506–24.

36. P. Ekman, W. V. Friesen, and P. Ellsworth, "Methodological Decisions," in P. Ekman, ed., *Emotion in the Human Face*, 2nd ed. (Cambridge, UK: Cambridge University Press, 1982), 7–21.

37. P. Ekman and W. V. Friesen, "The Repertoire of Nonverbal Behavior: Categories, Origins, Usage, and Coding," *Semiotica* 1 (1969): 49–98.

38. D. S. Berry and L. Zebrowitz-McArthur, "Perceiving Character in Faces: The Impact of Age-Related Craniofacial Changes on Social Perception," *Psychological Bulletin* 100 (1986): 3–18.

39. J. M. Montepare and L. Zebrowitz-McArthur, "Impressions of People Created by Age-Related Qualities of Their Gaits," *Journal of Personality and Social Psychology* 54 (1988): 547–56.

40. W. Wells and B. Siegel, "Stereotyped Soma-types," *Psychological Reports* 8 (1961): 77–78.

41. M. A. Collins and L. A. Zebrowitz, "The Contribution of Appearance to Occupational Outcomes in Civilian and Military Settings," *Journal of Applied Social Psychology* 71 (1995): 129–63.

42. B. Gillen, "Physical Attractiveness: A Determinant of Two Types of Goodness," *Personality and Social Psychology Bulletin* 7 (1981): 277–81.

43. J. Levav and J. J. Argo, "Physical Contact and Financial Risk Taking," *Psychological Science* 21 (2010): 804–810.

44. R. Heslin and T. Alper, "Touch: A Bonding Gesture," in J. M. Wiemann and R. P. Harrison, eds., *Nonverbal Interaction* (Beverly Hills, CA: Sage, 1983), 47–75.

45. S. M. Jourard, *Disclosing Man to Himself* (Princeton, NJ: Van Nostrand, 1968).

46. Levav and Argo, 804–810.

47. L. M. Kneidinger, T. L. Maple, and S. A. Tross, "Touching Behavior in Sport: Functional Components, Analysis of Sex Differences and Ethological Considerations," *Journal of Nonverbal Behavior* 25 (2001): 43–62.

48. E. T. Hall, *The Silent Language* (Greenwich, CT: Fawcett, 1959), and *The Hidden Dimension* (Garden City, NY: Doubleday, 1969).

49. J. K. Burgoon, D. B. Buller, and W. G. Woodall, *Nonverbal Communication: The Unspoken Dialogue*, 2nd ed. (New York: Harper & Row, 1996), 122.

50. K. Nishiyama, *Doing Business in Japan: Successful Strategies for Intercultural Communication* (Honolulu: University of Hawaii Press, 2000), 28.

51. M. L. Knapp, *Essentials of Nonverbal Communication* (New York: Holt, Rinehart and Winston, 1980), 7; M. L. Knapp and J. Hall, *Nonverbal Communication in Human Interaction*, 7th ed. (Belmont, CA: Wadsworth Cengage Learning, 2010).

52. S. E. Quasha and F. Tsukada, "International Marriages in Japan: Cultural Conflict and Harmony," in L. A. Samovar, R. E. Porter, and E. R. McDaniel, eds., *Intercultural Communication: A Reader*, 13th ed. (Boston: Wadsworth Cengage Learning, 2012), 129.

53. Ibid., 129.

54. Ibid., 129.

55. "You Are What You Drive: A Silver SUV Broadcasts a Very Different Message from a Green Sedan," *USA Weekend Magazine*, October 20, 2002, 20–21.

Chapter 6

1. H. A. M. Voorveld and M. van der Goot, "Age Differences in Media Multitasking: A Diary Study," *Journal of Broadcasting & Electronic Media* 57 (2013): 392–408.

2. S. R. Hiltz and M. Turoff, *The Network Nation: Human Communication via Computer* (Reading, MA: Addison-Wesley, 1993).

3. J. V. Pavlik and S. McIntosh, *Converging Media: A New Introduction to Mass Communication*, 3rd ed. (New York: Oxford University Press, 2013).

4. Ibid.

5. N. K. Baym, *Personal Connections in the Digital Age* (Malden, MA: Polity Press, 2010), 6–12.

6. P. B. O'Sullivan, S. Hunt, and L. Lippert, "Mediated Immediacy: A Language of Affiliation in a Technological Age," *Journal of Language and Social Psychology* 23 (2004): 464–90.

7. N. S. Baron, "Letters by Phone or Speech by Other Means: The Linguistics of Email," *Language and Communication* 18 (1998): 133–70.

8. R. L. Daft and R. H. Lengel, "Information Richness: A New Approach to Managerial Behaviour and Organizational Design," *Research in Organizational Behaviour* 6 (1984): 191–233.

9. J. B. Walther, "Interpersonal Effects in Computer-Mediated Interaction: A Relational Perspective," *Communication Research* 19 (1992): 52–90.

10. Ibid.

11. J. B. Walther, "Computer-Mediated Communication: Impersonal, Interpersonal, and Hyperpersonal Interaction," *Communication Research* 23 (1996): 3–43.

12. J. B. Walther, "Social Information Processing Theory: Impressions and Relationship Development Online," in L. A. Baxter and D. O. Braithwaite, eds., *Engaging Theories in Interpersonal Communication* (Newbury Park, CA: Sage, 2008), 391–404.

13. C. Haythornthwaite, "Social Networks and Internet Connectivity Effects," *Information, Communication & Society* 8 (2005): 125–47.

14. Ibid.

15. N. S. Baron, *Always On: Language in an Online and Mobile World* (New York: Oxford University Press, 2008).

16. L. Humphreys, "Mobile Social Networks and Social Practice: A Case Study of Dodgeball," *Journal of Computer-Mediated Communication*, 13, no. 1 (2007).

17. C. Haythornthwaite, "Strong, Weak, and Latent Ties and the Impact of New Media," *Information Society* 18 (2002): 385–401.

18. R. L. Daft and R. H. Lengel, "Information Richness: A New Approach to Managerial Behaviour and Organizational Design," *Research in Organizational Behaviour*, 6, (1984): 191–233.

19. S. E. Caplan, "Preference for Online Social Interaction: A Theory of Problematic Internet Use and Psychosocial Well-Being," *Communication Research* 30 (2003): 625–48.

20. S. E. Caplan, "Relations among Loneliness, Social Anxiety, and Problematic Internet Use," *CyberPsychology & Behavior* 10 (2007): 234–42.

21. S. E. Caplan, "Problematic Internet Use and Psychosocial Well-Being: Development of a Theory-Based Cognitive-Behavioral Measure," *Computers in Human Behavior* 18 (2002): 533–75.

22. Ibid.

23. B. S. Titsworth and K. A. Kiewra, "Organizational Lecture Cues and Student Notetaking as Facilitators of Student Learning," *Contemporary Educational Psychology* 29 (2004): 447–61.

24. MTV and The Associated Press, "The *MTV–Associated Press* Poll Digital Abuse Survey, September 23, 2009, http://www.athinline.org/MTV-AP_Digital_Abuse_Study_Full.pdf.

25. R. Spears and M. Lea, "Social Influence and the Influence of the 'Social' in Computer-Mediated Communication, in M. Lea (ed.), *Contexts of Computer-Mediated Communication*. (Hemel Hempstead: Harvester Wheatsheaf, 1992), 30–65.

26. CBS News, "Tyler Clementi's Parents Want Tougher Charges," March 23, 2011, http://www.cbsnews.com.

27. M. Knapp, J. Daly, K. Albada, and G. Miller, "Background and Current Trends in the Study of Interpersonal Communication," in M. L. Knapp and J. A. Daly, eds., *Handbook of Interpersonal Communication*, 3rd ed. (Thousand Oaks, CA: Sage, 2001), 3–20.

Chapter 7

1. B. Garner, *The Blair Garner Show*, syndicated country music radio show, February 16, 2018.

2. "Off-Eric," on *The Blair Garner Show*, February 16, 2018.

3. D. R. Harfield, personal conversation, January 29, 2015; J. Brownell, *Listening: Attitudes, Principles, and Skills*, 4th ed. (Boston: Allyn and Bacon, 2009, 151–52. Copyright © 2010 by Pearson Education; L. A. Janusik, "Teaching Listening: What Do We Know? What Should We Know?" *International Journal of Listening* 16 (2002): 5–39; and C. Coakley and A. Wolvin, "Listening in the Educational Environment," in M. Purdy and D. Borisoff, eds., *Listening in Everyday Life: A Personal and Professional Approach*, 2nd ed. (Lanham, MD: University Press of America, 1997), 179–212.

4. D. R. Harfield, CLP, unpublished manuscript based on International Listening Association Convention, Johnson City, TN, March 2011; W. Gallagher, *Rapt Attention and the Focus of Life* (New York: Penguin Press, 2009); and, N. Herrmann, *The Creative Brain* (Lake Lure, NC: The Ned Herrmann Group, 1993).

5. J. Brownell, *Listening: Attitudes, Principles, and Skills*, 4th ed. (Boston: Allyn and Bacon, 2009) 14; D. R. Harfield, personal conversation, January 29, 2015.

6. L. A. Janusik and A. D. Wolvin, "24 Hours in a Day. A Listening Update to the Time Studies," paper presented at the meeting of the

International Listening Association, Salem, OR, 2006; and R. Bohlken, "Substantiating the Fact That Listening Is Proportionally Most Used Language Skill," *The Listening Post* 70 (1999): 5.

7. S. Baker, "Identifying Communication Skills Necessary to Succeed in the Ever Changing and Competitive Workplace," unpublished Master's thesis, University of Northern Iowa, 2009.

8. National Association of Colleges & Employers, Job Outlook 2015: The Candidate Skills/ Qualities Employers Want, retrieved March 1, 2015, from www.naceweb.org/s10262014/candidate_skills_employer_qualities/.

9. R. Bohlken, "Substantiating the Fact That Listening Is Proportionally Most Used Language Skill," *The Listening Post* 70 (1999): 5; L. A. Janusik, "Teaching Listening: What Do We Know? What Should We Know?" *International Journal of Listening* 16 (2002): 5–39; and C. Coakley and A. Wolvin, "Listening in the Educational Environment," in M. Purdy and D. Borisoff, eds., *Listening in Everyday Life: A Personal and Professional Approach*, 2nd ed. (Lanham, MD: University Press of America, 1997), 179–212.

10. L. A. Janusik, "Teaching Listening: What Do We Know? What Should We Know?" *International Journal of Listening* 16 (2002): 5–39; and L. A. Janusik and A. D. Wolvin, "Listening Treatment in the Basic Communication Course Text," in D. Sellnow, ed., *Basic Communication Course Annual* (Boston: American Press, 2002).

11. L. A. Janusik and A. D. Wolvin, "24 Hours in a Day. A Listening Update to the Time Studies," paper presented at the meeting of the International Listening Association, Salem, OR, 2005.

12. M. Imhof and T. Weinhard, "What Did You Listen to in School Today?" paper presented at the 25th Annual Convention of the International Listening Association, Fort Myers, FL, April 2004.

13. "Priorities of Listening Research: Four Interrelated Initiatives: A White Paper Sponsored by the Research Committee of the International Listening Association, 2008." International Listening Association, 2008. Retrieved May 27, 2018, from https://listen .org/resources/documents/white_paper_prioritiesresearch.pdf.

14. A. D. Wolvin, *Listening in the Quality Organization*, (Ithaca, NY: Finger Lakes Press, 1999).

15. D. R. Harfield and M. L. Beall, Listening Online Class Learning Module 1, University of Northern Iowa, Spring 2018.

16. Ibid.

17. A. D. Wolvin, *Listening in the Quality Organization*, (Ithaca, NY: Finger Lakes Press, 1999).

18. D.R. Harfield and M.L. Beall, Listening Online Class Learning Module 2, University of Northern Iowa, Spring 2018.

19. D. R. Harfield, personal phone conversation, January 29, 2015.

20. L. A. Janusik, "Teaching Listening: What Do We Know? What Should We Know?" *International Journal of Listening* 16 (2002): 5–39.

21. D .R. Harfield, personal phone conversation, January 29, 2015.

22. Herrmann, *The Creative Brain* (Lake Lure, NC: The Ned Herrmann Group, 1993).

23. Ibid.

24. Ibid., and Harfield, personal phone conversation, January 29, 2015.

25. D. R. Harfield, and M. L. Beall, *Introduction to Effective Listening*, Learning Module 2, for online listening class, University of Northern Iowa, Spring 2018.

26. D. R. Harfield, and M. L. Beall, *Introduction to Effective Listening*, Learning Module 3, for online listening class, University of Northern Iowa, Spring 2018.

27. A. Wolvin, ed., *Listening and Human Communication: 21st Century Perspectives* (Boston: Blackwell Publishing, 2009).

28. M. Imhof, "Precognitive Strategies for Students," International Listening Association Convention presentation, March 2010.

29. Adapted from Judi Brownell, *Listening: Attitudes, Principles, and Skills*, 4th ed. (Boston: Allyn and Bacon, 2009), 148–50. Copyright © 2010 by Pearson Education. Reprinted by permission of the publisher.

30. "Empathy," Dictionary.com, retrieved March 13, 2012, from dictionary.reference.com/browse/empathy.

31. J. Brownell, *Listening: Attitudes, Principles, and Skills*, 4th ed. (Boston: Allyn and Bacon, 2009), 172.

32. R. Nichols, "Factors Accounting for Differences in Comprehension of Material Presented Orally in the Classroom," doctoral dissertation, University of Iowa, 1948.

33. "Self Perceptions and Personal Bias, Public Speaking: The ACA Open Knowledge Online Guide," retrieved March 12, 2012, from http://textcommons.org/node/122.

34. D. Harfield, personal communication, March 12, 2012.

35. Edward D'Angelo, *The Teaching of Critical Thinking* (Amsterdam, The Netherlands: B. R. Gruner, 1971), 7.

36. R. H. Ennis, "A Taxonomy of Critical Thinking Dispositions and Abilities," in J. Baron and R. Sternberg, eds., *Teaching Thinking Skills: Theory and Practice* (New York: Freeman, 1987).

37. The Foundation for Critical Thinking, retrieved April 5, 2018, from http://www.criticalthinking.org/pages/our-concept-of-critical-thinking/411.

38. M. L. Beall and D. R. Harfield, Module 5, Listening, for online listening class, University of Northern Iowa, Spring 2018.

39. C. Angove, "The Rise of Social Media in Organizations: How to Turn the Internet into Interactive Dialogue," unpublished Master's degree research project, University of Northern Iowa, May 2012.

Chapter 8

1. National Association of Colleges and Employers, "What Employers Seek on a Resume," December 11, 2017, accessed February 28, 2018, from https://www.naceweb.org/talent-acquisition/candidate-selection/what-employers-seek-on-a-resume/.

2. S. Adams, "The 10 Skills Employers Most Want in 2015 Graduates," November 12, 2014, retrieved February 28, 2018, from http://www.forbes.com/sites/susanadams/2014/11/12/the-10-skills-employers-most-want-in-2015-graduates/.

3. J. Swan, University of Northern Iowa, personal conversations, February 2015.

4. "Public speaking," Merriam-Webster Online Dictionary, retrieved February 14, 2015, from http://www.merriam-webster.com/dictionary/public%20speaking.

5. "Social media," Merriam-Webster Online Dictionary, retrieved February 14, 2015, from www.merriam-webster.com/dictionary/social%20media.

6. Students may wish to surf the web to find topics. Keying in "topics for speeches" on Google netted nearly 49 million hits in 0.30 second on March 15, 2018. Another site that also offers topics and help for choosing informative topics is http://www.myspeechclass.com/informativetopics2.html (this site adds topics weekly). There are similar sites for persuasive topics. YouTube is a source for useful video clips, and Hulu provides TV episodes. Many college and university speech communication departments publish lists on their own websites. Web searches, Facebook, and LinkedIn may give you information about people and how to contact them. Pinterest provides a wealth of information on a variety of topics of personal interest.

7. "Writing Guide: Informative Speaking," Colorado State University, retrieved February 27, 2015, from http://writing.colostate.edu/guides/guide.cfm?guideid=52. Many colleges have similar web pages with similar information.

8. Personal conversations with Japanese communication colleague Takehide Kawashima, December 2016. This is also true for other Asian countries. A good explanation of this phenomenon is found in Stella Ting-Toomey's *Face Negotiation Theory* Gudykunst, W.B., ed. Theories in intercultural communication. (Newbury Park, CA: Sage., 2005).

9. S. J. Lind, "Teaching Digital Oratory: Public Speaking 2.0," *Communication Teacher* 26, no. 3 (2012): 163–69.

Chapter 9

1. "Did you Know? Shift Happens (updated for 2018)" accessed February 24, 2018, from https://www.youtube.com/watch?v=u06BXgWbGvA.

2. G. Couros, "Why Social Media Can and Is Changing Education," *Connected Principals,* March 21, 2011, accessed February 25, 2015, from http://georgecouros.ca/blog/archives/1860.

3. Abdullah Al-Asmari, "My Saudi Arabia." This University of Northern Iowa graduate student shared insights about Saudi Arabia with the intercultural communication class. His presentation was about two and a half hours, and these remarks are adapted from that lecture.

4. Abdullah's remarks were in the form of a lecture presentation to the class, so additional information supplemented the information he provided for this example. The primary source was: "Middle East: Saudi Arabia," *The World Factbook,* Central Intelligence Agency, accessed June 18, 2012, from https://www.cia.gov/library/publications/the-world-factbook/geos/sa.html.

5. James Doubek, "Attention, Students: Put Your Laptops Away," transcript from NPR Weekend Edition, Sunday, April 17, 2016, Education, accessed March 20, 2018, from https://www.npr.org/2016/04/17/474525392/attention-students-put-your-laptops-away?utm_campaign=storyshare&utm_source=facebook.com&utm_medium=social.

6. Oprah Winfrey's Golden Globes Speech Transcript, accessed January 8, 2018, from http://www.harpersbazaar.com/culture/film-tv/a14551183/oprah-winfrey-golden-globes-speech-transcript/.

7. Ibid.

8. Ibid.

9. Adapted from remarks made in an oral defense of an unpublished Master's thesis by Anna Levina, "Recent Jewish Immigrants' Communication in Postville, Iowa: A Case Study," University of Northern Iowa, June 3, 2003.

10. Em Griffin, A. Ledbetter, and G. Sparks,"Axiology," in *A First Look at Communication Theory,* 8th ed. (Boston: McGraw-Hill, 2011).

11. "Africa's Orphaned Generations," UNICEF, 2011, accessed April 30, 2018, from https://www.unicef.org/sowc06/pdfs/africas_orphans.pdf.

12. Ibid.

13. Ibid.

14. Ibid.

15. Ibid.

16. Mission One Million, "History of the Organization," accessed April 30, 2018, from http://mission1m.org/.

17. "Orphans," UNICEF press center, accessed March 3, 2015, from www.unicef.org/media/media_45279.html.

18. "Africa's Orphaned Generations," UNICEF, 2011, accessed April 30, 2018, from www.unicef.org/sowc06/pdfs/-africas_orphans.pdf.

19. Ibid.

20. C. J. Loomis, "Warren Buffett Gives Away His Fortune," CNN Money, June 25, 2006, accessed March 3, 2015, from http://money.cnn.com/2006/06/25/magazines/fortune/charity1.fortune/.

21. "Africa's Orphaned Generations," Part 2, UNICEF, 2003, updated 2011, accessed April 30, 2018, from https://www.unicef.org/sowc06/pdfs/africas_orphans.pdf.

Chapter 10

1. Fast Facts: Hunger, World Vision Blog, June 3, 2011, accessed March 15, 2015, from http://blog.worldvision.org/causes/fast-facts-hunger/.

2. B. Senauer, "Ending Global Hunger in the 21st Century: Projections of the Number of Food Insecure People," *Applied Economic Perspectives and Policy* 23, no. 1 (2012): 68–81, accessed March 15, 2015, from http://aepp.oxfordjournals.org/content/23/1/68.short.

3. Smithsonian Institute and Museums, http://www.si.edu/, accessed March 15, 2015.

4. "Earth Day: The History of a Movement," accessed March 15, 2015, from http://www.earthday.org/earth-day-history-movement?gclid=CMvWp9THyMYCFQYJaQodD4QMzw.

5. T. Buzan, *Mind Maps at Work: How to Be the Best at Work and Still Have Time to Play* (New York: HarperCollins, 2004). Also, "How to Make a Mind Map in 8 Steps," accessed March 15, 2015, from https://www.google.com/search?q=%E2%80%9CHow+to+Make+a+Mind+Map+in+8+Steps.%E2%80%9D&espv=2&biw=1292&bih=690&site=webhp&tbm=isch&tbo=u&source=univ&sa=X&ei=_5s9VfGGPMijyATI4YH4AQ&ved=0CCQQsAQ.

6. Ibid.

7. "Eating Disorder Statistics," South Carolina Department of Mental Health, accessed March 15, 2015, from http://www.state.sc.us/dmh/anorexia/statistics.htm.

8. "Worldwide Orphan Facts, Figures and Statistics," SOS Children's Villages, accessed March 15, 2015, from http://www.sos-usa.org/our-impact/childrens-statistics.

9. J. Robinson, "Silent Assassin: The Ticking Time Bomb of Stress," HuffPost Healthy Living, accessed March 15, 2015, from http://www.huffingtonpost.com/joe-robinson/stress-screenings_b_3347483.html.

10. "Laughter Is the Best Medicine: Health Benefits of Humor and Laughter," HELPGUIDE. ORG, accessed March 15, 2015, from http://www.helpguide.org/articles/emotional-health/laughter-is-the-best-medicine.htm.

11. Ibid.

12. Lee Iacocca, cited in Glenn Van Ekeren, *Speaker's Sourcebook II* (Englewood Cliffs, NJ: Prentice Hall, 1994), 73.

13. "Laughter Is the Best Medicine: Health Benefits of Humor and Laughter," HELPGUIDE. ORG, accessed March 15, 2015, from http://www.helpguide.org/articles/emotional-health/laughter-is-the-best-medicine.htm.

14. Ibid.

15. "Choosing to Adopt," accessed March 15, 2015, from http://adoption.about.com/od/adopting/bb/befrdecideadopt.htm.

16. D. Zarefsky, *Public Speaking Strategies for Success,* 5th ed. (Boston: Allyn and Bacon, 2008), 222.

17. "What Are Sleep Deprivation and Deficiency?" National Heart, Lung, and Blood Institute, accessed March 15, 2015, from http://www.nhlbi.nih.gov/health/health-topics/topics/sdd/.

18. "Eating Disorders," National Institutes of Mental Health, accessed March 15, 2015, from http://www.nimh.nih.gov/health/publications/eating-disorders-new-trifold/index.shtml.

19. J. Rifkin, "The Bio Tech Century," delivered May 1998, City Club of Cleveland, OH, accessed March 15, 2015, from http://www.americanrhetoric.com/.

20. D. Zarefsky, *Public Speaking Strategies for Success,* 5th ed. (Boston: Allyn and Bacon, 2008), 222.

Chapter 11

1. Graham D. Bodie, "A Racing Heart, Rattling Knees, and Ruminative Thoughts: Defining, Explaining, and Treating Public Speaking Anxiety," *Communication Education* 59, 1 (January 2010): 70–105.

2. J. C. McCroskey, "The Communication Apprehension Perspective," in J. A. Daly and J. C. McCroskey, eds., *Avoiding Communication: Shyness, Reticence, and Communication Apprehension* (Beverly Hills, CA: Sage, 1984), 13.

3. Many sources identify "glossophobia," or "fear of public speaking," as one of our greatest fears. David Walleechinsky, Amy Wallace, Ira Basen, and Jane Farrow, in *The New Book of Lists,* (New York: Penguin Random House, 2006) say that 73 percent of Americans identify "fear of speaking" ahead of fear of spiders, snakes, and death.

4. X. Liao, "Effective Communication in Multicultural Classrooms: An Exploratory Study," unpublished Master of Arts thesis, University of Northern Iowa, May 2003.

5. Hugh Jackman, Pre-Oscars (2009) interview. YouTube. Accessed April 15, 2012, from http://www.youtube.com/watch?v=eRjPaTUD3N4.

6. K. K. Dwyer, *Conquer Your Speech-Fright: Learn How to Overcome the Nervousness of Public Speaking* (Belmont, CA: Wadsworth Publishing, 1997), 73–83.

7. Merriam Webster online dictionary, accessed April 1, 2015, from http://www.merriam-webster.com/dictionary/meditation.

8. M. Ricard, A. Luts, and R. J. Davidson, "The Mind of the Meditator," *Scientific American* (November 2014): 39–45.

9. S. Chaiken, "Communicator Physical Attractiveness and Persuasion," *Journal of Personality and Social Psychology* 37 (1979): 1387–97. Many

other current studies identify physical attractiveness as a factor in attending to another's speech. This article provides a more complete foundation for current work.

10. W. J. Seiler, "The Effects of Visual Materials on Attitude, Credibility, and Retention," *Speech Monographs* 38 (November 1971): 331–34; W. J. Seiler, "The Conjunctive Influence of Source Credibility and the Use of Visual Materials on Communicative Effectiveness," *Southern Speech Communication Journal* 37 (Winter 1971): 174–85; and P. Brett, "A Comparative Study of the Effects of the Use of Multimedia on Listening Comprehension," *System* 25 (March 1997): 39–53.

11. Ibid.

12. *Presentations That Persuade and Motivate,* The Results-Driven Manager Series (Boston: Harvard Business School Press, 2004).

13. William Germano, "The Scholarly Lecture: How to Stand and Deliver," *The Chronicle of Higher Education* Vol. 50, Issue 14, Page B15) (November 28, 2003).

14. Personal conversation with Dr. Victoria DeFrancisco, University of Northern Iowa, January 20, 2012.

Chapter 12

1. "Information," Merriam-Webster Dictionary, retrieved October 13, 2018, from https://www.merriam-webster.com/dictionary/information.

2. D. Zarefsky, *Public Speaking: Strategies for Success,* 5th ed. (Boston: Allyn and Bacon, 2008), 412.

3. Adapted from W. Fotheringham, *Perspectives on Persuasion* (Boston: Allyn and Bacon, 1966), 33.

4. Dr. D. Brownstein, "The Country's #1 Health Crisis," *Newsmax Health,* May 30, 2015.

5. C. Cudworth, "Sometimes It's the Junk in Your Head That Needs Cleaning Out," Takeaways, retrieved June 4, 2012, from http://fengshui.about.com/od/thebasics/qt/clearclutter.htm.

6. "Statistics about Depression," retrieved June 4, 2015, from http://psychcentral.com/blog/archives/2010/09/02/statistics-about-college-depression/.

7. G. Carlson, interviewed by Canadian Broadcasting Corporation staff at FM 89.3 Radio, Winnipeg, Manitoba, June 11, 2015; http://podcast.cbc.ca/mp3/podcasts/mbinfora-dio_20120611_71114.mp3.

8. American Diabetes Association, "National Diabetes Statistics Report, 2014," retrieved January 30, 2018, from http://www.diabetes.org/diabetes-basics/statistics/.

9. R. Alexander, "Does a Child Die of Hunger Every 10 Seconds? *BBC News,* June 17, 2013.

10. S. J. Crow, C. B. Peterson, S. A. Swanson, N. C. Raymond, S. Specker, E. D. Eckert, and J. E. Mitchell, "Increased Mortality in Bulimia Nervosa and Other Eating Disorders," *American Journal of Psychiatry* 166 (2009): 1342–46.

11. "Milestones," *Time,* May 28, 2012, 21; D. Martin, "Evelyn B. Johnson, Pilot and Instructor, Dies at 102," *New York Times,* May 12, 2012.

12. "'Smart Bomb' Drug Targets Breast Cancer," *NewsmaxMedia,* retrieved January 30, 2018, from http://www.newsmaxhealth.com/health_stories/herceptin_breast_cancer/2012/06/03/454338.html?s=al&promo_code=F185-1.

13. Mayo Clinic, "Eating Disorders: Symptoms," retrieved January 30, 2018, from http://www.mayoclinic.com/health/eating-disorders/ds00294/dsection=symptoms; also, "Eating Disorder Statistics," South Carolina Department of Mental Health, retrieved January 30, 2018, from http://www.state.sc.us/dmh/anorexia/statistics.htm.

14. Eligible Receiver, *Frontline,* PBS, retrieved January 30, 2018, from http://www.pbs.org/wgbh/pages/frontline/shows/cyberwar/warnings/.

15. S. Toulmin, *The Uses of Argument* (Cambridge, UK: Cambridge University Press, 1969), 94–145.

16. H. Clancy, "Exec Predicts Dead Calm for U.S. Wind Energy Production," GreenTech Pastures, retrieved January 30, 2018, from http://www.zdnet.com/blog/green/execpredicts-dead-calm-for-us-wind-energy-generation/21394.

17. J. McCroskey, retrieved June 4, 2015, from www.jamescmccroskey.com.

18. L. Talerico-Hedred, World Vision Blog, "Fast Facts: Hunger," retrieved January 30, 2018, from http://blog.worldvision.org/causes/fast-facts-hunger/.

19. South Carolina Department of Mental Health, "Eating Disorder Statistics," retrieved January 30, 2018, from http://www.state.sc.us/dmh/anorexia/statistics.htm.

20. K. German, B. E. Gronbeck, D. Ehninger, and A. H. Monroe, *Principles and Types of Speech Communication,* 17th ed. (Boston: Allyn and Bacon, 2010), 185–205.

21. M. Schwabe, "Volunteering with Bethel Missions in Guatemala," persuasive speech given at the University of Nebraska–Lincoln, used with permission.

22. George W. Bush, *Joint Session of Congress Speech,* September 20, 2001, retrieved March 23, 2018, from https://georgewbush-whitehouse.archives.gov/infocus/bushrecord/documents/Selected_Speeches_George_W_Bush.pdf.

Chapter 13

1. L. Stinson, "Unplugged for 40 Days," *Journal Star,* April 2, 2011, D1, D3.

2. Zephoria Digital Marketing, retrieved February 26, 2018 from https://zephoria.com/top-15-valuable-facebook-statistics/.

3. L. Stinson, "Unplugged for 40 Days," *Journal Star,* April 2, 2011, D1, D3.

4. Used with Permission from L. Stinson, "Unplugged for 40 Days," *Journal Star,* April 2, 2011, D1, D3."

5. 8 social media statistics for 2017, retrieved February 26, 2018 from https://oursocialtimes.com/7-social-media-statistics-for-2017/.

6. "18-24-Year-Old Smartphone Owners Send and Receive Almost 4K Texts per Month," retrieved November 3, 2014, from http://www.marketingcharts.com/online/18-24-year-old-smartphone-owners-send-and-receive-almost-4k-texts-per-month-27993/.

7. L. Raine, A. Lenhart, and A. Smith, "The Tone of Life on Social Networking Sites, *Pew Internet Reports,* February 9, 2012, retrieved February 16, 2012, from http://www.pewinternet.org/Reports/2012/Social-networking-climate.aspx.

8. M. L. Knapp and A. L. Vangelisti, *Interpersonal Communication and Human Relationships,* 6th ed. (Boston: Allyn and Bacon, 2009).

9. B. H. Spitzberg, "What Is Good Communication?" *Journal of the Association for Communication Administration* 29 (2000): 103–19; J. T. Woods, *Interpersonal Communication Everyday Encounters,* 7th ed. (Boston: Wadsworth Cengage, 2013), 30–33; K. Floyd, *Interpersonal Communication,* 7th ed. (New York: McGraw-Hill, 2011), 28–30.

10. C. R. Berger and R. J. Calabrese, "Some Explorations in Initial Interactions and Beyond: Toward a Developmental Theory of Interpersonal Communication," *Human Communication Research* 1 (1975): 98–112; and C. R. Berger, "Response–Uncertain Outcome Values in Predicted Relationships. Uncertainty Reduction Theory Then and Now," *Human Communication Research* 13 (1986): 34–38.

11. C. R. Berger, "Beyond Initial Interaction: Uncertainty, Understanding, and Development of Interpersonal Relationships," in H. Giles and R. St. Clair, eds., *Language and Social Psychology* (Oxford, UK: Blackwell, 1979), 122–44.

12. E. Griffin, *A First Look at Communication Theory,* 8th ed. (New York: McGraw-Hill, 2012).

13. D. E. Brashers, J. L. Neidig, S. M. Haas, L.W. Cardillo, and J. A. Russel, "'In an Important Way, I Did Die,'" Uncertainty and Revival among Persons Living with HIV or AIDS," *AIDS Care* 11 (1999): 201–19; D.E. Brashers, "Communication and Uncertainty Management," *Journal of Communication* 51 (2001): 477–97.

14. D. E. Brashers, "A Theory of Communication and Uncertainty Management," in B. Whaley and W. Samter, eds., *Explaining Communication Theory* (Mahwah, NJ: Lawrence Erlbaum, 2007): 210–18.

15. D.E. Brashers, "Communication and Uncertainty Management," *Journal of Communication* 51 (2001): 477–97.

16. Ibid., 477–97.

17. I. Altman and D. Taylor, *Social Penetration: The Development of Interpersonal Relationships* (New York: Holt, Rinehart & Winston, 1973); and M. L. Knapp and A. L. Vangelisti, *Interpersonal Communication and Human Relationships,* 6th ed. (Boston: Allyn and Bacon, 2009), 13–19.

18. W. Thibaut and H. H. Kelley, *The Social Psychology of Groups,* 2nd ed. (New Brunswick, NJ: Transaction Books, 1986), 9–30; and E. Griffin, *A First Look at Communication Theory,* 6th ed. (New York: McGraw-Hill, 2006), 122–25.

19. W. C. Schutz, *The Interpersonal Underworld* (Palo Alto, CA: Science and Behavior Books, 1966), 13–20.

20. K. Floyd, *Communicating Affection: Interpersonal Behavior and Social Context* (Cambridge, UK: Cambridge University Press, 2006).

21. R. F. Baumeister and M. R. Leary, "The Need to Belong: Desire for Interpersonal Attachments as a Fundamental Human Motivation," *Psychological Bulletin* 117 (1995): 497–529.

22. R. G. Kuijer, B. P. Buunk, J. F. Ybema, and T. Wobbes, "The Relation between Perceived Inequity, Marital Satisfaction and Emotions among Couples Facing Cancer," *British Journal of Social Psychology* 41 (2002): 39–56.

23. J. T. Wood, "Dialectical Theory," in *Making Connections: Readings in Relational Communication*, 2nd ed., eds. K. M. Galvin and P. J. Cooper (Los Angeles, CA: Roxbury, 2000), 132–38; L. A. Baxter, "Dialectical Contradictions in Relationship Development," *Journal of Social and Personal Relationships* 7 (1990): 69–88; and L. A. Baxter, "Thinking Dialogically about Communication in Interpersonal Relationships," in *Structure in Human Communication*, ed. R. Conville (Westport, CT: Greenwood, 1994).

24. L. A. Baxter and B. Montgomery, *Relation: Dialogues and Dialect* (New York: Guilford, 1996), 185–206.

25. L. A. Baxter, "Dialectical Contradictions in Relationship Development," *Journal of Social and Personal Relationships* 7 (1990): 69–88.

26. D. Fine, *The Fine Art of Small Talk* (New York: Hyperion, 2005).

27. A. L. Sillars and M. D. Scott, "Interpersonal Perception between Intimates: An Integrative Review," *Human Communication Research* 10 (1983): 153–76.

28. J. M. DeGroot, *Reconnecting with the Dead via Facebook: Examining Transcorporeal Communication as a Way to Maintain Relationships* (Doctoral dissertation, Ohio University, 2009). ProQuest Digital Dissertations, AAT 3371475.

29. J. W. Pennebaker, *Opening Up: The Healing Power of Expressing Emotions* (New York: Guilford, 1990).

30. V. J. Derlega, S. Metts, S. Petronio, and S. T. Margulis, *Self-Disclosure* (Newbury Park, CA: Sage, 1993), 74.

31. S. Petronio, "Communication Boundary Management: A Theoretical Model of Managing Disclosure of Private Information between Marital Couples," *Communication Theory* 1 (1991): 311; and S. Petronio and J. P. Caughlin, "Communication Privacy Management Theory: Understanding Families," in D. O. Braithwaite and L. A. Baxter, eds., *Engaging Theories in Family Communication: Multiple Perspectives* (Thousand Oaks, CA: Sage, 2006), 35–49.

32. S. Petronio, "The Boundaries of Privacy: Praxis of Everyday Life," in S. Petronio, ed., *Balancing the Secrets of Private Disclosures* (Hillsdale, NJ: Erlbaum, 2000), 9–15.

33. J. T. Wood, *Gendered Lives: Communication, Gender, and Culture*, 8th ed. (Belmont, CA: Wadsworth, 2009), 123–24.

34. D. Tannen, *You Just Don't Understand: Women and Men in Conversation* (New York: Quill, 2001).

35. C. K. Riessman, *Divorce Talk: Women and Men Make Sense of Personal Relationships* (New Brunswick, NJ: Rutgers University Press, 1990).

36. S. Petronio, "Communication Strategies to Reduce Embarrassment Differences between Men and Women," *The Western Journal of Speech Communication* 48 (1984): 28–38.

37. D. Lithwick, "Teens, Nude Photos and the Law," *Newsweek*, February 23, 2009, 18.

38. N. Gibbs, "Second Thoughts about Kids and Cell-Phones," *Time*, March 5, 2009, 56.

39. R. P. Hart and D. M. Burks, "Rhetorical Sensitivity and Social Interaction," *Speech Monographs* 39 (1972): 75–91.

40. S. W. Littlejohn and K. Foss, *Theories of Human Communication*, 9th ed. (Belmont, CA: Wadsworth, 2008).

41. J. C. McCroskey and T. A. McCain, "The Measurement of Interpersonal Attraction," *Speech Monographs* 41 (1974): 261–66.

42. M. A. Collins and L. A. Zebrowitz, "The Contributions of Appearance to Occupational Outcomes in Civilian and Military Settings," *Journal of Applied Social Psychology* 25 (1995): 129–63; and I. Van Straaten, R. G. Engels, C. Finkenauer, and R. W. Holland, "Meeting Your Match: How Attractiveness Similarity Affects Approach Behavior in Mixed-Sex Dyads," *Personality and Social Psychology Bulletin* 35 (2009): 685–97.

43. S. M. Andersen and A. Baum, "Transference in Interpersonal Relations: Influences and Affect Based on Significant Representations," *Journal of Personality* 62 (1994): 459–97.

44. M. A. Collins and L. A. Zebrowitz, "The Contributions of Appearance to Occupational Outcomes in Civilian and Military Settings," *Journal of Applied Social Psychology* 25 (1995): 129–63.

45. N. Angier, "Opposites Attract? Not in Real Life," *The New York Times*, July 8, 2003, F1, F6; and P. M. Buston and S. T. Emlen, "Cognitive Processes Underlying Human Mate Choice: The Relationship between Self-Perception and Mate Preferences in Western Society," *The Proceedings of the National Academy of Sciences* 100 (2003): 8805–10.

46. I. Van Straaten, R. G. Engels, C. Finkenauer, and R. W. Holland, "Meeting Your Match: How Attractiveness Similarity Affects Approach Behavior in Mixed-Sex Dyads," *Personality and Social Psychology* 35 (2009): 685–97.

47. W. M. Bernstein, B. O. Stephenson, M. L. Snyder, and R. A. Wicklund, "Causal Ambiguity and Heterosexual Affiliation," *Journal of Experimental Social Psychology* 19 (1983): 78–92; K. H. Price and S. G. Vandenberg, "Match-

ing for Physical Attractiveness in Married Couples," *Personality and Social Psychology* 5 (1979): 398–400; and M. Lea, "Factors Underlying Friendship: An Analysis of Responses on the Acquaintance Description Form in Relation to Wright's Friendship Model," *Journal of Social and Personal Relationships* 6 (1989): 275–92.

48. M. R. Parks and K. Floyd, "Making Friends in Cyberspace," *Journal of Communication* 45 (1996): 84; and J. B. Walther and M. R. Parks, "Cues Filtered Out, Cues Filtered In: Computer-Mediated Communication and Relationships," in *Handbook of Interpersonal Communication*, 3rd ed., eds. M. L. Knapp and J. A. Daly (Thousand Oaks, CA: Sage, 2002), 529–63.

49. A. Feingold, "Gender Differences in Effects of Physical Attractiveness on Romantic Attraction: A Comparison across Five Research Paradigms," *Journal of Personality and Social Psychology* 59 (1990): 981–93; and S. A. Meyers, "'Your Mother Would Like Me': Self-Presentation in the Personals Ads of Heterosexual and Homosexual Men and Women," *Personality and Social Psychology Bulletin* 19 (1993): 131–42.

50. J. Coupland, "Past the 'Perfect Kind of Ague'? Styling Selves and Relationships in Over-50 Dating Advertisements," *Journal of Communication* 50 (2000): 9–30.

51. M. R. Parks and K. Floyd, "Making Friends in Cyberspace," *Journal of Communication* 45 (1996): 85.

52. M. Knapp, *Social Intercourse: From Greeting to Good-Bye* (Boston: Allyn and Bacon, 1978), 3–28; and M. L. Knapp and A. L. Vangelisti, *Interpersonal Communication and Human Relationship*, 6th ed. (Boston: Allyn and Bacon, 2009), 33–37.

53. D. P. McWhirter and A. M. Mattison, *The Male Couple* (Englewood Cliffs, NJ: Prentice-Hall, 1998).

54. M. L. Knapp and A. L. Vangelisti, *Interpersonal Communication and Human Relationships*, 6th ed. (Boston: Allyn and Bacon, 2009), 33.

55. Ibid., 37–42.

56. Ibid., 39.

57. Ibid., 40.

58. Adapted from an article written by Jonathan Butler titled "The Donut Shop Experiment," in *The Front Porch Where People Share Life*, published by The Front Porch, LLC, © 2002.

59. L. Stafford and D. Canary, "Maintenance Strategies and Romantic Relationships: Type, Gender, and Relational Characteristics," *Journal of Social and Personal Relationships* 8 (1991): 217–42.

60. J. M. Tyler, R. S. Feldman, and A. Reichert, "The Price of Deceptive Behavior: Disliking and Lying to People Who Lie to Us," *Journal of Experimental Social Psychology* 42 (2006): 69–77.

61. J. T. Hancock, C. Toma, and N. Ellsion, "The Truth about Lying in Online Dating Profiles," *Proceedings of ACM ChI 2007 Conference on Human Factors in Computing Systems* (2007): 449–52.

62. Ibid., 451.

63. C. L. Toma and J. T. Hancock, "Reading between the Lines: Linguistic Cues to Deception in Online Dating Profiles," *Proceedings of ACM CSCW10 Conference on Computer-Support Cooperative Work* (2010): 5–8.

64. B. M. DePaul, J. J. Lindsay, B. E. Malone, L. Muhlenbruck, K. Chandler, and H. Cooper, "Cues to Deception," *Psychological Bulletin* 129 (2003): 74–118.

65. M. L. Knapp and A. L. Vangelisti, *Interpersonal Communication and Human Relationships*, 6th ed. (Boston: Allyn and Bacon, 2009), 43–47.

66. M. L. Knapp, R. P. Hart, G. W. Friedrich, and G. M. Shulman, "The Rhetoric of Goodbye: Verbal and Nonverbal Correlates of Human Leave-Taking," *Speech Monographs* 40 (1973): 182–98.

67. W. Wilmot and J. Hocker, *Interpersonal Conflict*, 8th ed. (New York: McGraw-Hill, 2011), 11.

68. Ibid., 33, 37.

69. R. A. Baron, "Attributions and Organizational Conflict," in *Attribution Theory: Applications to Achievement, Mental Health, and Interpersonal Conflict*, eds. S. Graha and V. Folkes (Hillsdale, NJ: Erlbaum, 1990), 185–204; and R. Cropanzano, ed., *Justice in the Workplace* (Hillsdale, NJ: Erlbaum, 1993), 79–103.

70. W. Wilmot and J. Hocker, *Interpersonal Conflict*, 8th ed. (New York: McGraw-Hill, 2011), 47.

71. Ibid., 101.

72. M. L. Knapp and A. L. Vangelisti, *Interpersonal Communication and Human Relationships*, 6th ed. (Boston: Allyn and Bacon, 2009), 384; K. Floyd, *Interpersonal Communication*, 2nd ed. (New York: McGraw-Hill, 2011), 375; A. C. Filley, *Interpersonal Conflict Resolution* (Glenview, IL: Scott, Foresman, 1975); D. D. Cahn, "Intimate in Conflict: A Research Review," in *Intimates in Conflict: A Communication Perspective*, ed. D. D. Cahn (Hillsdale, NJ: Erlbaum, 1990), 1–24; W. W. Cupach and D. J. Canary, *Competence in Interpersonal Conflict* (New York: McGraw-Hill, 1997); and R. Blake and J. Mouton, *The Managerial Grid* (Houston: Gulf Publishing, 1964).

73. A. L. Sillars, S. G. Coletti, D. Parry, and M. A. Rogers, "Coding Verbal Conflict Tactics: Nonverbal and Perceptual Correlates of the Avoidance–Distributive–Integrative Distinction," *Human Communication Research* 9 (1982): 83–95; and W. Wilmot and J. Hocker, *Interpersonal Conflict*, 8th ed. (New York: McGraw-Hill, 2011), 152.

74. Q. Wang, E. L. Fink, and D. A. Cai, "The Effect of Conflict Goals on Avoidance Strategies: What Does Not Communicating Communicate," *Human Communication Research* 38 (2012): 222–52.

75. J. Gottman and S. Carrere, "Why Can't Men and Women Get Along? Developmental Notes and Marital Inequities," in *Communication Relational Maintenance*, eds. D. Canary and L. Stafford (New York: Academic Press, 1994).

76. J. Gottman, *Why Marriages Succeed and Fail: And How You Can Make Yours Last* (New York: Simon and Schuster, 1994); and J. Gottman, *The Marriage Clinic: A Scientifically Based Marital Therapy* (New York: Norton, 1999).

77. K. Neff and S. Harter, "The Authenticity of Conflict Resolutions among Adult Couples: Does Women's Other-Oriented Behavior Reflect Their True Selves," *Sex Roles: A Journal of Research* (2002): 403–21.

78. A. L. Sillars and W. W. Wilmot, "Communication Strategies in Conflict and Mediation," in J. Wiemann and J. A. Daly, eds., *Communicating Strategically: Strategies in Interpersonal Communication* (Hillsdale, NJ: Erlbaum, 1994), 163–90.

79. J. S. Neuman and B. A. Baron, "Social Antecedents of Bullying," in S. Einarsen, H. Hoel, D. Zapf, and C. L. Cooper, eds. *Workplace Bullying: Development in Theory, Research*, 2nd ed. (London: CRC Press, 2010): 201–27.

80. W. Wilmot and J. Hocker, *Interpersonal Conflict*, 8th ed. (New York: McGraw-Hill, 2011), 163.

81. Ibid., 168–74.

82. S. W. Duck, "A Perspective on the Repair of Personal Relationships: Repair of What, When?" in S. W. Duck, ed., *Personal Relationships 5: Repairing Personal Relationships* (New York: Macmillan, 1984).

83. B. R. Burleson and W. Samter, "Effects of Cognitive Complexity on the Perceived Importance of Communication Skills in Friends," *Communication Research* 17 (1990): 165–82; W. Samter and B. R. Burleson, "Evaluations of Communication Skills as Predictors of Peer Acceptance in a Group Living Situation," *Communication Studies* 41 (1990): 311–26; B. R. Burleson, J. G. Delia, and J. L. Applegate, "The Socialization of Person-Centered Communication: Parent's Contributions to Their Children's Social-Cognitive and Communication Skills," in M. A. Fitzpatrick and A. L. Vangelisti, eds., *Explaining Family Interactions* (Thousand Oaks, CA: Sage, 1995), 34–76.

84. M. L. Knapp and A. L. Vangelisti, *Interpersonal Communication and Human Relationships*, 6th ed. (Boston: Allyn and Bacon, 2009), 403.

85. J. M. Reisman, "Friendliness and Its Correlates," *Journal of Social and Clinical Psychology* 2 (1984): 143–55.

86. E. P. Simon and L. A. Baxter, "Attachment-Style Differences in Relationship Maintenance Strategies," *Western Journal of Communication* 57 (Fall 1993): 423.

87. Ibid., 423.

88. Ibid., 428.

89. Ideas for this section are derived from a Parent Effectiveness Training workshop and from T. Gordon, *Parent Effectiveness Training* (New York: Wyden, 1970).

Chapter 14

1. S. A. Beebe and J. T. Masterson, *Communicating in Small Groups: Principles and Practices*, 11th ed. (Boston: Allyn and Bacon, 2015), 6–12.

2. G. Lumsden, D. Lumsden, and C. Wetthoff, *Communicating in Groups and Teams: Sharing Leadership*, 5th ed. (Belmont, CA: Wadsworth, 2010).

3. K. Adams and G. J. Galanes, *Communicating in Groups Applications and Skills*, 9th ed. (New York: McGraw-Hill, 2015), 10.

4. Ibid., 10–11.

5. B. S. Boneva, A. Quinn, R. Kraut, S. Kiesler, and I. Shklovski, "Teenage Communication in the Instant Messaging Era," in R. Kraut, M. Brynin, and S. Kiesler, eds., *Computers, Phones and the Internet: Domesticating Information Technology*, (New York: Oxford University, 2006): 201–18; J. B. Walther, T. Loh, and L. Granka, "Let Me Count the Ways: The Interchange of Verbal and Nonverbal Cues in Computer-Mediated and Face-to-Face Affinity," *Journal of Language and Social Psychology* 24 (2005): 36–65.

6. N. K. Baym, Y. B. Zhang, and M-C. Lin, "Social Interactions across Media: Interpersonal Communication on the Internet, Face-to-Face, and the Telephone," *New Media & Society* 6 (2004); 299–318.

7. J. Peter and P. M. Valenburg, "Research Note: Individual Differences in Perceptions of Internet Communication," *European Journal of Communication* 21 (2006): 213–26.

8. M. Buckingham and C. Coffman, "Item 9: Doing Quality Work," *Gallup Management Journal* [online], Spring 2002, retrieved on July 7, 2011, from www.gallupjournal.com/q12Center/articles/19990517.asp.

9. J. R. Katzenbach and D. K. Smith, "The Discipline of Teams," *Harvard Business Review* (March–April 1993): 111–20.

10. L. P. Stewart, P. J. Cooper, A. D. Stewart, and S. H. Friedley, *Communication and Gender*, 4th ed. (Boston: Allyn and Bacon, 2003), 44–50; D. N. Maltz and R. A. Borker, "A Cultural Approach to Male–Female Miscommunication," in J. J. Gumperz, ed., *Language and Social Identity* (Cambridge, UK: Cambridge University Press, 1982), 195–216; and E. Baird, "Sex Differences in Group Communication: A Review of Relevant Research," *Quarterly Journal of Speech* 62 (1976): 179–92.

11. B. F. Meeker and P. A. Weitzel-O'Neil, "Sex Roles and Interpersonal Behavior in Task-Oriented Groups," *American Sociological Review* 42 (1977): 91–105; R. L. Hoffman and N. K. V. Maier, "Quality and Acceptance of Problem Solutions by Members of Homogeneous and Heterogeneous Groups," *Journal of Abnormal and Social Psychology* 62 (1961): 401–07.

12. J. D. Rothwell, *In Mixed Company: Communicating in Small Groups and Teams* (Boston: Wadsworth, 2013), 32–35; J. C. McCroskey, V. P. Richmond, and R. A. Stewart, *One on One: The Foundations of Interpersonal Communication* (Englewood Cliffs, NJ: Prentice-Hall, 1986), 244–47; M. E. Roloff, "The Impact of Socialization on Sex Differences in Conflict Resolution" (paper presented at the annual convention of the International Communication Association, Acapulco, Mexico, May 1980); E. A. Mabry, "Some Theoretical Implications of Female and Male Interaction in Unstructured Small Groups,"

Small Group Behavior 20 (1989): 536–50; and W. E. Jurma and B. C. Wright, "Follower Reactions to Male and Female Leaders Who Maintain or Lose Reward Power," *Small Group Research* 21 (1990): 97–112.

13. J. Bond and W. Vinacke, "Coalition in Mixed Sex Triads," *Sociometry* 24 (1961): 61–65; B. A. Fisher, "Differential Effects of Sexual Composition Interaction Patterns in Dyads," *Human Communication Research* 9 (1983): 225–38; W. E. Jurma and B. C. Wright, "Follower Reactions to Male and Female Leaders Who Maintain or Lose Reward Power," *Small Group Research* 21 (1990): 97–112; and D. J. Canary and B. H. Spitzberg, "Appropriateness and Effectiveness Perceptions of Conflict Strategies," *Human Communication Research* 14 (1987): 93–118.

14. G. J. Galanes and K. Adams, *Effective Group Discussion*, 14th ed. (New York: McGraw-Hill, 2013), 147.

15. The Official Robert's Rules of Order Website, retrieved on February 10, 2018, from www.robertsrules.com.

16. T. Postmes, R. Spears, and M. Lea, "The Formation of Group Norms in Computer-Mediated Communication," *Human Communication Research* 26 (July 2000): 341–70.

17. R. A. Baron and N. R. Branscomber, *Social Psychology*, 13th ed. (Boston: Pearson, 2012), 392.

18. F. E. Fiedler, *A Theory of Leadership Effectiveness* (New York: McGraw-Hill, 1967); and P. Weissenberg and M. H. Kavanagh, "The Independence of Initiating Structure and Consideration: A Review of the Evidence," *Personnel Psychology* 25 (1972): 119–30.

19. M. Conlin, "Champions of Innovation," *Business Week*, June 2006, 19–26.

20. R. K. White and R. Lippitt, *Autocracy and Democracy: An Experimental Inquiry* (New York: Harper & Row, 1960), 26–27; and K. Adams and G. J. Galanes, *Communicating in Groups: Applications and Skills*, 9th ed. (New York: McGraw-Hill, 2015), 260.

21. L. G. Bolman and T. E. Deal, *Reframing Organizations: Artistry, Choice, and Leadership*, 2nd ed. (San Francisco: Jossey-Bass, 1997); and G. Morgan, *Images of Organizations*, 2nd ed. (Thousand Oaks, CA: Sage, 1997).

22. K. Adams and G. J. Galanes, *Communicating in Groups: Applications and Skills*, 9th ed. (New York: McGraw-Hill, 2015), 261; R. K. White and R. Lippitt, "Leader Behavior and Member Reaction in Three 'Social Climates,'" in D. Cartwright and A. Zander, eds., *Group Dynamics: Research and Theory*, 2nd ed. (New York: Harper & Row, 1960), 527–53.

23. K. Adams and G. J. Galanes, *Communicating in Groups: Applications and Skills*, 9th ed. (New York: McGraw-Hill, 2015), 259.

24. M. Conlin, "Champions of Innovation," *Business Week*, June 2006, 20.

25. V. Zarya, "The 2017 Fortune 500 Includes a Record Number of Women CEOs," *Fortune*, retrieved January 12, 2017, from http://fortune.com/2017/06/07/fortune-women-ceos/.

26. A. B. Gershenoff and R. J. Foti, "Leader Emergence and Gender Roles in All-Female Groups: A Critical Examination," *Small Group Research* 34 (April 2003): 170–96.

27. J. A. Kolb, "Are We Still Stereotyping Leadership? A Look at Gender and Other Predictors of Leader Emergence," *Small Group Research* 28 (August 1997), 370–93.

28. S. B. Shimanoff and M. M. Jenkins, "Leadership and Gender: Challenging Assumptions and Recognizing Resources," in R. Y. Hirokawa, R. S. Cathcart, L. A. Samovar, and L. Henman, eds., *Small Group Communication: Theory and Practice*, 8th ed., (Los Angeles: Roxbury, 2003), 184–98.

29. M. Loden, *Feminine Leadership or How to Succeed in Business without Being One of the Boys* (New York: Times Books, 1985).

30. S. C. Koch, "Evaluative Affect Display toward Male and Female Leaders of Task-Oriented Groups," *Small Group Research* 36 (2005): 678–703.

31. A. H. Eagly and B. T. Johnson, "Gender and Leadership Style: A Meta-Analysis," *Psychological Bulletin* 108 (1990): 233–56.

32. R. Sharpe, "As Leaders, Women Rule: New Studies Find That Female Managers Outshine Their Male Counterparts in Almost Every Measure," *Business Week 2000–2009*, retrieved July 14, 2009, from www.businessweek.com.

33. E. E. Duehr and J. E. Bono, "Men, Women, and Managers: Are Stereotypes Finally Changing?" *Personnel Psychology* 59 (2006): 459–71; A. H. Eagly and S. Sczesny, "Stereotypes about Women, Men, and Leaders: Have Times Changed?" in M. Barreto, M. K. Ryan, and M. T. Schmitt, eds., *The Glass Ceiling in the 21st Century* (Washington, DC: American Pscyhological Association, 2009), 21–47, and "Business Women Differ from Business Men in Style, Not Skill," 2008, retrieved on July 13, 2009, from www.coaching-for-new-women-managers.com/business-women.html.

34. D. Forsyth, M. Heiney, and S. Wright, "Biases in Appraisal of Women Leaders," *Group Dynamics: Theory, Research, and Practices* 1 (1997): 98–103; S. Shackelford, W. Wood, and S. Worchel, "Behavioral Styles and the Influence of Women in Mixed-Sex Groups," *Social Psychology* 59 (1996): 284–93; and A. Eagly, S. Karau, and M. Makhijani, "Gender and the Effectiveness of Leaders: A Meta-Analysis," *Journal of Personality and Social Psychology* 117 (1995): 125–45.

35. A. H. Eagly and S. Sczesny, "Stereotypes about Women, Men, and Leaders: Have Times Changed?" in M. Barreto, M. K. Ryan, and M. T. Schmitt, eds., *The Glass Ceiling in the 21st Century* (Washington, DC: American Pscyhological Association, 2009), 21–47.

36. G. J. Galanes and K. Adams, *Effective Group Discussion*, 14th ed. (New York: McGraw-Hill, 2013), 15–17

37. K. D. Benne and P. Sheats, "Functional Roles of Group Members," *Journal of Social Issues* 4 (1948): 41–49.

38. R. Y. Hirokawa, "Consensus Group Decision-Making, Quality of Decision and Group Satisfaction: An Attempt to Sort 'Fact' from 'Fiction,'" *Central States Speech Journal* 33 (1982): 407–15.

39. R. S. DeStephen and R. Y. Hirokawa, "Small Group Consensus: Stability of Group Support of the Decision, Task Process, and Group Relationships," *Small Group Behavior* 19 (1988): 227–39.

40. S. A. Beebe and J. T. Masterson, *Communicating in Small Groups*, 11th ed. (Boston: Pearson, 2015), 206–207.

41. W. Wilmot and J. Hocker, *Interpersonal Conflict*, 9th ed. (New York: McGraw-Hill, 2014), 13.

42. Ibid., 11.

43. K. Adams and G. J. Galanes, *Communicating in Groups: Applications and Skills*, 9th ed. (New York: McGraw-Hill, 2015), 229.

44. Ibid., 242–44.

45. R. V. Harnack, T. B. Fest, and B. S. Jones, *Group Discussion: Theory and Technique*, 2nd ed. (Englewood Cliffs, NJ: Prentice-Hall, 1997): 153–54.

46. J. Dewey, *How We Think* (Lexington, MA: Heath, 1910).

47. A. Beebe and J. T. Masterson, *Communicating in Small Groups*, 11th ed. (Boston: Pearson, 2015), 271.

48. D. S. Gouran and R. Y. Hirokawa, "Effective Decision Making and Problem Solving in Groups," in R. Y. Hirokawa, R. S. Cathcart, L. A. Samovar, and L. D. Henman, eds., *Small Group Communication*, 8th ed. (Los Angeles: Roxbury, 2003), 27–38.

49. B. J. Broome and L. Fulbright, "A Multistage Influence Model of Barriers to Group Problem Solving: A Participant-Generated Agenda for Small Group Research," *Small Group Research* 26 (February 1995): 25–55.

50. P. B. Paulus, ed., *Psychology of Group Influence*, 2nd ed. (Hillsdale, NJ: Erlbaum, 1989).

51. R. A. Cooke and J. A. Kernaghan, "Estimating the Difference between Group versus Individual Performance on Problem-Solving Tasks," *Group & Organizational Studies* 12 (September 1987): 319–42.

52. S. A. Beebe and J. T. Masterson, *Communicating in Small Groups*, 11th ed. (Boston: Pearson, 2015), 14.

53. I. L. Janis, *Groupthink: Psychological Studies of Policy Decisions and Fiascoes*, 2nd ed. (Boston: Houghton Mifflin, 1983); and J. D. Rothwell, *In Mixed Company: Communicating in Small Groups and Teams* (Boston: Wadsworth, 2013), 247–55.

54. P. E. Tetlock, R. S. Peterson, C. McGuire, S. Change, and P. Feld, "Assessing Political Group Dynamics: A Test of the Groupthink Model," *Journal of Personality and Social Psychology* 63 (1992): 403–25.

55. I. L. Janis, *Groupthink: Psychological Studies of Policy Decisions and Fiascoes*, 2nd ed. (Boston: Houghton Mifflin, 1983).

56. K. Adams and G. J. Galanes, *Communicating in Groups: Applications and Skills,* 9th ed. (New York: McGraw-Hill, 2015), 188–90.

57. S. J. Karau and K. D. Williams, "Social Loafing: A Meta-Analytic Review and Theoretical Integration," *Journal of Personality and Social Psychology* 65 (1993): 681–706; B. K. Latané and S. Harkins, "Many Hands Make Light the Work: The Causes and Consequences of Social-Loafing," *Journal of Personality and Social Psychology* 37 (1979): 822–32; B. G. Schultz, "Improving Group Communication Performance," in L. R. Frey, D. S. Gouran, and M. S. Poole, eds., *The Handbook of Group Communication Theory and Research* (Thousand Oaks, CA: Sage, 1999), 371–94; and S. A. Beebe and J. T. Masterson, *Communicating in Small Groups,* 11th ed. (Boston: Pearson, 2015), 82–83.

58. S. Sorensen, "Grouphate" (paper presented at the International Communication Association, Minneapolis, MN, May 1981).

Chapter 15

1. K. B. Barbour, F. B. Berg, M. Eannace, J. Greene, M. Hessig, M. Papworth, C. Radin, E. Rezny, and J. Suarez, *The Quest: A Guide to the Job Interview* (Dubuque, IA: Kendall/Hunt, 1991), 47.

2. R. B. Adler, M. M. Maresh-Fuehrer, J. Elmhorst, and K. Lucas, *Communicating at Work: Strategies for Success in Business and the Professions,* 12th ed. (New York: McGraw-Hill, 2019), 5

3. D. Grossman, LeaderCommunicatorBlog, The Grossman Group, March 8, 2017, www.yourthoughtpartner.com/blog, retrieved March 9, 2018, 1; and S. Ginsberg, "So Many Messages and So Little Time," *Business Outlook,* May 5, 1997, C1, cited in R. B. Adler, M. M. Maresh-Fuehrer, J. Elmhorst, and K. Lucas, *Communicating at Work: Strategies for Success in Business and the Professions,* 12th ed. (New York: McGraw-Hill, 2019).

4. M. T. Hora, "Beyond the Skills Gap," *NACE Journal,* February 1, 2017, 3.

5. Interview with Dr. Kelli Smith, former assistant director of career services, University of Nebraska, Lincoln, May 5, 2012.

6. C. J. Stewart and W. B. Cash Jr., *Interviewing Principles and Practices,* 15th ed. (New York: McGraw-Hill, 2018), 134.

7. "Your Ultimate Job Search Guide," a booklet prepared by the University of Nebraska Career Services, 2017–2018, p. 6; and Career Connections Nebraska, http://www.nebraska-careerconnections.org/students-college.htm, retrieved March 17, 2018.

8. B. Darrow, "LinkedIn Claims Half a Billion Users," Fortune, http://fortune.com/2017/04/24/linkedin-users/, retrieved April 8, 2018.

9. "Linkedin.com Site Info," *Alexa Internet,* retrieved March 16, 2018, from https://www.alexa.com/siteinfo/linkedin.com.

10. Ibid.

11. "Your Ultimate Job Search Guide," a booklet prepared by the University of Nebraska Career Services, 2017–2018, p. 9.

12. Ibid., 9.

13. Ibid., 15–29.

14. Ibid., 15–27.

15. Ibid., 17

16. Ibid., 18–19.

17. M. Valdes and S. McFarland, "Resume, References and Passwords, Please," *Lincoln Journal Star,* Sunday, March 25, 2012, B8.

18. "Your Ultimate Job Search Guide," a booklet prepared by the University of Nebraska Career Services, 2017–2018, pp. 26–27.

19. T. W. Dougherty, D. B. Turban, and J. C. Callender, "Confirming First Impressions in the Employment Interview: A Field Study of Interviewer Behavior," *Journal of Applied Psychology* 79 (1994): 659–65.

20. D. S. Chapman and P. M. Rowe, "The Impact of Videoconference Technology, Interview Structure, and Interviewer Gender on Interviewer Evaluations in the Employment Interview: A Field Experiment," *Journal of Occupational and Organizational Psychology* (2001): 279; C. J. Stewart and W. B. Cash Jr., *Interviewing Principles and Practices,* 15th ed. (New York: McGraw-Hill, 2018): 129–92; O. Crosby, "Employment Interviewing: Seizing the Opportunity and the Job," *Career Outlook,* U.S. Bureau of Labor Statistics (updated by Elka Torpey), April 2016, retrieved April 9, 2018, from https://www.bls.gov/careeroutlook/2016/article/pdf/employment-interviewing.pdf.

21. D. S. Chapman and P. M. Rowe, "The Impact of Videoconference Technology, Interview Structure, and Interviewer Gender on Interviewer Evaluations in the Employment Interview: A Field Experiment," *Journal of Occupational and Organizational Psychology* (2001): 279–298; C. J. Stewart and W. B. Cash Jr., *Interviewing Principles and Practices,* 15th ed. (New York: McGraw-Hill, 2018): 177–178.

22. J. Meyers, "The Ideal Job Candidate," *Collegiate Employment Institute Newsletter,* July 15, 1989, p. 6.

23. Ibid.

24. Ibid.

25. *The Endicott Report: Trends in the Employment of College and University Graduates in Business and Industry* (Evanston, IL: The Placement Center, Northwestern University, 1980), 8. In the May 2012 interview, Dr. Smith said that the rejection reasons companies give today are not different from what they were in 1980. Tina V., "Job Rejections: Reasons from an HR Point of View," tina-v.hubpages.com, September 20, 2012, https://www.localwise.com/a/292-15-reasons-to-reject-a-job-candidate (last retrieved March 30, 2018).

Text Credits

Chapter 1: p. 12, U.S. Census Bureau

Chapter 2: p. 52, Tannen, D. "You Just Don't Understand: Women and Men in Conversation." © New York: Morrow, 1990, 24–25.

Chapter 4: p. 80, Carroll, L. "Alice's Adventures in Wonderland, Through the Looking Glass, and The Hunting of the Smark." © New York: Modern Library, 1925. pp. 246–47; p. 84, Cushner, K., A. McClelland, and P. Safford. *Human Diversity in Education: An Integrative Approach.* 3rd ed. © New York: McGraw-Hill 2010; p. 86, Espy, W. R. "Guidelines: Reducing Bypassing." Based on News bulletins from W. R. Espy, "Say When," This Week, July 13, 1952, quoted in W. V. Haney, Communication and Organizational Behavior, 396; p. 90, Hall, E. T. "The Hidden Dimension." © Garden City, NY: Doubleday, 1966.

Chapter 7: p. 140, Wolvin, A. D. "Listening in the Quality Organization." © Ithaca, NY: Finger Lakes Press. 1999; p. 141, 144, 145, Depicted by Dwight R. Harfield, and used with permission; pp. 148–149, Adapted from Judi Brownell, *Listening: Attitudes, Principles, and Skills, 4e.* Published by Allyn and Bacon, Boston, MA, pp. 151–52. Reprinted by permission of the publisher.

Chapter 8: p. 180, Lind, S. J. "Teaching Digital Oratory: Public Speaking 2.0." Communication Teacher, 26, 3, 163–169. © 2012.

Chapter 9: p. 195, Oprah Winfrey's Golden Globes Speech Transcript, retrieved January 8, 2018 from http://www.harpersbazaar.com/culture/film-tv/a14551183/oprah-winfrey-golden-globes-speech-transcript; p. 198, Mission One Million. "Needs." © Mission One Million. Retrieved March 3, 2015; p. 199, "Africa's Orphaned Generations." © UNICEF, 2011; p. 200, Based on Africa's Orphaned Generations, Ch2, UNICEF, http://www.unicef.org/sowc06/pdfs/africas_orphans.pdf, retrieved March 31, 2012.

Chapter 10: p. 206, "Fast Facts: Hunger." © World Vision Blog; p. 208, "The History of a Movement." © Earth Day Network; p. 211, "Worldwide Orphan Fact, Figures and Statistics." SOS Children's Villages. © SOS Children's Villages; p. 212, Based on B. McEwen and G. Chrousos, "Stress: The Time Bomb in Your Body." Health Report. Retrieved May 20, 2012, from Stress.Newsmax.com; pp. 213–214, Seiler, William J. Based on "Laughter Is the Best Medicine: Health Benefits of Humor and Laughter." HELPGUIDE.ORG. © William J. Seiler; p. 215, Based on "Adoption Facts." from Very Well Family. © William J. Seiler; p. 217, Based on "What Are Sleep Deprivation and Deficiency?" National Heart, Lung, and Blood Institute; p. 217, Rifkin, Jeremy. "The BioTech Century." Delivered May 1998, City Club of Cleveland, OH. Retrieved March 15, 2015, from http://www.americanrhetoric.com; pp. 217–218, Based on "Eating Disorders," National Institutes of Mental Health; pp. 221–222, Sarah Johansen informative speech. Used with permission.

Chapter 11: p. 232, Based on Mulac, A. and A. R. Sherman, "Behavior Assessment of Speech Anxiety," *Quarterly Journal of Speech* 60, 2: 138. © April 1974; p. 251, Based on "Milestones," © Time, May 28, 2012: 21. & D. Martin, "Evelyn B. Johnson, Pilot and Instructor, Dies at 102," © New York Times, May 12, 2012; p. 252, Based on "'Smart Bomb' Drug Targets Breast Cancer." © NewsmaxMedia, June 3, 2012; pp. 252–254, Microsoft® Power-Point, Microsoft Office, Microsoft Corporation. Reprinted with permission; p. 253, Based on "Eligible Receiver." © Frontline, PBS; p. 254, Lincoln, Abraham. "The Gettysburg Address." November 19, 1863.

Chapter 12: p. 259, By permission. From Merriam-Webster.com © 2018 by Merriam-Webster, Inc. https://www.merriam-webster.com/dictionary/information; p. 272, Based on Mayo Clinic, "Eating Disorders: Symptoms." & "Eating Disorder Statistics." South Carolina Department of Mental Health; p. 284, Based on J. McCroskey. Retrieved June 4, 2015, from www.jamescmccroskey.com; p. 288, M. Schwabe, "Volunteering with Bethel Missions in Guatemala." Persuasive speech given at the University of Nebraska–Lincoln, used with permission.

Chapter 13: p. 302, Used with Permission from L. Stinson, "Unplugged for 40 Days," Journal Star, April 2, 2011, D1, D3; p. 304, Knapp, M. L. and A. L. Vangelisti. *Interpersonal Communication and Human Relationships. 6th ed.* © Boston: Allyn and Bacon, 2009; p. 308, Altman, Irwin and Dalmas Taylor. "Social Penetration: The Development of Interpersonal Relationships." Copyright © 1973 by Irwin Altman and Dalmas Taylor; p. 312, Petronio, S. "The Boundaries of Privacy: Praxis of Everyday Life," in S. Petronio, ed., *Balancing the Secrets of Private Disclosures.* © 2000 Hillsdale, NJ: Erlbaum 9–15; p. 325, Based on an article written by Jonathan Butler titled "The Donut Shop Experiment," in *The Front Porch Where People Share Life,* published by The Front Porch, LLC, © 2002; p. 336, Knapp, M. L. and A. L. Vangelisti. *Interpersonal Communication and Human Relationship. 6th ed.* © Boston: Allyn and Bacon, 2009, 33–37; p. 336, Duck, S. W. "A Perspective on the Repair of Personal Relationships: Repair of What, When?" in *Personal Relationships 5: Repairing Personal Relationships,* ed. S. W. Duck. © New York: Macmillan, 1984; p. 337, Based on E. P. Simon and L. A. Baxter. "Attachment-Style Differences in Relationship Maintenance Strategies." © Western Journal of Communication 57 (Fall 1993): 423.

Chapter 14: p. 319, Stephanie Whitlow, an honor student at Wayne State College in Wayne, Nebraska, with her permission; p. 358, "Reaching Consensus in Groups." Based on S. A. Beebe and J. T. Masterson. *Communicating in Small Groups,* 11th ed. 206–207. © Boston: Pearson, 2015; p. 364, Three Categories of Symptoms Leading to Group Thinking." Based on G. J. Galanes and K. Adams, *Effective Group Discussion, 14th ed.* 188–190. © New York: McGraw-Hill, 2013.

Chapter 15: p. 380, University of Nebraska-Lincoln. Used with permission; p. 380, "Employers Rate the Essential Need of the Career Readiness Competencies." Data from Job Outlook 2018, National Association of Colleges and Employers. This report can be found at https://www.naceweb.org/career-readiness/competencies/employers-rate-career-competencies-new-hire-proficiency; p. 381, University of Nebraska-Lincoln. Used with permission; p. 381, "Need vs. Proficiency of Career Readiness Competencies, by Percent of Respondents." Data from Job Outlook 2018, National Association of Colleges and Employers. This report can be found at https://www.naceweb.org/career-readiness/competencies/employers-rate-career-competencies-new-hire-proficiency; pp. 382–385, University of Nebraska-Lincoln. Used with permission; p. 357, Based on P. B. Paulus, ed., *Psychology of Group Influence,* 2nd ed. © Hillsdale, NJ: Erlbaum, 1989.

Index